RES MARITIMAE
CYPRUS AND THE
EASTERN MEDITERRANEAN FROM
PREHISTORY TO LATE ANTIQUITY

American Schools of Oriental Research

Archaeological Reports

Larry G. Herr, editor

Number 04
Res Maritimae
Cyprus and the Eastern Mediterranean from
Prehistory to Late Antiquity

Edited by
Stuart Swiny
Robert L. Hohlfelder
Helena Wylde Swiny

RES MARITIMAE

CYPRUS AND THE EASTERN MEDITERRANEAN FROM PREHISTORY TO LATE ANTIQUITY

PROCEEDINGS OF THE SECOND INTERNATIONAL SYMPOSIUM
"CITIES ON THE SEA"

Nicosia, Cyprus, October 18–22, 1994

Edited by

STUART SWINY
ROBERT L. HOHLFELDER
HELENA WYLDE SWINY

**Cyprus American Archaeological Research Institute
Monograph Series, Volume 1**

SCHOLARS PRESS • ATLANTA, GEORGIA

RES MARITIMAE
CYPRUS AND THE EASTERN MEDITERRANEAN FROM PREHISTORY TO LATE ANTIQUITY

edited by
Stuart Swiny
Robert L. Hohlfelder
Helena Wylde Swiny

© 1997

American Schools of Oriental Research

Library of Congress Cataloging in Publication Data
Res Maritimae : Cyprus and the eastern Mediterranean from prehistory
  to late antiquity / edited by Stuart Swiny, Robert L. Hohlfelder,
  Helena Wylde Swiny.
        p.   cm. — (American Schools of Oriental Research
  archaeological reports ; no. 04)
    Includes bibliographical references.
    ISBN 0-7885-0393-6 (cloth : alk. paper)
    1. Cyprus—Commerce—Mediterranean Region. 2. Mediterranean
Region—Commerce—Cyprus. 3. Shipping—Mediterranean Region—
History. 4. Middle Ages—History. 5. Commerce—History—Medieval,
500–1500.   I. Swiny, Stuart. II. Hohlfelder, Robert L.
III. Swiny, Helena Wylde. IV. Series.
HF3757.Z7M437   1998
382'.0939'37—dc21   97-40079
                                           CIP

Printed in the United States of America
on acid-free paper

∞

Contents

Preface

*R*es Maritimae is an apt title for a volume such as this which covers a range of topics concerned with "matters maritime" in the eastern half of the Mediterranean from the early Holocene through the Roman period—a 10,000 year time span. The twenty-six papers by multinational authors underscore the interdisciplinary nature of *Res Maritimae*. This congress focused on issues such as eustatic change, the exploitation of raw materials, trade, marine archaeology, ship iconography, ancient history—including some of its more flamboyant characters—and ranged from harbor technology to shipwrecks and seafaring.

It was on the veranda of the Cyprus American Archaeological Research Institute, commonly known as CAARI, one hot summer's afternoon in 1992 that the idea of organizing a conference devoted to the marine environment began to crystallize. Robert L. Hohlfelder, who had just finished his first underwater survey season at Paphos harbor, noted that Cyprus would be an ideal venue for the second scholarly gathering of the international symposium of "Cities on the Sea." (The first had been held in Haifa, Israel, September 22–29, 1986.) This idea appealed to Stuart Swiny, who had retained an abiding interest in maritime archaeology since his work on the Yassi Ada wreck in the 1960s. Furthermore, CAARI, recently housed in its renovated premises, was ideally suited to host such an event. Indeed, with this conference it emerged as a Mediterranean research center of consequence.

Late in 1992 scholars were canvassed in order to determine whether such a concept would be of interest to the academic community. It quickly became clear that this was indeed the case. Since no such gathering can be successful without the guiding hand of a knowledgeable Conference Secretary, we were fortunate that Helena Wylde Swiny, who played an important role in the "Kyrenia Ship" excavation, willingly accepted this position. *Res Maritimae* was then advertised in various archaeological journals, which resulted in the submission of papers from scholars specializing in Cyprus, Albania, Greece, Turkey, Syria, Lebanon, Israel and Egypt. In order to accommodate a program with thirty-three contributions, two keynote lectures, poster sessions and several field trips, a four day meeting was arranged from the 18th to the 22nd of October 1994.

The organizers took pleasure in welcoming so many speakers and attendants who were visiting Cyprus for the first time. As a result, and surely to the benefit of all who attended, the gathering was characterized by a lively and often humorous exchange of new ideas as well as the intermingling of established researchers, doctoral candidates and professionals with empirical knowledge.

Millennia of foreign domination have meant that despite its advantageous maritime position, only in the second half of the twentieth century have the inhabitants of Cyprus shown a sustained interest in the sea. Indeed, in the past decade the island has at long last come into its own, as it has developed into the fourth largest seafaring nation in the world. The same is true with respect to underwater archaeology. In the 1960s, when the field was becoming an accepted discipline rather than the domain of adventurers and treasure seekers, the Department of Antiquities of the Republic of Cyprus led the way by giving permission for the excavation of the "Kyrenia Ship," a Hellenistic merchantman that sank off the north coast of the island. The ensuing excavation and reconstruction made a major contribution to the development of underwater archaeology and its techniques. When the results of this project are published in full, Cyprus will finally be seen to have played a pioneering role in our understanding of ancient technology as well as maritime trade.

The Cyprus Ports Authority, well aware of this background, should be commended for celebrating its twentieth anniversary in 1993 by sponsoring *Cyprus and the Sea,* a symposium jointly organized with the Archaeological Research Unit of the University of Cyprus. The proceedings of this conference, bearing the same name, were published in Nicosia in 1995. This meeting and the resulting volume focusing on the island served to highlight the opportunity that existed for a more regional approach to the same general theme which was adopted by *Res Maritimae*. The latter gains in significance when seen in context with recent monographs such as *Sailing through Time: The Ship in Greek Art* (Athens 1995) and the three volumes of *Tropis* published since 1985 by the Hellenic Institute for the Preservation of Nautical Tradition, or symposia that have taken place on Cyprus and elsewhere in the region, such as *Cyprus and the Crusades* (Nicosia 1994) and *The Development of the Cypriot Economy* (1995), all of which add to the maritime picture.

The present anthology is a fitting sequel to *Mediterranean Cities: Historical Perspectives* (eds. I. Malkin and R. L. Hohlfelder, London 1988) and *Archaeology of Coastal Changes* (ed. A. Raban, Oxford 1988)—the two proceedings volumes of the first "Cities on the Sea" Symposium. *Res Maritimae* continues the study of port cities as gateways to land and sea transportation systems through which moved the people, trade and ideas of antiquity. It delves deeper into the ever changing physical and political milieu in which these cities thrived or foundered, adding another dimension to our understanding of that environmentally diverse, multicultural world known as the Mediterranean.

The editors gratefully acknowledge the interest and support of Ms. Marcelle Wahba, then Director of the United States Information Service in Nicosia, who was instrumental in obtaining a grant from the United States Information Agency to defray the administrative costs of the conference. Thanks are also due to the Bank of Cyprus, the British Council, Commercial Union Assurance (Cyprus) Ltd., Keo Ltd., Lanitis Brothers Ltd., Montanios & Montanios, Famagusta and S. J. Seraphim Ltd. for financial donations or gifts in kind. The United States Ambassador Richard Boucher and Ms. Carolyn Brehm graciously hosted a reception at their residence in honor of the conference and the Larnaca Branch of the Friends of the Cyprus Museum provided the refreshments in the Larnaca Fort.

It is a pleasure to record our appreciation for support received from the Director of the Department of Antiquities Dr. Demos Christou who offered the Larnaca Fort as a venue for the above-mentioned reception.

We wish to express our thanks to Professor Vassos Karageorghis and Mr. Cemal Pulak for their keynote lectures "Aspects of the Maritime Trade of Cyprus in Antiquity" and "The Bronze Age Shipwreck at Uluburun."

The value of the conference was certainly enhanced by the site tours conducted by Dr. Pierre Aupert, Professor Paul Āström, Dr. Olivier Callot, Dr. Maria Hadjicosti, Mr. A. H. S. (Peter) Megaw, Dr. Demetrios Michaelides, Professor Robert Hohlfelder and Professor Marguerite Yon. We thank them all, from the marshes of Kition to the parapets of Paphos, for describing their excavations in such detail.

We are most grateful to Professor R. Thomas Schaub, former chair of ASOR's Publication Committee, who enthusiastically embraced the idea of an independent monograph series for CAARI. He recognized the importance of such a publication outlet for research on the archaeology and history of Cyprus. Dr. Billie Jean Collins, ASOR Director of Publications, was unfailingly helpful during the long and complicated process of preparing the manuscript for publication.

In Boulder, Colorado, Ms. Pat Murphy of the staff of the History Department of the University of Colorado devoted long days to recomposing and sometimes deciphering the individual manuscripts of our contributors. Without her diligence, patience and professionalism, this volume could easily have withered away and joined the legion of proceedings volumes that never have seen the light of day.

We are sure that all the contributors to this volume would agree that it would be remiss not to mention the small, dedicated CAARI staff that strove so hard to make the conference itself a success: Ms. Bonny Bazemore, Program Coordinator of CAARI, spent many long hours on the word processor with the Conference Secretary printing up schedules, programs and communiqués; Ms. Vathoulla Moustoukki, CAARI Secretary, performed her usual magic and sought to fulfill everybody's requests, no matter how large or small; Mrs. Maria Stavrou, Librarian and Mrs. Diana Constantinides, the Getty Grant Librarian helped in many different ways, as did Mrs. Marita Anderson the ever versatile CAARI Archivist who prepared the abstracts for preconference distribution. Others too were key figures in the greater scheme of things; the goodwill and assistance of Mr. Roy Smith, Mrs. Fotoulla Christodoulou and Mrs. Georghia Nicolaou were contagious. Mrs. Lillian Craig, Honorary CAARI Trustee, Ms. Danielle Parks, Fulbright Fellow, Dr. Michael Given, Leverhulme Fellow, Mr. John Leonard, former Assistant Director of CAARI, and Ms. Malia Nemechek generously contributed their time and expertise.

Stuart Swiny
Robert L. Hohlfelder
Helena Wylde Swiny

Nomads of the Sea

MICHAL ARTZY

University of Haifa
Mt. Carmel
Haifa 31905
ISRAEL

"Nomads of the Sea" were fringe groups employed as economic mercenaries within established, yet varied political and economic systems of the Bronze Age. They became an essential part of a trade network, a position obtained because of their peculiar expertise: knowledge in navigation and prerequisites for successful maritime trade plus capital in the form of a boat. They served as intermediaries and brought their traditions to coastal settlements and along land routes of the economic hinterland. Thus, those who started out as hirelings carried out, in time, their own "sailors' trade" and the natural evolution to "entrepreneurial trade" and economic competition with their employers was a matter of time. When the economic situation was no longer favorable, the "Nomads of the Sea" (who, in the process, became merchants of the sea), reverted to marauding practices: they joined forces with pirates, and the image of "Sea Peoples" familiar to us from the Egyptian sources emerged.

In a meeting called "The Crisis Years: The 12th Century B.C.," scholarly discussion centered on a quest for a better understanding of this enigmatic period. While there is no doubt that there were great changes in the century under discussion, the crisis, as a few of those scholars who attended this conference mentioned, did not start in the 1100s B.C.E. Much old and new information pertaining to the period exists, and some, but not all, was treated and considered.[1] These data are scattered in various subdisciplines of the field, and are difficult to recover fully.[2]

The "crisis," if we are to retain the nomenclature, started much earlier and had, at first, little to do with the nineteenth century *Zeitgeist* of waves of migrations or the like, but rather with political and socio-economic changes coupled with possible climatic changes that eventually brought about the years of confusion and possible movement of peoples. During the Late Bronze period the eastern Mediterranean underwent social and economic changes that spawned a more complex society than the area had previously known. Varied social and cultural systems existed side by side. In their various maritime activities their relations were more intricate than an effort to maintain a military balance of power. The pursuit of economic superiority, influence, and survival brought the more powerful entities into contact with others who could

---

[1] As Horst Klengel writes of Syria, "the period beginning during the so-called Amarna Age about the middle of the 14th century and ending with the invasion of the 'Sea Peoples' in the early 12th century B.C.E. is the chapter of Syrian prehellenistic history which is the best documented so far" (Klengel 1992: 100). The data he speaks of are Syrian, but beside the Syrian, which included Ugarit, there are Hittite and Egyptian written sources. There are archeological sources and now additional maritime sources.

[2] Many of the participants in the meeting and the volume called *Crisis Years* (Ward and Joukowsky 1992) are no doubt the leading authorities on the topic in their areas of specialization, but, as often happens in meetings in which such an extensive topic as this is addressed, the scholars tend to make their contributions in their areas of expertise and leave the synthesis to the reader.

support them in their quest. Treaties and alliances were but one way to insure cooperation; another was to hire or use the offices of mercenaries and intermediaries.[3]

The symbiotic relationship of the greater powers with military or economic mercenaries or with smaller, militarily weaker groups bound by treaties and alliances could easily be broken. A dependency of the economic powers on others was a sure way for destabilization and disaster. The international economic system of the Late Bronze Age demanded security for the merchants and their merchandise for a profitable trade. Hirelings, who at times came from fringe groups, economic or geographical, could cause a ripple in a tenuous equilibrium. They could become an essential part of the trade network by virtue of their peculiar expertise and the requirements for a successful maritime trade. Those who started out as hirelings would in time carry out their own "sailors' trade," which in time would naturally evolve into "entrepreneurial trade" and economic competition with those who hired them.

The inherent economic weaknesses of the Hittite Empire,[4] as well as those manifest on the Syrian coast,[5] have been studied recently. Coastal Syria has been used for the model of the collapse of the Palace Economy by Liverani

and others (Liverani 1987: 69), while the inner parts of Syria were shown to belong to different economic spheres. While these spheres were most obviously linked to one another, the core influences were diverse. Thus, one cannot use Ugarit as a geopolitical model for Emar on the Euphrates, despite their trade contacts (Heltzer 1977: 207). While Assyria played a role in upper Mesopotamia in the 14th and especially the 13th century where Emar was economically involved, it was not so in the coastal zone. The collapse of the Hittite Empire in Anatolia contributed to the upheavals experienced in the coastal zone and less to the inner Syrian sites.

Turning to the Egyptians, upon whose texts much of the essential synchronism for these "crisis years" has been founded,[6] we necessarily have to start with Ramses III. His reign of 30+ years is sufficiently well-known to say that he was beset with serious external and internal problems (Lesko 1992).[7] We have the naval scene depicted on the walls of Medinet Habu and a papyrus attributed to the end of his reign that describes this pictorial event. These are the data most often quoted in any discussion of the "Sea Peoples."[8] They were the people responsible for all the anxiety at the end of the thirteenth century B.C.E. and the first years of the

---

[3] This statement is not meant to propose that the participants in the trade were equal to one another. There was a variety in the level of operation even within different systems.

[4] Güterbock and Hoffner presented some of the history of this issue in their papers at "Crisis Years" (Ward and Joukowsky 1992: 53–55 and 46–47). In their articles, they mention Otten (1983), whose work on the written sources in Hatti has since been replaced by other studies including their own, and Bittel's valuable archaeological study (Bittel 1983) with the added observations of Neve's more recent work (1989–90).

[5] Thirteenth century Ugarit was smaller than it was in the 14th century. It was small in size, militarily weak, but economically strong. During most of the thirteenth century it was under the suzerainty of the Hittites who required military contingents from Ugarit. The city seemed to have found a way out of dispensing with some of their men by making financial arrangements instead. By the end of the thirteenth century, before the fall of Ugarit, the merchant king was very young and, according to one letter written by the Hatti king to a prefect, was not very experienced (Lehmann 1979). For more data see Yon (1992), Klengel (1993), Heltzer (1982), and Astour (1981).

[6] Lesko summarized the Egyptian domestic affairs during the period and examined the Ramesside historical records. He says, "as an Egyptologist … I am reasonably content and even a bit smug that my field provides the essential synchronism upon which this whole conference is based" (Lesko 1992: 151).

[7] Weinstein collected the archaeological data which concerned the presence of the Egyptians in the Southern Levant (Weinstein 1992), especially during the reign of Ramses III. Weinstein wonders why exactly were the Egyptians so active in the region, which included the Jezreel Valley and perhaps the Jordan Valley. The answer is probably not the one he proposes, namely that Ramses III attempted to gather enough control in order to contain the military expansion by the "Sea Peoples." It is more probable that their involvement was economically based. The Egyptians would have had a share in the taxes and wealth emanating from the active regional trade which included Trans Jordan. One of the routes, via the Jezreel Valley, traversed this region in an east-west direction. From Megiddo it could take a southern route to Egypt or continue to the sea (Artzy 1994). This route, which we assume to be of great economic importance, could well have forded the Jordan river near Tell es-Saidiyeh. The route on the Trans Jordanian side met a north-south main route which reached Syria and eventually Emar on the Euphrates and Hattusha.

[8] We do not feel that it is necessary to reiterate the origin of the name. Others have done it in the past. Singer (1988: 239) collected a good bibliography pertaining to this question. Nancy Sandars' book introduces the topic as well (1978).

twelfth. If we believe this exaggerated and obviously sensational report, we have to admit that this group certainly got a bad press from Ramses III and his scribes.

But can we trust this report? How much of the report was the boasting of a king who had had his share of problems (Sandars 1978).[9] Not surprisingly, scholars working on the sections dealing with his northern campaign suggest that parts of the reliefs are probably copies of earlier materials and earlier Pharaohs (Lesko 1992: 152–53). Earlier Pharaohs faced problems caused by peoples from the north and west, including ones who came via the sea. Almost one hundred years earlier, Ramses II faced the Shardan on their war boats (Artzy 1987: 28), and Merneptah had to meet a massive attack of the Libyans and their allies (Lesko 1992). Ramses III, according to his own account, faced several attacks of which the most famous is the one commemorated in the naval battle. In one detail, however, the Harris Papyrus does not completely agree with the scene depicted on the wall at Medinet Habu. In the visual representation, the battle scene features many Egyptian boats, all of one type. The written account, on the other hand, notes that three different types of boats confronted the enemy. The three were the *br,* the *mns* and the *aha.* What we see in the depicted scene is probably the *aha,* the war boat, a term already used by Ramses II in his description of the naval attack by the Shardan that he so valiantly repelled (Artzy 1988: 184).[10] Likewise, the artist presents diverse groups of surprised adversaries with their different attributes, but all used the same type of boat. This is a strange occurrence, considering the supposed dissimilar origins of these invaders. One possible explanation is that there were indeed different boats participating in the battle, but only one was chosen to represent all types. Artistic expediency might have prevailed over historical accuracy.

Another example of the problematic nature of this account as an historical record is its mention of the fall of the Hittites. It is the only report to provide this information. We are informed that those who attacked Egypt had already sacked various other important states, among them the Hittites and Carchemish (Sandars 1978: 119). Of course Ramses boasts that these same enemies, who had been so successful elsewhere, were trounced by his own troops. The destruction of Hattusha, we must remember, is unlikely to have been carried out by ships. To the Egyptians, who could have grouped events together, the destruction of a site in Cilicia (a Hittite province) could have been interpreted as the demise of the whole of Hatti. Possible signs of Cilicia reverting to its natural maritime attitude, which included Cyprus and the Dodecanese, appear just at the time or a bit earlier, at the later part of the thirteenth century B.C.E.[11] The reliability of the Ramesside report has also been questioned because of its report that Carchemish fell. In fact, the city continued to exist under the direct rule of the Hittite family which had ruled there for at least four previous generations (Hawkins 1988: 102–3). It is a curious statement in another way, since Carchemish was situated in inland Syria wellbeyond the coast. As for Hattusha, the "Sea Peoples" did not have to exchange their boats for pack animals in order to attack and destroy it. The semi-nomadic Kashka, who had already caused havoc time and again in Hattusha and its countryside, were a much better choice for the agents of the final destruction of the Hittites. It is also possible that the report of the fall of Ugarit prior to the naval battle is not to be completely trusted. Although there is no doubt that Ugarit did fall in the first part of the twelfth century B.C.E. and was not resettled (Yon 1992: 111), the fate of contemporary coastal sites, such as Byblos, Tyre and Sidon, was completely different (Caubet 1992: 128–30). Thus a com-

[9] Sandars's book on the Sea Peoples is still a good source for laymen and scholars. Although we do not agree on several crucial points presented in the study, its usefulness cannot be overestimated. She says: "The language has been called "poetical" but is more justly described as "bombastic." It is a murky substitute for straightforward historical narrative, but that is something the ancient world never set out to give." It probably could not have been expressed in a clearer way.

[10] Could these same Shardan, who were vanquished by the forces of Ramses II, have become the shipwrights who instructed the Egyptians in the art of building the small, fast and maneuverable *aha* which is depicted almost a century later in the Medinet Habu Naval Scene of Ramses III?

[11] Indeed, ceramics that have been identified as Mycenaean IIIC1 or late Helladic IIIC1 (associated with the "Sea Peoples' " destruction) have been found on the Cilician coast of southern Anatolia, but, not surprisingly, not in the central part. There is little imported Mycenaean Ware associated with the Hittite Imperial levels at Kazanlı, Mersin and Tarsus. The appearance of an Aegean type of pottery in LBIIb level is not necessarily due to an invasion (Sherratt and Crouwell 1987). Mycenaean type pottery could well have been produced in Cyprus or in Eastern Greece, both of which would have been natural trading partners, being situated on similar maritime networks. When the Hittite control weakened, reversion to traditional trading patterns would have been a natural development.

plete destruction of Syria was not necessarily the case. On the contrary, it is probably not the case at all.[12]

The Rameside information has misled scholars for many years. Naturally, a written account of a contemporary narrator cannot be completely discounted, but one has to consider the circumstances of the period, Ramses' position, and his scribe's ability or motivation to relay the news accurately. Thus, just as we use other boastful scenes and reports of the Egyptian Pharaohs with caution, we should approach Ramses' report. As an historical record, it is problematic.

I will not dwell on the exact date of the battle, its locale, or the events immediately preceding or following it. These topics deserve a study of their own.[13] The thrust of this study primarily concerns the hundred years or so before the events described by the Egyptian scribes, a period that we feel contributed greatly to the "Crisis Years." The balance of power in the Levantine coast at the end of the fourteenth and during most of the thirteenth centuries B.C.E. was dominated by two main entities—the Egyptians and the Hittites in Anatolia. There were also other centers, such as Ugarit or Cyprus (or parts of it) for that matter, that might not have been equal to the two superpowers in military ability, but certainly were formidable economic powers. The competition for the markets necessitated centralized management to ensure the construction and maintenance of the

seagoing vessels, the upkeep of open routes and anchorage and the availability of required merchandise. The economic situation required adequate manpower, either local emissaries or individuals who could be hired for any and all assignments. Maintenance of available maritime routes and their outlets was an arduous chore. Maritime travel kept the mariners and merchants away from their homes for very long periods of time (sometimes years). There were always dangers associated with seafaring, even in the few navigable months of the year. Some vital maritime concerns, such as the building of the vessels, which we think of as being of foremost importance, were farmed out (Lambrou-Phillipson 1993: 170).[14] Ugarit either paid for, or hired others to fulfill tasks that its citizens did not wish to carry out.[15] Mercenaries may have been employed as guards (Heltzer 1983: 13) and as crews for ships engaged in the city's flourishing trade.[16]

The Egyptians, Hittites, and others involved in Mediterranean trade did the same. On a recently published papyrus found at el-Amarna, Aegean-looking soldiers wearing tusk helmets are represented (Parkinson and Schofield 1993). The papyrus is necessarily dated to the fourteenth century B.C.E.[17] Hood (1990: 233) mentions burials of foreigners containing amber in lower Egypt of the XIX–XX dynasties. Yet another place where we might meet the hirelings is in the el-Amarna letters in which the Mi-Shi people

[12] Annie Caubet collected much of the data pertaining to the Syrian sites (1992: 128–30). She shows that sites were occupied after the destruction of Ugarit. There was, however, a period of abandonment after the end of the twelfth century B.C.E. That is unlike Cyprus in which a continuation can be shown. We feel that this has more to do with the economic situation along the coast than with the advance of violent elements.

[13] The location of the battle has been often seen as being in the Delta, most recently see Bietak (1985: 217) or somewhere closer to Amurru, possibly in the modern northern Israel or Lebanon (Singer 1985: 109).

[14] Connie Lambrou-Phillipson cites the case of Ugarit, which purchased boats for its use in Byblos. She actually counts all the boats mentioned in Ugaritic texts and comes to the conclusion that they cannot be considered a *thalassocracy* in the modern sense (Lambrou-Phillipson 1993: 170).

[15] Yon mentions the estimates of population at between 6,000 and 8,000 urban inhabitants (Yon 1992: n. 2) and mentions an estimate of Liverani of 10,000 at the end of the Late Bronze Age. Heltzer (1976) estimates the rural population at no more than 25,000. We have to bear these numbers in mind when we consider the trade networks in which Ugarit was active.

[16] An interesting example of using hirelings can be gleaned from a situation in the Assyrian trade with Kanesh *Karum* that Larsen cites (1982: 43). A merchant named Enlil-bani lived in Kanesh as a representative of an Assyrian (probably family) firm some time in the nineteenth century B.C.E. He sent Kukkulanum, as his employee, a hireling, to deliver goods. Kukkulanum was entrusted with the goods and had to carry out his employer's wishes along the route. Kukkulanum had two young men, caravan boys, of whom one seems to have been the master's son who was sent to learn the trade. He, like the other young man, was not given a wage, but was given silver with which he could engage in small (personal) trade along the route. When they arrived they had to return the silver they got, interest free. In other words they could carry out a small lucrative trade of their own. It is quite likely that Kukkulanum not only watched the young and gave them advice, but could well have carried out an entrepreneurial trade of his own.

[17] How did these individuals find out where there might be employment? Temples and brothels, functioning like bars in later periods, might have been sources of such information.

are mentioned. When these letters were first published, their name was read as Mi-Lim, but already in 1953, their name was transcribed as Mi-Shi (Lambdin 1953: 75).[18] These people were actually hired mariners from the general area who acted in the sea around Byblos and Amurru as coastal guards for the Egyptian overlords. Interestingly, a boat model found in Byblos looks much like a Medinet Habu boat of the "Sea Peoples" without the birds' heads (Basch 1988: 67). We obviously do not know who produced the model and how it was used, but the general type was known.

The Hittites, the "land lubbers," must have had their hirelings, such as the sea going Lukka, who carried out much of the shipping for them and most probably engaged in other maritime adventures as well. Reading of the problems the Hittites had with a certain Piyamaradus, we might well feel that indeed he was such an hireling, an economic mercenary. Another group with whom the Hittites and other economic entities had their share of problems were probably the *Shikalayu,* or *Shiqala,* who were said to be living on boats and were named the "enemy" by the Hittite king (Lehmann 1979). In a letter written by the Hittite king to the vizier in Ugarit (since as he says, the reigning king was too young and inexperienced), the Hittite king asked to have a certain person, who was held captive by the *Shiqala,* ransomed and sent back to Hatti to be debriefed. Yon refers to the man as a possible Ugaritic spy (1992: 116).[19]

The topic of this study is the "Nomads of the Sea." The word nomad implies a carefree individual who roams the deserts in an unhindered manner, owing nothing to authority and expecting nothing in return. A model of more recent nomads proposed by E. Marx is, we feel, more realistic. Marx sees pastoral nomads as a specialized sector of a complex society, one which is not feasible in a subsistence economy. Nomads are susceptible to control by the state and in order to reduce their dependency on the state market they engage in additional economic ventures (Marx 1992: 256–57). Thus these nomads or semi-nomads who, were at times intermediaries, were also bandits, caravan leaders or mercenaries linking Arabia, the sown lands and the established political systems. One could easily imagine that these same intermediaries converged closer to the settled areas to sell meat and milk products and acquire manufactured goods and corn to meet their needs. Oren (1987: 77) who has carried out a comprehensive survey of the second millennium B.C.E. "Ways of Horus" in northern Sinai and southern Philistia says, "the distribution map of settlement in the New Kingdom is characterized by clusters of sites in which the central fort, or station, is surrounded by many smaller camp sites for caravans, and many seasonal encampments for the local inhabitants who lived in huts or in tents and depended for their protection and supplies on the Egyptian authorities in the main settlement." This model, likewise, could apply to maritime trade in the second millennium B.C.E. The intermediaries (hirelings) were the emissaries of the established economic systems, they served as the transporters of goods, traders and military mercenaries. When authority crumbled and could no longer supply the necessary economic safety, the intermediaries reverted to piracy and eventually settlement in areas that became known to them during their involvement in the trade. The "Peoples of the Sea" would thus have been the equivalent of the "Peoples of the Desert."

While the written sources of the period under discussion are limited, comparable historical situations where written substantiations do exist are used in this study. For the desert situation I look at the relationship between the later Roman Empire and the Saracens in Mayerson's work: "travellers, eremites, and papyrological documents record a number of transactions in which the Saracens provide transport or serve as messengers, guides, and sellers of ani-

---

[18] Lambdin pointed out that already in the Ebeling glossary in Knudson's edition of the el-Amarna letters (1915: 1550) the identity is questionable. Lambdin proposed the name Mi-shi that is to be equated with the Egyptian word *msh* "army, troops." They are mentioned in at least five texts, EA 101: 4,33; 105:27–; 108: 38; 110: 48, 52 and 126: 63). Säve-Söderbergh (1946: 60) still called them Mi-Lim. It is very likely that these people were hired for their task as a form of coast guard. It is hard to believe that any real Egyptians carried out that chore along the Byblos and Amurru coast, south of Ugarit. Altman has already shown the good relations between the family of Abdi-Ashirta and the Mi-Shi people (Altman 1977: 9). He proposes that these relations with the avowed enemy of Rib-Addi of Byblos, who was, according to his own protestations, a devoted servant of the Egyptian king (for other view on the letters of Rib Addi see: Liverani 1973), were understandable in view of the corruption rampant in the Egyptian camp. We would like to propose that the answer is in the nature of the employment of this group. As local fringe group they were hired by the Egyptians, when the pay was greater elsewhere, it was not hard for them to play the market for all its worth. This explains their ambivalent relationship with Rib-Addi and eventually the treatment of Abdi-Ashirta himself.

[19] If indeed he was a spy with the Shiqala, did he then speak their language? If, like the Mi-Shi people, they were from the area, there would have been little problem.

mals" (1989: 73).[20] For the maritime aspect, the amalgamated group, the Cilician pirates of the second and first centuries B.C.E., can be observed. N. Rauh, in his work on the Cilician Pirates (this volume), quotes Appian on this group: "Perhaps this evil had its beginning among the men of Cilicia Tracheia, who were joined by men of Syrian, Cyprian, Pamphylian and Pontic origin and those of almost all the Eastern nations, who, on account of the severity and the length of the Mithridatic war, preferred to do wrong rather than to suffer it, and for this purpose chose the sea instead of the land" (Appian: xiv, 92).

It was a hopeless, dire economic situation in which these people found themselves, but there was yet another element that added to their plight. In the first half of the second century B.C.E. Rome censured Rhodes economically. Rhodes, at that time, was in the center of the east-west economic maritime route, the entrepôt for grain, slaves and other merchandise. In the position of middleman, already in the third century B.C.E. (Berthold 1984: 82–83) it influenced others, such as the Cycladic islanders, and exercised some control in coastal Asia Minor where it gained a foothold. Following the Roman censure, Rhodes lost both Lycia and Caria while Delos, an Athenian dependent, became the free port in its stead. Scholars dealing with these events point to a period of confusion and lack of conscious purpose. This was coupled with the Roman policy of nonintervention in local rivalries, which they carried out as a policy after initially intervening as arbitrators. It was a major cause of the fused coastal Asia Minor to revert to a state of small precincts (Green 1993: 434–35). Following the censure, inhabitants of the southern coast of Anatolia, the fringe of the Seleucid and Ptolemaic empires who were employed as economic maritime hirelings, found partial employment as mercenaries in the internal Seleucid dynastic disputes. The diminishing economic possibilities were instrumental in their reversion to piracy, either as a full or part-time occupation. Plutarch describes these mariners and their bases: "In many places too there were regular fortified harbors and signal stations for the use of the pirates, and the fleets which put in at these places were admirably equipped for their own work with fine crews, expert pilots, and light, fast ships" (Plutarch: *Pompey,* 24). They were drawn from an international substrata of Maritime society and were called "Cilician," although this was not necessarily their place of origin. It was just one name to identify them as belonging to a certain clique, whether or not their descent was from Cilicia (Rauh, this volume). Pompey was sent by Rome to eradicate them and carried out the assignment with surprising speed. How he managed the complicated task has not been satisfactorily explained, although Green might have the answer which applies not only to the "Cilician Pirates," but our "Nomads of the Sea," of more than a thousand years earlier: "It does seem as though Pompey had perceived, and attempted to deal with some of the grim endemic problems that lay behind the social scourge of piracy; at least he had the common sense to realize that out-of-work pirates needed an alternative way of making a living" (Green 1993: 658).[21]

Rauh has shown (this volume) that the Cilician pirates and early modern pirates were similar in behavior as in their escape from socially established norms in their dress. They liked outlandish colors "gilded sails, the purple awnings, the silver oars" (Plutarch: *Pompey,* 24) and likened themselves to chiefs, kings and tyrants (Appian: xiv, 92). The much earlier "Sea Peoples," our "Nomads of the Sea," as portrayed at Medinet Habu, might also have been showing off their outlandish attire, which was fancied by the Egyptian artist and the exaggerated outcome was presented for his contemporaries' benefit and accepted by us verbatim.

Yet another picture with a slightly different twist can be discerned among the more recent nineteenth century pirates who might still be practicing their art in Southeast Asia, along the Malaysian Littoral. These people are scattered in small, separated groups over an extensive area and their total number, by the middle of the sixties of this century was

[20] Mayerson has recently published a volume of collected papers called: *The Near East in Late Antiquities* (Mayerson 1994).

[21] Using some of the descriptions of these "Cilician" pirates made by Appian, we cannot but see similarities to the period we are concerned with, namely the end of the Bronze Age. For instance: "… and thought that if they should all unite they would be invincible. They built ships and made all kinds of arms …They had forts and peaks and desert islands and retreats everywhere, but they chose for their principal rendezvous this part of the coast of Cilicia which was rough and harborless and rose in high mountain peaks, for which they were called by the common name of Cilicians" (Appian: XIV, 92). "The city of Rome felt this evil most keenly, her subjects being distressed and herself suffering grievously from hunger by reason of her own populousness. But it appeared to her to be a great and difficult task to destroy so large a force of seafaring men scattered everywhither on land and sea, with no fixed possession to encumber their flight, sallying out from no particular country or any known places, having no property or anything to call their own, but only what they might chance to light upon" (Appian: XIV, 93).

less than twenty thousand. They came into contact with many different people: Malay, Chinese, Burmese and Thai among others (Sopher 1977: ix). Sopher further stresses that "it is evident that the phenomenon of piracy among these [boat] people was a special cultural characteristic resulting from close contact and close political affiliation with Malays, and that the chief piratical groups were not in fact the sea nomads proper, but the island people with strand villages, sedentary fishing operations, occasional garden and orchard cultivation, and the capital and organizational ability to make and man for extensive sea raiding expeditions. In the vicinity of such groups, the sea nomads lived and traded; being economic and political dependents of the more powerful clans, they were utilized as boatmen, rowers, and even as warriors on the pirate boats, and it seems likely that such experiences led them to adapt some of the piratical techniques to their own contacts with strange boats" (Sopher 1977: 88). He further describes populations moving inward to safer ground to avoid the raids of the various marauders.

Returning to the Late Bronze period, we have to consider both the perpetrators and carriers involved in the eastern Mediterranean Trade. They were Egyptians or Hittites, merchants from Cyprus or Ugarit and other coastal sites, or for that matter a mixture of all of them—a polymorphic society that must be considered in the complex situation especially following the Peace of Kadesh. Whoever the perpetrators and financiers of the trade were, they were not necessarily those who carried it out. We propose that intermediaries, nomads or semi-nomads, were the important link between Arabia, the sown lands and the established political systems. Likewise, it was intermediaries who carried out a large part of the maritime transport, in the Bronze Age, especially the thirteenth century B.C.E. These middlemen, "Nomads of the Sea," constituted various gradations of fringe elements of maritime semi-nomads and coastal settlers. These were people to whom the boat was part of life and a long-term capital investment, even if it was not necessarily their home. They became the employees and the emissaries of the established economic systems, hired hands whose maritime expertise rendered them a meaningful element in the active international trade of the Late Bronze Age. Their womenfolk, children and others who were not actively involved in the trade remained behind continuing their diverse economic pursuits. This, of course, was the case during more or less settled periods. We would venture to add at this junc-

ture that, at times, artisans, such as metalsmiths or others who knew about the production of the purple dye, joined the sailors.

A window on a connection between an eastern overland supply route and a Mediterranean coastal distribution area may be seen in the anchorage site of Tel Nami, on the coast of Israel, some 15 km south of Haifa. The site was occupied in the Middle Bronze IIA and again in LB II, especially Late Bronze IIB, the thirteenth century B.C.E. Nami would not have been very successful as a purely agricultural site since it has little good arable land and suffers from high ground water level and swamping. The site must have been dependent on trade, especially sea trade, and very likely on the traffic of foreign commodities of a luxurious nature. Even if Nami served as a favored port for vessels plying the eastern Mediterranean coast, its exceptional affluence could not be due only to local, north-south coastal trade. Other sites existed along the coast and the competition would have been fierce. Its added role as an outlet for an overland route (fig. 1) would explain the remarkable prominence of the site in the LB IIB period (Artzy 1994).

The polymorphic society at Nami is well-represented by the different rituals seem to have taken place there. There are remains of Canaanite, Syrian, Cypriot and Aegean cults (Artzy 1991). A goddess with entwined snake legs appears on a gold pendant, a motif presently known only in Mitanni (Artzy 1994: 125). There are also Hittite hieroglyphs on a ring of a type known, among others, from Emar where many sealings of this type were found (Artzy 1995: 29).[22]

When approaching Nami from the sea, the mariners must have used navigational landmarks to find safe anchorage for their vessels. Such a landmark was probably the cavity in the Carmel Mountain carved out by the Me'arot River less than 4 km east of Nami. The jaw-like crevice, which is easily discernible from the sea, was probably the marker of Nami's location. Its shape might have lent the name MGR (*Mugar*) a Semitic word meaning "cave" to Nami (Artzy 1995: 33). Graffiti of boats appear on the cliffs in the area. The most common form is the "fan" or Akko-Kition type (fig. 2): a distinctive boat noted previously on a late thirteenth century altar from Tel Akko (Artzy 1987) and at Kition *Kathari*, in Cyprus (Basch and Artzy 1986). It is likely that these engravings were made by mariners, our "Nomads of the Sea," familiar with other parts of the eastern Mediterranean, who inscribed the images of their

[22] What language did this amalgamation of peoples communicate in? We assume that any pidgin language that may have included elements of coastal Canaanite, the language of Cyprus, and Mycenaean Greek would have. It would have been a kind of an eastern Mediterranean maritime *lingua franca*. At a later date the Cilician pirates, diverse as they were, knew and respected other groups they met.

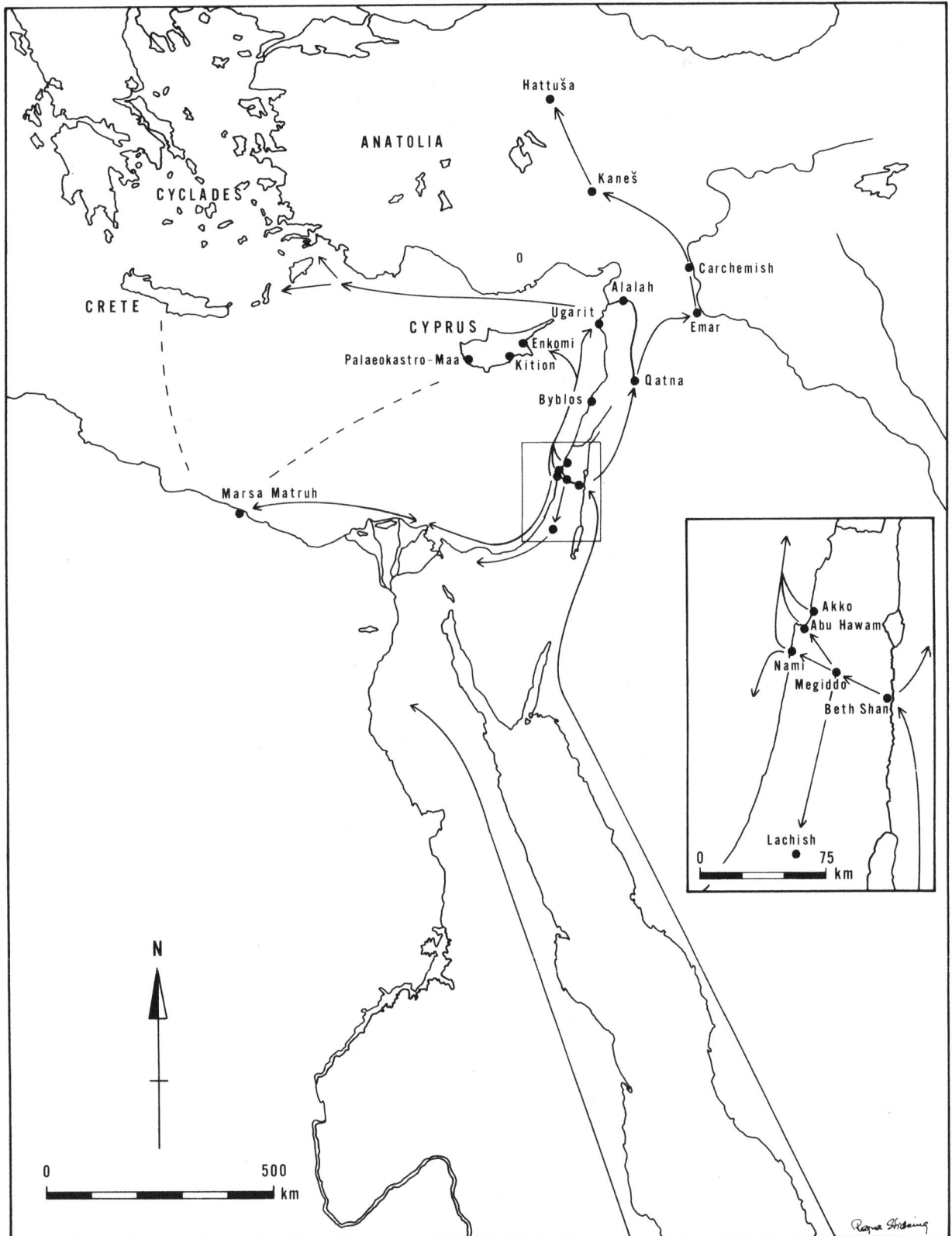

Fig. 1. Coast and Desert: Nami and its possible connections.

trade on the landmark to which they owed their safe arrival, a form of an *ex-voto* practice, or a terrestrial bench mark by the mariners to indicate a proposed route used as a supplementary path connecting the Carmel coast and the hinterland.

The incised boats are not limited to the Akko-Kition type. There are others, such as those similar to the "Sea Peoples" boats shown at Medinet Habu. Interestingly, not one on the Carmel ridge appears with two animal heads (which might or might not be duck heads).[23] But the most impressive boat in the area, as far as size, depth of incision and the positioning on the rocks is, no doubt, the boat of Aegean type that has been documented at Gazi, Tranaga and Dramesi in Beotia (fig. 3; Basch 1987: 142–147; 1994: 20–21). A similar type of boat has also recently been found in records from Teneida, the Dakhla Oasis, in the western Delta of Egypt (Basch 1994 and this volume). The Teneida record has more details than the one from the Carmel Ridge. It has men, whom Basch has shown to be Libyans, holding small ships in their hands. The boat is dated to Ramses II or Ramses III, thirteenth–early twelfth century, a time in which fortresses were constructed to keep the coasts and western borders of Egypt safe (Habachi 1980). The concurrent appearance of this type of vessel on the Carmel ridge and in Egypt should not be taken as a coincidence. The small boat models held by the mariners on the Teneida boat are of a familiar type, an outward inclined stem with an animal, probably a bird's head, on it.[24] There might be some jest in the presentation of these men, such as the emphasized nakedness combined with a most elaborate, cumbersome headdress for these active mariners. There may be some exaggeration—a little "artistic freedom"—in the rendering of the scenes by the artists involved with the production of this monument. In this case, the geographical position of the document should also be considered. The reason it was found so far inland might be because these mariners were settled by Ramses II quite a distance from the sea in order to keep them away from mischief and this document is a tribute to their former glory. This obviously recalls the settlement of the "Cilician" pirates by Pompey to keep them out

of harm's way. An alternative explanation is proposed by Basch (1994).

The significance of these "Nomads of the Sea" increased as the nature of the trade changed. When we think of a King's Trade, as Polanyi would have had it, we think of the king's merchant as beholden to the king, but doing his own business on the side. Whatever the main cargo was, there it was complemented by "sailors' trade," a trade of small objects, maybe some ceramics that took little space and even less tonnage which the sailors themselves could exchange along the coast for their own benefit (Artzy 1985a; 1985b). With the use of hired mercenaries, the main load was still the pay load for which they were hired, but the crew would have had more of a business interest of their own.[25] The Cape Gelidonya Shipwreck is a case in point. Among the ingots found on board were several types, oxhide, bun and of special interest at this juncture, the slab ingots, which are bronze rather than copper. The third type, the slab ingots, were small in size and weight and were all found in the vicinity of the "captain's cabin," where other personal pieces for daily use were also located (Bass 1967: 81–82). Bass felt that they might have been used as currency. Indeed, it is quite possible that the captain of the vessel and his sailors were involved in a trade distinct from the main cargo of the ship for their own benefit. We would call this type of trade "sailors' trade" verging on "entrepreneurial trade," which is a common practice of sailors world-wide even today. Some of the scrap metal from Nami is similar to that of the Gelidonya wreck, for instance, the pieces from incense stands (Bass 1967: 105; Artzy 1994: 126). Nami was most probably a recycling center of metals; the few people who inhabited the summit at Nami did not need to be extremely specialized to run such an operation. The same might be true of the purple dye industry, which used the murex shell, remains of which were found on the summit of the site.[26] There are remains of some of the goods that were conveyed and exchanged and possibly manufactured at Tel Nami. Besides scrap metal and the metal working tools, more than eighty bun ingots were found in the sea just 800 m north of the site. As previously mentioned, there are many signs of

[23] The artists of the scene in Medinet Habu may have taken a fancy to such protomes and decided to put two of them in their document, one on the stem and another on the stern. This is another case in question as to the authenticity of the Rameside record.

[24] We are not sure that they are models. If the mariners are serving as coast guards, or are pirates, these vessels might signify their pride in the booty captured by them. The appearance of these men suggests prowess and strength.

[25] For a similar case in a land caravan situation see footnote 14.

[26] The purple dye industry is thought to have originated in the Aegean, namely in Crete at least by the Late Bronze Age (Stieglitz 1994). One possible scenario is the transmission of the knowledge of the production from the Aegean to the Syro-Palestinian shores by these entrepreneurs. The production of the dye was not limited to technical knowledge, but required

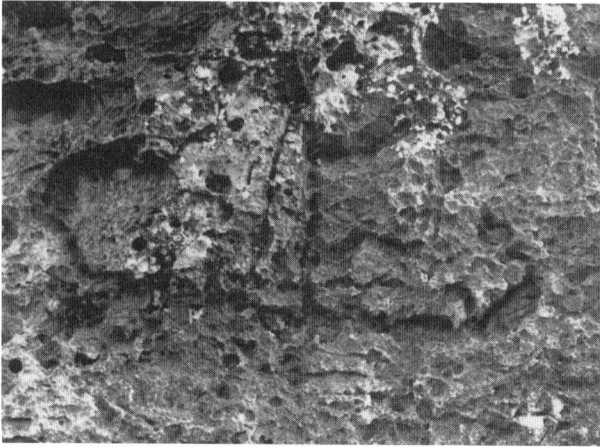

Fig. 2. "Fan" Type Boat from Nahal Me'arot.

Fig. 3. "Aegean" Type Boat from Nahal Me'arot.

intermediaries—nomads or semi-nomads functioning as caravan leaders, mercenaries or bandits.

Another commodity connected with transshipment of goods is the large jars, named Collared Rim Jars, or pithoi, found at the site. The Collared Rim jars have been the topic of numerous studies especially dealing with the settlement of the Israelites.[27] Collared Rim Jars first appear in the coastal region, in the thirteenth century B.C.E. before they materialize in the Israelite hill country. They appear in the Jezreel Valley in Megiddo, Beth Shean and in Trans Jordan. The situation, as proposed for the hill country and that of the end of the twelfth and eleventh centuries, should not be superimposed on the end of the thirteenth century, which was influenced by affairs well beyond the area.

The Nami jars include types that are comparable to those from the local hill country, Cypriot and possibly others as well. The tradition of collars on large ceramic vessels existed well before the thirteenth century B.C.E. in several areas of the eastern Mediterranean.[28] Pithoi aboard ships have appeared not only on the Uluburun wreck, where the one pithos on display in the Bodrum Museum happens to have a collar, but also at the Cape Iria wreck (Vichos, this volume). It is also known in pictorial representations of ships in the New Kingdom Period. In the Theban tomb of Kenamon, at least one large jar, or pithos (fig. 4), is presented in the fore area of one of the ships (Davies and Faulkner 1947: 43, pl. VIII; Daressy 1895: pls. XIV–XV). It is usually assumed that it was the drinking water container, but they appear in multiple numbers aboard one ship, as on the Uluburun wreck, where they were used for storage of other goods. Thus the earliest concentration of these Collared Rim Jars in Late Bronze IIB, the thirteenth century B.C.E., is at Tel Nami, a coastal site with little agricultural hinterland and the Carmel ridge behind it. Several jars display impressed holes on the handles or rims that have previously been accorded an ethnic connotation by archaeologists dealing with the Hill Country, Trans and Cis Jordanian Israelite settlement (Zertal 1994: 55). At Nami, alongside these imprinted marks are incised ones resembling

what is probably a main trade in which Nami was involved and from which it gained its wealth, namely the "silent trade" in incense, which tends to leave no material remains. As time passed, the dependence of the economic systems on these traders placed them in a position of power. The line differentiating the intermediaries from entrepreneurs, mercenaries and pirates was thin, as was that between desert

a recognition of the habitat of the murex shells. Since many were needed for a small amount of dye, many had to be collected at a time. The ancients kept the murex shells in captivity where they showed cannibalistic tendencies. This can be seen in a hole they drill into the shell of the victim (Spanier and Karmon 1987). It is possible that the shallow waters of the coast in what is later known as the Phoenician coast made it easier to locate the fields in which the murex could be collected and thus lent itself to smaller operations, entrepreneurial ones, as seen at Akko, Shiqmona (Karmon and Spanier 1988), Dor and possibly Nami among others.

[27] Many have dealt with this topic in the past and there will, no doubt, be many more studies in the future (see esp. Esse 1992).

[28] The practice may have started with an attempt to strengthen the area where the rim was attached to the main body of a ceramic vessel. In time it might have become an aesthetic addition.

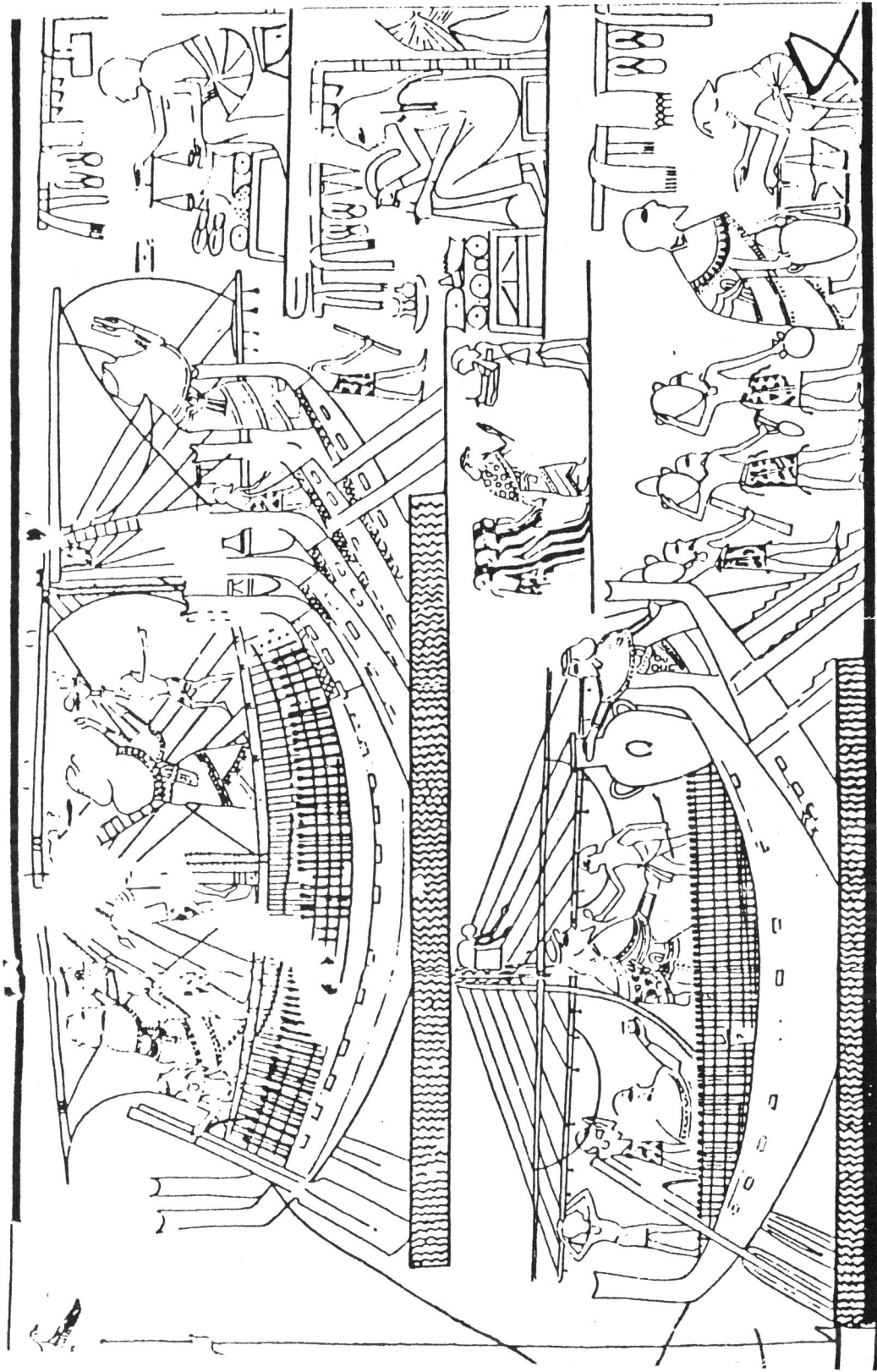

Fig. 4. Pithos aboard Boat. Drawing from Kenamon's Grave.

Cypro-Minoan signs that appear on Cypriot ceramics (fig. 5). The concurrent appearance of the Cypriot and the other marks, which are attributed to inland areas, may well be a reflection on the role of the anchorage of Tel Nami in maritime and inland trade, as well as on the people who carried it out.

As to those who used and introduced these vessels, or marks, to the hinterland, we cannot assign a particular ethnic identity, but there were plenty of groups on the move. There were coastal Canaanites and Syrian merchants, Egyptian, Cypriot, Aegean and coastal Anatolian mariners, the representatives of the system economies and the fringe mariner— "Nomads of the Sea" of various origins. One did not have to belong to any one group to employ a large jar.

In the process of changing from being "Nomads of the Sea" to entrepreneurs or merchants of the sea, these fringe groups were employed as economic mercenaries within the established, yet varied political and especially economic systems, and followed, usually, the recognized laws of trade in an international age. They served as intermediaries and brought their traditions to coastal settlements and along land routes to the economic hinterland. When the economic situation was no longer favorable, these same people reverted to marauding practices, and the image of "Sea Peoples" familiar to us from the Egyptian sources emerged. Hirelings, from fringe groups of economic or geographical nature, could cause a ripple in the tenuous equilibrium by becoming an essential part of a trade network, a position obtained because of their peculiar expertise: capital in shape of a boat and knowledge in navigation, prerequisites for a successful maritime trade. A combined set of roles of respectability and occasional pilfering became a way of life in the second part of the second millennium B.C.E. even to the heroes feted

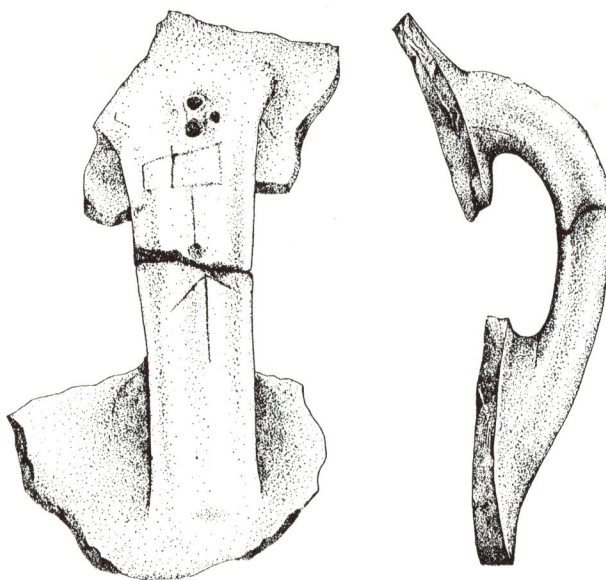

Fig. 5. Signs on Collared Rim Jars/*Pithoi* from Tel Nami.

in Homer's *Iliad* and *Odyssey*. It is impossible to indicate an exact date for each stage of the development. It is also hard to express the fluidity of the evolution to bar grams of roles. Those who started out as hirelings, carried out their own "sailors' trade" and a natural evolution to "entrepreneurial trade" and to economic competition with those who hired them, was a matter of time. It started, at least, by the fourteenth century, if not earlier, and continued to evolve during the thirteenth century B.C.E. The events of the twelfth century, the "Crisis Years," were the extension of that transition.

ACKNOWLEDGEMENTS

This paper would not have been written if it were not for the encouragement of those involved in *Res Maritimae* as well as Dr. S. Sherratt, Dr. A. Miller (Carmel Hospital in Haifa) and my co-workers at Nami Project. Thanks are due to the Israel Science Foundation and the Dorot Foundation for their financial support. Most of the work on this study was done while the author was a visiting scholar at Wolfson College, Oxford.

REFERENCES

Appian
1988   *Appian's Roman History,* in Loeb Classical Library, trans. H. White. Cambridge: Harvard University.

Altman, A.
1977   The Fate of Abdi Ashirta. *Ugarit Forschungen* 9: 1–10.

Artzy, M.
1985a   Merchandise and Merchantmen: On Ships and Shipping in the Late Bronze Age Levant. Pp. 135–40 in *Proceedings of the Second International Congress on Cypriote Studies,* Nicosia: Zavallis.

1985b   Supply and Demand: A Study of Second Millennium Cypriote Pottery in the Levant. Pp. 93–99 in *Production and Exchange in Aegean and Mediterranean Prehistory,* eds. A. B. Knapp and Tamara Stech, UCLA Institute of Archaeology Monographs 29. Los Angeles: University of California at Los Angeles.

1987   On Boats and Sea Peoples, *Bulletin of the American School of Oriental Research* 266: 75–85.

1988   Development of War/Fighting Boats of the IInd Millennium B.C. in the Eastern Mediterranean. *Report of the Department of Antiquities of Cyprus:* 181–86.

1991   Conical Cups and Pumice, Aegean Cult at Tel Nami, Israel. Pp. 203–6 in *Thalassa, the Prehistoric Aegean and the Sea, Aegeum VII,* eds. R. Laffineur and L. Basch, Liege: University of Liege.

1994   Incense, Camels and Collared Rim Jars: Desert Trade Routes and Maritime Outlets in the 2nd Millennium, *Oxford Journal of Archaeology* 13: 121–47.

1995   Nami: A Second Millennium International Maritime Trading Center in the Mediterranean. Pp. 17–41 in *Recent Discoveries in Israel: A View to the West,* ed. S. Giten. New York: Archaeological Institute of America Colloquia and Conference Papers 1.

Astour, M. C.
1981   Ugarit and the Great Powers in Ugarit. Pp. 3–29 in *Ugarit in Retrospect,* ed. G. D. Young, .Winona Lake: Eisenbrauns.

Åström, P.
1992   Continuity, Discontinuity, Catastrophe, Nucleation—some Remarks on Terminology. Pp. 17–30 in *The Crisis Years: The 12th Century B.C. from Beyond the Danube to the Tigris,* eds. W.

A. Ward and M. S. Joukowsky. Dubuque, Iowa: Kendall/Park.

Balensi, J.; Herrera, M. D.; and Artzy, M.
1993   Tell Abu Hawam. Pp. 7–14 in *Archaeological Excavations in the Holy Land, Revised Edition* ed. E. Stern, New York: Simon and Schuster.

Basch, L.
1987   *Le museé imagenaire de la marine antique.* Athens: Institute for the Preservation of Hellenic Nautical Traditions.

1994   Un Navire grec en Egypte à l'époque d'Ulysse. *Neptunia* 195: 19–26.

Basch, L., and Artzy, M.
1986   Ship Graffiti at Kition. Pp. 322–44 in *Excavations in Kition V,* eds. V. Karageorghis and Martha Demas. Nicosia: Department of Antiquities.

Bass, G. F.
1967   *A Bronze Age Shipwreck.* Philadelphia: Transactions of the American Philosophical Society 57.

1986   A Shipwreck at Ulu Burun (Kaş): 1984 Campaign. *American Journal of Archaeology* 90, 3: 269–96.

Berthold, R. M.
1984   *Rhodes in the Hellenistic Age.* Ithaca, NY: Cornell University.

Bietak, M.
1985   Response to T. Dothan. Pp. 216–19 in *Biblical Archaeology Today: Proceedings of the International Congress on Biblical Archaeology, Jerusalem, April 1984,* ed. J. Amitai. Jerusalem: Israel Exploration Society.

Bittel, K.
1983   Die archaeollogische Situation in Kleinasien um 1200 v.Chr. und wärend der nachfolgenden vie Jahrhunderte. Pp. 25–50 in *Griechenland, die Ägäis und die Levante während der Dark Ages." Symposium Zwettl 1980,* ed. S. Deger-Jalkotzy. SBWien 418.

Coubet, A.
1992   Reoccupatation of the Syrian Coast after the Destruction of the Crisis Years." Pp. 123–31 in *The Crisis Years: The 12th Century B.C. from Beyond the Danube to the Tigris,* eds. W. A. Ward and M. S. Joukowsky. Dubuque, Iowa: Kendall/Park.

Daressy, G.
1895   Une flottile phénicienne. *Revue Archéologique* 27: 286–92.

Davies, N. DeG., and Faulkner, R. O.
1947   A Syrian Trading Venture to Egypt. *Journal of Egpytian Archaeology* 33: 40–46.

Dever, W. G.
1992   The Late Bronze Age—Early Iron I Horizon in Syria-Palestine: Egyptians, Canaanites, Sea People," and Proto-Israelites. Pp. 99–110 in *The Crisis Years: The 12th Century B.C. from Beyond the Danube to the Tigris*, eds. W. A. Ward and M. S. Joukowsky. Dubuque, Iowa: Kendall/Park.

Dorsey, D. A.
1989   *The Roads and Highways of Ancient Israel*. Baltimore: Johns Hopkins University.

Esse, D. L.
1992   The Collared Rim Pithos at Megiddo: Ceramic Distribution and Ethnicity. *Journal of Near Eastern Studies* 51: 81-103.

Green, P.
1993   *Alexander to Actium*. London: Thames and Hudson.

Gruen, E. S.
1984   *The Hellenistic World and the Coming of Rome*. Berkeley University.

Güterbock, H. G.
1992   Survival of the Hittite Dynasty. Pp. 53–55 in *The Crisis Years: The 12th Century B.C. from Beyond the Danube to the Tigris*, eds. W. A. Ward and M. S. Joukowsky. Dubuque, Iowa: Kendall/Park.

Habachi, L.
1980   The Millitary Posts of Ramesses II on the Coastal Road and the Western Part of the Delta. *Bulletin de l'Institute Français d'Archéologie Orientale* 80: 12–30.

Hawkins, J. D.
1988   Kuzi Teshub and the Great Kings of Karkamis. *Anatolian Studies* 38: 99–108.

Heltzer, M.
1977   The Metal Trade of Ugarit and the Problem of Transportation of Commercial Goods. *Iraq* 39: 203–11.
1983   The Serdana in Ugarit, *Israel Oriental Society* 9: 9–16.

Hood, S.
1993   Amber in Egypt. Pp. 230–35 in *Amber in Archaeology*.(Proceedings of the Second International Conference on Amber in Archaeology, Librice 1990), eds. C. W. Beck and J. Bouzek.

James, F. W., and McGovern, P. E.
1993   *The Late Bronze Egyptian Garrison at Beth Shan: A Study of Levels VII and VIII*. University of Pennsylvania.

Karageorghis, V., and Demas, M.
1988   *Excavations at Maa-Paleokastro 1975–1986*, Nicosia: Zavallis.

1985   *Excavations at Kition V*. Nicosia: Department of Antiquities Cyprus.

Karmon, N., and Spanier, E.
1988   Remains of a Purple Dye Industry Found at Tel Shiqmona. *Israel Exploration Journal* 38: 184–86.

Klengel, H.
1993   *Syria: 3000–300 B.C.*, Berlin: Academie.

Knudzon, J. A.
1915   *Die El-Amarna Tafeln*, Leipzig.

Lagarce, J., and Lagarce, E.
1988   The Intrusion of the Sea Peoples and their Acculturation: A Parallel between Palestinian and Ras Ibn Hani Data. *Studies in the History and Archaeology of Palestine* III: 137–69.

Lambdin, T. O.
1953   The Misi-People of the Byblian Amarna Letters. *Journal of Cuneiform Studies* 7: 75–80.

Lambrou-Philipsen, C.
1993   Ugarit: a Late Bronze Age Thalasocracy? The Evidence of the Textual Sources. *Orientalia* 62: 163–70.

Larsen, M. T.
1982   Caravans and Trade in Ancient Mesopotamia and Asia Minor. *Bulletin of the Society for Mesopotamian Studies* 4: 33–45.
1987   Commercial Networks in the Ancient Near East. Pp. 47–56 in *Centre and Periphery in the Ancient World*, eds. M. Rowlands, M. Larsen and K. Kristiansen, Cambridge: Cambridge University.

Lehmann, G. A.
1979   Die Sikalaju—ein neues Zeugnis zu den 'Seevölker' Heerfharten. *UF* 11: 481–94.

Leonard, A., Jr.
1987   The Significance of Mycenaean Pottery Found East of the Jordan River. *Studies in the History and Archaeology of Jordan* III: 261–66.

Lesko, L. H.
1992   Egypt in the 12th Century B.C. Pp. 151–56 in *The Crisis Years: The 12th Century B.C. from Beyond the Danube to the Tigris*, eds. W. A. Ward and M. S. Joukowsky. Dubuque, Iowa: Kendall/Park.

Linder, E.
1981   Ugarit: A Canaanite Thalssocracy? Pp. 31–42 in *Ugarit in Retrospect*, ed. G. D. Young, Winona Lake, IN: Eisenbrauns.

Liverani, M.
1987   The Collapse of the Near Eastern Regional System at the End of the Bronze Age in Case of Syria. Pp. 66–73 in *Centre and Periphery in the Ancient World*, eds. M. Rowlands, M. Larsen and

K. Kristiansen, Cambridge: Cambridge University.

Marx, E.
1992   Are There Pastoral Nomads in the Middle East?
        Pp. 255–60 in *Pastoralism in the Levant.* eds.
        Bar-Yosef, O. and Khazanov, A. Madison: University of Wisconsin.

Mayerson, P.
1989   Saracens and Romans: Micro-Macro relationships. *Bulletin of the American Oriental Society*
        274: 71–79.
1994   *Monks, Martyrs, Soldiers and Saracens.* Jerusalem: Israel Exploration Society.

Merrillees, R. S.
1992   The Crisis Years: Cyprus, A Rejoinder. Pp.
        87–92 in *The Crisis Years: The 12th Century B.C.
        from Beyond the Danube to the Tigris*, eds. W.
        A. Ward and M. S. Joukowsky. Dubuque, Iowa:
        Kendall/Park.

Muhly, J. D.
1991   Egypt, the Aegean and Late Bronze Age Chronology in the Eastern Mediterranean: A Review
        Article. *Journal of Mediterranean Archaeology*
        4: 235–47.

Negbi, O.
1991   Were there Sea Peoples in the Central Jordan
        Valley at the Transition from the Bronze Age to
        the Iron Age? *Tel Aviv*: 205–43.

Negbi, O., and Negbi, M.
1993   Stirrup Jars Versus Canaanite Jars: Their Contents and Reciprocal Trade. Pp. 319–29 in *Wace
        and Blegen,* ed. Carol Zerner, Amsterdam: G.
        C. Giebens.

Neve, P.
1989   Bogazköy-Hattusha. New Results of Excavations in the Upper City. *Anatolica* 16: 7–19.

Oren, E. D.
1987   The 'Ways of Horus' in North Sinai. Pp. 69–120
        in *Egypt, Israel, Sinai—Archaeological and Historical Relationships in the Biblical Period,* ed.
        A. F. Rainey, Tel Aviv: Tel Aviv University.

Otten, H.
1983   Die letzte Phase des hethitischen Grossreiches
        nach den Texten. Pp. 13–21 in *Griechenland,
        die Ägäis und die Levante während der Dark
        Ages." Symposium Zwettl 1980,* ed. S. Deger-
        Jalkotzy. SBWien 418.

Parkinson, R., and Schonfield, L.
1993   Akhenaten's Army? *Egyptian Archaeology* 3:
        34–36.

Plutarch
1972   *The Fall of the Roman Republic,* trans. Rex
        Warner. New York: Penguin.

Redford, D. B.
1992   *Egypt, Canaan, and Israel in Ancient Times.*
        Princeton: Princeton University.

Sandars, N. K.
1978   *The Sea Peoples.* London: Thames and Hudson.

Säve-Söderbergh, T.
1946   *The Navy of the Eighteenth Egyptian Dynasty,*
        Uppsala Universitets Årsskrift 6.

Sherratt, A., and Sherratt, S.
1991   From Luxuries to Commodities: The Nature of
        Mediterranean Bronze Age Trading Systems. Pp.
        351–86 in *Bronze Age Trade in the Mediterranean,* Studies in Mediterranean Archaeology,
        Jonsered: Åströms.

Sherratt, S.
1994   Commerce, Iron and Ideology: Metallurgical
        Innovations in 10th–11th Century Cyprus. Pp.
        59–106 in *Proceedings of the International Symposium Cyprus in the 11th Century,* ed. V.
        Karageorghis. Nicosia: Leventis Foundation.

Sherratt, S., and Crouwel, J. H.
1987   Mycenaean Pottery from Cilicia in Oxford. *Oxford Journal of Archaeology* 6: 325–52.

Singer, I.
1985   The Beginning of Philistine settlement in Canaan
        and the Northern Boundary of Philistia. *Tel Aviv*
        12: 109–22.
1988a   Mereneptah's Campaign to Canaan and the
        Egyptian Occupation of the Southern Costal
        Plain of Palestine in the Ramesside Period. *Bulletin of the American Oriental Society* 269: 1–10.
1988b   The Origin of the Sea Peoples and Their Settlement on the Coast of Canaan. Pp. 239–50 in
        Society and Economy in the Eastern Mediterranean, eds. M. Heltzer and E. Lepinski, Leuven:
        Orientalia Lovaniensia Analecta 23.

Sopher, D. E.
1977   *The Sea Nomads.* Singapore: The National Museum.

Spanier, E., and Karmon, N.
1987   Muricid Snails and the Ancient Dye Industries.
        Pp. 179–92 in *The Royal Purple and Biblical
        Blue,* ed. E. Spanier, Jerusalem: Keter.

Stieglitz, R. R.
1994   The Minoan Origin of Tyrian Purple. *Biblical
        Archaeologist* 57: 46–54.

Tubb, J. N.
1988   The Role of the Sea Peoples in the Bronze Industry of Palestine Transjordan in the Late
        Bronze–Early Iron Age Transition. Pp. 99–112
        in *Bronze Working Centers of Western Asia,* ed.
        London: J. E. Curtis.

Ussishkin, D.
1985   Level VII and VI at Tel Lachish and the End of
        the Late Bronze Age in Canaan. Pp. 213–28 in
        *Palestine in the Bronze and Iron Ages, Papers
        Dedicated to Olga Tufnell*. ed. J. N. Tubb. Lon-
        don: Institute of Archaeology.

Ward, W. A., and Joukowsky, M. S. (eds.)
1992   *The Crisis Years: The 12th Century B.C. from
        Beyond the Danube to the Tigris*. Dubuque,
        Iowa: Kendall/Park.

Weinstein, J.
1992   The Collapse of the Egyptian Empire in the
        Southern Levant. Pp. 142–50 in *The Crisis
        Years: The 12th Century B.C. from Beyond the*
        Danube to the Tigris, eds. W. A. Ward and M.
        S. Joukowsky. Dubuque, Iowa: Kendall/Park.

Yon, M.
1992   The End of the Kingdom of Ugarit. Pp. 111–22
        in T*The Crisis Years: The 12th Century B.C. from
        Beyond the Danube to the Tigris*, eds. W. A.
        Ward and M. S. Joukowsky. Dubuque, Iowa:
        Kendall/Park.

Zertal, A.
1994   "To the Land of the Peizzites and the Giants":
        On Israelite Settlement in the Hill Country of
        Manasseh. Pp. 47–69 in *From Nomadism to
        Monarchy*, eds. I. Finkelstein and N. Naʾaman,
        Jerusalem: Israel Exploration Society.

Une représentation de navire de type égéen dans l'oasis de Dakhleh (Égypte) vers 1200 av. J.-C.

LUCIEN BASCH

Marine Academy Belgium
Avenue A. Huysmans 206, Bte 9
Bruxelles 1050
BELGIQUE

At the end of the thirteenth century B.C.E., a new type of ship that specialized in naval war appeared in the Aegean. An unpublished photograph of a representation of a ship of this type was taken in 1936 or 1937 by H. A. Winkler at Teneida, a village of the oasis of Dakhleh (Egypt). The crew shown on board the ship is Libyan. The whole picture seems to be an ex-voto engraved by a group of pirates on their way to or from Nubia or Kordofan, after the looting of at least four merchant ships, which are also represented.

Dans le domaine égéen—Grèce occidentale, archipel et Crète— l'iconographie du navire pendant l'Âge du Bronze s'est montrée généreuse: elle nous permet, malgré ses lacunes, d'être sûrs que la marine égéenne des origines fut affaire de tâtonnements: quatre ou cinq types d'embarcations coexistaient, dont certains, en termes d'évolution, menaient à des impasses technologiques (Basch 1991, *passim*). C'est dire que le sceau minoen trouvé à Platanos (Crète), daté de 1800 av. J.-C. environ (fig. 1), n'est, à cette époque, qu'un type de navire égéen parmi d'autres, mais promis, lui, à un avenir bimillénaire. Qu'a-t-il de particulier? D'abord, c'est un voilier, l'un des premiers en mer Égée. Mais, surtout, sa structure est différente de celle de ses contemporains; elle est caractérisée par une étrave verticale qui domine le prolongement de la quille, qui s'étend devant elle. Cette projection n'est évidemment pas un éperon, arme de guerre, d'ailleurs impensable sur un voilier, mais elle constitue un allongement «artificiel» de la coque au niveau de la carène, forme primitive de taillemer, peut-être, et sûrement une amélioration des qualités nautiques d'une coque apparemment trapue—et cela par un procédé très simple, certainement apparu pour la première fois en mer Égée.

À la fin de l'Âge du Bronze (HR III B et HR III C) se produit un phénomène d'importance majeure dans l'architecture navale européenne: la création du «vaisseau long», construit tout spécialement pour la guerre sur mer et qui descend en ligne directe du navire de Platanos, distinct du «vaisseau rond», destiné au transport.

On rencontre les deux types, ensemble, sur ce qui semble avoir été le montant d'un dromos d'une tombe de Dramesi (Béotie), identifiée par Blegen (1949) comme l'Hyria homérique (fig. 2). Se fondant sur la céramique trouvée dans la tombe, Blegen l'attribuait, à titre d'hypothèse, à l'HR I. Toutefois, cette date me paraît trop haute pour le type de vaisseaux incisés dans le montant; rien n'empêche que ces incisions aient été pratiquées à une date plus basse. Le vaisseau supérieur, sur la fig. 2, a, comme le navire de Platanos, une étrave verticale, qui domine une projection, ici fort courte, de la quille; il est doté d'un mât central et d'une voile. Mais cette fois, sa quille est absolument rectiligne (fig. 3), au contraire de celle du

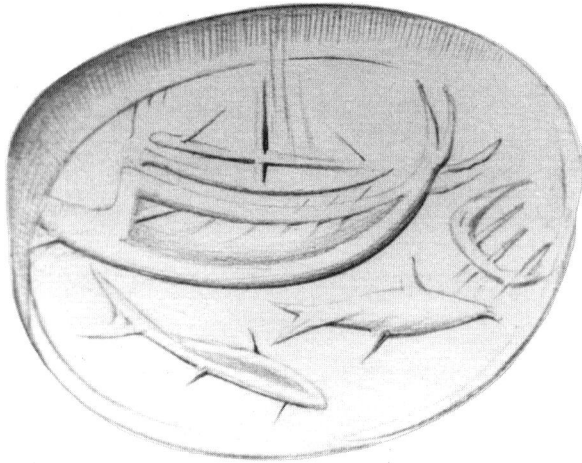

Fig. 1. Sceau de Platanós (Crète), vers 1800 av. J.-C. Musée d'Heraklion, n° 1079. Dessin: Piet De Jong.

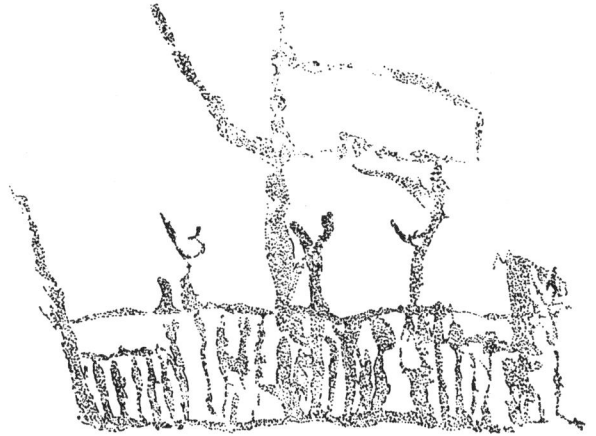

Fig. 3. Navire de guerre mycénien (navire du registre supérieur de la fig. 2).

Fig. 2. Graffiti incisés sur unpilier. Dramesi (Béotie), entre 1400 et 1200 av. J.-C. Musée de Scimatari.

Fig. 4. Navire peint sur un sarcophage trouvé à Gazi (Crète), vers 1200 av. J.-C. Musée d'Heraklion.

«vaisseau rond», dû sans doute à la même main et qui figure au-dessus de lui. La forme très allongée du «vaisseau long» donne à penser que sa propulsion pouvait aussi être assurée par des rames.

Les témoignages d'un type aussi caractéristique et aussi propre à l'Égée vont se multiplier à la fin de l'Âge du Bronze, c'est-à-dire à une époque où les Mycéniens, longtemps après avoir conquis la Crète, se montrent très actifs sur tous les rivages de la Méditerranée, surtout orientale. Je rappelle ici quelques types, bien connus.

En Crète: un navire peint sur un sarcophage de Gazi, daté de 1200 environ, présente la même étrave verticale s'encastrant dans une quille droite; la projection en avant de l'étrave est ici très prononcée (fig. 4).

À Chypre: un graffito d'Enkomi, vers 1200 av. J.-C. (fig. 5): l'étrave a disparu, mais il est aisé de la reconstituer.

En Grèce propre: une peinture sur une pyxis provenant de Tragana, près de Pylos, datant de 1150 av. J.-C. environ (fig. 6). Sur cet exemplaire, la projection est courte. On y remarque un «château de proue», de structure complexe, qui est certainement l'ancêtre des *ikria* des navires grecs de l'époque géométrique, qui servaient de postes de combat (fig. 7 et 8). Cette structure existe aussi sur le navire de Dramesi et celui d'Enkomi; il est absent de celui de Gazi.

Dans l'île de Milo, vers 1150 av. J.-C. (fig. 9); il convient d'observer qu'ici la jonction entre l'étrave verticale

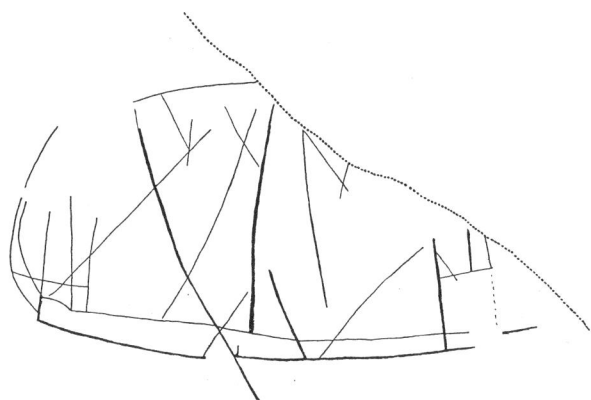

Fig. 5. Graffito d'Enkomi (Chypre), vers 1200 av. J.-C.

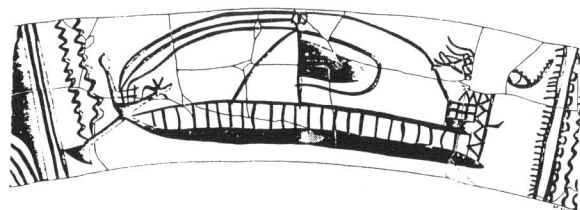

Fig. 6. Navire peint sur une boîte ronde. Tragana (près de Pylos), Grèce. Vers 1150 av. J.-C. Dessin: Professeur Korrès.

Fig. 7. Fragment de vase attique, 8e siècle av. J.-C. (Musée du Louvre, A 527). Noter le «château de proue», dominant l'éperon. Cet éperon a pour origine la projection de la quille des fig. 1 à 6, 9, 10, 13 et 14.

Fig. 8. Fragment de vase attique, 8e siècle av. J.-C. (Musée du Louvre, A 528). Combat sur le «château de proue». Un assaillant, monté à bord, a la gorge percée d'une flèche. La partie représentant l'éperon est manquante.

et la quille est une reconstitution due à S. Marinatos (1933: 219, fig. 10); elle est cependant hautement vraisemblable.

Signalons enfin la silhouette d'un navire de la même famille, réduite, à la façon d'un idéogramme, à ses éléments les plus caractéristiques, et par là d'autant plus intéressante, gravée dans un rocher du Mont Carmel, face à la mer, près de Haifa (fig. 10). Il fut publié, mais incompris, en 1971 (Wreschner 1971).[1] Ce graffito témoigne soit d'une incursion égéenne au Levant, soit d'une adoption de ce type de navire par un autre peuple méditerranéen.

La représentation d'un tel navire dans une oasis d'Égypte est autrement surprenante et est susceptible d'éclairer d'un jour nouveau un épisode de l'histoire de ce pays. Hans A. Winkler dirigea, en 1936 et 1937, sous les auspices de l'Egypt Exploration Society, et grâce à l'aide financière de Sir Robert Mond, une exploration systématique des déserts égyptiens, à la recherche de gravures rupestres. Une partie du résultat de ces expéditions fut publiée en 1937 et 1938 en deux volumes (Winkler 1937 et 1938), présentés comme un rapport préliminaire et contenant 199 photographies de ces gravures, ce qui ne représente qu'environ un dixième de la récolte photographique. Le choix de Winkler n'était pas neutre: il se portait avant tout

---

[1] Je suis très reconnaissant envers Mme le Dr M. Artzy, de l'Univeristé de Haifa, non seulement pour m'avoir signalé cet article, mais surtout pour m'avoir guidé sur le site ; il lui revient d'avoir correctement identifié ce graffito.

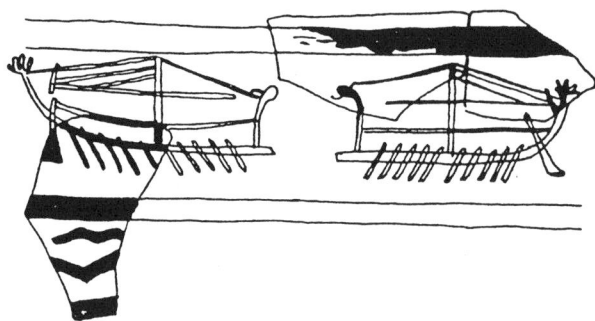

Fig. 9. Deux fragments de vase provenant de Phylacopi (île de Milo), vers 1150 av. J.-C. Reconstitution de S. Marinatos (1933: 219, fig. 10).

Fig. 10. Gravure rupestre, Mont Carmel (Israël). Probablement entre 1250 et 1150 av. J.-C.

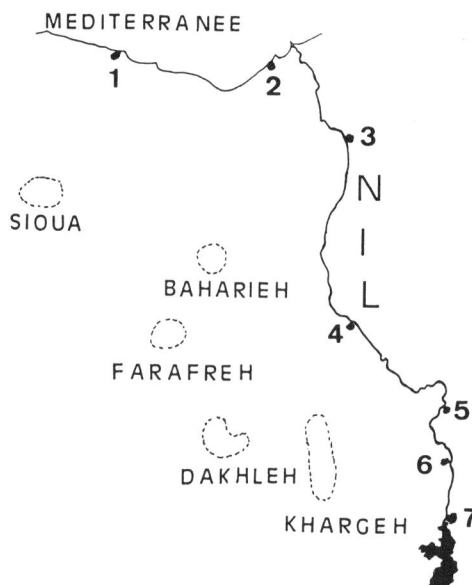

Fig. 11. Les oasis d'Égypte: 1: Marsa Matruh 2: Alexandrie 3: Le Caire 4: Asyut 5: Louxor 6: Edfou 7: Assouan.

images de navires, non relevées par Winkler (Giddy 1987: 279–81).

Le site exploré par ce dernier, et auquel il attribue le n° 69, est décrit par lui de la manière suivante:

> Several hills at the eastern end of the *hatîya* of Tenîda … Arabic inscriptions and *wusûm*. Ibex, ostriches; cattle, camels, horses, dogs. Crocodiles swallowing men. Men with bow, with shield and sword, with lance, with throwing irons, with pistols, with guns. Men on horseback, on camel-back. Row of fettered slaves. Naked women, some beside *angarêb,* the native bedstead. Human hand, outlines of feet, lines, probably gaming-boards. On the surface stone implements, ostrich-shells, postsherds (Winkler 1939: 8–9).

L'une de ces gravures (fig. 13), non publiée par Winkler, présente toutes les caractéristiques du «vaisseau long» minoen ou mycénien: quille longue et rectiligne, étrave rigoureusement verticale, devant laquelle la quille forme une longue projection, un «château de proue» important et un gouvernail (latéral) à pale triangulaire semblable à celles des fig. 4, 6 et 9. Si, comme toutes les gravures rupestres, l'image est forcément tracée avec un certain schématisme,

sur les gravures représentant des bateaux remontant à l'époque prédynastique, sur lesquels il fondait certaines théories relatives au peuplement de la vallée du Nil.[2]

Winkler repéra dans l'oasis de Dakhleh treize sites de gravures rupestres. Cette oasis (fig. 11 et 12) comprend seize villages, dont le chef-lieu, Mut. Dakhleh est relié à l'oasis de Kargeh par une piste immémoriale, le Darb el Gubbari, qui contourne, par le sud, un plateau (Abu Tartur) qui sépare les deux oasis (fig. 12). Le village de Teneida (on trouve d'autres graphies: Tineida, Tenîda), le plus oriental de l'oasis de Dakhleh, est situé sur cette piste; il s'agit d'un carrefour de caravanes et les rochers des environs sont couverts de gravures allant de la préhistoire à des images de trains. Leur inventaire par Winkler est certainement incomplet: à proximité de Teneida, le site de Halfat el-Bir a livré d'autres

[2] Je remercie ici très vivement Madame Patricia Spencer, Secrétaire de l'Egypt Exploration Society, pour m'avoir autorisé, en 1991, à examiner la totalité des photographies de l'expédition de H. A. Winkler, conservées au siège de la Society, à Londres, ce qui me permit de découvrir, à ma très grande surprise, le document inattendu présenté ici.

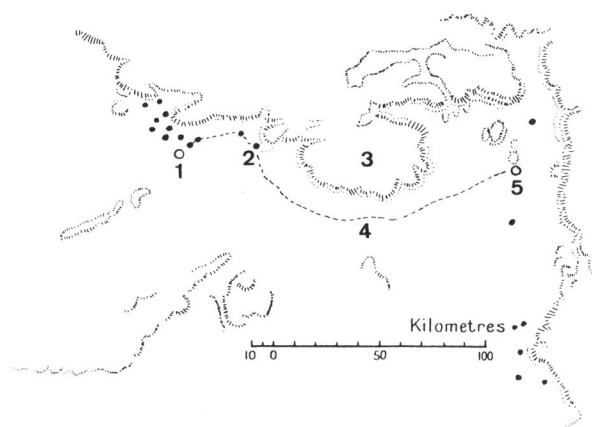

Fig. 12. Les oasis de Dakhleh et de Khargeh. 1: Mut, chef-lieu de l'oasis de Dakhleh. 2: village de Teneida. 3: plateau d'Abu Tartur. 4: piste de Darb el-Gubbari. 5: Qasr Khargeh, chef-lieu de l'oasis de Khargeh.

Fig. 13. Gravure rupestre. Teneida. Photo: Egypt Exploration Society.

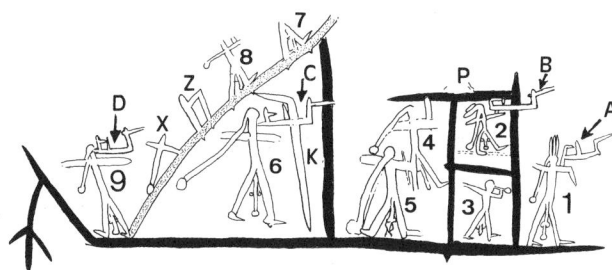

Fig. 14. Dessin d'après la fig. 13. En noir: traits appartenant au navire. En pointillé: hauban ? 1 à 9: personnages. A, B, C, D: modèles de navires. K : crosse de jet ou «gourdin de combat». X, Z: objets non identifiés.

elle est exceptionnelle par le soin des détails. Il semble, par ailleurs, qu'elle faisait partie d'un ensemble plus vaste. C'est précisément le soin apporté aux détails qui permet de se poser une série de questions.

— Le trait oblique en arrière du mât (en pointillés sur la fig. 14) représente-t-il un hauban ou un étai arrière? En tout cas, soit l'un, soit l'autre: une comparaison avec le navire de Tragana (fig. 6) s'impose. La présence de deux membres de l'équipage (les n° 7 et 8) debout sur ce cordage ne

contredit pas cette hypothèse: grimper dans le gréement est de toutes les époques; dès 2400 av. J.-C. environ, on en trouve, en Égypte, une représentation: un marin grimpant le long d'un étai (Landström 1970: 43, fig. 117). Ici, les personnages sont représentés debout, ce qui n'est pas la position d'un marin grimpant, mais il est compréhensible que la position réelle était difficilement réalisable dans une gravure rupestre. Quant aux «objets» X et Z, je ne suis pas parvenu à les identifier.

— À quatre des neuf membres de l'équipage (il en existait peut-être un dixième en P) est rattaché un objet chaque fois semblable (A, B, C et D), rattaché respectivement aux personnages 1, 2, 6 et 9. Cet objet n'est pas difficile à identifier, bien qu'il soit inattendu: il s'agit d'un modèle de bateau, pouvu d'un petit mât central, mais qui n'a rien de commun avec le navire principal de type égéen (fig. 15). La figure de proue de ces quatre bateaux est, dans tous les cas, une tête d'oiseau au bec exagérément allongé, évoquant une tête de canard. L'ornement de poupe est d'interprétation plus difficile: sur les navires A et B on songera à une courbure sans caractère animal ou anthropomorphique et sur les navires C et D à un profil humain stylisé, au nez proéminent. C'est à Chypre, et uniquement à Chypre, que l'on trouve tous les parallèles de ces extrémités (à une époque postérieure, il est vrai, mais les exemples de conservatisme dans l'ornementation à caractère plus ou moins magique sont nombreux): la tête d'oiseau, en proue ou en poupe (fig. 16 A, B) et l'ornement de poupe soit en profil humain stylisé (fig. 16 C), soit en forme de courbure purement géométrique (fig. 16 D) ou de courbure mi-géométrique, mi-animale (fig. 16 E).[3]

[3] Assez curieusement, c'est à Chypre que nous ramène cette extraordinaire cargaison de modèles réduits: Kinyras, roi mythique de Chypre à la fin de l'Âge du Bronze, qui avait offert à Agamemnon une cuirasse de bronze (*Iliade,* XI, 20), avait, d'après un récit légendaire, promis à Ménélas l'envoi de cinquante vaisseaux en vue de participer à la guerre contre

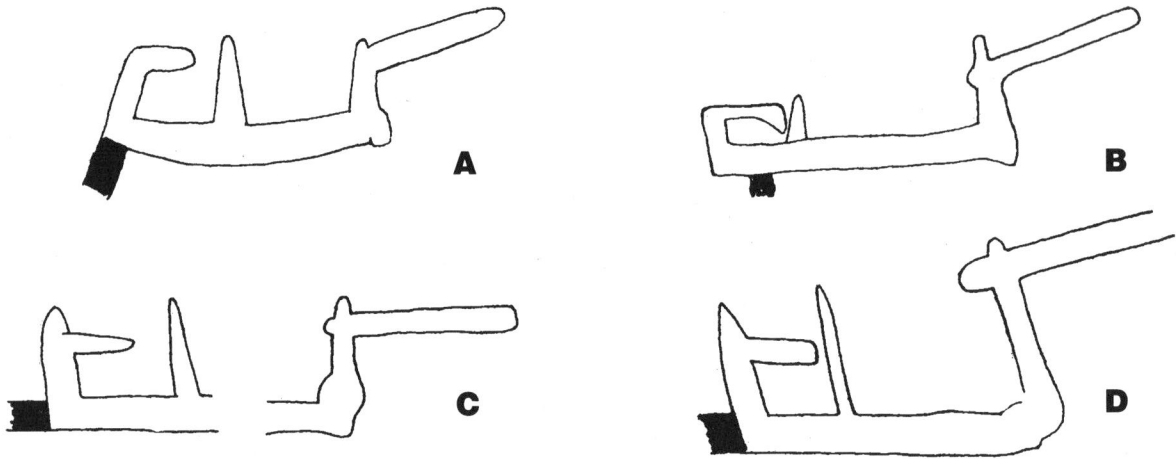

Fig. 15. Modèles A, B, C et D (cf. fig. 14). En noi: le lien qui rattache chaque modèle à un membre de l'équipage (respectivement: 1, 2, 6 et 9).

— Au point de vue typologique, le navire de Teneida est le plus proche de celui de Gazi par la longueur de la projection de proue et de celui de Tragana par l'importance du «château de proue». On voit ici qu'il était à deux étages. Le personnage n° 3, seul membre de l'équipage à ne pas porter de tresse, ne tient pas de modèle de navire; un examen très attentif montre qu'il porte à sa bouche une espèce de trompette, ce qui paraîtrait saugrenu sans les considérations de R. Rebuffat (1977) sur les pirates étrusques, appelés plusieurs fois (d'après des textes de Ménandre, d'Hésychius et de Photius: Gras 1977: 55, n. 17) «pirates-trompettes» (ληιστοσαλπιγκταί). L'usage de la trompette étrusque dans le but de créer la terreur était familier dans le monde antique, comme en témoigne, par exemple, l'*Énéide,* VIII, 524–30. Je ne songe évidemment pas à déduire de la présence de ce joueur de trompette une origine pré-étrusque pour le navire de Teneida: plus simplement, l'usage de cet instrument paraît être plus ancien qu'on pouvait le soupçonner et il est indicatif du caractère guerrier du navire (fig. 17).

— L'équipage n'a, de toute évidence, aucune caractéristique pouvant le rattacher au monde mycénien. Tous les personnages sont représentés absolument nus; l'auteur a insisté sur deux particularités: les parties sexuelles, figurées avec un luxe de détails qui permet de constater la pratique de la circoncision, et la chevelure des personnages 1, 4, 5, 6 et 9 (celle des n° 7 et 8 est perdue): une tresse gigantesque, terminée par une boule. À ma connaissance,

l'iconographie égyptienne ne connaît rien de semblable. Par ailleurs, il est frappant de constater que, selon Hérodote, quatre tribus libyennes, les Maces, les Machlyes, les Auses et les Maxyes, se distinguaient par le soin apporté à leur coiffure, différente pour chaque tribu (Hérodote IV: 175, 180 et 191); les Machlyes, en particulier, avaient pour signe distinctif de laisser pousser les cheveux sur la nuque. Ce qui achève de donner un caractère libyen à l'équipage est la présence, devant le personnage n° 6, d'un «bâton» à l'extrémité recourbée obliquement vers le haut (fig. 18); il s'agit d'une crosse de jet, arme primitive bien connue des Égyptiens. L'hiéroglyphe qui le désigne a exactement la même forme et, dans certains textes, il désigne un gourdin utilisé à des fins guerrières par les Libyens (Gardiner 1976: 513, hiéroglyphe T 14); ici, représenté surdimensionné, trônant au centre du navire, il a une valeur emblématique, celle qu'aurait pu avoir, en d'autres temps, un drapeau libyen.

L'un des membres de l'équipage se distingue encore plus nettement des autres que le n° 3: le n° 1, debout devant le «château de proue», c'est-à-dire occupant une position insigne, est le seul à porter, en plus de sa tresse, une coiffure qui semble être une couronne de plumes verticalement plantées. Si les représentations égyptiennes des habitants de Libye (Tehenou ou Temehou) les montrent régulièrement coiffés d'un nombre variable de plumes (de une à quatre: Bates 1914: 43 et 130, pl. I, II, III et V), celles-ci sont toujours très espacées et toujours plantées obliquement dans la chevelure. Ici, nous voyons trois plumes rigoureusement

---

Troie; toutefois, Kinyras tricha: il n'envoya qu'un seul vaisseau, qui transportait quarante-neuf modèles de navires en argile (références sur Kinyras: Lipinski 1992, *sub verbo*). Toutefois, je ne crois pas à une parenté entre la gravure rupestre et cette légende, mais plutôt à une singulière coïncidence.

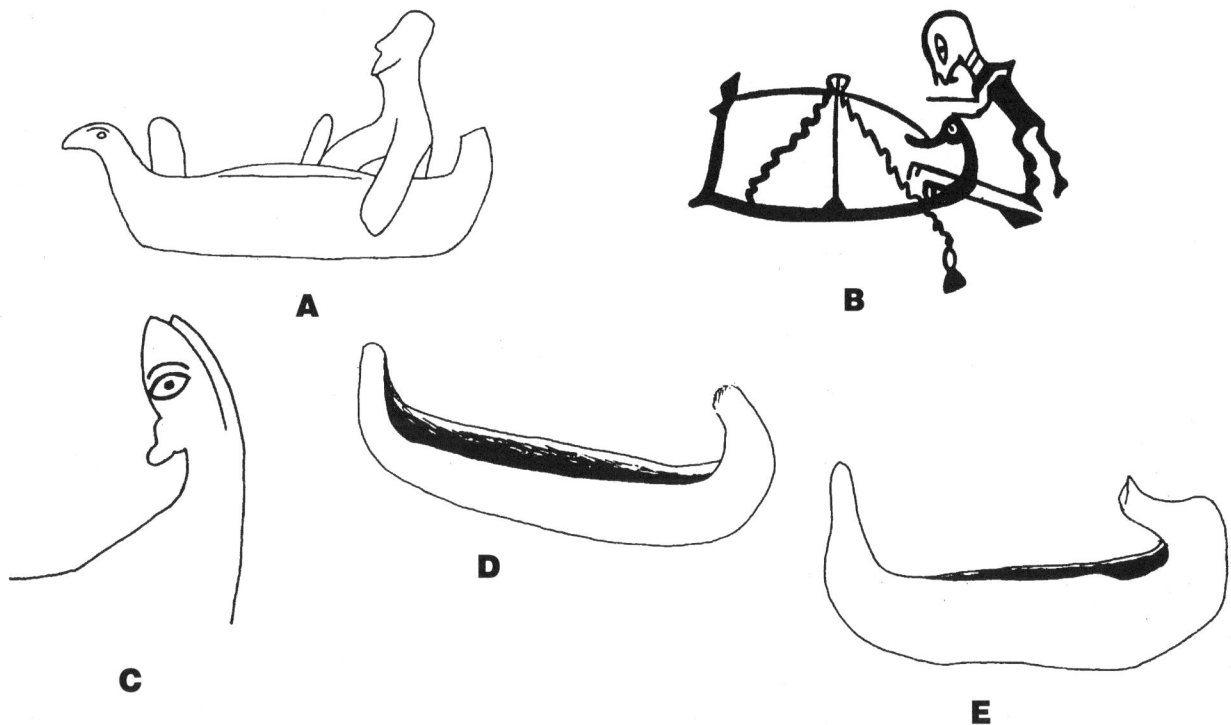

Fig. 16. A) Modèle chypriote, provenant probablement de Yialousa, vers 600 av. J.-C. Musée archéologique de Nicosie, n° 1937 / VI–8/3; B) Peinture de vase chypriote, vers 600 av. J.-C. Musée archéologique de Nicosie, n° 1947 / 1–16/1; C) «Figure de poupe» d'un modèle chypriote, provenant d'Amathonte. 6e siècle av. J.-C. Metropolitan Museum of Art, collection Cesnola, n° 74.51.1752; D) Modèle chypriote provenant d'Amathonte, vers 600 av. J.-C. British Museum, n° 94.11–1184; E) Modèle chypriote (provenance inconnue), vers 600 av. J.-C. Collection Pierides, Larnaca.

verticales, très semblables à la fameuse coiffure dite «couronne de plumes», caractéristique de certains Peuples de la Mer: les Peleset (ou Philistins), mais aussi les Tjeker et, peut-être, des Denyen et des Shekelesh (Sandars 1985: 134). Cette «couronne de plumes» ne semblait être connue qu'à l'est du Delta. Toutefois, D. B. Redford a fait observer que dans l'inscription célébrant la victoire de Ramsès III sur les Libyens en l'an 5 de son règne, sur son temple funéraire de Medinet Habu, figurent parmi les captifs deux chefs dont le nom n'est pas libyen (Redford [1992: 250] les rend par «Melie» et «Moschion», ce qui les rend proches du grec) et qui sont les seuls à porter la «couronne de plumes» à l'ouest du Delta (Kitchen 1983: 24, 14–15). Il n'est pas indifférent de noter que des tessons de céramique datés de l'HR III C représentant des personnages portant une coiffure similaire ont été trouvés à Cos (Morricone 1975: fig. 357 a–c).

À la réserve possible du personnage n° 1, il paraît assuré que tout l'équipage est formé d'un peuple habitant la Libye, mais je ne crois pas qu'il soit possible d'être plus précis; d'après W. Hölscher (1937), les Mashouash, alliés des Libyens, étaient circoncis, au contraire de ceux-ci, mais

G. A. Wainwright (1962) réfutait cette opinion. Je n'oserais départager ces auteurs.

* * * * *

Après cette analyse de la représentation du navire et de son équipage, se posent des questions relatives à leur importance dans l'architecture navale de la fin de l'Âge du Bronze et, enfin, à la signification de cette gravure rupestre dans une oasis égyptienne aussi éloignée de la mer.

Au point de vue de l'architecture navale, on ne peut manquer d'être frappé par la longueur remarquable de la «projection» qui prolonge la quille au-delà de l'étrave. L'art rupestre est forcément schématique et tend, pour cette raison même, à accentuer des caractéristiques qui semblaient importantes à l'auteur; j'incline, pour ce motif, à penser que la «projection» devait, dans la réalité, être en effet importante. Cet élément n'est d'ailleurs pas neuf à cette époque, si l'on considère l'importance de la «projection» du navire de Gazi. Il est communément admis que cette dernière «projection» n'est pas à proprement parler un éperon au sens d'une arme de choc, étant donné qu'il est

Fig. 17. Détail de la fig. 13: «château de proue».

surmonté d'une espèce de figure de proue qui serait nécessairement très endommagée en cas de rencontre brutale avec la coque d'un navire adverse. Sur le navire de Teneida, il n'existe aucune «figure de proue», pas plus qu'une structure quelconque qui serait forcément endommagée en cas de choc. Par ailleurs, la présence d'un personnage très particulier (cf. *supra*) debout sur la «projection» rend pratiquement inconcevable qu'elle ait été entièrement située sous l'eau: elle était probablement située au niveau de la mer, même si on la voit dans le strict prolongement de la quille, nécessairement sous-marine: dans la réalité, la projection pouvait être légèrement surélevée par rapport à la quille; c'est d'ailleurs ce que montre le navire de Gazi, et, un peu plus de quatre siècles plus tard, les navires de l'époque géométrique (cf. fig. 7). La «projection» du navire de Teneida aurait donc, théoriquement, *pu* jouer le rôle d'un véritable éperon.

Ce qui rend cette hypothèse incertaine est la fragilité apparente de cette longue aiguille, mais il faut noter qu'on retrouve cette même silhouette d'un éperon long et frêle sur un navire peint sur un vase du Géométrique Récent trouvé à Khaniale Tekke (Crète) (Boardman 1967: 73 et pl. 14, 21) (fig. 19). Sur cette dernière représentation, la nature offensive de l'éperon ne fait aucun doute: il est surmonté de deux *proembola* qui avaient manifestement pour but d'amortir le choc dans les parties hautes de l'étrave. On voit que, sur le plan technique, les arguments «pour» et «contre» s'équilibrent à peu près, mais un examen de la situation des forces antagonistes en présence dans la région du Delta et de la côte libyenne vers 1200 av. J.-C. me paraît ici utile.

Marsa Matruh, seul bon port de la Marmarique, doit nous intéresser particulièrement: situé à environ 250 km à l'ouest d'Alexandrie, à mi-chemin entre le Delta et la Cyrénaïque, relativement proche de l'extrémité orientale de la Crète et au débouché d'une piste menant à l'oasis de Siwah, Marsa Matruh fut, au cours de deux siècles au moins, un centre actif d'échanges commerciaux internationaux. Des fouilles, commencées au cours de l'hiver 1913/1914 et poursuivies en 1985, 1987 et 1989 ont livré, dans un îlot situé au centre de la lagune actuelle de Marsa Matruh (l'«îlot Bates») de la céramique chypriote, égyptienne, crétoise, mycénienne et cananéenne, datée du 14e et du 13e siècles av. J.-C. (Bates 1927; White 1986, 1989 et 1990). Tout indique que si ces contacts furent pacifiques et que des navires marchands chargés de marchandises diverses se rendaient fréquemment dans un port à l'ouest du Delta, cette même région fut certainement, dès le début du règne de Ramsès II, sinon plus tôt, l'objet d'incursions soit isolées, soit organisées, de pirates et de guerriers venus du nord. Deux textes éclairent cette situation:

1. La stèle d'Assouan de l'an 2 (Breasted 1906: 204–205, n° 478; Kitchen 1979: 6, 345) célèbre la victoire du Pharaon sur les «guerriers de la Très Verte». Le lieu d'origine de ces envahisseurs n'est pas précisé, mais l'intérêt du texte est de démontrer que l'Égypte était menacée par mer dès le début du règne.
2. Une stèle de Tanis, non datée, mais également du règne de Ramsès II et vraisemblablement à peu près contemporaine de la première, doit en être rapprochée. Étudiée par J. Yoyotte (1949), elle nous apprend que «les (gens des) Îles-qui-sont-au-milieu (de la Très Verte) sont sous sa crainte et viennent à lui avec les envois de leurs rois, (car la frayeur qu'il inspire) gouverne (?) leurs coeurs. Quant aux Shardanes au coeur rebelle, on ne savait les combattre de toute éternité; ils venaient (et leur coeur [?]) était confiant(?) … sur des vaisseaux-combattants-au-milieu-de-la-mer; on n'aurait su tenir devant eux » (Yoyotte 1949: 63).

La suite du texte est très mutilée, mais laisse entendre que les Shardanes furent écrasés. Je ne m'attarderai pas ici sur l'origine des Shardanes, question fort controversée et

Fig. 18. Détail de la fig. 13: personnage n° 6 et, devant lui, la crosse de jet ou «gourdin de combat».

d'ailleurs hors de mon propos, pour lequel il me suffit de souligner deux points très importants de ce texte.

1. Pour désigner les vaisseaux ennemis, le scribe est contraint d'utiliser une périphrase qui nous oblige à conclure, en premier lieu, que ces navires étaient construits spécialement en vue du combat sur mer (et non de vaisseaux marchands dotés d'archers) et, ensuite, que les Égyptiens ne disposaient pas de tels navires à cette époque.

2. Même si le texte pèche par une vanité habituelle dans ce genre de littérature, ce qui empêche, bien sûr, d'accepter littéralement «de toute éternité», il n'en reste pas moins que, ne serait-ce que pour célébrer la gloire de les avoir enfin vaincus, le Pharaon reconnaît que ces Shardanes venus de la haute mer avaient mené en Égypte des expéditions ou des razzias couronnées de succès, dès le début du règne au plus tard.

Les Shardanes ne devaient pas être les seuls à opérer en Égypte: on a remarqué plusieurs fois (Bérard 1927, 2: 378; Faure 1980: 190; Redford 1992: 250) que le récit fait par Ulysse des aventures des pirates qu'il avait menés par mer en Égypte (*Odyssée*, XIV: v. 246 et suiv.) reflète très vraisemblablement une réalité remontant au règne de Ramsès II ou de son successeur, Merneptah.

Aux textes éloquents de Ramsès II, il convient d'ajouter ses actes, peut-être bien plus éloquents encore. Des fouilles

ont fait apparaître que sous son règne furent construits douze fortins ou forteresses proches de la côte, de la région d'Alexandrie jusqu'à 50 km environ à l'ouest de Marsa Matruh, soit sur 300 km environ. Six de ces forts furent édifiés au sud de la future Alexandrie (ce qui me semble démontrer que ce site était considéré comme particulièrement sensible) et les six autres en Marmarique (Rowe 1953 et 1954; Habachi 1980; plan: Rowe 1954: 488). Pour ma part, je me rallie entièrement à la conclusion de L. Habachi:

> It can be said with our present state of knowledge, that Ramesses II was the first to be aware of the danger threatening Egypt from the strong Sea People,[4] and that he erected on the margin of the cultivated land on the coastal road in the west a line of temple-fortresses to defend the country, or at least to announce any danger from the Sea. Libyans were often tempted to attack Egypt, but they were always defeated; there was no need therefore, for any fortification to be erected in the West before the appearance of the Sea People. (1980: 30).

On ne peut s'empêcher de se demander si le dispositif de fortifications mis en place de manière méthodique par Ramsès II pouvait être pleinement efficace sans liaisons par mer entre ces diverses places fortes et il est tentant, pour des raisons de logique, de donner à cette question une réponse affirmative, même sans se dissimuler son caractère d'hypothèse. On peut pousser le raisonnement plus loin: si

---

[4] Une réserve de ma part ici: je remplacerais «the strong Sea People» par: des guerriers venus de la mer.

Fig. 19. Navire peint sur un vase de Khaniale Tekke (Géométrique Récent). D'après Boardman (1967; pl. 14, 21).

une telle flotte, nécessairement de guerre, existait, il lui fallait une base principale, située sur la côte. Celle-ci ne correspondrait-elle pas aux «ports submergés» d'Alexandrie, étudiés par G. Jondet (1916)? Les six forts au sud-est de l'actuelle Alexandrie s'expliqueraient d'autant mieux.[5]

Si Ramsès II, incontestablement conscient de la vulnérabilité des côtes d'Égypte exposées à une menace venue de la haute mer et certainement assez puissant pour établir un solide cordon défensif, a créé une marine de guerre spécialisée pour faire face aux envahisseurs venus de la Très-Verte, quels étaient les navires composant cette flotte? Dans son étude de la stèle de Tanis, J. Yoyotte observe qu'«on ne saurait attribuer aux faibles rois de la XIXe dynastie finissante la création de la puissante flotte militaire que paraît avoir possédée Ramsès III ..., on peut penser que c'est Ramsès II, à partir de sa nouvelle résidence du Delta appelée par un hymne (Anast., III, 7, 6 ...) "le port d'attache des archers des vaisseaux *(pdtyw mnsw)*" du roi, qui put mettre en échec l'audace des Shardanes par la création d'une marine de guerre et en garnissant de troupes les navires de commerce» (Yoyotte 1949: 69).

Munir d'archers des navires marchands *(mns)* est une chose, créer une marine de guerre composée de navires spécialisés, tels les «navires-combattants-au-milieu-de-la-mer» en est une autre; c'était même là la seule réponse adéquate, la première n'étant qu'une solution de fortune. Or les navires de Ramsès III représentés sur le temple de Medinet Habu sont, comme je le démontrerai, de véritables navires de guerre: il n'est pas inconcevable, loin de là, qu'ils eussent été inventés sous le règne de Ramsès II.

La vergue unique, sur ces navires de Ramsès III, est une innovation—et plus précisément un emprunt probablement fait à la Syrie, de même que le nid de pie, au sommet du mât.[6] Cette seconde nouveauté est la plus significative: le nid de pie, qui permet d'observer la côte de loin en mer serait dépourvu de sens si le navire était confiné aux eaux du Nil (toutes les autres représentations de navires purement égyptiens, y compris ceux de l'expédition de Pount, figurés au temple d'Hatshepsout à Deir el Bahari, ne montrent, au sommet du mât, que le calcet): ces navires-ci sont propres à la navigation en mer. Enfin, s'ils peuvent être propulsés par la voile seule, la «densité» des rameurs, très rapprochés, indique que le «moteur humain» était essentiel; ce qui confirme à quel point il l'était est le soin apporté à sa protection: une longue fargue dissimule presque complètement le corps des rameurs, dont on n'aperçoit que le sommet de la chevelure. L'étrave des navires de Ramsès III se termine par une tête de lion tenant dans sa gueule une tête d'Asiatique: simple emblème guerrier ou éperon destiné à frapper au-dessus de la flottaison, tel qu'il exista en Méditerranée du Moyen Âge jusqu'à la fin de l'âge des galères? Certains auteurs se sont prononcés en faveur de la seconde solution (Marx 1946 et 1948; Landström 1969: 23), d'autres expressément contre (notamment Gibson 1947). Une réponse certaine me semble impossible. Toutefois, il semble assuré que la défaite des navires combattus par la flotte de Ramsès III était assurée par leur chavirement

---

[5] Dans un livre récent, Claire Lalouette, professeur à l'Université de Paris-Sorbonne, écrit: «Touthmosis III, le premier, comprendra l'intérêt stratégique du site de l'île de Pharos, à l'ouest de la moderne Alexandrie, et commencera la construction d'un immense port d'accueil, que les Ramsès développeront» (1986: 153). C. Lalouette ne présente aucune référence à l'appui de cette affirmation ; je lui ai posé la question par écrit, mais n'ai reçu aucune réponse. S'il est bien établi que certaines expéditions de Touthmosis III vers la côte syrienne ou palestinienne eurent lieu par mer, j'avoue ne pas voir ce qui rattacherait cet «immense port d'accueil» à ce souverain, mais une attribution des vestiges décrits par G. Jondet (1916) à Ramsès II ne me paraît pas pouvoir être exclue.

A ce propos, il me paraît que Strabon s'est fait l'écho d'une très ancienne tradition dans sa description du port d'Alexandrie, lorsqu'il écrit que "les premiers rois d'Egypte .... prévenus contre tous les navigateurs, et surtout contre les Grecs, que l'exiguité de leur territoire portait à chercher et piller ailleurs ce qu'ils ne trouvaient pas chez eux, placèrent en ce lieu (la future Alexandrie) une garde avec ordre d'en défendre l'abord aux étrangers; ils donnèrent pour habitation à cette garde Rhakotis, qui forme maintenant la portion d'Alexandrie située au-dessus des loges de navires" (Strabon, 17, 1, 6 = 17.792).

[6] Ce qui semble bien démontrer cette origine est le relief du Musée de Berlin n° 24025, datant de la XVIIIe dynastie et trouvé à Saqqarah (Vinson 1994: 43, fig. 30): malheureusement mutilé (la coque est absente), il représente le déchargement d'amphores de type cananéen à bord d'un navire dont le gréement et le nid de pie sont identiques à ceux des navires de Ramsès III. Ce gréement devait donc être familier à l'Égypte dès le début de la XIXe dynastie.

(Nelson 1943; fig. 4: le navire N 2 commence à basculer, le navire N 3 a complètement chaviré). Dans son analyse de ce combat naval, H. H. Nelson attribue ce chavirement aux conséquences du jet d'un grappin par les marins égyptiens dans la voile du navire ennemi («grappling hooks into the enemy's sail» (Nelson 1943: 53). Il est certain, d'après le relief de Medinet Habu, que les Égyptiens ont utilisé le grappin (Nelson 1943: fig. 4; il est lancé de E 1 à N 1 et de E 3 à N 3), mais ce grappin n'aboutit pas dans la voile pour la très simple raison qu'aucun navire ennemi n'est représenté sous voile: toutes leurs voiles sont représentées carguées. Il est bien plus probable que la fonction du grappin était d'agripper le navire ennemi en vue de son abordage, non de son chavirement. En revanche, celui-ci pouvait être obtenu par des chocs (répétés?) contre la coque au moyen de l'«éperon» au-dessus de la surface de la mer—à la manière des béliers de la guerre terrestre.

Il est temps de replacer le navire de Teneida dans ce qui semble être son contexte: celui de la création de vrais navires de guerre en Méditerranée orientale. Il est certain que ce n'est pas là une invention égyptienne: l'Égypte n'a fait que répliquer à la fréquentation de ses côtes par des navires de guerre venus du nord. Il est tentant d'émettre l'hypothèse suivante: à une époque où l'architecture du navire de guerre est encore dans l'enfance et où des formes navales antagonistes coexistent, il est normal que l'on ait procédé à des améliorations par tâtonnements; aussi, la projection de la quille au-delà de l'étrave, typique des navires égéens et qui, à l'origine, était totalement dépourvue de caractère offensif, a-t-elle pu acquérir, de façon certainement très imparfaite, son caractère d'arme offensive plus tôt qu'on ne le pense généralement—en fait dès 1200 av. J.-C. environ? Le fait que les Égyptiens n'en ont pas équipé leurs navires en réplique n'est pas un argument contraire: d'abord parce que la «projection» du navire de Teneida, si elle était utilisée comme éperon, devait être très imparfaite, et ensuite parce que le rôle de la quille, toujours essentiel en cas de combat à l'éperon, était très différent en Égypte de ce qu'il était sur les «vaisseaux longs» égéens à quille rectiligne.

* * * * *

Il reste à déterminer quel fut le rôle exact du navire dont la représentation figure à Teneida et la raison pour laquelle elle fut gravée à cet endroit.

On sait qu'en l'an 5 du règne de Merneptah, les Libyens tentèrent d'envahir l'Égypte avec l'aide de peuples venus

nécessairement par mer: les Lukka, les Shardanes, les Teresh, les Shekelesh et les Eqwesh.[7] Une telle ligue suppose des contacts réguliers avec des peuples venus des rivages de l'Anatolie, de la Crète, des îles de la mer Égée ou de la Grèce continentale. La vue de navires similaires à celui de Teneida devait donc être familière aux habitants de la côte de la Libye actuelle.

Merneptah obtint une victoire totale, mais les Libyens firent une nouvelle tentative d'invasion, selon les sources égyptiennes officielles, en l'an 5 et en l'an 11 du règne de Ramsès III. Ces deux tentatives furent repoussées; les Libyens n'avaient plus pour alliés les peuples venus de la mer, mais les Mashouash, proto-berbères venus de Cyrénaïque, d'ailleurs devenus majoritaires lors de l'offensive de l'an 11. Lors du décompte du butin saisi après la victoire remportée en cette année, figuré à Medinet Habu, on voit apparaître un total de 239 épées de type mycénien (Grandet 1993: 209), ce qui démontre la poursuite de liens déjà anciens avec l'Égée.

L'équipage du navire de Teneida ne comprenant, à l'exception possible du pesonnage n° 1, que des habitants de la Libye, la question se pose de savoir si ceux-ci, au cours des guerres menées contre Merneptah et Ramsès III ont mené contre l'Égypte des opérations navales. Cela me paraît exclu pour l'invasion de l'an 5 de Merneptah, les contingents étrangers suffisant certainement pour armer les navires avec lesquels ils étaient venus. Quant aux deux autres tentatives libyennes, il n'est pas fait mention, dans les sources égyptiennes, d'interventions navales. Le navire de Teneida doit, dans ces conditions, être placé dans un contexte différent de celui des «guerres libyennes», celui de la piraterie.

L'argument essentiel à l'appui de cette hypothèse est celui des «modèles de navires» brandis comme des trophées: tous ces navires diffèrent complètement du navire de Teneida en ce qu'ils sont clairement des navires marchands et s'ils sont figurés au bout des bras de l'équipage, c'est, tout aussi clairement, parce qu'ils ont été capturés par lui. Or ce qui devait intéresser ces pirates était beaucoup moins le navire capturé que sa cargaison. Si une partie du butin pouvait être écoulée en Libye même, une autre, consistant en objets précieux de petite taille, pouvait probablement trouver acquéreur à meilleur prix bien plus au sud, en Nubie et au Soudan. Ces pirates ne pouvaient évidemment pas emprunter la voie de la vallée du Nil, mais il existait une route parallèle à celle-ci: l'itinéraire utilisant les pistes menant de Marsa Matruh et aboutissant au Kordofan par les oasis de Siwah,

---

[7] Il aurait été tentant de considérer les Eqwesh (ou Aqayouasha) comme des Achéens. Comme ils sont représentés dans l'iconographie égyptienne comme circoncis, l'identification est invraisemblable. Toutefois, D. B. Redford (1983), pour des raisons linguistiques, estime que les Eqwesh étaient originaires de l'île de Cos.

Baharieh, Farafreh, Dakhleh, Kargeh, Baris et Selima (Giddy 1987 et Vivian 1990, *passim*). On a vu la richesse du site de Teneida en graffiti de toutes espèces: elle ne s'explique que par l'attribution à ce lieu d'un caractère sacré ou magique où il était de coutume de graver des ex-voto. Et c'est ce caractère que me semble revêtir cette gravure rupestre: celui d'un ex-voto réalisé par des pirates chargés de leur butin, en route vers le sud, ou, l'ayant vendu avec profit, revenant vers le nord.

Il reste à savoir comment un équipage qui était sinon totalement, du moins très majoritairement, originaire de l'actuelle Libye, s'était procuré un navire de type égéen. Ceci reste une énigme, mais sa clef pourrait bien être le personnage à «couronne de plumes», debout devant l'étrave: son origine, on l'a vu, pourrait être différente et sa position, indiquant peut-être un «status symbol», pourrait indiquer une fructueuse opération conjointe entre le fournisseur (égéen ?) du navire, responsable de sa conduite en mer, et un équipage recruté en Libye.[8]

REFERENCES

Basch, L.
  1991   Carènes égéennes à l'âge du bronze. *Aegeum (Annales d'archéologie égéenne de l'Université de Liège)* 7 (= Thalassa, Actes de la 3e rencontre égéenne internationale de l'Université de Liège, Calvi, 23–25 avril 1990): 43–50.
  1994   Un navire grec en Égypte à l'époque d'Ulysse. *Neptunia* 195: 19–26.
Bates, O.
  1914   *The Eastern Libyans.* London: Frank Cass.
  1927   Pp. 125–97 in *Excavations at Marsa Matruh,* Varia Africana 4. Cambridge: Peabody Museum.
Bérard, V.
  1927   *Les navigations d'Ulysse.* Paris: Armand Colin.
Blegen, C. W.
  1949   Hyria. *Hesperia, Supplement* VIII: 39–42.
Boardman, J.
  1967   The Khaniale Tekke tombs, II. *Annual of the British School at Athens* 62: 57–75.
Breasted, J. H.
  1906   *Ancient Records of Egypt,* III. London-Leipzig.
Faure, P.
  1980   *Ulysse le Crétois.* Paris: Fayard.
Gardiner, A.
  1976   *Egyptian Grammar.* 3ᵉ édition. Oxford: Oxford University.
Gibson, C. E.
  1947   The Origin of the Ram. *The Mariner's Mirror* 33: 164–69.
Giddy, L. L.
  1987   *Egyptian Oases.* Warminster: Aris and Philipps.
Grandet, P.
  1993   *Ramsès III. Histoire d'un reigne.* Paris: Pygmalion/Watelet.

Habachi, L.
  1980   The Military Posts of Ramesses Ii on the Coastal Road and the Western Part of the Delta. *Bulletin de l'Institut Français d'Archéologie Orientale* 8: 13–30. Le Caire.
Hölscher, W.
  1937   *Libyer und Ägypter.* Ägyptologische Forschungen 4. Glückstadt-Hamburg.
Jondet, G.
  1916   *Les ports submergés de l'ancienne île de Pharos.* Mémoires de l'Institut Égyptien 7.
Kitchen, K. A.
  1979   *Ramesside Inscriptions, Historical and Bio-graphical,* II. Oxford.
  1983   *Ramesside Inscriptions, Historical and Bio-graphical,* V. Oxford.
Lalouette, C.
  1986   *Thèbes ou la naissance d'un empire.* Paris: Fayard.
Landström, B.
  1969   *Sailing Ships.* Haarlem.
  1970   *Ships of the Pharaohs.* London: Allen and Unwin.
Lipinski, E. (directeur de la publication)
  1992   *Dictionnaire de la civilisation phénicienne et punique.* Turnhout: Brepols.
Marinatos, S.
  1933   La marine créto-mycéniene. *Bulletin de Correspondance Hellénique* 57: 170–235.
Marx, E.
  1946   The First Recorded Sea Battle. *The Mariner's Mirror* 32: 242–51.
  1948   The Origin of the Ram. *The Mariner's Mirror* 34: 118–19.

[8] J'ai présenté une première version de cet article (Basch 1994), dont les conclusions divergent de celles exposées ici; ces dernières sont les seules que je maintienne.

Morricone, L.
1975   Coo — Scavi e scoperte nel «Serraglio» in
        località minore (1935–1943). *Annuario della
        Scuola Archeologica di Atene* 50–51 (1972–73;
        N.S. 34–5): 139–396.

Nelson, H. H.
1943   The Naval Battle Pictured at Medinet Habu.
        Journal of Near Eastern Studies 2: 40–55.

Rebuffat, R.
1977   Naissance de la marine étrusque. *Dossiers de
        l'Archéologie* 24: 50–57.

Redford, D. B.
1983   Compte-rendu de: W. Helck, Die Beziehungen
        Ägyptens und Vorderasiens zur Ägäis bis ins 7.
        Jahrhundert v. Chr. (1979). *Journal of the Ameri-
        can Oriental Society* 103: 481–83.

1992   *Egypt, Canaan and Israel in Ancient Times.*
        Princeton: Princeton University.

Rowe, A.
1953   A Contribution to the Archaeology of the West-
        ern Desert, I. *Bulletin of the John Rylands Li-
        brary* 36.1: 128–45.

1954   A Contribution to the Archaeology of the West-
        ern Desert, II. *Bulletin of the John Rylands Li-
        brary* 36.2: 484–500.

Sandars, N. K.
1985   *The Sea Peoples.* 2e édition. London: Thames
        and Hudson.

Vinson, S.
1994   *Egyptian Boats and Ships,* Shire Egyptology
        Series 20. Princes Risborough.

Vivian, C.
1990   *Islands of the Blest. A Guide to the Oases and
        Western Desert of Egypt.* Mokessen, PA: Trade
        Routes Enterprises.

Wainwright, G. A.
1962   The Meshwesh. *Journal of Egyptian Archaeol-
        ogy* 48: 89–99.

White, D.
1986   1985 Excavations on Bate's Island, Marsa
        Matruh. *Journal of the American Research Cen-
        ter in Egypt* 23: 51–84.

1989   1987 Excavations on Bate's Island, Marsa
        Matruh: Second Preliminary Report. *Journal of
        the American Research Center in Egypt* 26:
        87–126.

1990   The Third Season at Marsa Matruh, the Site of a
        Late Bronze Age Trading Station on the North-
        west Coast of Egypt. *American Journal of Ar-
        chaeology* 94: 330.

Winkler, H. A.
1938–   *Rock-Drawings of Southern Upper Egypt,* I
1939   (1938), II (1939). London: The Egypt Explora-
        tion Society, Oxford University.

Wreschner, E.
1971   Prehistoric Rock-Engravings in Nahal ha-
        Me'arot, Mount Carmel. *Israel Exploration
        Journal* 21: 217–18.

Yoyotte, J.
1949   Les stèles de Ramsès II à Tanis. *Kêmi* 10: 58–74.

Cyprus and Cilicia:
The Typology and Palaeogeography
of Second Millennium Harbors

LUCY K. BLUE

Institute of Archaeology
University of Oxford
36 Beaumont Street
Oxford, OX1 4XB
ENGLAND

There is a growing body of literature concerned with second millennium B.C.E. harbors and anchorage sites of Cyprus, and, to a lesser extent, Cilicia. One project in particular (Gifford 1978), has revealed a wealth of evidence relating to the palaeogeographic environment of the coastal littoral of Kition, in southeastern Cyprus. Through analyses of corehole samples taken from the area, Gifford was able to reconstruct the prehistoric coastline of Kition and ascertain the area of the Bronze Age harbor at Kathari.

This paper outlines a topographical typology of anchorage sites, and identifies the problems involved in interpreting their location in relation to their immediate coastal palaeogeographic environments during the second millennium B.C.E. A number of examples from both Cyprus and the Cilician delta are examined in order to demonstrate that, with enhanced geomorphological and archaeological analysis, a greater appreciation of the location of second millennium B.C.E. anchorage sites is realized. By assessing the contribution already made by archaeologists, in conjunction with geomorphologists, geologists, sedimentologists and geographers, an attempt is made here to clarify the problems of identifying the location, nature and extent of Bronze Age harbors in the eastern Mediterranean.

The point of this paper is a simple one: Modern maps are misleading when we consider ancient harbors, and an appreciation of ancient conditions requires both evidence and imagination. The point is obvious, but it is only with these considerations in mind that we can hope to recognize what Bronze Age harbors and anchorages looked like and where they were located. "Harbors, havens and anchorages of every type and technical quality are located at the waterline. The water-line is in a constant state of flux: almost everywhere along the eastern Mediterranean seaboard, the present waterfront is not the same as in the past, and it will change again in the future" (Raban,1995: 139). We need to consider what the coastal topography of the Bronze Age eastern Mediterranean was like, how it has changed and how it differs from what is depicted on mod-

ern maps. In order to achieve this goal I will first outline a topographical typology of anchorage sites based on one presented by Flemming (Muckelroy 1980: 162–63). He identified six main types of natural anchorages, which have been extended here to encompass the major types of anchorages around the shores of the eastern Mediterranean.

A. Anchorages on high energy, cliff-lined coasts (fig.1):
1. Natural bay (hundreds)
2. Almost enclosed bay e.g. Fethiye, southwest Turkey
3. Bays either side of an "anvil-shaped" headland e.g. Maa *Palaeokastro,* Cyprus
4. Lee of promontory e.g. Cape Kiti, Cyprus

5. Sheltered valley
6. Offshore island or reef e.g. Pseria, northeast Crete

B. Anchorages on low energy, low-lying coasts (fig. 2):
    1. Riverine (River mouth/Upriver) e.g. Israeli coast in this period
    2   Inland lake upriver e.g. Enkomi *Ayios Iakovos,* Cyprus
    3. Natural embayment e.g. Bronze Age harbor of Kition *Kathari,* Cyprus
    4. Deltaic e.g. Cilician delta, Turkey
    5. Lagoonal e.g. Hala Sultan Tekké *Vizaja,* Cyprus; Marsa Matruh, Egypt

This typology addresses harbors on two types of coastline. There are those on high energy, cliff-lined coasts, such as large parts of the Turkish coast, the northern Levant and parts of the coast of Cyprus that, due to the nature of the coastline, could still be identified and even utilized as anchorages today. However, low-lying coastlines, as we have learned from the work of geomorphologists such as Butzer (1971), Vita Finzi (1969, 1972), Erol (1967), Kraft et al. (1977) and Gifford (1978), have changed. We have to look beneath the alluvial valley, upstream of the prograding delta, in order to identify anchorage sites of the second millennium B.C.E. Fig. 3 is an approximate outline of the coastal palaeogeography of the eastern Mediterranean in the second millennium B.C.E. and helps to illustrate how and where the coastline has altered.

Low-lying coastlines have been impacted more greatly by the processes of geomorphological change than cliff-lined coasts since, and during, the second millennium B.C.E. This is not to deny the varying effects of sea level change and tectonic activity around the coasts of the eastern Mediterranean during this period, however, again, it is harbors on low-lying coastlines that are more affected by these processes. Due to the nature of such coastlines, the lateral displacement is much greater than the vertical. Additionally, since tidal amplitudes in the eastern Mediterranean are minimal, there is no mechanism to assist deposited coastal sediments out to sea. This is particularly noticeable along low-lying coasts where sediment accumulates in river outlets, particularly those of insignificant perennial flow, adding to the problems of siltation at river mouths.

With the aid of geomorphological analysis and drawing on a number of examples from both Cyprus and the Cilician delta, I will illustrate how it is possible to suggest localities for unidentified sites known to have played an important role in the eastern Mediterranean during the Middle and Late Bronze Ages.

CYPRUS

Larnaca Lowlands

An obvious example from Cyprus is the area of the Larnaca Lowlands, which has received much scholarly attention in the last twenty years. Two harbor sites were to play an important role in Late Bronze Age trade, well-positioned in the east of the island for contacts with the Levant, Egypt and Anatolia, Kition *Kathari* and Hala Sultan Tekké *Vizaja.* Both were occupied throughout the Late Bronze Age and acted as seaborne trade centers, as well as regional outlets for the distribution of copper. Evidence for copper smelting has been identified at both sites. Gifford (1985: 47, fig. 2) identifies the location of the Late Bronze Age sites of Kition *Kathari* and Hala Sultan Tekké *Vizaja* within a reconstruction of the Late Bronze Age (ca. 1300 B.C.E.) palaeogeography of the Larnaca Lowlands.

The two most active geomorphological elements of the Larnaca Lowlands coastal region during the Late Pleistocene and Holocene epochs, are, according to Gifford (1985: 45), the Tremithos River and its alluvial fan, and a natural salt pan just south of the modern city of Larnaca, known as the Larnaca Salt Lakes. The Tremithos River, primarily an agent of deposition, has carried millions of tons of alluvial sediment from the eastern foothills of the Troodos Massif down to the coast west of Cape Kiti. These deposited sediments have then been carried by currents and winds through a process of longshore drift around Cape Kiti and northward along the west side of Larnaca Bay, thereby altering the local coastal geography. Gifford (1985: 47) explains that the Salt Lake depression originated in the Late Pleistocene as "a discontinuous, shallow valley or trough between the toe of the Tremithos River's alluvial fan and earlier Pleistocene aeolian and marine rock units to the east."

The site of Hala Sultan Tekké *Vizaja* was located on the southwestern shores of a lagoon or marine embayment, still accessible to the sea, now known as the Larnaca Salt Lake (Gifford 1985: 47, fig. 2). During the late second millennium, the westward transgression of the sea caused by rising sea level, was reduced and net aggradation of the coastline seaward resulted. Northerly deposition of longshore drift sediments probably choked the eastern channel of the embayment of Hala Sultan Tekké, eventually cutting it off from the sea (Gifford 1985: 47–48). As stated by Åström and Engvig "It is highly probable that the present Salt Lake at Hala Sultan Tekké was a navigable harbor with an inlet from the sea in the Late Bronze Age. This is suggested by the situation of the Late Bronze Age town along its shore and by the many stone anchors found in the town" (1975:

1. NATURAL BAY.

2. ALMOST ENCLOSED BAY.

3. BAYS EITHER SIDE OF AN 'ANVIL-SHAPED' HEADLAND.

4. IN LEE OF A PROMONTORY.

5. SHELTERED VALLEY

6. Anchorage in Lee of island / offshore reef.

OFFSHORE ISLAND.

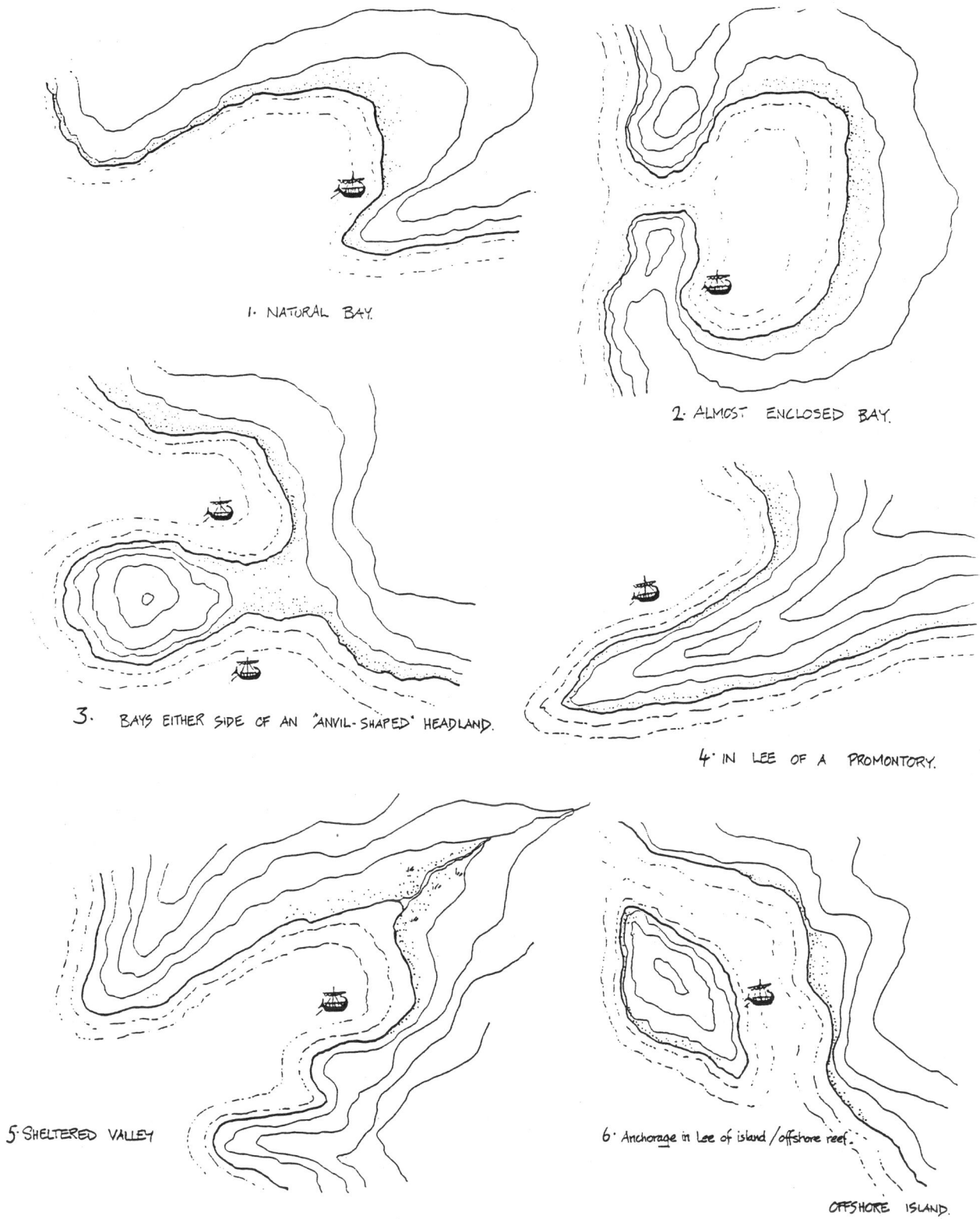

Fig. 1. Anchorages on high energy, cliff-lined coasts.

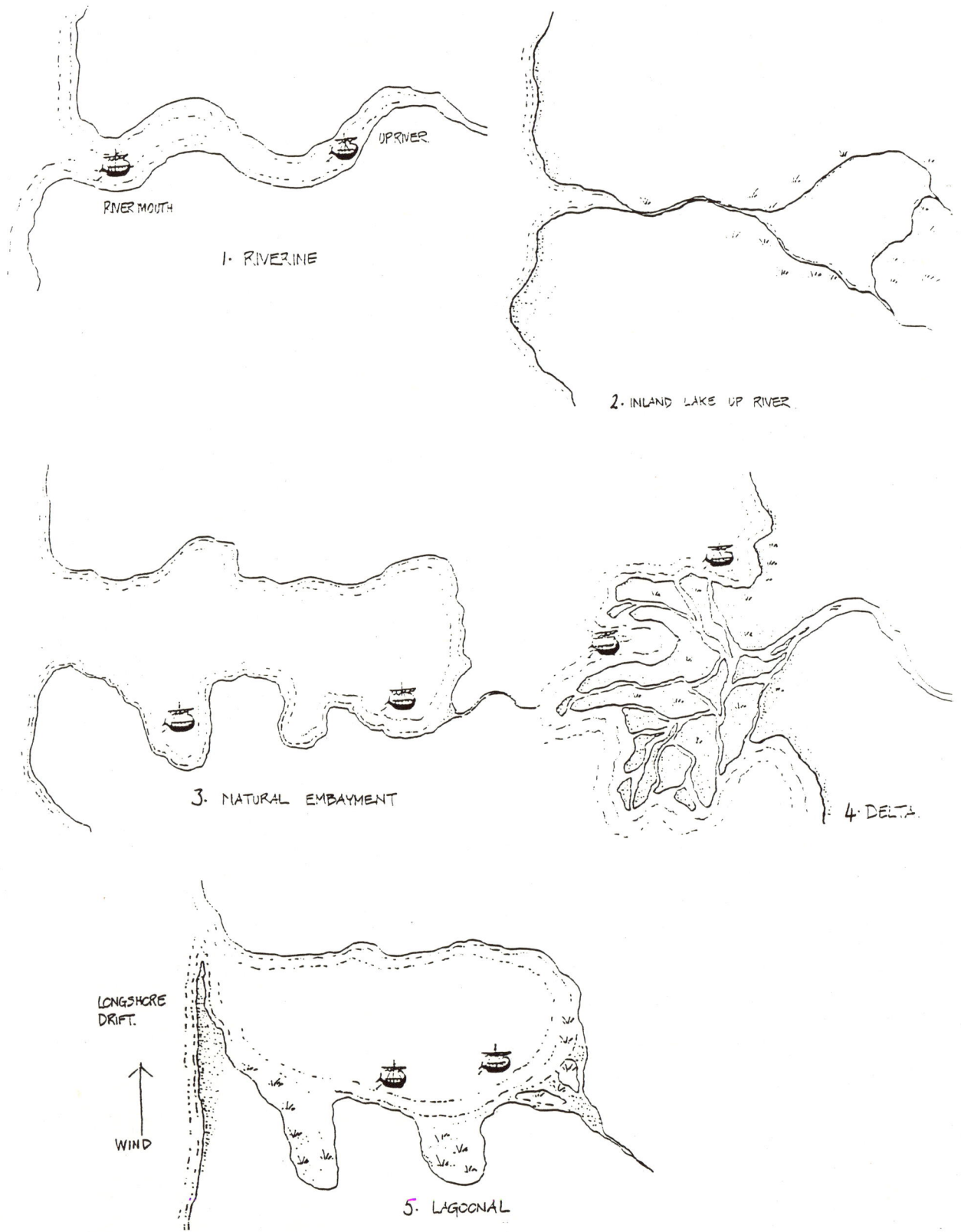

Fig. 2. Anchorages on low energy, low-lying coasts.

6). Slope wash from the land surface west of the Salt Lake depression also contributed to the infilling of the inlet (Gifford 1985: 48). Mollusca excavated from the Salt Lake from sealed Late Cypriot IIIA/1 levels support the theory that the lake must have been a lagoon at this period, soon to be cut off from the sea (Åström 1986: 68).

This process of northerly longshore transportation with the associated formation of sandbars and spits, combined with the progradation of slope wash deposits eastward, was also to affect the second millennium site of Kition, in the area of Kition *Kathari*. *Kathari* is located to the north of Classical Kition, on a low hill of marl bedrock which runs parallel to the present shoreline about 500 m away (Nicolaou 1976: 15). Marshy ground lies to the north and northeast of *Kathari* and is believed to have extended to the east and south east in antiquity (Gifford 1978: 56–83). This assertion is made by Gifford who in the 1970s took a number of corehole samples from the area of Kition (Gifford 1985a: 377, fig. 1), from which he was able to reconstruct the coastal palaeogeography of the Larnaca Lowlands and to ascertain the area of the Bronze Age harbor of Kition *Kathari*.

Nicolaou (1976: 74, fig. 16) outlines the approximate position of the coastline of Kition in prehistoric times. The area of marshy ground that lies to the north and northeast of the Bronze Age settlement is believed to have formed a bay that gradually silted up until the end of the Late Bronze Age when only a small inlet to the sea survived (fig. 4).

The bay and then the inlet are believed to have acted as the Bronze Age harbor of Kition *Kathari,* which shrank in size due to longshore drift. Corehole samples taken by Gifford (1978: 163, fig. 59, 1985a: 385, fig. 4) reveal a lagoonal environment present in this area until at least the Hellenistic period.

Akrotiri Peninsula

The second example in Cyprus is one that until recently, with the Maroni, Episkopi and Vasilikos valley surveys, had received little archaeological or geomorphological analysis; that of the Akrotiri Peninsula on the south coast. Unlike the area of the Larnaca Lowlands, which played an important role particularly in Late Bronze Age trade, this area of

Fig. 3. Possible coastal palaeogeography of the eastern Mediterranean in the second millennium B.C.E.

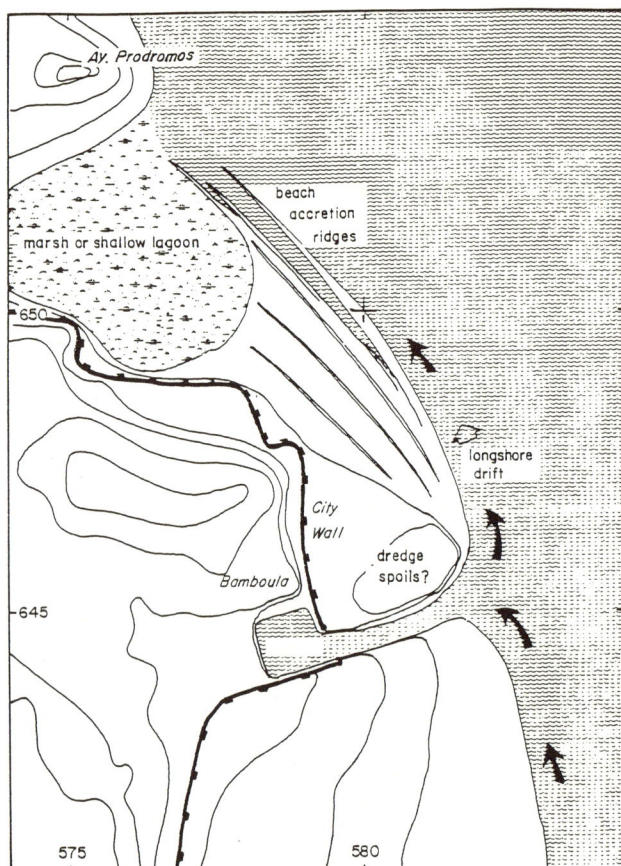

Fig. 4. Preliminary palaeogeography of the area around Kition in the second millennium B.C.E. After Gifford (1985a).

southern Cyprus does not appear to have been so prominent, except as an outlet for copper distribution. However, the picture that is currently emerging may perhaps change this view.

Swiny (1981: 51–87) first outlined the possibility of a land-based access or trade route, also relating to copper distribution nodes, that could well have been established in this period, channelling down the Kouris river valley, linking Morphou Bay, 70 km away in the northwest of the island, with sites along the south coast. Excavations in the Episkopi area have revealed a wealth of second millennium material including the Late Bronze Age sites of Episkopi *Phaneromeni* and *Bamboula,* as well as a line of copper production sites up the valley. A recent survey by Flourentzos (1991: 66) has revealed pottery parallels from sites on the north coast, such as the Linou-Katydhata area, with the Middle Bronze Age tombs of Alassa in the Kouris Valley.

The Kouris River, prior to modern damming at its head and tapping of several large springs near Alassa village, was one of the island's major rivers. The configuration of the shoreline in the areas of Episkopi-Akrotiri has been affected by the alluvial deposition of the Kouris River.

Based on this fact and assumptions made by Stanley Price (1980: 8) relating to the Akrotiri Salt Lake area, I suggest the following outline of the geomorphological processes that have affected the Akrotiri peninsula during and since the Bronze Age (fig. 5).

Stanley Price (1980: 8) stated that the "Akrotiri Salt Lake was probably formed as a result of seaward development of spits from mouths of (the) Kouris and Garyllis rivers eventually reaching (what was then) the offshore island (of Akrotiri) running west from the present Cape Gata and forming a tombolo, with an area of sea-water isolated as a salt-lake." Swiny (1981: 51–87) and Michaelides (1988: 1601) both testify to the large volume of sediment deposited at the mouth of the two rivers.

Although the assumptions of Stanley Price present a valuable introductory analysis of the pattern of geomorphological change in the area of the Akrotiri Salt Lake, the picture is more complex. Other factors must be taken into consideration. First, the littoral drift along the coast east of the Akrotiri peninsula is essentially easterly, which would not have encouraged the rapid southerly transportation of sediments from the Garyllis River mouth. In fact, the formation of the easterly spit that eventually linked the mainland to the island of Akrotiri, is not thought to have occurred until historic times (Nir 1993: 32), thereby leaving the eastern side of the peninsula open to the sea in the Bronze Age. However, prevailing winds on the west side of the Akrotiri peninsula are onshore, which prevent the River Kouris from prograding out into the sea, causing the build-up of sediment at the river mouth and forcing sediment to accumulate along the shore. This would correspond with Stanley Price's argument. The question of tectonic activity is not brought into Stanley Price's equation, despite the fact that localized fault activity is known to be present in the area, particularly along the south western side of Akrotiri Island, where Flemming and Webb (1986: 21) estimated a maximum subsidence of 1 m/1,000 years. Perhaps the problem is partially answered by aeolian deposition, wind blown deposits that have accumulated in the area of the Salt Lake. There can be no doubt that wind blown material has contributed considerably to the formation of the Akrotiri Salt Lake, particularly since the relative stabilization of sea level at the end of the Bronze Age. Geological maps clearly distinguish the Pleistocene marine deposits from those of recent alluvial and aeolian deposits that have accumulated in the area of the modern Salt Lake (fig. 5).

Bearing all these factors in mind, it is quite feasible that the infilling of the Akrotiri Salt Lake has occurred since

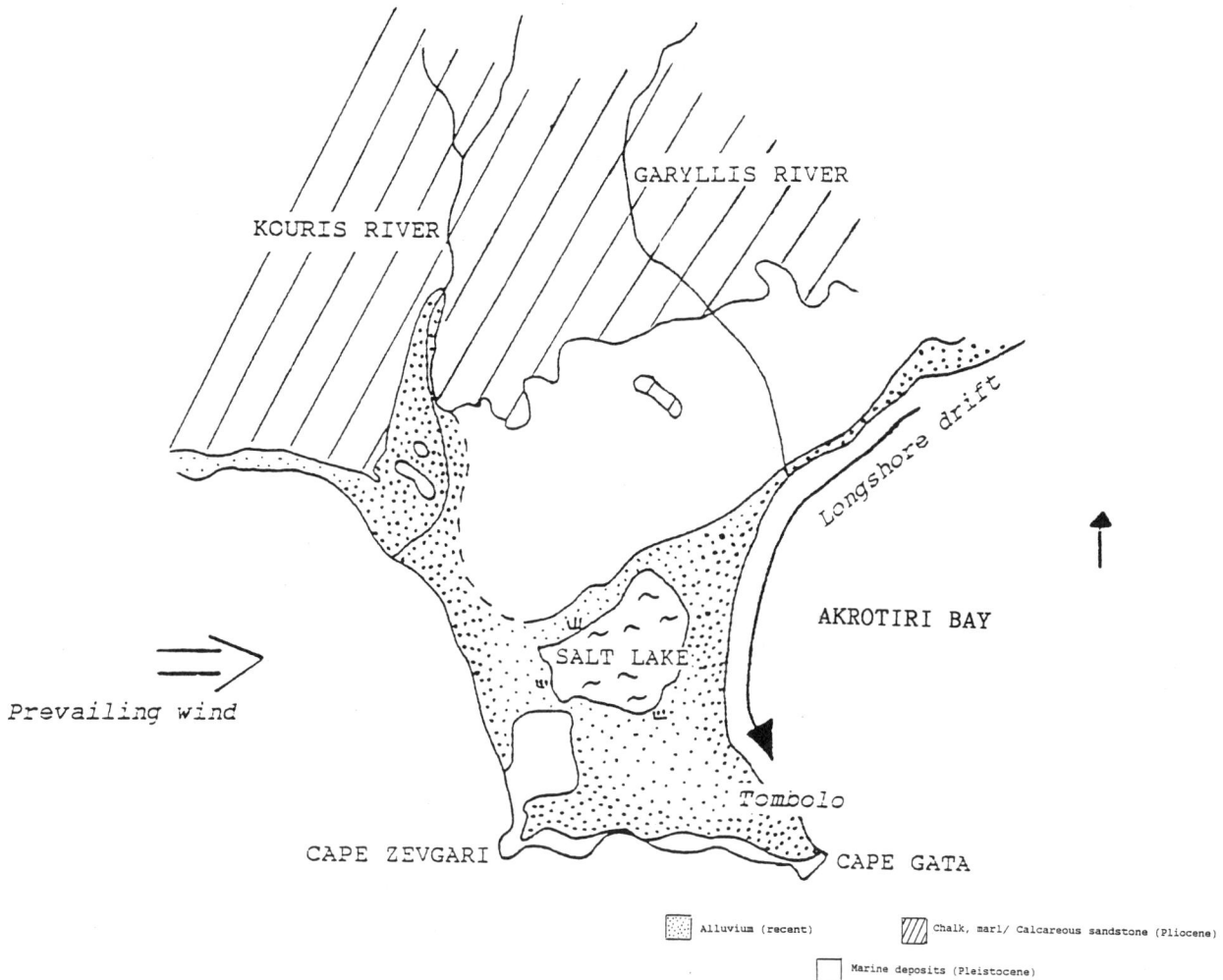

Fig. 5. Geology and prevailing maritime conditions of the Akrotiri Peninsula.

the Bronze Age and that prior to this period the area of the Salt Lake was a lagoon linked to the sea or a marine embayment providing sheltered anchorage behind the offshore island of Akrotiri.

The remains of a Hellenistic or Roman shipwreck have been identified some 150 m inland from the west coast of the peninsula (Heywood 1982: 164; Collombier 1987: 167), northwest of the modern town of Akrotiri, implying that this area was submerged during this period (fig. 6).

Furthermore, Gjerstad (1926: 15; Catling 1963: 161) identified a Late Bronze Age cemetery with associated pottery, near the modern village of Asomatos. The cemetery site of Asomatos *Phasouri* is currently located on the northern shores of the Akrotiri Salt Lake on the edge of the Pleistocene marine deposits. Heywood (1982: 166) states that the Late Bronze Age cemetery of Asomatos *Phasouri* was associated with a site of the same period. Thus, it is pos-

sible that the site of Asomatos *Phasouri* could well have utilised an extremely sheltered anchorage on the shore of a lagoon or marine embayment in the Late Bronze Age period.

Obviously a number of questions remain unanswered. No systematic corehole study of the Akrotiri Salt Lake has as yet been undertaken in order to ascertain the precise nature of the area during and since the second millennium B.C.E. Even if the area of the Akrotiri Salt Lake did offer shelter to vessels in this period, we have yet to determine the function of the harbor. What catchment area did it serve, and how did it relate to the possible anchorages at the mouths of the Maroni and Vasilikos valleys to the east and the Episkopi valley to the west? Further research needs to be undertaken to determine not only the typology of the anchorage at Akrotiri but also its function.

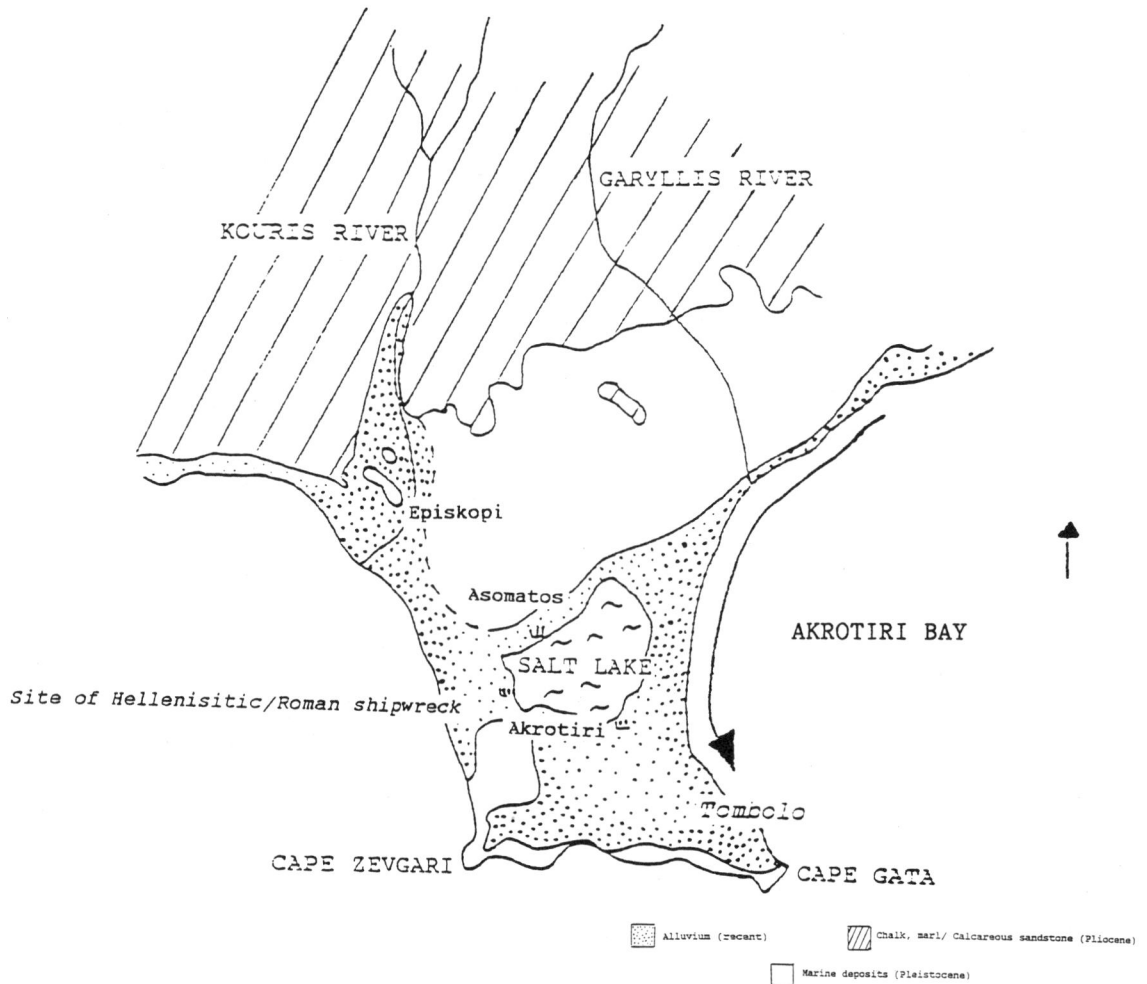

Fig. 6. Akrotiri Peninsula, locations of sites referred to in the text.

CILICIAN DELTA OF SOUTHERN TURKEY

The Cilician delta in southern Turkey is a crucial but relatively poorly investigated center of maritime trade, with links to the Hittite empire, the Levant and Cyprus.

Textual evidence certainly implies the existence of maritime activity and trade along the coastline of Cilicia (Gordon 1958: 28–31; Hoffner 1967: 21–22, 34–38; Linder 1981: 33–35; Astour 1981: 12–29). The Ugaritic and Hittite texts refer to trading activities between the two areas throughout the second millennium (KBo XII 42 rev. Col. III; PRU IV (17.130); RS 17.316), with particular reference to a coastal town believed to have been located in western Cilicia, called *Ura* (RS 20.213). This site has yet to be identified with a specific settlement, although Garstang (1943: 1–12) places it in the vicinity of the Bronze Age site of Silifke. It was known to have been the city that specialized in *tamkarutum*, foreign trade (RS 17.319); and is be-

lieved by Heltzer (1977: 203–11) to be the "real port of entry to the Hittite Empire." A Ugaritic tablet (RS 26.158) relates the shipment of grain to *Ura;* and a Hittite text (KBo XII 12) notes the shipment of metals such as silver, gold, copper, and tin to Ugarit. The rivers of the Cilician delta undoubtedly were an excellent means by which to transport products between the coast and the Anatolian plateau, via the Cilician Gates.

In order to analyze existing archaeological data and identify possible anchorage sites, it is important to understand the changes in the palaeogeography of the Cilician delta. It is composed of three slightly tilted fill terraces of Pleistocene age, surrounded at a lower level by a deltaic plain, believed by Erinç (1978: 87–108, fig. 3) to be of post-glacial date, prograding at a rate of 150–300 m/100 years, not necessarily a gradual or continuous process (fig. 7). Strabo (12.2.34) notes the rapid progradation of the delta in first century B.C.E. This deltaic growth is believed to have

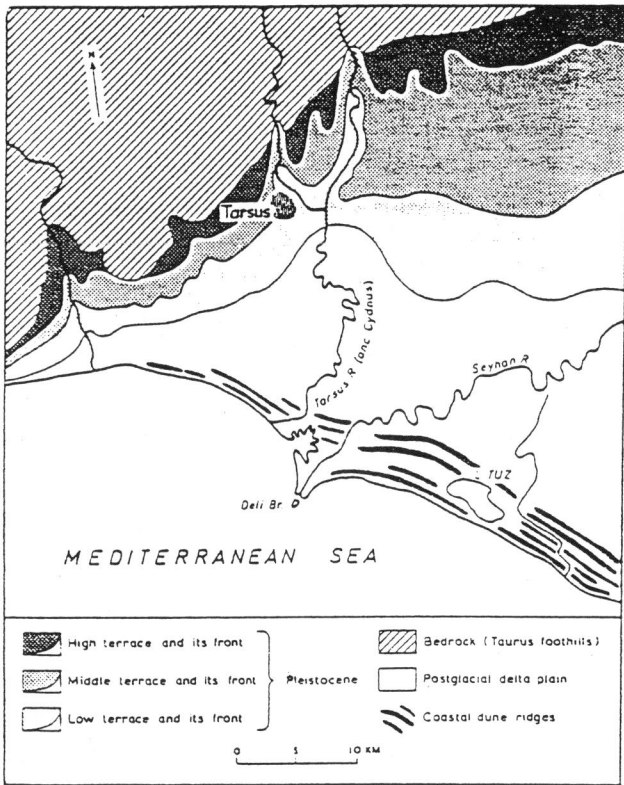

Fig. 7. The deltaic plain of Çukurova (Cilicia). After Erinç in Brice (1978: 101, fig. 3).

increased with the reduction in the rate of sea level rise around the end of the second millennium, "the effects of subsidence (thereby being) overcome by those of alluviation" (Russel 1954: 378, 382), and is therefore likely to have landlocked any harbors that functioned prior to this date, or buried them beneath deposits of alluvial sediment. As Evans (1973: 100) states, "the infilling and decline of many harbors is thus an almost inevitable consequence of their construction." Hence traces of harbors in deltaic regions are often slight and to be revealed require large scale excavation.

As a result of the unstable nature of the delta, settlement appears to have been largely restricted to higher ground around the Pleistocene terraces and Karataş/Misis Dağ promontory (Seton Williams 1954: 121–56).

One of the better known sites in the area of the Cilician delta is Tarsus or Gözlü Kule. The tell is presently situated some 15 km inland, not on the coastal delta, but on the lower fill terraces to the west of the coastal delta, with the nearby River Tarsus deeply entrenched (fig. 8). Excavated by Hetty Goldman (1950) in the 1930s and 1940s, Tarsus has revealed significant Bronze Age remains, with occupation levels dating from Neolithic times. Ceramic remains have revealed second millennium connections throughout the eastern Mediterranean (Astour 1965: 16). From textual evidence, Tarsus, Hittite *Tarsa,* is known to have been an ancient harbor. The exact location of the harbor is unknown

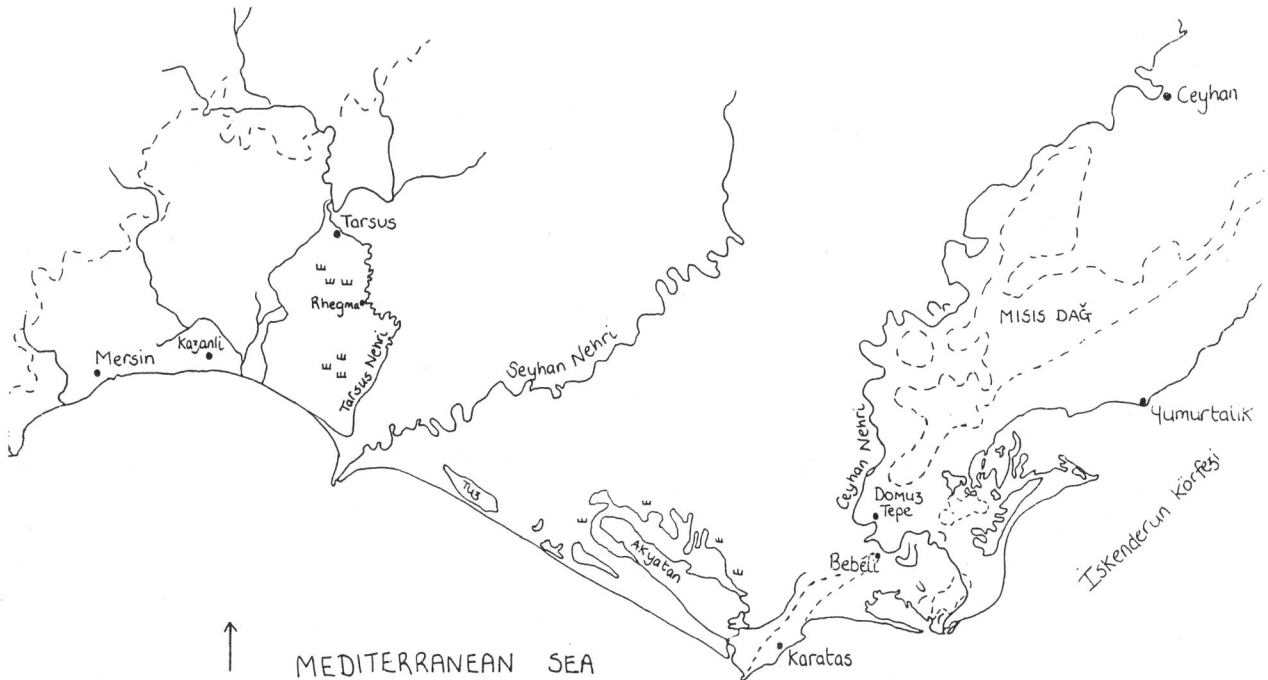

Fig. 8. Cilician Delta.

but geomorphological surveys by Evans (personal communication), demonstrate that it was situated to the southwest of Tarsus in a large marine embayment that was eventually drained as a result of tectonic uplift in the area of Tarsus and general silting up of the Tarsus (Kydnos) River, which drove the shoreline seaward. The harbor of Tarsus, known later as *Rhegma,* or marsh, was abandoned by Justinian prior to the sixth century A.D., at which point the river was diverted to its present channel east of the modern city (Stillwell 1976: 883–84). Sedimentary evidence suggests that the area of the ancient harbor is now drained marshland, covered with extensive plantations of eucalyptus trees that drain the swamps, and define the area of the lagoon prior to silting (Van der Have, personal communication).

Domuz Tepe, the second site that I would like to consider on the Cilician delta, is less well studied than Tarsus. It is presently situated 12 km from the coast on the eastern side of the delta, just on the western edge of the Karataş/Misis Dağ promontory, north of the present course of the Ceyhan River, which passes through a saddle to cross to the eastern side of the promontory at this point. Fig. 8 identifies the location of the site of Domuz Tepe.

Seton Williams (1954: 121, fig. 1) in her survey of 1951, lists Domuz Tepe among the important Middle and Late Bronze Age sites in the area, with traces of Mycenaean IIIC pottery (Mee 1978: 121–56) and Middle Cypriot III ware (Seton Williams 1954: 154).

Situated to the northwest of the modern town of Yeşilköy on the edge of a low, limestone plateau, commanding a good view over the flat Ceyhan River valley plain, the site extends over an area of roughly 100 by 150 m, and stands approximately 20 m high (fig. 9).

Although the river is now about half a kilometer to the west of Domuz Tepe, it is believed once to have passed much closer to the site (Bird 1985: 96). However, as a result of the Tarsus uplift, large quantities of sediment built up to the west of the Misis Dağ, causing the river baseline to rise to the lip of the saddle and ultimately forcing it through the saddle at Bebeli, to build its delta out into the İskenderun Gulf to the east, as opposed to directly south as was its previous course (Bird 1985: 96, fig. 53/1916; Evans 1971: 394). This change in the river course is very apparent on aerial photos (Gilbert, personal communication). The date of the change in the river course is not clear, although it is believed to have occurred sometime during the first millennium B.C.E. (Erol 1967: 98). Figure 10a shows the location of the ancient coastline. Just prior to the change in the river course Domuz Tepe would have been well situated in a sheltered position behind the dağ close to the mouth of the Ceyhan River. It is therefore possible that the site, located on the edge of the only area of high ground in an unstable marshy region, could have acted as a riverine harbor monitoring the movement of vessels entering the Ceyhan River. However, at this stage these assumptions are only specula-

Fig. 9. Domuz Tepe as photographed by the author in 1991, view from the east.

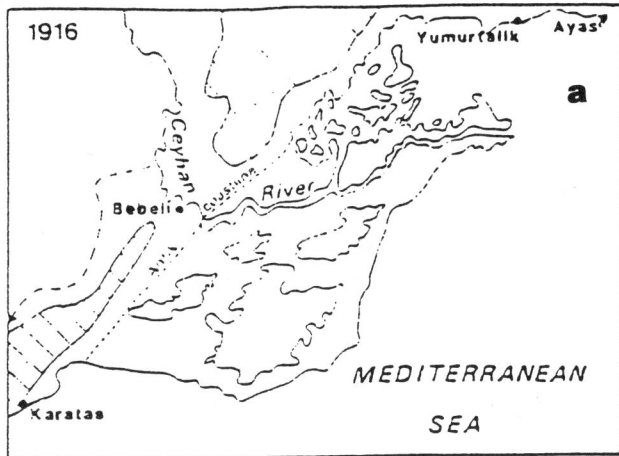

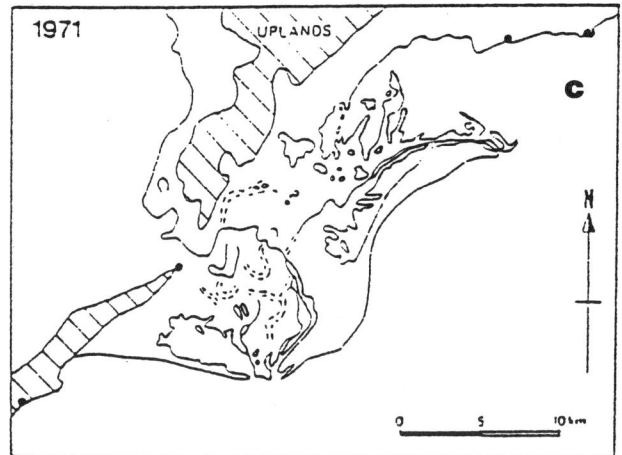

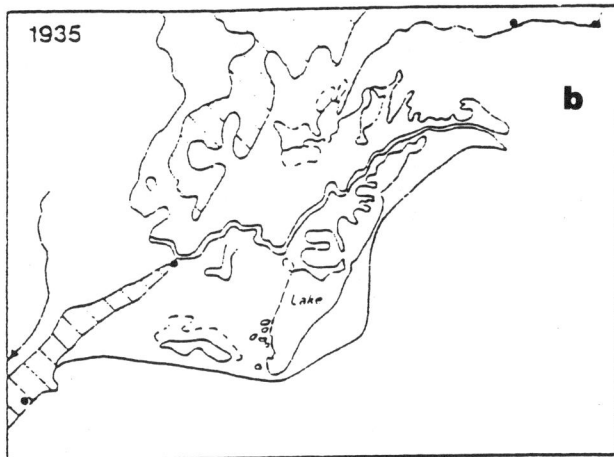

Fig. 10. Changes in the coastline of the Ceyhan delta, southern Turkey, following diversion of the river mouth southward in 1935. After Bird (1985: fig. 53).

tive and further research needs to be undertaken in order to ascertain the precise nature of the area during the second millennium B.C.E. and the function of the site of Domuz Tepe.

The moral of these examples is clear. The Bronze Age landscape, especially outlets to the sea and major arteries of trade, particularly on low-lying stretches of the coast, has largely disappeared. It is only with continued interdisciplinary investigation and observation of the coastal topography that we can begin to understand the palaeogeography of this area and make assumptions about the configuration of the Bronze Age coastline. One can almost say that a definitive characteristic of a Bronze Age harbor is that it is no longer in the same relationship to the sea. In order to identify the location of harbors of this period we have to reconstruct the landscape as it would have been in the Bronze Age.

REFERENCES

Astour, M. C.
1965   *Hellenosemitica: an Ethnic and Cultural Study in Western Semitic Impact on Mycenaean Greece*: 16. Leiden: Brill.
1981   Ugarit and the Great Powers. Pp. 3–29 in *Ugarit in Retrospect,* ed. G. D. Young. Winona Lake: Eisenbrauns.

Åström, P.
1986   Hala Sultan Tekke and its Foreign Relations. Pp. 63–68 in *Cyprus between the Orient and the Occident. Acts of the International Archaeological Symposium,* ed. V. Karageorghis. Nicosia: Department of Antiquities, Cyprus.

Bird, E. F. C.
1985   *Coastal Changes: A Global Review.* Chichester: Wiley.

Butzer, K. W.
1971   *Environment and Archaeology.* London: Methuen.

Collombier, A. M.
1987   Modifications des lignes de rivage et ports antiques de Chypre: état de la question. Pp. 159–72 in *Deplacemants des lignes de rivage en Mediterranée.* Colloques Internationaux du CNRS. Paris: Editions du Centre National de la recherche Scientifique.

Catling, H. W.
1963   Patterns of Settlement in Bronze Age Cyprus. *Opuscula Atheniensia* 4: 129–69.

Engvig, O. T. and Åström, P.
1975   *The Cape Kiti Survey. An Underwater Archaeological Survey. Hala Sultan Tekke II.* Studies in Mediterranean Archaeology 45: 2. Göteborg: Åströms.

Erinç, S.
1978   Turkey Since the Last Glacial. Pp. 87–108 in *The environment of the Near East and Middle East since the last Ice Age,* ed. W. Brice. London: Academic.

Erol, O.
1967   Observations on the Anatolian Coastline During the Holocene. Pp. 95–102 in *Convegno Internationale de Studi Sulle Antichita di Classe. 14–17 Oct. 1967.* Ravenna, Italy: Congress.

Evans, G.
1971   The Recent Sedimentation of Turkey and the Adjacent Mediterranean and Black Seas: A review. Pp. 385–406 in *Geology and History of Turkey,* ed. A. S. Campbell. Tripoli: Petrological Exploration Society of Libya.

1973   Recent Coastal Sedimentation: a review. Pp. 89–114 in *Marine Archaeology. Proceedings of the 23rd Symposium of the Colston Research Society, 1971,* ed. D.J. Blackman. London: Butterworths.

Flemming, N. C., and Webb, C. O.
1986   Tectonic and Eustatic Coastal Changes During the Last 10,000 Years Derived from Archaeological Data. *Zeit. Geomorph. N.F. Suppl.-Bd.* 62: 1–29.

Flourentzos, P. F.
1991   *Excavations in the Kouris Valley I. The Tombs.* Nicosia: Department of Antiquities, Cyprus.

Garstang, J.
1943   Discoveries at Mersin and Their Significance. *American Journal of Archaeology* 47: 1–12.

Gifford, J. A.
1978   *Palaeogeography of Archaeological Sites of the Larnaca Lowlands, SE Cyprus.* Ph.D. dissertation, University of Minnesota.
1985a   Potential Bronze Age Coastal Change in the Vicinity of Kition. Pp. 375–87 in *Excavation at Kition V:1. Text,* ed. V. Karageorghis & M. Demas. Nicosia: Department of Antiquities, Cyprus.
1985b   Palaeogeography of Ancient Harbour Sites of the Larnaca Lowlands, SE Cyprus. Pp. 45–48 in *Harbour Archaeology, Proceedings in the 1st International Workshop on Ancient Mediterranean Harbours Caesarea Maritima,* ed. A. Raban. BAR International Series 257. Oxford: B.A.R.

Gjerstad, E.
1926   *Studies in Prehistoric Cyprus.* Uppsala: A.-B. Lundequistska.

Goldman, H.
1950   *Excavation at Gözlü Kule, Tarsus.* Princeton, New Jersey: Princeton University.

Gordon, C. H.
1958   Abraham and the Merchants of Ura. *Journal of Near Eastern Studies* 17: 28–31.

Heltzer, M.
1977   Metal Trade of Ugarit and the Problems of Transportation. *Iraq* 39: 203–11.

Heywood, H. C.
1982   The Archaeological Remains of the Akrotiri Peninsula. Pp. 162–75 in *An Archaeological Guide to the Ancient Kourion Area and the Akrotiri Peninsula,* ed. H. W. Swiny. Nicosia: Department of Antiquities.

Hoffner, H. A., Jr.
  1967   A Hittite Text in Epic Style about Merchants. *Journal of Cuneiform Studies* 21–22: 34–38.
Kraft, J. C.; Aschenbrenner, S. E.; and Rapp, G. Jr.
  1977   Palaeographic Reconstructions of Coastal Aegean Archaeological Sites. *Science* 195: 941–47.
Linder, E.
  1981   Ugarit: A Canaanite Thalassocracy. Pp. 31–42 in *Ugarit in Retrospect,* ed. G. D. Young. Winona Lake: Eisenbrauns.
Mee, C.
  1978   Aegean Trade and Settlement in Anatolia in the Second Millennium B.C. *Anatolian Studies* 28: 121–56.
Michaelides, P.
  1988   The Ancient Port of Amathus (Cyprus)—its Construction, Foundation Conditions and Final Abandonment. Pp. 1597–1603 in *Engineering Geology of Ancient Works, Monuments and Historical Sites*, eds. C. Marinos and D. Koukis. Rotterdam: Balkema.
Muckelroy, K. (ed.)
  1980   *Archaeology Under Water.* New York: McGraw Hill.
Nicolaou, K.
  1976   *The Historical Topography of Kition. Studies in Mediterranean Archaeology* 43: 9–51, 71–85. Göteborg: Åströms.
Nir, Y.
  1993   *The Coasts of Cyprus.* Jerusalem-Nicosia: Geological Survey of Israel.

Raban, A.
  1995   The Heritage of Ancient Harbour Engineering in Cyprus and the Levant. Pp. 139–88 in *Cyprus and the Sea,* eds. V. Karageorghis and D. Michalides. Nicosia: University of Cyprus.
Russel, R. J.
  1954   Alluvial Morphology of Anatolian Rivers. *Annual Association of American Geographers* XLIV: 363– 91.
Seton Williams, V.
  1954   Cilician Survey. *Anatolian Studies* 28: 121–56.
Stanley Price, N. P.
  1980   *Early Prehistoric Settlements in Cyprus: A Review and Gazetteer of Sites c. 6500–3000 B.C.* BAR International Series 65. Oxford: B.A.R.
Stillwell, R. (ed.)
  1976   *The Princeton Encyclopedia of Classical Sites:* 883–84. Princeton: Princeton University.
Swiny, S.
  1981   Bronze Age Settlement Patterns in Southwest Cyprus. *Levant* 13: 51–87.
Vita Finzi, C.
  1969   *The Mediterranean Valleys. Geological Changes in Historical Times.* Cambridge: Cambridge University.
Vita Finzi, C.
  1972   Supply of Fluvial Sediment to the Mediterranean During the Last 20,000 Years. Pp. 43–46 in *The Mediterranean Sea: A Natural Sedimentation Laboratory,* ed. D. J. Stanley. Stroudsberg, PA: Dowden, Hutchinson and Ross.

The Concrete-Filled Barges of King Herod's Harbor of Sebastos

CHRIS BRANDON

Nautical Archaeology Society
Pringle Brandon Architects
10 Bonhill Street
London EC2A 4QJ
ENGLAND

Caesarea is located on Israel's Mediterranean coast halfway between Haifa and Tel Aviv and it was there that King Herod built the royal harbor of Sebastos between 21 and 10 B.C.E. The Roman harbor engineers who were brought in by Herod to help, developed a number of innovative design solutions to meet the short timescale for its construction.

The site, which now largely rests beneath the sea, is being excavated by Professor Avner Raban of the University of Haifa.

Excavations at the northern end of the main outer breakwater have revealed evidence of an unusual type of Roman harbor design. Enormous concrete blocks 7 × 14 m on plan and over 3.5 m high are set out on the seabed in a loose header arrangement. These blocks formed the foundation to the spine wall referred to by Josephus in both Jewish Wars *and* Jewish Antiquities. *They were cast within permanent wooden forms built by shipwrights using traditional shell-first ship building techniques.*

These caissons, or barges, were built on the shoreline and floated out to the site where concrete was added, sinking them onto the seabed. The "concrete" comprised two distinct layers of hydraulic pozzolana based mortar, sandwiching a weaker non-hydraulic lime mortar layer.

The Roman harbor engineers at Caesarea Maritima developed a number of innovative solutions in its construction to suit the particular site conditions and the demanding timescale imposed on the project by Herod.

The technical and logistical problems that these designers and contractors faced were enormous and numerous. Not only were there no natural features of any consequence to provide the basis of a harbor but also the site was very exposed and the conditions, even in the best seasons of Spring and Autumn, would have been difficult to work in as there were frequent heavy swells and breaking seas, made worse by shallower water than exists at present.[1] In addition they chose to import one of the basic raw materials for the construction of large parts of the harbor. Massive quantities of pozzolana powder and tufa were shipped in from Italy to be used in the making of hydraulic "concrete," and it is likely that the timber used as false work in forming the concrete was also imported.[2]

---

[1] Josephus describes the sea and coast conditions of this part of the coastline in both of his texts on the city (St. Thackeray 1927: 192–94; Marcus 1963: 160–62; translation by J. P. Oleson 1989).

[2] A very detailed and thorough analysis was carried out by J. P. Oleson and G. Branton at the University of Victoria to compare samples of pozzolana and tufa from Caesarea and Puteoli, and from volcanic quarries and Roman concrete buildings elsewhere in Italy and the Aegean. This proved beyond doubt that the material was imported from around the Bay of Naples to Caesarea (Oleson and Branton 1992: 58–63).

One of the most unusual and certainly the most innovative means by which the Romans managed to construct the harbor enclosure, which was over 800 m in its combined length, and speed up the process, was to build in parts of the southern breakwater open cellular structures that could be rapidly inundated by sand-bearing seawater and quickly become silted up.[3] Once these pockets were filled with sand they were sealed and capped with masonry to become part of the harbor breakwater. However, to be able to meet the timescale imposed by Herod it was necessary to work on many fronts at the same time. A. Raban has suggested that "construction islands" were set up at the outset of the project at key points around the planned outline of the harbor from which the infill sections could be extended.[4] Concrete platforms formed the bases of these "islands" and different techniques were evolved in the building of them, the variations in design being due mainly to site constraints, although evolution of design could also be a contributing factor.

In 1982, in area G (fig. 1), evidence of the original timber formwork for several large rectangular concrete blocks on the end of the northern breakwater provided details on how one version of these bases was constructed (Oleson 1989: 127–30). The wooden forms or caissons were 15 m × 11.5 m on plan and 2 m high, and consisted of a double wall of planking with a 23 cm gap between mounted onto a 29 × 29 cm sleeper beam. The interior of the form was strengthened by timber ties and struts but there was no bottom or floor to the caisson itself. The double wall provided the required floatation to move it from the shoreline out to the site where it could then be sunk into place after being filled with a pozzolana based concrete. The solidified concreted walls then provided a permanent containment for the fill of hydraulic concrete comprising the blocks that still largely remain *in situ*. These caissons are a combination and an adaptation of techniques described by Vitruvius.[5]

This paper will concentrate, however, on the particular design of a concrete filled timber caisson that was found in area K at the end of the main southern breakwater. Evidence of similar structures was found initially in 1990 and studied over the following seasons (Vann 1991: 132). This is a summary of the findings to date rather than a definitive statement, as the excavation and investigation are still continuing in the area.

Area K (fig. 1) covers an area 70 × 21 m at the northern end of the main southern breakwater and includes the two free-standing concrete bases which, it has been suggested, are the foundations for the yoked blocks supporting the statues described by Josephus.[6] The main area of the site consists of a chaotic pile of enormous tumbled concrete blocks, many still retaining the impressions of the formwork into which the concrete was poured, together with large *kurkar* (local sandstone) blocks.[7] This mound is spread across the

[3] Raban (1992a) describes how probes made into sand deposits within the harbor enclosure exposed accumulated layers of well-sorted grain size sediments, demonstrating the change of wave energies over the time span of the deposit. It is suggested that it took two to three years for the natural process to silt up the pockets. Once filled, they were covered with a layer of rubble, sealing the captured sediments and serving as a base for paving slabs for the promenade and floors to the storage vaults.

[4] Raban (1992a) proposes that the first feature the engineers built was an artificial island, situated where eventually the top of the main mole would be, some 500 m north-northwest of the top of the southern promontory and about 350 m due west of the stem of the northern one. Another one was installed half way along the curved line of the main mole at the turn of its course from the west to a northerly direction, and also one at the tip of the northern breakwater.

[5] Oleson believes that the caisson design at area G is a conflation of two major types of formwork described by Vitruvius, in an adaptation of the basic principles involved to a third type of situation. "The engineer knew from the start that he was working with a hydraulic concrete that could be poured directly in the sea water, but the character of the sandy sea bed and rubble breakwater foundation made it difficult to fix prefabricated forms in place by means of pilings. In consequence, bottomless, double-walled wooden forms were constructed on shore and floated out to their final destination. Once the footings had been cleared and levelled by divers, mortar was poured into the hollow sections of the double-wall, until the buoyancy was overcome and the form settled onto the prepared sea bed. While the inundated form was being filled with cement and aggregate, rubble was also dumped around the periphery to prevent shifting of the formwork prior to the curing of the concrete, or undermining of the final block. Although Vitruvius' single-walled forms were prefabricated, pounding their uprights into the harbour floor would have been a difficult and time consuming process" (Oleson 1988: 154–55).

[6] The towers at the entrance were described by Josephus in the first century: "At the harbour entrance there were colossal statues, three on either side, set up on columns. A massively built tower supported the columns on the port and two upright blocks of stone yoked together, higher than the tower on the other side" (St. Thackery 1927, translation by Oleson 1989).

[7] *Kurkar,* the local building stone, is a relatively soft and porous carbonate-cemented quartz eolianite sandstone (see Oleson and Branton 1992: 58–63).

site and rises from the current seabed depth of between 7–8 m to within 2 m of the surface. It had been assumed that this was the collapsed remains of the lighthouse structure or Drusion, described by Josephus as being the tallest and most magnificent of a series of towers built at intervals along the stone wall that encircled the harbor.[8] The location being at the mouth of the harbor made this a possible candidate for a lighthouse site and it was during the 1990 study of the concrete and masonry blocks by R. L. Vann, in an attempt to reconstruct the lighthouse, that the "K" type caissons were discovered (Vann 1991: 123–39).

Beneath this mound are the remains of concrete forms set out in a loose header arrangement across the site (fig. 2). Each block was originally 14 × 7 m on plan and approximately 4 m high. These concrete blocks were cast within a different design of shuttering to that found at area G. The wooden formwork, of which substantial parts still remain below the current seabed, consists of a single watertight skin built with a floor in the same manner as shell-first ship construction. All the timber planks were edge fixed with tenons set into mortises and transfixed with treenails. The interior was then stiffened with floor beams, stringers, ties and raking struts. The resultant rectangular "barge" could be floated out to the site in a similar manner to the caissons found at area G.

The development of this alternative design was the direct result of the uniqueness of the Area K site and the time restraints faced by the builders. The early completion of the main southern breakwater would have been crucial to the success of an expeditious building program, making the northern breakwater and internal jetties much easier to build within its lee. The site at the terminus of this main breakwater would obviously be a crucial point to establish a "construction" base at the outset of the project. However, it presented the designers with particular problems in working so far from shore and being subjected to difficult sea conditions of large swells and strong longshore currents.

The designers chose a rectangular barge that could weather the sea conditions and enable them to ship to site a quantity of concrete within it. Being rectangular they could be sunk side by side to form a solid foundation for the overlaying structure. The open-bottomed caissons would not have been suitable for the open sea as the double-walled floatation section would have been susceptible to being swamped and flooded from swells and breaking seas and would easily founder. Their use was consequently restricted to protected areas such as the northern breakwater.

To date three caissons have been studied in area K and are generally identical in construction.[9] There are only minor variations between them, which could be due to evolutionary improvements in design or simply to the fact that they were built by different shipwrights. These barges were rectangular, flat-bottomed craft 14 m long with a beam of 7 m and a height of approximately 4 m, and one at least had an inner central compartment 2.5 m wide and 6.5 m long (fig. 3). They were built with planking, edge fastened with mortises and tenons which were transfixed with treenails in the same manner as traditional shell-first ship construction. The pine boarding ranges in size between 19 cm to 26 cm deep by 8 cm thick on the sides of the caisson and 19 cm to 26 cm by 5.5 cm on the bottom and also on the walls to the inner compartment. No end joints in the planking have been seen and therefore it is not possible to say if they were scarfed, as would be expected in this method of construction.

The tenons, which are made from a hardwood, are on average 8 × 10 cm and spaced at 20 cm centers, although the upper boards on K5 have tenon spacing of 30 cm. The tenons are secured with 11 mm diameter treenails, and are arranged so that they are staggered from board to board. The planks were built up one by one rather than prefabricated and this is confirmed by the way the ends of the individual boards have been cut where let into the corner posts in sequence. Each board clearly has been cut separately and

[8] "When the submarine foundation was finished, he then laid out the mole above sea level, 200 feet across. Of this, a 100 ft portion was built out to break the force of the waves, and consequently was called the *prokumia*. The rest supported the stone wall that encircled the harbour. At intervals along it were great towers, the tallest and most magnificent of which was named Drusion, after the stepson of Caesar" (St. Thackery 1927, translation by Oleson 1989).

[9] The excavations at area K, which were begun there in 1990, have been carried out under the direction of Professor A. Raban of the University of Haifa, with logistic support from the Center of Maritime Studies of the University of Haifa and numerous dive volunteers from Israel, America and Europe. Excavation techniques had to suit the terrain which was covered in massive concrete and stone blocks. The first caisson to be excavated, K2, was the most straightforward as it was not completely buried beneath the mass of collapsed structure. However, to reveal the detail of the timber elements that comprised the original formwork, it was necessary to dig down through consolidated concrete by as much as 1.5 m.

This was not possible at K3 due to the extent of the overlaying concrete and tumbled masonry which was in excess of 4 m thick. Although some parts were in a somewhat fragmented state, marine growth had re-concreted it together. Conse-

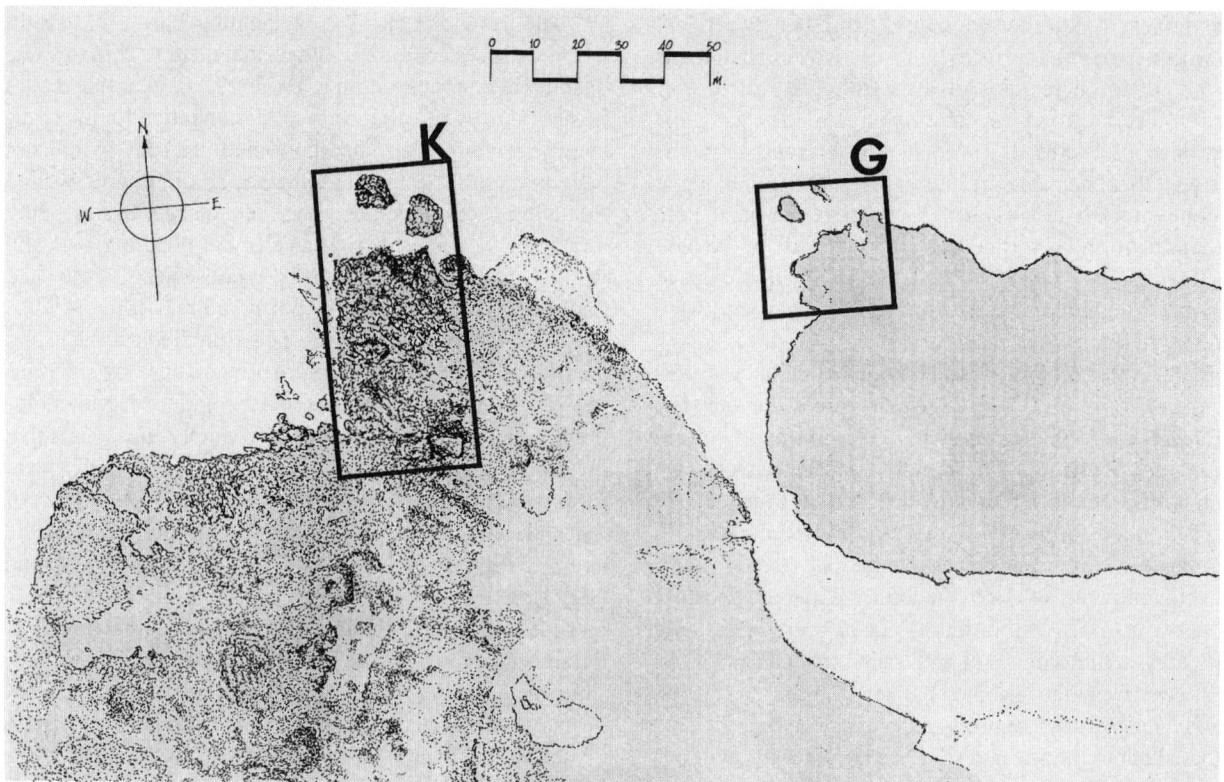

Fig. 1. Areas "G" and "K" either side of the entrance to the harbor.

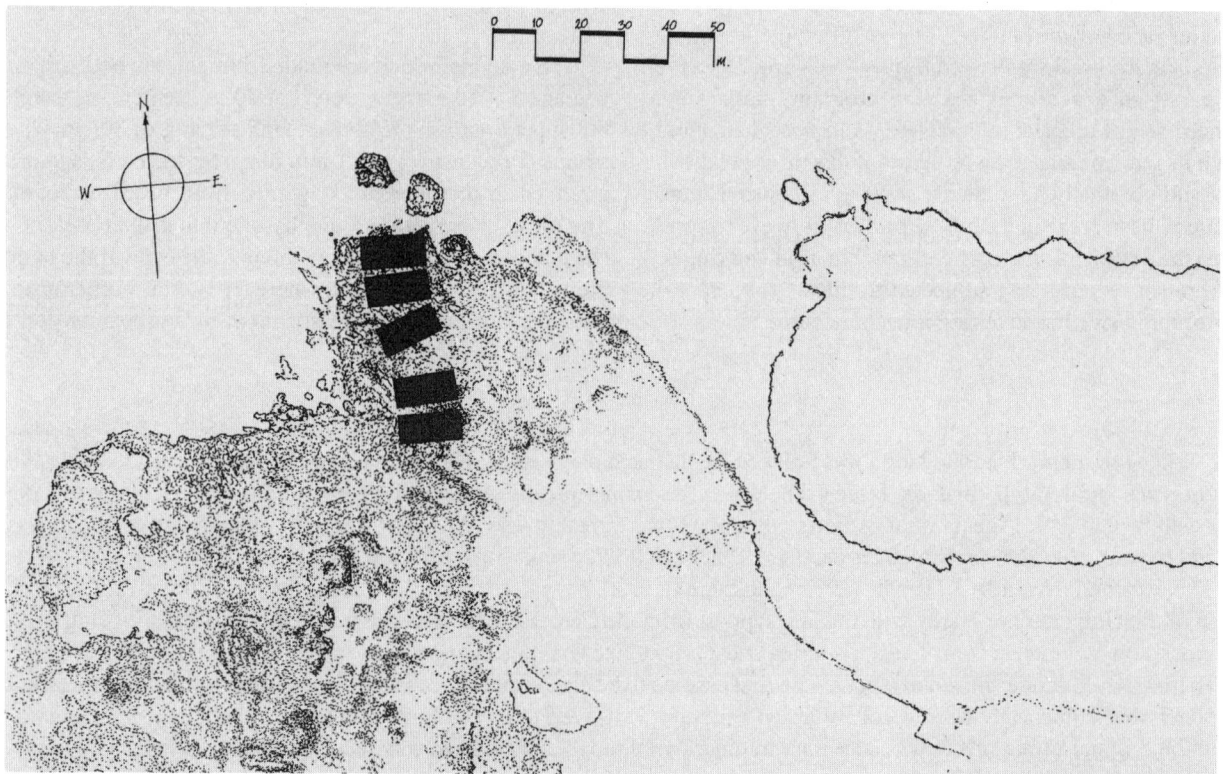

Fig. 2. Header arrangement of concrete blocks across the site.

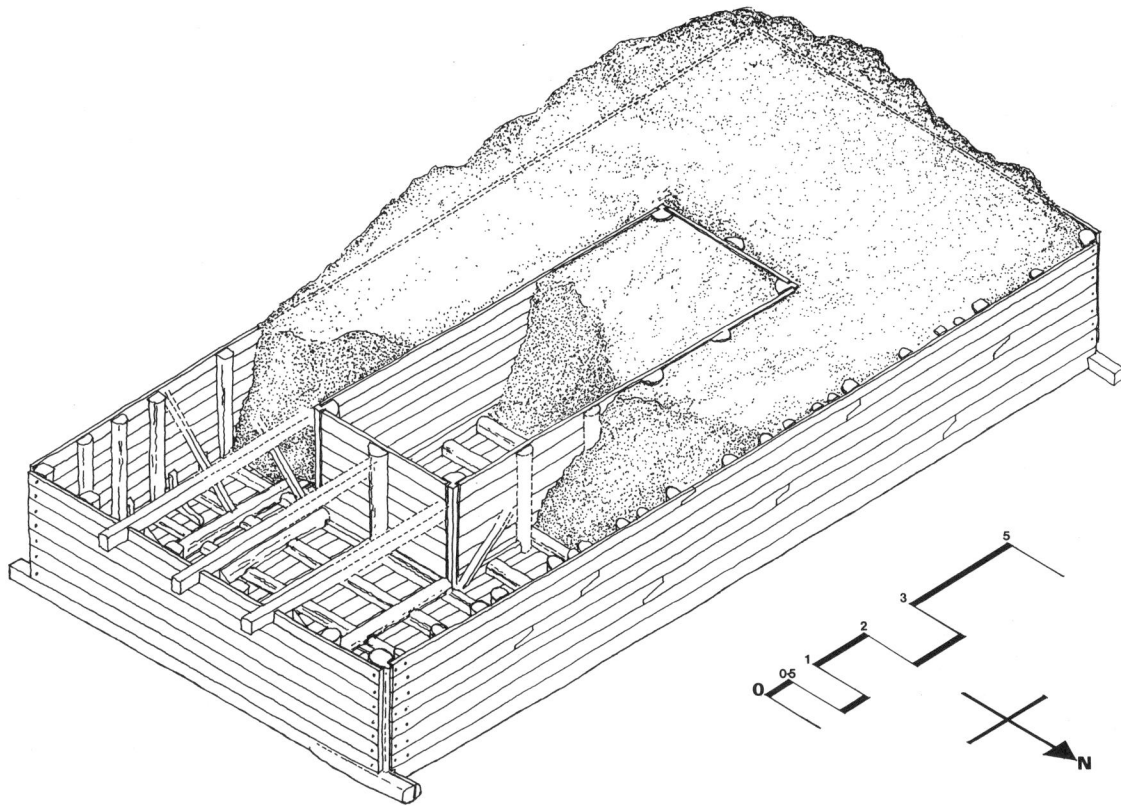

Fig. 3. Part reconstruction of a type "K" caisson.

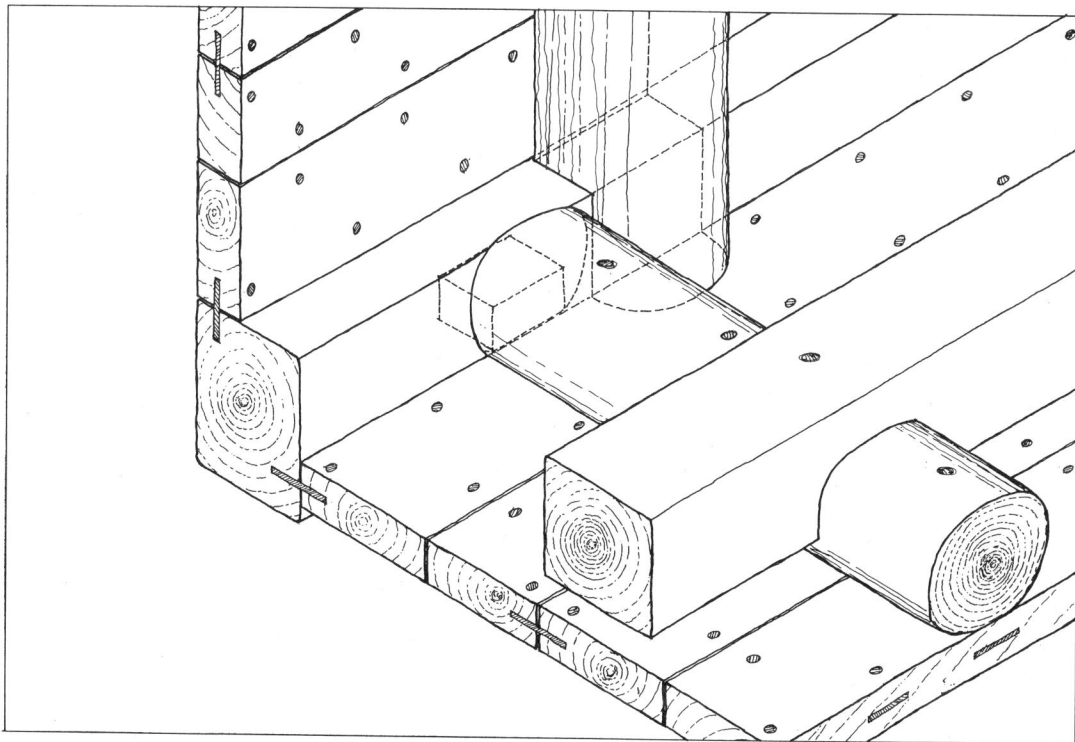

Fig. 4. Detail of junction of side and bottom planking and chine beam.

they do not quite line up one with each other. There is no evidence of any caulking material between the boards, although there are the remains of a lime-based cement slurry which has seeped out through the joint between the chine beam and the first plank and then solidified, thus effectively sealing the gap.

A 26 cm × 20 cm chine beam forms the junction between the side walls and the floor (fig. 4). The planking on the sides is fixed to the chine beam with mortise and tenon joints secured with treenails. This also applies to the floor planking that runs parallel to the chine. However, the ends of the bottom boards are set into the chine beam at bow and stern. This section is rebated along its length and in the case of K2 has mortises cut to take the projecting tenons that were cut into the ends of the boards (fig. 5), whereas K3 has a different design where the ends of the planks have been rounded on section and let into a similar rebate on the side of the chine (fig. 6). The floor frames comprise 20 to 25 cm × 20 cm rough-hewn pine sections (some still having bark adhering to them indicating that these were not secondary use timbers) set with an irregular spacing between each varying from 30 cm to 70 cm (fig. 7). The frames are fixed to the bottom planking with at least one treenail per board. The ends of the frames are set into the chine beam with a tenon that protrudes from the lower half of the frame (fig. 4). It is therefore apparent that the frames were fitted before the chine beam was offered up and fixed to the sides.

The inner face of the chine beam at the bow and stern, which projects down below the level of the bottom planking, has a firring piece set against it to protect it from damage when the structure was launched (fig. 8). This detail does not appear on the underside of the side chine beams, clearly indicating the method by which the caissons were launched.

The chine beam on the bow and stern projects out from the sides of the caisson by between 20 cm and 30 cm, and the complicated joint between the junction of the chine beams and the side wall planking is capped with a 4 cm × 5 cm quadrant section of timber which has been mitred and fixed around the chine beam (fig. 9). Stringers of approximately 25 cm diameter, with bark still adhering, were nibbed over the frames and transfixed to them with treenails (fig. 10). Timber knee sections provided stiffness to the junction of the side planking, chine beam and bottom planking and were fixed in place with treenails and iron pins (figs. 10 and 11).

Diagonal bracing or raking members provided rigidity between the inner compartment and the outer side wall planking. These raking props were braced off the frames, stringers or knees and secured at their heads by beams or directly onto the side frames. Beams positioned between the inner compartment and the outer side frames were set at approximately 2 m above the floor frames and projected through the side wall planking (fig. 10). This was above the water line of the "barge" when floating with an initial fill of approximately 0.5 m of concrete.

The inner cell, of which evidence remains in K2 but not in K5, is formed directly off the bottom planking and the floor frames are discontinuous either side of it. The function of the inner cell, which is built in the same watertight construction as the main part, can only be surmised. It could well have served as a central stabilising chamber to allow the barge to be loaded and sunk in a controlled manner. Within the compartment, the floor frames are similar to those that are outside it but are set into protruding edge beams onto which the corner posts and stringer are also fixed. A stringer runs on axis (approximately) and is nibbed onto the floor frames and fixed to them and to the edge beam of the inner compartment with treenails. The corner posts are formed from pine trunks into which rebates are cut to take the side planking. The posts are set onto the edge beam with a tenon that is wedged in place (fig. 12). The exterior "corner posts" are of a similar design to those found in the inner cell. The ends of the boards are let into the rebates running on either side of the "post" and are fixed in place with a combination of metal pins and treenails (fig. 9). This cut-

quently, in order to investigate the nature of the K3 structure and to examine its underside and compare its construction with that of K2, a vertical shaft was formed against the edge of the caisson and a tunnel was driven underneath it for a distance of 4 m.

In the other areas to the south of K2 and K3 the extent of the collapsed structure severely limited the sites where probes could be made. However, due to an erosion layer existing above the floor timbers on K5 it was possible, after the removal of some large blocks, to enter a labyrinth of tunnels that ran under the tumbled structure. With only a minimal amount of further excavation it was possible to uncover a large area of the caisson floor, although unfortunately erosion had obliterated all visible evidence of vertical structure. K8 was very badly broken up and there is evidence that this may have started in antiquity as excavations around the displaced fragments of the K8 caisson uncovered a wreck site dating to the first century C.E., and could only have got to where it did if it sank on top of an already broken up breakwater.

There is no apparent timber formwork remaining of K9, however, the concrete block does substantially remain, although split in half, and lies within the 14 m × 7 m footprint and has an overall height of approximately 4 m.

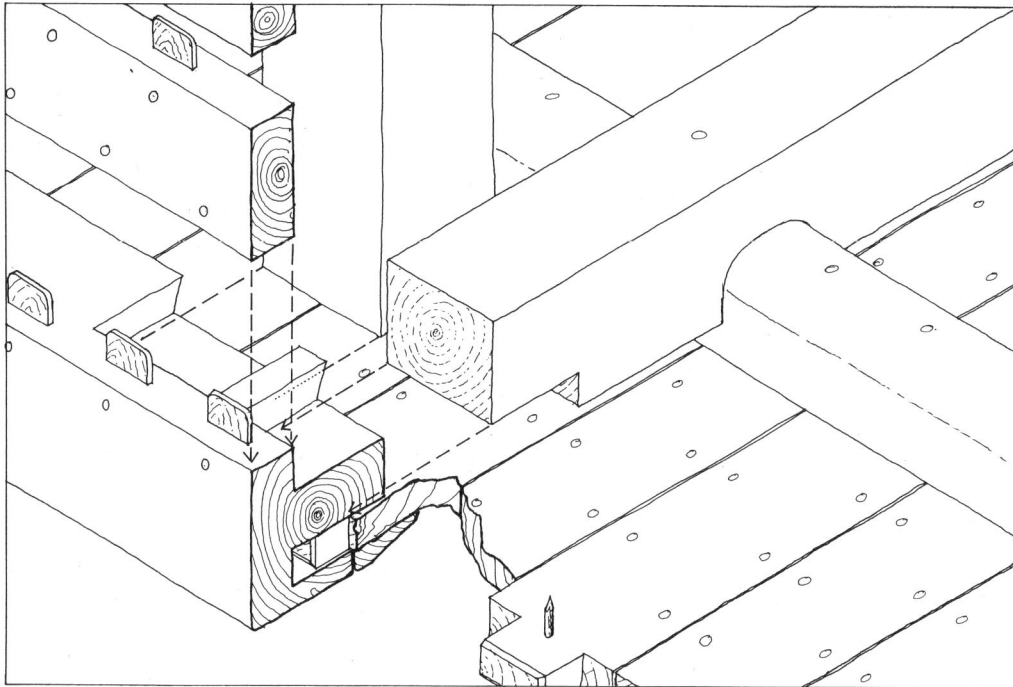

Fig. 5. Detail of the junction of the bow/stern chine beam and bottom and side planking, K-2.

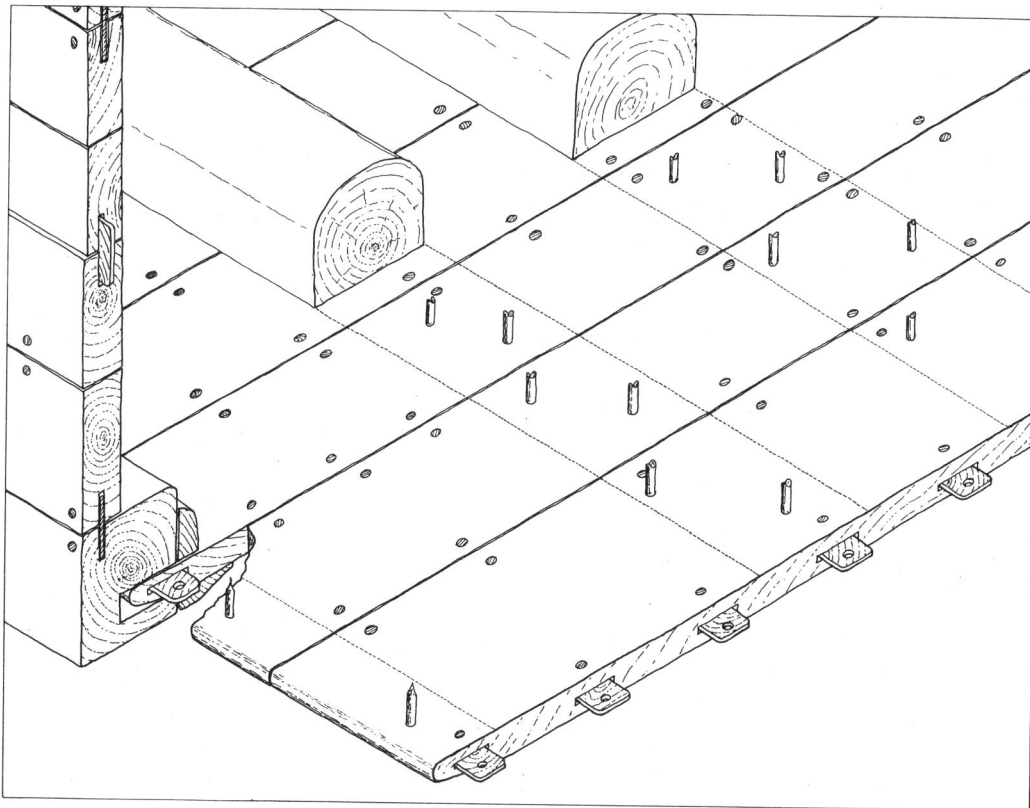

Fig. 6. Detail of the junction of the bow/stern chine beam and bottom and side planking, K-3.

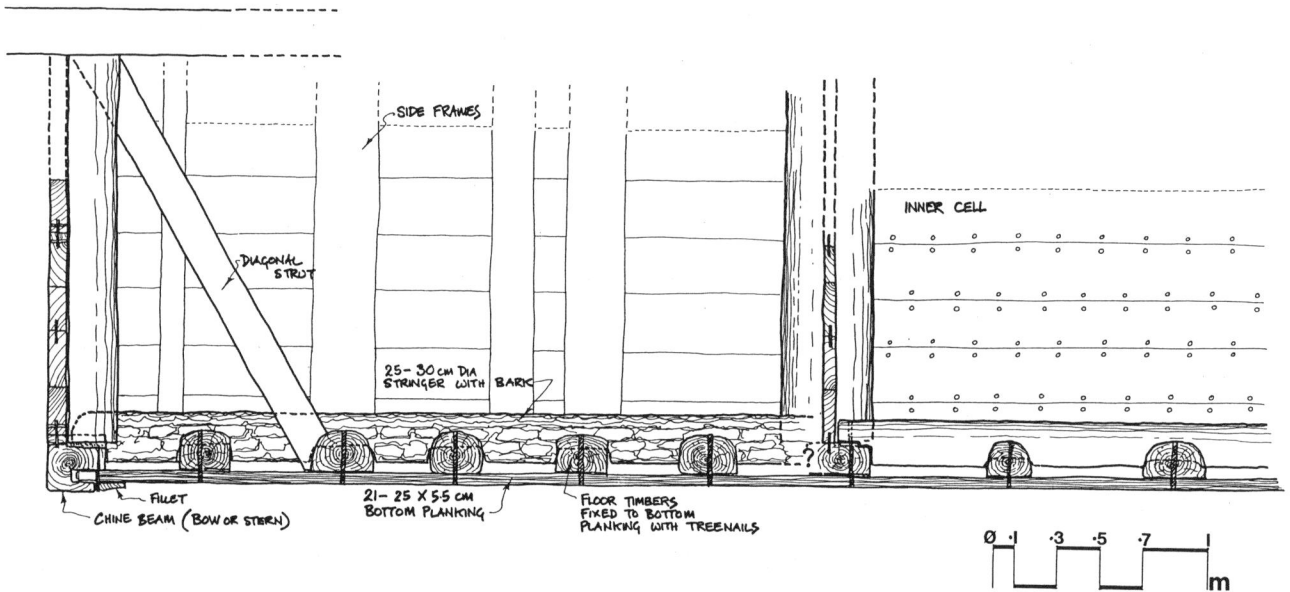

Fig. 7. East–west cross section through a typical type "K" caisson.

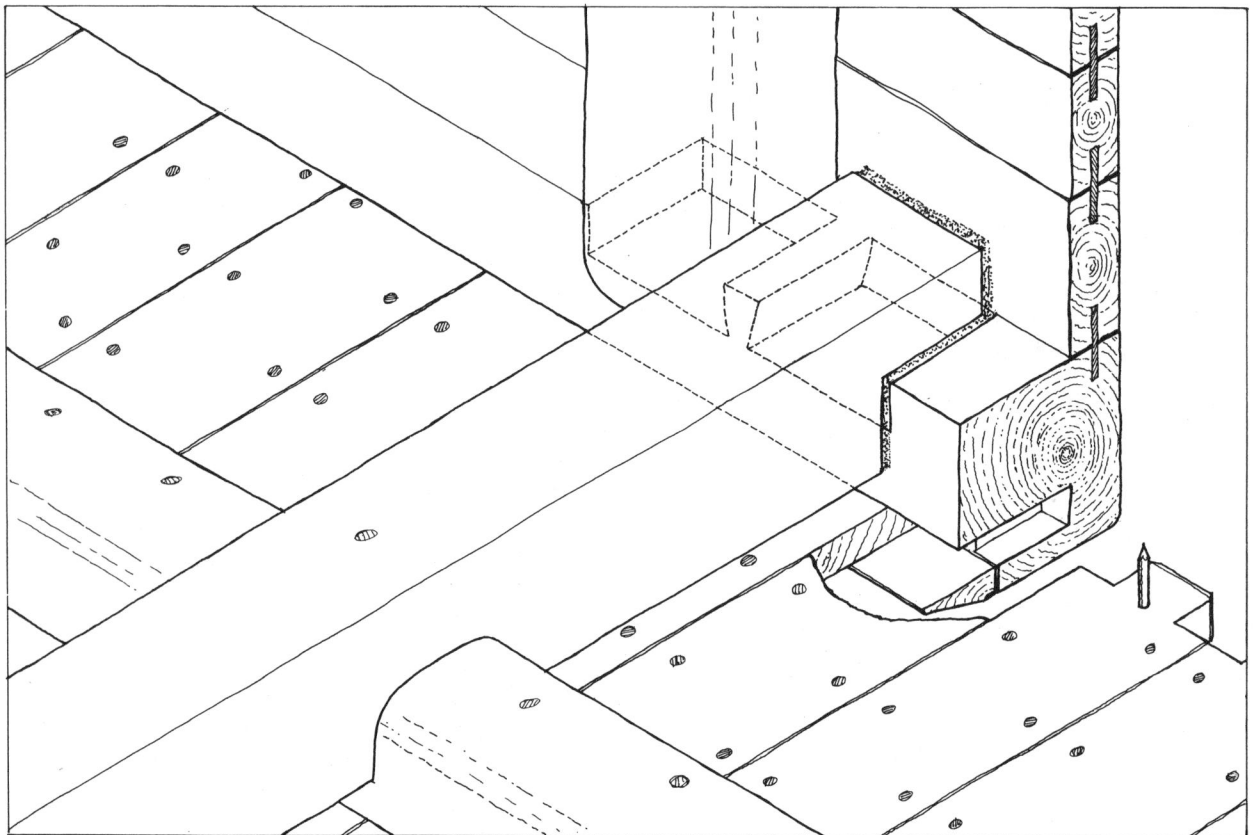

Fig. 8. Chine beam at bow/stern, K-2.

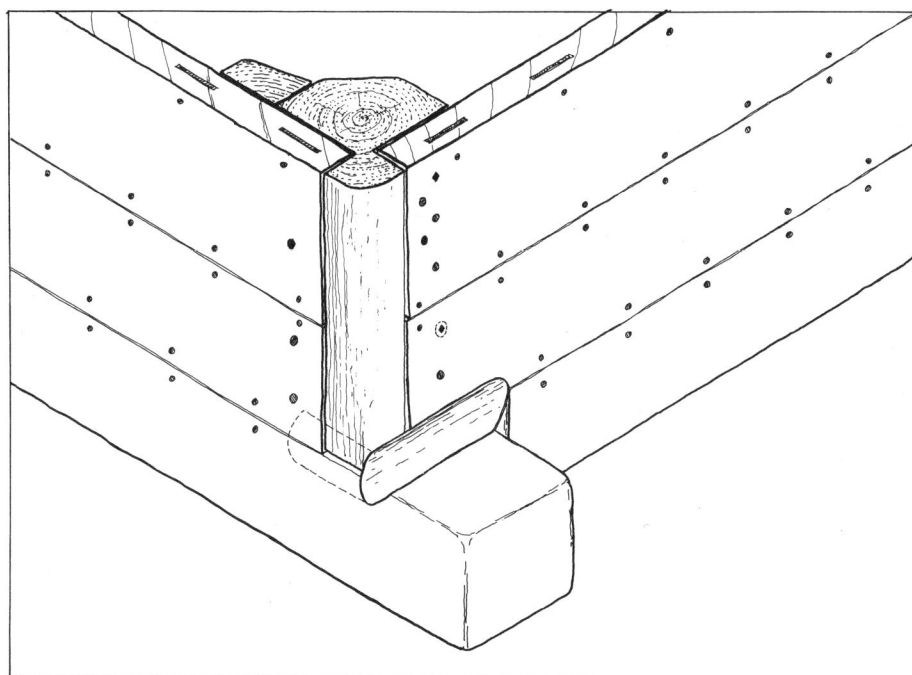

Fig. 9. Northeast corner of caisson K-5.

away post, however, leaves a weak nib that was broken off most of the corners that were excavated, and it is likely that this damage occurred in antiquity. The side frames range in size, shape and spacing, being either rectangular, square, semi-circular or quadrant shaped posts approximately 18 to 20 × 18 cm, and are fixed to the side planking with both treenails and metal pins. These side frames are notched into and over the chine beams where they project into the caisson (figs. 4, 5, and 8). There is also evidence that not all the frames extended over the whole height of the sides and some did not reach the chine.

Based on the evidence of the surviving structure, hypothetical reconstruction can be suggested. There is no doubt that the bottom planking was constructed first, and was probably set out on a raised "trestle" to enable the treenails to be trimmed as each board was fixed in place. A possible site for the "shipyard" is on the foreshore beside what is now Kibbutz Sdot Yam to the south of the ancient harbor where jetty-like structures have been found (Galili, Dahari, and Sharvit 1993: 61–77). From there the barges could be towed with the longshore current to their destination around the harbor enclosure. The floor frames would next be fitted onto the bottom planking, and the chine beams offered up to the sides and fitted over the tenons on the frames. The bow and stern chines were then added and the stringers let in on top of the frames and fixed into the bow and stern chine beams. The external corner posts were then erected and propped in

place while the side planking was built up board by board and cut to fit between the corner posts. Once the side walls had been completed and the side frames, diagonal props and cross beams added, the barge was then launched, probably on log rollers, bow or stern first. This procedure is confirmed by the evidence from the underside of the chine beam where a triangular closing fillet protects the downstanding edge of the chine beam and only appeared on the bow or stern.

The estimated weight of the empty barge is 70 metric tons, and it would have floated with a draught of approximately 0.5 m. It was then partially filled with a pozzolana-based concrete to a depth of approximately 0.5 m, which was allowed to cure before being taken out to the site. With this concrete layer in place, it would float with a draught of about 1.5 m.

The use of a hydraulic concrete in this lower portion indicates that the caisson was not entirely waterproof. The concrete both provided ballast and helped to seal the joints, particularly around the bottom edges. Once the concrete had hardened, the barge was towed to its pre-determined destination and moored in place while lighters brought lime mortar and lumps of tufa and limestone aggregate to be transferred therein. This lime mortar concrete was loaded in until the caisson settled onto the seabed which had previously been prepared with a rubble layer of concrete, tufa, and stone. At this point the freeboard was minimal and a pozzolana-

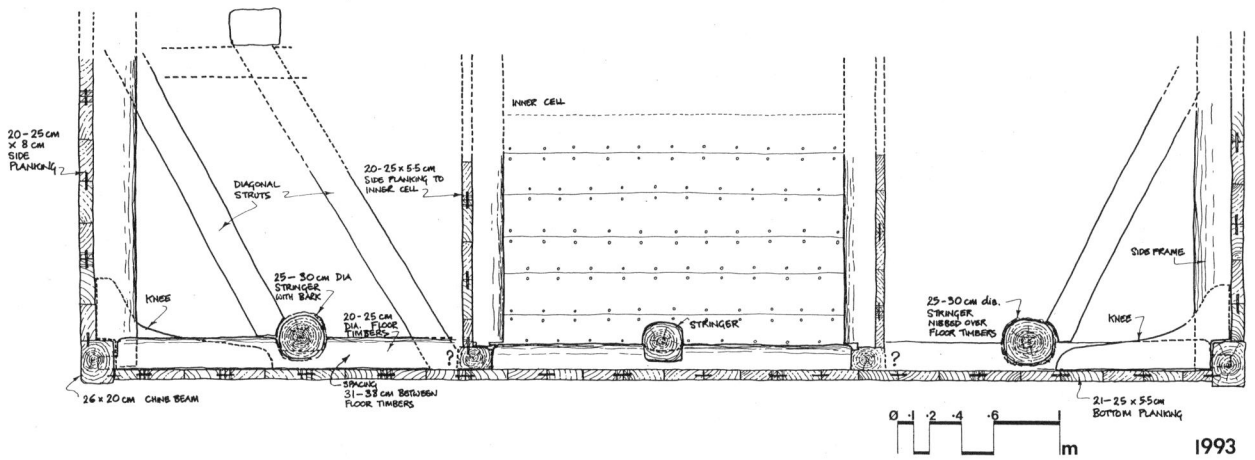

Fig. 10. North–south cross section through a typical type "K" caisson.

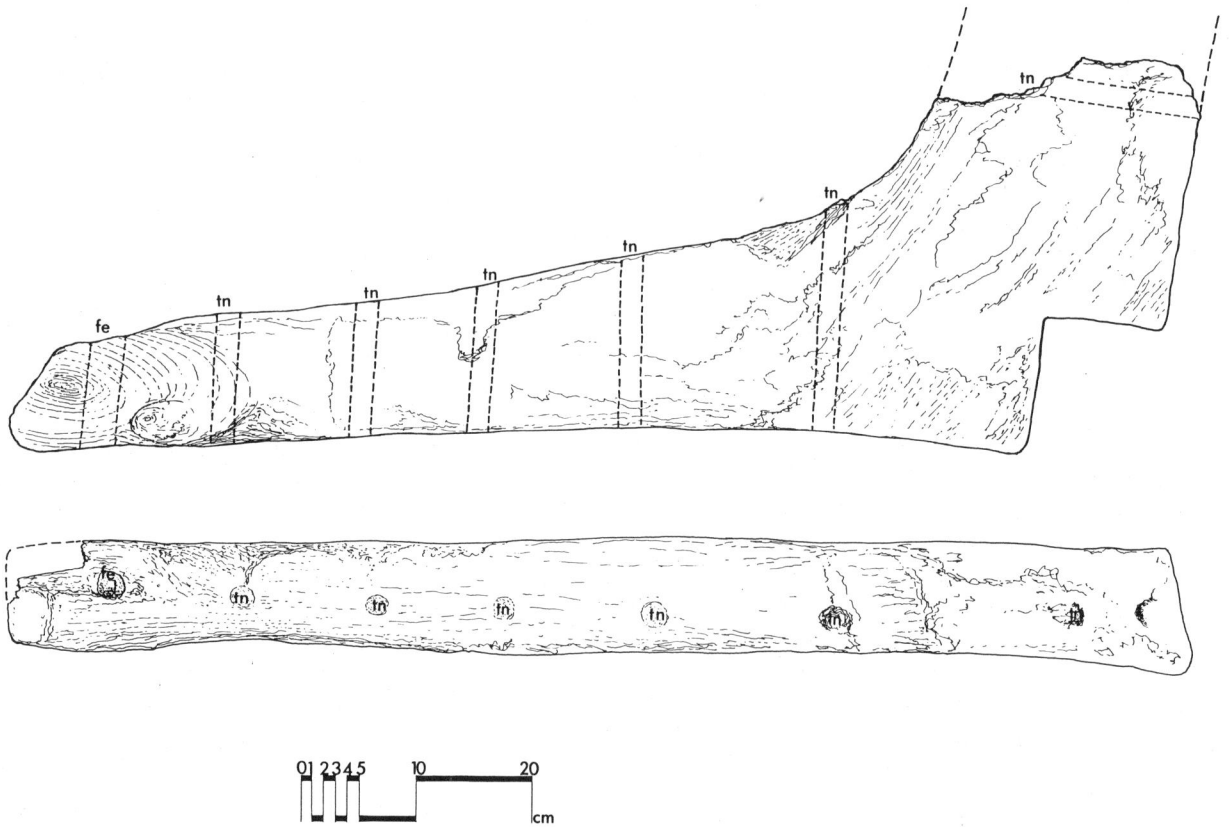

Fig. 11. Detail of knee from the north side of K-5.

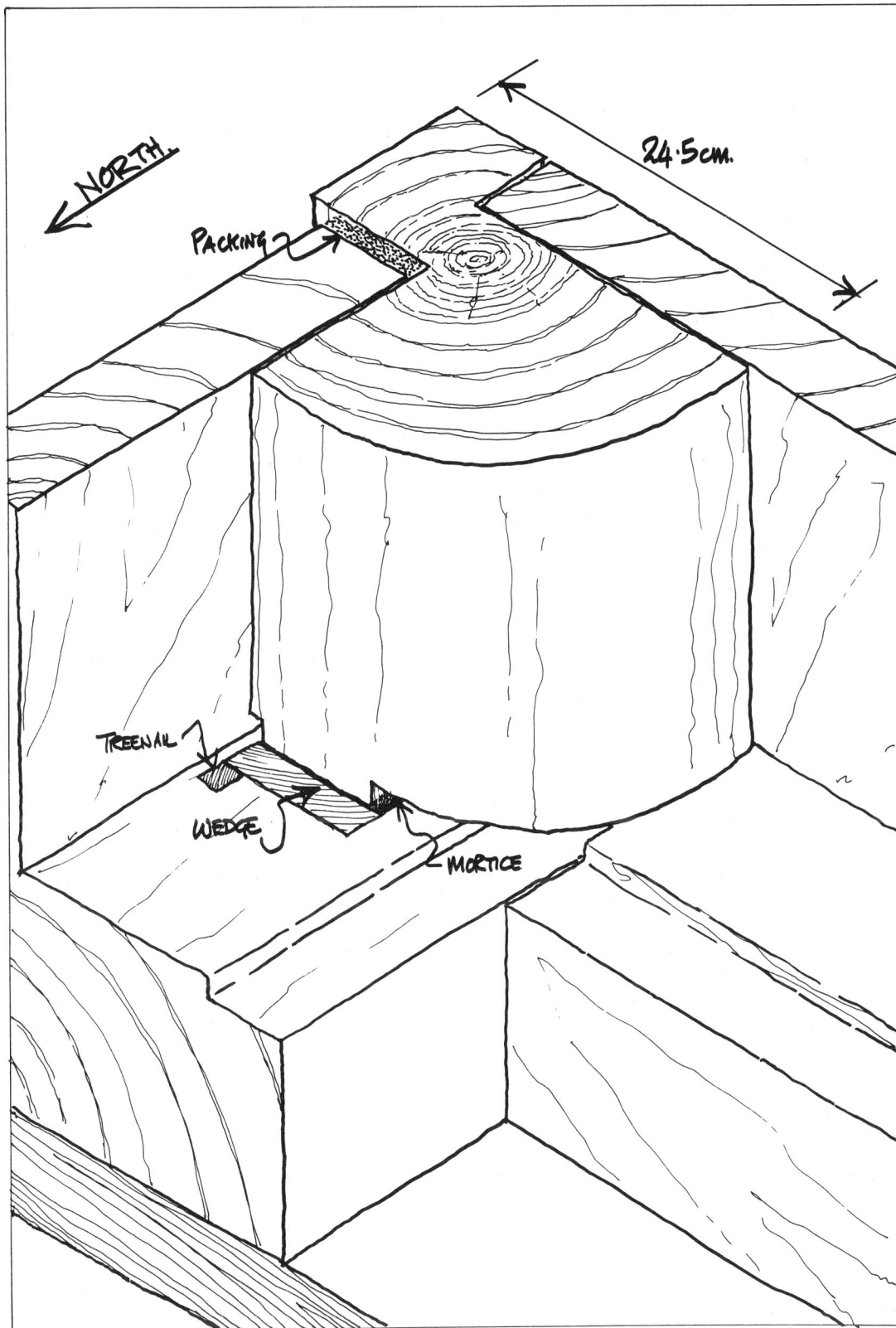

Fig. 12. Detail of northeast corner of inner cell of K-2.

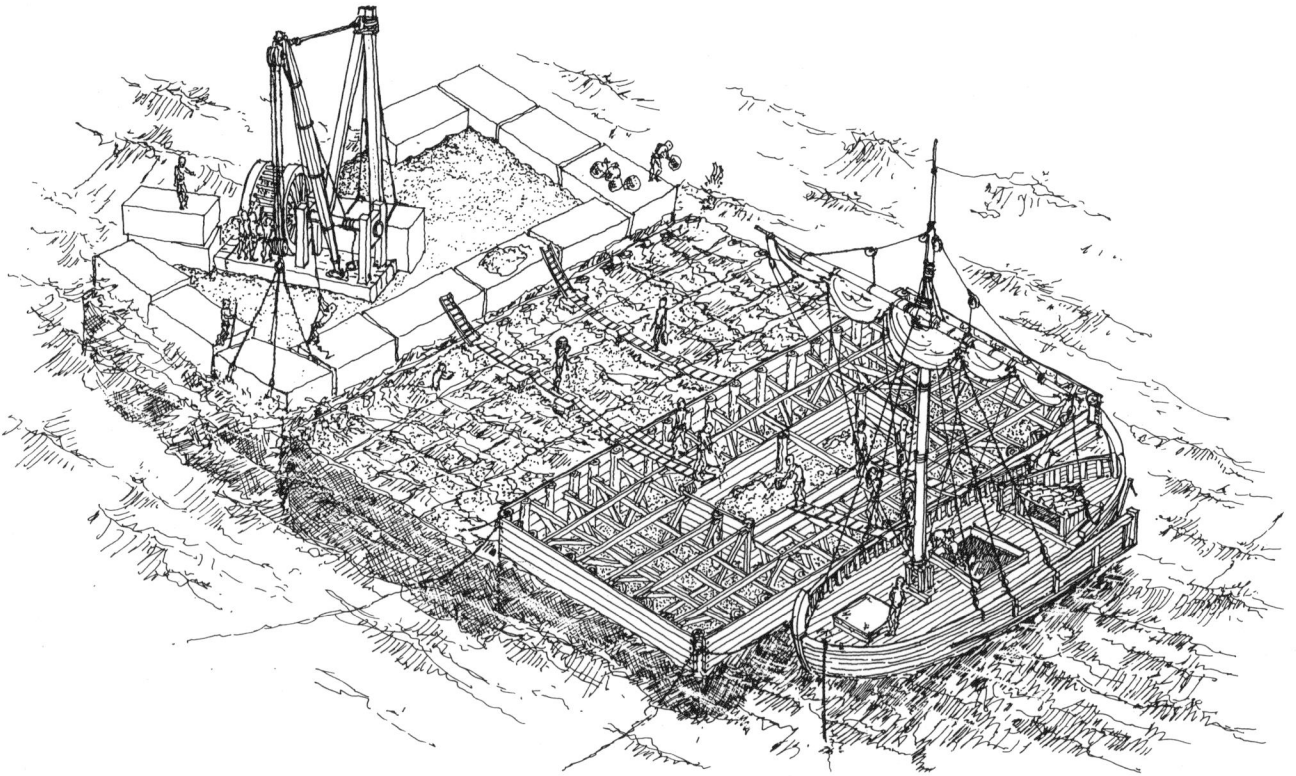

Fig. 13. Reconstruction sketch of the placement of concrete into a sinking caisson.

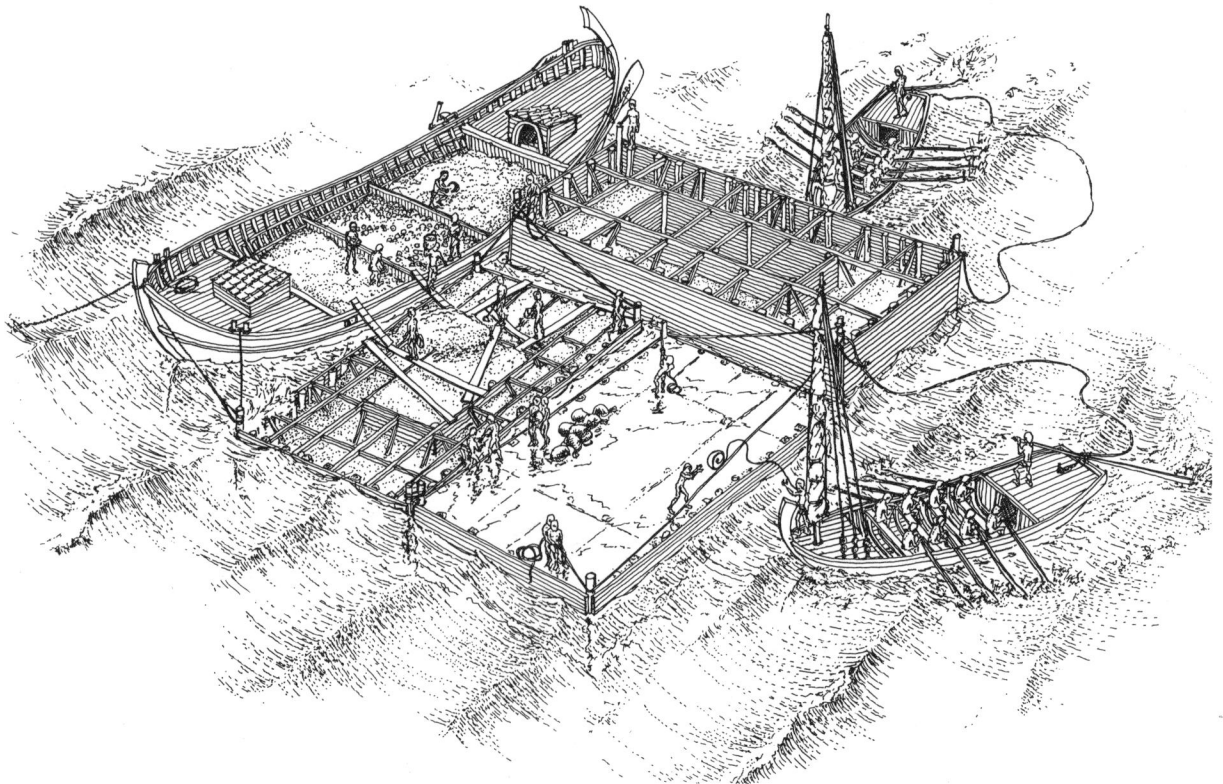

Fig. 14. Reconstruction sketch of the placement of concrete into a settled caisson.

rich mix was used to complete the fill.[10] It required only a further cap of 1.0 m of mortar and aggregate. The upper layer of hydraulic material was used to seal in the non-hydraulic layer and protect it from the seas, which would obviously break across the caisson, until such time as the rubble breakwater was added and the overlaying structure built on top (figs. 13 and 14).

Since the placement of the caissons does not appear to have been very precise, possibly due to mooring difficulties, it was necessary to infill between the blocks with additional concrete. If the gap was small, the concrete, placed in sacks, was dumped in the gap, such as between K2 and K3, or else the ends between caissons were blocked with prefabricated shuttering and concrete added as was the case in between K3 and K5, and between K5 and K8. This concrete would obviously have had to be placed in inundated forms, and therefore would need to have been hydraulic, which is confirmed by the *in situ* material, which consists of a pozzolana-rich mix. Once the blocks K2 to K9 had been set in place and the voids inbetween filled, they would have provided a platform 45 m long by 14 m wide. A rubble embankment was built up against the seaward side and a combination of cut blocks and rubble infill capped with stone paviors lined the leeward side.

Although there are examples from other Roman harbors of the use of mortise and tenon joints held together with treenails in the construction of formwork, particularly from North Africa, they do not show the ship construction detailing that is prevalent in the "K" type caissons.[11] There is no evidence of the use of comparably built barges in either contemporary texts or from other excavated sites. The caisson at Laurons (France), although built for a similar purpose, was more closely related to terrestrial carpentry-joinery technology than shipbuilding and was filled with rubble rather than concrete.[12] Later the architects/engineers who built the harbor at Portus outside Rome used redundant hulls of ships as permanent shuttering in the breakwater and also for the foundation to the lighthouse. This use provides the closest comparison to the Caesarea caissons. There are, however, no examples of concrete moles that have similar layering properties, where the block was made with a non-hydraulic core. In all likelihood the engineers were faced at the outset with material delivery problems. It would have taken some time to ship all the necessary pozzolana from the Bay of Naples area in Italy to Caesarea, and with the pressures of the harbor building program, decisions could well have been made deliberately to use a non-hydraulic lime mortar as a means of reducing the amount of imported material required in the construction of the harbor.

Unfortunately, this method of construction was inherently defective. The weak layer in the middle of the blocks became exposed due to seismic movements. Being in effect mass concrete, with little or no structural reinforcement, the blocks had no tensile strength, so any sagging or hogging action would have caused them to crack, allowing currents to wash through and erode the soluble centers, undermining the overlaying structures. This partly explains why the harbor so quickly fell into disrepair and why it would have been very difficult to rebuild (Raban 1992a: 111–24).

The remains of the caissons now lie at varying depths, generally sloping down from a depth of 7 m on the south to over 9 m at the north end. It is suggested that this variation in depth is due to a number of reasons, the principal ones being tectonic movement, variations in load along the length of the harbor wall, and the location of the fault lines. Now, as more of the lime-rich mortar in the central area of the blocks is exposed and sand levels vary on the seabed in different seasons, further erosion takes place causing the existing remains to fracture and become more jumbled as they shift during severe storms.

---

[10] Preliminary results from samples of concrete taken from K5 in 1994, which were tested by Technotrade Ltd Harpenden, show that the top and bottom layers of concrete contain high proportions of pozzolana and low lime, whereas the middle layer has a high lime and low pozzolana content. In the samples from the middle layer there were particles of burnt lime in the lime bound mix that had not rehydrated.

[11] Yorke and Davidson (1985: 157–64) describe examples of mortise and tenon jointed forms for inundated concrete structures along the North African coastline. However, none appear to comprise a barge-like structure.

[12] (Ximenes and Moerman 1985: 229–52). This article contains the description of a 22.9 m long by 2.2 m wide wooden caisson that was rubble-filled.

REFERENCES

Galili, E.; Dahari, U.; and Sharvit, J.
  1993   Underwater Surveys and Rescue Excavations along the Israeli Coast. *International Journal of Nautical Archaeology* 22.1: 61–77.
Marcus, R.
  1963   *Josephus, Jewish Antiquities, books XV–XVII,* Cambridge, MA.
Oleson, J. P.
  1988   The Technology of Roman Harbours. *The International Journal of Nautical Archaeology* 17.2: 154–55.
  1989   Area G: Northwest Tip of Northern Breakwater and Adjacent Tower. Pp. 127–30 in *The Harbours of Caesarea Maritima. Results of the Caesarea Ancient Harbour Excavation Project, 1980–1985, 1: The Site and the Excavations,* ed. A. Raban. BAR International Series 491. Oxford: B.A.R.
Oleson, J. P., and Branton, G.
  1992   The Technology of King Herod's Harbour. Pp. 58–63 in *Caesarea Papers. Journal of Roman Archaeology Supplementary Series Number Five,* ed. R. L. Vann. Ann Arbor.
Raban, A.
  1992a   Sebastos: the Royal Harbour of Caesarea Maritima—a Short-lived Giant. *International Journal of Nautical Archaeology* 21.2: 111–24.

  1992b   The Herodian Harbor of Caesarea: How it was Built and Operated. *Center for Maritime Studies News,* Report No. 19, Haifa.
St. Thackery, H.
  1927   *Josephus, The Jewish Wars against Rome,* Cambridge MA.
Vann, R. L.
  1991   The Drusion: a Candidate for Herod's Lighthouse at Caesarea Maritima. Pp. 123–39 in vol. in *The International Journal of Nautical Archaeology* 20.2: 123–39.
Yorke, R. A. and Davidson, D. P.
  1985   Survey of Building Techniques at the Roman Harbours of Carthage and some other North African Ports. Pp. 157–64 in *Harbour Archaeology: Proceedings of the First International Workshop on Ancient Mediterranean Harbours, Caesarea Maritima,* ed. A. Raban. BAR International Series 257. Oxford: B.A.R.
Ximenes, S. and Moerman, M.
  1985   The Roman Harbour of Laurons: Buildings and Structures. Pp. 229–52 in *Harbour Archaeology: Proceedings of the First International Workshop on Ancient Mediterranean Harbours, Caesarea Maritima.* ed. A. Raban. Oxford: BAR International Series 257. Oxford: B.A.R.

Sowing the Four Winds: Targeting the Cypriot Forest Resource in Antiquity

JULIA ELLIS BURNET

School of Biological Sciences
Macquarie University
Sydney, NSW 2109
AUSTRALIA

The impact of trade and exchange on the Cypriot forest resource has frequently been underestimated. While trees remain as part of an afforested landscape, little research into changes in composition and dynamic process has been undertaken, with the result that radical alteration in species dominance may pass unrecognized.

A two-fold approach is, therefore, necessary to

(i) redress an often unspoken bias in describing the resources utilized to initiate and maintain trade links between Cyprus and other Mediterranean countries. The traditional reliance on documentary sources—both Greek and Roman historical references and Homeric literature—distorts the study of environmental context and landscape relationships for early settlement sites.

(ii) gain an understanding of the economic value of forest products not only as raw materials harvested for shipbuilding and other heavy construction, for domestic purposes, for funerary and for ritualistic use, and for medicinal preparation, but also as necessary elements in resource control.

This paper examines those species most likely to have been under pressure from harvesting, indiscriminate or otherwise, and the resulting dramatic change in species patterning.

INTRODUCTION

Trade patterns depend at least in part on available commodities and their utilization. The natural resource wealth of Cyprus has been known since antiquity and trade links appear to have been established with the island as soon as seafaring technology had developed to a point where transportation costs would be minimized.

TEXTS AND LANDSCAPES

It has been customary in the past to rely heavily on ancient texts as an historical source in determining environmental relationships, commodity production, distribution and utilization. The use of textual material raises many fundamental problems, a principle issue being the range of ambiguities in the vocabulary of trees and timber in ancient literature. In Latin, for example, there is a difference between *materia,* wood used for building or craft making, and *lignum,* meaning fuel wood. In Greek, one word, *xylon,* covers wood of every description. A further difficulty is encountered in identifying species. Theophrastus (*HP* 3.8.2) knew that the names attributed to the various species of oak growing in Macedon differed from those given the same range of species growing on Mt. Ida in the Troad. Similarly, the Arcadian names for the main species of pine distinguished by the Greeks were the opposite of those accepted in the rest of Greece. However, as some of the examples presented by Theophrastus were based on hearsay, these discrepancies between species might be explained by the collation of information from various sources (Meiggs 1982: 18). Confusion between cedar and juniper can create additional problems. The Greek *kedros* and Latin *cedrus* do not always mean cedar. In Greek the word also includes the *Juniperus* spp, the *Cedrus* spp. being relatively unknown.

Tree names in Akkadian, Hebrew and Egyptian textual sources are even more controversial. The only secure word known in Akkadian is the word for cedar, *erinu*. The identification of pine, juniper and other important commercial trees, however, remains obscure. Loret (1916) and Glanville (1931: 16, 31) argued that the common term used by the Egyptians for imported wood (ash-wood), also pertained to fir, or possibly fir and pine rather than cedar (Meiggs 1982: 55).

A further difficulty is that most ancient writers appear to have borrowed freely from previous written works. Pliny the Elder, to whom is credited the more accurate descriptions of ancient Cyprus (Meiggs 1982), relied on the works of Theophrastus (ca. 370–288/5 B.C.E.), a pupil of Aristotle, and on the oral tradition ascribed to Homer. Pliny's plagiarism can be detected clearly in his description of the palm (*NH* 13.33), which is almost identical to the one by Theophrastus. Pliny's original contribution to the botanical corpus was thought to be his record of the largest cedar known to have been growing on Cyprus at that time. It was reported to have been harvested to provide the mast for a galley commanded by Demetrius Poliorcetes (ca. 300 B.C.E.), and is reputed to have had a recorded length of 130 feet (*NH* 16: 203-206). The same account, however, is related in Ezekiel (*Ezekiel* 27: 7).

From the above it appears that the relevant Mediterranean literature is inadequate for the identification of tree species pertaining to specific locations or the utilization of timber resources. Botanical species appear to have been referenced by writers who have little knowledge of botanical science, a fact deplored by Dioscorides during the first century C.E. (Riddle 1985). Furthermore, some authors, including Theophrastus, Eratosthenes and Strabo, relied on oral accounts as the source of their descriptions or based their scholarship on documentary sources in the library at Alexandria. Nibbi (1994) not only reviews the error in species identification in ancient textual sources but cites the continuation of misinformation in current literature. Setting aside these traditional references, several sources are available and can be regarded as of critical importance in understanding environmental factors related to timber utilization

and export. They are, first, the epigraphic evidence such as the association occurring in the third century B.C.E. between the Sacred Grove at Kourion and the god Apollo. An inscription indicates that the sanctuary at that time was dedicated to Apollo Hylates, Apollo of the Woodlands (Sinos 1990: 20).[1] No oaks grow in the vicinity of the sanctuary today, but in the shaded, moist areas of the aqueduct head adjacent to the temple many ground cover species associated with a sheltered forest canopy can be found *in situ*.

Secondly, the artistic representations by indigenous craftsmen, such as those on cylinder seals, clearly depict tree forms that can sometimes be readily identified. Ohnefalsch-Richter (1893: 101–41) identified eleven forms of stylized tree on cylinder seals from Cyprus. The oldest shows a realistic representation of a tree or branch that Richter attributed to one of the native conifers. The simplified form of the tree, however, precludes positive identification. Other examples discussed by Ohnefalsch-Richter are of interest for they appear to suggest that the harvesting of lower tree limbs became progressively severe. Unlike the natural conifer, which is self-pruning in dense forest stands where lateral limbs are lost close to the bole, the artificial pruning of branches leaves a stump retained by the tree, which becomes fixed by resin and creates a very knotted structure in the timber. A final form in Ohnefalsch-Richter's list of types is undoubtedly a palm tree. With the further development of a distinctive glyptic craft during the Late Cypriot Bronze Age another type of tree representation, described as the "bouquet tree" (Poroda 1948), becomes a unique addition to the collection.

The third source is comprised of the dynastic lists, including accounting systems, maintained by strong centralized governments. Although this source does not often specify country of origin, or applies an archaic name form, such as Alashiya (Petrie 1898: 44–48; Moran 1992: 104–13), through accurate identification of the species recorded the country of origin might be determined. These records include references to the importation of cedar from the temple list of Ramses III (ca. 1195–1164 B.C.E.). A reconstruction of a temple stele by Hayes (1949) reads: "(I) ap[proached (?)] ... [ced]ar (of) the Plateaus of Cedar ... which (I) made, cutting (down) the tree(s)" (Ward 1971: 63). From the Palermo Stone (recto vi; 2–4) we read: "Bring forty ships filled (with) cedar logs ... shipbuilding (of) cedar wood, one Praise-of-the-Two-Lands ship, 100 cubits (long), and (of) *meru* wood, two ships, 100 cubits (long)

---

[1] The epithet *"Hylates"* derives from the ancient Greek word YLN—Hyle meaning woodland or forest. This has been ascribed to Stephanus Byzantius of the fifth century C.E. who described an extensive forest located in the area of the sanctuary under this name.

... making doors of the royal palace (of) cedar wood" (Pritchard 1950: 227). Pritchard notes that the word translated as cedar probably applied to that species and other coniferous woods also, and may be applied to any timber transported by sea.

Alternatively, another method of determining the complexities of biodiversity and cultural interaction in antiquity is to examine the landscape to assess the unique qualities of tree species associated with that landscape, and make some correlations, albeit tentative, between these factors and the remains of wood from ancient artifacts. The largest assemblage of extant wooden material in the Mediterranean region has been excavated at sites in Egypt. The combination of extensive and prolonged trading links with other nations and the dry climatic conditions experienced along the Nile have contributed to the preservation of a wealth of wooden material, the species identification of which demonstrates examples of early trading.

The ancient afforested environment comprising part of the natural resource of Cyprus was dominated by three primary factors: geological parent material, aspect or exposure, and the incidence and frequency of wild-fire. Secondary factors include rainfall, elevation, and the impact of free-range grazing, including fallow deer and moufflon, replaced later by goats.

Using these primary factors, I have projected a mosaic of forest cover that is radically different in perception from that traditionally described. The pattern defined is one of different ecological associations. By using environmental reconstruction, based on an understanding of the composition and dynamic structure of the forest, the vegetation pattern that emerges is dominated by those species with a natural affinity for the sedimentary rock formations that occupy two-thirds of Cyprus.

The Mesaoria was characterized by an open woodland composed of the *Cupresses sempervirens* (cypress) with dense riparian cover over streams (Holmboe 1914: 201). This cover was rich in species composition, *Platanus orientalis* (Oriental plane), *Alnus orientalis* (alder), *Laurus noblis* (bay), with *Nerium oleander* (oleander), *Myrtus communis* (myrtle) and *Rubus sanctus* (blackberry) as substrata species, *Pteris* (ferns) and *Rubiaceae* (cleavers or bedstraw) as ground cover plants. The riparian cover inhibited the rapid flow of water and may have induced areas of swamp. Frankel (1974) suggested that the original internal communication routes between settlements in the island's interior lay away from river lines and, in light of the riparian cover extant in isolated locations, this appears most plausible. The substrata vegetation on the hills surrounding the Mesaoria contain valuable food resources, *Olea europea* (wild olive), *Pistacia terebinthus* (terebinth), *Capparis spinosa* (caper) and *Crataegus azarolus* (haw-

thorn berries), all of which contribute to a rich and varied diet over changing seasonal conditions.

This substrata extends into the pillow lavas of the Troodos foothills where the now dominant pine *Pinus brutia* (Calabrian pine) was probably originally contained. A major role in antiquity of the *Pinus brutia* was that of a gossan indicator, the species growing well in the vicinity of copper-ore-carrying seams (Constantinou 1992). *Pinus brutia* is light-demanding, and intolerant of species competition, thus rendering it an important species for the establishment of secondary forest cover.

Higher in the mountains, the forest would have had co-dominant species representing deciduous hardwoods, the *Quercus lusitanica* (Royal oak) with the *Pinus nigra* (black pine), on the serpentine and gabbro formations with a good representation of *Juniperus oxycedrus* (prickly juniper), a species now severely depleted due to raised soil temperatures after ground cover and substrata disappearance (Polycarpou 1954). The *Cedrus brevifolia* (cedar) are thought to have been confined to the diabase geological formations at high altitudes (Chapman 1934) although it is now known that they can grow in a wide range of situations. Cedars require good canopy shade during early development and this factor is the most critical for natural regeneration.

The forests of the coastal areas included *Quercus calliprinos* (oak), *Juniperus phonecia* (Phonecian juniper) and *Cupresses sempervirens* again with complex associations in the substrata. The valley floors carried the riverine associations of *Platanus orientalis* and *Alnus orientalis* with an understory of *Pteris* and *Rubus* in moist areas, *Cistus villosus* (cistus) and *Origanum majorana* (marjoram) on the slopes or in open spaces beneath the *Pinus brutia* canopy. *Olea europea*, *Vitis vinifera* (wild grape), and *Ficus carica* (fig) occurred within these forest stands, which are still present in scattered, isolated areas and are well-represented in the archaeological record (Kyllo 1982; Colledge 1980; 1981; 1982).

WOOD TAXONOMY— TIMBER QUALITY AND POTENTIAL USE

An examination of these tree species from a different perspective, namely the study of the internal structure of the timber, may define the use made of the forest resource and its importance as a trade commodity. This factor is particularly pertinent for species selected for ship building (Theophrastus *HP* 7.1).

In the living tree, wood performs a threefold roll of support, conduction and storage. Sapwood transports sap to the upper areas of the tree and acts to conserve or store food. Sapwood lumber is light colored and always nondurable in character. Heartwood contributes support to the living tree and functions as a repository for metabolic waste products. It frequently has a dark appearance and is in some species naturally resistant to biological degradation (Wenger 1984: 567).

Sources of variation affecting wood products are density, specific gravity, static bending, proportional limit, modules of rupture, modules of elasticity, and stress in compression. The specific gravity of timber is the ratio of the density of oven dried wood to the density of water at four degrees celsius where the density of water is 1.0 g/cm³. Density is the weight or mass of a unit volume of wood. In the metric system, density and specific gravity are numerically identical. Density, therefore, relates to the basic wood structure of tree species and their variable moisture content. The presence of extractives in wood cells can have a major effect upon the density of the wood. This is an important factor relating to some of the pine species indigenous to Cyprus, as they are very high in mineral and extractable substances, such as resin, which add to the weight of a timber length, but reduce its strength.

Mechanical properties of wood define its action as a natural engineering material under load or stress, such as, for example, the performance of ship keels or ribs in heavy seas. Static bending is measured by loading a beam at a slow, constant rate, typically resulting in deflections of fracture of 2.5 cm per minute. Proportional limit is the limit of proportionality between load (stress) and deformation (strain). With an increase in load beyond the proportional limit, deformation increases by a greater percentage than the load. Stressing beyond the proportional limit results in permanent deflection. Modules of rupture are the measure of the breaking strength of a beam expressed in terms of stress per unit area. It is determined by computing the fiber stress in the outer fibres of a beam at maximum load and serves as a practical strength comparison for different species of timber. Modules of elasticity are a measure of the stiffness or rigidity of a beam or column. It is the ratio of stress to corresponding strain below the proportional limits. Other mechanical properties that are frequently measured are maximum stress in compression parallel to grain, compression strength perpendicular to grain, sheer strength parallel to grain, compression strength perpendicular to grain, sheer strength parallel to grain, impact bending strength, tensile strength perpendicular to the wood grain, and hardness (Wenger 1984).

All wood substance, regardless of the species from which it comes, has about the same density. The difference in density that occurs between species arises from the cellular structure of wood and depends on the size of the cells, the thickness of the cell walls, and some other relatively minor factors.

Wood in the green state contains a substantial quantity of moisture that varies considerably between heartwood or sapwood, and again with great differences between species. The amount of moisture in a piece of wood accordingly affects the weight of the wood. Most species of wood, even when green, float in water. The buoyancy of wood is due to air contained within the cells. When wood is kept submerged, the air within the cells is gradually expelled by water, with the result that it becomes heavier and finally sinks.

The rate at which wood will absorb water when continuously exposed to it varies with species, whether it is sapwood or heartwood; the length of the piece, size of cross section, and other factors. Whereas one species may become waterlogged after a relatively short period of exposure, another may remain underwater many years without absorbing so much water that it becomes heavy enough to sink. The heartwood of most species is much more impermeable than the sapwood. Thin boards or short sections absorb water more rapidly and become waterlogged sooner than thick long pieces. Since water diffuses or moves most easily in the longitudinal direction, the wood close to the end surfaces of submerged lumber will normally have a much higher moisture content than wood 0.3 m or more from the ends.

For these reasons it is extremely difficult to calculate the weight of water that a given ship or boat will take on if continuously afloat over a period of years. The problem of doing so is further complicated by the fact that, in hull planking for example, drying continues from the inboard face even though the outboard face is in continuous contact with water. Under such conditions, solid planking never becomes saturated, particularly if of an impermeable species such as cedar. On the other hand, keels are usually thick enough so that, if made of heartwood of a hardwood species, they can remain in water for years without becoming waterlogged. By contrast, sapwood may become waterlogged very quickly.

The specific gravity of a piece of wood is an excellent index of the amount of wood substance the piece contains and, therefore, is also an index of its strength properties. Average specific gravity-strength relationships based on a large number of species of both hardwood and softwood varieties show that some properties, such as maximum crushing strength parallel to grain, increase approximately in proportion to the increase in specific gravity, although in a few cases some species increase more rapidly. Again, although there appears to be a general correlation between specific gravity and strength, the rule does not hold true for all species, particularly those whose wood contains relatively large amounts of resin, gum, and other extractives, which add to the weight but do not contribute equally to the strength as would a like amount of wood substance. In addition, species vary in the structural arrangement of their fibers. For these reasons, two species that average the same specific gravity may exhibit different strength characteristics.

Conditions of growth often cause wide variations in weight of a species of wood; some trees grow faster, some are more vigorous. Trees with wide annual rings have grown more rapidly than trees with narrow rings. In soft woods, as a general rule, exceptionally slow-growth or fast-growth material is lighter in weight and weaker than normal-growth stock. In hard wood, fast growth is generally indicative of good strength properties, although slow growth does not necessarily mean weakness. Locality of growth, within the normal range of growth of a species, has relatively little effect on the quality of lumber.

All wood subjected to normal use conditions contains a degree of moisture. The exact quantity of moisture depends on the amount of seasoning the material has received and from the perspective of long-term usage, the atmospheric and related conditions to which it is exposed. The strength of wood is intimately related to the amount of moisture it contains. As wood dries, most strength properties are increased. On the other hand, there are great differences in the strength of different species of wood at the same moisture content. A relationship also exists between the strength of woods at the same moisture content and their weight, the drier woods being stronger.

A final important point is that wood shrinks most in the direction of the annual growth rings (tangentially), about half to two-thirds as much across these rings (radially), and very little, as a general rule, along the wood grain (longitudinally). Typically, the heavier species of wood shrink more across the grain than the lighter ones. When freedom from shrinkage is more important than hardness or strength, for example, in the planking of small boats, a light-weight species would ideally be chosen. When it is important to combine hardness with strength or low shrinkage, as in the case of tree-nails, some exceptional species such as the *Quercus* spp. and *Alnus* spp. would be selected.

Table 1, on the mechanical properties of the most important commercial species within the Cypriot environment, aids in the demonstration of their cultural association through trade potential and desirability. The figures quoted in Table 1 represent new and as yet unpublished research (Burnet). Previous data was gleaned from sources as diverse as the University of Thesalonika (Tsoumis 1991) and the South African Forestry Department in Pretoria (1977). However, both sets of figures appear to be derived from Kollmann (1951). The figures presented in Table 1 were prepared by Peter Chapman, Research Division, State Forests of New South Wales (1995), from small specimens of wood supplied by Mr. Alexandrou, Principal, Cyprus Forestry College, Prodromos. As noted, some difficulty was encountered due to the small size of some specimens. The analysis overall is the first to be conducted as a comparison of Cypriot species.

The wood of the *Pinus brutia* is harder than that of most other pines and after seasoning is more inclined to surface check or splitting (a form of drying degrade often related to excessive temperatures) than other species. For this reason slow seasoning is of great importance for maximum wood utilization. Timber from relatively young trees, those of about fifty years growth, is hard and heavy, and consequently very strong. Timber from the *Pinus brutia* was used in construction as flooring, doors and ceilings, for ship building and musical instruments. Its bark was important for the tanning of hides.

The timber from the *Cupresses sempervirens* is fine, even and straight-grained. The relatively high figure quoted for hardness reflects these fiber qualities and its lack of retained sap and resin. Growth rings are distinct and young timber can be knotty. A fragrant scent repels insects. The timber dries rapidly and well with little degradation or splitting. It is easily worked and finishes well but it is difficult to make a clean bore unless the timber length is well supported. Likewise it is difficult to mortise. These factors reflect the density of the wood (Wenger 1984: 585). The timber is liable to termite and marine-borer attack (Bolza and Keating 1972) if planking is subjected to a stagnant water anchorage. Timber from the *Cupresses sempervirens* was used in the ancient Near East for construction, shipbuilding, mummy cases, religious carvings, and the doors of sanctuaries and religious structures (1 *Kings* 5:22; 2 *Chronicles* 3:5). The doors of St. Peter's in Rome were hung for over 1100 years without showing signs of decay (Record and Hess 1943: 7).

The *Platanus orientalis* (often confused with the sycamore by North American authors) was utilized for durability and strength although the wood weight was lighter than most *Quercus* spp. Principal uses were for chariot axles and hubs of wheels, including water wheels. It was used in the construction of Egyptian coffins and mummy cases. The wood grain is usually irregular, fairly easy to work, finishing smoothly but likely to warp unless carefully seasoned (Record and Hess 1943: 428).

The wood from the *Juniperus* spp. was used in ship construction as ribbing because the natural curvature of branches from mature trees attained ideal proportions for this purpose. The berries were used in a wide range of medicinal preparations as demonstrated from the excavation of a 3rd Dynasty Egyptian grave (Manniche 1989).

TABLE 1. Sample mean test results

Botanical Name	Compress-ion Strength	Bending MOR	Bending MOE	Shear Strength	Density	Moisture Content
	(MPa)	(MPa)	(MPa)	(MPa)	(kg/m3)	0%
Acer obtusifolium	68	154	13,190	17.7	771	10%
Arbutus andrachne	93	172	15,700	22.0	934	10%
Cedrus brevifolia	56	86	6,890	12.7	593	11%
Cupressus sempervirens	50	94	7,880	13.6	521	11%
Crataegus azarolus	56	117	10,440	13.8	699	11%
Juniperus oxycedrus ©	53	105	7,190	15.5	572	11%
Juniperus Oxycedrus (p)	65	109	8,940	14.9	714	10%
Laurus nobilis	67	141	8,050	16.5	785	10%
Myrtus communis	80	154	13,910	19.7	911	9%
Olea europea	65	51	7,390	23.8	1,053	6%
Pinus brutia	50	82	6,800	13.5	677	9%
Pinus nigra	37	82	5,710	10.8	513	11%
Pistacia lentiscus	78	147	10,400	15.4	953	9%
Pistacia terebinthus	59	94	8,620	21.9	971	9%
Platanus orientalis	62	120	11,180	15.8	699	9%
Quercus coccifera	88	193	13,260	22.6	1,050	9%
Quercus lusitanica	82	145	11,900	22.0	1,074	10%
Ceratonia siliqua	63	90	8,100	17.5	844	9%

UTILIZATION AND COMMERCIAL EXPLOITATION

The exploitation of the Cypriot forest resource that began during the Bronze Age was the result of internal and external economic and political strategies. The trade system of the eastern Mediterranean moved towards the development of urban nodes in strategic locations (Kreutz 1976). The dominance of water transport in the expansion of metropolitan nodes in the eastern Mediterranean periphery meant that Cyprus needed to maintain a dual economy, one based on the seaboard and thus within the trading system, and the other on a self-sufficient agricultural economy. The whole eastern Mediterranean from the fourteenth to twelvth centuries B.C.E. underwent a period of unprecedented international contact and stimulation in trade (Smith 1965). Evidence from the widespread distribution of trade items and the adoption and adaptation of foreign goods is well-documented (Knapp 1992). I would, therefore, suggest that while

the production and export of copper as a major trading commodity is undeniable, trade in timber as a second major resource is also of critical importance when assessing the complexities of foreign economic relationships, some of which relied more heavily on the Cypriot timber supply than on its copper production.

In particular, during the latter half of the 18th Dynasty (1567–1304 B.C.E.), Egyptian control over the Levant was weakened by the rise of the Hittite Empire, with the eventual loss of the Syrian ports and suzerainty over Lebanon and Palestine. By the end of the 19th Dynasty (1304–1195 B.C.E.), Egypt had lost control over all the major areas that had previously supplied ship-building timber. Alternatively, Cyprus had plentiful supplies of timber within easy access of natural harbors and sites. Particularly, Hala Sultan Tekké and Kition show clear signs of contact with Egypt during the Late Bronze Age (Peltenberg 1985). It appears logical on the grounds of accessibility, supply and demand, together with established trading contacts, that by the time of Ramses

III (1198–1167 B.C.E.), Egypt was obtaining foreign timbers from Cyprus.

A rich forest resource can be utilized in many different ways, four of which appear particularly pertinent to the trade and tribute relationships connected with Cyprus. In selecting these four aspects of forest utilization, I have tried to show how the forest resource as a whole was exploited. Although only a brief overview can be given here, I propose that the forest should be conceived as a source of a range of materials. The four areas of utilization are heavy construction, domestic requirements, funerary and ritualistic use, essential oil and medicinal preparations.

HEAVY CONSTRUCTION

Heavy construction demands a timber equal to the loads that will be applied transversally to the length of the beam. The strength of the beam is determined by its resistance to bending and this is proportional to the width of the beam and the square of its depth. The greater transverse thickness is therefore placed in the direction in which the weight is applied. Long struts or columns of wood are liable to yield, not by direct crushing, but by cross-breaking due to lateral bending. All timber lengths used in building construction need to be thoroughly seasoned.

The shape and dimensions of timber utilized for shipbuilding is governed by its natural curvature or length. Compass timber, that is, timber with a natural curvature, is used chiefly in the framework of ships. As a rule, the curvature should be uniform throughout the piece, or greatest at one-third from its ends. The most valuable curved woods have a camber of between 2.5 and 1.5 cm per meter. Kneed timber is formed where a bough parts from the tree trunk. The primary use of knee-pieces is in the ribbing of vessels. Long, straight pieces of timber are used for keels. Large compass-timbers of lengths above 8 m and with a diameter greater than 30 cm are essential for this role. Mast and spar wood must be straight and as cylindrical as possible. Coniferous wood was utilized for masts and those of the greatest dimensions were harvested for this purpose.

Most of the timber used in shipbuilding is compass timber, more abundant in complex, uneven-aged forests. For the development of quality mast woods, trees from a very different forest stand were harvested. Slow, prolonged and uniform growth is required and the trees must be closely grown in an even-aged stand until their full height is attained. Only a certain percentage of trees growing under optimum conditions in an even-aged forest stand will attain the dimensions required for masts.

Wood species from fifty-nine Mediterranean shipwrecks have been identified (Parker 1992: 26) and although there seems to be no obvious pattern in the use of species,

ship frames were usually of *Quercus* spp., *Ulmus* spp. (elm), or *Pinus* spp., planks most often of *Pinus* spp. or *Cupresses sempervirens* frequently called "fir" (Post 1899), the keel often of *Quercus* spp., and tree-nails from a range of woods including *Quercus coccifera*, *Olea europea*, and *Ceratonia siliqua* (carob). Parker suggests that the wrecks offer no clear evidence for the exhaustion of timber resources.

Timbers from the Maʾagan Michael (ca. 430–390 B.C.E.) shipwreck in Israel indicate a light structure mostly of *Pinus brutia* (Parker 1992: 248). The Kyrenia wreck discovered off the north coast of Cyprus was likewise principally of *Pinus halepensis* with a pulley-block of *Morus* (mulberry), tenons and false keel of *Quercus cerris* (Steffy 1985: 87; Parker 1992: 232). Lying in the Sea of Galilee to the south of Kibbutz Ginosar, the Ginosar wreck's keel was of cedar and jujube, with cedar planking and oak tenons (Parker 1992: 194). The diverse species used in the Ginosar wreck suggest timber reuse.

DOMESTIC UTILIZATION OF TIMBER

Combs, utensil boxes, spindles and chairs are all items of domestic use made from timber. Moderately hard, fine and homogeneous woods in which neither the annual growth rings or the medullary rays are too prominent are suitable for this purpose. *Quercus* spp., *Juniperus* spp. and *Olea europea* are primary woods utilized for these objects.

Wood used in musical instruments has special qualities and characteristics: the higher the key, the finer the woody zones should be. Such timber is often isolated within a forest and it is rare that an entire tree specimen could be used because only the fine-zoned parts tend to be suitable. All wood used for such purposes must be thoroughly seasoned.

The timber utilized by wheelwrights in the construction of chariots needed to be even-grained, long-fibered, tough and dense, and free from knots. Wheels, axles and shafts are the principal components of the wheelwright's craft. The wheels consist of the nave, spokes, felloes and tires. The nave or hub is made generally from the timber of the *Quercus* spp. or *Platanus orientalis* as the wood needed to be hard and dense so as to prevent the loosening of the spokes, which were mortised into it the nave. The felloes, mortised together in a circle, were generally of split wood. Whenever possible, naturally curved wood was chosen and, as the pieces are only short, there may have been an ample supply of timber with the suitable curve. Sawn felloes are much weaker than those split from wood with a natural curve. A bent rim used in light chariots may have been made from one piece of steamed, split wood, *Quercus* spp. or *Acacia raddiana* (acacia) being the species most often employed. Spokes were made from a thoroughly tough and strong timber, not subject to shrinkage in hot, dry weather. Poles required strong, straight timber lengths, and the axles were usually fashioned from *Quercus* spp. or *Platanus* spp.

FUNERARY AND RITUALISTIC USE

Sarcophagi and coffins of cedar have been identified with the funerary practices of Egypt (Lucas 1948: 488–90; Meiggs 1982: 409) and appear closely associated with the 18th Dynasty. Merrillees (1968) noted the presence of Cypriot Base Ring pottery found in the burials of the professional or middle classes from sites throughout Egypt. Finds excavated by Kanawati (1984) from the Saqqara tombs northwest of Teti's Pyramid also include Cypriot Base Ring ware. Forty burials were recorded from this site, over half of them in wooden coffins (Kanawati 1984: 59). The juxtaposition of wooden coffins and Cypriot pottery may suggest a correlation between two imported commodities: the Base Ring ware, and the single-width timber used in the coffin construction, a feature indicative of imported timbers.

Burial number 9, located above the northeast corner of the Mehi tomb at Saqqara, consisted of a well-preserved wooden coffin with only a few planks displaced from the lid that had been skillfully joined. The planks extended from the raised foot to the shoulders onto which the separately made head fitted. Likewise the beard, wig and arms were fixed into place with wooden tenons. A nearby wooden anthropoid coffin had a lid carved from a single length of timber (Kanawati 1984: 67-69). A quantity of Cypriot pottery was recovered from about one third of the burials excavated at this site.

To date, very little work on the identification of timber species associated with archaeological deposits has been undertaken. The importance of species identification through polarization microscopy, electron microscopy and other techniques as an archaeological tool has wide, and far reaching applications that provide information regarding the structure of cell walls and other diagnostic features hidden to light microscopes. The crystalline nature of cell walls consists of a thin primary wall and a much thicker secondary one, the latter made of three layers. The smallest visible building units of cell wall are the fibrils, which appear string-like under the electron microscope. The orientation and weaving of fibrils vary between species, which can thus be isolated.

MEDICINAL AND COSMETIC PREPARATIONS

In the fourth century B.C.E., Aristotle wrote:

> it was found on the island of Cyprus that there was a mountain larger and higher than all others, which was

called Troodos, where there were many different kinds of plants useful for the art of medicine, and if I attempt to talk about each one individually, time will not be sufficient to tell everything (Ph. 266)

The role of Cyprus as a supplier of medicinal herbs was well-known and most probably a trading system in this commodity was already established before Aristotle's time. Dioscorides visited Cyprus in the first century C.E. to collect herbs and mineral extracts (Riddle 1985) and Galen also comments on the medicinal herbs of the island (*De Antidotis* 14. 7). The export of herbs from Cyprus is tentatively suggested by extracts from the Linear B texts and from cargoes excavated from ancient shipwrecks. Coriander found on the Uluburun wreck seems certain to have been of Cypriot origin (Bass: 1991) and terebinth resin used for embalming, incense and perfume was also carried on the Uluburun wreck in large quantities (Haldane 1990: 57).

Decoration on the Mastaba of 'Ankhm'ahor' at Saqqara includes a processional scene of gift bearers. The third bearer has a basket with two looped handles attached to the top edge, which the hieroglyphics beside identify as "best cedar oil." Another adjacent sequence also depicts a bearer with an enormous, elegantly shaped jar with a small lug and curved, slender handle reaching from the vessel shoulder to the broad rim crowning a slender neck (Badawry 1978: 32).

The demand for volatile oil used in the embalming process may have opened a market for the range of plant extracts available from species growing in forest substrata not available in Egypt. The number and variety of these species cannot be covered here in a comprehensive manner, but a few recorded in the pharmacological texts of ancient Egypt, the Levant—principally in Biblical texts—and from the early *materia medicas* of Greece as well as from tomb excavations are outlined briefly. The mention of oil in the Amarna correspondence (Petrie 1898: 45–47) emphasizes the Egyptian need for oil imports. The paucity of the forest resource in Egypt was recorded by Theophrastus (*HP* 4: 3–5) and it is reflected in the lists of imports recorded.

The *Crataegus azarolus* produces medicines from both flowers and fruit mostly used in the treatment of heart complaints. The *Cupresses sempervirens* is rich in resinous compounds and the fruit or cones have been used medicinally since antiquity in the treatment of anemia and glandular fever. The *Juniperus* spp. has been used medicinally and as an aromatic for both cosmetic and culinary purposes. The *Lauris noblis* produces fragrant oil used in the treatment of rheumatism. The *Lavandula stoechas* (Mediterranean lavender) of the Makheras Forest is well-known for its aromatic, antiseptic, and medicinal properties and is still harvested locally. *Myrtus communis* is also very rich in fragrant oil and has been widely used in perfumery and as an antiseptic. The *Papaver* spp. (poppy) was, as noted above

(Merrillees 1968), a primary export believed to be so valuable that a distinctive pottery style was developed to contain its precious contents. The *Pistacia*, both *terebinthus* and *lentiscus*, and the *Salvia willeana* (Cypriot sage), also produced elements utilized medicinally (Georgiades 1992).

CONCLUSION

Madon (1881) contributed an insightful account on forest resource depletion in observing that to make masts and spars for ships mature trees had to be selected. Likewise, the planking required in vessel construction requires strong lengths that can only be supplied by mature trees from which the sapwood must be eliminated. Timber for construction also demands well-grown trees. Fellings to produce lumber for export of necessity would be confined to fully mature specimens, because young trees are unsuitable. In an uneven-aged forest stand the felling of mature trees would release the younger pole and sapling age group and provide them with a wider resource pool, that is, nutrients and available moisture, enabling them to attain strong onward growth.

Extensive canopy gaps in an uneven aged forest also promote the natural regeneration of some species, particularly the pines, but can inhibit the regeneration of juniper and cedar as the rise in soil temperature damages early root development (Polycarpou 1954).

It is probable that the demand for agricultural land encroached more on the forest reserve than indiscriminate harvesting of the resource itself, moreover the exploitation of the forest substrata may have created an internal imbalance in the forest dynamic. Substrata species are mostly of the hardwood variety and would provide premium fuel for ceramics, lime plaster and copper production. The landscape cannot be viewed as a simplified pattern of degradation sequence since the former mosaic and the present vegetative cover continue the evolutionary sifting of species in a form of dynamic flux constantly responding to the demands placed on the ecological resource of specific localities. Local knowledge of habitat requirements and the need to sustain the forest resource has been recorded by Theophrastus (*HP* 8.8.1) who cited the command of Cypriot kings to protect trees and not cut them down. This edict may possibly represent the earliest record of forest management, but it is also a significant characteristic of a cultural system in which trees signified wealth and stability.

REFERENCES

Badawry, A.
1978   *The Tomb of Nyhetep-Ptah at Giza and the tomb of "Ankhim" Ahokat Saggara.* Berkeley: University of California.
Bass, G. F.; Pulak, C.; Collon, D.; and Weinstein, J.
1991   The Bronze Age Shipwreck at Ulu Burun: 1986 Campaign. *American Journal of Archaeology* 93: 1–29.
Bovill, A. K.
1920   *Report on the natural resources and the present development of the forests of Cyprus.* Nicosia: Govt. Printing Office.
Casson, L.
1971   *Ships and Seamanship in the Ancient World.* Princeton: Princeton University.
1980   Two Masted Greek Ships. *International Journal of Nautical Archaeology* 9: 68-69.
1991   *The Ancient Mariners,* 2nd ed. Princeton: Princeton University.
Chapman, G. W.
1934   *A Reconnaissance Report for Paphos Forest* [unpublished].
Colledge, S.
1980   Plant species from Kissonerga *Mylouthkia*—Feature 16.3, in E. J. Peltenburg, Lemba Archaeological Project, Cyprus, 1978: Preliminary Report. *Levant* XII: 18–20.
1981   Kissonerga *Mylouthkia* 1979: Paleobotanical Report, in E. J. Peltenburg, Lemba Archaeological Project, Cyprus, 1979: Preliminary Report. *Levant* XIII: 47.
1982   Lemba *Lakkous* 1980—Flora, in E. J. Peltenburg, Lemba Archaeological Project, Cyprus, 1980: Preliminary Report. *Levant* XIV: 53.
Constantinou, G.
1992   Ancient Copper Mining in Cyprus. Pp. 13–24 in *Early Metallurgy in Cyprus, 4000–500 B.C.,* eds. J. D. Muhly; R. Maddin; and V. Karageorghis. Nicosia: Pierides Foundation.
Fisher, W. R.
1908   *Schlich's Manual of Forestry* vol. V, 2nd ed. London Bradbury: Agnew and Co.
Frankel, D.
1974   Inter-site Relationships in the Middle Bronze Age of Cyprus. *World Archaeology* 6: 23–43.
Frost, H.
1965   *Under the Mediterranean.* Englewood Cliffs, NJ: Prentice-Hall.

Galen
  1821–   *De Antidotis*, trans. C. G. Kuhn, from ancient
  1833   Greek. Leipzig.
Georgiades, C.
  1987   *Flowers of Cyprus II: Plants of Medicine.*
           Nicosia: Cosmos.
  1992   *Flowers of Cyprus I: Plants of Medicine.* 2nd
           ed. Nicosia: Stavrinides.
Glanville, S. R. K.
  1931   Records of a Royal Dockyard of the Time of
           Tuthmosis III: Papyrus British museum 10056
           Part I. *Zeitschrift für Ägyptische Sprache und
           Alterumskunde* 66: 105–21.
Haldane, C. W.
  1990   Shipwrecked Plant Remains. *Biblical Archae-
           ologist* 53.1: 55–60.
Hayes, W. C.
  1949   Career of the Great Steward Henenv under
           Nebhepetre Mentu-hotpe. *Journal of Egyptian
           Archaeology* 35: 43–49.
Holmboe, J.
  1914   *Studies in the Vegetation of Cyprus.* Bergen: John
           Griegs.
Jane, F. W.
  1956   *The Structure of Wood.* 2nd ed. Completely re-
           vised by K. Wilson and D. J. B. White. London:
           Adam and Charles Black.
Johnstone, P.
  1972   Bronze Age Sea Travel. *Antiquity* 46: 269–74
Kanawati, N.; El-Khouli, A.; McFarlane, A.; and Maksoud,
N. V.
  1984   *Excavations at Saqqara north-west of Teti's
           pyramid.* Sydney: Macquarie University Ancient
           History Documentary Research Centre.
Keating, W. G., and Bolza, E.
  1982   *Characteristics, Properties and Uses of Timbers
           South-East Asia, Northern Australia and the Pa-
           cific,* vol. I. Melbourne: Inkarta.
Knapp, A. B.
  1992   Bronze Age Mediterranean Island Cultures and
           the Ancient Near East. Part 2. *Biblical Archae-
           ologist* 56: 112–28.
Kollmann, F.
  1951   *Technologie des Holzes und der Holzwerkstoffe.*
           Berlin: Springer.
Kreutz, B. M.
  1976   Ships, Shipping and the Implication of Change
           in the Early Mediterranean. *Viator* 7: 79–109.
Kyllo, M.
  1982   The Botanical Remains. Pp. 90–93 in *A Subter-
           ranean Settlement in Cyprus,* ed. E. J. Peltenberg.
           Warminster: Aris and Phillips.

Lavers, G. M.
  1969   The Strength Properties of Timbers. *Bulletin* 50:
           Second ed. London: Her Majesty's Stationery
           Office.
Loret, V.
  1916   Quelques notes sur l'arbre. *Annales du Service
           des Antiquités d'Egypte* 16: 33–51.
Lucas, A.
  1948   *Ancient Egyptian Materials and Industries.* 3rd
           ed. London: Edward Arnold.
Madon, P. G.
  1881   *Forest Conservation in the Island of Cyprus.* [Re-
           printed Nicosia: Nicosia Govt. Printing Office,
           1930.]
Manniche, L.
  1989   *An Ancient Egyptian Herbal.* London: British
           Museum Publication.
Meiggs, R.
  1982   *Trees and Timber in the Ancient Mediterranean
           World.* Oxford: Clarendon.
Meikle, R. D.
  1977   *Flora of Cyprus,* vol. 1. Kew: Royal Botanical
           Gardens.
  1985   *Flora of Cyprus,* vol. 2. Kew: Royal Botanical
           Gardens.
Merrillees, R. S.
  1968   *The Cypriote Bronze Age Pottery Found in
           Egypt.* Lund: Studies in Mediterranean Archae-
           ology.
  1987   *Alashia Revisited.* Paris: Gabalda et Cie.
Moran, W. L.
  1992   *The Amarna Letters.* Trans. William L. Moran.
           Baltimore: John Hopkins University.
Nibbi, A.
  1994   Some Remarks on the Cedar of Lebanon. *Dis-
           cussions in Egyptology* 28: 35–52.
Ohnefalsch-Richter, M.
  1893   *Kypros: the Bible and Homer.* London: Asher
           & Co.
Parker, A. J.
  1992   *Ancient Shipwrecks of the Mediterranean and
           the Roman Provinces.* BAR International Series
           580. Oxford: B.A.R.
Peltenburg, E. J.
  1985   Rammeside Egypt and Cyprus. Pp. 150–79 in
           *Acts of the International Archaeological Sym-
           posium: "Cyprus Between the Orient and the
           Occident,"* ed. V. Karageorghis. Nicosia: De-
           partment of Antiquities.
Petrie, W. M. F.
  1898   *Syria and Egypt from the Tell El Amarna Let-
           ters.* London: Methuen.

Pliny the Elder
1938   *Natural History* in Ten Volumes. Trans H. Rackham and W. H. S. Jones, from Latin. Loeb Classical Library. Cambridge, MA: Harvard University.

Polunin, O. and Huxley, A.
1981   *Flowers of the Mediterranean.* London: Chatto & Windus.

Polycarpou, A.
1954   *Classification of Forests into Crop Types and the Preparation and Interpretation of Stock Maps in Cyprus.* Nicosia: Forest Department.

Poroda, E.
1948   Cylinder seals of the Late Cypriote Bronze Age. *American Journal of Archaeology* 52: 178–98.

Post, G. E.
1899   Fir. *Dictionary of the Bible,* ed. James Hastings. Edinburgh: T & T Clark.

Pritchard, J. B.
1950   *Ancient Near Eastern Texts.* Princeton: Princeton University.

Record, S. J., and Hess, R. W.
1943   *Timbers of the New World.* London: Oxford University.

Riddle, J. M.
1985   *Dioscorides on Pharmacy and Medicine.* Austin: University of Texas.

Sinos, S.
1990   *The Temple of Apollo Hylates at Kourion and the Restoration of its Southwest Corner.* Athens: Leventis Foundation.

Smith, W. S.
1965   *Interconnection in the Ancient Near East.* London: Newhart.

South Africa, Department of Forestry
1977   *Bulletin* 48: 14–17.

Steffy, J. R.
1985   The Kyrenia Ship: an Interim Report on its Hull Construction. *American Journal of Archaeology* 89: 71–101.

Strabo
1929   *The Geography* in Eight Volumes. Trans. H. L. Jones, from Latin. Loeb Classical Library. Great Britain.

Theophrastus
1916   *Historia Plantis* in Two Volumes. Trans. Sir Arthur Hart from ancient Greek. Cambridge, MA: Harvard University.

Thirgood, J. V.
1981   *Man and the Mediterranean Forest: a History of Resource Depletion.* London: Academic.

Tsoumis, G.
1968   *Wood as Raw Material.* Oxford: Pergamon.
1991   *Science and Technology of Wood.* New York: Chapman & Hall.

Ward, W. A.
1971   *Egypt and the East Mediterranean World 2200–1900 B.C.* Beirut: American University of Beirut.

Wenger, K. F.
1984   *Forestry Handbook,* 2nd ed. New York: John Wiley.

Les Hangars du Port de Kition
(Ve–IVe s. av. J.C.)

OLIVIER CALLOT

Maison de l'Orient Méditerranéen
Fédération d'Unités
Université Lumière Lyon 2
Centre National de la Recherche Scientifique
7 rue Raulin
F – 69007 Lyon
FRANCE

The harbor installations excavated at Kition Bamboula *display three main building phases attributed to the fifth and fourth centuries B.C.E. This artical concentrates on the first, best-preserved phase. To date, the excavations have uncovered six sheds 30 m in length, each furnished with a ramp to support the ship's hull. A series of pillars built between the sheds clearly indicates that the original plan included a roof.*

In addition to describing the in situ *remains, with the help of a reconstruction based on the evidence preserved from the fifth century B.C.E., the author attempts also to explain their mode of operation. Of particular interest is how the warships of the Kings of Kition, about 30 m long and weighing approximately 30 tons, could have been hauled under cover up these slipways.*

Si de très nombreuses installations destinées à abriter des bateaux sont connues sur tout le pourtour de la Méditerranée, celles d'époque classique demeurent rares. De surcroît, il s'agit souvent d'aménagements sommaires destinés à des navires de commerce. En revanche les installations construites pour abriter des vaisseaux de guerre dans des ports fermés sont extrêmement rares.[1]

En fait le seul exemple qui, jusqu'à ces dernières années, avait fait l'objet d'une étude sérieuse est celui des hangars de Zéa au Pirée (Dragatzes et Dörpfeld 1885: 63–68).

Cependant si les reconstitutions sont particulièrement évocatrices, les vestiges eux-mêmes sont bien pauvres.[2] De ce fait, les installations mises au jour à Kition (Larnaca, Chypre) sont de très loin les mieux conservées et autorisent, avec assez peu de risques d'erreur, des propositions de reconstitution.

Dès 1987, la mission de Kition *Bamboula*, dirigée par Marguerite Yon, mettait au jour au Nord de la fouille de curieux aménagements, qui furent d'abord interprétés comme les fondations d'un grand édifice d'époque classique

---

[1] Je ne parlerai pas ici de ports comme ceux de Carthage ou d'Apollonia qui appartiennent à des périodes plus récentes qu'à Kition.

[2] Il y a aussi, tout récemment, le cas de Thasos (Simossi 1994: 163–78). L'identification avancée est possible, mais les misérables vestiges paraissent tout de même insuffisants pour les reconstitutions proposées.

(rapports de la mission dans Yon 1985: 939; 1986: 853–54). Mais en 1987, la découverte des premières rampes permettait d'affirmer que nous étions en présence d'installations portuaires situées sur un des côtés d'un bassin fermé (rapport dans Yon 1988: 829–30; in press): elles devaient abriter la flotte de guerre des derniers rois de Kition, Milkyaton et Pumayyaton (Yon 1992: 243–60). Les campagnes successives permirent d'étendre le secteur fouillé[3] et, bien sûr, de se faire une idée beaucoup plus claire des aménagements de ce port et ce, malgré les difficultés dues à la proximité de la nappe phréatique.

Dans cet article je n'aborderai que l'aspect architectural de ces installations portuaires.[4] Puis, dans une seconde partie, je tenterai d'évoquer leur fonctionnement. J'ajouterai aussi que la fouille n'est pas achevée et qu'il demeure encore bon nombre d'incertitudes qui seront, bien entendu, signalées.

La partie actuellement dégagée de ces installations occupe une surface au sol d'environ 1400 m², mais il est assuré que, dans l'antiquité, elles avaient une extension nettement plus importante (fig. 1).

Au nord d'une vaste place qui a pu être en relation avec le sanctuaire de Melkart ou d'Astarté à l'époque classique, on trouve un long mur de soutènement orienté d'est en ouest. Il est construit en assises régulières de pierres de taille avec tous les trois lits une assise de règlage en dalles de gypse. Au sud, il retient une terrasse, haute à l'origine d'environ 3 m. Tous les 6 m, ce mur est renforcé par des contreforts sur ses deux faces. Au sud, ils sont noyés dans du remblai et ne sont donc visibles que du côté nord.

Ces contreforts définissent des travées larges de 5,20 m—6 m d'entraxe—dans lesquelles ont été construites des rampes pour des bateaux. Dans l'état actuel de la fouille, six des ces rampes ont été entièrement ou partiellement dégagées. A l'ouest, les restes d'un mur continu dans sa partie sud et probablement fait d'une succession de murets au nord, doit correspondre à la limite occidentale de cet ensemble. En revanche, à l'est, il ne subsiste à peu près plus rien, et la possibilité que d'autres rampes aient existé de ce côté reste parfaitement envisageable. Elles doivent être complètement détruites au sud, mais probablement mieux conservées au nord où elles sont plus profondément enfouies.

Ces installations présentent trois états principaux. Toutefois c'est le premier, daté probablement de la fin du Ve siècle, qui demeure le plus important et le mieux conservé.

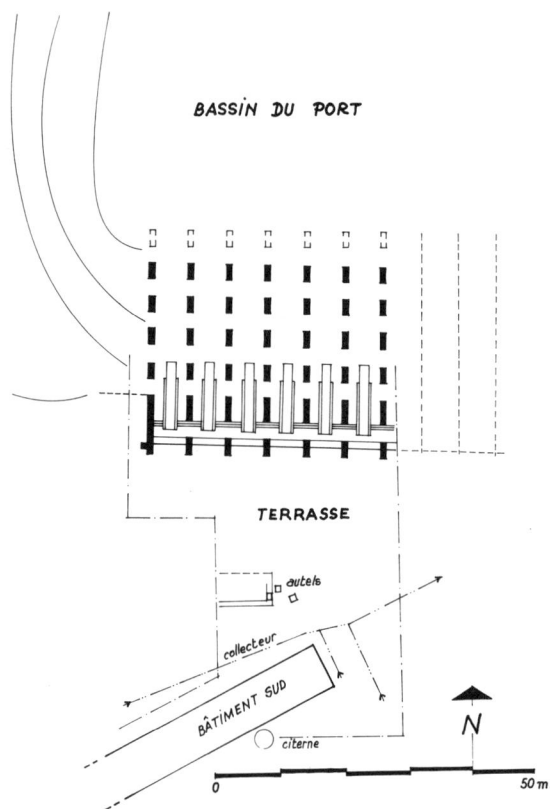

Fig. 1. Plan d'ensemble de l'état I (reconstitution).

DESCRIPTION ARCHITECTURALE

Le premier état (Ve siècle)

Chaque rampe, construite sur un plan rectangulaire allongé du nord au sud, mesure 10,50 m de longueur sur 1,80 à 1,90 m de largeur (fig. 2, 3 et 4). Au sud elles sont hautes d'environ deux mètres, puis descendent vers le nord en suivant une pente d'environ 13°. Elles sont portées par deux murs de soutènement à l'est et à l'ouest, construits en blocs soigneusement maçonnés au plâtre. Le remplissage intérieur est constitué par un solide blocage de moellons grossiers liés au plâtre. Enfin l'ensemble est recouvert d'un enduit de plâtre blanc. Certaines rampes portent par endroits des taches de peinture rouge venant des bateaux ou de la toiture. Sur chacun des côtés longs du tablier on trouve deux

---

[3] Rapports dans Yon (1989 et suiv.); cf. état de la question dans Calvet (1993: 125–29) avec bibliographie des travaux de la mission.

[4] Le point de vue archéologique et historique a déjà été présenté par M. Yon au colloque *Cyprus and the Sea, Nicosie 25–26 sept. 1993* (Actes à paraître, avec bibliographie récente sur le sujet).

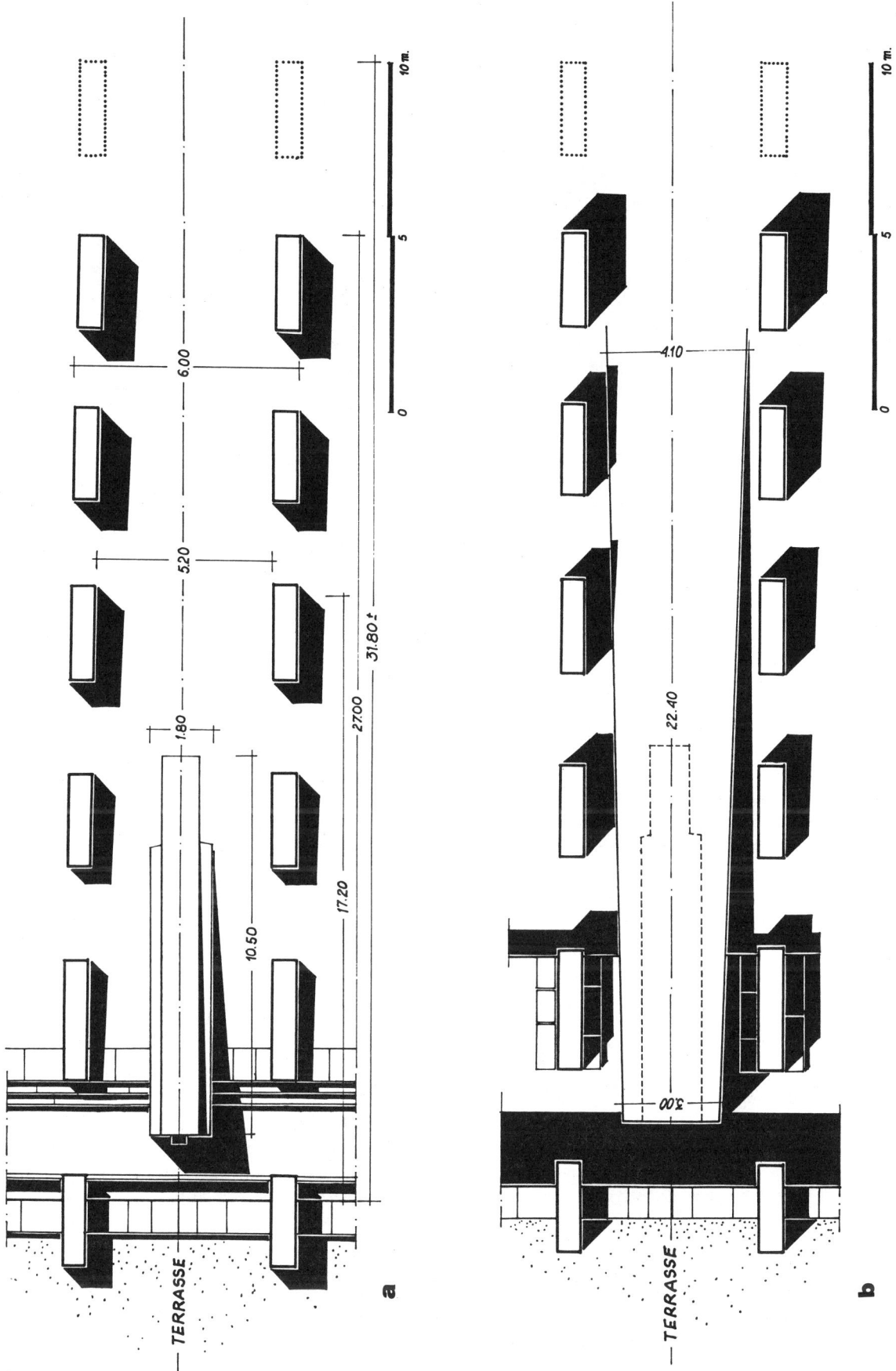

Fig. 2. Reconstitution d'une travée: a) État I; b) État II.

Fig. 3. Rampe de l'état I (face sud).

grosses rainures larges d'une trentaine de centimètres. Elles étaient probablement destinées à assujettir un bâti en bois qui sera évoqué plus loin. On notera aussi sur les faces sud de chacune des rampes une petite console en pierre probablement destinée à caler un étai (fig. 4).

En alternance avec les rampes, et présentant le même entraxe de 6 mètres, on trouve des alignements nord-sud de murets, placés dans l'axe des contreforts du soutènement de la terrasse (fig. 5). Comme ce dernier, ils sont édifiés en pierres de taille avec des assises de réglage faites de dalles de gypse. Ces murets, épais de 0,80 m, sont longs en moyenne de 2,50 m sauf ceux du sud qui ont 3,50 m. Ils sont espacés de 2 m à 2,50 m les uns des autres. Leur rôle était double: ils servaient d'abord de base à des poteaux, certainement en bois, qui supportaient la couverture de chacune des travées. Ensuite, et c'est ce qui explique leur curieuse forme allongée, ils servaient à caler des étais inclinés qui maintenaient en place les coques des navires lorsqu'ils étaient tirés sur les rampes; le dispositif adopté sera décrit plus loin.

La circulation entre les rampes et le soutènement de la terrasse était assurée au sud par un passage est-ouest large de 1,20 m, qui courait tout le long des installations. Dans chaque intervalle entre les contreforts du soutènement, ce passage était doublé par des sortes de cuves allongées, limitées par des parapets faits de dalles placées de chant;

aucune d'elles ne possède le moindre système d'écoulement. Le rôle de ces aménagements qui ne paraissent pas avoir été des bassins nous échappe encore. On notera aussi, au sommet des faces internes des contreforts, de gros logements destinés à recevoir des pièces de bois horizontales.

La circulation nord-sud se faisait entre les rampes et les piliers. On y accédait au sud par trois marches faites de belles dalles de gypse. Puis chaque passage, au sol de terre battue, descendait en pente douce vers le bassin du port.

Sur le schéma de la fig. 2, chacune des travées est longue d'environ 25 m. Toutefois, comme la fouille n'est pas achevée, il est encore impossible de dire s'il existait plus au nord une ou plusieurs autres séries de murets-piliers.

Enfin la couverture, portée par des poteaux en bois, devait être une toiture en bâtière placée au-dessus de chacune des travées. La charpente, d'une portée de 6 m, était naturellement en bois et faite d'une succession de fermes simples. Elle était couverte en grandes tuiles plates peintes en rouge dont nous avons retrouvé de nombreux fragments. Comme on peut le voir sur la reconstitution de la fig. 6, je propose une toiture en deux parties. En effet, si elle avait été d'un seul tenant, sa partie nord aurait été haute de près de 11 m, ce qui l'aurait rendue instable tout en nécessitant l'emploi de très grandes pièces de bois; cela paraît tout à fait inutile.[5]

---

[5] A mon avis, c'est une toiture de ce type qu'il faudrait restituer également sur les installations de Zéa au Pirée, plutôt que la toiture inclinée que l'on voit sur les plans ou la maquette. En effet personne ne semble avoir pensé aux difficultés techniques que pose une telle toiture, surtout si elle est installée sur de hautes colonnes de faible diamètre.

Fig. 4. Rampe de l'état I, avec console pour un étai.

Le deuxième état (début du IVe siècle)

Il correspond à un remaniement assez profond de l'ensemble. On constate en effet que certains murets-piliers situés entre les rampes ont été en partie reconstruits, ce qui voudrait dire que la toiture a du s'effondrer dans des circonstances qu'il est encore impossible de préciser.

L'essentiel des travaux de reconstruction correspond à un élargissement, et surtout à un allongement des rampes (fig. 2 et 7). Elles sont désormais longues au minimum de 25 m, larges de 3 m au Sud et 4 m au nord, et hautes de 2,50 m à 3 m au sud. Je rappellerai encore que, la fouille n'étant pas achevée au nord, nous ignorons s'il existe, de ce côté, une sixième, voire même une septième rangée de piliers, ce qui porterait la longueur des travées à un peu plus de 30 m.

Ce réaménagement pourrait correspondre à un abaissement du niveau de la mer qui aurait nécessité un allongement des rampes. Mais on constate aussi que ces nouvelles rampes ont un profil différent de celles du premier état. Ceci pourrait indiquer que c'est la forme des navires qui aurait changé au IVe siècle. Il est encore difficile de répondre à ces deux questions.

Les travaux ont été exécutés de deux façons différentes. D'abord à l'est, les trois premières rampes connues ont été doublées sur toute leur longueur par des murs de pierres maçonnées avec un remplissage de gravats provenant de démolitions (fig. 7). Quant aux sols des rampes, ils étaient en terre battue avec un profil nettement bombé. En revanche, les rampes occidentales sont doublées à l'est et à l'ouest par des murs en briques crues, disposées sur un seul parement, avec un remplissage fait des mêmes gravats de démolition.

L'emploi de ce matériau de moins bonne qualité, et surtout beaucoup moins résistant (en particulier en milieu humide), pourrait indiquer qu'il a fallu achever ce réaménagement de façon hâtive, mais aussi avec des moyens financiers limités.

L'allongement et surtout le rehaussement des rampes ont entraîné un changement du niveau des sols qui les entouraient. Au nord, le sol en terre battue du premier état a plus ou moins été maintenu. En revanche, au sud, il a été fortement exhaussé. Pour cela, on a édifié des murets en pierres sèches à l'extrémité nord de la première rangée de piliers et remblayé tout le secteur méridional. Contrairement à celui du premier état, le sol du second état ne présentait pas une surface horizontale, mais il s'élevait progressivement d'est en ouest. Des dalles de gypse, disposées au pied des murets-piliers de la première rangée au sud, étaient destinées à caler la base des étais qui maintenaient les bateaux sur les rampes. En revanche, pour les autres piliers, c'est le dispositif du premier état qui continuait à être utilisé. Enfin la couverture, certainement reconstruite, devait être à peu près identique à celle du premier état.

Le troisième état (IVe siècle)

Les travaux de cette troisième phase ne sont vraiment visibles que sur la rampe située le plus à l'Ouest. Toutefois quelques vestiges un peu plus à l'est pourraient faire penser que ce troisième état concernait au moins les trois dernières rampes du côté occidental. Cependant la fouille de ce secteur n'est pas achevée; aussi la reconstitution de cet état reste-t-elle encore très hypothétique.

Fig. 5. Muret-pilier de l'état I, avec trous pour les étais.

Au sud, le sol autour de la rampe a été fortement exhaussé et se trouve désormais au même niveau que le sommet du soutènement, donc que celui de la terrasse. Quant au sommet de la rampe, il dépassait ce sol d'au moins 1,50 m; elle était donc située à environ 4,70 m au-dessus du sol du premier état. La partie nord n'a pas encore été dégagée et nous ignorons donc la longueur de cette rampe. Mais on peut supposer qu'elle avait à peu près la même longueur que celles du second état, soit 25 m ou plus avec, bien entendu, une pente nettement plus prononcée, ce qui n'est pas sans poser bien des problèmes pour lesquels il est encore impossible de donner des réponses. Enfin certains aménagements pourraient laisser supposer que cette rampe a été couverte avec, là aussi, de réelles difficultés, vu sa hauteur et sa très forte pente.

En définitive cette unique rampe, si haute, si raide et si mal construite, pose tant de problèmes qu'on est réellement en droit de se demander si elle servait encore à supporter un bateau.

FONCTIONNEMENT

A la suite de cette description, je souhaiterais aborder mon second point: celui du fonctionnement de ces installations, en me limitant ici aux hangars du premier état qui, notons-le, sont les mieux construits, mais aussi les mieux préservés.

Imaginons un navire de la flotte militaire royale de Kition rentrant au port à la suite d'une longue course. Peut-être avait-il subi quelques avaries et sa coque, gorgée d'eau, se trouvait alourdie. Aussi fallait-il le tirer sous un hangar pour le faire sécher, mais aussi pour procéder aux différentes réparations.

Nous sommes peu renseignés sur la silhouette des navires de guerre phéniciens de la fin du Ve siècle.[6] Toutefois les dimensions des hangars, qui paraissent très voisines de celles des *néoria* du Pirée, permettent de supposer sans trop de risques d'erreur que les navires de guerre de Kition avaient à peu près le même gabarit que les trières athéniennes.[7]

Avant d'être tiré sous son hangar, le navire devait être démâté et les rames retirées. Se pose alors une question difficile: comment tirait-on la coque sous son abri? Il faut en effet se rappeler que ces navires mesuraient près de trente mètres de longueur et que, quand ils arrivaient gorgés d'eau, ils devaient peser plus de trente tonnes.

Voyons donc comment on a pu procéder dans le premier état.

Il y a d'abord l'aménagementes sols et des rampes. En effet il est inconcevable que les navires aient été tirés directement sur la terre puis, plus loin, sur les rampes elles-mêmes. Que se soit dans l'antiquité ou à des périodes plus récentes, on connaît de nombreux aménagements destinés à supporter les bateaux qu'on tirait à terre. Il s'agit dans la

---

[6] Basch (1987: 319–20) donne quelques exemples, en particulier, les monnaies de Sidon ou de Byblos.
[7] Sur les trières athéniennes voir, en particulier, Casson (1973), ou Basch (1987).

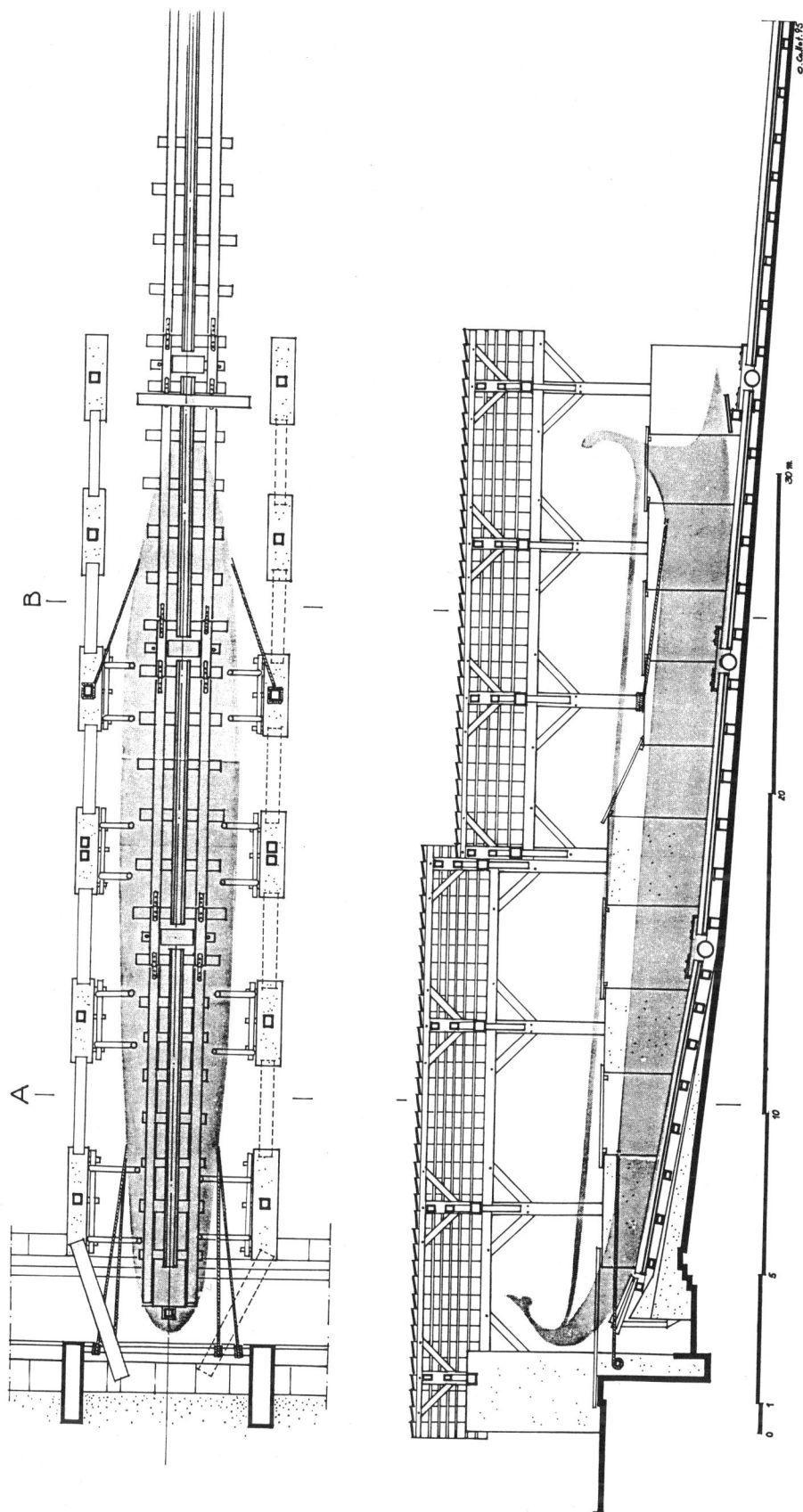

Fig. 6. Essai de reconstitution de l'état I: plan, et coupe longitudinale.

Fig. 7. Rampes des états I et II.

plupart des cas de sortes de traîneaux, que les spécialistes nomment *vasa,* ou de rails en bois appelés *scala.* D'autres dispositifs consistaient à faire glisser les coques sur des traverses creusées d'une échancrure centrale dans laquelle s'adaptait la quille du navire.

Le dispositif que je propose aux fig. 6 et 8 est bien sûr hypothétique, mais il s'inspire de ces différentes méthodes. La voie que devait suivre la coque pour être installée dans son hangar comporte deux tronçons. Le premier, au nord, est en terre et correspond au rivage du port dont les eaux devait atteindre la première rangée de piliers des hangars. On peut imaginer là une suite de traverses en bois maintenues latéralement par des poutres longitudinales. Peut-être avait-on disposé au centre de ce rail une sorte de glissière qui permettait de guider la quille saillante du navire. Il est probable que ce rail se prolongeait au nord en dehors du hangar dans les eaux mêmes du bassin. Ainsi la coque flottant encore en partie y était engagée et tirée vers la rampe à l'intérieur du hangar. Toutefois, il faut se rappeler le poids considérable de ces navires (près de 30 tonnes). Aussi ai-je pensé à un procédé fort simple utilisé dans des installations modernes qui ont fort bien pu exister dès l'antiquité.[8] Il s'agit de gros rouleaux en bois maintenus dans les parties latérales du rail. Ainsi disposés, ils permettaient à la coque, non plus de simplement glisser dans la partie centrale, mais de rouler, ce qui, notons-le, devait diminuer considérablement les efforts. Ces rouleaux ne devaient pas être nombreux et les trois que j'ai restitués à la fig. 6 paraissent tout à fait suffisants. Le second tronçon correspondait à la rampe elle-même; on devait y trouver un dispositif un peu différent. Dans les rainures qui bordent les côtés longs on adaptait deux longues poutres (ou plusieurs éléments assemblés), elles-mêmes reliées par des traverses. Elles devaient porter la prolongation de la glissière centrale qui maintenait la quille. Enfin, pour éviter que les poutres latérales ne s'écartent, on peut restituer des tirants métalliques qui les reliaient entre elles.

A présent voyons par quel moyen les coques étaient tirées à leurs places, en rappelant encore leurs dimensions et leurs poids.

On pourrait, par exemple, imaginer des cabestans ancrés dans le sol de la terrasse. Dans le secteur où ce sol est encore conservé, nous n'avons pas trouvé la moindre trace de tels aménagements. Il faut toutefois remarquer que le soutènement qui retient la terrasse est doublé, sur toute sa longueur, par une large et profonde tranchée de fouille du siècle dernier qui à fait disparaître tous les restes architecturaux.[9] Est-ce à son emplacement qu'étaient

[8] Des installations de ce type existent à la Callelongue à Marseille. Je remercie Antoinette Hesnard pour les documents qu'elle a bien voulu nous fournir: voir Hesnard 1994, avec bibliographie récente. Je remercie aussi H. Frost de ses suggestions.

[9] Sur les fouilles anciennes à Kition *Bamboula,* voir récemment Salles (1993: 17–18).

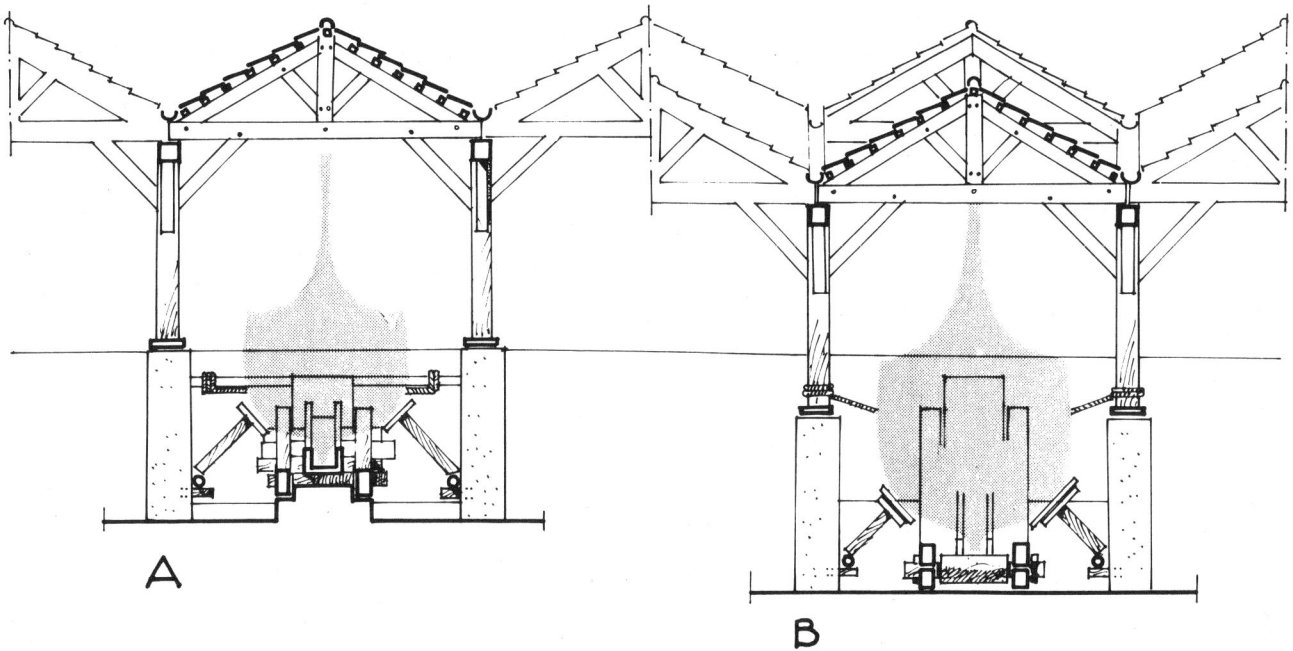

Fig. 8. Essai de reconstitution de l'état I: coupes transversales.

installés les cabestans? Cela paraît bien difficile, car ils se seraient trouvés bien près du rebord de la terrasse.[10]

Reste alors la solution la plus simple et qui ne laisse aucune trace: la traction animale ou humaine, pour laquelle la vaste surface constituée par la terrasse pouvait parfaitement convenir. Pourtant je doute fort de la traction animale car, pour déplacer un navire de trente tonnes, il aurait fallu un attelage de près de 80 paires de boeufs; on imagine bien mal un tel ballet sur la terrasse au sud.

En revanche la traction humaine est, elle, parfaitement envisageable. En effet, 100 à 120 hommes sont suffisants pour tirer de tels navires et, notons-le, ce chiffre est inférieur à un équipage de trière qui comptait en moyenne 200 hommes.[11] Au début de la manœuvre, les hommes chargés de hâler la coque se trouvaient sous le hangar. Mais lorsque celle-ci commençait à s'engager sur la rampe, une partie d'entre eux devait monter sur la terrasse pour terminer l'opération.

Une dernière question se pose: celle de l'étaiement des bateaux pendant qu'ils étaient halés et, surtout, lorsqu'ils étaient en place sous leurs hangars. La glissière qui maintenait la quille permettait une certaine stabilité, mais ce n'était cependant pas suffisant pour empêcher la coque de déverser, en particulier si elle n'était pas maintenue dans sa partie supérieure. On peut très bien imaginer que des hommes, postés sur les murets-piliers et équipés de sortes de gaffes, s'employaient à maintenir la coque en bonne position. L'accès au sommet de ces murets-piliers était aisé depuis la terrasse par des passages en planches qui devaient se prolonger d'un pilier à l'autre (fig. 6 et 8). On notera d'ailleurs que, lorsque le bateau était en place, c'est aussi depuis ces murets-piliers qu'on pouvait accéder au pont du navire.

Lorsque la coque avait atteint son emplacement définitif, on disposait des étais pour caler les côtés longs. Nous avons retrouvé, proches de la base des murets-piliers, des séries de trois logements cylindriques où devaient être scellées des pièces de bois: elles formaient des sortes de consoles sur lesquelles on plaçait une pièce horizontale qui permettait de caler le pied des étais (fig. 5, 6 et 8). Ce dispositif, qui paraît un peu compliqué à première vue, s'explique facilement. En effet il était impossible de placer les étais à

---

[10] Cependant, bien que peu convaincu par ce procédé, je ne peux pas l'exclure complètement. Les recherches entreprises sous les constructions hellénistiques au sud du soutènement n'ont, pour le moment, donné aucun résultat. Mais il faudra attendre un dégagement plus important pour affirmer définitivement qu'il n'y a jamais eu de cabestans.

[11] La question du déplacement de lourds bateaux a été très bien étudiée pour le passage de l'isthme de Corinthe (Raepsaet 1993: 233–61; voir en particulier l'annexe de M. Tolley 257–61).

la base des murs où ils se seraient enfoncés dans le sol trop humide.[12] Au nord, du côté de la proue, on devait disposer des cales dont nous n'avons naturellement pas retrouvé la moindre trace. En revanche les aménagements sont beaucoup plus clairs du côté de la poupe. La rampe est une indication par elle-même. On pourrait s'étonner de trouver sous ce hangar une rampe qui ne correspond même pas au tiers de la longueur du bateau. En fait elle n'était là que pour porter la poupe, qui devait être nettement relevée par rapport au corps central de la coque, directement posée sur le sol de la plage.

Grâce à elle il est d'ailleurs possible d'esquisser avec une relative précision le profil du navire qu'elle portait. On rappellera encore les petites consoles placées aux extrémités sud des rampes de ce premier état. Elles devaient servir de base à des étais supportant les poupes qui, à cet endroit, devaient être en porte-à-faux. Il y avait aussi les poutres en bois situées entre les contreforts du soutènement de la terrasse au sud. On devait y accrocher des cordages qui retenaient les bateaux. Enfin on peut noter qu'il était possible d'accrocher d'autres cordages aux poteaux qui soutenaient la toiture (fig. 6 et 8).

A partir de ce moment, les coques des trières étaient calées sous un abri bien aéré; elles pouvaient sécher tranquillement tandis que l'on procédait au diverses réparations nécessaires avant un prochain départ.

* * * * *

Voici en quelques mots ce qu'il est possible de dire, pour le moment, sur ces installations. Bien des points restent encore dans l'ombre, mais espérons que les prochaines campagnes, malgré les difficultés dues à l'eau, vont permettre de répondre aux dernières questions. Nous aurons alors un ensemble tout à fait exceptionnel et on ne peut que souhaiter qu'une restauration des ruines et une mise en valeur du site permettent de le conserver.

REFERENCES

Basch, L.
1987   *Le musée imaginaire de la marine antique,* Athènes: Institut Hellénique our la préservation de la tradition hautique.

Calvet, Y.
1993   Kition, Mission française, in *Kinyras, l'archéologie française à Chypre,* M. Yon éd., Lyon: Travaux de la Maison de l'Orient.

Casson, L.
1971   *Ships and Seamanship in the Ancient World.* Princeton: Princeton University.

CRAI
        Comptes Rendus de l'Académie des Inscriptions et Belles Lettres. Paris.

Dragatzes, I. et Dörpfeld, W.
1885   *Praktika tes Archaiologikes Hetaireias.*

Hesnard, A.
1994   Une nouvelle fouille du port de Marseille, place Jules-Verne. *CRAI* 1994: 195–216.

Raespsaet, G.
1993   Le diolkos de l'Isthme à Corinthe: son tracé, son fonctionnement. *BCH* 118: 233–61.

Salles, J.-F.
1993   *Kition-Bamboula* IV, *Les niveaux hellénistiques.* Paris: Editions Recherches sur les Civilisations.

Simossi, A.
1994   Les Néoria du port de Thasos. Pp. 63–178 in *Mélanges offerts à Claude Vatin,* Travaux du centre Camille Julian n°17. Aix-en-Provence.

Yon, M.
1985   Chronique des fouilles à Chypre: Kition-Bamboula. *BCH* 109: 939–41.

1986   Chronique des fouilles à Chypre: Kition-Bamboula. *BCH* 110: 851–55.

1988   Chronique des fouilles à Chypre: Kition-Bamboula. *BCH* 112: 827–30.

1989   Chronique des fouilles à Chypre: Kition-Bamboula. *BCH* 113: 824–26.

1992   Le royaume de Kition (époque classique). *Studia Phoenicia* IX: 243–60.

1993   Le port de guerre de Kition (Chypre). *Dossiers Archéologie et histoire: Marine antique,* n° 183: 40–41.

---

[12] Pour le second état (dont je n'étudie pas ici le fonctionnement) on rappellera que l'exhaussement des sols avait enterré la base de la première rangée de murets-piliers au sud. De ce fait, le dispositif pour l'étaiement des coques se trouvait enfoui. On y a remédié en disposant, à la base des murets, des dalles de gypse (fig. 2) qui empêchaient que le pied des étais ne s'enfonce dans le sol humide. Si ce dispositif est efficace, on constate néanmoins qu'il est beaucoup plus sommaire que celui du premier état, comme le sont d'ailleurs tous les aménagements de la seconde phase.

1995   Kition et la mer à l'époque classique et hellénistique. Pp. 119–30 in *Cyprus and the Sea*, eds. V. Karageorghis and D. Michalides. Nicosia: University of Cyprus.

in press   Kition et la mer. *Actes du Symposium européen Flotte et commerce dans la Méditerranée. Ravello 1989.*

KYRENIA II:
The Return from Cyprus to Greece
of the Replica of a
Hellenic Merchant Ship

GLAFKOS A. CARIOLOU

Captain of KYRENIA II (1986–1990)

According to information passed on by Hesiod in his Works and Days, *"there is nothing pleasant about sailing in April, in the so-called spring sailing season, and it is hard to escape coming to grief; yet still and even so, men in their shortsightedness do undertake it."*

The Hellenic Institute for the Preservation of Nautical Tradition, with a carefully prepared experiment, investigated the sailing routes of antiquity and the performance under sail of commercial sailing vessels dating to ca. 400 B.C.E.

An almost eighty percent authentic replica of an ancient merchant ship, called the KYRENIA II, sailed over 520 Nautical Miles (N.M.) via the ancient port of Paphos on Cyprus, to Rhodes, Astypalea and Syros with its final destination being the harbor at Zea (Piraeus). The dates of this voyage were April 7–26, 1987.

The results are very useful to the field of Nautical Archaeology as they include the planning of the voyage, the preparation of the ship and crew, the sailing performance of the vessel and other aspects of navigation and seamanship. They also provide an insight into the vast amount of knowledge possessed by the ancient Greek mariners and shipbuilders.

INTRODUCTION

On Saturday, the 20th of November, 1965 Andreas Cariolou, my late father, who was on a dive gathering sponges, discovered the wreck of an ancient merchant ship of the fourth century B.C.E. at a depth of 30 m off the northern coast of Cyprus. With him, I took the first black and white photographs of a small mound of amphoras, which was all that protruded from the sandy bottom. A few years later, a team of archaeologists and divers under the leadership of Michael Katzev managed to bring the finds to the surface and, with the assistance of Richard Steffy (1985, 1994), the ship's hull was reassembled in the castle of my home town of Kyrenia. I personally worked as a diver on the underwater excavation in the summers of 1967 to 1969.

Project Origin

As one may correctly assume, a deep sentimental connection drove me to become involved in the KYRENIA II project and thanks to the Hellenic Institute for the Preservation of Nautical Tradition, and the Greek Ministry of Culture, I present my findings here.

Objectives

The objectives of the return trip of KYRENIA II[1] from Cyprus to Greece were fourfold:

---

[1] For the first voyage of KYRENIA II in 1986 see Katzev (1990) and Tzalas (1987). See also the video tapes "The Ancient Ship of Kyrenia: Captain and Sailors Three," National Geographic Production; "Kyrenia II: Greece to Cyprus" an RVTV/Transvideo Co-Production in collaboration with the Hellenic Institute for the Preservation of the Nautical Tradition, Piraeus, Greece.

1) To investigate and test the possibility of sailing west, back to Greece in the wintertime, when the winds are most favorable and blow from the east,[2] and to determine the possible duration of the trip in antiquity.

2) To test the feasibility of sailing the vessel with only four men as crew members and of handling the vessel at night.

3) To test and investigate the performance and capabilities of the vessel in general as well as under adverse conditions.

4) To try to obtain as much information as possible in order to aid archaeological research as well as maritime studies.

Planning the Voyage

Using statistical analysis of meteorological data provided by the Cyprus Meteorological Department (Meteorological Service 1986) it was decided that the trip should commence on the 1st of April 1987 because of the high probability of strong Easterly winds during this month. These winds are the result of the so-called Atlas or Desert Depressions, usually forming over the Atlantic ocean near the Atlas mountain region and the coast of East Africa from January to May each year. These depressions pass over the dessert picking up hot dry air. With the center of a cyclonic system over Egypt they usually move eastward, causing a strong easterly gradient in the area between Paphos, Cyprus and Mandraki, Rhodes.

The Optimum Route

Due to political reasons it was necessary to avoid the coast of Turkey and Turkish occupied northern Cyprus, thus sailing to the harbor of Kyrenia had to be excluded. This partially effected the authenticity of the trip. Sailing 230 Nautical Miles (N.M.) from Paphos to Rhodes became a navigational exercise that was probably not encountered by the sailors of the Kyrenia Ship in antiquity. Using a polar diagram and other records, including those of the 1986 trip from Greece to Cyprus, a probable route was formed with thirty-four alternatives. The choice of each route totally depended on the wind direction. The optimum route, i.e. that with the least number of tacks, was as follows: Limassol, Paphos, Rhodes, Nisyros, Denousa (a small island east of Naxos), Syros, Kythnos, Kea, Sounion, Phleva (a small island off Sounion), to Phaleron (Piraeus). This route gave a linear distance of 520 Nautical Miles (N.M.). We estimated

a sailing time of twelve to fifteen days to cover this journey.

The Navigation Plan

The Navigation Plan of the voyage contained the port of departure, the port of arrival, the compass courses, the distance, the favorable wind direction, the wind direction limits and finally the totally unfavorable wind direction or "No sail" limits. It was calculated that wind with an "average" direction commencing at 140 degrees and ending at 067 degrees was unfavorable to sail and from 240 degrees to 330 degrees was a "No sail" situation. The plan of the voyage was submitted to and approved by the Hellenic Institute for the Preservation of Nautical Tradition.

Safety—Security—Towage—Scientific Escort

By courtesy of the Greek ship owner Mr. Latsis, the offshore tug "Ellas" (45 m L.O.A., 5 m draft, and capable of 13 knots maximum speed) was to be our escort/safety vessel. The tug was to provide towage in and out of ports as it was difficult, if not impossible, to maneuver a square-rigged vessel in and out of the small modern day harbors in this area. It also served as a base station for the accompanying researchers, scientists and archaeologists.

PREPARATION OF THE SHIP

Ship's Condition

On the 8th of February we commenced the maintenance of KYRENIA II at the Kyrenia Nautical Club, Limassol, Cyprus, inside a specially constructed building, which housed the entire ship with lowered mast. The KYRENIA II had remained after the previous trip in the moderately polluted waters of the port of Limassol for a period of forty-three days. As a result, 11.5% (0.84 sq m) of the total keel surface that was submerged (7.28 square meters) had been superficially affected by woodworm, which had penetrated the thick outer covering of pine-resin/pitch. Upon detailed examination, 7.9% (0.42 square meters) of the first planks on both sides of the rabbet line had also been attacked by woodworm. In addition, most of the submerged hull had a thickness of 2 mm of marine growth over the pitch. The ancient ship had had a 2 mm thick plating or lead-sheathing placed on top of the pitch, which offered a degree of protection. It was decided to protect the hull with modern antifouling paint.

---

[2] For an interesting article on seasonal wind patterns in the eastern Mediterranean see Murray (1995).

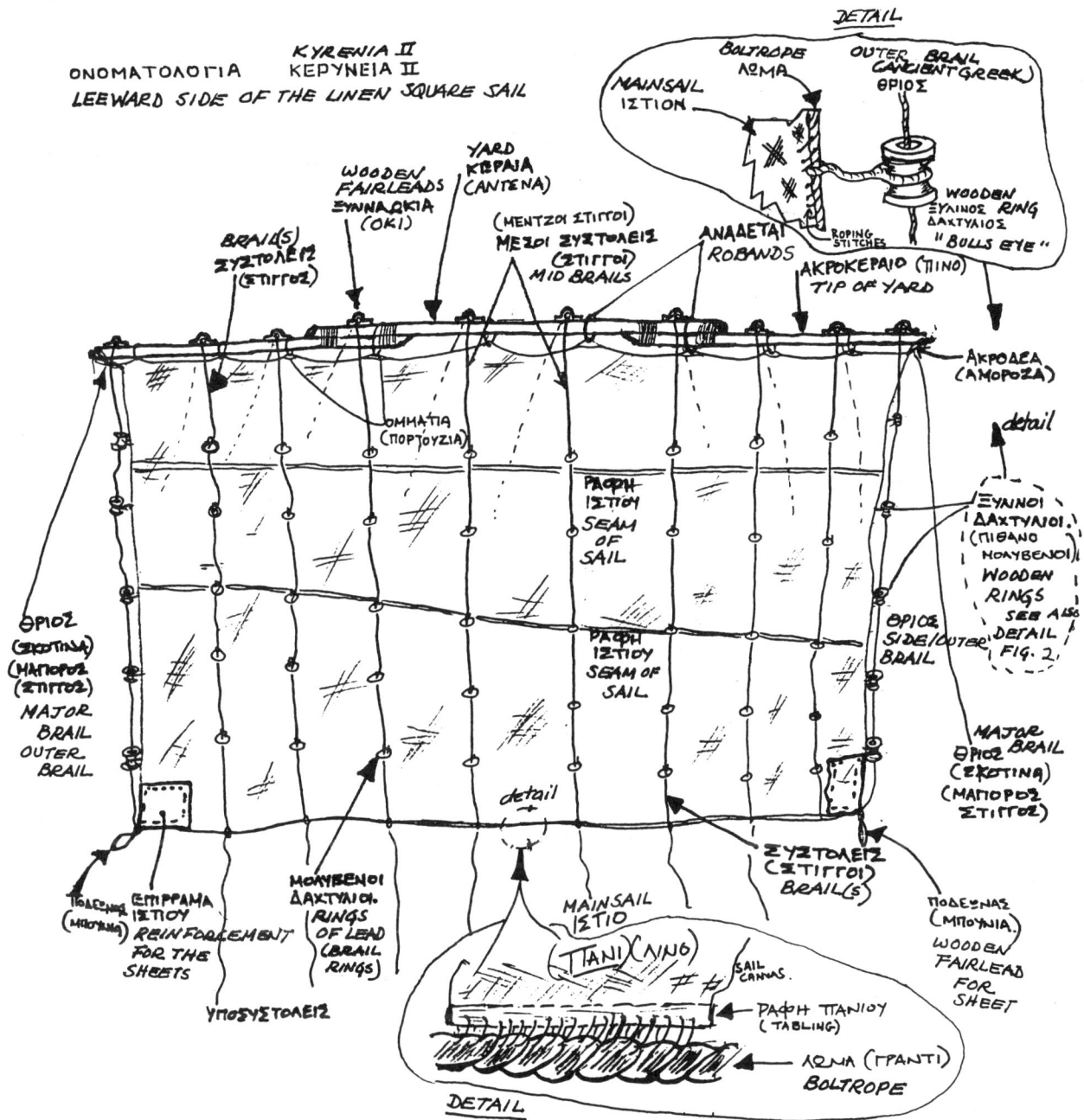

Fig.1. Leeward side of the linen square sail with details of rigging. Sketch from author's log.

Antifouling Treatment

Three coats of protective chemical were applied inside and outside the hull below the waterline, prior to applying the antifouling, in order to protect the wooden hull from worm action. Most of the hull below the waterline was painted with black (so as to follow the ancient tradition color-wise) antifouling paint. However, four areas were treated with only the ancient method of protective coating, a mixture of pine/pitch and linseed oil, in order to test and measure the different methods of protection and degrees of fouling.

Rigging—Sail—Refurbishment and Repair

The main halyard (ΥΠΕΡΑ-ΜΑΝΤΑΡΙ) and seven of the sail brails (ΣΥΣΤΟΛΕΙΣ ΙΣΤΙΟΥ) were changed, including the two major brails (ΘΡΕΙΟΣ) (fig. 1). The sail tabling (reinforcing) (ΡΑΘΗΜΑΝΙΟΥ) was checked and re-sewn on the boltrope (ΛΩΜΑ ΙΣΤΙΟΥ) where necessary (detail, fig. 1). The stitching was reinforced around the brail rings (ΔΑΚΤΥΛΙΟΙ ΜΟΛΥΒΔΟΥ)/fairleads on the sail (fig. 2 with details). The halyard block system (ΕΠΑΡΤΗΣ ΥΠΕΡΑΣ) was changed from a ratio of 1:2 to 1:3, and was tested along with the steering arm or tiller, (ΛΑΓΟΥΔΕΡΑ) (fig. 3). Two broken stanchions were replaced. The wooden rings (ΞΥΛΙΝΑ ΔΑΧΤΥΛΙΔΙΑ) of the major brail (figs. 1 and 2 details) were respliced. Finally the entire vessel, as well as all the ropes and blocks were thickly coated with linseed oil. The total area treated, below the first wale, was 64.8 square meters. To complete these refittings and all other work on the hull, we spent a total of 281.9 man-hours.

The Crew: Captain and Crew of Four

A crew of five was selected, four to be the working crew and one to act as a replacement in case of an emergency. They were:
- Nikos Mertiris, age 40, a professional seaman with trawler fishing experience both in the Atlantic and the Mediterranean.
- Kostas Agathangelou, 39, a proficient seaman from the town of Kyrenia, a quay master in Limassol port, who distinguished himself by his excellent humor and cordial character.
- Stamatis Chrisafitis, 27, an experienced sailor from the island of Hydra, student of naval architecture at the Metsovian Polytechnic, who had rowed on Tim Severins' "Argo" experiments and had been a crew member of the KYRENIA II's 1986 trip to Cyprus.
- George Pahitis, 28, a good sailor and a coastal naviga-

tor, from the town of Kyrenia, who has a degree in Hotel Administration and now proven cooking abilities under rough sea conditions.
- Glafkos A. Cariolou, 35, a marina and boat yard director, from the town of Kyrenia, with twenty-five years of sailing and navigation experience.

Each crew member, with the exception of Nikos Mertiris, had already had a minimum of fifty hours of experience and training on board KYRENIA II.

THE TRIP

KYRENIA II was relaunched on the 1st of April 1987 (fig. 5). We departed from Limassol on the 7th of April with a crew of four; calm weather and *completely* calm seas; so we had to be towed to Paphos!

With a long-range forecast for an Atlas Depression we left Paphos with *all* crew on board. There were light, westerly, unfavorable winds. We sailed on a starboard tack, in anticipation of the Easterly, on a course heading to Alexandria for approximately 50 N.M. out of Paphos. We then changed to a port tack, which headed us towards the coast of Anatolia, the ancient Tristomon, and Cape Gelidonya.

The anticipated Atlas Depression arrived, which caused gusting easterly winds of 53 knots and waves up to 3.5–4 m in height. In spite of the fearsome roar of the eastern Mediterranean, KYRENIA II, with no significant problems, successfully arrived on the 12th of April, four days after departure, in Mandraki, Rhodes.

We departed from this harbor on April 14th, after having reinforced KYRENIA II's rigging and prepared for lower temperatures as well as having waited for favorable weather. After having sailed a distance of 124 N.M. in adverse weather conditions, we ran, close hauled, into a storm near the island of Amorgos, which gusted to 55 knots (10 Beaufort). During this storm most of the lead brail rings came off the sail and one of our two quarter rudders broke on its loom and thus most of the close-haul capability of the sail was lost. In spite of the storm, however, the freeboard of the vessel (1.5 m) proved to be adequate to prevent swamping by the rough seas.

Canvas and awnings were kept stowed as we had to be able to move swiftly at night when visibility was less than 50 m. Temperatures were close to zero due to the wind-chill factor. Handling the sail and natural-fiber ropes at night without sailing gloves was an extremely difficult task.

After sailing to the lee of the island of Amorgos and into safer waters, we were towed southeast to Astypalea where we sought refuge in the harbor of Skala. We waited there four days before the wind force decreased to a reasonable level. Our damages were repaired in 24 hours. The loom was fixed and the new steering oar tiller was reinforced.

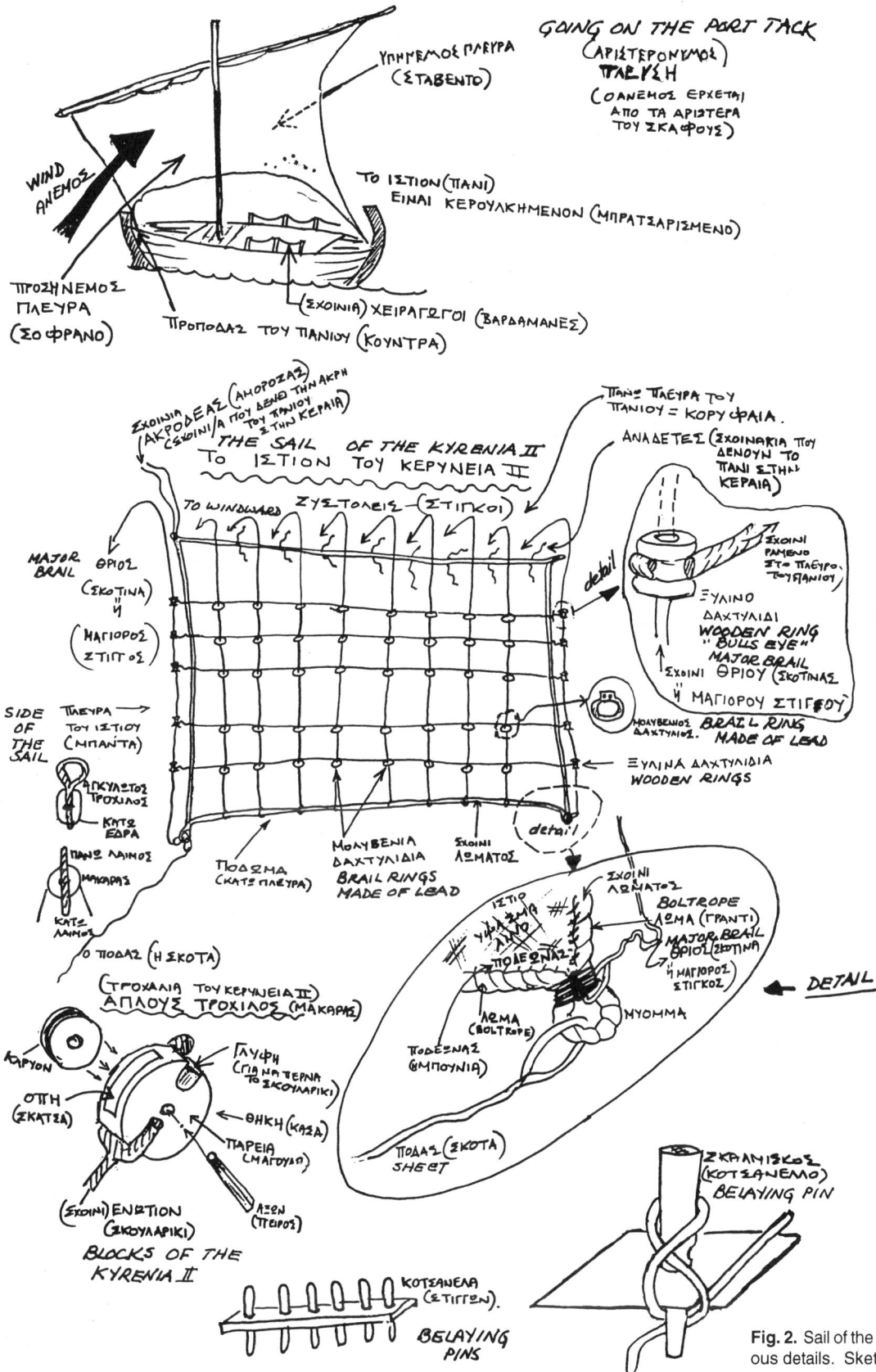

Fig. 2. Sail of the KYRENIA II with various details. Sketch from author's log.

_ ΟΝΟΜΑΤΟΛΟΓΙΑ " ΚΕΡΥΝΕΙΑ ΙΙ"

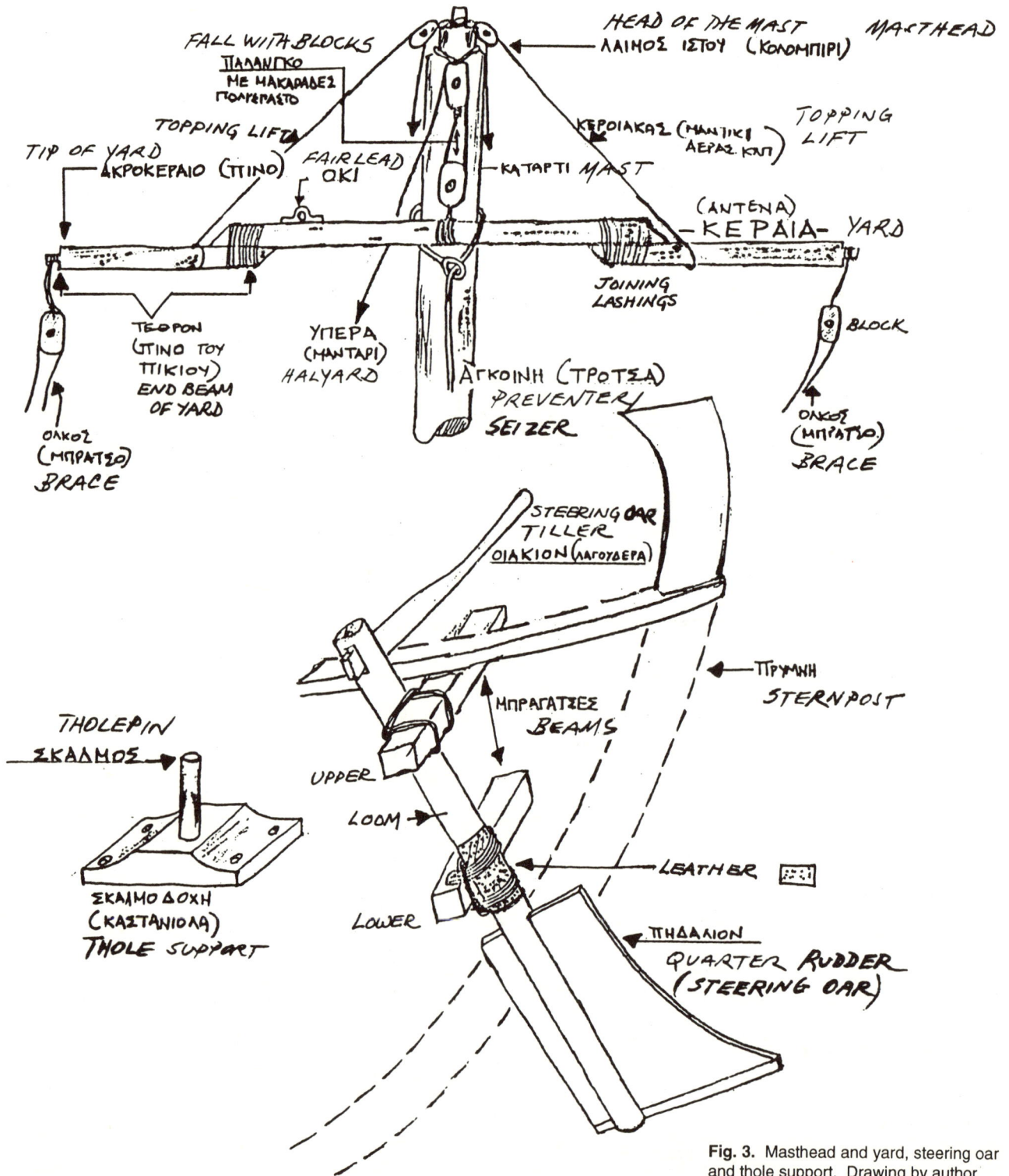

FALL WITH BLOCKS
ΠΑΛΑΓΚΟ ΜΕ ΜΑΚΑΡΑΔΕΣ ΠΟΛΥΣΠΑΣΤΟ

HEAD OF THE MAST   MASTHEAD
ΛΑΙΜΟΣ ΙΣΤΟΥ (ΚΟΛΟΜΠΙΡΙ)

TOPPING LIFT
ΚΕΡΟΙΑΚΑΣ (ΜΑΝΤΙΚΙ ΑΕΡΑΣ ΚΛΠ)   TOPPING LIFT

TIP OF YARD
ΑΚΡΟΚΕΡΑΙΟ (ΠΙΝΟ)

FAIRLEAD
ΟΚΙ

ΚΑΤΑΡΤΙ MAST

(ANTENA)
-ΚΕΡΑΙΑ- YARD

JOINING LASHINGS

ΤΕΘΡΟΝ (ΠΙΝΟ ΤΟΥ ΠΙΚΙΟΥ) END BEAM OF YARD

ΥΠΕΡΑ (ΜΑΝΤΑΡΙ) HALYARD

ΑΓΚΟΙΝΗ (ΤΡΟΤΣΑ) PREVENTER/ SEIZER

BLOCK

ΟΛΚΟΣ (ΜΠΡΑΤΣΟ) BRACE

ΟΛΚΟΣ (ΜΠΡΑΤΣΟ) BRACE

STEERING OAR
TILLER
ΟΙΑΚΙΟΝ (ΛΑΓΟΥΔΕΡΑ)

ΠΡΥΜΝΗ STERNPOST

ΜΠΡΑΓΑΤΣΕΣ BEAMS

THOLEPIN
ΣΚΑΛΜΟΣ

UPPER

LOOM

LEATHER

ΣΚΑΛΜΟΔΟΧΗ (ΚΑΣΤΑΝΙΟΛΑ) THOLE SUPPORT

LOWER

ΠΗΔΑΛΙΟΝ QUARTER RUDDER (STEERING OAR)

Fig. 3. Masthead and yard, steering oar and thole support. Drawing by author.

After we had departed from Astypalea on April 20th, we were forced to stop, for the third time, at the port of Syros due to encountering head winds of 40 knots, which broke one of the steering oars off the island of Delos. But we had sailed 110 N.M. non-stop.

At Syros we had the opportunity, with the assistance of the local shipyard, to overhaul KYRENIA II with a new forebeam, two totally repaired and reinforced steering oars and other minor repairs and improvements.

We departed from Syros on the 25th of April after having waited four days once again for weather conditions to improve. After sailing 10 N.M. we entered into the flat calm of an anticyclone. As we were now heavily pressed for time we decided that we had to be towed to Zea Marina at Piraeus, instead of sailing the leg from the island of Yaros (18 N.M. northwest of Syros) via Kythnos to our final destination. We arrived at Zea on the 26th of April 1987 at 02:40. The total duration of the trip had been 20 calendar days.

Actual Distances—Sailing versus Towing

From Limassol, Cyprus to Zea, Greece, we sailed a distance of 495 N.M., 70% of the total voyage, and we were towed for a distance of 212.5 N.M., 30% of the voyage. We had actually sailed for 181 hours and 15 minutes (84.5%) and we were towed for 33 hours and 15 minutes (15.5%). We were able to follow the best possible rhumb line route for approximately 75% of the trip.

Weather Conditions

From Cyprus to Rhodes we had mostly light variable head winds with temperatures up to 22 degrees C. and zero octas (0/8) cloud coverage. When we were 100 N.M. east of Rhodes, there was a sudden change. A low over Egypt, moving slowly east caused an easterly pressure gradient. It became partly cloudy, 3 octas, (3/8 cloud coverage) with drizzle and wind from 100 degrees with a force of 45–53 knots (10 Beaufort). The sea was very rough and visibility was 3 N.M. or less. From Rhodes to Astypalea conditions were mainly unfavorable with head winds and complete cloud coverage, low temperatures (10–12 degrees C) and almost continuous rain. Low clouds and fog made the voyage after the island of Kos more difficult and dangerous. Out of Amorgos we entered a violent storm of gusting head winds up to 55 knots (10 Beaufort) with very low visibility, rain and high waves.

The leg from Astypalea to Syros was sailed in fair weather with sunny, clear skies and light to moderate, favorable winds. It was only out of Delos that we experienced head winds gusting up to 40 knots (8 Beaufort).

The anticyclone encountered from Syros to Zea caused a complete calm with clear skies and comfortable temperatures.

In conclusion, we had either very light or very strong winds! We had two storms of 10 Beaufort, 53 and 55 knots from 100 degrees and 340 degrees respectively and one strong wind of 40 knots from 230 degrees.

Measuring Instruments and Services

A minimal number of instruments were carried by KYRENIA II and the tug "Ellas." On board the KYRENIA II were:

1) One wind speed indicator (cup impeller type of horizontal rotation) calibrated in knots. All of the wind speed readings represented Apparent or Relative wind speed. The anemometer was positioned on top of the stern post, away from any unwanted airflow.

2) One electromechanical Log/Speedometer that recorded the vessel's speed through the water. The impeller was towed from the stern approximately 3 m off the centerline of the vessel in order to avoid any interference with hull turbulence. The speed scale was from 0–12 knots. The same instrument was also used to record the total distance travelled.

3) One stationary steering compass used to record the ship's heading.

4) One handbearing compass that was used to determine the azimuth bearings of a) the approximate apparent wind direction, b) the leeway or the angle between heading and actual course, c) the angle of drift.

5) An improvised clinometer that had been hand-made by Stamatis Chrisafitis and was located on the bulkhead inside the stern cabin. The scale was in 5 degree increments and covered angles of heel up to 45 degrees port and starboard.

6) A traditional scale capable of weighing materials up to 300 kg (kantari).

7) A tape measure for general measurements and a complete selection of tools for a wood joiner or carpenter.

8) For draft measurements, three positions were marked by a chisel on the hull to indicate the vertical distance between that point and the bottom-most point of the keel. All three points were marked on the port side of the vessel, and included: a) a stern mark with the figure 350 on the top of the rail, b) the greater depth mark with the figure 270 on the gunwale, and c) the stem mark with the figure 253 on top of the rail near the bow. These figures indicated the exact vertical distance in centimeters from the bottom of the keel to the carved point or mark. Measuring the distance between these

ΗΜΕΡΟΛΟΓΙΟ "ΚΕΡΥΝΕΙΑ ΙΙ"

ΣΗΜΕΙΩΣΕΙΣ

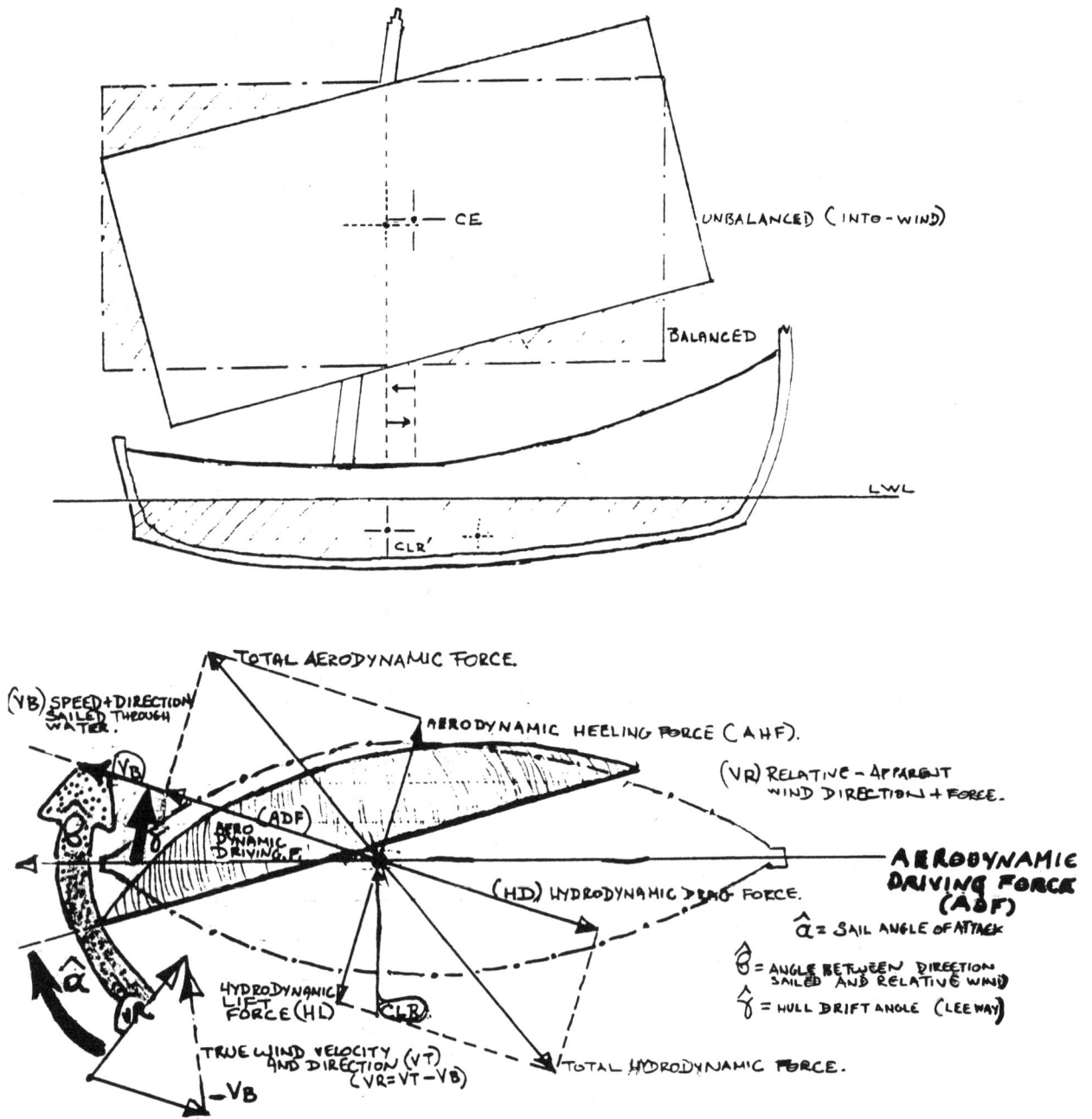

Fig. 4. Improved sailing performance. Drawing by author.

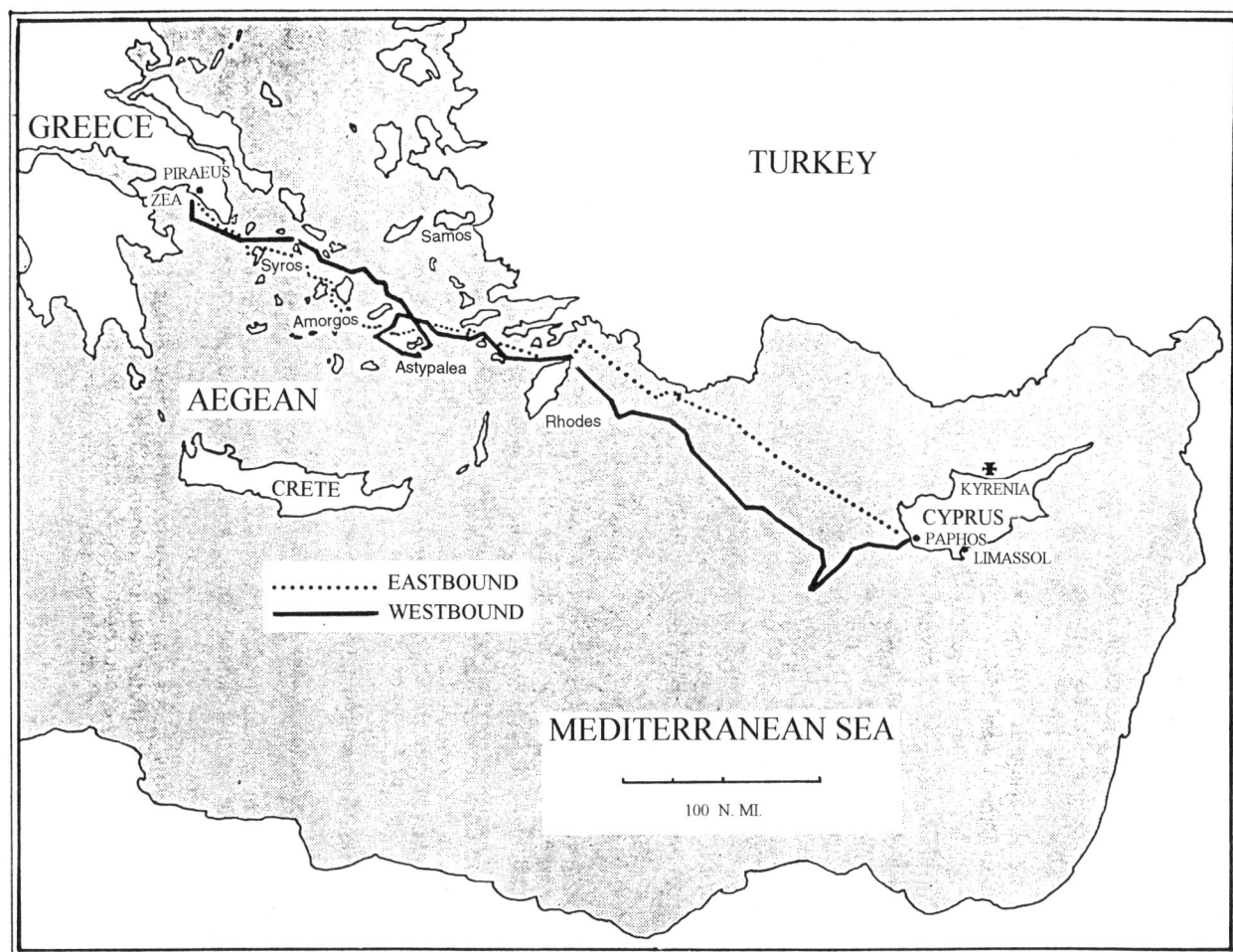

Fig. 5. Voyage of the KYRENIA II. After Katzev (1987).

points and the sea surface in the calm waters of each mooring site at a zero clinometer reading, gave us the exact draft of the vessel and the cargo loading balance, as well as a good idea of the vessel's trim.

9) Our normal electronic wristwatches and stopwatches were used for timing, noon-sights and other navigational purposes and saved us from having to use a sun-clock!

Safety Equipment and Navigation

Safety equipment carried on board consisted of one marine VHF radio with another reserve radio, fourteen life jackets, one life raft capable of holding ten people and two parachute flares.

Navigational instruments and procedures were kept to a minimum in an effort not to vary greatly from assumed authentic circumstances. We have no significant information as to what navigational instruments were used by our ancestors. For navigating we used the stationary compass

of the vessel, a hand bearing compass, three sea charts, a simple plastic sextant, our wristwatches, the nautical almanac and a star chart.

From Paphos to Rhodes we used both dead reckoning and astronavigation as this is a stretch of approximately 200 N.M. with no visible land. The Sun, Venus, Arcturus, the Moon and Polaris were used extensively. From Rhodes to Sounion and Piraeus usual coastal navigation procedures were adequate during the daytime. Navigating the Aegean during daylight hours is comparatively easy as it is usual to see another island before you loose sight of your port or island of departure. However, at night with strong winds, heavy seas, fog and low cloud, without an engine or radar and very limited sailing performance capability, navigation and sailing gives one a nasty feeling, similar to that produced by playing Russian roulette!

The vessel moves at a speed of 8–12 knots without one having accurate knowledge of the distance from navigation dangers and nearby islands. When and if land is sighted under these circumstances, it would probably be impossible to avoid a crash or calamity. It was found that navigating in the open sea, far from the islands and land, was much easier during the night than the day. One always had a wide choice of stars for guidance. It was, and is, much safer to navigate amongst the islands during the daytime.

Sailing Performance

KYRENIA II has a square sail with a horizontal breadth of 11.18 m and a vertical height of 5.6 m. The sail area equals 62.6 sq m. The dry weight of the sail was 61 kg It is attached on the yardarm by 12 robands (ΑΝΑΔΕΤΕΣ). On the leeward side of the linen sail (figs. 1 and 2) there are eight vertical rows of lead brail rings facing up and down. From the boltrope on the foot of the sail we spliced eight brails (ΣΥΣΤΟΛΕΙΣ), which pass through each of the five rings attached on the sail in a vertical row (one on top of the other). The brail then passes over the yardarm (ΚΕΡΑΙΑ) on the windward side, through the wooden fairleads (ΟΚΙΑ) of the yardarm, and ends up on the after deck secured on the brail belaying pins (ΚΟΤΣΑΝΕΛΑ). On the port and starboard sides of the sail there are five wooden rings or "bulls eyes" spliced on the boltrope through which the rope of the outer buntline or outer brail or clew garnet (ΘΡΕΙΟΣ/ ΜΑΓΓΙΟΡΟΣ ΣΤΙΓΓΟΣ) is passing in the same manner as through the lead rings.

The clew and tack of the sail are controlled by two long sheet ropes (ΠΟΔΑΣ) passing through two wooden fairleads (ΠΟΔΕΩΝΑΣ) giving a ratio of 1:2 to the pulling of the sheets. The rotation of the yardarm is controlled by the port and starboard braces (ΟΛΚΟΙ) (fig. 3) passing through a block giving a 2:1 purchase. On the vertical plane the movement of the yardarm is controlled by the port and starboard topping lifts (ΚΕΡΟΙΑΚΕΣ) passing through their respective blocks (fig. 3). The yardarm weighs 80 kg and has a length of 11.6 m.

Prismatic Coefficient and Metacentric Height

The prismatic coefficient of the vessel is approximately 0.627. The beam to depth ratio is 2.68. The metacentric height of the vessel was not measured but this should have been fairly high as the return or recovery to the vertical plane of the mast after wave induced inclination was very quick. It would be further improved with additional weight-cargo loaded on board. (No inclination test was done.) The approximate freeboard was 1.5 m at all times.

THE SAIL OR THE PLAN OF THE SAIL

During the storm that we encountered 100 N.M. east of Rhodes, we were able to sail with full sail area, without using the sail downhauls, at speeds up to 12 knots, at an almost dead run or open broad reach course. The superiority (compared to contemporary triangular mainsails) of the plan or form of a square sail during this storm was very clear as regards the balance of the hydro and aerodynamic forces exerted on the hull and sail. We found to our surprise that periods of up to 15–30 minutes would pass without any course adjustment being necessary when we had both steering oar tillers lashed during the storm.

In view of the low aspect ratio of the sail form, compared to contemporary sails, the usual rolling effect experienced in modern yachts when on a run was not present or it was comparatively little. In spite of waves with an approximate height of 3.5–4.5 m, we experienced no particular problems. The run was so smooth that in one case, with winds gusting up to 50 knots, it was possible to climb to the top of the mast and replace the badly worn yardarm preventer or seizer (ΤΡΟΤΣΑ/ΑΓΚΟΙΝΗ) (fig. 3).

The close-hauled ability and performance of the vessel was influenced in a negative way mainly by the following parameters:
1) Low sail aspect ratio approximately 1:5.
2) The external depth of the actual keel, which is only 21 cm. (There was no practical keel effect).
3) The C.L.R. (center of lateral resistance) of the vessel is well aft of the C.E. (center of effort).
4) The general hydrodynamics of the hull form, specifically due to the lack of a deeper keel, was regarded as not suitable for sailing close-hauled.

[Note: the L.W.L. (length at the waterline) equals 14.5 m, the L.O.A. (length over all) equals 14.8 m, the C.L.R. is estimated to be at a point approximately 7.2 m, measured from the bow, the C.E. is approximately 1.42 m forward of the C.L.R., thus giving a "negative lead of approximately 9.8%.]

Many other parameters must have affected the close-hauled sailing ability, such as the actual tailoring of the sail, the angle of the yardarm, the shape and handling of the steering oars, the trim or loading method of the vessel, and even the position of the crew. Sailing close-hauled required skill, coordination and speed, which all took us considerable time and effort to master. The best close-hauled angle was achieved off the island of Delos, south of Mykonos, where we were able to sail at a relative angle of 51 degrees between the heading of 283 degrees and the true wind direction of 232 degrees, with a true wind speed of 23.4 knots. The vessel's water speed was 6.8 knots on a port tack and at an angle of heel of approximately 20 degrees. Due to sea surface conditions it was not possible to measure the leeway. However, the estimated angle of drift was 10 degrees. (The above gave us a close-hauled ability or angle between the course and the true direction of wind equal to approximately 60 degrees.) This could reasonably be compared to contemporary yachts, which have a normal close-hauled ability from 40 to 50 degrees to the true wind direction.

The same on course stability was observed on a close-hauled tack as mentioned before. On this course there was a very slight tendency to go off the wind. Damage to the steering oars always occurred when sailing close-hauled. By aligning the steering oars on the island of Syros, I believe we at least minimized the effect of short period waves and the effect of the hydrodynamic drag. We did not, however, have much chance to investigate and test this new steering arrangement.

The following procedures for improving the sailing performance at close-haul were carried out (fig. 4):

1) To try to achieve a higher aspect ratio for the sail form, we a) lifted the yardarm higher on the mast by approximately 70–80 cm, and b) inclined the yardarm when sailing as close-hauled as possible, with the after arm or leeward arm as high as possible, thus increasing the height(s) of the sail plan form by 1.10 m, which in turn raised the aspect ratio from 1.5 to 1.7. In this case the tack of the sail was very tightly secured to the windward end of the fore-deck cross-beam.

2) To try to balance the sailing performance, we transferred the cargo forward in order to move the center of lateral resistance (C.L.R.) forward to meet the center of effort (C.E.), and inclined the mast further aft in an effort to move the C.E. aft so as to meet the C.L.R.

3) The sailing performance of the KYRENIA II was improved immensely by the introduction of downhauls (ΥΠΟΣΥΣΤΟΛΕΙΣ), in an effort to flatten the sail and to improve the close-haul ability.

Tacking (ΑΝΑΣΤΡΟΦΗ)

Tacking was found to be difficult but possible. We successfully tacked twice without using oars in winds between 2–4 Beaufort. Tacking in winds above 4 Beaufort proved difficult and very dangerous for the integrity of the sail, and therefore was not practiced.

Gybing (ΥΠΟΣΤΡΟΦΗ)

Gybing was the most frequently used method to go about, changing from a port to a starboard tack. The procedure was easy in winds up to 5 Beaufort, but above that it requires skill and perfect coordination. A gibe may be carried out in wind forces up to 10 Beaufort without serious problems. In general the sailing performance dramatically improved with the use of sail downhauls or brail hitches (ΥΠΟΣΥΣΤΟΛΕΙΣ) as mentioned above.

Rolling

Rolling was found to be less than that experienced on modern yachts under sail.

Heeling

Heeling in winds up to 30–35 knots at close-haul was approximately 25 degrees.

Yaw

The yaw was negligible in comparison to modern yachts and almost non-existent.

Hogging

No proper measurements were taken but there was no apparent hogging.

Plank Sheering

We did not detect any apparent plank sheering.

Leaking

When at zero degrees of heel the vessel did not leak. At 8–12 degrees of heel, the port side third frame from the after bulkhead (on the wale scarf) leaked considerably. This was repaired using oakum, animal fat, leather and a lead patch.

Broaching

Even with the sail reefed or "brailed" it was easy to avoid broaching, and no tendency to broach was observed. However, on two or three occasions we passed from the broaching position without any considerable problem.

Swamping

In spite of rough conditions, swamping was not experienced and we did not find it necessary to use a canvas "spray deck" when the vessel was unloaded.

Longitudinal and Transverse Strength

No measurements were taken, but I can confirm that the hull had substantial flexibility.

Twisting

None was observed. Twisting and slight hogging was noted only during split seconds when we were hit by the escorting ships "Ellas" and "Aedon" (a minesweeper) on two different occasions. During the collisions considerable flexibility of the shell-construction was conspicuous. However, there was immediate, total, recovery. No leakage was observed following the impacts.

Hull Speed

In theory, the hull speed should be approximately 9 knots. However, in practice with approximately 45–50 knots of true wind speed on a run or broad reach we averaged 11.98 knots for a period of 5.8 hours over a distance of 69.49 N.M. During this period the maximum speed must have been just over 12 knots!

Vibrations

We did not feel vibrations of any frequency on the hull or the rigging under any conditions.

Main Weakness

This was the steering oars. They had the tendency to break at speeds of above 5 knots and during close-hauled tacks. This was slightly counteracted by the realignment of the two steering oars so that their projected hydrodynamic axis was brought parallel with the center line of the vessel (fig. 4).

Moisture Effect

With high atmospheric humidity, moisture and rain, the sail and ropes often became saturated with water, with a subsequent increase in sail and rigging weight. Handling had to be slower and performed with greater care. As the result of a heavier and flatter sail, the sailing performance when close-hauled with a good wind (5 Beaufort) improved, whereas performance was adversely affected in lighter winds. A slight increase in rolling was observed as a result of the heavier sail and rigging.

Rowing Performance

This vessel was certainly not designed to be rowed over a distance! A lot of muscle, body weight and skill was required. KYRENIA II could be rowed with two or four standing oarsmen. The oars are balanced by lead weights and the four oars weigh 21.75, 30.00, 22.00, and 27.50 kg respec-

tively. They are 6.12 m long. The oars had to be trimmed to the correct loom length so as to avoid the collision of opposing oars. Four competent oarsmen can row this 16 ton vessel (without cargo) at a speed of 0.75 knots with the yardarm raised, the sail fully reefed or brailed-up in an absolute calm. Under these conditions or with a very light breeze the ship could be accurately controlled and maneuvered inside a port. With a wind of approximately 5–7 knots (2–3 Beaufort) the vessel cannot be controlled at all by the oars only.

The Rigging

The standing rigging consisted of 30 mm diameter natural-fiber (hemp and manila) rope. It consisted of a backstay (ΠΑΡΑΤΟΝΟΣ) and two shrouds (ΕΠΙΤΟΝΟΥΣ) on each side of the mast. For the running rigging, there was an inner and outer forestay (ΕΣΩ ΠΡΟΤΟΝΟΣ—ΕΞΩ ΠΡΟΤΟΝΟΣ) used according to the sail and yard position. The inner forestay was used with strong winds when the down hauls were all released together with the outer forestay, and the sail was used like a spinnaker. The topping lift halyards (ΚΕΡΟΙΑΚΕΣ), the yardarm halyard and block system (1:3 purchase) as well as the preventer or seizer (ΑΓΚΟΙΝΗ/ΤΡΟΤΣΑ) completed the running rigging (fig. 3). We also had a bosun's chair halyard.

It was observed that both the forestay and backstay did very little work and the inner forestay could be removed for future trials. The joining lashings of the yardarm (fig. 3) allowed the two end beams of the yard to bend forward on the horizontal plane.

SAILING

Close-hauled

We installed eight sail down-hauls (ΥΠΟΣΥΣΤΟΛΕΙΣ) in order to fully utilize the square sail. The tack of the sail was tied as low as possible on the upper side of the forebeam on the windward side. Two thick ropes under tension were positioned between the inboard part of the forebeam, ending on each side of the aft part of the vessel, diagonally crossing the boat at a point just forward of the mast.

This rope served as the attaching base for the downhauls. The tension of the downhauls would start at maximum tension next to the tack and continue decreasing until the last two or three down hauls which were left either loose or with very little tension. The best sailing results were observed when a sail "groove" was achieved on the sail surface, commencing from the tack and ending on the leeward side of the yardarm.

Broad Reach—Running (ΦΟΡΟΣ—ΕΠΙΦΟΡΟΣ—ΟΥΡΙΟΔΡΟΜΙΑ)

The inboard downhauls were still used with low tension so as to try to place the foot of the sail right below the yardarm.

Tacking (ΑΝΑΣΤΡΟΦΗ)

As already stated, one of the most difficult procedures was tacking the boat. It required training, fitness, good knowledge and high coordination. It also became more difficult in a strong wind. The procedures we followed were:

1) We attempted to achieve a maximum boat speed on the particular course.
2) Both steering oars were turned, but not too much; a wide turn was necessary.
3) One person was responsible for the braces, a second crew member for the downhauls, the third for the tack of the sail and the fourth on the clew of the sail. No one was actually needed to steer as the tillers were lashed and left in a turning position.
4) The topping lifts were slackened.
5) On the fore side of sail, the luff was made tight.
6) As the vessel turned into the wind, the tension on the clew was increased by the manual force of a crew member, thus presenting a full flat sail plan form.
7) When the vessel's bow was on the eye of the wind, all downhauls were immediately released and the "braceman" slowly turned the yardarm, but stopped as soon as the yardarm was 90 degrees to the wind.
8) As soon as the yardarm rotation commenced, the clew and tack of the sail were untied. As the vessel turned, the yardarm was rotated. During the rotation the "tackman" held the sail, which lay above him, as flat and as tight as possible while the "downhaul-man" was doing exactly the same thing, as he was positioned by the mast. The forepart of the sail was tensioned, while the afterpart was flapping in the wind. The other half of the sail, from mast to leech, had to be loose to present as little surface as possible to the wind.
9) The vessel sometimes drifted astern, before turning to the required side.
10) As soon as the bow passed into the new tack, the rotation of the yardarm was continued. The previous "clewman" quickly ran to the forebeam and very tightly tied down the old clew, which now becomes the tack. The "downhaul-man" pushed the sail in front of the mast against the wind and kept the sail tightly down while the rest of it was flapping. As soon as a positive tack was established, the sail was set as in the previous tack.

DANGER! With strong winds, the sail will turn and be blown against the mast, so care must be taken so as not to break the yardarm. So, in a strong wind it is necessary to brail the after half of the sail before one commences the tack. All the crew members must stand and put their weight on the side of the turn if possible. Gybing was much easier, as has already been explained, and this is what we did most of the time, and under most weather conditions.

Additional Sail Area

An additional piece of sail was added below the original but it needed extensive adjustment before it could become a suitable sail part.

Steering

Steering was carried out by two steering oars of 59.5 and 61.5 kg The upper point was lashed forward of the upper beam and the lower point on the afterside of the lower beam (ΜΠΡΑΓΑΤΣΑ) (fig. 4).

We found that the turning maneuver was very slow. The extension of the after lower beam, to meet a position where it brings the two steering oars parallel to the center line of the vessel, is expected to improve the turning and general steering performance.

An alteration to the after edge of the blades definitely will improve steering further.

Steering oars broke in heavy seas and swell on a close-hauled tack at a high speed, when the hydrodynamic forces were increased. The breaking point was always at the uppermost end of the blade where it joins with the loom of the steering oar. The addition of steel collars, on the island of Syros, reinforced the oars and improved the situation.

The steering oars were usually lashed together by their tillers and very little adjustment was necessary during the voyage. Pulling up one steering oar improved speed when on a reach, broad reach, or when running. However, it was not advisable to lift a steering oar when close-hauled, as this increased leeway and the burden on the single oar that was being used. It was difficult to determine which steering oar should best be drawn up and which to leave down.

When sailing with little wave action, it was better to lower the leeward steering oar, but with moderate swell it was better to use the windward steering oar, as there was less possibility for it to break. Changing a steering oar took approximately 30 minutes in Force 6 and relashing approximately 15 minutes. In addition, we decided to rig a seat for the helmsman during his long standing hours.

Cargo

Thirty-five amphoras were loaded on board, together with all the other paraphernalia. The loading of each amphora took approximately 35 seconds, and unloading took approximately the same length of time, using two crew members on the mole and two on board. Each empty amphora weighed 10.1 kg (They were exact replicas). Full of wine the same amphora would have weighed approximately 43.5 kg.

When observing the loading space necessary for the 35 amphoras it was very difficult to imagine the cargo of 404 amphoras that were found upon the ancient Kyrenia ship, which was a comparatively small vessel. By looking at pictures of the loaded vessel, even if we assume that the 35 amphoras covered 1/5th of the available cargo area, then 5 times 35 equals 175 amphoras *only* as cargo. The first layer would take approximately 175 amphoras and the second presumably the same number, which would bring a total of 350 amphoras. We therefore believe that there must have been a third layer of 54 amphoras standing high above the level of the gunwale. With an approximate total empty weight equal to 10.1 kg × 404 equals 4,080.4 kg or a full weight of 43.5 kg × 404 or 17,574 kg.

In spite of all the storms encountered during the voyage, no movement of the cargo was observed.

LIFE ON BOARD

A list of provisions was prepared with the advice of Michael and Susan Katzev on the basis of what had been found on board the ancient Kyrenia ship, and what was known to have existed in the fourth century B.C.E. From these foodstuffs we prepared the following meals:

Breakfast. The mornings usually started with dried bread, *paximadi,* Cyprus *halloumi* cheese, honey and olives, chased down with wine and plenty of almonds.

Lunch. At noon fish, literally swimming in olive oil, was served with an ocean of lentils or beans called *mouchendra,* with onions and garlic, together with lots of wine and *paximadi.*

Dinner. At night, *halloumi* and dried salted meat, mainly pork, was eaten with *paximadi,* together with a deadly liquid known as *zivania,* which is made out of grape pips. It may not have existed at all in antiquity, but it is a very well known and highly respected strong drink in present day Cyprus.

We allowed ourselves the luxury of sleeping bags, as the expense of being dressed or equipped with ancient wintertime attire and sleeping facilities was not within our financial capabilities. We slept mainly inside the after or forward quarters, having covered both decks with low cost canvas and the forward quarter with a curtain also made of canvas.

"Caulking the steering beam" was the expression encrypted by our crew of "ancients" for visiting the "toilet" ("ΚΑΛΑΦΑΤΙΣΜΑ ΜΠΡΑΓΑΤΣΑΣ!"). This task was easily performed while under sail from the lower after-beam or the forebeam, depending on the urgency of the situation, irrespective of wind direction or strength or conditions of humidity.

Health and Morale

Sailing a replica of a 2,500 year old sailing vessel is a hard exercise even for a well-trained modern day sailor/racer. We believe that this exercise kept us healthy and far from the usual wintertime flu or other similar ailments, in spite of being wet, cold, without sleep and completely exposed to the elements on an almost continuous basis.

The spirit of the crew was excellent at all times, and of course we look forward to doing such a trip again, one day, even with a force 17; that is if we are sailing back home to Kyrenia!

CONCLUSIONS AND AFTERTHOUGHTS

It is highly probable that vessels sailed from west to east from the Aegean into the eastern Mediterranean basin, i.e. to Asia Minor, Cyprus, Syria, Israel, Palestine and even as far as Egypt, during the months of June to February. But it is highly unlikely that these vessels were able to return to the Aegean, sailing from east to west, during the same period.

Vessels sailed from the eastern Mediterranean into the Aegean, i.e. from east to west, only in the period of March, April and May during the Easterlies, if the Atlas Depressions existed at that time. However, the probability of sailing across to Egypt in order to return into the Aegean in the summertime must be investigated. The trip would take much longer.

When determining the placement of towns with ports/harbors great consideration was taken—apart from other parameters—of the prevailing wind, as communication and trade links depended a lot on sailing ships.

The requirements of harbor design in antiquity were seriously different from those of today. The positioning of the port entrance was of prime importance. It was probably sited in such a way as to allow an ancient vessel to sail in from the direction of the prevailing wind either on a broad-reach or running.

The ancient sailors were well-aware of the average wave length in the Aegean and they most probably took this into consideration when designing the Length on the Waterline

(L.W.L.) of their vessels. Due to their limited close-hauled sailing performance, vessels had to have a very high stern and a lower stem, contrary to contemporary naval architecture. This was because they would probably change to a "running" tack whenever they were fighting a storm. Sailing with the wind behind or after a storm with just a small storm jib or even no sails at all and a drogue towed at the end of a 300–400 m rope tied to the stern is nowadays still the best way to escape a force 10!

Most probably it was due to their understanding of storms and bad weather strategy, i.e always fighting the storm with the high stern against the breaking waves, that the anchor was dropped astern rather than from the bow.

The seemingly "wrong" relationship between the Center of Lateral Resistance (C.L.R.) and the Center of Effort (C.E.), which had a tendency to sail off the wind, was prob-ably done on purpose in order to prevent broaching in a heavy storm. The vessel always presented a high sea-worthy stern to the heavy breakers of any storm even with the steering oars safely withdrawn. (In a storm even with no steering oars, the vessel will safely sail "after the storm" on a running tack with the wind and waves behind her high stern.)

Sailing vessels, of the same age as the Kyrenia ship, must have had a much better steering system than the one we used on the KYRENIA II. The steering system used on ancient merchant ships remains a research challenge! Commercial sailing vessels of antiquity were probably towed, rowed and/or assisted by smaller rowing vessels or "tenders" in and out of a harbor. We feel that it would have been prudent and seaman-like to carry on board, or tow behind us, such a rowing boat or tender.

REFERENCES

Katzev, M. L.
1990   An Analysis of the Experimental Voyages of KYRENIA II. Pp. 245–56 in Proceedings of the 2nd International Symposium on Ship Construction in Antiquity. *Tropis II*. ed. H.E. Tzalas, Athens: Hellenic Institute for the Preservation of Nautical Tradition.

Meteorological Service
1986   *A Study of the Surface Winds in Cyprus*. Meteorological Paper Series No. 8, Fourth Edition. Nicosia: Ministry of Agriculture, Natural Resources and the Environment. Meteorological Service.

Murray, W. M.
1995   Ancient Sailing Winds in the Eastern Mediterranean. Pp. 33–45 in *Proceedings of the International Symposium, Cyprus and the Sea*, eds. V. Karageorghis and D. Michaelides, Nicosia: University of Cyprus.

Steffy, R. J.
1985   The Kyrenia Ship: An Interim Report on its Hull Construction. *American Journal of Archaeology* 89: 71–101.
1994   *Wooden Ship Building and the Interpretation of Shipwrecks*. College Station: Texas A&M University.

Tsalas, H.
1987   *Kyrenia Ship Exhibition: A Voyage into Time and Legend aboard the Kyrenia Ship*. Athens National Archaeological Museum. Athens: Hellenic Institute for the Preservation of Nautical Tradition.

The Origins of the *Polis*:
The View from Cyprus

NANCY DEMAND

Department of History
Indiana University
Bloomington, IN 47405
U.S.A.

This paper considers the challenge posed to two theories of the origins of the polis *by the exclusion of the Cypriot kingdoms from the category of* polis. *These theories find the origins of the* polis *in continuity with the Mycenaean past and in Phoenician influence. The Cypriot kingdoms offer excellent examples of both conditions; as non-*poleis, *they thus serve as counter-examples to these theories, but they have been excluded from discussion. This paper considers two possible reasons for this exclusion: Gjerstad's classification of the kingdoms as Oriental despotism, and the current popularity of Athenocentric ideological definitions of the* polis. *It argues that the Cypriot kingship was not significantly different from other early Greek kingships, and that the ideological definitions of the* polis *are chronologically vague and conceptually confused. In conclusion, some promising trends that would include Cyprus in the investigation of the early Greek state are considered.*

THE ORIGINS OF THE *POLIS:*
THE VIEW FROM CYPRUS

By the Iron Age in Cyprus, cities on the sea—Greek-speaking cities with the exception of Kition—had become the focal points for economic and cultural life. These were cities of Mycenaean descendants subject to strong influences from Phoenician culture both through trade and from their neighbor Kition. Given this background, these cities would seem to offer a good testing ground for two recently popular theories of the origins of the Greek *polis:* that it arose from Phoenician influence, and that it developed out of continuity with the Mycenaean past. Yet none of the *polis*-historians takes the Cypriot cities into consideration. In fact, everyone seems to agree that the Cypriot cities were not *poleis;* thus Nicholas Coldstream states explicitly that "no *polis* system ever took root" in Cyprus (1990: 59).

This, then, is the question raised in this paper: why are the Cypriot cities not considered by those who speculate on the origin of the *polis,* since these cities provide clear instances of conditions that many of these scholars consider vital, such as continuity with the Mycenaean past and Phoenician influence. The paper begins with a brief summary of the two theories of continuity and Phoenician influence, then considers possible reasons for the exclusion of Cyprus, with a brief digression defending the Cypriot kingdom as a respectable Greek state-form, and concludes by noting some recent trends in a more inclusive direction.

RECENT THEORIES OF THE
ORIGINS OF THE POLIS

A number of historians locate the origins of the *polis* in the surviving remnants of Mycenaean culture. A good example is offered by Donlan's recent article, "The Pre-state Community in Greece" (1989).[1] Donlan (1989: 5) claims

---

[1] See too Donlan and Thomas (1993), Thomas (1976; 1977); Maddoli (1970); Andreev (1979); van Effenterre (1985); I. Morris (1991); S. Morris (1992).

that "the transition to the city-state was a predictable and uniform political process," which he traces back to the remnants of the disintegrating Bronze Age kingdoms that had as their focal point the *polis,* or fortified settlement, under the rule of a local leader, the *basileus.* According to Donlan, this process of *polis* formation was exported to Asia Minor with Mycenaean immigrants, beginning around 1050 B.C.E. (1989: 20). Such communities "eventually, and more or less simultaneously, evolved into city-states," and the occurrence of this process independently in diverse regions is "a compelling indication that the embryo of the *polis*-state existed by about 1050 B.C." (1989: 20). Donlan identified the transition from pre-state to *polis* by the appearance of the formal political institutions of the assembly, council and law court, which he dates to the early decades of the eighth century B.C.E. (1989: 20).[2] Kingship ended, however, only around 700 B.C.E.; thus for about a century, kingship and *polis* overlapped, a situation that Donlan does not consider incompatible with *polis*-status.

While Donlan incorporated the Greek settlements in Asia Minor into his scheme, he did not consider similar Mycenaean settlements on Cyprus. But surely Cyprus presents a challenge to his theory: if the *polis* developed out of the Mycenaean tradition, if its embryo existed in the Mycenaean diaspora in 1050 B.C.E., why did it not develop in Cyprus, where that tradition was strongest and most unbroken?

The second theory of the origins of the *polis,* that of Phoenician influence, first gained widespread interest when A. Snodgrass adopted it in his popular book, *Archaic Greece* (1980).[3] Almost contemporaneously with Snodgrass' book, Drews (1979) provided a more specific scenario suggesting the form that Phoenician influence took and the route by which it was communicated.[4]

Drews noted Thasos and Pithecusae (but not Cyprus) as possible points of Phoenician influence upon the Greek *polis,* but he argued instead for a rather tenuous route by way of Crete to Sparta. The beginning of the trail in Crete is supported by the discovery of the Tekke bronze bowl with its Phoenician inscription, which reinforces earlier evidence of Phoenician presence; the influence then passed by way of Kythera to the Eurotas valley. According to Drews, Phoenician influence was expressed chiefly in political form in the institutions of the *gerousia,* or council of elders, and the dual kingship. Tradition assigned the establishment of the *gerousia* to approximately 750 B.C.E., and Drews suggested that Phoenician councils may have inspired it "in some vague way" (1979: 49). In the case of the dual kingship, he claimed only that there are "some grounds" for the assertion of Phoenician influence, based on extended conjecture about the nature of the Phoenician model.[5] He admitted, however, that there were no Phoenician parallels for either the life-long tenure nor the hereditary nature of the Spartan kingship. From these Phoenician political ideas borrowed by Sparta, Drews claimed that "the new system was instituted, and a new era dawned in Greek political history" (1979: 58). In other words, the *polis* was born.

My intention here is not to jettison either of these explanatory models for the rise of the Greek state. Rather, I want to look more closely at the underlying assumption that creates the problem, namely that the Cypriot states can for some reason be dismissed as irrelevant to the history of the *polis.*

DEVELOPMENT OF THE STATE IN DARK-AGE CYPRUS

The oldest reasoning underlying the exclusion of the Cypriot kingdoms from *polis* status lies in precisely that Near Eastern factor to which the second group of historians attributed the origins of the *polis,* their Phoenician connections. This view goes back to E. Gjerstad (1948: 446, 452, 498–500) with his classification of the Cypriot kingdoms not as *poleis* but as "Oriental despotisms." His view of Phoenician influence as a pernicious factor, preventing the development of the *polis,* is still widely accepted today (Maier and Karageorghis 1984; Rupp 1985; and Barceló 1993: 230).

Kingship itself cannot be the issue. For the Greeks themselves there was no question that kingship was compatible

---

[2] Other defining characteristics of the *polis* suggested by Donlan include "an integrated community, central place, elaborated ranking, and an incipient central organization" (1989: 26); "formal machinery of organization, regulation, and coercion" that technically define a state; and transition from personal chiefdom to impersonal state (1989: 18).

[3] Suggested in 1960 by Oliver (1960: 56).

[4] Drews has been followed by S. Morris (1992); two other recent proponents of Phoenician influence, Gschnitzer (1988; 1993), and Bernal (1993), are vague about the exact route.

[5] Drews' actual claims are very carefully phrased: "If the Spartan dyarchy did originate in the eighth century, it is not impossible that the inspiration for it came from Phoenicia" (1979: 53).

with *polis* status. In fact, Aristotle ranked it among the best forms of government, (*Pol.* 1279a 28–30, 1288a 8–33), and Plato's Philosopher King was offered as a model for Greek *poleis* (*Rep.* 473c–e, *Pol.* 293c–d). In regard to Cyprus in particular, Isocrates freely used the term *"polis"* in referring to the kingdom of Salamis.[6] Modern scholars have been less broad-minded. Drews, whose study of Greek kingship focuses on its limited, non-absolutist nature, dismissed Cyprus with a footnote (1983: 6, n. 14), while Carlier (1984: vi, 486), whose study of Archaic Greek kingship counted fifty-six such kings, excluded the Cypriot kingships specifically on the grounds that they were too close to the Syro-Phoenician model.

In fact, it may be that the Cypriot kings in the post-Bronze Age world were little different from the early Greek *basileis* that these scholars described. At least that is the case with the picture of the Late Bronze Age starting point, admittedly contested, that has been sketched by RMerrillees (1992).[7] He argued that Late Bronze Age Cypriot settlements were probably autonomous under a very elementary form of government that dealt with such necessities as dispute resolution, defense, and the regulation of land and water resources. There were kings, but they were not absolute in power (so too Rupp 1985; 1988). He also suggested that merchants also played a role in government, whether as an "elite," or collectively, perhaps serving as a rudimentary form of council. In such a scenario, the Cypriot states approximated the early *polis* in which *basileis* were not absolute rulers but formed part of an essentially aristocratic government.

For the Geometric period, two scenarios of Cypriot kingship have been suggested. Like the proponents of continuity in the origins of the *polis,* F.-G. Maier and V. Karageorghis (1986: 156–58) have argued for continuity from the Achaean settlement, although in this case "Mycenaean" kingship was gradually transformed not into a *polis* but into the type of an "Oriental Despotism." Most scholars agree with this picture of continuity,[8] although, in contrast, D. Rupp (1985) has posited an absolute break, with the emergence of the state only in the mid-eighth century B.C.E. as a consequence of the increase in social stratification that resulted from uneven exploitation of the commercial opportunities offered by the Phoenicians in Kition.[9] He also saw the new Cypriot state as an adaptation of Oriental despotism.

Evidence for the Geometric and Archaic Cypriot kings comes mainly from cemeteries, and especially from the Royal Tombs at Salamis (Karageorghis, 1948, 1967a, 1969). Finds in the burials at Salamis document the wealth and Near Eastern contacts of these early rulers by their rich grave offerings and sacrifices of horses and chariots and even of servants. Although finds with similar, if less spectacular, princely features have been found elsewhere on the island,[10] it was the evidence from Salamis burials especially that have provided the evidence for the model of Oriental despotism. But Salaminian society, at least in death, does not appear to have been characterized by the sharp division between the king and his subjects that the Oriental Model presupposes.[11] Among the Royal Tombs there were gradations in wealth, with relatively poorer burials, such as Tombs 19 and 31,

---

[6] Isocrates, *Evagoras,* 49-50, 52-57, listing Greeks who left Greece to live in Cyprus because they found his rule more equitable than that at home; *Nicocles* 9, 19, 24, 31; Cyprians, the best constitution, 13. Aeschylus, *Suppliants,* 282, in which the women are referred to as "Kyprios charaktēr, long cited as evidence for the Greek view of Cyprus as foreign (Maier 1989: 18), involves a textual problem and probably does not refer to Cyprus at all. See Hadjistephanou (1990), and K. Hadjioannou (1985).

[7] Muhly (1972) and Knapp (1985) argue that the island was a unitary state in the Bronze Age, based upon their identification of it with Alashiya in Near Eastern texts; contra Merrillees (1987).

[8] Based on the congruity of later legends of kingdom foundations with the archaeological material (Gjerstad 1944; Fortin 1980); the survival of the Mycenaean term for king, "anaktes"; and writing.

[9] Rupp (1985; 1987; 1988); Rupp credits Tatton-Brown (1979: 70) with the suggestion.

[10] Burials with similar princely features at other sites on Cyprus include tombs at Tamassos: Tombs 1, 2, 9, 79, 103 and 312 (Gjerstad, 1948: 39 and 42, figs. 11.7, 12 and 13); "Königsgräuber," (Buchholz 1973: 322–37) and (1978: 177–200); Amathus, Tomb 306, (Karageorghis 1981: 10–18). An early Cypro-Archaic tomb found near Kouklia (Palaipaphos) had an unusually wide dromos and contained chariot equipment and the skeletons of horses (Karageorghis 1963; 1967b). Built tombs with fine ashlar masonry include examples from Idalion (Karageorghis 1964: 28–84); Kition—Chapel of Ayia Phaneromeni, seventh/sixth century (Karageorghis 1976: 142–44); Trachonas (Karpas area), and Xylotymbou (Gjerstad 1948: 40, figs. 12.3 and 5).

[11] Thus Karageorghis says of the kings, "No doubt they were considered superhuman, and their power in life over their subjects must have been absolute." (1982: 530–31).

which contained only sacrificed asses without vehicles or gear. Karageorghis (1969: 73) suggested that these may have been the graves of "an intermediate class of noblemen or wealthy citizens." In contrast to the built tombs called "Royal," the burials of ordinary citizens have been discovered in the mostly rock-cut tombs of Cellarka. But these non-royal graves also reveal gradations of status, with the wealthier burials displaying such "royal" characteristics as the horse-sacrifice of Tomb 10 and the servant-sacrifice of Tomb 83. Their form is adapted from the form of the Royal Tombs, and one is even a built tomb like the Royal Tombs. Karageorghis (1969: 127) suggested that the richest and largest of these tombs, Tomb 105, may have been that of a citizen who was wealthy "but not of such rank as to entitle him to burial in the 'royal' part of the cemetery." This view from Salamis is supported by Rupp's (1989: 356–60) analysis of burials from other sites, which found evidence for a tripartite social structure in which a middle-level or non-governing elite sought to emulate the behavior of their betters.

It is interesting to compare the burials of the early Cypriot kings with the burial of the so-called Hero of Lefkandi (Popham et al. 1993: 85–92, 97–101), for the Lefkandi burial shows that some of the marks attributed to Oriental despotism were to be found in mainland Greece some two hundred years before the burials in the Tombs of the Kings (1000–950 B.C.E.). In this rich cremation burial, the ashes were deposited in a bronze urn, identified as an heirloom from Cyprus by the excavators (Popham et al. 1993: 86–92), in a pit in the floor of a monumental building constructed shortly before the burial. The cremated male was accompanied by an inhumed woman, possibly sacrificed (Popham et al. 1993: 21), as well as by a chariot and the sacrifice of horses. After the burial the building itself was partially dismantled and buried in a tumulus. Other, similar but less spectacular burials elsewhere in Greece and Crete, including numerous horse sacrifices, demonstrate that the Lefkandi burial was not an anomaly.[12] No one, however, classifies these notable signs of prestige in burial as marks of Oriental despotism.

In the Classical period, a clue to Cypriot political institutions is provided by the inscription from Idalion, dated 478–470 B.C.E., in which the king and the city *(polis)* acted jointly to hire physicians to treat the wounded during a siege (Buck, 1955: 210–12, n. 20). Gjerstad (1948: 498, 499) remarks that "this indicates some sort of democratic constitution," but immediately adds that this "may be due to Athenian influence" and points out that under the successors of Evagoras and Nicocles the government "rapidly degenerated into a system of police terror," as evidenced by various anecdotes of tyrannical excesses.[13] While Gjerstad (1948: 499) alluded to the nature of such anecdotes as political invective, he still maintained "that these stories give a true picture of the degenerate state of Cypriote kingship at the end of the Cypro-Classical period." He did not acknowledge the fact that these tales have parallels in the stories of the ruling tyrants of cities of indisputable *polis* status, such as Corinth and Syracuse.[14]

DEFINITIONS OF THE *POLIS*

The second possible cause for the exclusion of Cyprus from the study of the early *polis* seems to be conceptual confusion over the definition of the *polis* itself. The recent trend in the search for the earliest *polis* has been away from the traditional identification based on urbanistic features such as population growth, fortifications, temple, or agora, and toward its identification in ideologico-political terms. For example, I. Morris (1991: 48) defines the essence of the *polis* as the idea of a citizen estate, *"a community of citizens,* not a mass of subjects under a differentiated elite." His definition excludes kingship, specifying that, "If the citizens became subjects, their community ceased to be a *polis"* (1991: 27). He does allow, however, for tyrannical and oligarchical rule (1987: 186). Similarly, K. Raaflaub (1993: 44) in a recent survey of work on the origins of the *polis,* identified the essence of the *polis* as a mentality, a "sense of community and identification with it."

Since the extension of self-government was a gradual process and mentality is difficult to document, political definitions are often vague about the onset of the *polis* or put its origins surprisingly late, as late as the reforms of Solon (Hölkeskamp, 1992: 104–7) or even Cleisthenes (Morris, 1987: 8, 171, 209–10). Morris, in fact, postulated a double beginning of the Athenian *polis*, the first in the eighth century B.C.E., the second in the sixth century B.C.E., on the

---

[12] Knossos: Catling (1978–79: 46); Naxos: Lambrinoudakis and Zapheiropoulou (1983; 1984; 1985); Atlante (East Locris): cited in Deger-Jalkotzy (1991: 62, n. 62). Horse burials: Kosmetatou (1993).

[13] References to Cypriot tyranny: Athen. VIII 149 e, f; 352 d; Diog. Laert. IX, 10.58–9; Plut. *Moralia* 449 E; Plin. *Nat. hist.* VII, 23; Valer. Max. III, 3, ext. 4; Cic., *Tusc. disp.* II, 22; *De nat. deor.* III, 333.

[14] On the cultural bias in the work of Gjerstad, and some of its effects on his interpretations of early Cypriot history, see Reyes (1994: 3–4); on the weight of later evidence from political invective (1994: 25).

basis of his analysis of burial customs as an index of an egalitarian mentality. Similarly, but on more general grounds, Raaflaub (1993) posited two phases of *polis* formation: a "crystallization" in the eighth century B.C.E., and an "integration" in the seventh and early sixth centuries B.C.E. The shifting and amorphous nature of political definitions, and the fuzzy conceptual basis upon which they rest, reveal an ideological approach that is made quite explicit in Ian Morris' statement that "the most compelling reason" for the study of Greece is its "comparative value for understanding contemporary arguments about liberty and equality" (1993: 216).

MORE PROMISING NEW DIRECTIONS

Thus at the central core of *polis* studies today are scholars engaged in an ideologically-driven search for the origins of the *polis* as an ideal type, who have fallen into the old trap of construing the Greeks as the forerunners of their own political ideals. On the periphery, however, there are some promising trends that could foster the incorporation of Cyprus into the investigation of the development of the

early Greek state. These include the radical questioning of the concept of the *polis* itself by W. Gawantka (1985); Reyes' (1994) reinvestigation of the evidence for Gjerstad's interpretation of Cypriot history as a series of foreign dominations; and other efforts that question the unique character of the *polis* and place it into a broader geographical context. Thus C. Morgan (1991) has called for more attention to the non-*polis* forms taken by the Greek state, especially the *ethnos*. In a broader context, S. Morris (1992) has situated the *polis* within the continuum of state-forms that arose in the Near East in the Iron Age, including the Phoenician and Israelite kingdoms. A research agenda framed in these terms would clearly include Cyprus. Finally, J. Velasco (1994) put the *polis* into the even wider context of an ancient world that included pre-Roman Spain. A similar inclusiveness seems to mark the agenda of the new research program of the Copenhagen Polis Centre.

Whatever its formulation, we need a new approach to the *polis* that will allow the Cypriot kingdoms their ancient place in the broad spectrum of Greek state-forms. As prime examples of the influence of both Bronze Age continuities and Phoenician influence, they should be at the forefront of any study of the development of the Greek state.

REFERENCES

Andreev, J. V.
  1979   Könige und Königsherrschaft in den Epen Homers. *Klio* 61: 378–79.
Barceló, P.
  1993   *Basileia, Monarchia, Tyrannis. Historia Einzelschrift #79.* Stuttgart: Franz Steiner.
Bernal, M.
  1993   Phoenician Politics and Egyptian Justice in Ancient Greece. Pp. 241–61 in *Anfänge politischen Denkens in der Antike,* ed. Kurt Raaflaub. Munich: R. Oldenbourg.
Buchholz, H.-G.
  1973   Tamassos, Zypern, 1970–1972. *Archäologischer Anzeiger* 88: 322–37.
  1978   Tamassos, Zypern, 1974–1976. *Archäologischer Anzeiger* 93: 177–200.
Buck, Carl D.
  1955   *The Greek Dialects.* Chicago: University of Chicago.
Carlier, P.
  1984   *La royauté en Grece avant Alexandre.* Strasbourg: AECR.
Catling, H. W.
  1978–   Archaeology in Greece, 1978–79. *Archaeological Reports* 25: 3–46.
  1979

Coldstream, J. N.
  1990   The Geometric Period. Pp. 47–64 in *Footprints in Cyprus,* 1st ed. 1982, ed. Sir David Hunt. London: Trigraph.
Deger-Jalkotzy, S.
  1991   Diskontinuität und Kontinuität: Aspekte politischer und sozialer Organisation in mykenischer Zeit und in der Welt der Homerischen Epen. Pp. 53–66 in *La Transizione dal Miceneo all' alto Archaismo: dal palazzo alla citta,* eds. D. Musti, *et al.* Rome: Consiglio Nazionale delle Ricerche.
Donlan, W.
  1989   The Pre-state Community in Greece. *Symbolae Osloenses* 64: 5–29.
Donlan, W., and Thomas, C. G.
  1993   The Village Community of Ancient Greece: Neolithic, Bronze and Dark Ages. *Studi Micenei ed Egeo-Anatolici* 31: 61–71.
Drews, R.
  1979   Phoenicians, Carthage and the Spartan Eunomia. *American Journal of Philology* 100: 45–58.
  1983   *Basileus: The Evidence for Kingship in Geometric Greece.* New Haven: Yale University.

Fortin, M.
    1980   Foundation de Villes grecque à Chypre:
            Légendes et Découvertes archéologiques. Pp.
            25–44 in *Melanges d'Études anciennes offerts à*
            Maurice Lebel, eds. J.-B. Caron, M. Fortin, and
            G. Maloney. St-Jean-Chrysostome, Quebec: Edi-
            tions du Sphinx.

Gawantka, W.
    1985   *Die sogenannte Polis: Entstehung, Geschichte*
            und Kritik der modernen althistoischen
            Grundbegriffe der griechische Staat, die
            griechische Staatsidee, die Polis. Stuttgart:
            Steiner.

Gjerstad, E.
    1944   The Colonization of Cyprus in Greek Legend.
            Opuscula Archaeologica 3: 107–23.
    1948   *The Swedish Cyprus Expedition* IV: 2: *The*
            Cypro-Geometric, Cypro-Archaic and Cypro-
            Classical Periods. Stockholm: The Swedish
            Cyprus Expedition.

Gschnitzer, F.
    1988   Die Stellung der Polis in der Politischen
            Entwicklung des Altertums. *Oriens Antiquus* 27:
            287–302.
    1993   Phoinikisch-karthagisches Verfassungsdenken.
            Pp. 187–98 in *Anfänge politischen Denkens in*
            der Antike, ed. Kurt Raaflaub. Munich: R.
            Oldenbourg.

Hadjioannou, K.
    1985   On the Interpretation of the ΚΗΠΡΙΟΣ
            ΧΑΡΑΚΤΗΡ of Aeschylus. Pp. 509–13 in
            Praktika of the Second Cyprological Congress
            I. Nicosia: Hetaireia Kypriakōn Spoudon.

Hadjistephanou, C. E.
    1990   ΚΥΠΡΙΟΣ ΧΑΡΑΚΤΗΡ in Aeschylus'
            Supplices 282–3: A New Emendation and Con-
            textual Interpretation. *Hermes* 118: 282–91.

Hölkeskamp, K. J.
    1992   Written Law in Archaic Greece. *Proceedings of*
            the Cambridge Philological Society 38: 87–115.

Karageorghis, V.
    1963   Une tombe de Guerrier à Palaepaphos. *Bulletin*
            de Correspondance Hellenique 87: 265–300.
    1964   Excavations in the Necropolis of Idalion, 1963.
            Report of the Department of Antiquities Cyprus,
            28–84.
    1967a   *Excavations in the Necropolis of Salamis* I
            Nicosia: Department of Antiquities.
    1967b   Nouvelles tombes de Guerriers à Palaepaphos.
            Bulletin de Correspondance Hellenique 91:
            202–47.
    1969   *Salamis. Recent Discoveries in Cyprus.* New
            York: McGraw Hill.

    1976   *View From the Bronze Age. Mycenaean and*
            Phoenician Discoveries at Kition. New York:
            Dutton.
    1981   Chronique des Fouilles à Chypre en 1980. *Bul-*
            letin de Correspondance Hellenique 105: 10–18.
    1982   Cyprus. Pp. 511–33 in *Cambridge Ancient His-*
            tory III. Pt. 1. Cambridge: Cambridge Univer-
            sity.

Knapp, A. B.
    1985   Alashiya, Caphtor/Keftiu, and Eastern Mediter-
            ranean Trade: Recent Studies in Cypriote Ar-
            chaeology and History. *Journal of Field Archae-*
            ology 12: 231–50.

Kosmetatou, E.
    1993   Horse Sacrifices in Greece and Cyprus. *Journal*
            of Prehistoric Religion 7: 31–41.

Lambrinoudakis, C.; Gruben, G.; and Koppes, M.
    1983   Anaskaphi Naxou: Sangri. *Praktika of the*
            Archaiologikes Hetaireias for 1983: 297–98.

Lambrinoudakis, C., and Zapheiropoulou, F.
    1984   Naxos. *Ergon of the Archaiologikes Hetaireias*
            for 1984: 74–79.
    1985   Naxos. *Ergon of the Archaiologikes Hetaireias*
            for 1985: 56–62.

Maddoli, G.
    1970   Δᾶμος ε βασιλῆες: contributo allo studio delle
            origini della polis. *Studi Micenei ed Egeo-*
            Anatolici 12: 27–36.

Maier, F. G.
    1989   Palaces of Cypriot Kings. Pp. 16–27 in *Cyprus*
            and the East Mediterranean in the Iron Age: Pro-
            ceedings of the Seventh British Museum Classi-
            cal Colloquium, Cyprus, 1988, ed. V. Tatton-
            Brown. London: British Museum Publications.

Maier, F. G., and Karageorghis, V.
    1984   *Paphos: History and Archaeology.* Nicosia: A.
            G. Leventis Foundation.

Merrillees, R. S.
    1987   *Alashia Revisited.* Paris: J. Gabalda.
    1992   The government of Cyprus in the Late Bronze
            Age. Pp. 310–28 in *Acta Cypria: Acts of an In-*
            ternational Congress on Cypriote Archaeology
            held in Göteborg on 22–24 August 1991.
            Jonsered: Åströms.

Morgan, C.
    1991   Ethnicity and Early Greek States: Historical and
            Material Perspectives. *Proceedings of the Cam-*
            bridge Philological Society 37: 131–63.

Morris, I.
    1987   *Burial and Ancient Society.* New York: Cam-
            bridge University.
    1991   The Early Polis as City and State. Pp. 25–57 in
            City and Country in the Ancient World, eds. J.

Rich and A. Wallace-Hadrill. New York: Routledge.

1993 Response to Papadopoulos (I) The Kerameikos Stratigraphy and the Character of the Greek Dark Age. *Journal of Mediterranean Archaeology* 6: 207–21.

Morris, S.
1992 *Daidalos and the Origins of Greek Art.* Princeton: Princeton University.

Muhly, J. D.
1972 The Land of Alashiya: References to Alashiya in the Texts of the Second Millenium B.C. and the History of Cyprus in the Late Bronze Age. Pp. 201–19 in *Proceedings of the First International Congress of Cypriot Studies 1969: Nicosia.* Nicosia: Hetaireia Kypriakon Spoudon.

Oliver, J. H.
1960 *Demokratia, the Gods and the Free World.* Baltimore.

Popham, M. R.; Calligas, P. G.; and Sackett, L. H.
1993 *Lefkandi* II *The Protogeometric Building at Toumba.* London: Thames and Hudson.

Raaflaub, K.
1993 Homer to Solon: The Rise of the Polis: The Written Sources. Pp. 41–105 in *The Ancient Greek City State: A Symposium on the Occasion of the 250th Anniversary of the Royal Danish Academy of Sciences and Letters, July 1–4, 1992,* ed. M. H. Hansen. Copenhagen: Munksgaard.

Rupp, D. W.
1985 Prolegomena to a study of stratification and social organization in Iron Age Cyprus. Pp. 119–31 in M. Thompson, M. I. Garcia, and F. J. Kense, eds., *Status, Structure and Stratification: Current Archaeological Reconstructions: Proceedings of the Sixteenth Annual Conference.* Calgary: University of Calgary Archaeological Association.

1987 Emergence of the State in Iron-Age Cyprus. Pp. 147–68 in *Western Cyprus: Connections,* ed. D. W. Rupp. Göteborg: Åströms.

1988 The 'Royal Tombs' at Salamis (Cyprus): Ideological Messages of Power and Authority. *Journal of Mediterranean Archaeology* 1: 111–39.

1989 Puttin' on the Ritz: Manifestations of High Status in Iron Age Cyprus. Pp. 336–62 in *Early Society in Cyprus,* ed. E. Peltenburg. Edinburgh: Edinburgh University Press in association with the National Museums of Scotland and the A. G. Leventis Foundation.

Reyes, A. T.
1994 *Archaic Cyprus: A Study of the Textual and Archaeological Evidence.* Oxford: Clarendon.

Snodgrass, A.
1980 *Archaic Greece.* Berkeley: University of California.

Tatton-Brown, V. A.
1979 The Archaic Period. Pp. 70–107 in *Cyprus BC: 7000 Years of History.* Exhibition Catalogue, ed. V. A. Tatton-Brown. London: British Museum.

Thomas, C. G.
1976 From Wanax to Basileus. *Hispania antiqua* 6: 187–213.

1977 The Dorians and the Polis. *Minos* 16: 216–18.

van Effenterre, H.
1985 *La Cité en grecque. Des origines à la défaite de Marathon.* Paris: Hachette litterature.

Velasco, J. A. S.
1994 City and State in Pre-Roman Spain: the Example of Ilici. *Antiquity* 68: 89–99.

Tectonics and History at Phalasarna

FRANK J. FROST

Department of History
University of California, Santa Barbara
Santa Barbara, CA 93106
U.S.A.

The Classical and Hellenistic city of Phalasarna lay on the far northwest corner of Crete and was virtually ignored by Greek and Roman writers except for the information in two texts that it had a "closed harbor." Captain T.A.B. Spratt of the Royal Navy was the first visitor to realize that this harbor was now 200 m from the sea and had been raised about 7 m by some great geological upheaval. Excavation since 1986 has revealed some of the fortifications and other structures around the harbor and has helped to support the theory that Phalasarna was taken by the Romans during the campaign of Metellus Creticus in 68–67 B.C.E.

At the same time, geomorphological reconstruction of the effects of two tsunamis by Paolo Pirazzoli has made it possible to associate the geological record with literary descriptions of the same events. One stratum of large stones in the silted harbor may be dated to C.E. 66; the more extensive stratum, which probably coincided with the uplift of all western Crete, is probably from the tsunami recorded by Ammianus Marcellinus, dated to 21 July 365.

On a summer day in 1859, Captain T. A. B. Spratt of the Royal Navy stood on a ridge in northwestern Crete and sketched the rugged acropolis and the coastal plain of the ancient harbor town of Phalasarna.[1] The remains of massive fortifications testified to the previous existence of the town, but otherwise Spratt had difficulty matching the terrain over which he was walking with the few literary descriptions surviving from antiquity. According to the geographer Skylax, "Phalasarna is the last city on the cape toward the sunset and has an enclosed harbor." A much later third-rate poet named Dionysios, son of Kalliphon, had only heard of the city: "They say there is a city in Crete, Phalasarna, lying toward the sunset, having an enclosed harbor.[2] But the end of the bay on which Phalasarna lay could never have been interpreted as a harbor, open as it was to a continual western swell, and there

was not even a beach upon which a ship could be hauled. But as Spratt walked along the shores of this corner of western Crete he observed a prominent wave notch etched upon every cliff he could see, six to seven meters *above* the present sea level. Spratt was an educated man and like his contemporary Charles Darwin was aware of recent discoveries of the geological processes that could change the face of the earth. He had already noted evidence of uplift further to the east in Crete, where structures associated with maritime activity in ancient times now lay inland from the sea. Here he could conclude that the relentless waves had long ago hammered the cliffs of far western Crete at an even higher sea level (Spratt 1865: II 227–35). The visible evidence made it almost certain that a gigantic upheaval of the western half of the island had taken place long after the city of Phalasarna had been founded. To his practiced mariner's

---

[1] For excavation to date, see Hadjidaki (1988: 463–79); Frost and Hadjidaki (1990: 513–27). Testimonia and extant inscriptions in Guarducci (1939: ch. 19).

[2] Skylax 47 (Müller 1855: I 427); Dionysios 120 (Müller 1855: I 242).

eye the existing walls of the ruined town seemed to enclose a large basin with a narrow entrance to the south, now covered with dense brush. In the center was a flat area about the size of a playing field. If he envisioned this space flooded by a higher sea level it all made sense.

This was the picture of Phalasarna as it appeared to its excavator Elpida Hadjidaki in 1986. Hadjidaki was no stranger to this coast. She had grown up a few dozen kilometers to the east in Chania and had visited the site many times. As an experienced underwater archaeologist attached to the Greek Archaeological Service, she had hoped to investigate an ancient harbor for the doctoral dissertation she was writing for me at Santa Barbara. Now here was her harbor—but on dry land 200 meters from the sea. Like Spratt before her she could envision the ancient harbor spread out before her beneath the soaring slopes of the acropolis. She also could appreciate a unique opportunity. Unlike most sites in the ancient Greek world Phalasarna had been deserted and never reoccupied. No modern, Turkish, or Byzantine structures would complicate the reconstruction of the city's past. But with no literary references to fall back on, the past of Phalasarna would have to be deduced entirely from excavation and from the geological record.

During the last seven years excavation has been able to reveal some of Phalasarna's history. The sheer scale and extent of the fortifications and public buildings suggest that the Phalasarnians, like so many other Cretan coastal communities, derived much of their revenue from piracy (fig. 1). The resources of the Livadian coastal plain could clearly never have provided either the capital or the labor force for such public works. So far as can be determined by associated pottery, the military architecture of some distinction first appeared in the fourth century B.C.E. A striking round tower formed the corner between the sea wall and the curtain wall that formed the eastern defense of the harbor. The architect designed a molding that separated the foundation from the upper courses of the tower, of which nine courses of ashlar masonry are completely or partially preserved (fig. 2). An internal cross wall strengthened the tower for probable use as an artillery platform. The line of the curtain wall running northeast is clear but the tower that occupied the northeast corner has not yet been cleared, nor is it possible to determine how it was connected to the main north tower. The north tower itself was obviously built at the same time as the round tower, as it has an identical molding meant to be viewed at the same eye level as the round tower's molding, even though they are across the harbor from each other. A broad double wall runs from the north tower in a westerly direction towards the acropolis and a complex of buildings we now call the industrial zone. Here we cleared a building containing four basins carved from single rectangular blocks of sandstone and then plastered (fig. 3). Similar basins have been found in bath houses elsewhere in the Greek world but these appear to have been used for processing clay, to judge from the quantity of clay found in them when they were excavated.[3]

Two separate trenches along the margins of the ancient harbor have exposed the quays at which the commerce of Phalasarna was loaded and unloaded. Along the eastern edge of the harbor a quay was constructed of massive sandstone blocks which would have allowed ships to dock directly alongside. Sockets and grooves towards the back of the quay indicate that doors led eastward, perhaps into a warehouse set against the eastern fortifications. At the northern end of the harbor an exploratory trench exposed another quay, leading one to speculate that much of the circuit of the harbor was lined with wharves. One of the blocks of this quay had been drilled to provide a hole for a mooring line.

Hadjidaki and a few visiting archaeologists had once speculated that a large field north of the harbor walls might actually be a second, internal harbor. But a trench begun in 1988, instead of turning up marine deposits, revealed a long wall trending off to the northeast (fig. 4). Tests performed on the bottom deposits proved that sea water had never entered this basin and that in antiquity it had contained fresh, or brackish water. It now seems likely that with the higher water table of ancient times this area may have been either a lagoon or a seasonal marsh created by runoff from the acropolis and by springs that no longer flow. The Phalasarnians evidently built this long wall to reclaim land on one side of the wall and to stabilize the shore of the lagoon on the other, perhaps as a water supply. This must have been an impressive engineering project, for the foundations were obviously laid a meter and a half under water.

The pirates of Phalasarna eventually started a fight they could not finish. In 1987 we were looking for the harbor entrance that obviously lay somewhere inland from a small cove along the present coastline. Tumbled masonry and dense brush obscured the possible line of the entrance at all points and eventually we started a trench at what seemed to be the likeliest spot. After two days we began to encounter huge worked blocks of masonry the same size as those in

---

[3] For baths of the same type, obviously for rinsing off rather than immersion, see Ginouvès (1962: 38–44 and figs. 14, 16–17, 23). Into the round sump at the lower end of our baths was fitted a sheet of lead, possibly to lift out sand and pebbles as they were rinsed out of the clay.

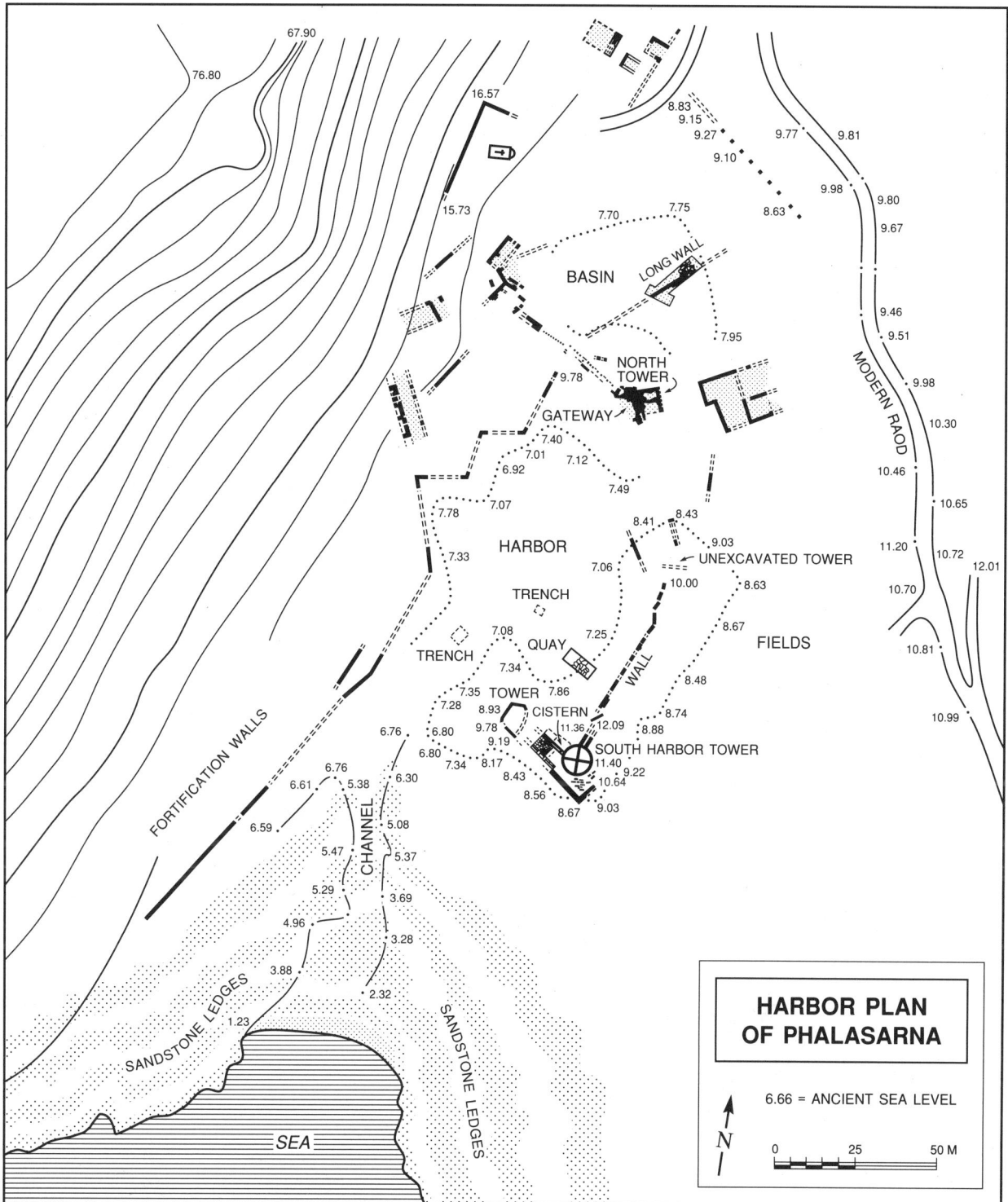

Fig. 1. Harbor Plan of Phalasarna. Not included on this plan are extensive fortifications to the north and the remains of three public buildings on the acropolis.

Fig. 2. The round tower from the west.

Fig. 3. The four basins. To the right are the remains of a broken one.

the city wall and the seawall. It did not seem that any possible reconstruction of the walls near the entrance could have resulted in an accidental collapse of blocks into this one spot and it now seems more and more likely that the harbor had been deliberately blocked. The culprits are easy to identify. In the late 70s B.C.E. Marcus Antonius, the father of the triumvir, was entrusted with an expedition against the Cretan pirates. He was defeated in a sea battle and humiliated but several years later the Romans launched their famous campaign to eliminate piracy in the Mediterranean for once and for all. The overall campaign was assigned to Pompey but Caecilius Metellus was specifically designated by the Senate to deal with the Cretans. He was completely successful and within two years had either reduced or accepted the surrender of all the Cretan pirate cities. It is our theory that the Romans reduced Phalasarna as a preliminary strike before their siege of Kydonia, the modern Chania (Frost 1989: 15–17). In addition to the blockage in the harbor entrance, we have found several catapult balls in the defenses of Phalasarna; one of them bears the inscription "X X," which we believe indicates 20 Roman pounds.[4] At the north tower there were obvious preparations for a siege. The original, fourth century B.C.E. tower, with its decorative molding, was stripped of the finely cut ashlar masonry blocks with which it had been faced, leaving only the rubble which had formed the interior. Then a higher tower was erected to the west, jammed right up against the molding of the original tower, indicating that a sense of urgency had rendered aesthetic considerations obsolete (fig. 5). Out at the northern end of

---

[4] At 9.0 kilos the stone is actually too heavy; 20 Roman *librae* would be approximately 6.5 kilos.

Fig. 4. The long wall.

the long wall in the lagoon we found a hastily built rubble wall containing decorative architectural elements. Finally, on the outer face of the eastern harbor curtain wall, someone carved a dedication to the nymph Akakallis, a deity of western Crete. The inscription can be dated to the first century B.C.E. (e.g., Guarducci 1939: 93 no. 5; 222, no. 3; etc.; on Akakallis see Frost 1996).   This dedication may have been a desperate expedient in the face of the Roman threat, but it didn't work. The uppermost horizon of settlement at Phalasarna ends in the mid-first century B.C.E. and we believe the Romans forced the inhabitants to relocate on the other side of the bay, where signs of a later settlement have

Fig. 5. View of earlier north tower (right).

been found. At any rate, with the harbor ruined, Phalasarna had been put out of business as a port city.

But where the history of Phalasarna ends the eventful geological record begins. The island of Crete lies along the southern and southwestern arc of the Aegean tectonic plate. The margin between this plate and the African plate is active, with the African plate diving under the Aegean plate. The ancient wave notch on the cliffs along the acropolis clearly shows the record of seismic activity. Where the sea laps the rock one will find a band of calcareous algae, which can live only on those few centimeters of interface between air and water. When the water either rises or subsides the algae at that level die off and cease to absorb ^{14}C from the environment. A well established chemical procedure can measure the rate of decay of radiocarbon in the concretions of the algae in the same way any other organic material can be carbon dated. For more than ten years Paolo Pirazzoli, of the Centre National de Recherche Scientifique has been measuring relative sea level changes all over the world, but particularly in the Mediterranean, using these procedures; we are indebted to him for the reconstruction that follows. Here at Phalasarna he can show the greatest changes known in the world over relatively short periods.[5]

For about 800 years prior to the Christian era there were several minor but abrupt upward adjustments of sea level— or more accurately, subsidences in the land—which can be seen by the progression of notches up the face of the cliff. The topmost notch indicates an increasingly rapid series of subsidences, dated from about mid-second century B.C.E. to mid-first century C.E. This sea level then stabilized, but in the fourth century C.E. the African plate gave a great heave and the enormous lithic block bearing Crete and the small island of Antikythera to the northwest was uplifted from 9 m at the southwest corner of Crete to 6.6 m at the site of Phalasarna.

A trench dug in the center of the harbor of Phalasarna demonstrates the geological history of the site, as shown in schematic drawings (fig. 6). With the entrance to the harbor partially blocked after the Roman victory, seawater continued to circulate but the waves began to wash marine sediments gently into the basin (fig. 6a). Silting was rapid, as can be shown by about 90 cm of marine residue mixed with sea shells that accumulated in little over a century.

Then occurs a layer of larger stones, some the size of a large watermelon (fig. 6b). Neither rains nor normal waves washed these stones into their present position. For an ex-

planation we must turn to literary accounts. It is most probable that an event mentioned by Philostratos in his life of Apollonios of Tyana explains the violence of the waves that moved these rocks into place. The holy man Apollonios happened to be in Gortyn, in about 66 C.E., during the later years of Nero's reign, when a great earthquake shook the countryside, the sea receded almost a mile, and an island came out of the sea north of Crete (Philostratos, *Vit. Apol.* 4.23–34). There at Gortyn the Italian excavators have found a stratum of destruction dating from the Neronian era (Di Vita 1979–80: 435–36). This was evidently not a major tectonic displacement; it was just a hiccup, but enough to cause widespread destruction and to slosh the seas around a bit.

The earthquake of 66 C.E. resulted in a slight subsidence of the land (less than 10 cm) rather than an uplift and for about 70 years waves washing into the basin continued to lay down marine sediments. At that time, however, the entrance to the basin seems to have sealed completely and for the next two centuries or more, terrestrial sediments drifted into the basin borne by wind or rain falling on the slopes of the acropolis (fig. 6c).

Then came the tectonic paroxysm that raised western Crete from 6 to 9 m above the existing sea level (fig. 6d). Such an event did not pass unnoticed. The Roman historian, Ammianus Marcellinus, writing in the later fourth century C.E., says

> Twelve days before the kalends of August [21 July 365], when Valentinian was consul with his brother, a little after daybreak … the whole of the firm and solid earth was shaken and trembled, the sea with its rolling waves was driven back and withdrew from the land, so that in the abyss of the deep thus revealed men saw many kinds of sea creatures stuck fast in the slime; vast mountains and deep valleys, which Nature, the creator, had hidden in the unplumbed depths then first saw the light of day …. Later the great mass of waters, returning when it was least expected, killed many thousands of men by drowning; and by the swift recoil of the eddying tides a number of ships foundered.[6]

Ammianus added that waves carried ships at Alexandria and at Methone in the southwest Peloponnese far inland where some ended up perched on top of buildings.

Looking out over the present site of Phalasarna we can imagine something very like the description of Ammianus: the sea inconceivably receding for a mile or more, fish left

---

[5] Pirazzoli et al. (1982); Pirazzoli (1986). The reconstruction that follows is based on the work of Pirazzoli et al. (1992).

[6] Am. Marc. 26.10.15–19. Many other ancient writers testified to the violence of this event all over the eastern Mediterranean (Jacques and Bousquet 1984).

c. A.D. 50

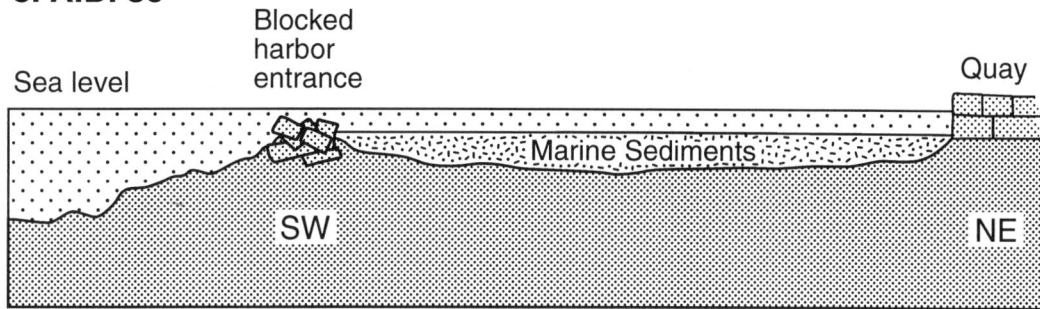

c. A.D. 66

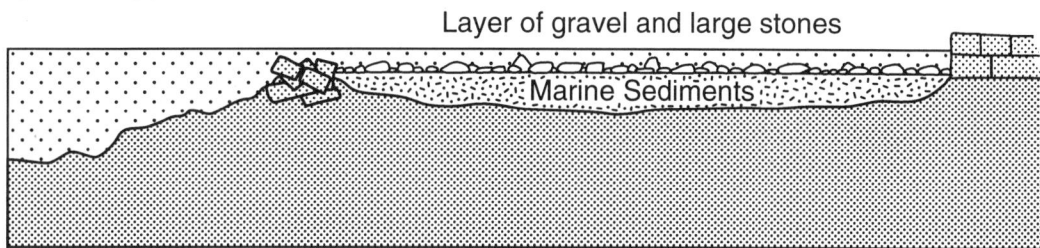

c. A.D. 350

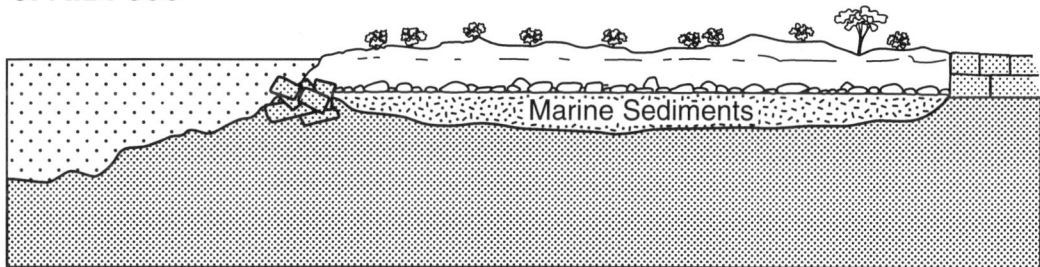

c. A.D. 365 − Present

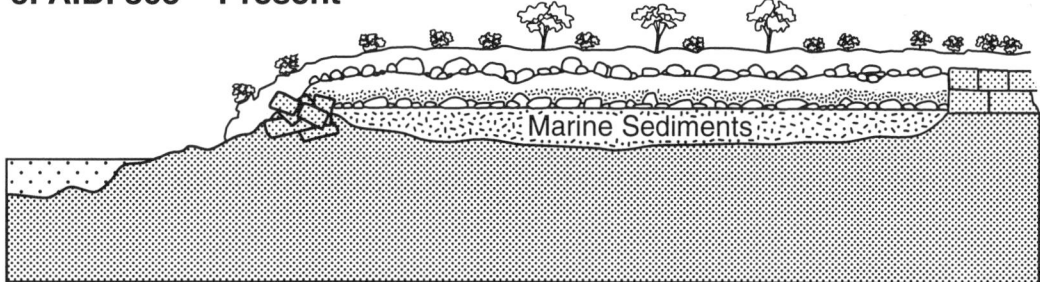

Fig. 6. Geological history of the harbor at Phalasarna. Vertical scale exaggerated.

flopping in the rocks and weed of the sea bottom, the toppling of all but the most sturdy buildings and walls, blinding clouds of dust, frantic bleating of sheep and goats—all of this observed only by the very few shepherds who still found reason to visit the surrounding hillsides. The round tower on the seaward side was slapped with a force like a giant hand. The top four courses of masonry on the eastern side fell neatly in unison and lie in orderly ranks on the surrounding slope. The sea rolled away from the coastal shelf to the west and piled up for a moment in a dome of waters off the coasts of southern Greece. Then gravity reasserted control and the sea flowed back in all directions, imperceptible to mariners perched on the swells out at sea but with growing violence as the wave front approached the shores of the Mediterranean to the north, west, and south. To the east Crete was the closest and the tsunami struck here first. The great round tower—or at least the lower surviving courses—was structurally so strong that it stood like an island in the flood. But it was covered with mud full of sea shells and round beach pebbles that were left high and dry when the waves receded. What the tsunami had done of course was to roil up the sea bottom on its journey back through the shallows until by the time it hit land it was a thick chowder of sand, shells, sea creatures of all kinds, and stones of all sizes up to boulders the size of sofa cushions. The great wave towered over the sea wall and harbor fortifications, rolled through the silted harbor, and carried with it a deposit of stones and boulders. Rolling northward through the harbor the wave slid up the slope of the northern edge of the harbor and then receded, leaving marine deposits containing masses of shells 2 m above what had once been the sea level, as can be seen above several walls where the debris was trapped by the masonry.

Paolo Pirazzoli and his colleagues have removed mollusk shells from the various strata of the harbor trench and radiocarbon dated them (fig. 7). The sandstone bedrock of the ancient harbor bottom was approximately 5 m above what is now the present sea level. Samples of shells taken about 10 cm above the bottom were dated to 522–340 B.C.E. Shells taken from the level just below the tsunami stratum of 66 C.E. were dated to 41 B.C.E.–145 C.E. Just before the tsunami stratum a band of about 10 cm is relatively free of marine life, indicating that sedimentation in the basin had nearly reached the existing sea level and had thus nearly cut off the circulation of seawater. But the earthquake of 66, as noted, caused increased subsidence of the land and marine

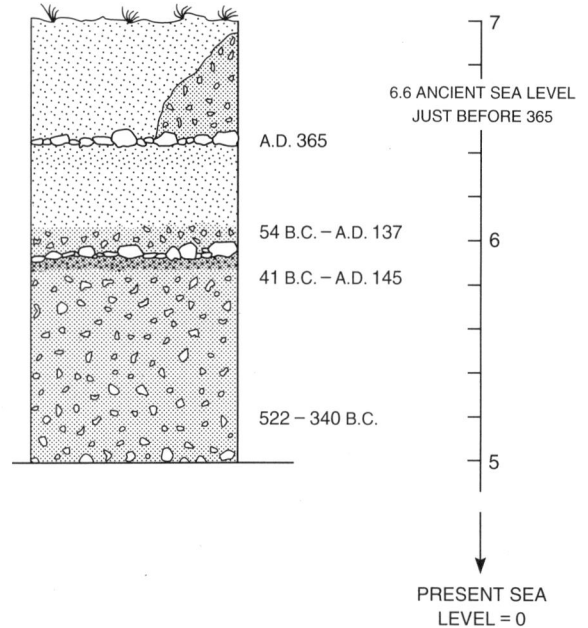

Fig. 7. Cross-section of the harbor trench at Phalasarna showing various strata. After Pirazzoli et al. (1992).

sediments once more accumulated on top of the tsunami stratum. Shells taken from directly above this stratum were dated to 54 B.C.E.–137 C.E., a radiocarbon date that is statistically identical to the date of the shells just below the tsunami level. At this point, marine life ceased to be deposited and succeeding sediments are all terrestrial, borne by wind or rain.

At the top of fig. 7, I have drawn *exempli gratia* a typical anomaly in the record caused by the sloshing of marine muds propelled by the great tsunami of 365 C.E. During the 1993 season a team from Coventry University analyzed foraminifera taken from such tsunami deposits. They confirmed that the species dominant in muds deposited by the high energy of a tsunami came from depths greater than the inner coastal shelf. Species of foraminifera deposited under quiet water conditions, on the other hand, are characteristic of the shallow waters of the inner shelf (Dawson 1996: 199–210). The presence of deep water foraminifera can thus be considered diagnostic of tsunami conditions and other reasons for anomalous deposits of marine sediments on dry land—dredging, for instance—can be discounted.

REFERENCES

Dawson, A. G.
1996   The Geological Significance of Tsunamis. *Zeitschrift für Geomorphologie* 102: 199–210.

Di Vita, A.
1979–   I terremoti a Gortina in età romana e protobi-
1980   zantina. *Annuario della Scuola archeologia di Atene* 57–59: 435–40.

Frost, F.
1989   The Last Days of Phalasarna. *Ancient History Bulletin* 3: 15–17.
1996   Akakallis, a Divinity of Western Crete. *Ancient World* 27: 54–58.

Frost, F., and Hadjidaki, E.
1990   Excavations at the Harbor of Phalasarna in Crete. *Hesperia* 59: 513–27.

Ginouvès, R.
1962   *Balaneutikè*. Paris: Boccard.

Guarducci, M.
1939   *Inscriptiones Creticae* II. Rome: Libreria dello Stato.

Hadjidaki, E.
1988   Preliminary Report of Excavation at the Harbor of Phalasarna in West Crete. *American Journal of Archaeology* 92: 463–79.

Jacques, F., and Bousquet, B.
1984   Le raz de marée du 21 Juillet 365. *Mélanges de l'Ecole française de Rome* 96: 423–61.

Müller, K.
1855   *Geographi graeci minores* I. Paris: Didot.

Pirazzoli, P.
1986   The Early Byzantine Tectonic Paroxysm. *Zeitschrift für Geomorphologie* Suppl. Band 62: 31–49.

Pirazzoli, P.; Thommeret, J.; Thommeret, Y.; Laborel, J.; and Montaggioni, L.
1982   Crustal Block Movements from Holocene Shore-lines. *Tectonophysics* 86: 27–43.

Pirazzoli, P.; Ausseil-Badie, J.; Biresse, P.; Hadjidaki, E.; and Arnold, M.
1992   Environmental Changes at Phalasarna Harbor, West Crete. *Geoarchaeology* 7: 371–92.

Spratt, T. A. B.
1865   *Travels and Researches in Crete*. London: Van Voorst.

Seafaring, Trade Routes, and the Emergence of the Bronze Age: Urban Centers in the Eastern Mediterranean

Hara Georgiou

Oinois 96
Glyphada 16674
GREECE

The position and orientation of bays and inlets played a part in the creation, development and trading focus of settlements in the Aegean islands and the eastern Mediterranean.

Geography and geomorphology, as it differed from island to island, affected the development of each location and its trade outlook in various ways. Of importance also were the distances from other trading sites, both insular and mainland, and from the sources of raw materials crucial to the economy.

Winds and currents, harbor exits and entries, will have dictated destinations and approaches. The Aegean seafarer of the Bronze Age would have used his knowledge and his considerable navigational skills to make the best use of the wind, weather and geography for his commercial profit.

Current theoretical work focusing on trade routes is based primarily on the distribution of metals and pottery exchanges/ imports between a handful of well-known sites. While the ultimate exchange of commodities is undeniable, such theories are inadequate to explain the variety of trade and the types of communication that must have existed.

Sailors were actively plying the waters of the Aegean and the eastern Mediterranean before the Neolithic period. Judging by the distribution of artifacts, their methods of transport and knowledge of the seas improved steadily during the Bronze Age.[1] Shipbuilding, sailing and navigation were powerful and important tools and I will demonstrate that the navigators of the Late Bronze Age were highly capable, otherwise they could not have been so effective.

GEOGRAPHY AND WEATHER

A number of factors can complicate navigation in the Aegean. To those who envision journeys as island hopping or coast hugging, this relatively closed sea studded with so many islands and landmarks may appear to be ideal for sailing. Yet it is a rather unpredictable body of water due to the land masses and high mountains as well as weather fronts influenced by three continents.

Navigation in the Aegean is a complex affair. Finding and identifying position and direction is and always has been important. Even in the recent past, those who ventured out on the high seas in small boats were likely to miscalculate their position at night or during conditions of reduced visibility such as storms or fog. Similarly, a dead calm, by night or day, with no landmarks in sight can result in loss of steering control, drifting and confusion. In addition to the above caveats, wind direction will not always allow for the following of a true or planned course, thus adjustments have to be made and calculated. Traveling time obviously

---

[1] Buchholz (1988: 187–228), discusses Cypriot mines and the increase of production and trade in the LBA.

depends on the weather and not on the skipper's wishes even in the case of short distances. Although arrival before nightfall is certainly preferable, it can never be taken for granted.

The Aegean has many uninhabited small islands and rock masses.[2] In ancient times beacons did exist on headlands and promontories of inhabited islands but could not have been maintained as they are today,[3] therefore it was imperative for the master of a ship to be an experienced navigator.

NAVIGATION TECHNIQUES

To peruse maps and weather patterns and to trace theoretical voyages are agreeable pasttimes and much important information can be gleaned, but to put this information to practical use is quite another matter. Before the widespread availability of the compass and electronic equipment, traditional fishermen and sailors handed down this information from one generation to the next.

The prevailing winds and currents as well as the preferred routes and approaches to land will have been much as they are for the modern sailor. A system based on the directional names of the winds, the forerunner of a geometrical windrose, is still widely used in Greece today and is likely to be very ancient. A simple version of a windrose is clearly known in Homer where the same four winds are repeatedly mentioned.[4] The imaginary east-west axis is approximately parallel to the length of the Mediterranean, an important reference point that is given further emphasis by the daily movement of the sun. The origin of each wind coincides with a point on the circle of the horizon (later with a cardinal compass point). Besides direction, wind force obviously is another variable with recognizable characteristics. More important however, is that one is taught by observation that each wind has a definite feel or quality such as relative humidity and odor, and is accompanied by a distinctive behavior of the waves.

Wave action will change with increasing proximity to a shore as will the color of the water whether by day or night. The proximity of land can be recognized by a number of physical characteristics because the frequency and nature of the waves changes. For example, close to a rocky shore, waves deflect and are choppy whereas they will have a more regular periodic movement outside of a bay or sandy beach. In general, swells on the open seas and in channels have greater regularity than waves closer to land. Signs in the sky, including the presence and behavior of birds, will announce increases and shifts in the wind best not ignored, and these observations are reinforced by reading cloud forms and direction.

Tides are not important in the Aegean, but sea currents combined with wind speeds can influence progress under sail. Some of the major currents reach speeds of 2 knots. A boat may be virtually stationary when sailing against a strong current in a light or variable breeze. Sometimes, the shortest distance between two points as calculated on a map can actually be the longest when sailing against the current. The Kaphireas current and its effect on Kea is a case in point.[5] Conversely, sailing with the current in a strong wind can increase speed substantially. Use of the current without the assistance of sails, paddles or oars to reach a specific destination is not practicable since a means of propelling the vessel is required to reach the current and then to leave it or link up with another current. Such planning can easily go awry with the advent of a sudden, contrary wind. Thus any control over destination at sea precludes the sole use of currents for propulsion.[6]

Wind shifts can be caused by land masses, especially islands. For example, the effect of a north wind on an egg-shaped island like Kea will be to deflect to a northwesterly on the east side and northeasterly on the west. Valleys will create local wind conditions on island coasts by funneling action. Land masses separated by narrow channels such as the small group of islands east of Melos or the Paros-Naxos

---

[2] For example, Piperi between Kythnos and Seriphos, Serphopoula, Patroklos near Sounion, Fleves off Vouliagmeni, Nata off Ermoupolis, and countless others.

[3] For Bronze Age Keos, see Troullos (Caskey 1971).

[4] Od. V.292–299: Evros (E), Notos (S), Zephyros (W), Boreas (N).

[5] Sailing from Makronissos to Kea in a north or northwesterly, you will make better time by heading north along the east coast of Makronissos and then east after overreaching Ay. Nikolaos harbor. Returning to Makronissos, speed is increased by sailing with the current down the west coast of Kea before heading west. Likewise, the Antimelos current complicates the approaches to Adamas harbor on Melos (Georgiou 1993).

[6] On the basis of the behavior of currents in the Aegean, I do not believe that seafaring in the Neolithic period, which involved specific ports of call such as the obsidian quarries of Melos, could have depended on currents alone for propelling vessels.

passage can create local winds and wind velocities unrelated to conditions just a few miles away.[7]

These are but a few of the many physical phenomena that the trained sailor learns to observe and interpret without instruments and charts.

TECHNICAL ADVANCES IN SHIP DESIGN AND RIGGING

The sailing vessels of the Bronze Age had a single rectangular or square sail that many archaeologists believe could only be used in following winds. Thus the misconception persists that prehistoric seafarers in the Aegean sailed north or south depending on the season, preferably during the warmer months,[8] a premise that is not entirely accurate.

The designs of boats and rigging allowed for considerable flexibility. Late Bronze Age boats in the Aegean were designed for speed under sail and indeed, sailors had many options besides running before the wind (Georgiou 1991: 61–67). The small sail area is justified by the need to operate cautiously in the seasonal winds of the Aegean and does operate to windward.[9] The possible angle of sailing is important to any consideration of how and where they sailed. The ability to control direction and destination opens possibilities not to be expected in simple theoretical linear routing patterns.

Winter wind forces are usually more intense than the summer *meltemi* winds and are just as often southerlies as north-westerlies. While summer gales may often reach 9 or 10 Beaufort conditions they do not usually last for many days. In addition, the milder water temperatures in summer make a considerable difference in a storm. Long hours of exposure to the wet and the cold with inadequate protection from the elements can be very debilitating and much greater endurance is needed to sail in stormy conditions and especially at night in any season but high summer.

Winter winds do not die at night as they do characteristically during a *meltemi*. This is a northeasterly wind in the northern Aegean and the Cyclades, but farther south, in Cyprus, it blows from a north-westerly direction due to the position of the island relative to the Asian continent. In effect, all winds occur in all seasons although with different intensity and frequency.

Weather patterns do not provide convincing arguments in defense of seasonal sailing activity. Many scholars assume that Bronze Age boats were laid up all winter long. Today, Greek fishing fleets are never inactive during the entire winter and boats are usually repaired in the spring when the air is drier, not in the winter. Hesiod is habitually quoted to support the lack of winter sailing in all periods of antiquity. However, theories based on the maritime activities of later periods may not be relevant to island communication in the Aegean Bronze Age when the circumstances and the needs were different. Island communities which have ceased to be autonomous economic units will naturally remain in contact with each other and the nearest mainland points whenever the weather permits.

It is clearly important to apply different standards to inter-island traffic and to long distance traffic. If sea travel can take place year round in the Aegean or the Saronic Gulf despite spells of bad weather, this does not necessarily mean that voyages to Cyprus and beyond would have been undertaken with the same regularity.

Sailing during the Bronze Age was not an amateur or random affair (Georgiou 1993). A reconstruction of methods of navigation used in the Aegean can be attempted by using Homeric and epigraphic sources (Höckmann 1982; Betts 1973; Kenna 1960; Marinatos 1933; Casson 1971; Bass, et. al. 1989; Morgan 1988; Barber 1987; Georgiou 1993; Palaima 1991: 273–311). To be sure, critical consistency and circumspection are advised when using Homer to illustrate anything earlier than the Iron Age, yet we return time and again to the *Odyssey* and the *Iliad* because they are among the earliest Greek texts about the sea and include references to celestial navigation as well as information about night sailing.[10] In the *Odyssey*, long distance travel is

---

[7] Certain ports such as Kamares on Siphnos and Mykonos are extremely difficult to enter or leave due to wind conditions. At Kamares, the long, narrow approach is framed by abrupt cliffs rising to great heights. Very few people today know how to enter this harbor safely under sail.

[8] For a recent treatment of this theory using charts, the Med. Pilot, theoretical sailing information, and some Strabo see Lambrou-Phillipson (1991: 11–21). She believes that winter south winds would not be exploited and argues that celestial navigation was unknown (1991: 13).

[9] The KYRENIA II, although differently rigged and with a single upper yard, sailed closer to windward than expected. Katzev (1990: 245–56; 255): remarkable ability to sail into the wind. Roberts (1991: 59): brailing allowed hull forms unsuited to propulsion by sail the opportunity to extend their cruising range and to be sailed in a wide range of directions other than before the wind. Georgiou (1991: 67): reconstruction of sail reduction is not correct.

[10] For examples see Od.II.413 ff.; Od. II.434; Od. III.1–5, Od. III.177–178; Od. V.33–35; Od. V.269–282; Od. IX. 82; Od. XII.279 ff.; Od. XIII. 29 ff.;Od. XIII 70–95; Od. XV.296; McGrail (1991) 87–90 discusses seafaring and navigational skills in Homer and the BronzeAge.

frequently preferred to short hauls, something which would entail night travel. It is in fact much easier to sail on a star-lit, moonless night because the stars assist in keeping a bearing. The eyes become accustomed to nuances of color and can perceive lights on the horizon and land masses at greater distances much more clearly than in moonlight.

A means of computing time by the stars is described in three different passages. Two occur in the *Odyssey* and the third is in a speech by Odysseus in the *Iliad*. The passages are clearly formulaic, yet they do make clear that the night was divided into watches and that the hour of the night was recognized by observing the movement of certain prominent stars. All three passages refer to the same time of the night before dawn, stressing the third watch:

1. Il. X 251–254 (The shield of Achilles is problematic in date). Odysseus responds: "Son of Tydeus... let us depart for the night is ending, dawn is near, the stars have turned their course; more than the two thirds of the night have passed; only one third remains."
2. Od. XII.312: "We were at the end of the two thirds of the night and the stars had begun their descent."
3. Od. XIV.483: Description of the night after the meal of Odysseus and the Eumaeus—Odysseus is speaking in recollection of another night: "In the third period (watch) of the night when the stars had turned their course (passed their zenith)."

The watches are based on the timing of the sequence of clock or decan stars that are first recorded on Egyptian Middle Kingdom coffin lids (Leach 1954: 115, Neugebauer 1957: 83, Leitz 1989). The "hour" of the night is determined by the rising of the decan that is listed in the proper decade of the month. Each star or star group rises heliacally with a difference of plus or minus ten days in relation to the adjacent group thus giving the name "decade" to the group and "decan star" to the first star in each decade (Neugebauer 1954: 796; Neugebauer and Parker 1960). In addition, Babylonian texts give us information about the night watches (Neugebauer 1954). The consecutive risings of the decans were probably used as early as 2500 B.C.E. as a star clock to indicate the hours of the night.[11] The times of star rises were

also used to mark the seasons, as for instance, the rising of Sirius with the Sun announced the rising of the Nile.

To return to the Homeric citations, the third watch is when the current decan star and those stars in front of it have all passed the meridian and are descending. This method of calculating watches presupposes an understanding of the concept of the zenith as well as the ability to identify and estimate the movements of decan stars.

In summation, the decan clock is described in the Homeric texts, and its use in the Mediterranean, if not in Greek speaking territories demonstrably predates the eighth century B.C.E. The navigational systems and the knowledge of astronomy attested in the Homeric texts are ultimately derived from Egyptian and Babylonian systems of the Middle and Late Bronze Age. The introduction of this knowledge into the Aegean area can most certainly have occurred before the eighth century B.C.E. (Snodgrass 1974: 114–25; Finley 1977; Davies 1984; Hainsworth 1984; Foxhall and Davies, eds. 1984: passim; Davies and Foxhall 1984: 177–83; Morris 1986: 81–138 for bibliography).

The ability to understand and apply the decanal system suggests some measure of navigational sophistication. Thus, seafarers as described in Homer were effectively prepared for night travel, which included navigation by the stars as well as the knowledge of harbors and the ability to find landfall in the dark. Can we not infer that earlier travelers had at least learned to identify certain stars to help them keep a course?

Simple navigational aids of the kind recorded in the Homeric epics are well-documented in other seagoing and preliterate cultures.[12] The star clock would not pose too much of a problem in calculating time unless long ocean voyages were involved. Seventeen days is the longest recorded time in the Homeric texts for a passage without landfall. Calypso's island may belong to the realm of fantasy, but a trip of seventeen days' duration is not inconceivable. The Kyrenia ship sailed in September from Piraeus to Paphos. In generally mild weather the journey took 25 days and included many stopovers. The trip north in April took 19 days, including stopovers in variable weather (Katzev 1990: 245–56). However, there is no technical reason why the round trip could not have been made in the same season

---

[11] On Middle Kingdom coffin lids the decanal constellations are arranged in ten day intervals throughout the year forming 36 columns with 12 lines each for the 12 hours of the night. Approximately twelve decans covered the interval between dusk and dawn. The year has 360 days or 36 decans. The name of the specific decan moves up one line from column to column creating a diagonal pattern. These sequences will vary according to the season due to the revolution of the earth. Star time increases by four minutes each day.

[12] See Thomas (1987: 73–115) for Micronesian navigation.

and it is not necessary to assume a six-month layover. In a typical modern sailboat the trip takes approximately ten days one way, including stopovers.[13]

CYPRUS: LOCATION OF PORTS

Islands have to be approached by sea, thus geography will influence anchorages and the development of harbor towns (Blue, this volume). It is important to know the prevailing winds that will affect approaches and anchorages.

One might expect major ports to be located on the north coast of Cyprus during the Late Bronze Age coinciding with the increase of Mycenaean trade goods on the island (Åstrom 1986: 63–68). Yet this does not appear to be the case. The north coast may well have better access to mineral resources and it might be closer to Rhodes and Crete, but it is not safe due to the prevailing wind direction and geomorphology. Chrysochou Bay offers no shelter in bad weather and Morphou Bay is a dangerous anchorage in north winds.[14] The detailed contours of the coast have admittedly changed, but surely not the prevailing winds. On Cyprus, the current works in a counterclockwise direction but the wind will affect its speed.[15]

Despite the possible use of harbors associated with specific inland activities on the bays of Morphou and Chrysochou , the important anchorages of Cyprus are and have always been open roadsteads and anchorages in bays and inlets on the south and southeast coasts located between Famagusta, Larnaca, Limassol and Paphos (Baurain 1984: 10–12). Yet even Paphos is not safe in southeasterly gales when anchorages in the lee of the Akrotiri peninsula are preferable. In addition, the coast north of Paphos presents

many problems that complicate an approach from this direction. The reef between Cape Drepanum and Paphos is the site of many wrecks. The Maa peninsula is the only exception on this coast, and conforms to a much favored Bronze Age pattern of a settlement on a promontory (Georgiou, in press).

Historical testimony eloquently corroborates the preference of the south coast for stopovers (Grivaud 1990: 23–25). In the fifteenth century, Venetian pilgrim transports heading to the Levant usually anchored at Paphos and Limassol, more rarely at Episkopi, Larnaca or Famagusta. On the way back, they would stop at Larnaca for supplies. Other ports of call, including Kyrenia, are rarely mentioned. Prior to the 1960s Kyrenia harbor was not safe in northerly winds and gales and was quite similar to Chania harbor in orientation and structure. Thus the north coast was avoided and all the stops were limited to the southern sites (Grivaud 1990: 23–25). This is due to the inhospitable configuration of the coast as well as the prevailing winds.[16] In stormy conditions, Venetian ships preferred to continue on to Kastellorizo, Rhodes or Crete.

All these factors will have affected the movement of ships in the region and the preferred ports of call. The southern ports of Cyprus were undoubtedly important intermediary stations for Late Bronze Age ships traveling to or from Egypt and the eastern Mediterranean littoral (Whittaker 1992: 30–34). These issues have been illuminated by the important results of the work at Uluburun and the identification of the objects on the ship (see Pulak, this volume). Much previous discussion about who traded where and why is now out of date.[17] The same ports also served traffic to points farther West.[18]

[13] From Aegina via Paros, Rhodes or Kastellorizo to Paphos.

[14] Marion with a harbor presumably somewhere near the modern Polis was used at a later date because of its proximity to the mines. Tomba tou Skourou must have been approached from Morphou Bay. However, both sites are exceptions.

[15] The easterly current on the north coast of Africa turns northeastward and northward on the coasts of Palestine and Syria. On the southern coast of Turkey the current generally sets westward, its rate increasing as the distance from the coast of Syria becomes greater.

[16] Winter winds are variable and occur from all directions but northwesterlies are the most frequent. In spring, winds are still variable although northwesterly winds predominate and southeastery winds (scirocco-khamsin) are more frequent than in winter. In summer, light to moderate northwesterlies are steady and persistent. These are equivalent to the northeasterly meltemi in the northern and central Aegean. In autumn, northwesterlies decrease somewhat. Late August, September and October have frequent calms. Strong winds are likely to blow from November and April, whereas there are no gales from May and October. March is the most inclement month with gales ranging from southwest to northwest lasting about three days and raising heavy seas.

[17] See Altman (1988: 230) for a discussion of problems that Aegean seafarers had to face when approaching Egypt and the Levantine coast.

[18] See Vagnetti (1986: 213) for a direct link between Italy (esp. Sicily and Sardinia) and Cyprus, independent of the Aegean, in the latest phases of the BA. See also Cline (1994: 63 and 106).

CONCLUSIONS: THE EFFECT ON ISLAND SETTLEMENT

Island settlement is related to geography. If an island has many possible ports it is more likely that there will also be a larger number of important settlements in use diachronically. A variety of physical factors will have influenced site location. These include:

1. Geographical configuration
2. Proximity to mines, quarries and other important resources
3. Proximity to fresh water source
4. Strategic location/defensive position

In some instances, Bronze Age sites in the Aegean developed inland (Knossos) or were located on inaccessible coasts with no harbor, such as Phylakopi (Georgiou 1993: 353–55). Other sites developed near a major harbor, such as Ayia Irini, Keos and presumably Akrotiri, Thera.

Much obfuscation has resulted from recent articles featuring desk top navigation to illustrate theoretical and symbolic aspects of prehistoric trade and exchange. Many reconstructions are sorely lacking in the practical element. Common pitfalls are calculations about average nautical miles per day traveled and average time needed for sea passages between two points. Furthermore, points are usually chosen because of geographical proximity and the presence in the archaeological record of non-local goods. While the presence of foreign objects is testimony to contacts, it cannot tell us much about trade and certainly less about trade routes. For this purpose, the shipwrecks provide more specific information from their cargo and it is from the study of the latter that we will begin to get a clearer view of trading patterns and not on land excavations. A shipwreck is a time capsule preserving the evidence of very recent contacts and in its stratigraphy can provide a sequence in the loading of the cargo. The Cape Iria ship is an excellent case in point (see Vichos, this volume).

Aegean lead weights are among the most significant objects for the analysis of contacts (Petruso 1992: 64–68). They represent a physical as well as a conceptual relationship between sites where they are found. Whereas their appearance at a number of sites establishes the relationship of these sites to each other, it cannot under any circumstances illustrate the means and method by which they reached their destination via theoretical trade routes.

Given the geographical spread of island groups, routing would have been a complex issue, quite possibly lacking any predictable pattern, but with known ports of call. There is a great difference between the identification of a sea route or trading route and the determination of a destination. Whereas I do not dispute the existence of ports of call, I do dispute the identification of specific trade routes based on the archaeological information available at present (Davis 1979: 146).

Our knowledge of the prehistory of most of the Aegean islands is exceedingly sparse and changes each year.[19] Are we to add another line or another bead to the "strings" or create subsidiary "strings" each time a new site yields non-local material? This approach has too many limitations. It would seem that all such speculation is premature and misleading because it fosters facile and attractive theories that have repercussions long after they have ceased to be valid.

Flexible approaches will indeed have to be found to explain and clarify communications between the Aegean and the eastern Mediterranean. At present it would be best to concentrate on recognizing ports of call without complicating the picture by trying to recreate trade routes. The Bronze Age knowledge of shipbuilding, seafaring, and navigation all contribute to an understanding of Bronze Age maritime activity. This maritime activity is a central factor in the development of coastal sites and cities, many of which retain their importance today for the very same reasons.[20]

---

[19]Excavations in 1994 at Mykonos have uncovered a large and important tholos tomb, testimony to important LBA habitation, previously undocumented.

[20] "The greater the motivation to travel, migrate or invade, the more complex become the results of this interaction" (Merrilees 1986: xxv–xxx).

REFERENCES

Admiralty Hydrographic Department, Great Britain
1949   *Mediterranean Pilot V. Comprising the Coasts of Libya, Egypt, Palestine and Syria, the Southern Coast of Turkey, and the Island of Cyprus.* London: Taylor, Garnett, Evans & Co.

Altman, A.
1988   Trade between the Aegean and the Levant in the Late Bronze Age. Some Neglected Questions. Pp. 229–39 in *Society and Economy in the Eastern Mediterranean (ca. 1500–100 B.C.),* eds. M. Heltzer and E. Lipinski. Orientalia Lovaniensa Analecta 23.

Åström, P.
1986   Hala Sultan Teke and its Foreign Relations. Pp. 63–68 in *Acts of the International Archaeological Symposium, "Cyprus between the Orient and the Occident,"* ed. V. Karageorghis. Nicosia, 8–14 September 1985. Nicosia: Department of Antiquities.

Barber, R. L. N.
1987   *The Cyclades in the Bronze Age.* London: Duckworth.

Bass, G. F.; Pulak, C.; Collon, D.; and Weinstein, J.
1989   The Bronze Age Shipwreck at Ulu Burun, 1986 Campaign. *American Journal of Archaeology* 93: 1–29.

Barrain, C.
1989   Chypre et la Mediterrannee au Bronze Recent. Synthese Historique. *Etudes Chypriotes,* 6. Paris.

Betts, J. H.
1973   Ships on Minoan Seals. Pp. 325–28 in *Marine Archaeology. Proceedings of the 23rd Symposium of the Coloston Research Society held in the University of Bristol, 4–8 April 1971,* ed. D. J. Blackman. London.

Buchholz, H. G.
1988   Der metallhandel des zweiten Jahrtausends im Mittelmeer. Pp. 187–228 in *Society and Economy in the Eastern Mediterranean (ca. 1500–100 B.C.),* eds. M. Heltzer and E. Lipinski. Orientalia Lovaniensa Analecta 23. Leuven: Peeters.

Caskey, J. L.
1971   Investigations in Keos, Part 1: Excavations and Explorations, 1966–1970. *Hesperia* 40: 358–96.

Casson, L.
1971   *Ships and Seamanship in the Ancient World.* Princeton: Princeton University.

Cline, E. H.
1994   *Sailing the Wine-Dark Sea. International Trade and the Late Bronze Age Aegean.* BAR International Series 591. Oxford: B.A.R.

Davies, J. K.
1984   The Reliability of the Oral Tradition. Pp. 87–110 in *The Trojan War. Its Historicity and Context. Papers of the First Greenbank Colloquium, Liverpool,* eds. L. Foxhall and J.K. Davies. Bristol: Bristol Classical.

Davis, J. L.
1979   Minos and Dexithea: Crete and the Cyclades in the Later Bronze Age. Pp. 143–57 in *Papers in Cycladic Prehistory,* eds. J. L. Davis and J. F. Cherry. Los Angeles: University of California.

Finley, M. I.
1977   *The World of Odysseus.* Second Edition. London: Chatto and Windus.

Foxhall, L., and Davies, J. K. (eds.)
1984   *The Trojan War. Its Historicity and Context. Papers of the First Greenbank Colloquium, Liverpool.* Bristol: Bristol Classical.

Georgiou, H. S.
1991   Bronze Age Ships and Rigging. Pp. 61–71 in *Thalassa. L'egee prehistorique et la mer. Aegaeum 7. Annales d'archaeologie egeenne de l'Universite de Liege,* ed. R. Laffineur. Liège: Université.

1993   A Sea Approach to Trade in the Aegean Bronze Age. Pp. 353–64 in *Wace and Blegen, Pottery as Evidence for Trade in the Aegean Bronze Age, 1939–1989* (A Conference Sponsored by the American School of Classical Studies and the British School of Archaeology at Athens, December 2–3, 1989), ed. C. Zerner. Amsterdam: J. C. Gieben.

in press   The Role of Maritime Contacts in the Urban Development of the Prehistoric Cyclades. In *International Symposium, Kea-Kythnos, Historical and Archaeological Research, June 1994,* ed. L. Mendoni.

Grivaud, G. (pub.)
1990   Voyageurs Occidentaux à Chypre au XVeme Siecle. *Excerpta Cypria Nova,* Vol. 1. Sources et Etudes de l'Histoire de Chypre XV. Nicosie: Centre de Recherches Scientifiques.

Hainsworth, J. B.
1984   The Fallibility of an Oral Heroic Tradition. Pp. 111–35 in *The Trojan War. Its Historicity and*

Context. Papers of the First Greenbank Colloquium, Liverpool, eds. L. Foxhall, and J. K. Davies. Bristol: Bristol Classical.

Höckmann, O.
1982 Schiffe des Minos. Schiffbau und Seefahrt im alten Kreta. *Romisch-Germanisches Zentralmuseum Arbeitsbericht,* 1: 8–12.

Katzev, M. L.
1990 An Analysis of the Experimental Voyages of KYRENIA II. Pp. 245–56 in *Proceedings of the Second International Symposium on Ship Construction in Antiquity,* Tropis II, ed. H. Tzalas. Athens: Hellenic Institite for the Preservation of Nautical Tradition.

Kenna, V. E. G.
1960 *Cretan Seals, with a Catalogue of the Minoan Gems in the Ashmolean Museum.* Oxford: Oxford University.

Lambrou-Phillipson, C.
1991 Seafaring in the Bronze Age Mediterranean: The Parameters Involved in Maritime Travel. Pp. 11–21 in *Thalassa, Aegaeum 7,* ed. R. Laffineur. Liège: Université.

Leach, E. R.
1954 Primitive Time Reckoning. Pp. 110–27 in *A History of Technology. I: From Early Times to Fall of Ancient Empires,* eds. C. Singer; E. J. Holmyard; and A. R. Hall. Oxford: Clarendon.

Leitz, Christian
1989 Studien zür Aegyptischen Astronomie. *Aegyptologische Abhandlungen* 49.

Marinatos, S.
1933 La marine créto-mycénienne. *BCH* 57: 170–235.

McGrail, S.
1991 Bronze Age Seafaring in the Mediterranean. Pp. 87–90 in *Bronze Age Trade in the Mediterranean* (SIMA) Vol. XL. Göteborg: Åströms.

Merillees, R. S.
1986 Summary and Conclusions. Pp. xxv–xxx in *Acts of the International Archaeological Symposium, "Cyprus between the Orient and the Occident,"* ed. V. Karageorghis. Nicosia: Department of Antiquities.

Morgan, L.
1988 *The Miniature Wall Paintings of Thera: a Study in Aegean Culture and Iconography.* Cambridge Classical Studies, Cambridge University.

Morris, I.
1986 The Use and Abuse of Homer. *Classical Antiquity* 5: 81–138.

Neugebauer, O.
1954 Ancient Mathematics and Astronomy. Pp. 785–803 in *A History of Technology. I. From Early Times to Fall of Ancient Empires,* eds. C. Singer; E. J. Holmyard; and A. R. Hall. Oxford: Clarendon.
1957 *The Exact Sciences in Antiquity.* Second Edition. Providence: Brown University.

Palaima, T. G.
1991 Maritime Matters in the Linear B Tablets. Pp. 273–310 in *Thalassa. Aegaeum 7,* ed. R. Laffineur.

Petruso, Karl M.
1992 *Ayla Irini: The Balance Weights. An Analysis of Weight Measurement in Prehistoric Crete and the Cycladic Islands.* Mainz: von Zabern.

Roberts, O. T. P.
1991 The Development of the Brail into a Viable Sail Control for Aegean Boats of the Bronze Age. Pp. 55–60 in *Thalassa. Aegaeum 7,* ed. R. Laffineur. Liège: Université.

Snodgrass, A. M.
1974 An Historical Homeric Society? *Journal of Hellenic Studies* 94: 114–25.

Thomas, S. D.
1987 *The Last Navigator.* New York: Holt.

Vagnetti, L.
1986 Cypriot Elements Beyond the Aegean in the Bronze Age. Pp. 201–16 in *Acts of the International Archaeological Symposium, "Cyprus between the Orient and the Occident,"* ed. V. Karageorghis. Nicosia, 8–14 September 1985. Nicosia; Department of Antiqutiites.

Whittaker, H.
1992 Contacts between the Aegean and the Levant in the Late Bronze Age. Pp. 27–34 in *Hydra: Working Papers in Middle Bronze Age Studies* 10.

The Classical Shipwreck at Alonnesos

Department of Maritime Antiquities
Erechthion 59
Athens 11742
GREECE

The largest Classical shipwreck known in the world was discovered recently near the island of Alonnesos, one of the northern Sporades, in the Aegean Sea. It is a Greek cargo ship, sunk sometime in the late fifth or the early fourth century B.C.E., at a depth of 30 m underwater. It was loaded with wine amphoras from the town of Mende on the Macedonian coast, as well as from the island of Skopelos, both places famous in antiquity for the quality of their wines, which were exported all across the Greek world, and to the Black Sea. A large quantity of Athenian black-glaze symposium tableware discovered on the ship suggests that it traded black-glaze containers as well as wine. A full scale excavation of the shipwreck with the Department of Maritime Antiquities under my direction began in August 1992, and will continue for a number of years. This is the largest and most important underwater project yet undertaken by the Department.

INTRODUCTION

Some time in the late fifth century B.C.E., a large Greek cargo ship sank off the southern coast of the island of Alonnesos, in Classical times called Ikos (Strabo 9.436; *PW* "Ikos," 1991) in the northern Sporades (fig. 1). It was discovered recently and reported to the Greek Department of Marine Antiquities.[1] A preliminary survey took place in the fall of 1991, and a full scale survey and excavation began in August 1992 and continued through 1993. It is the largest project yet carried out by the Greek Department of Underwater Antiquities, the first Classical ship to be excavated in Greek waters, and the largest ship of the Classical period to be studied to date.[2]

SITUATION BEFORE EXCAVATION

When first encountered by us in the fall of 1991, the Alonnesos wreck lay on the gently sloping sandy and rocky sea-floor between 22 and 30 m deep. It was marked by large quantities of amphoras apparently arranged in many layers, which formed a mound 25 m long and 10 m wide (fig. 2).

During the preliminary survey, four amphoras were brought to the surface for examination. The amphoras were used for transporting wine around 400 B.C.E., and originated from the ancient maritime town of Mende in Macedonia, and from the island of Peparethos, modern Skopelos. Mende was colonized in 730 B.C.E. by the Eretrians, and was one of the most important Greek colonies in the Chalkidike penin-

---

[1] The wreck was discovered by a Greek fisherman, Dimitris Mavrikis, who initially reported it to the Department of Maritime Antiquities. A further report to the Department was made later by Peter Winterstein, director of the German Association for Underwater Archaeology, DEGUWA, emphasizing the size and importance of the wreck.

[2] The scientific personnel taking part in the excavation were: archaeologists, E. Hadjidaki, E. Spondilis, D. Haniotis, A. Simosi, S. Asimakopoulou, C. Agouridis, D. Sotirakis, E. Mantzouka, G. Koutsouflakis, T. Gartagani, V. Lazari, G. Mavrofridis, F. Mantziou, M. Goutzamani, A. Ritzonis, E. Kaggelari, P. Skarpelou, and the student archaeologists C. Papachristopoulou, M. Tsopela, K. Sigler, and K. Tretheway; architects: N. Lianos, K. Tagonidou, V. Koniordos, T. Nakasis,

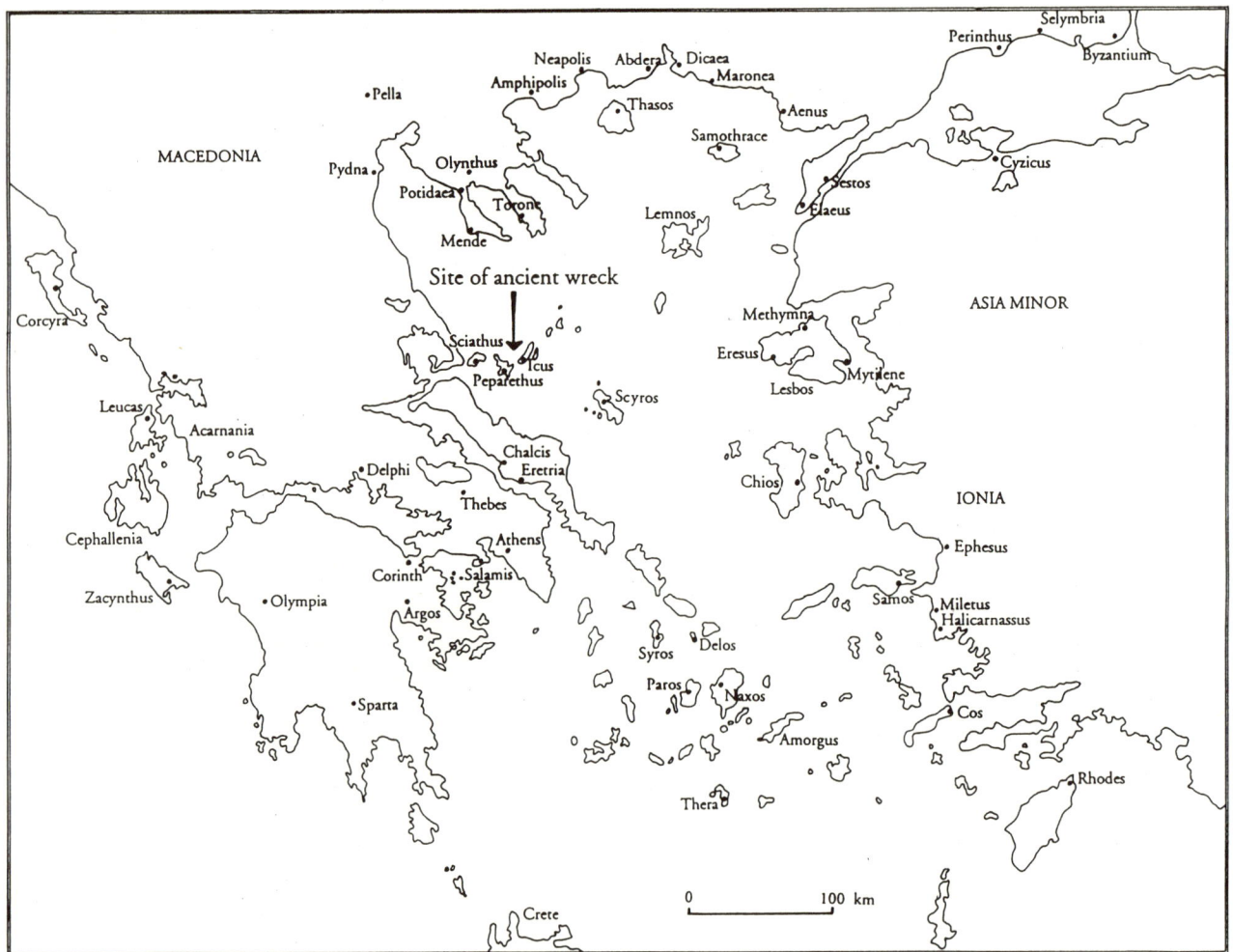

Fig. 1. Map of Classical Greece with wreck site off Alonnesos.

sula (Hicks 1882: no. 35, 49; 80; *PW* 1937 "Mende," 778–79). Peparethos is a Greek island in the northern Sporades (Strabo, 9.5.16; Hicks., 1882 inscriptions no. 24, 27; no. 30, 41; no. 35, 49; no. 48, 80; no. 81, 140; *PW* 1937 "Peparethos," 552–59) and together with Mende was among the ancient communities which produced and exported wine to the Black Sea area from the middle of the fifth century B.C.E. (Σοφοκλῆς, Φιλοκτήτης, v. 548–549, Loeb Classical Library, 1919, vol. II; Ἀθηναῖος, Δειπνοσοφισταί 1.29a, d–e, Loeb Classical Library, 1927, vol. I; Δημοσθένης, ΠΡΟΣ ΤΗΝ ΛΑΚΡΙΤΟΥ ΠΑΡΑΓΡΑΦΗΝ, xxxv, 35, edition "Les belles lettres,"

Paris, 1954; Eisman 1987: 37–52; Brashinski 1984: 105–7; Doulgeri-Intzessiloglou and Garlan 1990: 361–92; Monahoff 1989; Empereur and Garlan 1992: 19–21).

The Mendean type of amphora was rather short (height 0.65 m) and quite distinct from the Peparethian one. It had a pear-shaped body that ended in a long flared toe; the handles and the neck were short, the rim of the mouth flaring outwards. The Peparethos type was longer (height 0.85 m) and narrower, with a conical body that terminated in a moderately tall foot with a button on the bottom; the handles and neck were long and had a thick curled-over lip (fig. 3).

and the student A. Vaitsos; geologists-oceanologists: E. Hahamidou, V. Masoura; biologist: N. Nikodimou; topographer: G. Baksevanakis, D. Karantaidis; chemist: A. Katsi; computer operator: E. Saiti; photographers: P. Vezirtzis, G. Tsialikis, and C. Platt on behalf of National Geographic.

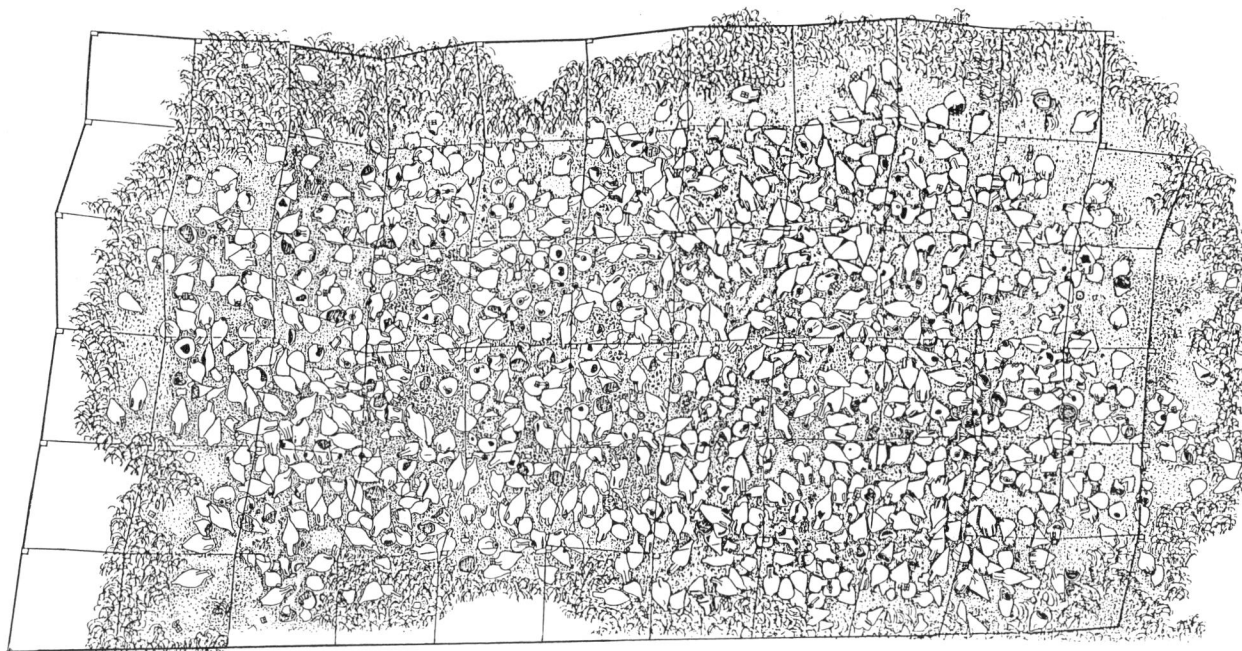

Fig. 2. Plan of wreck. D. Karantaidís and V. Koniordos.

RESULTS OF FIRST TWO SEASONS (1992, 1993)

Much of the first season, during the summer of 1992, was devoted to laying the groundwork for excavation. The wreck is not particularly close to the island of Alonnesos itself, but lies off a small uninhabited island, Peristera. We built a small village on the bare rocks that consisted of four wooden sheds, bathroom facilities, and three additional platforms. Diving took place from a floating platform.

The main scientific task of our first season was to survey the wreck thoroughly. The starting point was the laying down of a rope grid, consisting of 2 × 2 m sections. This grid was mainly useful for orienting the divers and precise measurements were not based upon it. Two complementary surveying methods were employed simultaneously. The first involved laying down a network of 92 fixed points, spaced roughly 2 m apart, whose depths were determined by a bathymeter. The horizontal distance between each fixed point and four or five of its near neighbors was carefully measured. The surface of the wreck was then photographed piece by piece in small sections (fig. 4), with at least three fixed points in each photograph. We then developed a computer program that utilizes the collection of distance measurements to find a best fit to the locations of the fixed points. The program also provides an estimate of the error in each measurement, a feature that enabled us to discard a number of distances that were patently wrong. This software was available on the site in 1993 and measurements were re-

taken when they were in dispute. Finally, all of the objects in each photograph were traced over on a digitizing tablet and stored in a Computer Aided Design program. The fixed points were used to relate one image to the other (fig. 5). The second method used to map out the site is a standard type of photogrammetry, relying upon fairly expensive specialized machinery. This method was employed by Dimitri Karantaidis, visiting from the Ministry of Macedonia and northern Thrace (fig. 2). The results of the two methods were essentially the same.

While the measurements were being taken for use in photogrammetry, we labeled all of the 1000 amphoras lying on the surface of the wreck. There were three other surface finds of note. Part of a ship's anchor was found 25 m from the main wreck, and possibly belonging to it. It is a lead strengthening piece that held wooden arms against the shank of the anchor (fig. 6) (Kapitan 1984: 33–44, fig.1). We also found one small black-glaze bowl and a heavy-walled cup/skyphos of the type that came into being ca. 420 B.C.E., and ceased production around 380 B.C.E. (fig. 7) (AGORA XII, pl. 27, fig. 6 between 617 and 621 and XII part I, 112; ΑΡΧΑΙΟΛΟΓΙΚΟ ΔΕΛΤΙΟ, Athens Ministry of Culture v. 19, 1964, Χρονικά, pl. 65a).

Following the survey, excavation was completed on two sections, each measuring 2 × 2 m—the wreck is covered by seventy-two such sections. From this small area, the density of finds was impressive: 150 wine amphoras were removed from the first three layers. The upper layers came

Fig. 3. Amphoras from Peparethos (left) and Mende (right). Photograph by P. Vezirtzis.

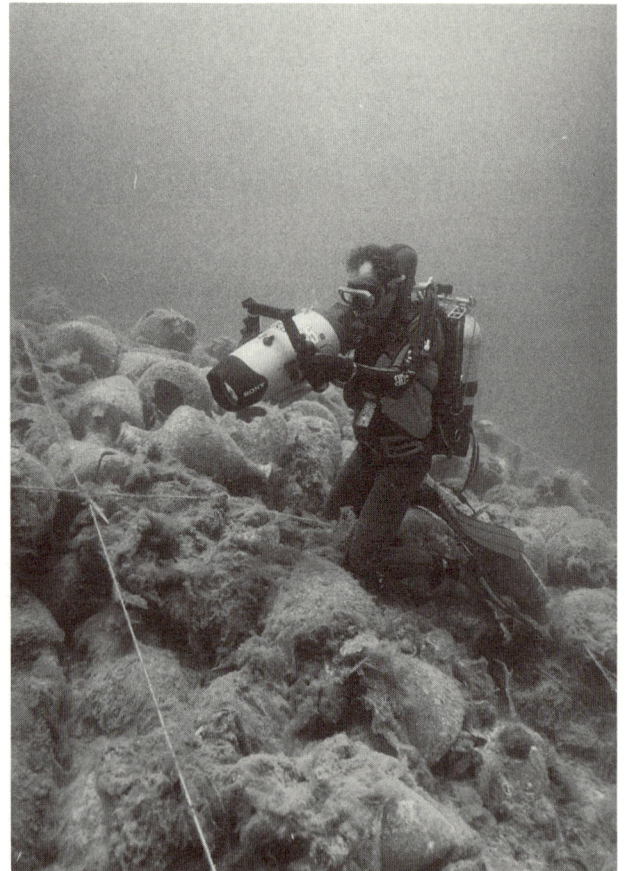

Fig. 4. Diver with videocamera during photogrammetry. Photograph by G. Tsialikis.

from Peparethos and the lower ones from Mende, with the sizes of the amphoras varying between 65 and 85 cm. The third layer also contained ten black-glaze kylikes with stamped rays enclosed within three bands (fig. 8), some with engraved stars in the center (fig. 9) (AGORA XII, part 2, pls. 22–23, fig. 5, between nos. 483 and 496), eighteen black-glaze plates and bowls (fig. 10), a wine mug (fig. 11) (AGORA XII, part 2, pl. 11, no. 215; ΑΡΧΑΙΟΛΟΓΙΚΟ ΔΕΛΤΙΟ, Athens Ministry of Culture v. 41, 1986, Χρονικά, pl. 33c), one lekanis with a lid (fig. 12) (AGORA XII, pl. 69, fig 13, no. 1555), an oinochoe similar to the one found at Olynthus, although not identical (fig. 13) (OLYNTHUS V, pl. 166, no. 733) and many additional pieces of broken fineware dating to between 425 and 380 B.C.E. An additional source for similar kylikes is Bakalakis (1990: 643–50).

As for metal objects, we found the lower body and the rim of a double-handled bronze bucket (bell situla) with Ionian decoration along the rim (fig. 14), very similar to the one excavated in a Macedonian tomb dating to the last quarter of the fifth century B.C.E., or beginning of the fourth century B.C.E. (Romiopoulou 1989, 194–98, pl. 45).[3] Right

next to the bucket we found one bronze ladle, and various short nails.

All of the black-glaze vessels belong to Symposium table-ware. The deep black-glaze has the fine appearance of the best Athenian ware, and analysis of the clay showed that the vessels originated in Athens.[4]

It seems that the ship was carrying a cargo of black-glaze containers as well as Mendean and Peparethian wine. Excavation stopped after having cleared two trenches down to the rocky bottom. No major pieces of the ship's hull were uncovered in these trenches. However, some small fragments of wood appeared, and were carbon dated to 425 B.C.E., and considerably larger chunks could be observed in adjacent unexcavated trenches.

---

[3] For more bronze situlae found in Macedonia see ΤΑΠΑ (1979: 80, type 332, pl. 47); Maragou (1985: 166, pl. 264); Andronikos (1992: 210 pl. 176); Greek Ministry of Culture (1980: pls. 17–19 and 26, 156 type 107, 163 type 123, and 170 type 135).

[4] Selected ceramics were analyzed at the nuclear research center "Demokritos" by Dr. G. Maniatis, and were found to have originated in Athens.

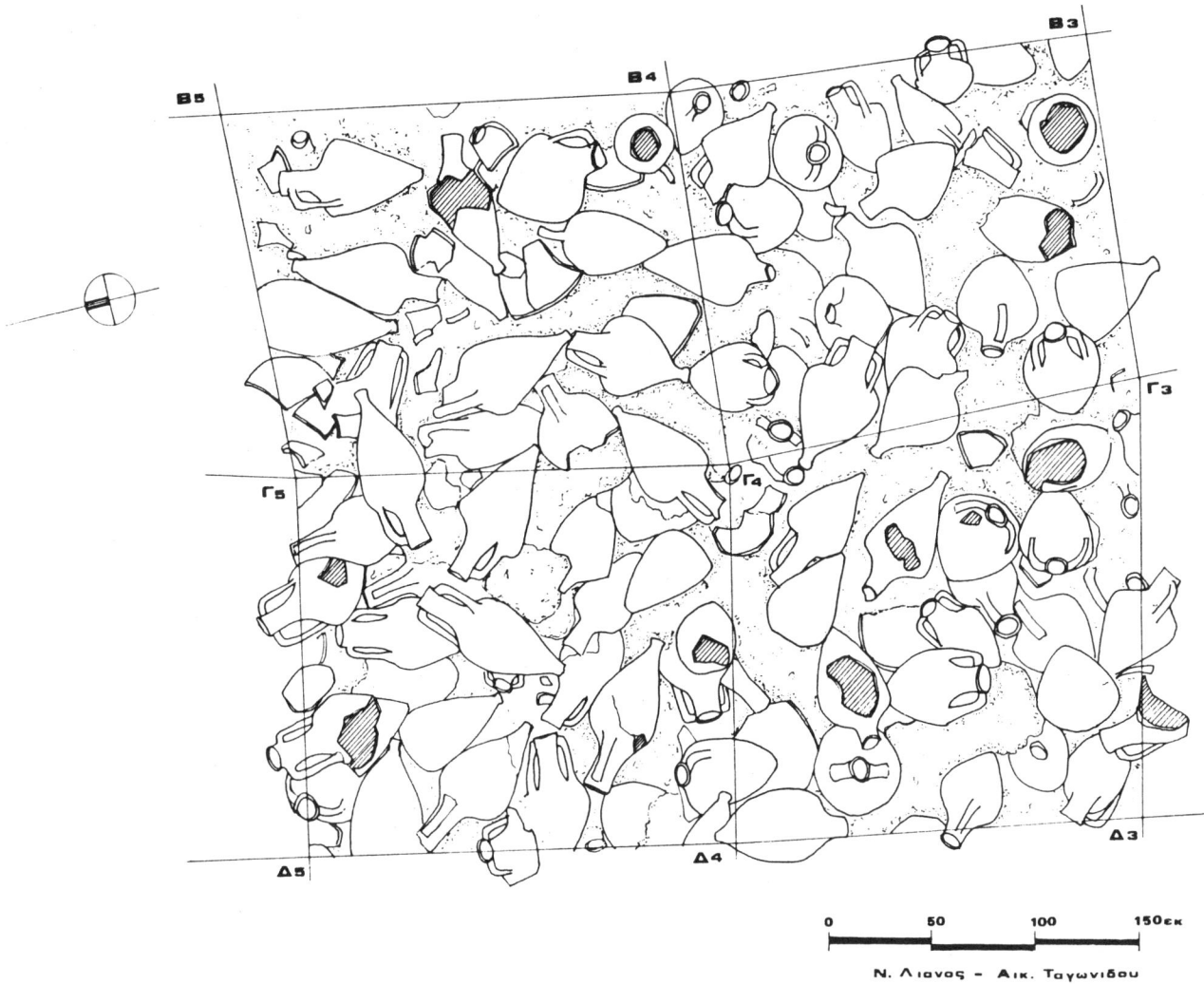

Fig. 5. Detail of plan of wreck: photogrammetric drawing of four sections. Drawing by N. Lianos and K. Tagonidou.

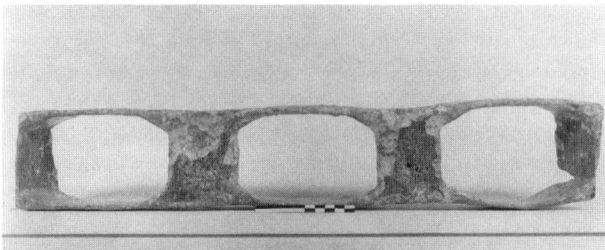

Fig. 6. Lead collar from part of a wooden anchor. Photograph by P. Vezirtzis.

CONCLUSIONS

The excavation of a Classical shipwreck is important because so few have ever been excavated anywhere in the world. The most famous is the Kyrenia Ship, which dates to around 350 B.C.E., and which was excavated by Michael

Fig. 7. Cup/skyphos. Photograph by P. Vezirtzis.

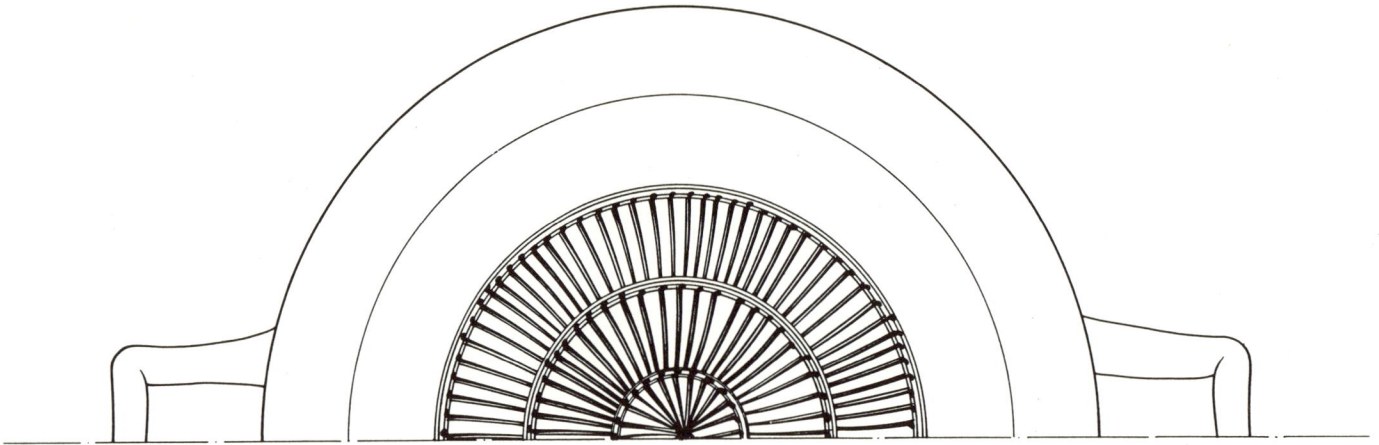

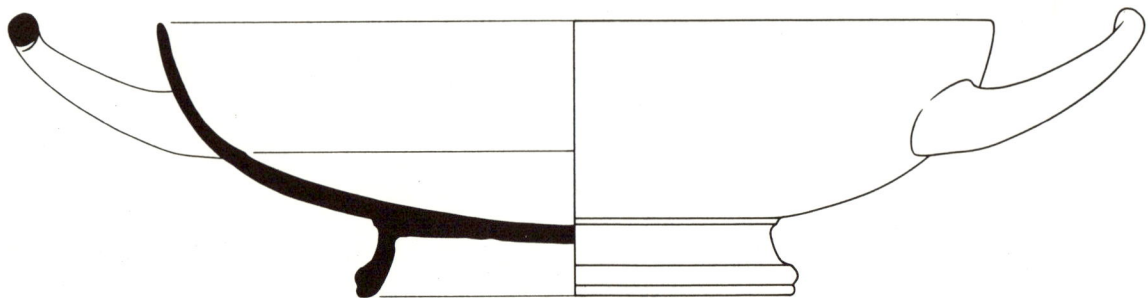

Fig. 8. Drawing of kylix with rays. Drawing by S. Piskardelis.

Katzev off the north coast of Cyprus in the late sixties and early seventies (Swiny and Katzev 1973; Katzev 1970). Large portions of the wood were recovered, making it possible to reconstruct the ship almost in its entirety (Katzev 1971; 1985; 1987). The Porticello wreck was excavated by Cynthia Eisman off the coast of Sicily (Eisman 1987). In this case some of ship's cargo remained, dating to exactly the same period as that of Alonnesos, and also containing wine amphora from Mende. Unfortunately, too little wood remained to allow reconstruction of the ship itself. The Ma'agan Michael wreck, excavated by Elisha Linder in Israel and found to be in a remarkable state of preservation, has the same size as the Kyrenia Ship; namely, 15 m long and 4 m wide (Linder 1992; 1993). A shipwreck of similar dimensions, but dating to the late sixth century B.C.E., was found well-preserved, buried in the silted harbor of Marseille in France, and is being excavated by Patrice Pomey (Pomey

and Hesnard 1993; Historical Museum of Marseille 1993). The ship was also 14 m long, and 4 m wide; it is part of an ongoing excavation, and a full report is in preparation. The wreck found at Alonnesos is considerably larger than any of these, and we have reason to hope that it is well-preserved, since the amphoras follow the outline of the ship, and are embedded in a partly sandy sea bottom that may have protected much of the wood.

There has been some disagreement about the size of merchant ships during the Classical period, with literary and archaeological evidence seeming to conflict. It was argued that ships carrying over 1500 amphora and weighing over 75 tons did not appear until the first century B.C.E. (Torr 1894: 25; Noettes 1935: 49 and 69–70; Parker 1992). Casson (1971: 171; 1994: 66), however, argues that the size of Classical merchant ships was frequently underestimated, and that burdens of up to 150 tons were not uncommon from the

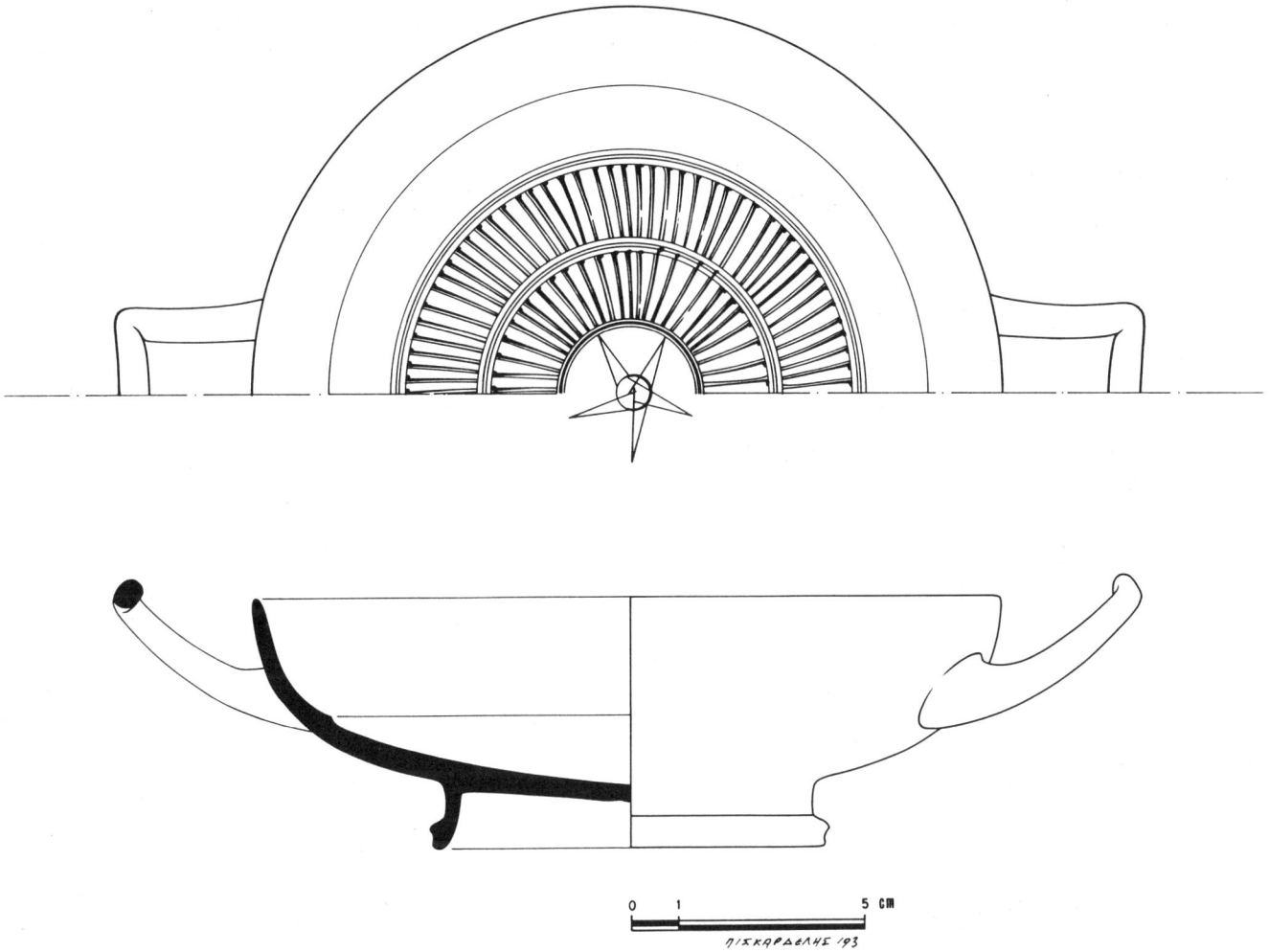

Fig. 9. Drawing of kylix with engraved star in center. Drawing by S. Piskardelis.

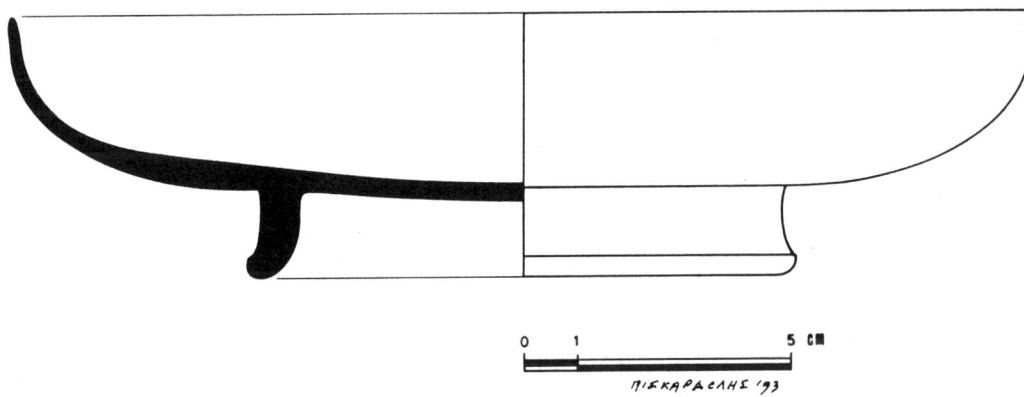

Fig. 10. Drawing of plate. Drawing by S. Piskardelis.

Fig. 11. Wine mug. Photography by P. Vezirtzis.

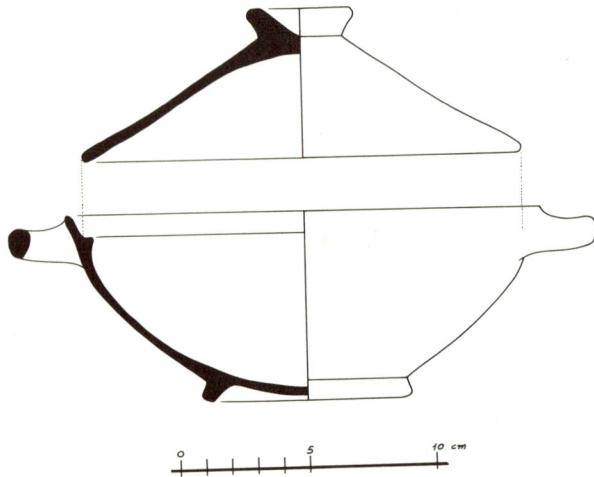

Fig. 13. Drawing of oinochoe. Drawing by S. Piskardelis.

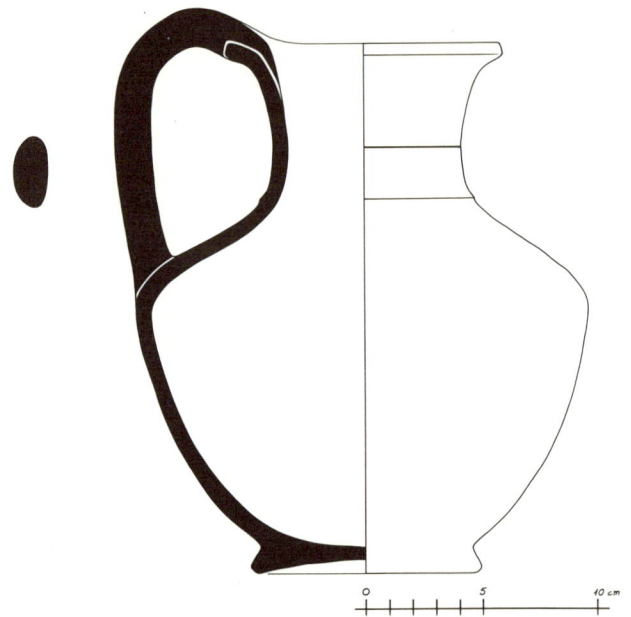

Fig. 12. Drawing of lekanis. Drawing by S. Piskardelis.

Fig. 14. Rim of bronze bucket (bell situla) with double handles. Photograph by P. Vezirtzis.

fifth century onwards. Our excavation supports this latter view. The surface layer alone contains one thousand amphora, weighing approximately 30 kg each. There are four layers, so a total of four thousand amphora, leading to a cargo certainly over 120 metric tons. This proves that the Greeks preceded the Romans in the construction of large cargo vessels.

Our best guess for the moment is that the ship started out in Athens with a cargo of black-glazed ware, and found its way to Mende, where it acquired a cargo of wine, continued down to Peparethos, took on additional cargo, and then sank. These conclusions are based on the stratigraphy of the cargo.

The eighteen largely intact plates that were excavated from the two trenches were all located beneath three or four layers of amphora, in an excellent state of preservation, sometimes stacked one within the other (fig. 15). In order to account for their surviving the sinking of the ship, one must assume that they were packed in wooden crates, prob-ably in a subfloor, the crates and protective floor now having disintegrated. Furthermore, charcoal found underneath some of the plates suggests that the ship sank due to fire. Was it piracy, or was it an accidental fire that caused the sinking of the ship? Further excavation will enable us to answer these questions, as well as how the Greeks sailed during the time of the Peloponnesian War and how the latter affected sea commerce.

Fig. 15. Black-glaze plates as found underwater. Photograph by S. Piskardelis.

REFERENCES

Andronikos, M,
1992   ΒΕΡΓΙΝΑ. Athens: Εκδοτική Αθηνών.
Bakalakis, G.
1990   Pp. 643–50 in Οἶνος Ισμαρικός. Thessalonike: University of Thessalonike.
Brashinski, I. B.
1984   *Research in Ancient Trade.* Leningrad: HAYKA (in Russian).
Casson, L.
1971   *Ships and Seamanship in the Ancient World.* Princeton: Princeton University.
1994   *Travel in the Ancient World.* Baltimore: Johns Hopkins University.
Doulgeri-Intzessiloglou A. and Garlan, Y.
1990   Vin et Amphores de Peparethos et D'Ikos. *Bulletin de Correspondance Hellenique* 114: 361–89.
Eisman, C.
1987   *The Porticello Shipwreck, A Mediterranean Merchant Vessel of 415–385 B.C.* College Station: Texas A & M University.

Empereur, J. Y. and Garlan, Y.
1990   Les atelier amphoriques grecs. Pp. 19–21 in LES AMPHORES GREQUES, les problemes de l'evolution du metier et de la commerce dans l'antiquité, eds. V. I. Kats and S. I. Monakhov. Saratov: Saratov University.
Greek Ministry of Culture
1980   *The Search for Alexander, an Exhibition.* Athens: Greek Ministry of Culture.
Hicks, E. L.
1882   *A Manual of Greek Historical Inscriptions.* Oxford: Clarendon.
Kapitan, G.
1984   Ancient Anchors—Technology and Classification. *International Journal of Nautical Archaeology* 13: 33–44.
Katzev, M. L.
1970   Resurrecting the Oldest Known Greek Ship. *National Geographic* 137: 841–57.
1974   Last Harbor for the Oldest Ship. *National Geographic* 146: 618–25.

1987   *Kyrenia II: An Ancient Ship Sails Again* (pamphlet). Athens: Hellenic Institute for the Preservation of Nautical Tradition, Piraeus.

Lefebvre des Noëttes, R.
1935   *De la marine antique a la marine moderne: la revolution du gouvernail.* Paris: Masson & Company.

Linder, E.
1992   Ma'agan Michael Shipwreck—Excavating an Ancient Merchantman. *Biblical Archaeology Review* 18: 24–35.
1993   Il Relitto di Ma'agan. *ARCHEO* VIII, 9: 98–109.

Maragou, L.
1985   Αρχαία Ελληνική Τέχνη. Athens: Goulandris Museum.

Monahoff, S.
1989   *Amphoras from the Tavric Peninsula of the 4'th to 2'd c B.C.,* Saratov: Saratov University (in Russian).

Musées de Marseille
1993   *Le Temps des Decouvertes: Marseille, de Protis a la reine Jeanne.* Marseille: Musées de Marseille.

Parker, A. J.
1992   Cargoes, Containers and Stowage: the Ancient Mediterranean. *The International Journal of Nautical Archaeology* 21: 89–100.

Pomey, P. and Hesnard, A.
1994   Marseille, Place Jules-Verne. Pp. 110–15 in *BILAN SCIENTIFIQUE DE LA REGION PROVENCE-ALPES-COTE D'AZUR,* Marseille: Ministère de la Culture et de la Francophonie.

Robinson, D. M.
1933   *Excavations at Olynthus, V, Mosaics, Vases and Lamps.* Baltimore: Johns Hopkins University.

Romiopoulou, K.
1989   Finds from Late Classical Tombs in Thessalonike. Pp. 194–218 in ΦΙΛΙΑ ΕΠΗ. Athens: ΑΡΧΑΙΟΛΟΓΙΚΗ ΕΤΑΙΡΕΙΑ (in Greek).

Sparkes, B. A., and Talcott, L.
1970   *The Athenian Agora, Results of Excavations Conducted by the American School of Classical Studies at Athens. Volume XII: Black and Plain Pottery of the 6th, 5th, and 4th Centuries B.C., Parts 1 and 2.* Princeton: The American School of Classical Studies at Athens.

Steffy, J. R.
1985   The Kyrenia Ship: An Interim Report on its Hull Construction. *American Journal of Archaeology* 89: 71–101.

Swiny, H. W., and Katzev, M. L.
1973   The Kyrenia Shipwreck: A Fourth-Century B.C. Greek Merchant Ship. Pp. 339–59 in *Marine Archaeology,* Colston Papers 23, ed. D. J. Blackman. London: Butterworths.

TAPA
1979   Θησαυροί της Αρχαίας Μακεδονίας. Thessalonike: Archaelogical Museum of Thessalonike.

Torr, C.
1894   *Ancient Ships.* Cambridge: Cambridge University.

Postclassical Effects on Classical Shoreline Sites: Straton's Tower/Caesarea Maritima, Israel and Torone, Chalkidike, Greece

T. W. HILLARD
J. L. BENESS

School of History, Philosophy, and Politics
Macquarie University
New South Wales
AUSTRALIA 2109

The two sites observed, both subject to rises in relative sea level, present two contrasting examples of the effects of postclassical processes on classical sites.

This paper argues that Caesarea's north bay provides a likely anchorage for Straton's Tower and presents the results of an underwater survey of the area in 1988 and 1990. The topography of any ancient anchorage has probably been obscured by coastal processes set in train by the building of Herod's spectacular artificial harbor to the south. As a result, part of the land site has collapsed into the sea (and into the putative anchorage).

At Torone, where first impressions of a probable anchorage might have suggested a similar interpretation, initial survey and excavations indicate that spillage from the adjoining land site has not occurred to any significant degree and that a rise in relative sea level has inundated a terrestrial site. An anchorage site, if it is to be found in that area, is to be sought further off shore.

CAESAREA'S NORTH BAY, AN ANCHORAGE OF HELLENISTIC STRATON'S TOWER?
(T. W. HILLARD)

Since the pinpointing of its position in 1960, the greatest amount of maritime archaeological interest in the port facilities of Caesarea Maritima has understandably focused on Sebastos, Herod's imposing artificial harbor complex named like the city it served after the Roman emperor Caesar Augustus and likewise built between 22 and 10 B.C.E. Sebastos utilized the full resources of Herod's wealth, imagination and state-of-the-art Roman marine technology (Joseph. bJ. 1. 408–14; Ant. 15. 331–41; cf. Oleson 1985; Oleson and Branton 1992; and Brandon [this volume]).

Straton's Tower, the settlement that formerly occupied the site chosen by Herod for his exhibition-city, was also a recognised anchorage of some significance, even if overshadowed by Dora and Ptolemais (Acco) in the north and Joppa (Jaffa), Ashkelon and Gaza to the south.[1] It was

[1] On Straton's Tower generally (and for a bibliography of earlier modern scholarship), its history and the problems of its location see Raban (1992a), and Roller (1992). The city served a rich hinterland, the products of which would have repaid a trading sojourn (Roller 1982: cf. Ringel 1975: 22–23; Holum et al. 1988). For a registration of Straton's Tower in

founded perhaps in the fourth century B.C.E. and possibly further developed during Ptolemaic occupation of this part of the Levantine coast. It is known to us as the point at which Zenon, an agent of Apollonios (treasurer to Ptolemy II Philadelphos), disembarked in 259 B.C.E. to commence a business tour of Judaea, the Transjordan and the Galilee. He re-embarked at Ptolemais.[2] After the third century B.C.E, it was swallowed by the Syrian empire until, with the gradual disintegration of Seleucid power, it became (with Dora, 12 km to the north) one of the bases of the local tyrant Zoilos (Joseph. Ant. 13. 324–35; cf. Levine 1975: 9).[3] He lost power (and Straton's Tower) to the expanding Hasmonean state just before the beginning of the first century B.C.E. Whether the port was utilized by the Hasmoneans is not known; there are some indications that the city was.[4]

Where was the original harbor located? An obvious site for an anchorage will have always been (or so it seems) the one developed subsequently by Herod. Here there was the advantage of an indentation in the coastline (where a rivulet had once emptied into the sea) and a small promontory to its immediate south. This promontory afforded some measure of protection from the prevalent southwesterly winds and features a rock outcrop that is the highest point on the visible coast. Although the assumption ought not to be made that the name of the town necessarily refers to an actual tower, this high point could have provided an essential lookout, desirable in the best circumstances but all the more so along coastlines infested, as this one was at the time, with pirates; and perhaps even the place for a lighthouse.[5] At the very least, it provided a navigational reference point. Following the discovery in 1976 of a submerged round tower just off the present shoreline within the Crusader fortress, Raban has further argued that there had been a Hellenistic *limen kleistos* here on the site where there is certain evidence of a later Herodian inner harbor.[6] But this anchorage (even with a sheltered inner basin) would not have been adequate by itself for the purposes of trade on any great scale.

The find of a stone anchor indicates that the larger bay to the south of the promontory was also utilized from at least the thirteenth century B.C.E. although there is no evidence that it was ever developed.[7] No matter how much activity might have occurred in its vicinity it must have remained a fair weather anchorage only. (Even more recent work has given attention to the coastline further south within the lee of *kurkar* islets, but that takes us even further from the probable site of the Hellenistic settlement.)

Hellenistic times, see the Zenon papyri PC2 59004 (mid-third century B.C.E.) and the citation of Artemidoros of Ephesos (ca. 100 B.C.E.) by Stephanos of Byzantion, s.v. Doros. To this may be added, Strabo 16.2.27. L.I. Levine (1975: 149, n. 43) points out that the settlement does not rate a mention in the late second century Letter of Aristeas. Nor, for that matter, does it figure in the Periplus of Ps.-Scylax (ca. 350 B.C.E.). On the relative strength of Ptolemais/Acco, Kashtan 1986: 103. Note that when the Romans, newly arrived in Palestine in the 60/50s B.C.E., bolstered the independence of the coastline cities, Straton's Tower was not granted, as were Dora, Joppa, Gaza and Ashkelon, the right to mint coins. On the other hand, see Raban (1992a: 17–18).

[2] Zenon papyri loc. cit.; cf. Ringel (1975: 23–24). The earlier significance of Straton's Tower as a trading station may be evidenced by the recognition in Athens of its possible founder, the philhellene Straton I (Levine 1975: 6; 145–46, nn. 16–18). But this much (i.e. the identity of its founder) is contentious (cf. Roller 1992: 23).

[3] Raban (1987: 71–88) has argued that it was during the tyrannate of Zoilos that Straton's Tower received the fortifications excavated by the Italian Mission to the site between 1959 and 1964 and still visible to the north of the city. Blakeley (1984) assigns the walls to Herod. For a continuation of the debate, see Raban (1992a); Blakeley (1992). For an alternative suggestion (reconciling the evidence and arguments on both sides of the debate) see Hillard (1992). Raban (1992a) has discerned traces of this wall (suggesting its southernmost line) within the crusader fortress.

[4] Levine (1975: 9; 149, n. 44); cf. Applebaum (1975: 62–64). There is no hard archaeological evidence for such an occupation.

[5] Hohlfelder (1983); though see Roller (1982: 50, n. 10); cf. Raban (1992a: 15–17) on the name Pyrgos (Tower)/ Migdal. South of Ashkelon it was the absence of distinguishable landmarks (with the exception of Mt Casium), which was the feature of the coastline considered most needful of note and which made, in that respect at least, this stretch of coastline treacherous (Pryor 1989: 82).

[6] For the most recent accounts of this feature, Raban (1987; 1989: 177–81 ["Area T1: Round Tower"]; 1992a: 10).

[7] Oleson et al. (1984: 286–88). In the eighteenth century, this bay was mistaken for Herod's Sebastos (Vann 1992; 278 fig. 5; 279) and this belief continued, in some quarters, into the twentieth century (Vann 1992: 287). On the possibility of its use in antiquity see Raban (1992b: 70).

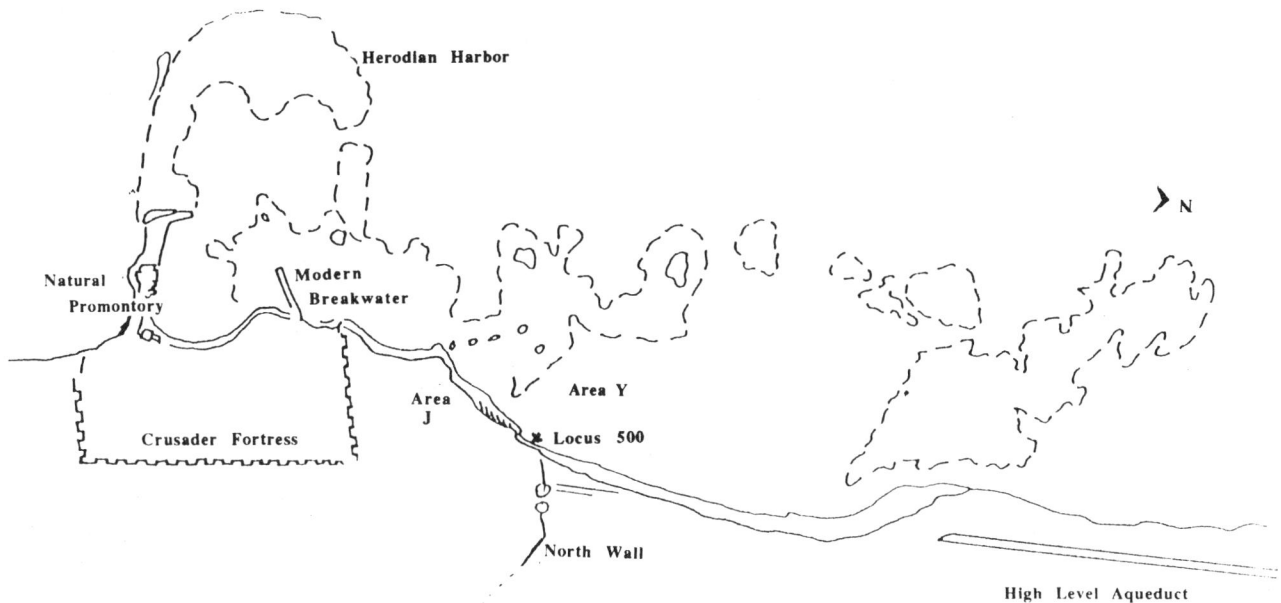

Fig. 1. A sketch map of the shoreline at Caesarea. The dotted lines marking submerged features, artificial and natural.

There is, on the other hand, more evidence of commercial development (in the Hellenistic period) to the north.[8] Finds in the much larger northern bay, now deepened (in the sense that it appears to be an even more significant indentation than it would have been in early antiquity) by the post-Herodian coastal process (on which, see below), suggest that there was continued shipping in that area from the Bronze Age through the Crusader period. The Caesarea Ancient Harbour Excavation Project (hereafter CAHEP) excavated a Roman shipwreck site (CAHEP Area Y) in the southern sector of the bay (see fig. 1). Systematic investigation of the wreck has revealed a merchant vessel of the late Republican or Augustan era, about 40 m in length and measuring 12 m in the beam, the largest from that period after the better-known Madrague de Giens ship.[9]

Over a six year period from 1975, Shelley Wachsmann and Kurt Raveh as Inspectors of Nautical Archaeology conducted a number of surveys along the coastline for the Israel Department of Antiquities. The results of those surveys are as yet unpublished but files held at CONRAD (the Center of Nautical and Regional Archaeology, Dor) were generously made available to the author. Around the area of the wreck site (CAHEP Area Y), Raveh reported the recovery of lead sheeting, bronze artifacts (scales, miniature bells), numerous marble finds including one 0.3 m fragment of a leg from the kneecap to above the ankle (identified as Hellenistic), and a crusader sword. With the exception of the last item, these finds may be classified as "Roman."

Anchors, of course, are the most common evidence of shipping. North of the wreck site, Raveh reports a heavier concentration of Byzantine, i.e. iron, anchors; to the south, stone anchors. It appears that earlier shipping, for obvious reasons to be outlined below, concentrated on the southern sector of the bay. At the extreme south end of the bay, about 500 m north of what became the main harbor, traders may have taken advantage of a smallish natural cove, partially sheltered by a line of off-shore *kurkar* rock outcrops, a reef that in antiquity may well have been a solid ridge.[10] In 1988, these "islands" were accurately mapped by CAHEP by means of a laser transit[11] (an interim sketch map based on

[8] This ties in well with Raban's argument that the earlier fortifications of the site did not encompass the southern area of the shoreline.

[9] Fitzgerald and Raban 1989: 184–190 ("Area Y: Roman Shipwreck"). For a further bibliography and brief description of the finds, see the registration in Parker (1992: 413), to which might be added Steffy (1994: 71 and 261, n. 31).

[10] Such breakwater reefs formed the simplest type of protection, long utilized along this coastline (Blackman 1982: 197–99; cf. Raban 1985: 11–44; for Sidon, see Blackman 1982: 199 fig. 9).

[11] This project was undertaken by Steven Sachs (University of Maryland) and the author. The results of that mapping are as yet unavailable.

aerial photography is provided in fig. 1) and a preliminary probe of the area was initiated. Earlier surveys and excavations on land had shown a higher concentration of Hellenistic sherds to the north of the Crusader fortress indicating perhaps that the Hellenistic settlement had tended to spread northwards rather than southwards of the area of the "main" (i.e. Herodian) harbor (Roller 1980: 35–42; 1983: 61–66).[12] This theory was further strengthened by the discovery of a partly submerged sea wall which runs along the north face of CAHEP's Area J. This was identified as a pre-Herodian harbor installation, possibly a quay, similar to those of Phoenician date at Athlit and Acco (Oleson et al. 1984: 301, and fig. 20; Raban 1987: 74–76, with figs. 7 and 8; Raban 1992a: 11, fig. 4; 13–14, figs. 7 and 8 [for plans]; fig. 10 [placing the quay in the context of Area J]). A trench subsequently opened in Area J next to this "loading quay" "produced the largest quantity of Hellenistic pottery yet discovered at Caesarea," and suggested commercial activity in this vicinity.[13] Subsequent seasons confirmed this impression (cf. Raban et al. 1980: 249–52 [on Area J–3]).

A preliminary search of the off-shore area in 1988 revealed, about 100 m north of CAHEP's Area J and about 20 m west (seaward) of the current beach line, a platform of ashlar blocks (CAHEP Area W, locus 500), mostly headers, its upper surface lying about 60 cm below sea level (Hillard 1989). This construction was oriented on a north-south axis. Similarities with the east-west structure adjoining Area J invite speculation that the two were connected in function if not physically, and perhaps marked the Hellenistic shoreline. This further suggests that the anchorage was larger than might have been expected. It certainly offered more than one modest loading quay nervously sheltering from southwesterlies at the southernmost point of the bay, and perhaps boasted docking facilities along more than 25 m of the shoreline and extending further north even than the east-west line of the (later?) fortification wall of the city.

A survey was also made of the *kurkar* "islands" that formed an outer barrier and afforded some measure of protection to the cove.[14] A 120 m north/south section was drawn of the line of four islands extending northwards from the outermost point of a "Byzantine breakwater" (built, apparently, to protect the commercial installations of Area J as the relative sea level rose in the Imperial period). At present, these islands, separated in three instances by distances of 16.5, 34.5 and 20.5 m, and just projecting above the surface of the water, provide limited shelter indeed (figs. 2 and 3: the "islands" are represented by the numbers 4; cf. fig. 4 for the north/south section). There is clear evidence, however, of these islands having been undercut by wave action and one clear instance where a shelf has toppled. There is reason to believe, therefore, that in antiquity they formed part of a more substantial ridge.[15] The protection afforded by such a feature would have been enhanced by a lower sea level.[16]

It is even possible that the island curtain was artificially reinforced at some stage.[17] In 1981, Wachsmann and Raveh found at a depth of 5 m and between two of the islands a seeming row of ashlar blocks, perhaps part of a wall, perhaps a jetty, or, "to be on the safe side" (Raveh), part of a ballast.[18] Extending from the northernmost of the four islands, they identified a wall 2 m wide and oriented in the direction of a larger islet to the north.[19] The author was unfortunately unaware of these earlier findings at the time of

[12] For a summation of earlier finds, see Vann "Straton's Tower" in Raban (1989: 25–27; cf. Raban 1992a: 20–21; though see also the persistent reservations of Roller 1992: 24).

[13] Holum et al. (1988: 44; cf. Oleson et al. 1984: 301–2; Vann "Straton's Tower" in Raban 1989: 26). The material dated from the third to the second centuries B.C.E. suggests that the port did not languish under Seleucid control of the coast; though the significance of the finds, as noted above, is still debated (Raban 1992a; Roller 1992).

[14] The author was assisted in this survey by J. L. Beness (then of the University of New England, Australia) and L. Ritchie/Vann (University of North Carolina).

[15] On the possibility of the reef's deterioration since antiquity, see Raban (1992a: 21, citing Neeve et al. 1978), adding the hypothesis that a submergence of the sea floor just west of the reef caused by a longshore fault line has further exposed the *kurkar* islets to stronger wave energies.

[16] On the rise of relative sea level at the site see Raban (1983: 250).

[17] The "plugging" of gaps in such off-shore reefs with rubble is noted elsewhere (Blackman 1982: 196 and 209, n. 80 for further reference).

[18] Photographs were taken on June 28th, 1981 (CONRAD Caes. 1330, Dive Sheet no. 163. Picture nos. 14 14 10; 14 14 11). They are now held by the Department of Antiquities in Jerusalem. The dimensions of the blocks (60 × 20 × 20 cm; 80 × 30 × 20 cm) perhaps suggest Roman work.

[19] CONRAD Caes. 829. Dive Sheet 115. Picture 140 006.

Fig. 2. Panorama of Caesarea's north bay: 1) Area J; 2) Partially submerged structure (possibly a quay); 3) Remains of a Byzantine breakwater; 4) *Kurkar* islands.

Fig. 3. Panorama of Caesarea's north bay: 1) *Kurkar* islands The dotted line represents the line of the E-W profile. The furthest figure, behind the group on the right, stands at the location of the mosaic pavement.

the 1988 probe and during a shorter reconnaissance conducted in 1990 (with J. L. Beness) was unable to locate these items. The protection provided by such a barrier might have been relative. Not all ports needed to be safely enclosed to qualify as commercial termini. The idea of ships coming to grief within a harbor itself was not a strange one to entrepreneurs or law-makers.[20] The Classical world had learned to live with less than ideal conditions inside harbor areas. Note, for example, the command of the god Asclepius

to Aelius Aristides (as treatment of one of the latter's many ailments) that he await a time "when the harbor waves were swollen by the south wind and ships were in distress, [and then] sail to the other side, eating honey and acorns from an oak tree, and vomit." (Aristides 47. 65 Keil)

A probe was made of the depth of this "cove" (which shipping could only have utilized by turning in from the north and sailing southward along the lee side of the islands). Depth was gauged along an east/west axis at 5 m

---

[20] Digest 14.2.4. Captains who plied this otherwise (nautically) safe coastline (i.e. with regard to sailing a mile or so offshore) were accustomed to negotiating dangerous islets, reefs and banks in the approach to anchorages. Even the well-developed harbor site of later Acre (anc. Ptolemais) tested navigational skills (Pryor 1989: 81–82).

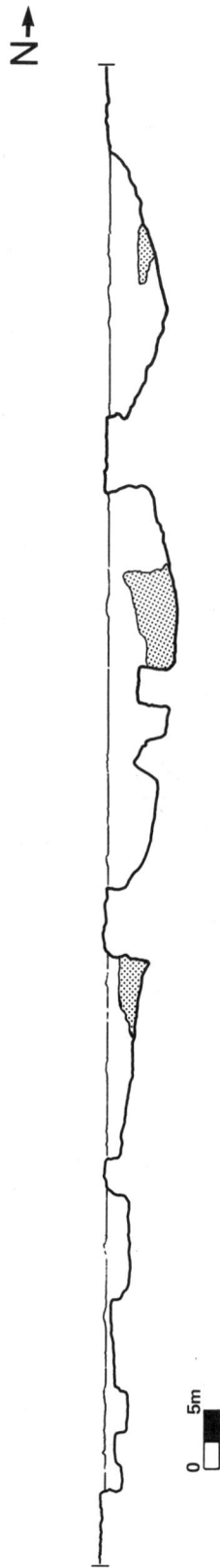

Fig. 4. A north/south section of the *kurkar* reef at Caesarea.

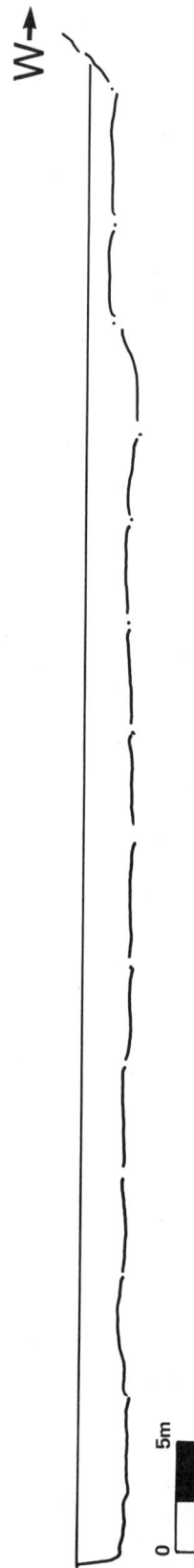

Fig. 5. An east/west section of the present depth of the putative anchorage.

intervals and an east/west section drawn (fig. 5).[21] The area is at present uniformly shallow, rarely being more than 2 m. (At one point it was 2.18 m and at another, its deepest, 2.33 m.) A sub-bottom profile was obtained with the use of a compressed air jet and found to follow similar contours of depth, the sand being only 18 to 50 cm deep. The deepest draft in the area, then, given the present profile, would be 2.61 m. This would be lessened by a lower relative sea level in the Hellenistic period.

Two alternative conclusions might follow from this. One is that the quays were serviced only or primarily by lighters, while the merchant ships anchored in the deeper central part of the bay or outside the island barrier.[22] A fully-operational port did not necessarily require a draft deep enough to take all ocean-going cargo ships. The other possibility, not mutually exclusive of the first, and the one that I favor here, is that the cove had the benefit of a deeper draft in ancient times and had been subsequently filled with spill from the considerable post-Herodian coastline erosion. The construction of Herod's harbor formed an artificial barrier along the line of the off-shore currents. The harbor structure dammed the longshore sand transport from the south and produced a wave diffraction that then gouged the "starved" beaches to the north. This was first described by Rim and Inman, as an explanation for the collapse of the last 2 km of the High Level aqueduct on its northern approach to the city.[23]

The force of the latter process is annually evidenced by the undercutting of the shoreline by winter storms that have strewn this area with heavy rubble. This disintegration of the terrestrial site into the sea is evident at a number of places along the shoreline, most spectacularly perhaps where the north wall of the Crusader fortress is collapsing. During the 1988 season, at a point on the heights directly above the area of the north bay being surveyed, a salvage excavation was undertaken of a mosaic floor, probably Early Byzantine, found cut by a modern dirt roadway along the edge of the embankment ca. 7.5 m above sea level (Area J–3): its

fragmentary state suggesting an undercutting of the cliff face at a point not considered dangerously precipitous in late antiquity.[24] In the preliminary probe of the north bay it was not possible to ascertain whether the sub-surface levels struck were bedrock or tightly compacted rubble. The latter seems more probable. In its afterlife this basin was in the nature of a closed lagoon on three sides, with no current to flush the area regularly to prevent silting and to help disperse the heavier rubble that strong westerly waves were now bringing down on the area.

There is every reason to suspect that this cove (the southernmost section of Caesarea's north bay) served as an anchorage, if not the anchorage, to Straton's Tower, its natural topography obscured by postclassical intrusion. There are some, most significantly R. Stieglitz, the director of excavations in Area J, who would gibe at the classification of this area as a harbor, though there is no reason to posit anything so developed as that suggested in some publications.[25] Those with doubts would allude to Strabo's implicit reference to Straton's Tower having a [single] landing place (prosormon echon). This might be too heavy a weight to place on Strabo's second-hand (and certainly by the time of any putative revised edition, out-of-date) account; though if literality is demanded, why not the north bay, since only a modest anchorage need be envisaged by Strabo's text? The northern anchorage seems to have continued in use even after the building of Herod's harbor to the south. The shipwreck excavated by CAHEP seems to me at least to be evidence of this, or at least that the anchorage was in use at the time when Herod's harbor was being constructed. This means that Herod had either looked to the use of this area as a preliminary to his major harbor works or that this basin had escaped the more general decay from which Straton's Tower was said to be suffering before Herod turned his attention to the site.[26] Shipping activity in the general area of Caesarea probably continued to follow well-established patterns, i.e. shipping continued to use the northern bay. A nineteenth century Admiralty map (reproduced in the Sur-

[21] In this survey, the author was assisted by (Dr.) J. J. McInerney (then a graduate student at the University of California, Berkeley).

[22] Such a service trade could still be seen in operation along this coastline at the end of the last century.

[23] For a convenient account of the argument, see Nir (1985), citing Rim (1951) and Inman (1974: 2049–62); and Inman (1978). The differing views of Neeve et al. (1973), favoring tectonic action as the reason for deterioration here, must be acknowledged.

[24] This was supervised by R. Stieglitz, the director of excavations in Area J (Raban et al. 1990: 252 and pl. 27 D).

[25] E.g. Raban (1992b: 72) implicitly suggesting a link up with the walls of Straton's Tower; cf. Holum et al. (1988: 46, fig. 24). In fact, Raban (1992b) envisages the more modest open anchorages outside Herod's Sebastos as operating independently of the latter and "only during calmer seas in late spring and early fall" (serving the municipal needs of the city, which he goes so far as to say Sebastos did not).

[26] Josephus bJ 1. 408. For speculation about the reasons for this decay see Hillard (1992: 47–48).

vey of Western Palestine 1882) indicates a mole of pillars (doubtless a Crusader construction on the analogy with the breakwater or jetty of columns found within the Crusader fortress) where the outer (Byzantine) wall of Caesarea reaches the shore in the north bay (Vann 1992: 285, fig. 11). Raveh reports a short quay of pillars at this point (which he orients north/south: the Admiralty map draws an east/west mole) that joins up at its southern end with an older ashlar construction.[27]

For what it is worth, rabbinical literature preserves the story of Rabbi Bar Kappara "walking up and down the cliffs by the sea at Caesarea when he saw a ship that had been wrecked in the ocean and a proconsul emerging from it naked."[28] In context, it is clear that the exegetical elucidations of Ecclesiastes 11.1 (of which this is one) conform to certain (probably apocryphal) motifs; but the item is clearly intended to have some topographical credibility, especially with the addition of such gratuitous detail as the cliffs. The anecdote is clearly not set in the main harbor, and the northern bay offers the only location at Caesarea where one might observe such a mishappening from an eminence of any height while "walking"; and the passage, if we place any credence in the item, suggests that shipping of some importance could come to grief in this area.

THE "HARBOR" AT TORONE?
(T. W. HILLARD AND J. L. BENESS)

The conditions that presently prevail in Caesarea's north bay that obscure the ancient topography and that are likely to continue doing so without heavy excavation, are surely the result of interference with the shoreline environment. As a result, a disintegrating land site has invaded the sea. At Torone, the opposite has happened. Our work there began as a search for the port facilities, which must have been more than average given ancient reports (to which we will return later).[29] Torone, practically at the southern tip of Sithonia, the middle promontory of the Chalkidike, provides an unbroken archaeological sequence from the Neolithic through to the Byzantine period, and impressive evidence of its postbyzantine occupation, during part of which time it served as a Turkish station contested by Turks and Venetians in AD 1659. From the beginning it was the sea that must have determined the city's significance. Artifactual evidence shows that by the Early Bronze Age (possibly by the late Neolithic) the settlement was not an isolated one, but rather a point well-integrated into a northern Aegean network embracing Lemnos and the Troad.[30] Excavations from 1992 of an impressive fourth century B.C.E. merchant ship at Alonessos that E. Hadjidaki describes (this volume), and specifically its cargo of amphoras from the Chalkidike provide a forceful reminder, if one was needed, of the flourishing trade in the area. Remnants (unfortunately unpublished) of seaborne trade in the form of late fifth century Mendean amphoras were discovered closer to Torone, near the southeast corner of Sithonia, in 1977—and perhaps again in 1981.[31]

A distinctive feature of the site is the "Lekythos," a small peninsula presently rising some 13 m above sea level

---

[27]This installation is at least 300 m north of CAHEP's Area J. The shoreline utilized may have been quite a lengthy stretch. The possibility that earlier observers were looking at some disintegration from the outer reach of the Byzantine walls could be entertained.

[28]Ecclesiastes Rabba XI 1 (quoted from Midrash Rabbah, translated under the editorship of R. H. Freedman and M. Simon (London, Soncino Press, 1939, 285); cf. Levine (1975: 55–56 and 187, n. 109). I thank Robert Hohlfelder for drawing my attention to this passage.

[29]After reconnaissance of the site by the two authors in 1990, underwater work has been conducted at Torone in 1993 and 1994 as a *synergasia* with the Greek Ephoria of Underwater Antiquities under the aegis of the Australian Expedition to Torone, itself conducted under the auspices of the Athens Archaeological Society and the Australian Archaeological Institute at Athens and directed by Professor Alexander Cambitoglou with Dr. J. K. Papadopoulos as Deputy Director. (Record of the Australian excavations there from 1975 can be found regularly in *To Ergon* and in *Praktika* 1984. A further introduction to the site is provided by Cambitoglou and Papadopoulos 1988.)

The Ephoria team was led by Chr. Samiou and N. Lianos. The Australian team has consisted of the authors, T. Sprent (surveyor), C. Coroneos and T. Smith. Any speculation that follows owes much to discussion with colleagues, but should not be assumed to be one of confident consensus. The underwater investigation of Torone is in its early stages. The authors will bear responsibility for any retractions that may need to be made in the light of further discoveries.

[30]For a study of early trade routes correlating data on sea currents and wind patterns (Liritzis 1988: see esp. 242 on the northern Aegean). Further afield, silver found in Mycenae's shaft graves has been argued to derive from the Chalkidike (Stos-Gale and Macdonald 1991: 271–79, cf. 280).

[31]Touchais (1982: 578 [from a press release]; cf. Parker 1992: 406–7). On the probable importance of Torone as a port in the trading networks of the Black Sea, Aegean and, beyond that, the wider Mediterranean, see Papadopoulos (1989: 79–81).

Fig. 6. The Lekythos, seen from the east across the north bay.

and joined to the mainland by a narrow isthmus, which served in Classical times as part of the city's inner fortifications (fig. 6). To the south rises the Anemomylos (90 m) which served as the Classical city's acropolis (seen rising to the left of fig. 7). Further to the south and towering over both is the Vigla (230 m), which was fortified in the Hellenistic period (fig. 8).

Torone will be best known to Classical scholars for events in the winter of 424/423 B.C.E. when, "protected" by an Athenian garrison, it was taken by the Spartans (one of the fruits of Brasidas' Long March). The Athenians were caught napping in the agora: some escaped by land; others to two Athenian ships that were anchored in the vicinity and thence to the Lekythos. When it fell, the Athenians who could escaped to the ships. In the following year, it was retaken by the Athenian general Kleon. Its occupancy was contested a number of times throughout the fourth century B.C.E., but it seems to have become a significant Macedonian garrison in the third and second centuries B.C.E., probably to guard one of the main sea routes to Kassandreia—and Thessaloniki (once the Potidaea canal had been opened).

In 169 B.C.E., C. Marcius Figulus, commander of a Roman fleet in a war that would see in the following year the effective destruction of Macedonian power, after an unsuccessful siege of Kassandreia, put in near Torone (together with the fleet of King Eumenes), began a siege of the place, but abandoned it on observing its strong defense force (Liv. 44.12.7–8). In the division of Macedonia that followed the battle of Pydna in 168 B.C.E., the harbor(s?) of Torone, together with three others to be found in the Chalkidike *(portus ad Toronen ac montem Atho Aeneamque et Acanthum),* were considered alongside the populous urban centers of Thessalonica, Cassandrea and the fertile lands of Pallene as one of the assets of the area (Livy 45.30.4).

It might have been thought that the focus of Livy's assessment (even if reference is made there to a plurality of harbors at Torone, which the Latin allows) is likely to have been the sheltered bay of Porto Koufo, even though approximately 3 km to the south of Torone, still considered to be one of the most magnificent natural harbors in the Mediterranean (Heikell 1982: 238; cf. Meritt 1923: 453–4), with depths of 40 to 60 m in some places and sheltered in almost all conditions, and which Thucydides places "in the territory of the Toronaeans," when he says that Kleon put in there (Thuc. 5.2). (Its position might be located in fig. 8, behind the wide massif of the Vigla [center] in the bay framed by the mountains rising to the left of the photograph.)

Yet this might be doubted. The inclusion in Livy's assessment, of the relatively featureless shoreline of Ierissos Bay (on which lay Acanthus), sheltered though it may be,[32]

---

[32] Not to mention the modest anchorages to be found around Mt. Athos, and the port of Aenea, fifteen Roman miles to the south of "Thessalonica" on the Thermaic Gulf, which one suspects was included in this register rather because of the richness of its hinterland (Liv. 44.10.7; cf. 44.32.8) and/or as a focus for pious tourism, being a city founded by Aeneas and at which annual sacrifice was offered to him (Dionys. Hal. 1.49.4; Liv. 40.4.9).

Fig. 7. The Lekythos and Anemomylos.

suggests that spectacular natural advantages were not the criteria. And Thucydides' incidental description of the site (5.2–3) distinctly and plainly differentiates *Koufos* from "the harbor of Torone,"[33] when he describes Kleon's fleet as having sailed out of the former and around to the latter.

Where, then, was the "harbor" of Torone—or, at least, the anchorage which Thucydides might have described as such?[34] A few possibilities might be considered (though we may confess now that we tentatively favor the sheltered portion of the bay to the immediate northeast of the Lekythos, lying off that part of the shoreline seen to the center left of fig. 6 and to the center of fig. 7). A small sandy bay to the south of the Lekythos provided a roadstead within the protection of Torone's walls (a portion of it is shown in figs. 9 and 10) but is exposed and offers poor shelter in many conditions. Thus, it had the advantage of being enclosed to the landward side but could not have served as an all-weather anchorage.

No definitive statement about the anchorages of Torone will be able to be made until a systematic investigation is conducted of the now dry flood plain behind the north beach (until recent times a marsh) (figs. 11 and 12) where currently are to be found on a rock outcrop the remains of the early Christian basilica of Agios Athanasios (the vague outline of the Lekythos can be discerned towards the left of fig. 11). Older members of the local community remember small craft moored in this area (or at least claim to have been told of such). Similar dried marshes exist in a number of bays to the north, perhaps suggesting that the relative sea level was higher in fairly recent times, although it must be noted that the plain at Torone was also fed by fresh water from the inland. The underwater investigations of 1993 and 1994 (on which more immediately below) seem to suggest rather that the relative sea level was even lower in antiquity, *perhaps* diminishing the likelihood that the area was a bay or lagoon at that time. (The evidence, however, is not necessarily indicative of a gradually transgressive water level, namely of the sea encroaching upon the land in a steady one-way manner.) Deep silting would need to be demonstrated—and may well be by future investigation. The possibility that this area served some maritime function cannot yet be ruled out, though it can be said that ships anchored in this vicinity might seem to have provided a poor escape route for fleeing Athenians who wanted to reach the Lekythos. Certainly after the fall of the latter, the ships by which the surviving Athenians fled were "at sea"; i.e., in

[33] Following the now generally accepted emendation of Thucydides' text by Pluygers and Leake. This is quite different to readings one might find in older translations such as Jowett's.

[34] Torone is probably to be characterized as a port rather than a harbor (on which important distinction, see Rickman 1985, 1988).

Fig. 8. The Vigla,Torone.

open water.[35] It is hoped that drilling in this area will be a project of a future season.

Whatever the opportunities that should be found to have been offered in the area of the plain, it would be surprising if the shoreline to the immediate north of the Lekythos was not utilized. The wide sandy bay to the north of the ancient town and especially its southernmost reaches along (and in the lee of) the isthmus to the Lekythos would have offered safe anchorage at most times of the year. The sheltered nature of the southernmost sweep of this broad bay and, in particular, the quietude in almost all conditions of a short space of shoreline from the rocky face of the Lekythos itself southeast for a distance of approximately 100 m (only after which, it might be noted, a sand beach begins), together with its convenient proximity to the fortified town, has led previously to the sensible assumption that this locality was likely to have served as an ancient roadstead. The Lekythos shields it from any southerly fetch (likely to be the most troublesome) or westerly winds, only refracted (and then comparatively modest) waves reaching the area. The cape off Destinika to the north shields it from the direct effect of northerlies. The mountains to the east protect it in

large degree from that quarter. A further advantage of such an anchorage would have been the fact that a ship under sail approaching from the southern end of Sithonia has only to round the point of the Lekythos to be in sheltered water; and to be within 100 m of the anchorage. The fact that the shoreline in this area was in some sort of public use may be further suggested by the possible indications of a gate that opened from the city wall onto this district.[36]

This probability was in the minds of the authors when they snorkelled over the site in 1990. Within fifteen minutes in the water a line of ashlar blocks had been discerned lying *in situ* at approximately a depth of 1.5 m about 38 m off shore, and running roughly parallel to the shoreline. The blocks form a single (jogged) line, but were embedded in a thicker wall of conglomerate which at first sight appeared cement-like and which ran right across the area in roughly the same line. (It was subsequently identified as natural.) Initially it was thought that we may have had here the remnants of port facilities, with the construction acting as some sort of outer protection for a sheltered anchorage between it and the present shoreline.[37]

[35] Thuc. 4.115.3: the Athenians fled "to the sea and the ships."

[36] The remains of an impressive wall (designated Wall C by the Australian Expedition) may still be observed along the shoreline here. Its solid foundations give way at one point to looser fill, suggesting that the projecting blocks at that point may not have been load bearing.

[37] All that was needed was the discovery of the trophy which, according to Thucydides, Kleon set up "near the harbor" (5.3). Indeed, three other blocks were observed at one point (and recorded in initial sketches) abutting the inner face of this

Fig. 9. The south bay at Torone, showing collapse of ruins into the bay.

First impressions might have suggested that this site replicated Caesarea's north bay in many respects. Clearly there has been spillage of architectural remains from the Lekythos and from the isthmus into the sea. This is particularly the case in the more weather-beaten south bay, where collapse from the mediaeval fortification is still visible above

Fig. 10. The south bay (detail).

wall, apparently *in situ,* cut in such a fashion as to suggest an intended concentricity. Imagination ran wild. (In fact, their actual function still has not been determined.)

Fig. 11. The now dry floodplain, looking towards the north bay.

the water (see figs. 9 and 10), but is also manifest to the north. Limestone fragments and ashlar masonry can be seen lying underwater from the top of the Lekythos, and the uniformly shallow area off the isthmus, which particularly interests us here, is strewn with rubble (see fig. 13).

Excavation disabused first impressions. A full account of the work of the *synergasia* may be found in Samiou et al. (1995) and elaboration is neither necessary nor appropri-

ate here. It can be reported, however, that within the first hours of a systematic exploratory search and survey of the area, the line of a wall had been found in a few centimeters of water, and this was followed by a number of others (to at least a distance of 25 m off-shore), all of them visible from the surface in clear conditions and with minimal clearing (with present indications being that some of these at least belonged to the antique period). It was clear that no heavy

Fig. 12. The floodplain, viewed from the isthmus of the Lekythos.

Fig. 13. Rubble and fallen masonry littering the submerged site to the immediate north of the isthmus, lying in a depth of 0.5-1 m.

rubble had significantly altered the natural topography of the site, indeed that scarcely any evidence suggests major interference to that topography, particularly within the region up to 20 m from the present shore[38]; and that this, almost certainly all of it, was a submerged terrestrial site. At Torone the sea has invaded what was at one time the land site, the dimensions of which will be better understood after the completion of our investigation of the line of conglomerate (two distinct lines crossing the site have now been discerned), which we now believe to be beachrock formed

Fig. 14. Ashlar masonry in outer line of conglomerate at a depth of approximately 1.75 m.

[38] Notwithstanding such features as, at one point, an apparently collapsed pavement of worked blocks, seemingly in secondary use, which may belong to the Medieval or early modern period.

along previous shores. The exact relationship between the latter and the line of ashlar masonry first observed in 1990 and with other features (one of which is shown in fig. 14) since discovered has yet to be determined.

The most likely interpretation at this stage is that of tectonic disturbance[39]; and one explanation for the fact that there is only a superficial layer of rubble over the site (where, indeed, it appears) and of the fact that only the lines of walls can now be observed will be the prompt salvage of any usable building material by the local population from what would have been at most waist-deep water. The investigation, then, has so far revealed what was once a gradually-sloping plain (gradient approx. 1:20) outside the city wall,

which was in commercial or domestic use. Shipping, if it used this area, must have ridden at anchor off this plain,[40] still adequately sheltered, utilising the gradually-sloping sea bottom for another 20 m beyond, before the steep drop-off that reaches a depth of 10 m within the next twenty. One interesting ramification of these findings, yet to be resolved, is the possible challenge to any conception of the site based on Thucydides' description of the "narrow" neck joining the Lekythos to the mainland. The isthmus, if the apparent evidence of earlier shorelines and a change in relative sea levels of ca. 1.75 m is valid, was at one time at least twice as wide as it is presently. At both sites we are challenged to conceptualize these particular areas afresh.

REFERENCES

Alexandersson, T.
1972   Mediterranean Beachrock Cementation: Marine Precipitation of Mg-Calcite. Pp. 203–23 in *The Mediterranean Sea: A Natural Sedimentation Laboratory*, ed. D.J. Stanley. Stroudsburg, PA: Dowden, Hutchinsons and Ross, Inc.

Applebaum, S.
1975   Hellenistic Cities of Judaea and its Vicinity. Some New Aspects. Pp. 62–64 in *The Ancient Historian and his Materials. Essays in Honour of C. E. Stevens on his Seventieth Birthday*, ed. B. Levick. Gregg International: Westmead, Farnborough, Hants, UK.

Blackman, D. J.
1982   Ancient Harbours in the Mediterranean. *International Journal of Nautical Archaeology* 11: 79–104 (Part 1); 185–211 (Part 2).

Blakely, J. A.
1984   A stratigraphically determined date for the inner fortification wall at Caesarea Maritima. Pp. 3–38 in *The Answers Lie Below: Essays in Honor of Lawrence Edmund Toombs*, ed. H. O. Thompson. Lanham, MD: University Press of America.

1992   Stratigraphy and the North Fortification of Herod's Caesarea. Pp. 26–41 in *Caesarea Papers. Straton's Tower, Herod's Harbour, and Roman and Byzantine Caesarea*, ed. R. L. Vann. *Journal of Roman Archaeology*, Supp. Ser. 5. Ann Arbor.

Cambitoglou, A.
1984   Torone. *Praktikates en Athenais Archaiologikes Etaireias* 140: 40–65.

Cambitoglou, A., and Papadopoulos, J. K.
1988   Excavations at Torone, 1986: A Preliminary Report. *Mediterranean Archaeology* 1: 180–217.

Fitzgerald, M., and Raban. A.
1989   Area Y: Roman Shipwreck. Pp. 184–90 in *The Harbours of Caesarea Maritima. The Results of the Caesarea Ancient Harbour Excavation Project, 1980–1985*. BAR International Series 491. Oxford: B.A.R.

Guidoboni, E.
1989   Catalogo. Area mediterranea. Pp. 622–717 in *I terremoti prima del Mille in Italia e nell' area mediterranea*, ed. E. Guidoboni. Bologna: SGA Storia-Geofisica-Ambiente.

[39] Record of the relatively common disturbance in this region in antiquity and since can be found in the chronicle of Guidoboni 1989; and, more specifically in that provided by Papazachos and Papazachou.

[40] Beaching might not have been an option here. The absence of a beach for the 100 m of shoreline that especially interests us might be significant. Sand deposits only begin to the east of this area (i.e. towards the more exposed area of the bay). While lithification of beachrock may occur under beach deposits (and occurs under different conditions at different sites; Alexandersson 1972; cf. Hopley 1986), the evidence at Torone might suggest that the process there was the result of a general lack of wave action within this relatively small protected area. This observation is consistent with the absence of such conglomerate in the relatively exposed small bays to the south of the Lekythos and the formation of beach in those small inlets. Thus, conditions conducive to beaching at the suggested landing place might not have been present.

Heikell, R.
1982   *Greek Waters Pilot.* St. Ives, England: Imray Laurie Norie and Wilson Ltd.

Hillard, T. W.
1989   A Hellenistic Quay in Caesarea's North Bay? *Mediterranean Archaeology* 2: 143–46.
1992   A mid–1st c. B.C. date for the walls of Straton's Tower? Pp. 42–48 in *Caesarea Papers. Straton's Tower, Herod's Harbour, and Roman and Byzantine Caesarea,* ed. R. L. Vann. *Journal of Roman Archaeology,* Supp. Ser. 5. Ann Arbor.

Hohlfelder, R. L.
1983   The Caesarea Coastline Before Herod: Some Preliminary Observations. *Bulletin of the American Schools of Oriental Research* 252: 67–68.

Holum, K. G.; R. L. Hohlfelder; R. J. Bull; and A. Raban
1988   *King Herod's Dream. Caesarea on the Sea,* New York and London: W. W. Norton & Co.

Holum, K., and A. Raban.
1993   Caesarea. Identification, History, Exploration and Excavation. Pp. 270–72 in vol. 1 of *The New Encyclopedia of Archaeological Excavations in the Holy Land,* eds. E. Stern, A. Lewinson-Gilboa, and J. Aviram. The Israel Exploration Society. Jerusalem: Carta.

Hopley, D.
1986   Beachrock as a sea-level indicator. Pp. 157–74 in *Sea-level Research: A Manual for the Collection and Evaluation of Data,* ed. O. van de Plassche. Norwich: Geo Books.

Inman, D. L.
1974   Ancient and Modern Harbours: A Repeating Phylogeny. *Proceedings of the 14th Coastal Eng. Conf.* Copenhagen.
1978   The Impact of Coastal Structures on Shorelines. *Coastal Zone* 78, vol. 3: 2265–72.

Kashtan, N.
1986   Ptolemais-Acco as a main maritime city during the Hellenistic-Roman period. P. 103 in *Cities on the Sea - Past and Present. First International Symposium on Harbours, Port Cities and Coastal Topography. Summaries,* ed. A. Raban. Haifa.

Levine, L. I.
1975   *Caesarea Under Roman Rule.* Leiden: Brill.

Liritzis, V. McG.
1988   Seafaring, Craft and Cultural Contact in the Aegean during the 3rd Millenium BC. *International Journal of Nautical Archaeology* 17: 237–56.

Meritt, B. D.
1923   Scione, Mende and Torone. *American Journal of Archaeology* 27: 447–60.

Neeve, D.; N. Bakler; S. Moshkovitz; A. Kaufman; M. Magaritz; and R. Gofna
1973   Recent Faulting along the Mediterranean Coast of Israel. *Nature* 245: 254–56.

Neeve, D.; E. Schachnai; J. K. Hall; N. Backler; and Z. Ben Avraham
1978   The Young (Post Lower Pliocene) Geological History of the Caesarea Structure. *Israel Journal of Earth Sciences* 27: 43–64.

Nir, Y.
1985   The Destruction of the Roman High Level Aqueduct and the Herodian Harbour at Caesarea. Pp. 185–94 in *Harbour Archaeology. Proceedings of the 1st International Workshop on Ancient Mediterranean Harbours, Caesarea Maritima 24–28/6/83,* ed. A. Raban. BAR Internatinal Series 257. Oxford: B.A.R.

Oleson, J. P.
1985   Herod and Vitruvius: Preliminary Thoughts on Harbour Engineering at Sebastos. Pp. 165–72 in *Harbour Archaeology: Proceedings of the First International Workshop on Ancient Mediterranean Harbours, Caesarea Maritima 24–28/6/83,* ed. A. Raban. BAR International Series 257. Oxford: B.A.R.

Oleson, J. P., and G. Branton
1992   The technology of King Herod's harbour. Pp. 49–67 in *Caesarea Papers. Straton's Tower, Herod's Harbour, and Roman and Byzantine Caesarea,* ed. R. L. Vann. *Journal of Roman Archaeology,* Supp. Ser. 5. Ann Arbor.

Oleson, J. P.; R. L. Hohlfelder; A. Raban; and R. L. Vann
1984   The Caesarea Ancient Harbour Excavation Project (CAHEP): Preliminary Report on the 1980–1983 Seasons. *Journal of Field Archaeology* 11: 281–305.

Papadopoulos, J. K.
1989   Roman amphorae from the excavations at Torone. *Archaiologike Ephemeris:* 67–103.

Papazachos, B., and Papazachou, C.
1989   *Hoi Seismoi tes Helladas.* Thessaloniki Οι Σεισμοί της Ελλάδας (Εκδόσεις ΖΗΤΗ): Zete.

Parker, A. J.
1992   *Ancient Shipwrecks of the Mediterranean and the Roman Provinces.* BAR International Series 580. Oxford: B.A.R.

Pryor, J. H.
1989   Winds, Waves, and Rocks: The Routes and the Perils Along Them. Pp. 71–85 in *Maritime Aspects of Migration,* ed. K. Friedland. Cologne.

Raban, A.
1983   Recent maritime archaeological research in Is-

rael. *International Journal of Nautical Archaeology* 12: 229–51.

1985   The Ancient Harbours of Israel in Biblical Times. Pp. 11–44 in *Harbour Archaeology: Proceedings of the First International Workshop on Ancient Mediterranean Harbours, Caesarea Maritima 24–28/6/83*, ed. A. Raban. BAR International Series 257. Oxford: B.A.R.

1987   The City Walls of Straton's Tower: Some New Archaeological Data. *Bulletin of the American Schools of Oriental Research* 268: 71–88.

1989   *The Harbours of Caesarea Maritima. Results of the Caesarea Ancient Harbour Excavation Project, 1980–1985.* BAR International Series 491. Oxford: B.A.R.

1992a   In Search of Straton's Tower. Pp. 7–22 in *Caesarea Papers. Straton's Tower, Herod's Harbour, and Roman and Byzantine Caesarea*, ed. R. L. Vann. *Journal of Roman Archaeology*, Supp. Ser. 5. Ann Arbor.

1992b   Kaisareia e pros Sebasto limeni: two harbours for two entities? (Καισαρεια ἡ προς Σεβαστῶ λιμένι). Pp. 68–74 in *Caesarea Papers. Straton's Tower, Herod's Harbour, and Roman and Byzantine Caesarea*, ed. R. L. Vann. *Journal of Roman Archaeology*, Supp. Ser. 5. Ann Arbor.

Raban, A.; Hohlfelder, R. L.; Holum, K. G.; Stieglitz, R. R.; and Vann, R. L.

1990   Caesarea and its Harbours: A Preliminary Report on the 1988 Season. *Israel Exploration Journal* 40: 261–56.

1993   Maritime Caesarea. Pp. 286–91 in vol. 1 of *The New Encyclopedia of Archaeological Excavations in the Holy Land*, eds. E. Stern, A. Lewinson-Gilboa, and J. Aviram. The Israel Exploration Society. Jerusalem: Carta.

Rickman, G. E.

1985   Towards a Study of Roman ports. Pp. 105–14 in *Harbour Archaeology. Proceedings of the First International Workshop of Ancient Mediterranean Harbours, Caesarea Maritima 24–28/6/83*, ed. A. Raban. BAR International Series 257. Oxford: B.A.R.

1988   The Archaeology and History of Roman Ports. *International Journal of Nautical Archaeology* 17: 257–67

Rim, M.

1951   Sand and Soil in the Coastal Plain of Israel. A Study of the Rate of Accumulation. *Israel Exploration Journal* 1: 33–48.

Ringel, J.

1975   *Césarée de Palestine. Étude Historique et Archeologique.* Paris: Editions Ophyrs.

Roller, D. W.

1982   The Northern Plain of Sharon in the Hellenistic Period. *Bulletin of the American Schools of Oriental Research* 247: 43–52.

1983   The Problem of the Location of Straton's Tower. *Bulletin of the American Schools of Oriental Research* 252: 61–66.

1992   Straton's Tower: Some Additional Thoughts. Pp. 23–25 in *Caesarea Papers. Straton's Tower, Herod's Harbour, and Roman and Byzantine Caesarea*, ed. R. L. Vann. *Journal of Roman Archaeology*, Supp. Ser. 5. Ann Arbor.

Samiou, Ch.; Lianos, N.; Beness; J. Lea; Coroneos, C.; Hillard, T.; Smith, T.; and Sprent, T.

1995   The Underwater Survey of Torone: A Preliminary Report of the 1993 Season. *Mediterranean Archaeology* 8: 89–100.

Steffy, J. R.

1994   *Wooden Ship Building and the Interpretation of Shipwrecks.* College Station, TX: Texas A & M University.

Stos-Gale, Z. A., and C. F. Macdonald

1991   Sources of Metals and Trade in the Bronze Age Aegean. Pp. 249–88 in *Bronze Age Trade in the Mediterranean*, ed. N. H. Gale. *Studies in Mediterranean Archaeology* 90. Jonsered: Åstroms.

Touchais, G.

1982   Chronique des fouilles en 1981. *Bulletin de Correspondance héllenique* 106: 529–635.

Vann, R. L.

1992   Early Travelers and the First Archaeologists. Pp. 275–90 in *Caesarea Papers. Straton's Tower, Herod's Harbour, and Roman and Byzantine Caesarea*, ed. R. L. Vann. *Journal of Roman Archaeology*, Supp. Ser. 5. Ann Arbor.

Mediterranean Maritime Landscapes: Transport, Trade, and Society on Late Bronze Age Cyprus

A. BERNARD KNAPP

Department of Archaeology
University of Glasgow
Glasgow G12 8QQ
SCOTLAND

How are a society's cultural and cognitive features or its political and economic institutions related to its maritime trading patterns? What roles did coastal settlements play in intra-island social development and dynamics? Was access to Cyprus's natural resources or other sources of wealth and prestige dictated and controlled by a coastal political organization, or by inland élites? To answer these questions, this study proceeds first by introducing the concept of the ideational maritime landscape, and then the maritime landscape of Late Bronze Age Cyprus. As one part of the Mediterranean maritime landscape, Cyprus's coastal centers are evaluated in light of several recent studies that deal with settlement hierarchies, and with factors of metallurgical production, transport, and wealth. The unifying themes of this study are the movement of people and goods throughout the maritime landscape, the routes they followed, and the social, economic, and ideological relationships involved in such movements.

LANDSCAPES

Recent work across several disciplines—archaeology, geography, history, anthropology—converges on the concept of the landscape, and in particular the social landscape (Bender 1993; Crumley and Marquardt 1990; Daniels and Cosgrove 1988). Landscape encompasses both the conceptual and the physical, bringing together themes, usually separated, that are vital for understanding human history. The landscape approach includes several features that may be regarded as an advance over studies concerned solely with settlement patterns (e.g., Parsons 1972; Trigger 1968). The entire landscape becomes the focus of concern. Using information derived from geomorphological studies, Geographical Information Systems' analyses, satellite imagery, and the like, it is now possible at least to attempt reconstructing the entire formational history of the landscape, rather than of settlement patterns alone (Rossignol and Wandsnider 1992). In this context, it is also important to embrace notions of the ideational and social, so that we may consider the way in which people interacted with the landscape, moved through it, and conducted within it those political and economic activities that so affected their lives.

Archaeologists have only recently begun to consider past landscapes in theoretical terms (e.g., Darvill et al. 1993), as opposed to a multitude of methodological studies on landscape formation and transformation. Although several different types of landscape have been canvassed (e.g., rural, urban, ceremonial, and maritime), these variations may be subsumed, for the sake of discussion, under two general categories: the cultural and the social. If we wish to read the cultural landscape, it must be viewed as a record of dynamic interactions between natural and human factors, each of which may modify, confuse, or destroy the landscape record (Shapiro and Miller 1990: 98–99). The notion of a cultural landscape in archaeology assumes that past patterns have created or influenced the present pattern through some predictable continuity (i.e., a uniformitarian approach), an assumption that neutralizes the historical and social factors that generated the landscape. Landscapes are shaped by human action, for instance in creating homes or shelters, clearing forests, draining swamps, building harbor facilities, etc. In turn, such factors shape human action, by encouraging various forms of land use, maritime activity, transport, or communications. The systematic study of the interplay between human action and changing landscape patterns—urban, rural, or maritime—has helped to raise archaeological sensitivity to the complexity of human adaptation, the diversity of regional contacts and interaction, and the rapidity with which such adaptations and interactions may change (Trigger 1989: 286).

In one sense, then, the landscape may be regarded as a spatial manifestation of the way people relate to their environment, and project culture onto nature (Crumley and Marquardt 1990: 73). In this view, however, past landscapes are regarded as palimpsests of settlement strategy, subsistence pursuits, maritime activity, or even trading patterns (Barker 1991: 1; Bradley 1993: 5–6). In most respects, such a naturalistic view regards the landscape as the passive stage on which the human drama is acted out. Landscapes, however, are much more complex, dynamic, and historically contingent (Meinig 1979: 2).

Human geographers seek meaning in the landscape as a "repository of human striving" (Tuan 1971: 184). Ingold (1993: 152) suggests that we should regard the landscape as "an enduring testimony to the lives and works of the past generations who have dwelt within it, and in so doing, have left there something of themselves." Such an approach to the study of the landscape is in fact social, and places real people, not passive natural or cultural determinants, at the center of the landscape sphere. Alcock's (1993) study of the sacred landscape in Roman Greece demonstrates that the location and significance of certain sanctuaries, as well as the role of cult, helped to articulate provincial social relationships, and served as a strategy to induce civic competition and ensure civic survival. The concept of a ritual landscape overturns the prevailing, passive view of the landscape, and instead considers how the landscape, as a source of the sacred and symbolic, may serve to establish social identity and power, and to reinforce socio-economic and religious institutions.

Landscapes may be mythologized, ritualized, socialized, or visualized and reappraised in terms of other peoples' relationship to the land (Bender 1992: 742). Landscapes are not just created by but are creative of specific social, historical, and cultural configurations. People engage with a landscape on the basis of such factors as gender, age, class, and religion, and they orientate themselves in landscapes that are significant socially and culturally because they link past activities to present experience. Neither cultural nor social landscapes are neutral: they are constructed by human actors whose aim is to perpetuate or change existing politico-economic relations. The landscape, therefore, is not some ready-made, naturally-given substrate on which a cultural design or mental template is imposed. It is never complete, nor is it built or unbuilt; rather it is a social expression, perpetually under construction (Head 1993: 486–89; Ingold 1993: 162).

MARITIME LANDSCAPES

Maritime space involves a greater radius of human action than its terrestrial counterpart, and an important part of the maritime cultural landscape may be regarded as social in nature (Westerdahl 1992). The waterfront, for example, often reveals a unique, human openness to outside impulses. In Medieval and later times, it was taboo to enter certain harbors. Islands often enjoyed magical sanctions or special jurisdiction, but just as often suffered economic deprivation or social isolation (Braudel 1972: 148–54). Transit points and maritime centers are sites where farmers and merchants meet mariners and sea traders, and where economic and cultural traditions may mingle or clash. Through the careful assessment of settlement patterns and/or the distribution of wealth and imports, it may even be possible to postulate or locate harbor sites or other structures (e.g., quays, breaker walls) related to maritime activity or to maritime movements in alternation with land-based transport. On the level of the maritime cultural landscape, the relationship between piracy and settlement location has long been touted but seldom demonstrated. Coastal locations require only that the resident population have some interest in the sea, whether it be piracy, trade, subsistence, or communications with some larger polity. Bronze Age merchants and mariners also had to be concerned with coastal currents and prevailing winds, offshore reefs and inshore rocks, suitable landfalls, taxation and duties (Altman 1988; Pryor 1988: 12–24). Other aspects of the maritime cultural landscape that may be especially relevant in the Mediterranean include the pattern and network of sailing routes, shipwrecks, maritime ports (and their toponyms), and other coastal constructions or remains of human activity, whether underwater or on land.

TRANSPORT:
SHIPWRECKS AND SAILING ROUTES

Compared to the results of research carried out in Melanesia and Oceania generally (e.g., Irwin 1992; Terrell and Welsch 1990), our knowledge about forms of Late Bronze Age maritime transport is quite limited, and dependent on evidence such as ships' models of clay or lead (Westerberg 1983); rough depictions or incised outlines of ships (Basch and Artzy 1985; Broodbank 1989); detailed but fragmentary wall-paintings of Cycladic or Aegean sailing ships and oared vessels (Doumas 1992); the reasonably well-preserved barque of an Egyptian pharaoh (Patch 1990); and the physical remains of Bronze Age ships (most importantly the Uluburun, Cape Gelidonya, and Cape Iria shipwrecks) (Bass 1967; Bass et al. 1989; Karageorghis 1993; Pulak 1992, 1993). It is customary to discuss the economic functions of a ship, but a more holistic view should also consider a vessel's social or ceremonial functions (Morgan 1988: 143–45; Broodbank 1989: 335–37).

Other questions that must be asked, but for which I can provide few answers, are: could essential materials such as timber, pitch, material for sails, cordage for rigging, and the requisite metals freely cross cultural, political, or economic boundaries? Or did legal prohibitions mean that such materials had to be provided within the confines of each maritime polity (Pryor 1988: 10)? To what extent did climate, technology, or other constraints affect the transport of products and people within the Bronze Age Mediterranean (McGeehan-Liritzis 1988; Pryor 1988: 12–24)? Is it possible that dynamic, social elements such as experience, dependability, and communications outweighed constraints such as the distance to markets, or the availability of resources (Curtin 1984: 15–37)?

Our understanding of sailing routes is conditioned to a certain extent by contemporary information on currents, wind directions, seasonal patterns, and the like (see Flemming 1992 on tide-gauge records and a Mediterranean archaeological database), and therefore requires that we make uniformitarian assumptions about climatic and meteorological conditions—that is, we must assume that conditions which prevailed during, say, the 15th century B.C.E. are not appreciably different from those that obtain during the twentieth century C.E. In this regard, it is necessary to point out that, in terms of plate tectonics and volcanism, the Mediterranean coastline is amongst the world's most active (Flemming 1992: 248–49). Our knowledge of Bronze Age ports, sailing routes, and even shipwrecks is also affected by mean sea-level change which, because of local subsidence or aggradation, varies considerably in each coastal region (Flemming 1992: 263–66, and fig. 8.1; Flemming and Webb 1986; Jeftic et al. 1992). If we do assume uniform meteorological conditions, then we may agree with the consensus of opinion that many ships would have hugged the Levantine or Anatolian coastlines as they travelled from south to north, and from east to west, following the anticlockwise currents. However, open-sea crossings were essential in order to reach islands such as Cyprus and Crete, or the Balearics in the western Mediterranean. Georghiou

(1991: 61–62) argues that maritime trading "was not a haphazard activity limited by seasons, weather conditions, or time of day." In addition, smaller, independent cycles of maritime activity, run by different carriers, would always have existed (Sherratt and Sherratt 1991: 358). Given the importance of maritime trade and efficient communications by sea for the Bronze Age economies of the eastern Mediterranean, is it perhaps too simplistic to think that merchants and mariners only traveled south in the summer and north in the winter, dependent on the prevailing winds? On the other hand, Hesiod (*Works and Days,* 618–631) advises his readers (translation Evelyn-White 1982: 49–51):

> truly gales of all kinds rage. Then keep ships no longer on the sparkling sea ... Haul your ship upon the land and pack it closely with stones all around to keep out the power of the winds that blow damply, and draw out the bilge-plug, so that the rain of heaven may not rot it. Put away all the tackle and fittings in your house, and stow the wings of the sea-going ship neatly, and hang up the well-shaped rudder over the smoke. You yourself wait until the season for sailing is come, and then haul your swift ship down to the sea

Similarly, the Medieval Spanish Muslim pilgrim Ibn Jubayr, departing from Acre on 18 October 1184, wrote (translated in Pryor 1988: 1):

> the east wind does not blow except in spring and autumn and ... no voyages can be made and merchants will not bring their goods to Acre. The spring voyages begin in the middle of April ... The autumn voyages are from the middle of October, when the east wind sets in motion. ... There is no other suitable time, for the winds then vary, that from the west prevailing.

Pryor (1988: 3–7) maintains that in the twelfth century C.E., commercial shipping rarely took to sea between November and mid-March; to navigate sailing ships successfully, it was important to utilize seasonal variations in weather patterns and to be familiar with localized meteorological phenomena. The most important rule of thumb for commercial shipping under sail, in any period, was to travel in moderate conditions with the wind abeam or astern. Meteorological conditions combined with the technological limitations of ancient-Medieval merchant ships meant that the preferred shipping routes were always situated along the coasts and chains of islands in the north Mediterranean. Scattered along these Mediterranean sea lanes were ports or naval bases whose control represented the key to maritime politico-economic power. We may expect a similar situation for the international era of the Late Bronze Age in the Mediterranean.

Shipwrecks, generally speaking, provide our most important material resource and—depending on their condition—may shed critical light on several features of the maritime landscape (sailing routes, traded goods, port of origin). In more recent, historical situations, it is important to know the difference between the spot where the ship foundered and its ultimate resting place (Westerdahl 1992: 8), but this knowledge is seldom possible when dealing with prehistoric wreck deposits. If literary references are taken at face value, being shipwrecked was a relatively common occurrence in antiquity. Indeed, Parker's (1992) catalogue of 1189 shipwrecks dating from the Bronze Age to about C.E. 1500 provides the material witness of this. And while that number represents a notable sample, it is surely a very conservative estimate of the total number of wrecks in the Mediterranean. Both natural factors and human predation were to blame: although the Mediterranean offers ideal sailing conditions in summer, in autumn or winter the sea may become uncomfortable or dangerous with hardly any notice (Parker 1992: 3; Pryor 1988: 13–21).

The status of shipwrecks as time-capsules is not always as significant as it is with the Uluburun, Cape Gelidonya, or Cape Iria deposits; in areas where numerous wrecks have been found, possibly only the ballast should be considered as a closed find (Westerdahl 1992: 7). When a wreck deposit can be regarded as a closed group, we have an example of what Muckelroy (1980: 108) termed "exchange frozen in time," where the material recovered (organic, nautical, mineral) is often unique, or at least not the usual terrestrial archaeological fare. The ship's cargo provides striking evidence for ancient trade, a sample of exchanged goods in transit from one port to another (Parker 1992: 3). The overall distribution of wrecked cargos for later periods, especially the Hellenistic and Roman, may shed some light on trading patterns generally, but Bronze Age evidence is far too limited for such an end. One noteworthy find of Parker's study, however, that may have some relevance for Bronze Age trade patterns, is that shipping was fairly balanced between single (or "bulk") and compound cargoes; less than five percent of the ships included in the study could be regarded as "tramps" or general cargo carriers (Parker 1992: 20–21).

How are a society's socio-cultural features, or its political and economic institutions, related to its maritime trading patterns? Can any social or economic factors be correlated with the maritime landscape? If so, how do they articulate with one another to produce a particular maritime pattern? Was access to Cyprus's natural resources or other sources of wealth and prestige dictated and controlled by a coastal political organization, or by inland elites?

In an attempt to deal with these questions, the remainder of this paper focuses on the maritime landscape of Late Bronze Age Cyprus, and considers the role that coastal settlements played in intra-island social development and dynamics. As one part of the Mediterranean maritime landscape, Cyprus's coastal centers are evaluated in light of recent studies that deal not only with settlement hierarchies, but also with factors of production, transport, and wealth. The unifying themes involved are the movement of people and goods throughout the terrestrial and maritime landscapes, the routes they followed, and the socio-economic relationships involved in such movements.

Settlement and Society on Late Bronze Age Cyprus

Building on the work of Catling (1962) and Keswani (1993), and taking into account evidence from more recent excavations and intensive surveys, it is possible to propose a four-tiered settlement model for Late Bronze Age Cyprus (Knapp 1997):

(1) primary coastal centers (commercial, ceremonial, administrative, production functions);
(2) secondary inland towns/transit points (administrative, transport, some storage functions);
(3) tertiary inland sites (ceremonial, production, transport, some storage functions); and
(4) agricultural support villages (production, storage, transport functions), and mining sites and pottery-producing villages (production function).

By itself, presumed site function is inadequate to distinguish and elaborate on a site hierarchy. Yet the present scheme has the virtue of distinguishing peripheral, inland sites involved mainly in production activities (e.g., Ambelikou, Apliki, and Sanidha) from all other site types, particularly from the coastal maritime centers, or the secondary transit points. Like most archaeological models, designed as dynamic constructs whose configuration will change as new data emerge, this settlement model for Bronze Age Cyprus is far from perfect. Primary centers like Kalavasos *Ayios Dhimitrios* and Alassa *Pano Mandilares/ Paleotaverna* not only have a multiplicity of functions (overlapping with those of secondary and tertiary centers) but an inland location much closer to the mines than the coastal centers. They may have controlled directly the mining, production and transport of copper, and were likely involved in agricultural production (olive oil). They would have functioned commercially as administrative and trans-shipment points. Alternatively, it could be argued that their functions revolved more tightly around administrative, metallurgical and ceremonial (Alassa) factors, and that the commercial and political functions were filled by Maroni *Tsaroukkas* (Manning et al. 1994) or a still unidentified port settlement at the mouth of the Vasilikos Valley (for Kalavasos), and Kourion (for Alassa) (Christou, this volume). This would parallel the situation at certain Levantine or Aegean trade centers (e.g., Ugarit, Gaza, Pylos, Knossos, Phaistos) that had separate harbor facilities (Raban 1991: 134). Moreover, the existence of imported prestige goods not just at inland centers, as we might expect, but also at sanctuary sites (e.g., Athienou—Dothan 1993: 132–33) and agricultural villages (e.g., Mathiati—Hadjicosti 1991) indicates that these sites were involved in wider networks of regional exchange (although imports may have reached them indirectly—Webb and Frankel 1994). Finally, if the coastal or near-coastal sites of Maa *Palaeokastro* and Pyla *Kokkinokremmos* actually had defensive functions, they do not sit well with the proposed settlement hierarchy.

The production and exchange relations that linked sites of different size, function, and location on Late Bronze Age Cyprus were highly complex, perhaps fluid, and subject to the motivations and whims of individual or collective human action. In the move to establish political alliances or economic hegemony, the capacity to manipulate social relations is no less important than the ability to control access to resources in demand. And there is still a need to come to grips more specifically with the issue of internal *vs* external communications, transport, and trade. The existence of "all these imponderables" (Merrillees 1992: 324) does not mean that we should forego the responsibility of attempting social or historical reconstructions. Rather it must be accepted that these variant data demand an interpretive framework that facilitates further discussion and evaluation. Interpretive parameters may have to be altered, reduced, or eliminated as new data and new understanding are acquired.

Any attempted social or economic reconstruction of the Late Bronze Age must deal with the fact that most material upon which interpretations are built derives from the period between about 1300–1200 B.C.E. (LC IIC in conventional terms). In other words, the comparative lack of stratigraphic evidence from settlements and from currently available survey data alike means that, in considering the settlement system of the first three to four centuries of the Late Bronze Age, it is necessary to extrapolate in part from the much more abundant evidence of the penultimate century of the Bronze Age. Interpreting the earlier stages, however, is facilitated in part by using documentary evidence related to *Alashiya* (Muhly 1972, 1989; Knapp 1996).

On the basis of the current archaeological record, Enkomi *Ayios Iakovos* still appears to be a dominant and independent power throughout the course of the LC I period (about 1600–1400 B.C.E.). That some form of centralized political organization still existed 300 years later (at Enkomi, or elsewhere), during the course of the fourteenth century B.C.E., seems indisputable on the basis of the Amarna

letters from *Alashiya*. And yet, sometime during the centuries 1400–1200 B.C.E., it is equally clear from the diversity of evidence from several sites that the island's various mineral, material, and exotic resources increasingly came under the control of local elites, who were able to stipulate the terms of production and trade. Several thirteenth century B.C.E. urban centers shared a very similar material culture, were involved in many of the same production activities (metallurgical, agricultural, crafts), constructed comparable public buildings in their respective sites (e.g., Alassa *Palaeotaverna,* Kalavasos *Ayios Dhimitrios,* Maroni *Vournes,* and Enkomi *Ayios Iakovos),* and made use of commonly understood symbols of group identity (e.g., "common" and "elaborate" style cylinder seals, Aegeanizing motifs on pottery and on seal impressions). If all of this information on economic organization and social structure is fed back into consideration of a site hierarchy, it seems clear that, at least by the LC II period, there existed a new and distinctive settlement structure that reflected site size, location, and (presumed) function.

Growing evidence for increased copper-ore processing at what may be regarded as elite areas in several LC II sites (Kalavasos *Ayios Dhimitrios,* Maroni *Vournes,* Kition *Kathari,* Hala Sultan Tekké *Vyzakija,* Alassa *Pano Mandilares)* suggests local production managed by local elites. Meanwhile, sites such as Analiondas *Palioklichia* and Aredhiou *Vouppes* would have served as agricultural support villages (Webb and Frankel 1994; Knapp et al. 1994), an integral part of the settlement system proposed by Catling for the Late Bronze Age (1962: 144–45). In such villages, surplus agricultural produce (grains, olive oil) would have been collected, processed, and redistributed, whether to mining sites or up the hierarchy to secondary or primary centers. Production sites such as Apliki *Karamallos* and Sanidha *Moutti tou Ayiou Serkhou* fulfilled the basic production needs of the economy, both in terms of raw materials and finished goods.

As intensified copper production and trade brought Cyprus within the eastern Mediterranean economic orbit by the beginning of the Late Bronze Age, the newly-built, primary, port cities developed into trade emporia with concentrated populations and specialized craftspeople. The social dynamics and market potential of Cypriot maritime centers (e.g., Enkomi *Ayios Iakovos,* Hala Sultan Tekke *Vyzakija,* and Kition) ensured that various domestic products (pottery, copper ingots) as well as imported goods (ivory, tin ingots, Aegean and Levantine pottery) were readily available (Åström 1986; Lagarce and Lagarce in Courtois et al. 1986: 59–199). The spatial configuration of these primary maritime centers, and their nearby satellite communities, is not at odds conceptually or schematically with the settlement hierarchy proposed here. Ideally, we might expect such sites to have provided a good source of fresh water, and a suitably sheltered anchorage or a beach for drawing up ships. Some ports may have developed because they offered safe havens from climatic elements or human predators, even if they lacked berthing or beaching features. There is no reason to assume that insular Bronze Age harbor sites should be located at regular or predictable intervals (unlike mainland ports or anchorages, often located to suit the daily needs of sailors who travelled perhaps 30–40 km per day on long-distance sea journeys) (Harden 1971: 33; Pryor 1988: 5–6; Westerdahl 1992: 7). If anything, the distribution of sites in Cyprus might lead us to predict the existence of a port site in the northwest, either around Polis/Marion or Karavostasi/Soli, and another along the north coast, perhaps near Kyrenia.

Approximate Distance in km between Major Late Cypriot Maritime Centers

Enkomi–Kition	80
HST–Maroni	40
Maroni–Kourion	60
Kourion–Palaepaphos	25
Palaepaphos–Maa	40

In order to consider more carefully the location of ports, inland centers, and industrial sites, a postgraduate student at the University of Sydney (Ms. Lita Diacopoulos) has established a database of all Bronze Age sites, coastal and inland, their most common material components (including imports and luxury goods), and their precise location in space, in relation to topographic and geological factors. Evaluating all these data by using GIS and computer mapping, it should be possible not only to verify or modify the proposed settlement hierarchy, but also to examine more critically the relationship between imports and luxury goods, inland settlements, and maritime centers.

Careful analysis of topographic features, and of environmental processes such as alluviation, tectonic uplift or subsidence, may make it possible to define "natural" harbor basins, and then to predict more specifically the likely location of coastal ports or anchorages (Blue, this volume). Another likely source of relevant information is the study of place names (Westerdahl 1992: 9–11), e.g. of wrecks, individual ships, harbors *(limani, pyla),* ship types, "nationality" names *(Poinikes),* names of warning *(thanatos, kolasi),* or of authority *(Ayios, Panayia, Apostelos, Akhiropiitos* "made without hands"—north coast monastery/church said to have been brought intact by the Virgin Mary from Anatolia, *Aphrodision, Episkopi),* migrant names, and names of temporary trading places *(Pharos, Potamos, Zygi* "weight scale for carobs") or places that refer to temporary trading rights and special jurisdiction *(Palaeokastro).*

Most "primary" sites in the settlement hierarchy of Late Bronze Age Cyprus (Enkomi, Kition, Hala Sultan Tekke, perhaps Kourion and Palaepaphos) should be regarded as maritime centers, even if they quite obviously served terrestrial functions as well. The important point is that the maritime component was not simply an extension of the terrestrial but rather was a critical and economically vital aspect of the site's very existence. Abundant imports at such sites make it clear that they were commercial centers and key nodes of communication, both within and beyond the island. Some clearly served production and ceremonial functions as well. Most were situated at the mouth of perennial rivers, or river drainages, but if we presume a climate similar to that of the present day, riverine transport could not have been used to bring goods to the coastal ports. Sites like Kition and Hala Sultan Tekke (Åström 1986; Collombier 1988)—the latter situated on an embayment and providing an ideal harbor for Bronze Age ships—formed a waterfront economic zone that could only have been served internally by overland transport.

A comprehensive picture of the maritime cultural landscape, at least in the Cypriot case, must include the inland towns and the transport routes that brought raw materials and agricultural produce to the coastal emporia (Keswani 1993; Knapp 1997). Any production/distribution system must somehow overcome the friction of distance. Elites, for example, often reproduce their position by locating fixed points of the economic infrastructure where transport and communication costs may be minimized (Paynter 1983: 265); I have referred to such sites above as "transit points." Luxury goods may be important in such systems, but only when elites control production and distribution, and when the transport system is efficient enough to make such goods available throughout the system (Santley and Alexander 1992: 25). The secondary and tertiary centers were chiefly administrative and ceremonial communities established at strategic communication nodes, where the production or movement of copper, exchanged goods, and agricultural products could be controlled. Theses sites served as transshipment points that facilitated the articulation of localized production and trade with regional and interregional systems. Raw materials or agricultural goods shipped from the periphery "up" the settlement hierarchy would have been collected ("bulked") and stored in such sites, while specialized goods moving downward from the primary coastal centers also were collected and dispersed ("break-of-bulk") there (cf. Santley and Alexander 1992: 26).

The ownership of productive land may have increased social stratification amongst farmers and within the agricultural areas, and led to social or politico-economic inequalities (Webb and Frankel 1994). Local elites who emerged from this process would have controlled production, storage, and distribution factors at agricultural villages (e.g., Analiondas *Palioklichia* and Aredhiou *Vouppes*), perhaps in alliance with more powerful leaders in the secondary and primary town centers. Economic relations between the primary and secondary or tertiary centers may have been based on tribute, perhaps in the form of copper from the distant periphery, or of subsistence goods from the near periphery (Keswani 1993: 79; Webb and Frankel 1994).

Some inland settlements (notably the tertiary sites in the proposed hierarchy) may also have formed part of what Alcock (1993: 172–214) has termed the "sacred landscape." Because many secondary or tertiary sites were situated on routes between the mining areas and the coastal centers, it is possible that an elite ideology, expressed through local cults, would have helped to articulate various relationships between the production-oriented periphery (inland) and the consumption- or distribution-oriented core (coastal). The location of "rural sanctuaries," in other words, was not haphazard, but rather was closely linked to human settlement in the landscape.

By the time of the transition from LC IIC to LC IIIA, about 1200 B.C.E., several key settlements in this system had been destroyed or abandoned, as had lower-tier settlements like Analiondas *Palioklichia* and Apliki *Karamallos*. The widespread collapse throughout the eastern Mediterranean and Aegean clearly affected external demand (especially for copper), which in turn would have fragmented the settlement hierarchy on Cyprus. The same factors that affected the primary and secondary or tertiary centers would also have disrupted the agricultural and mining villages, and thus almost certainly destabilized the unique system that interlinked and maintained the components of a hierarchical settlement system.

The large maritime centers (e.g., Enkomi, Kition, Palaepaphos) that survived the destructions and abandonments around 1200 B.C.E. may represent the stabilization of authority at a few key sites (Sherratt 1992: 326–28). These enduring maritime centers would have displaced the smaller administrative or ceremonial centers, and managed newly emerging Cypriot contacts overseas, from the Levant to the central Mediterranean (Smith 1987; Knapp 1990). The destructions around 1200 B.C.E. could indicate either (1) a return to more centralized political and economic structure, or (2) a general pattern of coastal raiding characteristic of eras that enjoy thriving maritime trade. In fact, both situations may have prevailed, and in truth the matter cannot be decided finally on the basis of the current archaeological record.

CONCLUSION

Archaeologists have often made limiting and inappropriate assumptions about the mobility of individuals, commodities, ships, and even communities throughout the landscape (Perlès 1992). A great deal of energy and expertise has been invested in the explanation of Mediterranean landscapes (e.g., Cherry et al.; van Andel and Runnels 1987), but little attention has been given explicitly to the maritime landscape. Synthesis and comparison on a much larger scale than that of individual surveys or excavations are now both possible and worthwhile, and regional patterns or rhythms of change may be examined on their own terms. Different degrees of maritime proficiency will have prevailed in different areas, but neither the material evidence nor the documentary record can resolve just how the centers of maritime knowledge and power established their prominence, or why their locations changed repeatedly through time. Trade, prestige and power were interlinked in a system where success was contagious. Mediterranean trade systems were in a continuous process of transformation: consumer or supplier demand and maritime technology enabled regional trade networks to be linked to a wider, common circulation system that moved common commodities as well as high-value goods (metals, oxhide ingots) between participating polities. Standardized values—as seen in bronze and stone weights (Kalavasos *Ayios Dhimitrios*), disk weights (Akrotiri on Thera), and the 30 kg copper oxhide ingots (Courtois 1983; Budd et al. 1995; Michailidou 1990; Petruso 1984)—would have facilitated long-distance trade, and served to stabilize a system in which politico-economic relations were always changing. The knowledge, experiences, and modes of communication wielded by Bronze Age Mediterranean traders and raiders were important sources of social power in themselves, invisible commodities, as it were, that motivated trade and continually transformed the Mediterranean maritime landscape.

ACKNOWLEDGEMENTS

This study was written while the author held an Australian Research Fellowship, funded by the Australian Research Council (Department of Employment, Education and Training, Commonwealth Government of Australia). I am most grateful for their support. I also wish to thank Dr. Stuart Swiny, former Director of the Cyprus American Archaeological Research Institute (CAARI), Nicosia, who made it possible for me to participate in the *Res Maritimae* conference. The superb library at CAARI facilitated completion of the research.

REFERENCES

Alcock, S. E.
1993   *Graecia Capta: The Landscapes of Roman Greece.* Cambridge: Cambridge University.

Altman, A.
1988   Trade between the Aegean and the Levant in the Late Bronze Age: some neglected questions. Pp. 229–37 in *Society and Economy in the Eastern Mediterranean (c. 1500–1000 B.C.)*, ed. M. Heltzer and E. Lipinski. Orientalia Lovaneinsia Analecta 23. Leuven: Peeters.

Åström, P.
1986   Hala Sultan Tekke—an international harbour town of the Late Cypriote Bronze Age. *Opuscula Atheniensia* 16: 7–17.

Barker, G.
1991   Approaches to archaeological survey. Pp. 1–9 in *Roman Landscapes: Archaeological Survey in the Mediterranean,* eds. G. Barker and J. Lloyd. British School at Rome, Archaeological Monograph 2. London: British Schoool at Rome.

Basch, L., and Artzy, M.
1985   Ship graffiti at Kition. Pp. 322–36 (Appendix II) in V. Karageorghis and M. Demas, *Excavations at Kition* V(1). Nicosia: Department of Antiquities.

Bass, G. F.
1967   *Cape Gelidonya: A Bronze Age Shipwreck.* Transactions of the American Philosophical Society 57.8. Philadelphia: American Philosophical Society.

Bass, G. F.; Pulak, C.; Collon, D.; and Weinstein, J.
1989   The Bronze Age shipwreck at Ulu Burun: 1986 campaign. *American Journal of Archaeology* 93: 1–29.

Bender, B.
1992   Theorising landscapes, and the prehistoric landscape of Stonehenge. *Man* 27: 735–55.

Bender, B. (ed.)
1993   *Landscape: Politics and Perspectives.* Oxford: Berg.

Bradley, R.
1993   *Altering the Earth.* Society of Antiquaries, Scotland, Monograph 8. Edinburgh.

Braudel, F.
1972   *The Mediterranean and the Mediterranean World in the Age of Philip II.* Vol. 1. New York: Harper and Row.

Broodbank, C.
1989   The longboat and society in the Cyclades in the Kyros-Syros culture. *American Journal of Archaeology* 93: 319–37.

Budd, P.; Pollard, A. M.; Scaife, B.; and Thomas, R. G.
1995   Oxhide ingots, recycling and the Mediterranean metals trade. *Journal of Mediterranean Archaeology* 8: 1–32, 70–75.

Catling, H. W.
1962   Patterns of settlement in Bronze Age Cyprus. *Opuscula Atheniensia* 4: 129–69.

Cherry, J. F.; Davis, J. L.; and Mantzourani, E.
1991   *Landscape Archaeology as Long-Term History: Northern Keos in the Cycladic Islands from Earliest Settlement to Modern Times.* Monumenta Archaeologica 16. Los Angeles: UCLA Institute of Archaeology.

Collombier, A. M.
1988   Harbour or harbours of Kition on southeastern coastal Cyprus. Pp. 35–46 in *Archaeology of Coastal Changes.* British Archaeological Reports, ed. A. Raban. International Series 404. Oxford: B.A.R.

Courtois, J.-C.
1983   Le trésor de poids de Kalavasos-Ayios Dhimitrios 1982. *Report of the Department of Antiquities, Cyprus*: 117–30.

Courtois, J.-C.; Lagarce, J.; and Lagarce, E.
1986   *Enkomi et le Bronze Récent à Chypre.* Nicosia: Leventis Foundation.

Crumley, C. L., and Marquardt, W. H.
1990   Landscape: a unifying concept in regional analysis. Pp. 73–79 in *Interpreting Space: GIS and Archaeology,* eds. K. M. S. Allen, S. W. Green, and E. B. W. Zubrow. New York: Taylor and Francis.

Curtin, P. D.
1984   *Cross-Cultural Trade in World History.* Cambridge: Cambridge University.

Daniels, S., and Cosgrove, D. E.
1988   Introduction: iconography and landscape. Pp. 1–10 in *The Iconography of Landscape: Essays on the Symbolic Representation, Design and Use of Past Environments,* eds. D. E. Cosgrove and S. Daniels. Cambridge: Cambridge University.

Darvill, T.; Gerrard, C.; and Starton, B.
1993   Identifying and protecting historic landscapes. *Antiquity* 67/256: 563–74.

Dothan, T.
1993   Mediterranean archaeology. *Biblical Archaeologist* 56: 132–34.

Doumas, C.
1992   *The Wall-Paintings of Thera.* London: Thera Foundation.

Evelyn-White, H. G.
1982   *Hesiod: The Homeric Hymns and Homerica.*

Loeb Classical Library. Cambridge: Harvard University.

Flemming, N.C.
1992   Predictions of relative coastal sea-level change in the Mediterranean based on archaeological, historical, and tide gauge data. Pp. 247–81 in *Climatic Change and the Mediterranean,* eds. L. Jeftic, J. D. Milliman, and G. Sestini. London: E. Arnold.

Flemming, N.C., and Webb, C.O.
1986   Tectonic and eustatic changes during the last 10,000 years derived from archaeological data. *Zeitschrift für Geomorphologie, Supplement* 62: 1–29.

Georgiou, H.
1991   Bronze Age ships and rigging. Pp. 61–71 in *Thalassa: L'Égée Préhistorique et la Mer.* Aegaeum 7, ed. R. Laffineur and L. Basch. Liège: Université de Liège.

Hadjicosti, M.
1991   The Late Bronze Age Tomb 2 from Mathiatis (new perspectives for the Mathiatis region). *Report of the Department of Antiquities, Cyprus:* 75–91.

Harden, D.
1971   *The Phoenicians.* Penguin: Harmondsworth.

Head, L.
1993   Unearthing prehistoric cultural landscapes: a view from Australia. *Transactions of the Institute of British Geographers* n.s. 18: 481–99.

Ingold, T.
1993   The temporality of the landscape. *World Archaeology* 25: 152–74.

Irwin, G.
1992   *The Prehistoric Exploration and Colonisation of the Pacific.* Cambridge: Cambridge University.

Jeftic, L.; Milliman, J. D.; and Sestini, G. (eds.)
1992   *Climatic Change and the Mediterranean: Environmental and Societal Impacts of Climatic Change and Sea-Level Rise in the Mediterranean Region.* London: E. Arnold.

Karageorghis, V.
1993   Le commerce chypriote avec l'occident au bronze récent: quelques nouvelles découvertes. *Comptes Rendus de l'Académie des Inscriptions et Belles-Lettres* (Avril-Juin): 577–88.

Keswani, P. S.
1993   Models of local exchange in Late Bronze Age Cyprus. *Bulletin of the American Schools of Oriental Research* 292: 73–83.

Knapp, A. B.
1990   Entrepreneurship, ethnicity, exchange: Mediterranean inter-island relations in the Late Bronze Age. *Annual of the British School at Athens* 85: 115–53.

1997   *The Archaeology of Late Bronze Age Cypriot Society: A Study of Settlement, Survey and Landscape.* University of Glasgow, Department of Archaeology, Occasional Paper 4. Glasgow.

Knapp, A. B. (ed.)
1996   *Sources for the History of Cyprus. Volume 2: Near Eastern and Aegean Texts from the Third to the First Millenmia B.C.* Institute of Cypriot Studies, Albany: State University of New York.

Knapp, A. B.; Held, S. O.; Johnson, I.; and Keswani, P.S.
1994   The Sydney-Cyprus Survey Project—second preliminary season (1993). *Report of the Department of Antiquities, Cyprus:* 329–43.

Manning, S. W.; Steel, L.; Jansen, H.G.; Conwell, D.H., Sewell, D.; Swinton, A.; and Collon, D.
1994   Tsaroukkas, Mycenaeans and Trade Project: Preliminary Report of the 1993 Season. *Report of the Department of Antiquities, Cyprus:* 83–106.

McGeehan-Liritzis, V.
1988   Seafaring, craft and cultural contact in the Aegean during the 3rd millennium B.C. *International Journal of Nautical Archaeology and Underwater Exploration* 17: 237–56.

Meinig, D. W.
1979   Introduction. Pp. 1–7 in *The Interpretation of Ordinary Landscapes,* ed. D. W. Meinig. Oxford: Oxford University.

Merrillees, R. S.
1992   The government of Cyprus in the Late Bronze Age. Pp. 310–29 in *Acta Cypria 3: Acts of an International Congress on Cypriote Archaeology held in Göteborg* (22–24 August 1991), ed. P. Åström. Studies in Mediterranean Archaeology and Literature, Pocketbook 120. Jonsered: Åströms.

Michailidou, A.
1990   The lead weights from Akrotiri: the archaeological record. Pp. 407–19 in *Thera and the Aegean World* 3, eds. D.A. Hardy, C.G. Doumas, J.A. Sakellarakis, and P. M. Warren. London: Thera Foundation.

Morgan, L.
1988   *The Miniature Wall Paintings of Thera. A Study in Aegean Culture and Iconography.* Cambridge Classical Studies 19. Cambridge: Cambridge University.

Muckelroy, K.
1980   Two Bronze Age cargoes in British waters. *Antiquity* 44: 100–9.

Muhly, J. D.
1972   The land of *Alashiya*: references to *Alashiya* in the texts of the second millennium B.C. and the history of Cyprus in the Late Bronze Age. Pp. 201–19 in *Acts of the First International Cyprological Congress,* ed. V. Karageorghis. Nicosia: Department of Antiquities, Cyprus.

1989   The organisation of the copper industry in Late Bronze Age Cyprus. Pp. 298–314 in *Early Society in Cyprus,* ed. E. J. Peltenburg. Edinburgh: Edinburgh University.

Parker, A. J.
1992   *Ancient Shipwrecks of the Mediterranean and the Roman Provinces.* British Archaeological Reports, International Series 580. Oxford: B.A.R.

Parsons, J. R.
1972   Archaeological settlement patterns. *Annual Review of Anthropology* 1: 127–50.

Patch, D. C.
1990   *Reflections of Greatness: Ancient Egypt at the Carnegie Museum of Natural History.* Pittsburgh: Carnegie Museum of Natural History.

Paynter, R. W.
1983   Expanding the scope of settlement systems. Pp. 233–75 in *Archaeological Hammers and Theories,* eds. J.A. Moore and A.S. Keene. New York: Academic.

Perlès, C.
1992   Systems of exchange and organization of production in Neolithic Greece. *Journal of Mediterranean Archaeology* 5: 115–64.

Petruso, K. M.
1984   Prolegomena to Late Cypriot weight metrology. *American Journal of Archaeology* 88: 293–304.

Pryor, J. H.
1988   *Geography, Technology, and War: Studies in the Maritime History of the Mediterranean, 649–1571.* Cambridge: Cambridge University.

Pulak, C.
1992   The shipwreck at Uluburun, Turkey: 1992 excavation campaign. *Institute of Nautical Archaeology Newsletter* 19: 4–11, 21.

1993   The shipwreck at Uluburun, Turkey: 1993 excavation campaign. *Institute of Nautical Archaeology Newsletter* 20: 4–12.

Raban, A.
1991   Minoan and Canaanite harbours. Pp. 129–46 in *Thalassa: L'Égée Préhistorique et la Mer.* Aegaeum 7, eds. R. Laffineur and L. Basch. Liège: Université de Liège.

Rossignol, J., and Wandsnider, L. (eds.)
1992   *Space, Time, and Archaeological Landscapes.* New York: Plenum.

Santley, R. S., and Alexander, R.T.
1992   The political economy of core-periphery systems. Pp. 23–49 in *Resources, Power, and Interregional Interaction,* eds. E. M. Schortman and P. A. Urban. New York: Plenum.

Shapiro, G., and Miller, J. J.
1990   The seventeenth-century landscape of San Luis de Talimali: three scales of analysis. Pp. 89–101 in *Earth Patterns: Essays in Landscape Archaeology,* eds. W. M. Kelso and R. Most. Charlottesville: University Press of Virginia.

Sherratt, A. G., and Sherratt, E. S.
1991   From luxuries to commodities: the nature of Mediterranean Bronze Age trading systems. Pp. 351–86 in *Bronze Age Trade in the Mediterranean,* ed. N. H. Gale. Studies in Mediterranean Archaeology 90. Göteborg: Åstroms.

Sherratt, E. S.
1992   Immigration and archaeology: some indirect reflections. Pp. 316–47 in *Acta Cypria 2: Acts of an International Congress on Cypriote Archaeology held in Göteborg* (22–24 August 1991), ed. P. Åström. Studies in Mediterranean Archaeology and Literature, Pocketbook 117. Jonsered: Åströms.

Smith, T. R.
1987   *Mycenaean Trade and Interaction in the West Central Mediterranean.* British Archaeological Reports, International Series 371. Oxford: B.A.R.

Terrell, J., and Welsch, R. L.
1990   Trade networks, areal integration, and diversity along the North Coast of New Guinea. *Asian Perspectives* 29: 155–66.

Trigger, B. G.
1968   The determinants of settlement patterns. Pp. 53–78 in *Settlement Archaeology,* ed. K.C. Chang. Palo Alto, CA: National Press Books.

1989   *A History of Archaeological Thought.* Cambridge: Cambridge University.

Tuan, Y.F.
1971   Geography, phenomenology, and the study of human nature. *Canadian Geographer* 15: 181-92.

Van Andel, T. H., and Runnels, C. N.
1987   *Beyond the Acropolis. A Rural Greek Past.* Stanford: Stanford University.

Webb, J. M., and Frankel, D.
1994   Making an impression: storage and staple finance at Analiondas *Paleoklichia. Journal of Mediterranean Archaeology* 7: 5–26.

Westerberg, K.
1983   *Cypriote Ships from the Bronze Age to c. 500 B.C.* Studies in Mediterranean Archaeology, Pocketbook 22. Göteborg: Åströms.

Westerdahl, C.
1992   The maritime cultural landscape. *International Journal of Nautical Archaeology and Underwater Archaeology* 21: 5–14.

Harbor Terminology in Roman Periploi

John R. Leonard

Department of Classics
State University of New York at Buffalo
Buffalo, NY 14260
U.S.A.

Roman writers of Periploi, especially Strabo and the anonymous Stadiasmus, use various terms in describing harbors and other commercial centers, including ἐπίνειον (epineion), ἐμπόριον (emporion), λιμήν (limen), ὅρμος (hormos), ὕφορμος (hyphormos), πρόσορμος (prosormos), portus, and statio. Do these ancient Greek and Latin words represent distinct, recognizable types of maritime facilities, or were they merely general terms employed indiscriminately by authors of the Roman period to describe harbors of diverse physical form and composition? Moreover, do ancient harbor terms represent a useful archaeological tool for coastal surveys and the excavation of Roman harbor sites? This paper addresses these questions and examines four ancient Greek harbor terms in particular, λιμήν, ὅρμος, ὕφορμος, and πρόσορμος, as they relate to the natural topography and archaeological remains of Cypriot and Cretan maritime sites. Textual, archaeological, and geomorphological evidence is considered, as well as contemporary harbor terminology in English.

The history of ports is, in great measure, the history of civilization. It is not too much to say that the Mediterranean was a cradle of civilization largely because it was a nursery of maritime trade.

F. W. Morgan (1958: 150)

INTRODUCTION

A recurring and troublesome question for readers of ancient Greek and Latin geographical texts is the exact meaning of numerous terms used by writers to describe harbors and other commercial centers around the coasts of the Mediterranean and adjacent seas. Roman Periploi written in Greek, in particular, contain a wide range of terms for such maritime facilities, including ἐπίνειον (epineion), ἐμπόριον (emporion), λιμήν (limen), ὅρμος (hormos), ὕφορμος (hyphormos), and πρόσορμος (prosormos).[1] Latin texts contain terms of similar function, but these are less frequent and fewer in number, consisting primarily of *portus* and *statio* (Rougé 1966: 117–18) (Tables 1, 2). Do the various ancient Greek terms for harbors found throughout Roman Periploi carry specific meaning, and if so, what information or mental image do writers of Periploi

[1] Periploi (sing.: periplous) are defined in the *Oxford Classical Dictionary* (2nd ed., s.v. "Periploi") as "a) reports of navigations by pioneers along unexplored coasts, b) manuals for the use of navigators, which collected and systematized the information of previous travellers. The term primarily referred to sailings round an enclosed basin like the Mediterranean and Black Seas, but was also applied to continuous navigations along any kind of coast." The Latin term *periplus* is defined in the *Oxford Latin Dictionary* (Combined ed., s.v. "periplus") as "a voyage round the coast (in quot., as the title of a geographical work)."

Transliterations are provided for ancient Greek harbor terms, following each term's first appearance in the text; these transliterations should not be confused with Latin harbor terms, which are italicized. See also Table 1.

The author extends his gratitude to Dr. D. Christou, Director of the Cypriot Department of Antiquities, as well as to past Directors Mr. A. Papageorgiou and Mr. M. Loulloupis, for their support of the Cyprus Coastal Survey, upon which

intend to convey when they report that a particular coastal place is an ἐπίνειον or has a ὅρμος? The way in which harbor terms are used by Roman writers such as Strabo, Josephus, and especially the anonymous author of the *Stadiasmus Maris Magni* (hereafter Stadiasmus) suggests that they probably were distinguishable terms, each of which conveyed, at least to some readers, a distinct meaning. Reconstructing these meanings today remains problematic, however, for the internal evidence of the texts is often circumstantial and ambiguous. The body of evidence that may hold the greatest potential for illustrating the meaning of ancient Greek harbor terms is the topographical (i.e. archaeological and geomorphological) evidence of eastern Mediterranean coastal sites themselves.

Although comparison of known ancient harbor sites with the particular ancient Greek terms used to describe them may appear straightforward, how much can we truly expect to learn from ancient Greek terms? Do the ancient terms reflect actual topographical or functional features of harbors, particularly those features that may still be recognizable today? Moreover, is the expectation of such specialized harbor terminology realistic? For example, do harbor engineers today use specialized terminology to refer to distinct types of maritime facilities? And how do we equate ancient Greek harbor terms with contemporary English terms? The aim of this paper is to address these questions and to provide an initial, thought-provoking examination of four ancient Greek terms, λιμήν, ὅρμος, ὕφορμος and πρόσορμος, as they relate to the natural topography and archaeological remains of Cypriot and Cretan maritime sites. Cyprus holds particular significance for the study of ancient Greek harbor terms, since the island's numerous natural and artificial harbor facilities are described in Roman Periploi with greater variety and evident specificity of terms than those of other Mediterranean areas.

HARBOR TERMINOLOGY IN ANCIENT TEXTS

Among the ancient Greek texts that provide evidence for maritime facilities, Roman Periploi are the most informative—and tantalizing. The places enumerated in these texts are usually listed in the order in which travelers would have encountered them as they sailed along the coasts. Periploi, such as that of Stadiasmus (ca. first to fourth century C.E.), may have served as navigational guidebooks similar to modern *Mediterranean Pilots,* for they occasionally include such additional details as available drinking water, the presence of dangerous reefs, or the disturbance of a particular wind (cf. Haslam 1976). For the modern study of ancient harbors, however, Periploi are inconsistent sources of information, because of the brevity or variability of their harbor descriptions. Ancient writers frequently provide many details for some sites, while only passing references to others, even when dealing with important maritime centers such as the Achaian city of Corinth. The Augustan geographer Strabo (*Geog.* 8.6.22), for example, reports that Lechaion, "[which the Corinthians] ... use for the trade ... from Italy, ... lies beneath the city, and does not contain many residences" (Loeb ed.).

Strabo (*Geog.* 8.6.25) then goes on to provide a more replete account of neighboring Sicyon, describing the city's political history, topography, and eventual inland refoundation on the acropolis. He does not discuss the harbor itself, however, except to note that "the old settlement [on the plain], which has a harbor (λιμήν), is a naval station (ἐπίνειον)" (Loeb ed.).

Ptolemy's *Geography* (second century C.E.) and Pliny's *Natural History* (first century C.E.) both offer textual evidence for Mediterranean coastal sites, consisting primarily of enumerated place-names, but the use of harbor terms by these authors (in ancient Greek and Latin, respectively) is sparing. In the specific case of Cyprus, neither Ptolemy (*Geog.* 5.14.1–7) nor Pliny (*Nat. Hist.* 5.129) includes any harbor terms in his description of the island.

Josephus, in his historical narrative (ca. 75–79 C.E.) concerning the Jewish wars, includes a lengthy description of the Herodian harbor of Caesarea Maritima (*J.W.* 1.408–415). He terms the harbor a λιμήν and provides numerous details on the facility's design, dimensions, and methods of construction. Again, however, the variable nature of literary harbor evidence is apparent within this text as well, for, in a subsequent reference to another Judean harbor, Anthedon, Josephus describes it merely as having been destroyed, then later rebuilt and renamed Agrippeion by King Herod (*J.W.,* 1.416).

portions of the present discussion are based. Heartfelt thanks are also due Prof. V. Watrous and Ms. H. Blitzer for their generous assistance and invaluable advice, particularly during the writer's brief 1994 visit to eastern Crete. Final revisions of the manuscript were completed in part in Cyprus, where the author extends special thanks to the CAARI Regulars for their stimulating input, including Dr. S. Swiny, Mrs. M. Stavrou, Ms. S. C Fox, Prof. R. L. Hohlfelder, and especially our conference organizer and editor, Mrs. H. W. Swiny, whose tireless dedication to Res Maritimae and willingness to share her knowledge of Cypriot archaeology are deeply appreciated. Illustrations were prepared by Ms. J. Ravenhurst, Ms. S. C. Fox, and Ms. K. Barth.

The terms λιμήν and ἐπίνειον both refer generally to a harbor, but ἐπίνειον is commonly interpreted more specifically as "naval station." Rougé traces the origin of this particular understanding of ἐπίνειον to the late tenth century C.E. *Suda,* but notes that in its earlier usage (by authors including Herodotus, Thucydides, Strabo, Pausanias, and Dio Cassius), ἐπίνειον refers to the commercial port of another town, or at least to a harbor that is dependent economically upon a town located some distance away (Rougé 1966: 109–10). Lehmann-Hartleben implies a similar meaning when he states, "Das Wort Epineion hat immer die Bedeutung des Seeplatzes einer bestimmt umschriebenen Region, sei diese nun ein Stamm, eine Landschaft oder eine Stadt (1923: 24, n. 1)." When this original meaning of ἐπίνειον is restored to Strabo's above-cited description of Sicyon, the passage takes on new and broader significance. Before the tenth century C.E., then, the term ἐπίνειον does not represent a particular topographical type of harbor facility. Rougé emphasizes, "nous n'avons trouvé nulle part ailleurs ce terme utilisé pour désigner l'équipement portuaire" (1966: 110). Nevertheless, since ἐπίνειον may denote a harbor with a commercial function, the term does imply the possible presence of quays and warehouses.

Ἐμπόριον, as well as the Latin *portus* and *statio,* are also terms that relate to the economic or commercial function of harbors. Rougé suggests, based upon the evidence of Diodorus Siculus (5.38.5), Strabo (*Geog.* 4.181), Themistius (*Or.* 10.135 c, d), and the *Periplus of the Erythraean Sea* (4, 6, 7, 8), that an ἐμπόριον (Latin: *emporium*) is a collection and transshipment center, where local and foreign goods are received and sold wholesale to exporters or local vendors (1966: 108). An ἐμπόριον may be either a distinct quarter within a large port or a completely separate establishment not necessarily located near the sea (Rougé 1966: 108–9). The term ἐμπόριον, then, indicates a commercial center in a general sense, and therefore cannot be considered a true harbor term.

A *portus* is a large, enclosed harbor that also served as a wholesale market, with warehouses for the storage of imported or soon-to-be-exported merchandise (Rougé 1966: 117–18). A *statio* is an unenclosed, undeveloped anchorage that served as a subsidiary market, where often merchants of similar origin gathered (Rougé 1966: 117–18). Servius (*In Aen.* 2.23) and Isidorus of Hispalis (*Orig.* 14.8.39–40) note that a *portus* is a facility for long-term layover, such as during winter months, while a *statio* offers only temporary refuge (Rougé 1966: 117). The Roman engineer Vitruvius (*De Arch.* 5.12.1) uses the term *portus* in a general sense, meaning a place where ships can find shelter from the weather. Later in his brief discourse on harbors, Vitruvius (*De Arch.* 5.12.2) describes the development of a natural anchorage *(statio)* into an artificial harbor protected by breakwaters *(portus).*

The terms ἐπίνειον, ἐμπόριον, *portus,* and *statio,* then, may be important in understanding a harbor site's archaeological record, for they suggest the possible existence on the site of quay and warehouse remains. *Portus* and *statio* also provide some sense of a harbor's overall topography, for these terms appear to indicate the form (either natural or artificial) of the harbor and the probable presence or absence of breakwater remains. Nevertheless, the terms ἐπίνειον and ἐμπόριον do not represent topographical types of harbors, while ἐπίνειον, ἐμπόριον, *portus,* and *statio* together (because of their relative infrequency in ancient Greek and Latin geographical descriptions) only supply the characteristics of a limited number of known Roman harbor sites. The ancient Greek terms λιμήν and ὅρμος, on the other hand, appear repeatedly in Periploi of the Roman period, and therefore hold greater potential for widespread archaeological significance. The additional use in Periploi of ὕφορμος and πρόσορμος seems to indicate the existence of a full range of technical terms, which may prove informative to archaeologists who survey coastlines and excavate Roman harbor sites. The specific meaning and potential archaeological value of the four terms, λιμήν, ὅρμος, ὕφορμος and πρόσορμος, will first be considered textually, then through the topographical evidence of known harbor sites in Cyprus and Crete.

Λιμήν, as the term appears in ancient literature, represents both a general designation for harbor facilities and the specific term employed by ancient writers to indicate a well-protected, relatively large port (Rougé 1966: 115–16). In general, the term λιμήν may refer to any type of harbor whether large or small, while specifically, from the perspective of Latin terminology, λιμήν is the equivalent of a *portus* (as opposed to a *statio*). When a particular place is designated ἀλίμενος (alimenos), the locality in question is intended to be understood as completely lacking in any sort of maritime facilities. Often, a qualifying adjective is combined with the general term λιμήν to indicate the particular nature of a harbor. For example, with respect to Cypriot harbors, Strabo (*Geog.* 14.6.3) notes that Kition has a λιμήν κλειστός, a "closed harbor," while Stadiasmus (310) describes Melabron as a λιμήν θερινός, a "summer harbor" (figs. 1, 2, 3). Λιμήν in its specific sense of a port, does not represent the sort of facility that provides secure shelter in all weather conditions: that rare type of facility, as Rougé argues (1966: 113–14, 116), is designated by the equally uncommon term πάνορμος (panormos), a derivative of the term ὅρμος.

Ὅρμος is one of the most informative of ancient Greek harbor terms, from an archaeological standpoint, for the term's inherent meaning testifies to a harbor facility's overall topography. The word ὅρμος according to Liddell and Scott's *Greek-English Lexicon* (9th ed., s.v. ὅρμος; hereafter: Liddell and Scott), carries the sense of a circular object

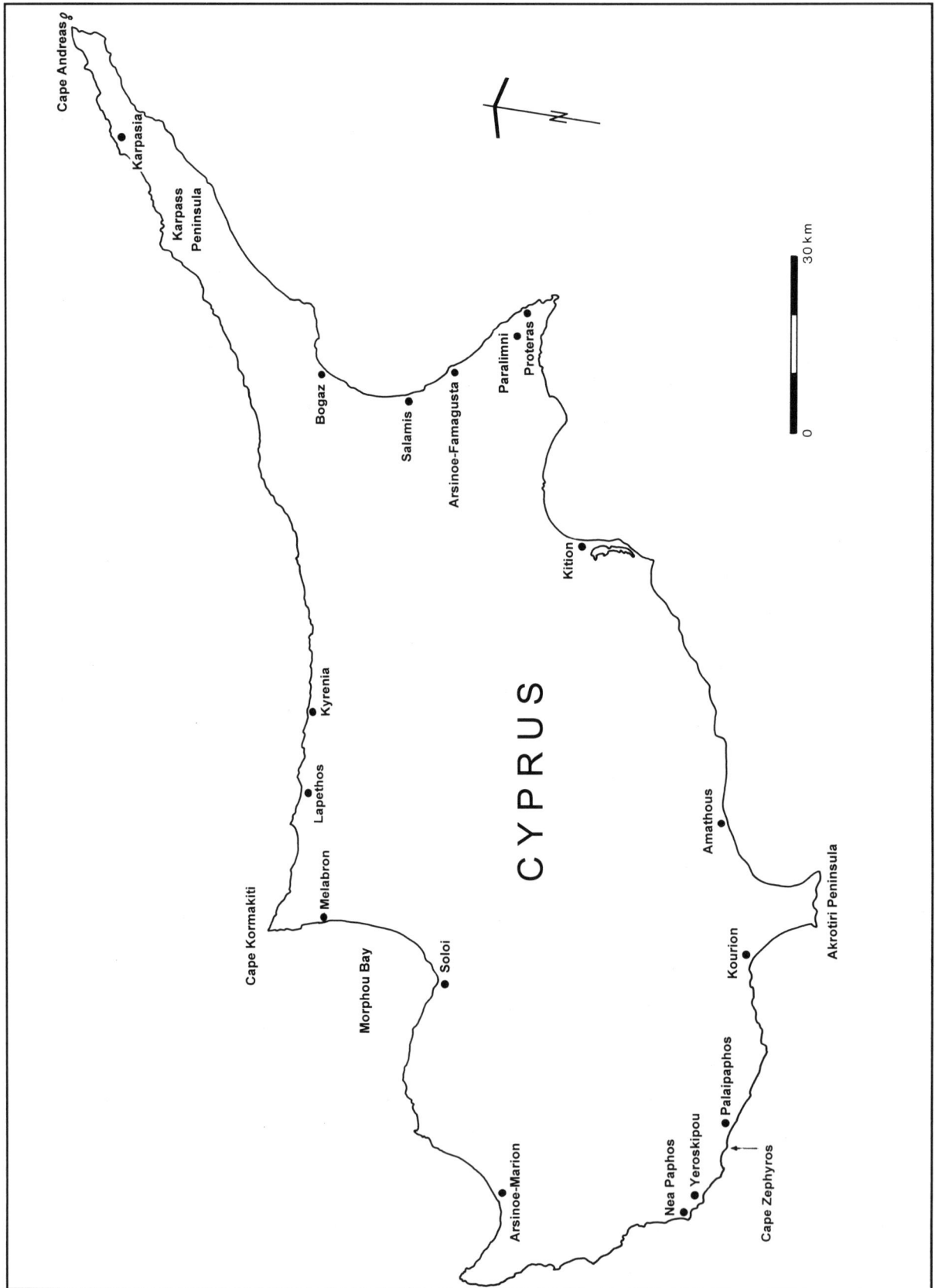

Fig. 1. Cyprus: Coastal sites mentioned in text.

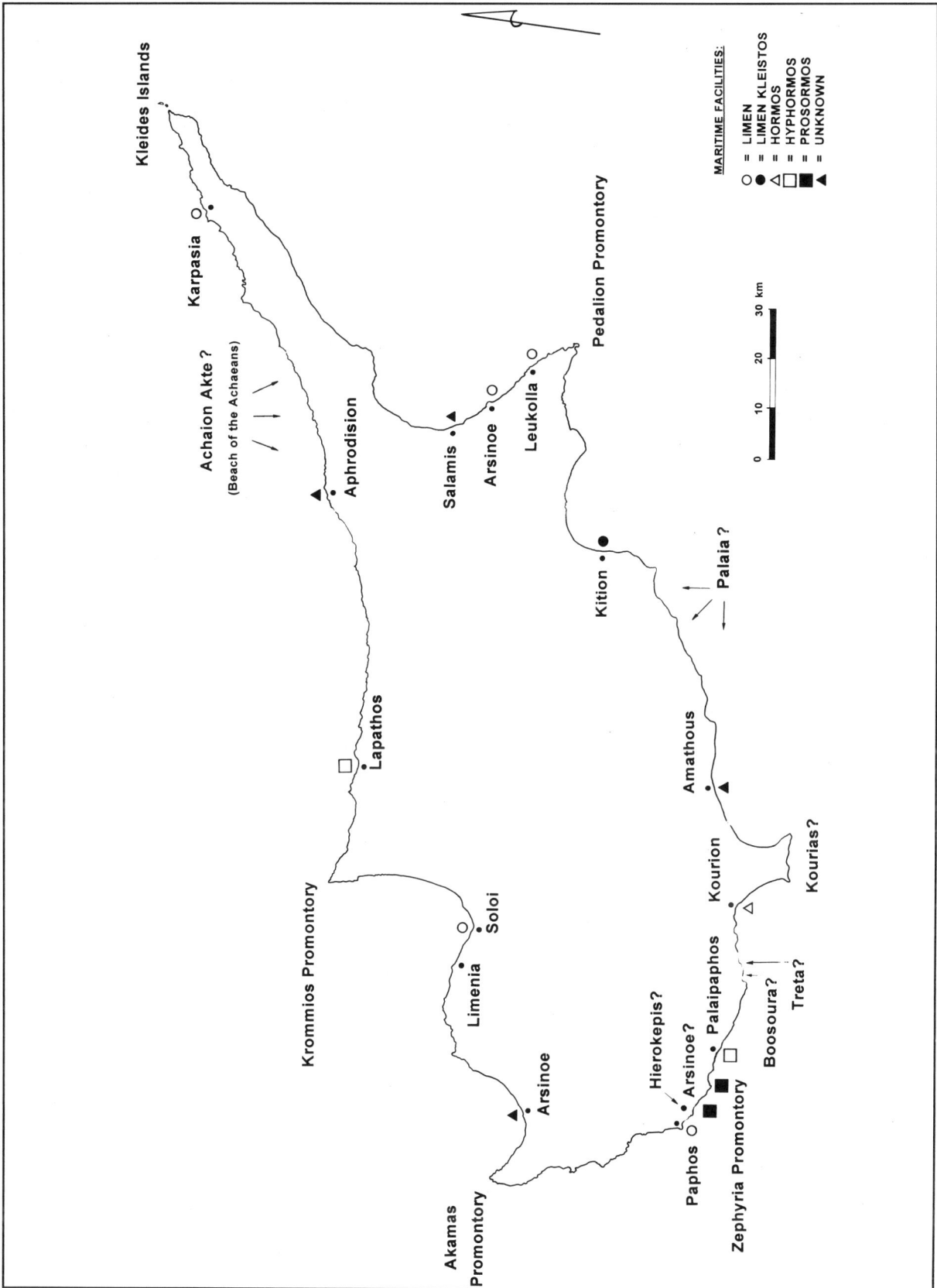

Fig. 2. Coastal Cyprus of Strabo.

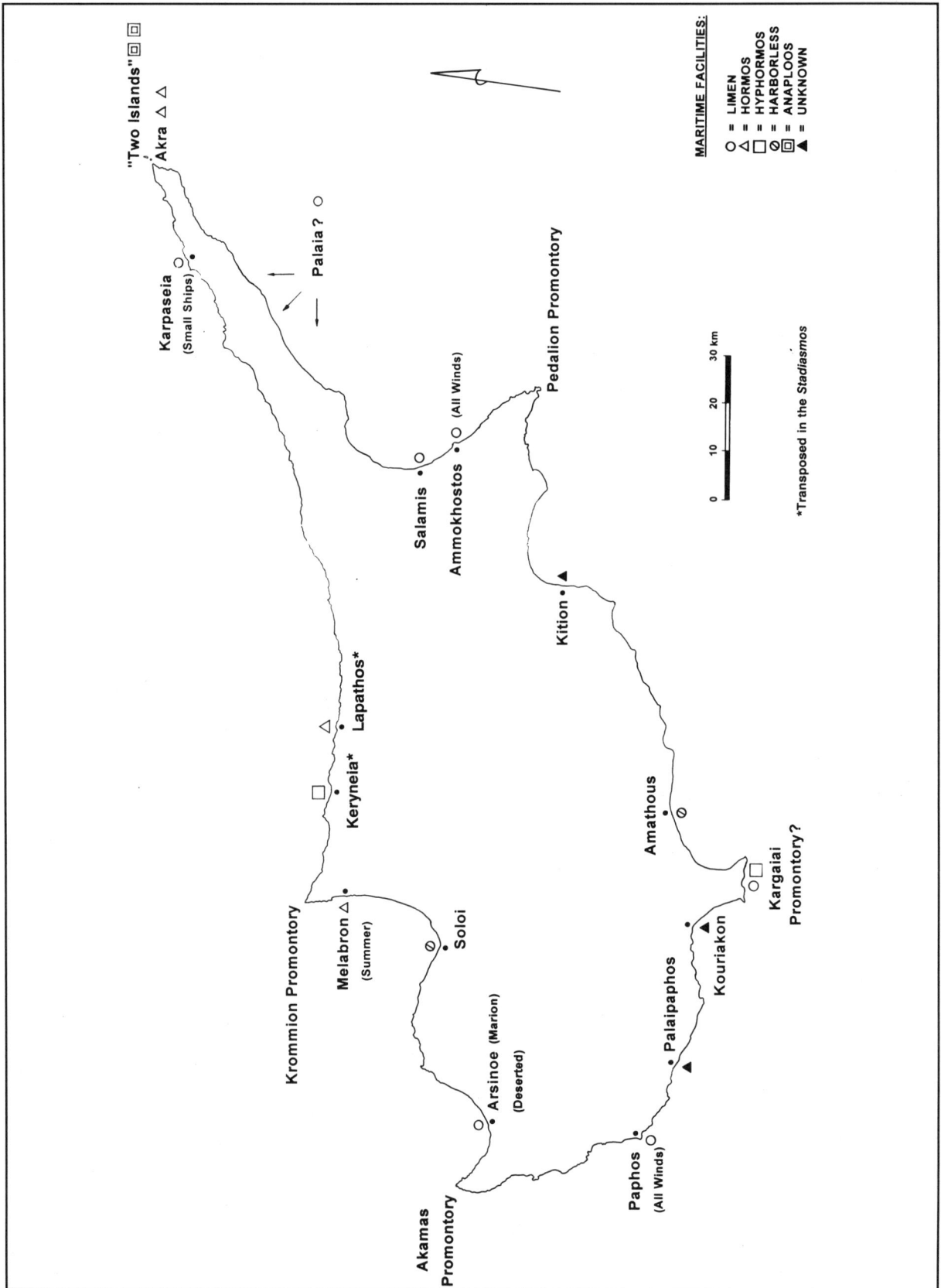

Fig. 3. Coastal Cyprus of Stadiasmos.

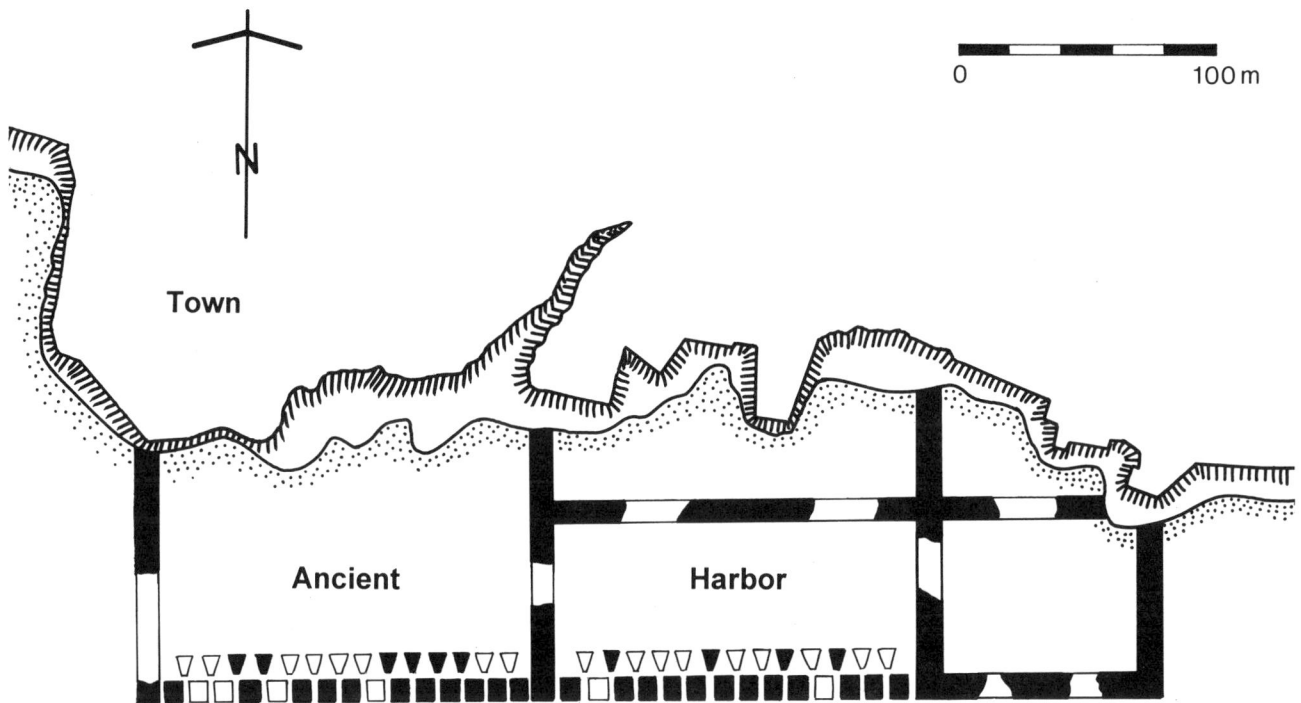

Fig. 4. Puteoli, Itali. After DuBois (1907: fig. 20).

or activity, such as a necklace, collar, or ring dance. When this sense is combined with the word's secondary meaning of "anchorage," "haven," or "refuge," the resulting meaning is a harbor with breakwaters or natural headlands that exhibit an enclosed, ring-like configuration. In a related meaning that stems from this sense of enclosure, ὅρμος may also refer to an inner basin within a harbor facility. Strabo (*Geog.* 5.4.6), for example, describes Puteoli (modern Pozzuoli) in Italy as:

> [A city that] has havens (ὅρμους) ... made by the hand of man, a thing made possible by the natural qualities of the sand .... By mixing the sand-ash with the lime, they can run jetties out into the sea and thus make the wide open shores curve into the form of bays, so that the greatest merchant ships can moor therein with safety (Loeb ed.).

The remains of these harbor basins at ancient Puteoli were recorded in the early 1900s by DuBois (fig. 4), who witnessed at that time features of the Roman harbor now obscured or destroyed by natural forces or modern development (DuBois 1907: fig. 20).

Josephus (*J.W.* 1.410), in his description of Caesarea Maritima, further illustrates this idea of inner basins when he reports that King Herod "constructed a harbor (λιμήν) larger than the Peiraios, including other deep roadsteads (ὅρμους) within its recesses" (Loeb ed.).

Ὅρμος is not always applied so specifically, however, for in at least one instance (Dio Cass. 74.12) the term appears, like λιμήν, as a general designation for a harbor (Rougé 1966: 114). Also like λιμήν, qualifiers are sometimes combined with ὅρμος, such as θερινός (summer), παντοίαις ναυσίν (for all ships), πλοίοις μικροῖς (for small ships), and τοῖς ἐτησίοις (for [use during] the northwest summer winds) (Rougé 1966: 113). Whether the term ὅρμος in such descriptive combinations refers to a harbor in general, or more specifically to a harbor with an enclosed, circular shape, cannot be determined solely from the texts; future archaeological examination of the harbor sites themselves may eventually resolve this question.[2]

Derivatives of the term ὅρμος, in addition to the aforementioned πάνορμος, include ὕφορμος and πρόσορμος. The meaning of these two terms remains largely obscure, however, for although they do appear from the texts to refer to anchorages subordinate in nature to those harbor facili-

[2] For references to specific ὅρμοι that appear with qualifiers in *Stadiasmus Maris Magni,* see Rougé (1966: 113, nn. 6–9).

ties represented by the term ὅρμος (in its specific sense) (Rougé 1966: 115), the actual topography of a ὕφορμος or a πρόσορμος cannot be established without additional information. The term ὕφορμος appears frequently in Periploi, especially that of Stadiasmus, while πρόσορμος is a rare term used only by Strabo in descriptions of southern Anatolian, Cypriot, Levantine, and North African anchorages.[3]

To summarize, the four terms λιμήν, ὅρμος, ὕφορμος, and πρόσορμος, as they are presently understood from ancient Greek texts alone, contain only limited archaeological value. Ὅρμος may hold the greatest potential as an archaeological tool, for this term indicates either a natural or artificial harbor of enclosed, circular shape, or an internal basin within a harbor. Archaeologists forearmed with this literary evidence should plan their strategies for the survey or excavation of known ὅρμος sites to account for the possible remains of breakwaters or internal manmade or natural divisions between basins. The terms λιμήν, ὕφορμος, and πρόσορμος, however, are less informative: λιμήν represents either a natural or artificial harbor of indeterminate size and character, or, more specifically, a natural or artificial port that may have been equipped with warehouses for the temporary storage of trade goods. Ὕφορμος, and πρόσορμος, in comparison with λιμήν and ὅρμος, represent anchorages of smaller size or inferior protection. To begin to gain a fuller understanding of these four harbor terms, literary and archaeological evidence for harbor sites in Cyprus will first be considered.

CYPRIOT ANCIENT HARBORS AND TERMINOLOGY

Ancient Greek harbor terms are used to designate Cypriot harbor facilities in three Periploi of widely ranging date: the probable mid-fourth century B.C.E. text of Pseudo-Scylax and the two Roman works of Strabo (Augustan period) and Stadiasmus (dating somewhere in the first through fourth

centuries C.E.).[4] Neither Pliny the Elder (*Nat. Hist.* 5.129), in the first century C.E., nor Ptolemy (*Geog.* 5.14.1–7), in the second century C.E., refers specifically to the island's harbors, although both writers enumerate Cypriot coastal towns.

The Cypriot Periplous of Pseudo-Scylax (103) (fig. 5) provides only limited assistance in the study of ancient harbor terminology, for the author employs one term, λιμήν, in his description of the island's various harbors (Leonard 1995a: 230, fig. 2). Nevertheless, he does report that Salamis and Soloi each have a λιμήν χειμερινός (a winter harbor), while the former's harbor is also a λιμήν κλειστός (a closed harbor).

Strabo (*Geog.* 14.6.3) (fig. 2) enumerates the Cypriot communities or harbors of Lapethos, Aphrodision, Karpasia, Salamis, Arsinoe (the later Famagusta), Leukolla, which may be located southeast of Paralimni (Leonard 1995a: n. 8), Kition, Palaia (location unknown), Amathous, Kourion, Palaipaphos, Cape Zephyria, Arsinoe (location unknown), Nea Paphos, Arsinoe (Marion), and Soloi. He further reports that Karpasia, Arsinoe-Famagusta, Leukolla, Nea Paphos, and Soloi each have a λιμήν; Kition has a λιμήν κλειστός; Kourion has ὅρμος; Lapethos and Palaipaphos each have a ὕφορμος; and Cape Zephyria and Arsinoe (between Cape Zephyria and Nea Paphos) each have a πρόσορμος. Strabo mentions no maritime facilities for the remaining towns of Aphrodision, Salamis, Amathous, and Arsinoe-Marion. Perhaps these towns did not possess operational harbors at the time of Strabo's writing, in the late first century B.C.E. or early first century C.E.[5]

Stadiasmus (297–317 C.E.) (fig. 3) enumerates Nea Paphos, Palaipaphos, Kouriakon (possibly Kourion), Amathous, Ammochostos (Famagusta), Salamis, Palaia (location unknown), Arsinoe (Marion), Melabron, Soloi, Kyrenia, Lapethos, Karpasia, and Kition. He describes Ammochostos, Salamis, Palaia, Arsinoe-Marion, and Karpasia as each having a λιμήν, and provides additional information about several of these facilities: the λιμήν at

---

[3] The seven πρόσορμοι cited by Strabo in his *Geography* include the following coastal places: 1) near the Dracanon Promontory on the island of Ikaria (14.1.19); 2) one of the three Chelidoniae Islands off the coast of Lycia (14.3.8); 3) Arsinoe in Cilicia (14.5.3); 4,5) Cape Zephyria and Arsinoe in Cyprus (14.6.3); 6) Straton's Tower (Caesarea Maritima) in Judea (16.2.27); and 7) Zephyrion in Cyrenaica (17.3.22).

[4] For dates of Pseudo-Scylax, Strabo, and Stadiasmus, see discussion and bibliography in Allain (1977: 53, 66, 68); Pirazzoli et al. (1992: 375); and Hadjidaki (1988: 467–68, n.13).

[5] Remains of an ancient harbor have been found at Amathous, dating to the late fourth century B.C.E., but this facility may have already gone out of use by 294 B.C.E. (Hermary 1993: 172). According to the excavators, the lack of late Hellenistic and Roman High Imperial material on the site may indicate a period of abandonment, until the sixth to seventh centuries A.D. when brief reoccupation of the shoreline is indicated by the presence of two wells (Empereur and Verlinden 1986a: 907; 1987a: 759). See also Empereur (1985; 1995); Empereur and Verlinden (1986b; 1987b).

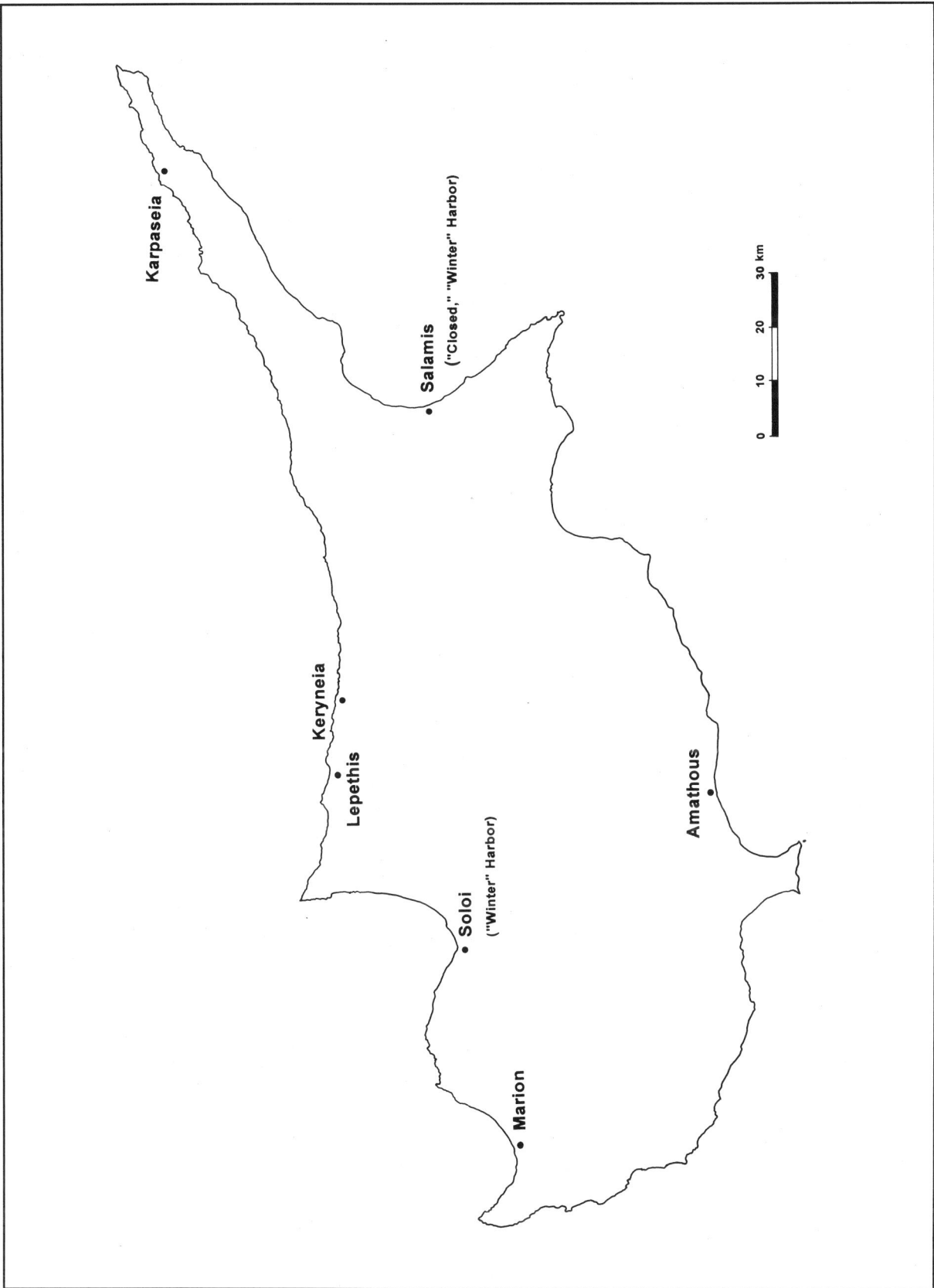

Fig. 5. Coastal Cyprus of Pseudo-Scylax.

Arsinoe (Marion) is deserted (ἔρημος), that at Karpasia is only suitable for small ships (πλοίοις μικροῖς), and both of these harbors are disturbed by northern winds (χειμάζει βορέου); the λιμήν at Ammochostos is suitable for all winds (παντὶ ἀνέμῳ), but this harbor has reefs in its basin—beware (ἔχει δὲ ἐν τῇ καταγωγῇ χοιράδας· διαφυλάττου).[6]

Stadiasmus further reports that the city of Nea Paphos (297) has a triple harbor suitable for all winds (λιμενα τρίπλουν παντὶ ἀνέμῳ, Lapethos (313) has a ὅρμος, Melabron (310) has a ὅρμος θερινός (a summer ὅρμος), Kyrenia (312) has a ὕφορμος, and Amathous (302) and Soloi (311) are harborless (ἀλίμενοι). Stadiasmus mentions no harbor facilities for Palaipaphos, Kouriakon, and Kition.[7] Perhaps when the Periplous was written, at some point between the first and fourth centuries C.E., these towns no longer possessed operational harbor facilities, or had ceased to be regular ports of call for travellers sailing along the island's southern coast.[8]

Three other places along the Cypriot coast are also noted by Stadiasmus: Kargaiai (303), which may represent the Akrotiri Peninsula (Leonard 1995a: n. 20, fig. 6); Akra (Cape Andreas) (307); and two islands lying near Akra (Kleides Islands) (307). Stadiasmus reports that Kargaiai is peninsular (ἀκρωτήριον) and has a λιμήν, a ὕφορμος, and fresh water; Akra has two ὅρμοι, both with fresh water; and the two islands near Akra each have an ἀνάπλοος

(anaploos), an anchorage of indeterminate topography where, judging only from the rare term itself, ships can withdraw from the winds and find shelter.[9]

The harbor terms used by Strabo and Stadiasmus for describing Cypriot harbors convey (on the basis of their textual interpretation discussed above) certain *a priori* impressions of the harbor sites' individual topographies. Subsequent consideration of archaeological and geomorphological evidence from the harbor sites themselves may confirm or dispel these impressions, as well as provide further insight into the meaning of the various terms. For example, Karpasia, Salamis, Kition, Nea Paphos, Arsinoe (Marion), Soloi, Arsinoe-Famagusta (Ammochostos), Leukolla, and Palaia are each reported to have a λιμήν, which, in the term's specific sense, may be translated "port." These cities, with the possible exception of Kition, Leukolla, and Palaia, were among the island's largest centers, and their harbor facilities may indeed have served as commercial ports.

The archaeological remains of harborworks have been recorded, or their presence at least noted, at several of the Cypriot λιμήν sites, including Karpasia, Salamis, Kition, Nea Paphos, and Soloi (du Plat Taylor 1980; du Plat Taylor and Megaw 1981; Flemming 1974; Papageorghiou 1990, 1991; Hohlfelder and Leonard 1994; Leonard and Hohlfelder 1993; Nicolaou 1966: 98; Des Gagniers and Tinh 1985: plans B,C). The ancient harbor at Arsinoe-Famagusta has never been studied, while that which served Arsinoe-Marion still

---

[6] The meaning of καταγωγῇ is problematic, but definitions given in Liddell and Scott (s.v. καταγωγῇ) include: "bringing down from (the high sea)," "halting-place," "place of rest," "lodging," and "shelter." Καταγωγῇ is translated "entrance" in Wallace and Orphanides (1990: 135).

[7] Mlynarczyk suggests that Stadiasmus ignores the anchorage at Palaipaphos, described by Strabo (*Geog.* 14.6.3) as a ὕφορμος, because the Stadiasmus account is "a typical Periplous, a guide for sailors, who were interested most in safe landing places provided with drinking water. Palaipaphos ... evidently was not considered such a place" (1990: 31).

[8] For Kition and Kouriakon during the Roman Period see below.

[9] Ἀνάπλοος is defined in Liddell and Scott (s.v. ἀνάπλοος) as "sailing upstream," a "canal (from the sea to an inland harbor)," "putting out (to sea)," and a "sailing back" or a "return." Unless the topography of the Kleides Islands has changed since antiquity, or been partially obscured by a rise in surrounding sea level, these rocks all seem too small to have had any actual canals or narrow channels leading into them away from the sea. A channel does exist *between* the Kleides Islands, however, through which perhaps ancient ships passed before anchoring in the lee of the islands (cf. Green 1973: fig. 5).

Alternatively, perhaps the term ἀνάπλοος referred to an anchorage that was reached by sailing against the current. The *Mediterranean Pilot* notes that the strength and direction of the currents in the vicinity of the Kleides Islands depend on the prevailing wind (Haslam 1976: 110, sect. 570). Also, the largest island ("Kleides Islet"), "should be rounded at a distance of at least 1 mile, as the current may attain a rate of 1.5 knots and confused seas build up after strong winds; the strength and direction of the current may differ from one side of the islet to the other" (Haslam 1976: 110, sect. 570).

Based on the example of the Kleides Islands, then, ἀνάπλοος might refer not to a particular type of harbor topography, but to the way in which sailors must approach the haven (against the current or "upstream"). The ἀνάπλοος at the Kleides Islands, furthermore, could have been on either side of the small archipelago, depending upon the wind and currents.

remains to be located. Although none of these λιμήν sites have yet produced structures identified as seaside warehouses, Karpasia, Salamis, Nea Paphos, and Soloi do have ancient breakwaters extending into the sea (du Plat Taylor 1980: fig. 2; Flemming 1974: 169–70, fig. 5; Leonard and Hohlfelder 1993: fig. 2; Nicolaou 1966: 98; Des Gagniers and Tinh: plans B, C).

The λιμένες at Karpasia and Nea Paphos consist of natural bays that were further enclosed by ashlar and rubble breakwaters. The breakwaters at Karpasia (fig. 6), installed evidently in the late fifth or early fourth century B.C.E. and subsequently improved during the Hellenistic period by the addition of quays, were built upon natural rock outcroppings (du Plat Taylor 1980: 154–56, 199). The breakwaters at Nea Paphos (fig. 7), on the other hand, constructed originally perhaps in the late fourth century B.C.E., appear to have been founded directly upon the seabed (Hohlfelder 1995: 194; Leonard and Hohlfelder 1993: 367–68). The harbor of Nea Paphos was probably a λιμήν κλειστός, at least in its original Hellenistic phase, with the city walls extending along the breakwaters to a fortifiable entrance (Hohlfelder 1995: 194; Hohlfelder and Leonard 1994: 46–47; Mlynarczyk 1990: 102). None of the historical sources, however, specifically mention such an enclosed configuration at Nea Paphos, and the architectural remains evident today suggest that by Roman times the harbor had either deteriorated or been altered from its original fortified design.[10] Whether the internally subdivided, triple harbor, mentioned by Stadiasmus, reflects the original Hellenistic design or a later Roman development can only be determined through continued archaeological study of the harbor.

The λιμήν at Soloi (fig. 8), merely by its location within Morphou Bay, was largely protected from southern and western winds. Breakwaters were installed, nevertheless, to provide ships with even greater security, particularly from northern and northwestern winds. The date of the harbor's construction remains unknown, but Pseudo-Scylax's earlier description (103) of a winter harbor (λιμήν χειμερινός) at Soloi may indicate that breakwaters capable of sheltering ships from the northern and northwestern summer winds had not yet been installed in the mid-fourth century B.CE.. The present internal area of the harbor appears from site plans to be small, but alluvial deposits from the Kambos and other nearby rivers may have gradually choked the

harbor's internal basin (Des Gagniers and Tinh 1985: plans B, C). This may explain Stadiasmus' later description of Soloi (311) as harborless (ἀλίμενος).

The λιμήν at Salamis (fig. 9), which lay near the mouth of the Pedieos River, may have consisted of a natural haven further protected by at least one ashlar and rubble breakwater (Hill 1940: 11–12, 129; Nicolaou 1966: 96; Flemming 1974: 169–70, fig. 5). This harbor, initially termed a λιμήν κλειστός by Pseudo-Scylax (103), suffered from extensive siltation due to the outflow of the Pedieos and nearby Yialias Rivers. The insidious effect of this natural process, combined with the importance of having an operational harbor, may explain not only why Nea Paphos eventually replaced Salamis as the island's capital in the second century B.C.E., but also why Strabo omits any reference to harbor facilities at Salamis in the Augustan period. Stadiasmus' subsequent description of a λιμήν at Salamis (305) may indicate that the harbor had been included in the urban renewal that followed destructive earthquakes in the first and fourth centuries C.E.

The λιμήν κλειστός at Kition also consisted of a natural inlet from the sea, beside which shipsheds were built at the end of the fifth century B.C.E. or in the first quarter of the fourth century B.C.E. (Nicolaou 1976a: fig. 17; Gifford 1985; Karageorghis 1989: 824–26; Papageorghiou 1990: 964–65, fig. 86; 1991: 812, fig. 46; Salles et al. 1993: 28; Yon 1995: 125). This natural inlet or bay at the foot of Bamboula hill appears to have been used until the third century B.C.E., when the harbor began to decline and the silting site fell largely into abandonment until the Medieval Period (Salles et al. 1993: 30–31). As in the harbor at Amathous (see above, n. 5), the archaeological record at Kition so far indicates only occasional use of the immediate shoreline during the Roman Period (Calvet 1993: 27), although the actual Roman harbors at both sites may yet remain to be discovered. Strabo's description of a λιμήν κλειστός at Kition, then, may be based upon outdated information, while Stadiasmos' failure to mention a harbor facility at all is perhaps an indicator of the city's relative decline during the Roman Period.

At various times in Cypriot Roman history, then, Karpasia, Nea Paphos, Soloi, and Salamis probably served as regional centers equipped with relatively large, well-protected λιμένες or ports.[11] Palaia and Leukolla, although simi-

---

[10] Vitruvius (5.12.1), whose early Imperial treatise, *De Architectura,* often reflects prior Hellenistic practices, describes generally the construction of enclosed harbors, the mouths of which may be blocked with chains. The mouth of the harbor at Nea Paphos may have also been flanked by a lighthouse standing on the *terminus* of the western breakwater (see Leonard et al. 1995).

[11] The role of Kition harbor in Cypriot Roman history remains uncertain, although maritime commercial activity probably continued there to some degree either within the silting harbor itself or somewhere nearby.

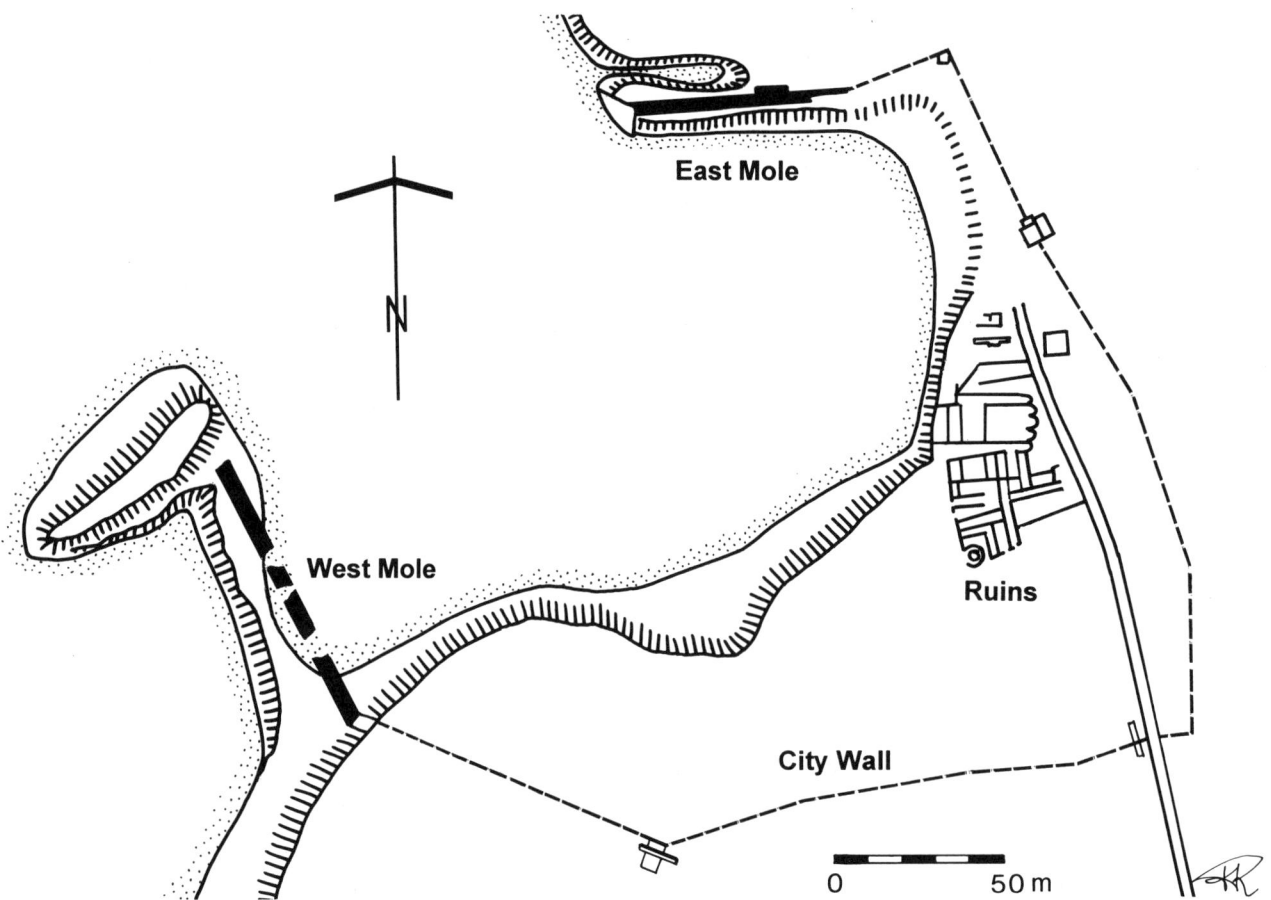

Fig. 6. Karpasia, Cyprus. After du Plat Taylor (1980: fig. 2).

larly identified as λιμένες, appear to have been smaller communities with only minor harbor facilities. Strabo (*Geog.* 14.6.3) refers to Palaia (fig. 2) merely as a small town (πολίχνη), while Stadiasmus (305a) (fig. 3) reports it is a village that has both a λιμήν and water (χώμη ἐστὶ καὶ λιμένα ἔχει καὶ ὕδωρ). Strabo (*Geog.* 14.6.3) enumerates Leukolla merely as a λιμήν (ˉειτ ἄλλος λιμήν Λεύκολλα), while Stadiasmus fails entirely to include it in his Periplous. The location of ancient Palaia has not yet been determined, perhaps in part because the historical sources give conflicting accounts of its position on the Cypriot coastline: either between Kition and Amathous (Strabo, *Geog.* 14.6.3) or along the southern littoral of the Karpas Peninsula (Stadiasmus, 305a–307). The site of Akrotiri, on the Karpas Peninsula northeast of Bogaz, may have been Roman Palaia (known previously as Knidos?), for archaeological remains found there range in date from the Late Bronze Age through Byzantine Period (Bouzek 1988: 71). Furthermore, the mole of an ancient harbor has been observed nearby in the sea (Bouzek 1988: 73).

Artificial harbor remains have not yet been found in the area of Paralimni, however, where Leukolla may once have stood (Leonard 1995a: n. 8). The widespread presence of pottery sherds scattered along the seabed in the vicinity of Paralimni and Protaras indicate Roman maritime activity, but the site of an actual harbor so far remains elusive. Based upon such insufficient evidence, Palaia and Leukolla could either have been artificial harbors or simple natural anchorages. Until further information does become available, Strabo's and Stadiasmus' identifications of Palaia and Leukolla probably should be viewed as examples of the abstract term λιμήν, meaning a harbor in the general sense.

The term ὅρμος, based upon Cypriot archaeological evidence, represents medium-sized or small harbors protected by artificial breakwaters or natural headlands. Strabo (14.6.3) describes the harbor at Kourion as ὅρμος, where submerged architectural remains indicate the existence in antiquity of an artificial harbor formed by at least one breakwater (figs. 10, 11; Leonard 1995a: 236, 238). This poorly

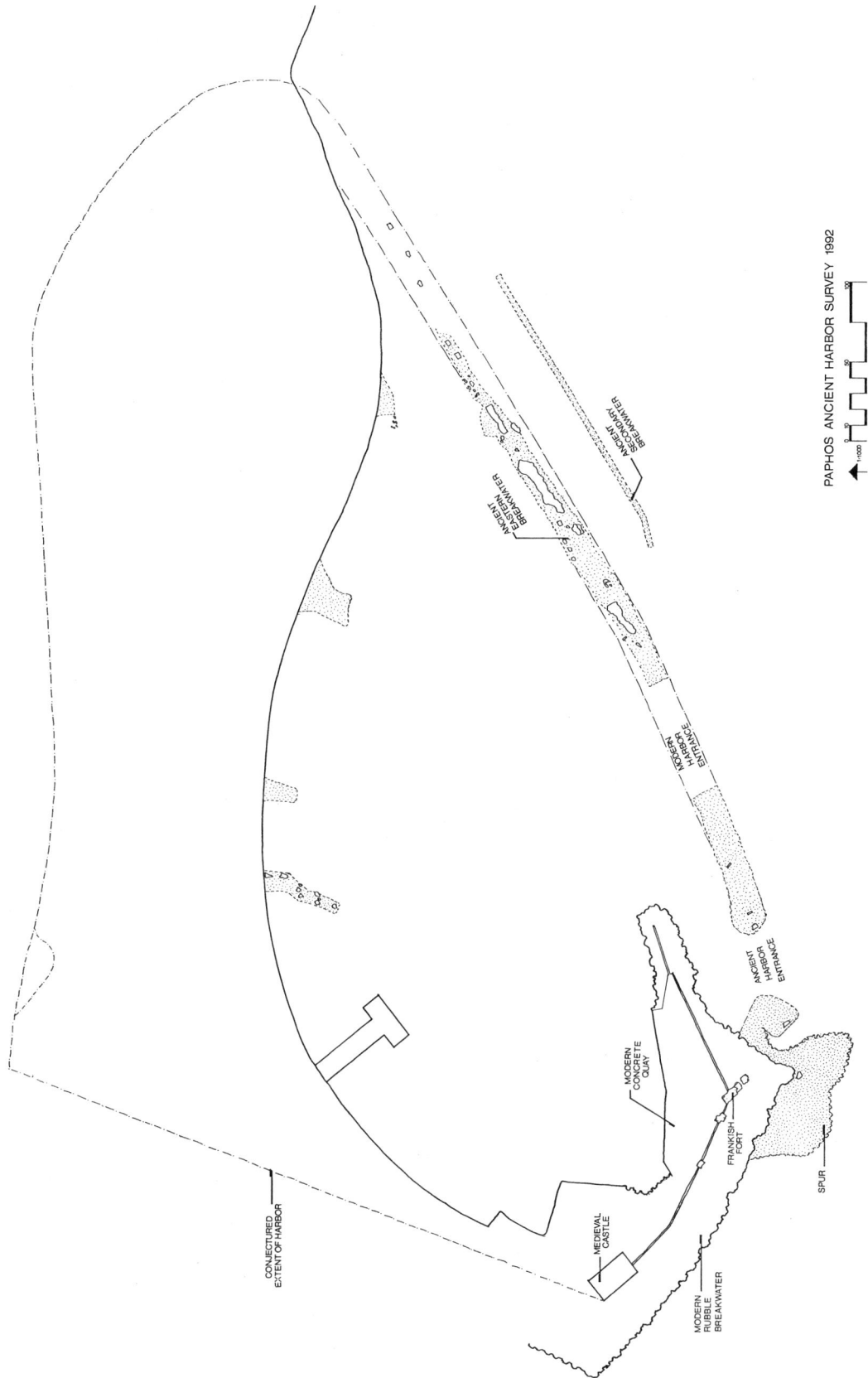

PAPHOS ANCIENT HARBOR SURVEY 1992

ANCIENT SECONDARY BREAKWATER

ANCIENT EASTERN INNER BREAKWATER

MODERN HARBOR ENTRANCE

ANCIENT HARBOR ENTRANCE

CONJECTURED EXTENT OF HARBOR

MODERN CONCRETE QUAY

MEDIEVAL CASTLE

FRANKISH FORT

SPUR

MODERN RUBBLE BREAKWATER

Fig. 7. Nea Paphos, Cyprus.

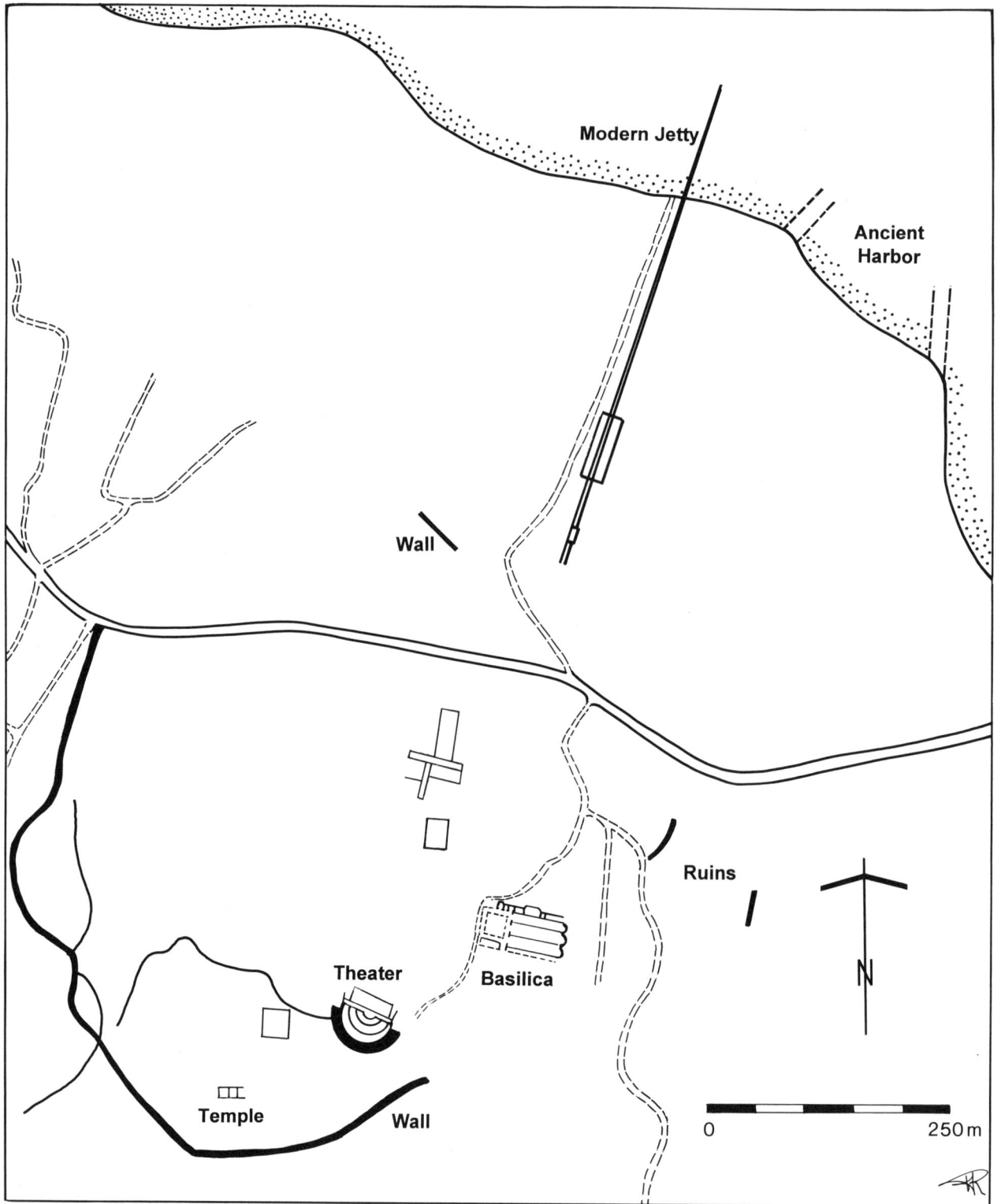

Fig. 8. Soloi, Cyprus. After Des Gagniers and Tinh (1985: plans B, C).

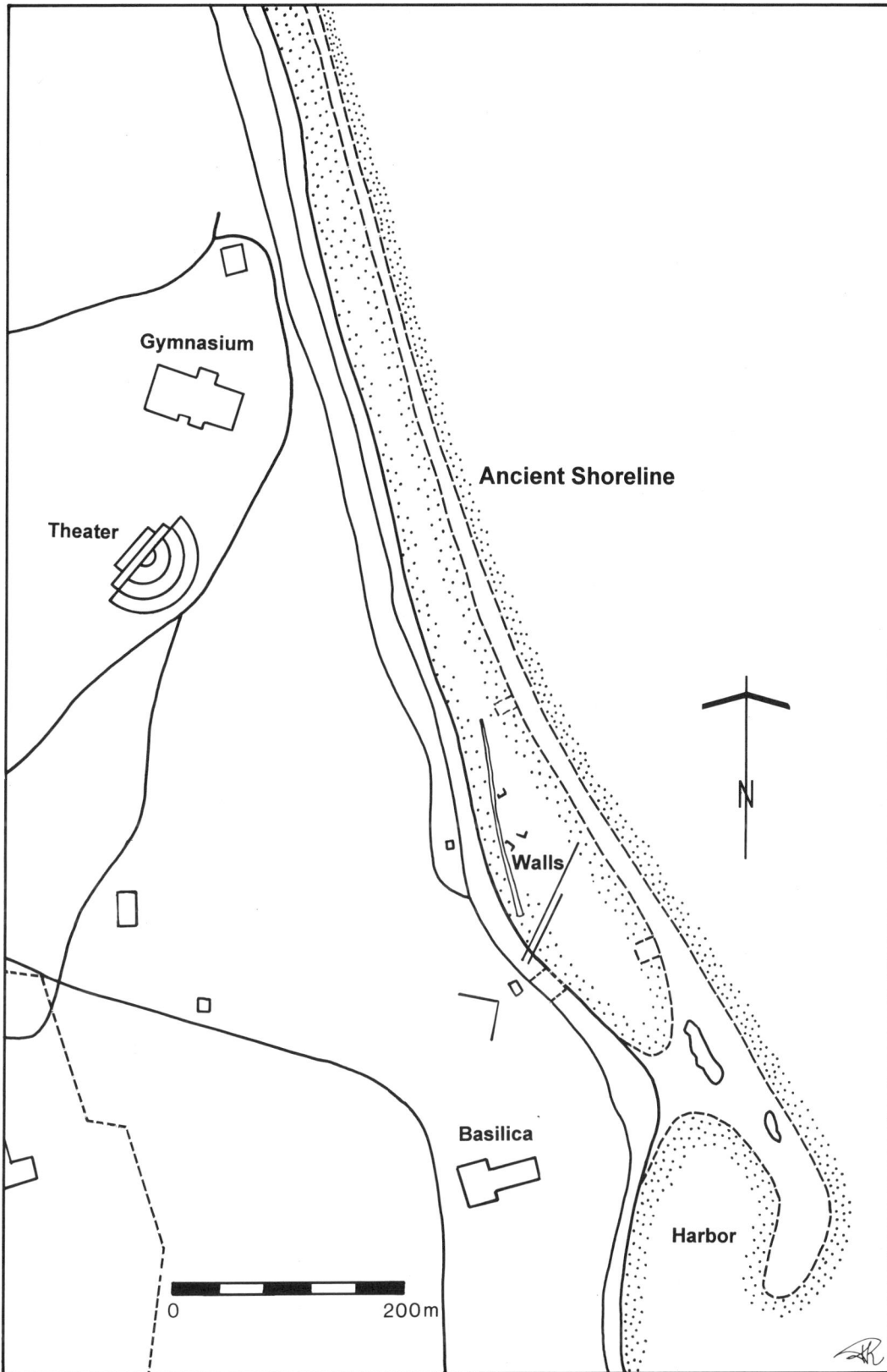

Fig. 9. Salamis, Cyprus. After Frost (1974: fig. 2).

preserved mole of indeterminate date, which appears to have
been constructed of ashlar blocks and rubble, projects acutely
from the present shoreline (cf. Swiny 1982: map 2). The
area once enclosed by this harbor probably included the now-
silted beach area and adjacent sandy flatland that extends
inland to the base of the neighboring cliffs. This internal
area, originally bounded on the land side by the concave,
southwestern slopes of the overlooking acropolis, and on
the sea side by at least one breakwater previously extending
further seaward, would have constituted a roughly circular
basin aptly reflected in the term ὅρμος.

If the "Kouriakon" of Stadiasmus (302, 303, 316) (fig.
3) is indeed to be identified with Kourion, as its position in
the enumeration suggests, then Stadiasmus' lack of reference to a harbor there may indicate that Kourion's ὅρμος
had gone out of use by the time the Periplous was written.[12]
Furthermore, although alluvial siltation caused by outflow
from the nearby Kouris River may have played some role in
the decline of Kourion harbor, the facility's ultimate fate,
like that of the city itself, was probably decided by destructive earthquakes in the 330s and 340s C.E., with a final in-
sult in 365 C.E. (Soren 1981: 122; 1986: 400–1; Soren and
Lane 1981: 178–82).[13] In this case, Stadiasmus' silence concerning harbor facilities at Kourion might constitute negative evidence in support of a later, fourth century date (post-
330s C.E.) for the Periplous itself. Such speculations, however, while worthy of consideration, can only be confirmed
through continued study of the textual and archaeological
evidence.

Cypriot examples of ὅρμοι also include Lapethos and
Melabron (south of Cape Kormakiti on Morphou Bay)
which Stadiasmus (313, 310) (fig. 3) describes as cities
with a ὅρμος and ὅρμος θερινός (a summer ὅρμος), respectively. Lapethos and Melabron, like Kourion, probably
had middle-sized Roman harbors of some importance.
Lapethos (fig. 12) was equipped with an artificial harbor
formed by two breakwaters: a long northern arm that angled
twice to enclose the inner basin, and a short southern arm
that projected directly from the shore, leaving only a narrow entrance open to the southwest (Nicolaou 1976b: fig.
1). This man-made harbor may have been built after the
Augustan period, for Strabo describes Lapethos as a
ὕφορμος or a minor, probably natural, anchorage. Caution
must be exercised in using Strabo's descriptions for dating
purposes, however, since the information upon which he
based his geographical accounts may have been old at the
time of writing (Pirazzoli et al. 1992: 387). The Periplous
of Stadiasmus, which seems—from its detailed coastal description and specificity of harbor terms—likely to have been
a relatively up-to-date navigational handbook, provides at
least a *terminus ante quem* (albeit not precise) for the construction of the ὅρμος at Lapethos.

The ὅρμος at Melabron (fig. 1) may simply have been
a natural facility, for the only architectural remains preserved
there are those of the town on the adjacent shore (Nicolaou
1966: 98).[14] Stadiasmus' report of a ὅρμος θερινός suggests that Melabron's harbor probably lay open to southern
and western winds. Unless the remains of artificial break-

---

[12] Müller (1855: CXXVIII, S.211) suggests that Κουριακόν and Κρομμυακόν may be contracted forms of Κουριὰς
ἄκρα and Κρομμύου ἄκρα or Κουριὰς ἄκρον and Κρομμύου ἄκρον. The geographical proximity of Krommyakon and
Melabron, as described in *Stadiasmus Maris Magni* (310), does indeed indicate that "Krommyakon" ought to be identified
with Cape Krommyon (modern Cape Kormakiti) on the north coast. The peninsula on the south coast (modern Akrotiri
Peninsula), however, which Pliny and Ptolemy call "Kourias," appears in *Stadiasmus Maris Magni* (303) under the name
"Kargaiai":

᾿Απὸ δὲ τοῦ Κουριακοῦ ἐπὶ Καργαίας στάδιοι μ΄· ἀκρωτήριόν ἐστιν ἔχον λιμένα, ὕφορμον, καὶ ὕδωρ.
From Kouriakon to Kargaiai is 40 stadia. [Kargaiai] is a peninsula which has a λιμήν, a ὕφορμος, and water.

(The fact that the epithet qualifies Kargaiai, not Kouriakon, is demonstrated by numerous other passages in the Periplous
[exs. 310–314], in which the epithet qualifies the ultimate locality named in the previous sentence.). It does not seem
reasonable, then, to interpret "Kouriakon" as also referring to Kourias (Akrotiri Peninsula). Instead, Kouriakon should
perhaps be understood to represent Κουριὸν ἄκρον, the headland or bluff upon which stands the city of Kourion.

[13] Several early Christian basilicas were constructed at Kourion. beginning in the late fourth century C.E., but the extent
to which the city was rebuilt and repopulated after the C.E. 365 earthquake remains unknown. For the latest discovery of a
basilica at Kourion, see Christou (this volume).

[14] Note, however, that an Italian survey team in the 1970s, led by L. Quilici and S. Quilici Gigli, may have found traces
of an ancient harbor and of a nearby lighthouse at the site of Palaekastro (Quilici and Quilici Gigli 1972–73: 12, 45, 54–56).
Additional work must be undertaken at Melabron, nevertheless, before the harbor's natural or artificial topography and
functional history are understood.

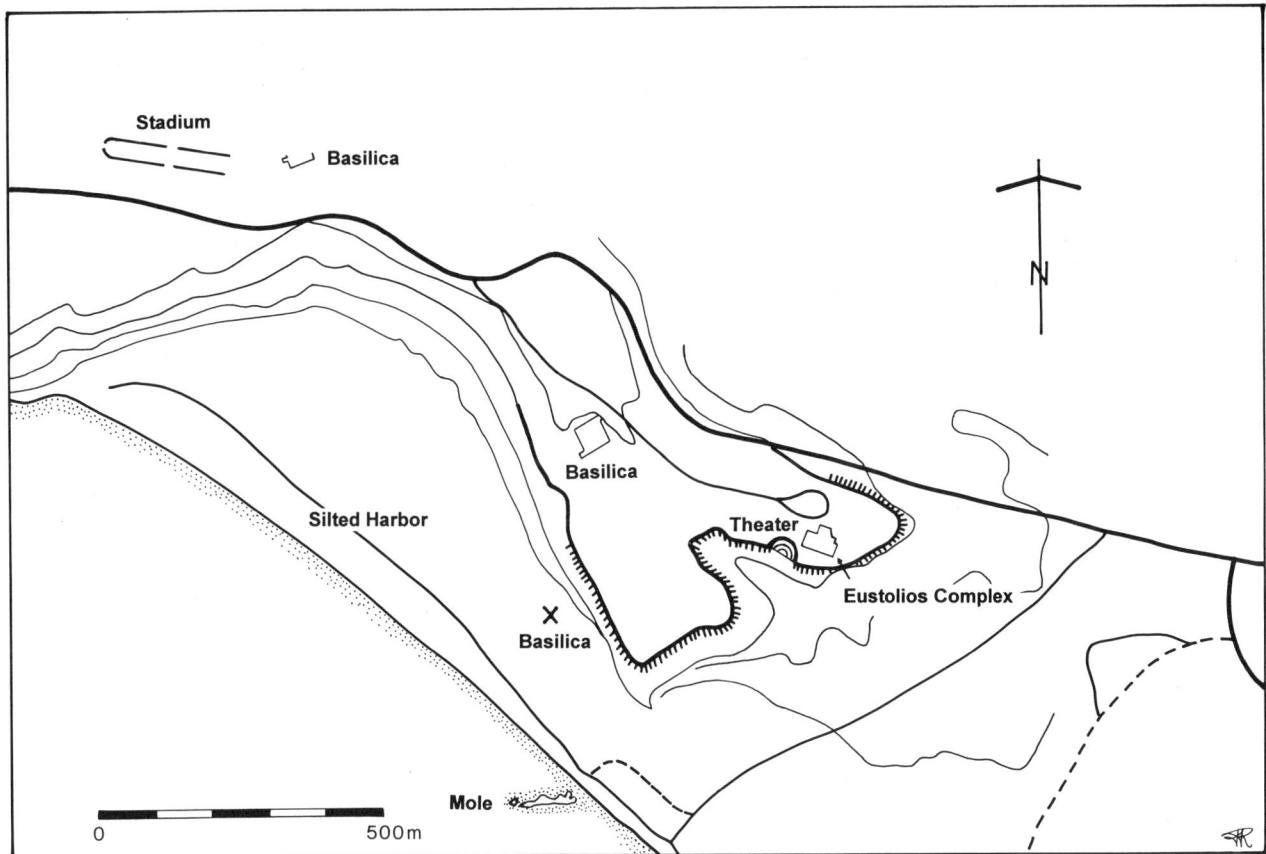

Fig. 10. Kourion, Cyprus. After Swiny (1982: map 2).

waters are eventually discovered at the site of Melabron, the description of a ὅρμος at Melabron should probably be interpreted as indicative of the facility's natural topographical setting, either in a circular bay or rounded river mouth now silted.

Ὅρμος is also employed by Stadiasmus (307) in describing two harbors at Akra, the remote promontory (now known as Cape Andreas) located at the tip of the Karpas Peninsula (fig. 1). In this case, the term ὅρμος probably reflects the natural topography of two enclosed (roughly circular) coves located on opposite sides of the cape, in one or the other of which ships could seek shelter depending upon the direction of the wind. Although the exact locations of two such ὅρμοι have not yet been identified, evidence for anchoring during antiquity has been discovered during underwater archaeological survey around the cape (Green 1969, 1973).

The term ὕφορμος, based upon Cypriot archaeological evidence, is less clear-cut in its meaning than λιμήν and ὅρμος. Palaipaphos, identified by Strabo (*Geog.* 14.6.3) (fig. 2) as having a ὕφορμος, appears to have had an anchorage that was not only inferior to those harbors described as ὅρμοι, but also never enclosed with artificial harborworks. Similarly, the ὕφορμος at Kargaiai (Kourias,

Akrotiri Peninsula), reported by Stadiasmus (303) (fig. 3), also seems to have been a minor, natural anchorage. The exact location of this anchorage remains uncertain, however, for there are several possible locations around the Akrotiri Peninsula (fig. 13): in the lee of the eastern coast (now known as Ladies' Mile Beach); off the western coast, where there can be seen on shore a scatter of Roman artifacts including pottery sherds, corroded coins, and glass fragments; within the confines of what is now the salt lake in the middle of the peninsula, but which in Roman times may have been a lagoon open to the east; or, lastly, in a southern bay (now known as Dreamer's Bay) where possible Roman warehouses are preserved on shore, and a submerged ancient breakwater lies in the sea (Heywood 1982: 167; Leonard 1995a: 227, n. 20, fig. 7). The last location appears the *least* likely candidate, for Stadiasmus also reports that Kargaiai has a ὅρμος, a description that best suits this artificial harbor at Dreamer's Bay. Without additional evidence, then, the ὕφορμος at Kargaiai can only be envisioned presently as an anchorage of natural, but otherwise indeterminate, topography.

The sense of the term ὕφορμος as a natural anchorage appears at odds with the evidence of Lapethos and Kyrenia, however, where the remains of man-made breakwaters have

Rubble Scatter

Buoy

Large Block

Kourion Mole
1990-1991
Scale: 1:300 (approx.)

Poseidon Grass

Rubble Scatter

Sand Beach

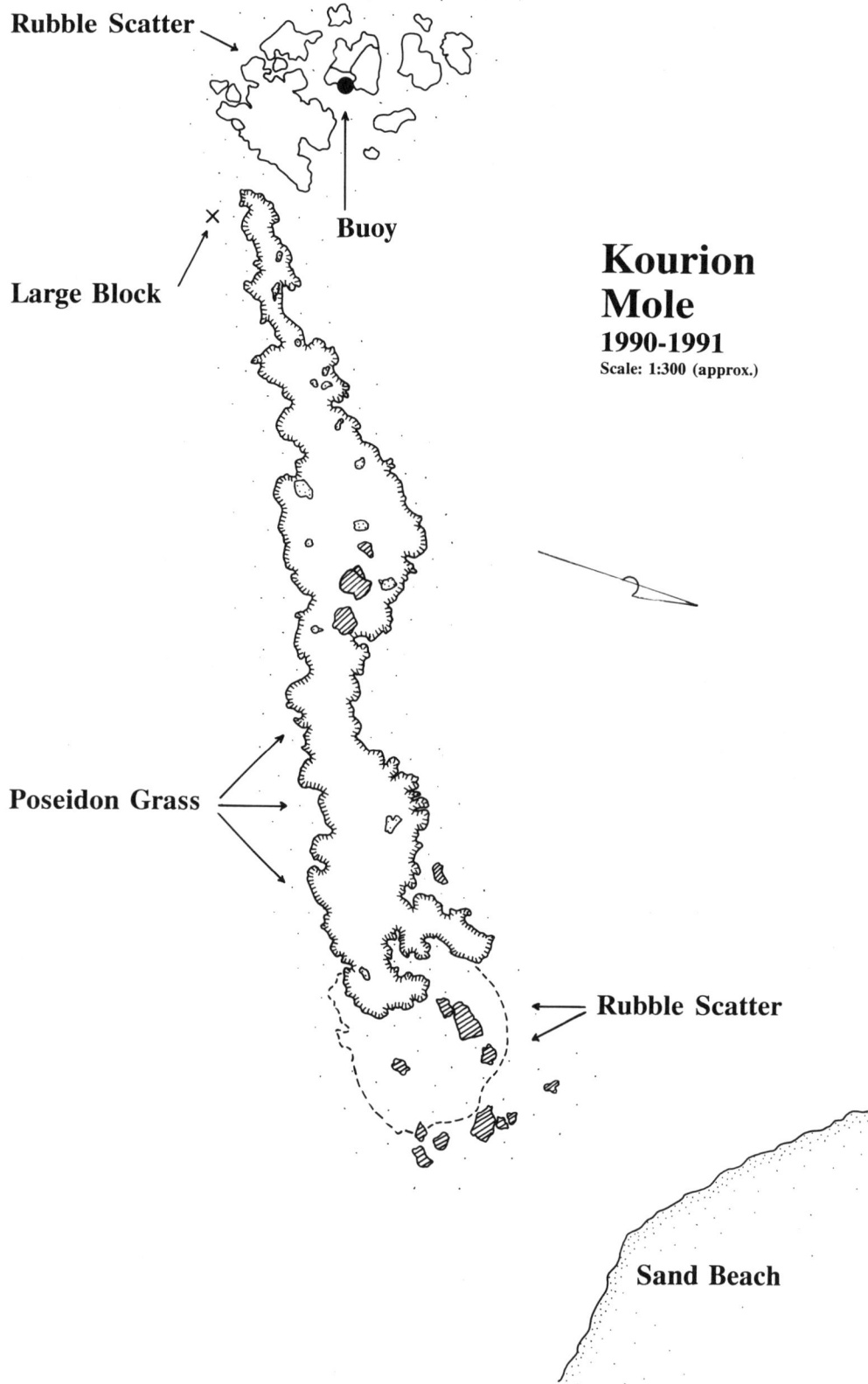

Fig. 11. Kourion, Cyprus.

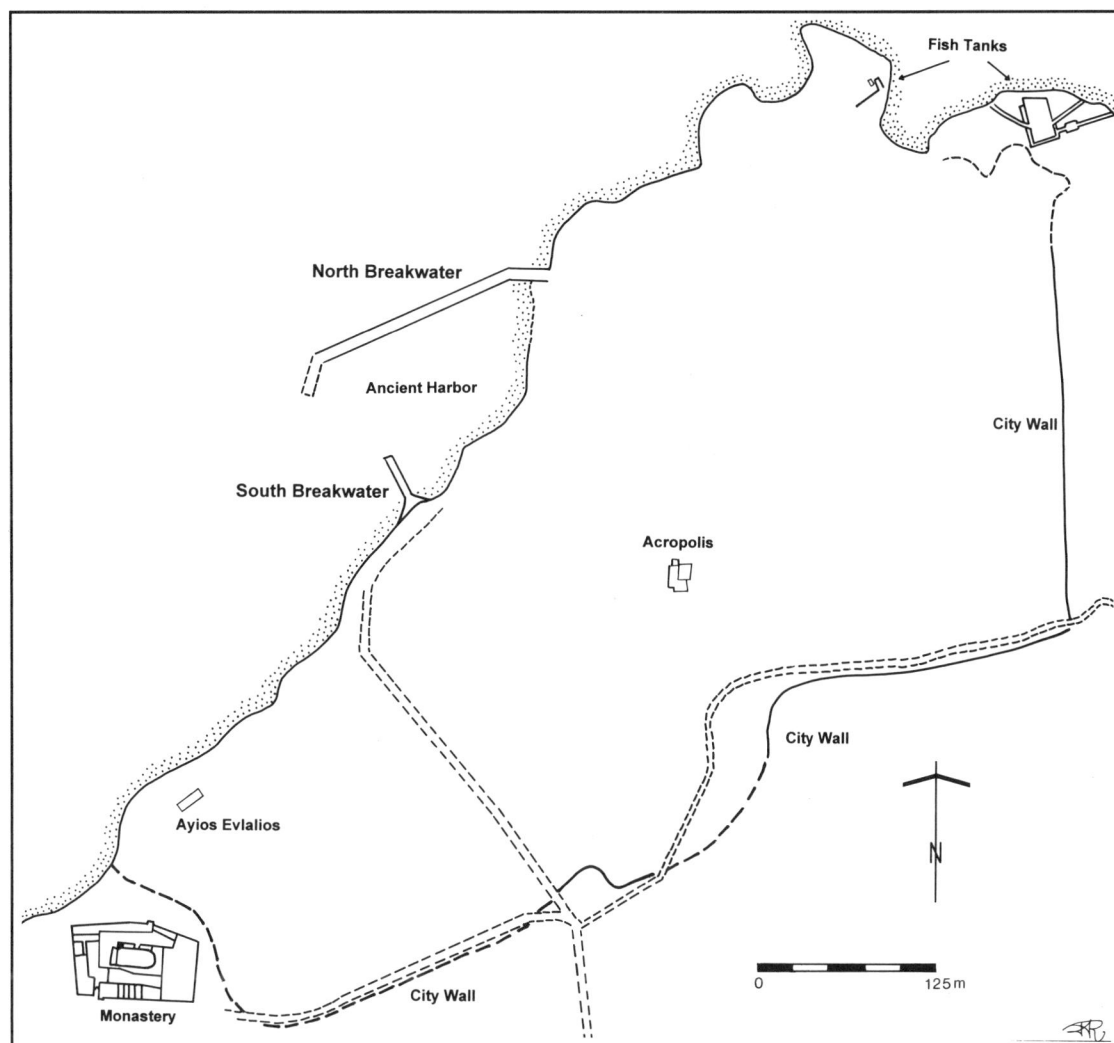

Fig. 12. Lapethos, Cyprus. After Raban (1995, fig. 39).

been found. In the case of Lapethos (fig. 12), Strabo's description (*Geog.* 14.6.3) of a ὕφορμος, as suggested above, may predate the building of the artificial harbor, which is apparently the facility described later by Stadiasmus (313) as a ὅρμος. The situation at Kyrenia, which is omitted completely by Strabo and subsequently described by Stadiasmus (312) as having a ὕφορμος, remains impossible to reconstruct without further information on the ancient harborworks' date of construction.[15] Stadiasmus may have been referring to a natural anchorage at Kyrenia, which had not yet been enclosed with breakwaters, or more likely to an anchorage situated among or outside the decaying ruins

of the artificial harbor, which had earlier succumbed to natural forces or human inattention. Only the eventual study of the ancient harbor itself at Kyrenia may lead to a clearer understanding of Stadiasmus' identification there of a ὕφορμος. In general, despite the ambiguity introduced by the examples of Lapethos and Kyrenia, the term ὕφορμος should probably be understood to mean a natural anchorage.

The final term, πρόσορμος, which also appears to mean a minor, natural anchorage, is used by Strabo (*Geog.* 14.6.3) in describing Cape Zephyria and the Arsinoe located between this cape and Nea Paphos (fig. 2). The to-

---

[15] The ancient harbor at Kyrenia, according to Yiannis Cleanthous, sometime Custodian of St. Hilarion and Kyrenia Castles, appears to consist of Hellenistic as well as Roman remains (personal communication: 27 June, 1995).

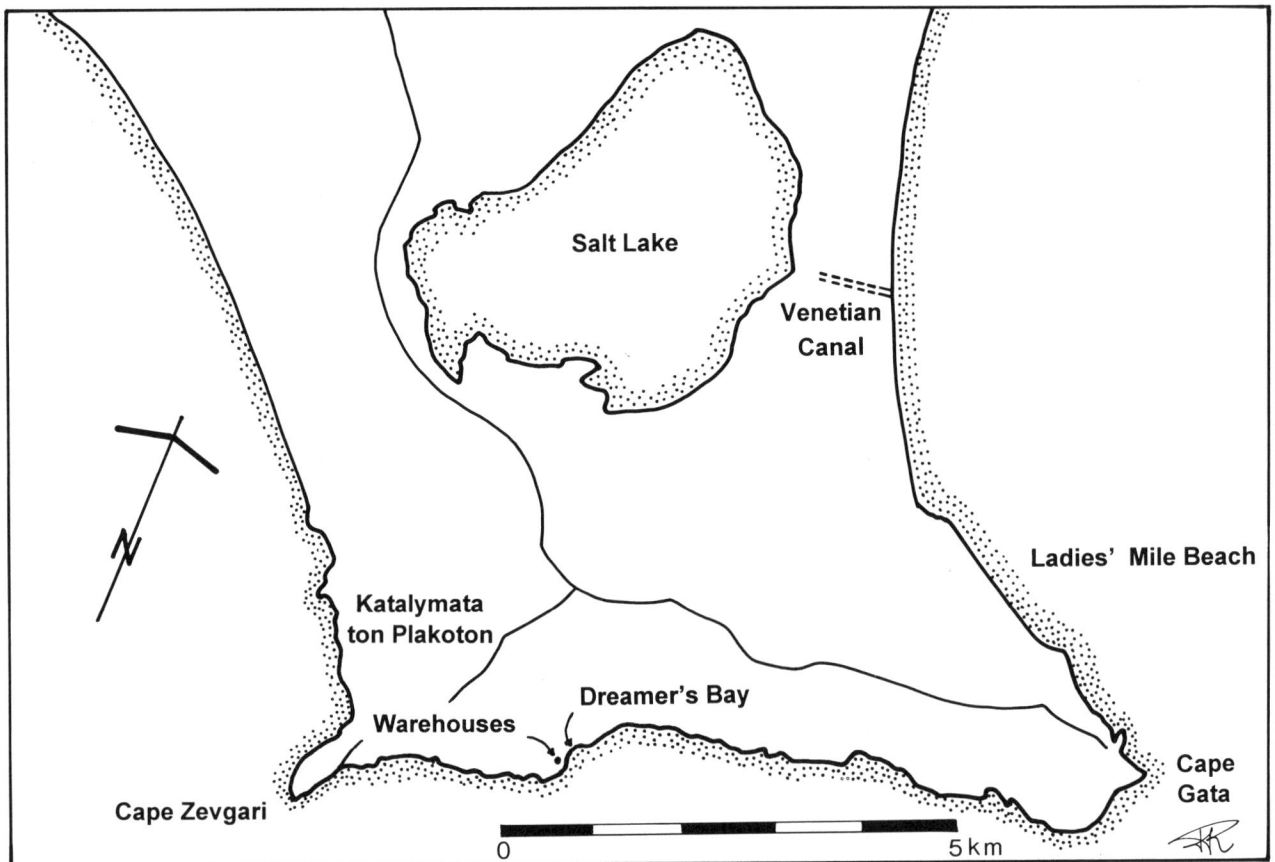

Fig. 13. Akrotiri Peninsula, Cyprus

pography of the southwestern Cypriot coast seems to support this understanding, for no traces of ancient harborworks have yet been found in the vicinity of Cape Zephyria (now Cape Zephyrus or Zefyros Point on official Cypriot maps) or between Cape Zephyria and Nea Paphos. Although the exact locations of these two πρόσορμοι have not yet been confirmed archaeologically, the anchorage at Cape Zephyria probably lay on the eastern (lee) side of the point,[16] while that belonging to Arsinoe may have lain below the modern village of Yeroskipou, in the lee of either the Moulia Rocks or the small point of land opposite these islets (fig. 14). Yeroskipou, judging at least from the similarity in place names, may have been the ancient Ἱεροκηπίς reported by

Strabo (*Geog.* 14.6.3), which appears from his description to have been Arsinoe's inland neighbor:

> and to another Arsinoe, which likewise has a landing-place (πρόσορμος) and a temple and a sacred precinct. And at a little distance from the sea is Hierocepis (Loeb ed.).[17]

Archaeological evidence attesting to ancient shipping in the vicinity of the Moulia Rocks was recently recorded in 1994 by the Paphos Ancient Harbor Exploration Project (Hohlfelder 1995b; see also Hohlfelder and Leonard 1994; Leonard and Hohlfelder 1993). Numerous concreted body

---

[16] There may have existed a small settlement near Cape Zephyria in Roman times, for archaeological survey in the area has revealed rock-cut rectangular basins, perhaps of Roman date and intended for the manufacture of fish paste, as well as two necropolis sites, Timi-Styllarka (Early Roman, Late Roman) and Timi-Vounaros (Hellenistic, Early Roman, Late Roman) (Rupp 1981: 266, nos. 75, 76, 77; 262; figs. 3–6). See also Mlynarczyk (1990: 114–15).

[17] Mlynarczyk, in her discussion of the *chora* of Nea Paphos, comments, "Hierokepis located undoubtedly at the spot of the modern Yeroskipou" (1990: 29).

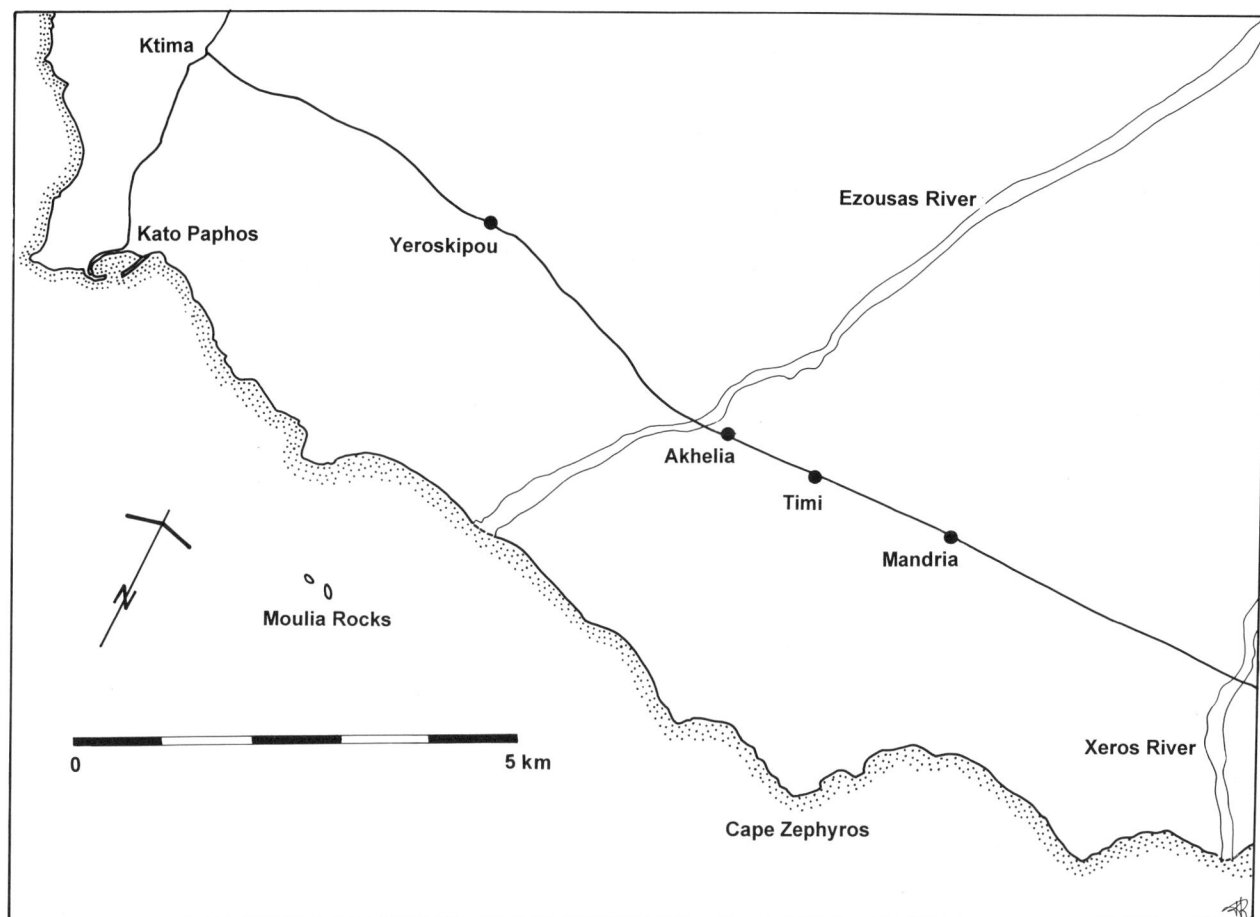

Fig. 14. Southwestern Cyprus: Moulia Rocks, Yeroskipou.

sherds and jar-tops belonging to Hellenistic and Roman transport amphoras lie submerged on and around the Moulia Rocks, probably representing both the usual refuse discarded from ships at anchor and the spilled cargoes of ships that may have been forced onto the rocks by the winds (Hohlfelder 1995b).[18]

Comparative modern evidence for the existence of viable anchorages near Yeroskipou Village is provided by the testimony of longtime Paphian residents, who recall seeing ships using the shelter of the Moulia Rocks as an alternative anchorage to the harbor at Paphos as recently as the 1960s and 1970s. The *Mediterranean Pilot,* furthermore, reports:

Anchorage may be obtained in summer by a vessel unable to enter Port Paphos, 3 cables E of Moulia Rocks in a depth of 13 m (43 ft), sand and mud. This is the best anchorage off this coast; the holding ground is good and there is fair shelter from W winds (Haslam 1976: 102, sect. 5.12).

Likewise, the anchorage in the lee of the small point opposite the Moulia Rocks served as an exportation port for carobs and possibly other local goods through at least the 1950s (Christodoulou 1959: 100, fig. 58).

Still another possible location for the anchorage of ancient Arsinoe, however, lies slightly further east near the modern village of Akhelia, perhaps within or somewhere

[18] The greatest concentration of ancient pottery yet recorded at the Moulia Rocks is located within an underwater cave in one of the Moulia Rocks themselves, where the cave's ceiling consists of concreted fragmentary amphoras (see Hohlfelder 1995b). Mlynarczyk notes the Moulia Rocks may represent the island of Noumenios reported by Stadiasmus (298–99), and the two islands (mistakenly) identified as Hiera and Cepia by Pliny (*Nat. Hist.*, 5.131) (Mlynarczyk 1990: 30).

near the mouth of the Ezousas River. Peristianis suggests that the modern Cypriot name Akhelia (pronounced *Ashelia;* note also that the village was previously called *Arshelia*) comes from the ancient name "Arsinoe" (Peristiani 1910: 403, cited in Mlynarczyk 1990: 114). The discovery in 1980 of a Roman *villa rustica* near Akhelia village provides more tangible evidence that an ancient settlement may indeed have been located somewhere nearby (Karageorghis 1981: 43).[19] Future archaeological study of the coastal areas below Yeroskipou and Akhelia villages may eventually be able to shed further light on the location and topography of ancient Arsinoe and its πρόσορμος.

CRETAN ANCIENT HARBORS AND TERMINOLOGY

Although the term πρόσορμος does not appear in geographical descriptions of Crete, ancient writers who describe the island's harbors do use ἐπίνειον, ἐμπόριον, λιμήν, ὅρμος, and ὕφορμος. A brief examination of several Cretan harbors, in comparison with their textual descriptions, provides further insight for the understanding of ancient Greek harbor terms, particularly ὅρμος and ὕφορμος.

Cherronesos (modern Chersonisos) (figs. 15, 16), where the substantial remains of Roman breakwaters now lie partly obscured by modern harborworks, is described by Stadiasmus (349) as having a λιμήν (Sanders 1982: 144, 146, fig. 53, pl. 64). Strabo (*Geog.* 10.4.14), however, in his earlier reference to Cherronesos, mentions only the city's role as the ἐπίνειον, or commercial port, of nearby Lyktos. Strabo's description of Crete differs markedly from his description of Cyprus, for (unlike Stadiasmus) the Augustan author does not provide a thorough, systematic Periplous of the Cretan coastline. Furthermore, Strabo uses only the single term ἐπίνειον in describing those harbors included in his Cretan account. In the case of Cherronesos, ἐπίνειον emphasizes the harbor's external connections or function, whereas λιμήν (used by Stadiasmus) suggests the facility's internal workings as a port.

The λιμήν at Cherronesos, evidently a less extensive Roman replacement for a previous Classical or Hellenistic installation, was built into the southeastern lee of a natural headland, and was therefore ideally situated to provide refuge from winds of all quarters (Leatham and Hood 1958–59: 269–70, fig. 2; Sanders 1982: 144, fig. 53). The harbor consisted of two breakwaters: a southern mole that projected directly eastward from the shore; and an eastern mole that abutted the protective headland at its northern end and angled inward 90° at its southern end, thereby creating an entrance channel between the two breakwaters that lay open to the east (Leatham and Hood 1958–59: fig. 2, pl. 64:a–d). Rectangular stone bollards located on the eastern mole (observed by Sanders in the 1970s, but now lying buried beneath modern harborworks) attest to berths where ships could tie up while their goods were unloaded or their holds refilled (Sanders 1982: 144). The remains of another quay, equipped with at least four more bollards, are also preserved adjacent to the shore inside the southern mole (Leatham and Hood 1958–59: 267–8, fig. 2:4; Sanders 1982: 146, fig. 53:D).

Lebena (fig. 16) was also a coastal center through which trade goods were shipped in Roman times, for Strabo (*Geog.* 10.4.11) describes this place as the ἐμπόριον of Gortyna. Although Strabo fails to mention specifically the existence of a harbor, he does imply that Lebena (*Geog.* 10.4.11), like Matalon, is an ἐπίνειον:

> [Gortyna] is ninety stadia distant from the Libyan sea at Leben (sic), which is its trading-center (ἐμπόριον); it also has another seaport (ἐπίνειον), Matalon, from which it is a hundred and thirty stadia distant. (Loeb ed.)

Stadiasmus (321) also refers to Lebena, but, like Strabo, fails to mention a harbor. Nevertheless, Lebena did have harbor facilities, consisting of a natural cove protected by headlands on the north and west, but which lay open to the south and east (Sanders 1982: fig. 59).

Phalasarna and Hierapydna (modern Ierapetra) are each reported by Stadiasmus (319, 336) as having a ὅρμος. Furthermore, Stadiasmus notes that Phalasarna is also an ἐμπόριον and an ancient city. The earlier work of Strabo is less informative, however, for he merely refers in passing to the two cities, without mentioning the existence of a harbor at either place (Phalasarna: *Geog.* 10.4.2; 10.4.13; Hierapydna: *Geog.* 10.3.19–20; 10.4.3). Phalasarna's harbor (figs. 15, 17) consisted of an inland rock-cut basin connected to the sea by a main access channel and a secondary possible desilting channel, both of which originally may have been narrow natural fissures (Pirazzoli et al. 1992: 377). Excavations conducted at Phalasarna between 1986 and 1988 have revealed the artificial harbor was already in use by the fifth and fourth centuries B.C.E., when it was fortified with walls and towers (Hadjidaki 1988: 473; Frost 1990: 524; Pirazzoli et al. 1992: 372, 375, 377, 385; Frost, this volume). Pseudo-Scylax (47) alludes to the enclosing for-

---

[19] Mlynarczyk supports the connection between Arsinoe and Akhelia, and furthermore interprets a third century B.C.E. dedicatory inscription to Aphrodite found in Akhelia as suggestive of a sanctuary located in the area (1990: 114–15).

CRETE

Samonion
Promontory

Olous

Hierapydna

Cherronesos

Knossos

Gortyna

Lebena

Matalon

Phalasarna

30 km

0

N

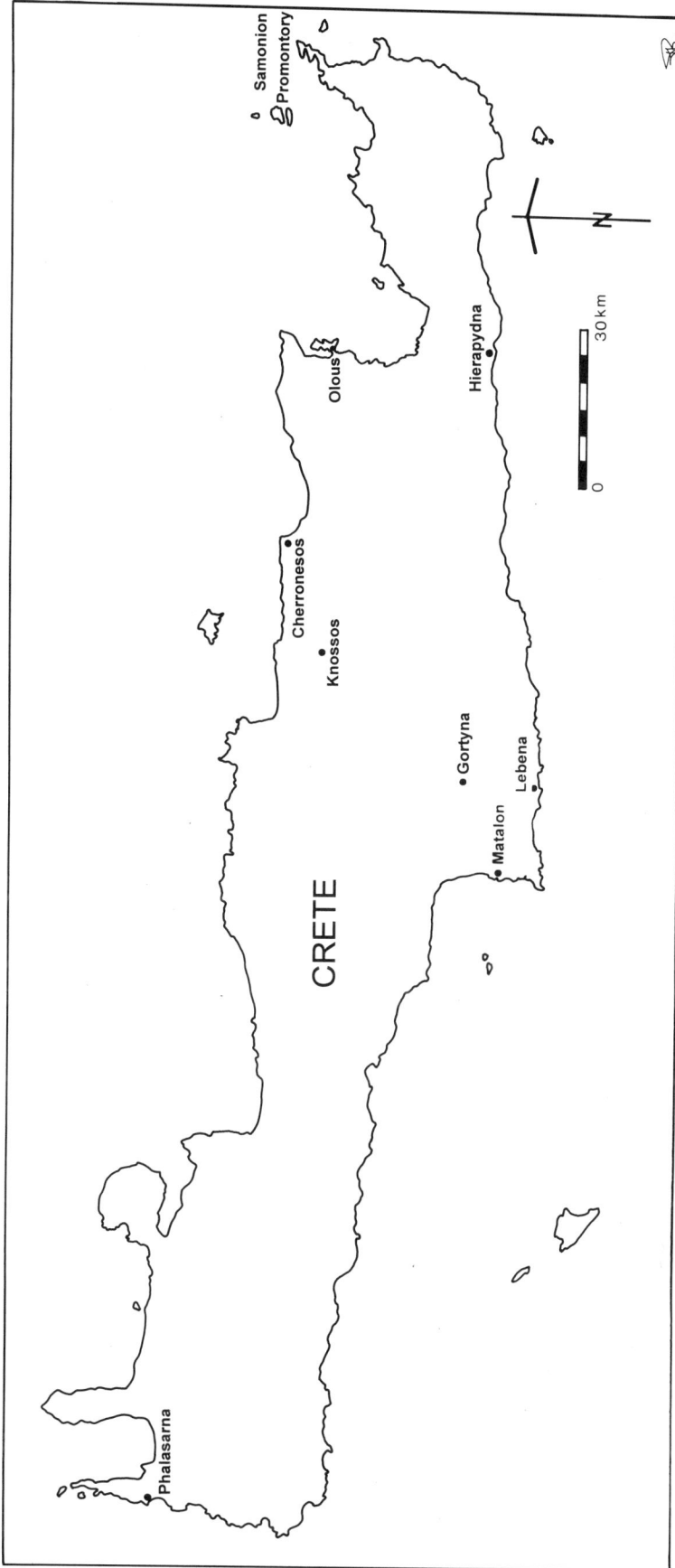

Fig. 15. Crete: Sites mentioned in text.

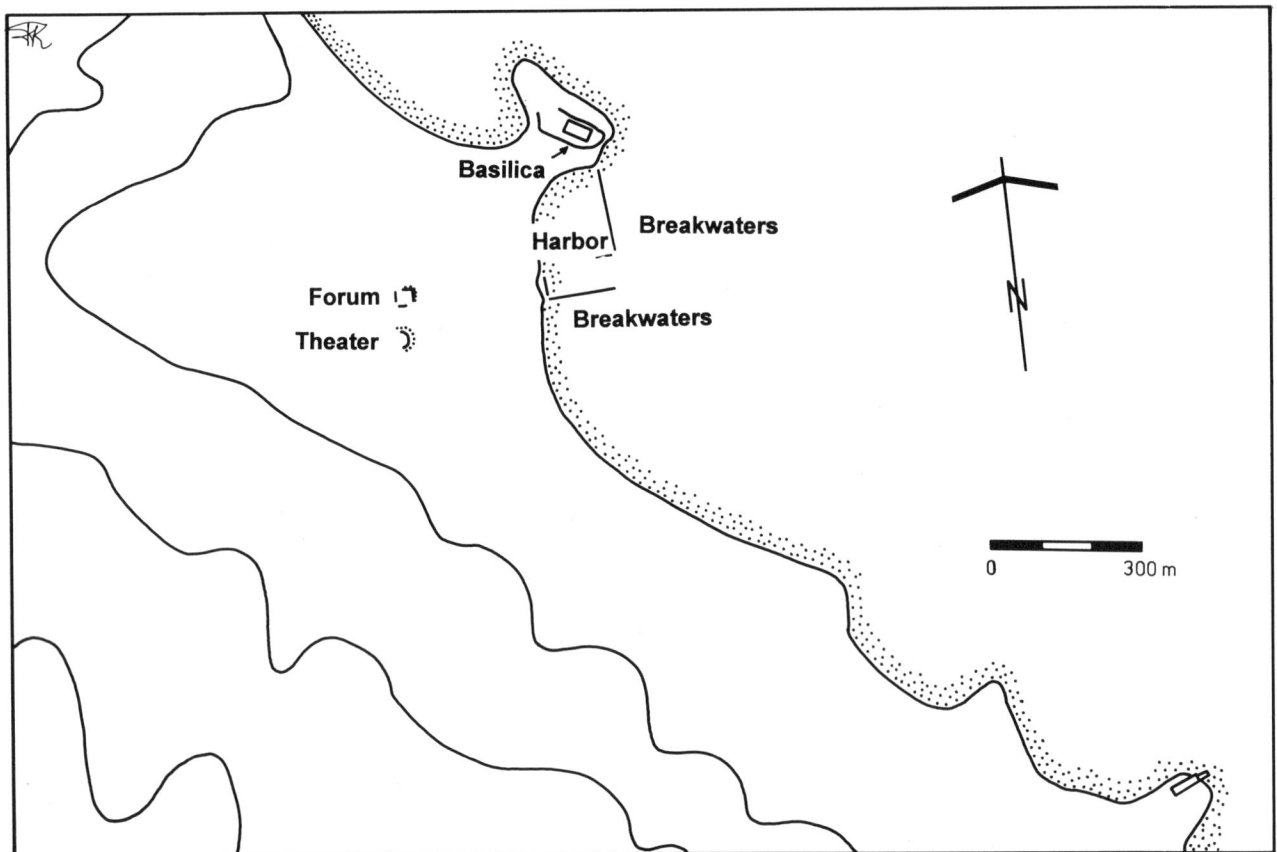

Fig. 16. Cherronesos, Crete. After Sanders (1982: fig. 53).

tifications and narrow defensible entrance when he notes in the mid-fourth century B.C.E. that Phalasarna is a λιμήν κλειστός.

Phalasarna's harbor was eventually put out of commission through the intentional blockage of the entrance, an action perhaps undertaken by the Romans in 67 B.C.E. (Hadjidaki 1988: 476). Subsequently, the rapidly silting harbor was further obstructed, and finally raised above sea level, as a result of severe earthquakes in 66 and 365 C.E. (Pirazzoli et al. 1992: 390; Frost, this volume). If Stadiasmus' report of a ὅρμος refers to harbor facilities at the abandoned harbor town of Phalasarna itself, then the subject of the description cannot have been the artificial harbor that lay abandoned and silting, but the natural cove that remained at its mouth. This inlet, although not as protected as the artificial harbor, probably continued to serve as an occasional refuge for passing ships even after the tectonic uplift of the mid-fourth century. Stadiasmus' additional description of an ἐμπόριον, however, seems ill-suited to Phalasarna, due to the harbor town's apparent lack of Roman occupation. In describing Phalasarna, then, Stadiasmus may have either been mistaken about the ἐμπόριον, or, more likely, been referring to a neighboring settlement that had

developed since the abandonment of the original harbor town. The site of one such Roman settlement, located 4 km south of Phalasarna, was discovered in 1987 (Hadjidaki 1988: 468, n. 22). The occurrence in antiquity of two adjoining settlements of similar name is exemplified by sites such as Palaipaphos and Nea Paphos in Cyprus, which are separated by approximately 16 km. Further archaeological study in the neighborhood of Phalasarna may eventually clarify the area's occupational history and maritime role during the Roman period.

The case of the ὅρμος at Hierapydna (figs. 15, 18) is more straightforward, for the remains of its rubble breakwaters may still be seen protruding from beneath modern concrete harborworks. Sanders sketched the outline of the ancient breakwaters in the 1970s, before construction of the massive marina in the west and the smaller quay in the east (Sanders 1982: fig. 49). Judging from Sanders' illustration, as well as from that of Lehmann-Hartleben in the earlier part of the century (1923: plan 37), the ancient harbor at Hierapydna was an artificial facility of generally circular shape that was similar in scale to the Cypriot ὅρμος at Lapethos. The breakwaters, whose date of foundation remains unknown, were built into the eastern lee of a small

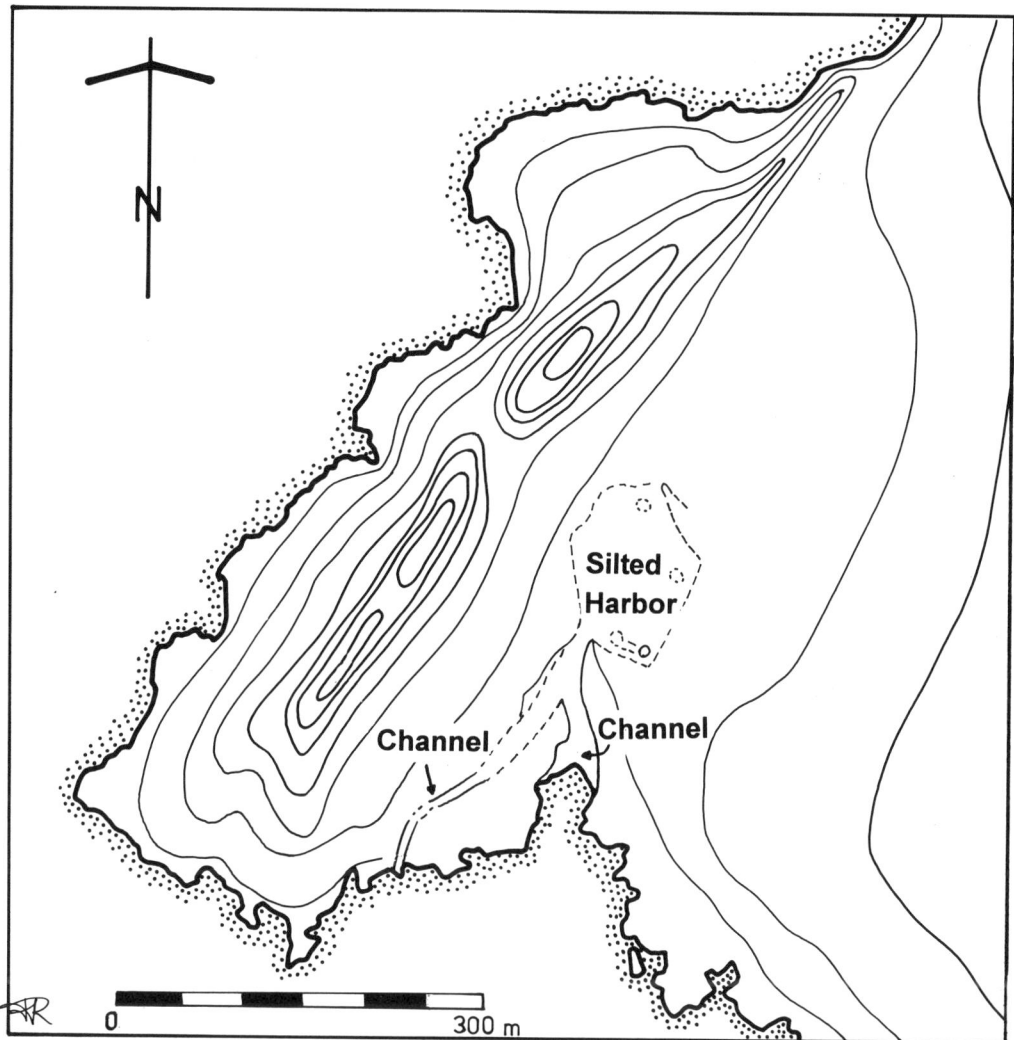

Fig. 17. Phalasarna, Crete. After Meyers (1992: fig. 34.1).

promontory, with an entrance channel left open to the east. The full extent of the once-enclosed basin, as well as the location of the inner, secondary basin discussed by Lehmann-Hartleben, can only be determined through additional archaeological study of the ancient harbor site (Lehmann-Hartleben 1923: 201–2).

Two Cretan examples of ὕφορμοι cited by Stadiasmus, include Olous (350) and the Samonion Promontory (318) (fig. 15). Strabo does not include Olous in his description, and mentions the Samonion Promontory (*Geog.* 10.3.20; 10.4.2–3; 10.4.5) without any reference to harbor facilities. The Roman city of Olous (fig. 19) originally extended from the mainland onto the peninsula, and may have had harbors on either (or both) side(s) of the isthmus (Sanders 1982: 141). No artificial harborworks have been found at this site, nor do they appear ever to have existed. The natural bays flanking the isthmus, particularly that in the north, must have provided adequate protection during most wind conditions.

The Samonion Promontory (modern Sideros Peninsula) (fig. 15) is described by Stadiasmus (318) as projecting toward the north. He further reports:

ἔςτι δὲ ἱερὸν Ἀθηνᾶς·. ἔχει ὕφορμον καί ὕδωρ·. τὰ δὲ ἄλλα ἠφανισμένα (318).

There is a temple of Athena. [The promontory] has a ὕφορμος and water. The others are destroyed (or hidden from view).

Stadiasmus refers in this passage, as in his description of the Cypriot promontory Akra (307), to the *tip* of the Samonion Promontory. A small partially submerged building, perhaps the remains of the ancient temple, was observed there by the nineteenth century English traveller, Captain T.A.B. Spratt (Sanders 1982: 138). The ὕφορμος was almost certainly a natural cove, but whether this anchorage lay on the eastern or western side of the cape remains un-

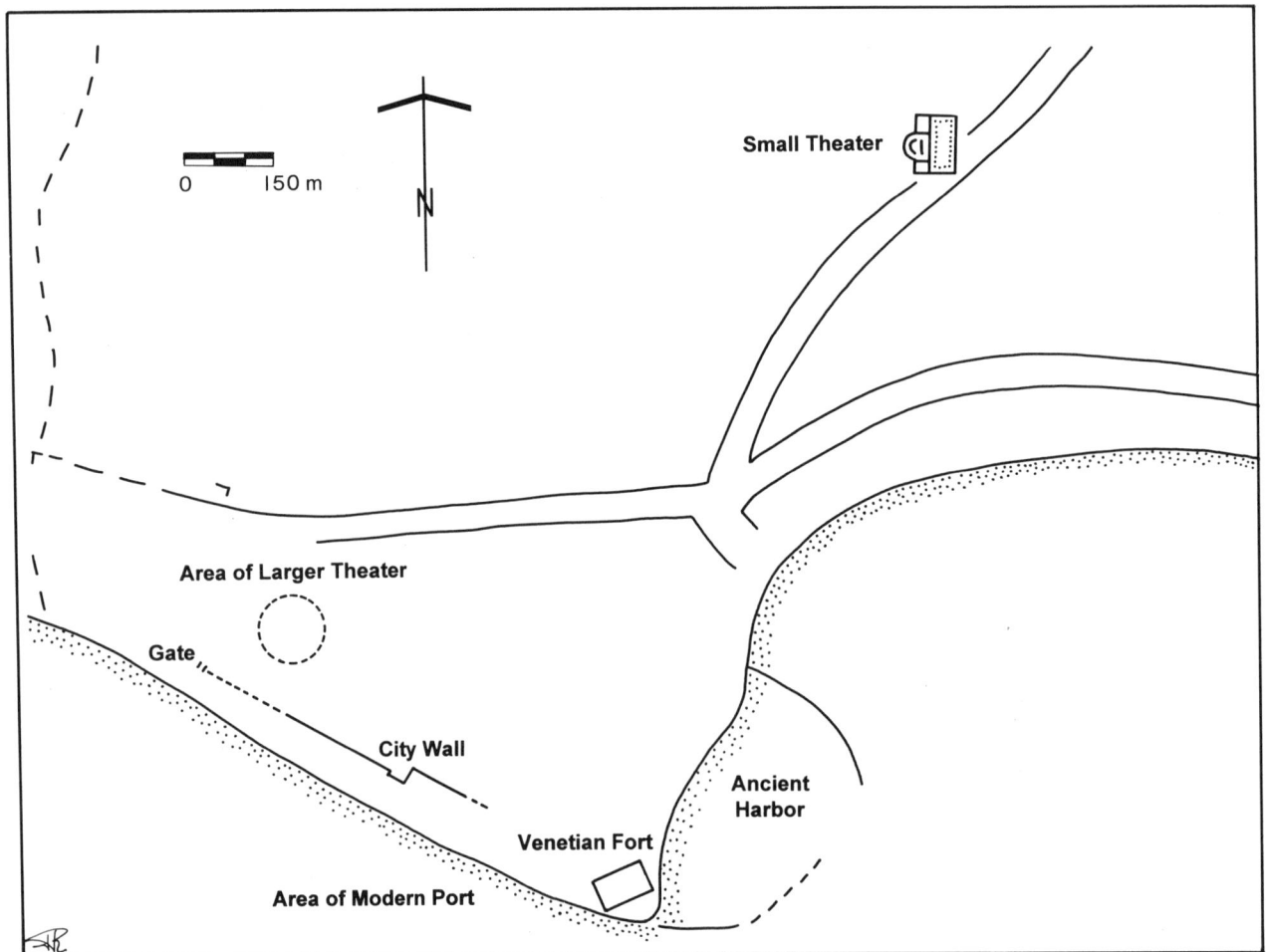

Fig. 18. Hierapydna, Crete. After Sanders (1982: fig. 49).

known.[20] Ancient ships, at various times, may have sought shelter on both sides of the cape, depending upon the direction of the wind.

Stadiasmus' final statement, "The others are destroyed (or hidden from view)," is particularly intriguing, for he may be referring to buildings, cities (as Müller 1855: 505 suggests), or even harbors that had previously been destroyed or submerged as a result of earthquakes and tectonic subsidence. Unlike the island's western end, Crete's eastern coast appears to have subsided gradually, with an abrupt, localized drop in post-Roman times (Pirazzoli 1988: 173–74). Stadiasmus' elliptical statement, then, may constitute ancient evidence for earthquake activity and resultant tectonic subsidence in eastern Crete.

In summary, examination of ancient harbor sites in Cyprus and Crete indicates that topographical differences do exist between harbor facilities designated by different terms in ancient Periploi. The most significant distinctions appear to be the overall scale and shape of individual harbors and the degree to which they were developed artificially during antiquity. The occasional use of λιμήν and ὅρμος as general harbor terms, however, as well as the discrepancies that occasionally seem to exist between maritime facilities' textual descriptions and their actual topography, give rise to the question: Just how exact and consistent can we expect ancient terminology to have been? In an attempt to address this problem, contemporary harbor terminology in English will next be considered as comparative modern evidence for the use of ancient harbor terms.

---

[20] Today, the *terminus* of the Sideros Peninsula is accessible only to military and other official personnel.

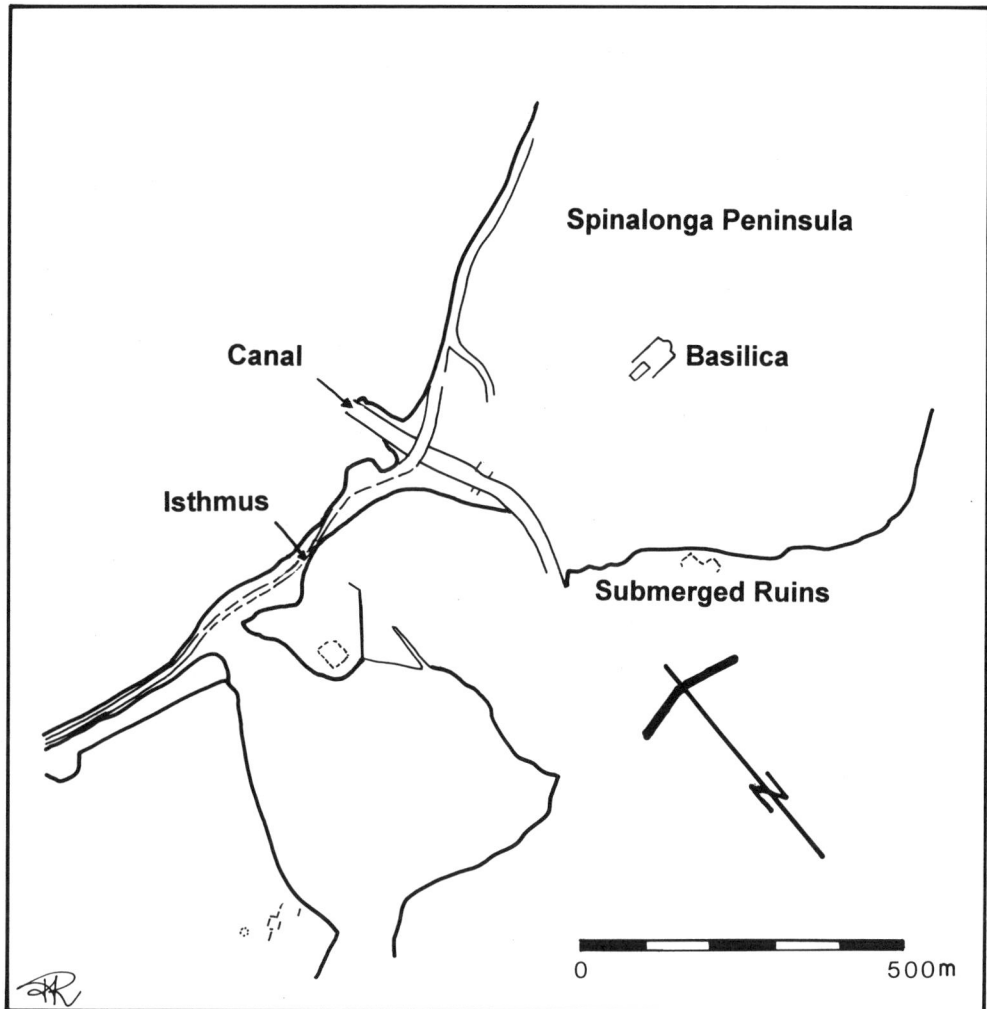

Fig. 19. Olous, Crete. After Meyers (1992: fig. 31.1).

CONTEMPORARY HARBOR TERMINOLOGY

Most harbor engineering textbooks and manuals found today in university libraries were originally published in the late nineteenth or early twentieth centuries, when shipping was rapidly expanding in response to European and American industrial development (see bibliography). In several cases (e.g., Du Plat Taylor 1934; Quinn 1961), these engineering texts reflect an interest or at least a concern on the part of their authors for the earliest history of harbors and the pre-modern evolution of commercial ports.[21] Perhaps this awareness and appreciation for the history of ancient harbors and shipping, particularly in the Mediterranean, stems from the emphasis that still existed a century ago on classical education, or perhaps from a collective sense among early modern harbor engineers that in defining their newly revitilized field they must address its history and development from earliest times.

Although this concern for historical perspective is not universal among late nineteenth and twentieth century harbor engineers, another fundamental aspect that receives more attention in contemporary harbor engineering texts is the definition of technical terms. Many harbor engineering manuals (e.g., Shield 1895, Cornick 1960–69) are strictly practical in nature and limited to the principles involved in the planning, construction, equipping, and management of modern industrial ports. Those texts that do address the more academic questions such as harbor terminology and classi-

[21] Du Plat Taylor's treatise holds particular interest for the study of ancient harbors because of its introductory chapter, an historical overview entitled "The Harbors of the Ancients," which includes detailed sketches of harbor sites in the central and eastern Mediterranean (1934: 1–21, figs. 1–19).

fication, however, offer important insight for the historical study of Greco-Roman harbors and maritime trade.[22] Because many of the most valuable harbor engineering texts of the past hundred years are now long out of print or relatively difficult to find in research libraries, definitions and other relevant points cited below are often reproduced here in full, with the intent that this contemporary comparative data may be to some degree more accessible to students of ancient harbors.

Perhaps one of the most useful harbor engineering texts for archaeologists and historians is the far-reaching study by Quinn (1961), who distinguishes himself from other authors in his thoughtful definition of technical terminology and various types of harbor facilities. Quinn describes a "harbor" as

> a water area partially enclosed and so protected from storms as to provide safe and suitable accommodation for vessels seeking refuge, supplies, refueling, repairs, or the transfer of cargo (1961: 71).

Cunningham (1908), in a more general definition, suggests

> a harbor is primarily a place of rest and refuge—a place where safety and hospitality are to be found (1908: 9).

A "port," on the other hand, according to Quinn, is

> a sheltered harbor where marine terminal facilities are provided, consisting of piers or wharves at which ships berth while loading or unloading cargo, transit sheds and other storage areas where ships may discharge incoming cargo, and warehouses where goods may be stored for longer periods while awaiting distribution or sailing (1961: 72).

This complex facility serves a surrounding geographical hinterland, for, as Quinn further states,

> the terminal must be served by railroad, highway, or inland-waterway connections, and in this respect the area of influence of the port reaches out for a considerable distance beyond the harbor (1961: 72).

Similarly, Bown also defines a "port" as

> a place which provides terminal facilities for ships ...

their cargoes ... and ... passengers. For this reason, a port is designed to look two ways—outwards to the sea, river, lake or canal on which it stands, and inwards over the hinterland which it serves (1955: 15).

Morgan's description of a "port," although more general, also refers to this intermediary position or role:

> A port is a place equipped to facilitate the necessary relations between ships, as agencies of sea transport, and the land (1958: 13).

Furthermore, Morgan notes that

> in a study of the physical setting of ports it is convenient to regard a port as normally comprising two main sections: the harbor and the port proper (1958: 26).

One of the most definitive statements on the function of a "port," however, is that found in a preliminary report by the United Nations Conference on Trade and Development (UNCTAD) Secretariat (1969), entitled, *Development of Ports; Improvement of Port Operations and Connected Facilities:*

> A port is essentially the point at which goods in transit are transferred from one medium of transport to another. On the seaward side, the port is concerned with a flow of ships which bring in cargo for discharge, ... take on cargo, and ... then depart. On the landward side, cargo is brought by road or by rail to the port and ... transferred into ships ... [or alternatively] cargo discharged from the ships is removed by land transport. In order that the operations should be efficient, both sides of the port must be considered. Between the land transport and the sea transport lie the storage and handling areas of the port, and in the organization of these a like degree of efficiency must be attained if the whole port is to operate as an efficient unit (1969: 4).

Maritime facilities of a simpler nature include "roadsteads," "off-shore moorings," and "anchorage areas." Cunningham notes that natural or artificial conditions may constitute a "roadstead," which is an area lying

> within a tract of water not necessarily enclosed in any way, even partially, but adjacent to or not far distant from the coastline, where there is good holding-ground for

---

[22] The significance of modern harbor engineering treatises for the historical study of Greco-Roman harbors and terminology first became clear to the present author through the work of G.E. Rickman, particularly his farseeing paper *Towards a Study of Roman Ports* (1985). Rickman (1985: 105) cites Quinn's (1961) definitions of "harbor" and "port" as a prelude to his discussion of the social and economic aspects of Roman harbor studies.

anchors and some protection from the onset of heavy seas (1908: 9).

Similarly, an "anchorage area," according to Quinn, is

> a place where ships may be held for quarantine inspection, await docking space while sometimes removing ballast in preparation for taking on cargo, or await favorable weather conditions . . . Anchorages are usually located away from the marine terminal and adjacent to main channels so as to be near deep water but out of the path of the main traffic. They may be in naturally protected areas or protected from the wind and waves by breakwaters (1961: 74).

An "off-shore mooring," however, is an anchorage without man-made protection from the elements, for, in Quinn's words, this type of facility is located

> where it is not feasible or economical to construct a dock or provide a protected harbor. Such an anchorage will consist of a number of anchorage units, each consisting of one or more anchors, chains, sinkers, and buoys to which the ship will attach its mooring lines. These will be supplemented in most cases by the ship's bow anchors. Bulk cargo is usually transported to or from the ship by pipeline or trestle conveyor, while other cargo may be transferred by lighter (Quinn 1961: 73–4).

In summary, a harbor may be either a protected water area for ships—in a general sense—or a constituent area within a larger port facility. A port is a multifunctional facility that accommodates ships and passengers, provides temporary storage for trade goods, and serves as a regional collection or distribution point, through which trade goods and passengers move on their way to or from places either across the water or within a particular hinterland. The simplest maritime facilities are roadsteads, anchorage areas, and off-shore moorings, which consist either of water areas with good holding-ground and at least partial protection for ships, or more exposed water areas equipped with artificial mooring aids. Roadsteads may be independent facilities, while anchorage areas and off-shore moorings are associated with ports.

In addition to defining common technical terms, contemporary harbor engineers also undertake to classify har-

bors according to their topography and function. Quinn initially divides harbors into three general categories: natural, seminatural (requiring only limited improvement), and artificial (entirely man-made) (1961: 71).[23] He then identifies various types of facilities, including harbors of refuge, military harbors, commercial harbors, ports, ports of entry, ocean ports, inland-waterway ports, and "free ports," which serve as international trading centers free from the usual customs restrictions (1961: 71–73).

Morgan also makes the distinction between natural and artificial harbors, but notes,

> it is, broadly speaking, the harbor which is worth distinguishing as artificial, for the port works of any port are inevitably artificial (1958: 49).

Morgan first classifies harbors by their topography, including, for example, fiords, embayed volcanoes, coral harbors, off-shore bar and spit harbors, island-protected harbors, ports on tidal estuaries and rivers, converging breakwater/jetty harbors,[24] and detached breakwater harbors (1958: 33–54). He then groups ports by function, including primitive lighter ports, naval, commercial, fishing, and ferry ports, ports of call, transshipment ports, entrepôt and free ports, "outports" (large ports built near older, smaller ports), coastwise and short-sea ports, and finally tramp, tanker, and liner ports (1958: 70–8). Furthermore, while ports also function occasionally as temporary harbors of refuge,

> a sheltered bay or roadstead without any port installations can serve just as well. These harbors, [however], have lost much of their significance with the decline of sailing ships (Morgan 1958: 73).

Shaler (1895) approaches harbor classification from a more specialized, topographical perspective, for this particular author groups harbors according to their geological formation. Shaler's classification includes lagoon, sand-spit, and crater harbors, as well as coral-reef, lake, and sea harbors (1895: 187–222). Vigarié, on the other hand, while mentioning port types previously discussed by authors such as Morgan (1958), also classifies port facilities as regional, industrial, and commercial (1979: 86).

Bown's (1955) classification is noteworthy as well, for it includes several additional port types distinct from those

---

[23] Cf. the typology of Bronze Age harbors by Blue, this volume. Note also that Mlynarczyk reports the existence of an unpublished work, completed in 1973 by H. Lebrun, "regarding the classification of Cypriot ports" (Mlynarczyk 1990: 102, n. 160; 177).

[24] H. Lebrun's unpublished classification (see above, n. 23) includes a similar category *"des ports installés dans un site naturel favorable et constitue de môles convergeants"* (Mlynarczyk 1990: 102, n. 160).

of other authors. Bown classifies maritime facilities according to their physical characteristics and principle types of trade. Within the first group, he includes sea, river, canal, and lake ports, natural harbors, artificial ports, open or tidal ports, and enclosed ports (1955: 33). The second, functional group consists of entrepôt, transshipment, and coal-shipping ports, bulk oil terminals, bunkering stations, and fishing, passenger, and coastwise ports (1955: 33).

Finally, the *Mediterranean Pilot* series, which, along with its imitators, probably remains the closest modern parallel to the Mediterranean Periploi of Stadiasmus and other ancient geographers, contains terminology similar to that prescribed by contemporary harbor engineers. Volume 5 in the series, for example, covers the coasts of the eastern Mediterranean and includes a table entitled, "Ports and Principal Anchorages" (Haslam 1976: 8–10, sects. 1.97–1.103). Larnaca, Limassol, and Famagusta (Cyprus) are listed here as "commercial harbors" under the column heading, "Type of port or anchorage, and remarks" (Haslam 1976: 9, sect. 1.100). Elsewhere in the table, Alexandria (Egypt) is listed as a "commercial harbor and naval base"; Marsa Matruh (Egypt) and Marmaris (Turkey) as a "sheltered anchorage" and a "secure anchorage," respectively; and Sour (Israel) as a "secure anchorage for small vessels," a description particularly reminiscent of Stadiasmus' account (314) of Karpasia in Cyprus (Haslam 1976: 8, sects. 1.98–9; 10, sect. 1.103).

The definition of harbor terms and classification of maritime facilities, undertaken by Quinn, Morgan, Cunningham, Bown, and other contemporary harbor engineers, testify to at least some degree of terminological specificity during the modern era. Morgan cautions, however, with respect to classification, that ports are frequently multifunctional, and types of ports based on function, therefore, will often represent only one aspect of a port (1958: 79). He further stresses:

> Thus when we appear to classify ports by giving them names we must remember that we are not doing so in a strictly scientific sense (1958: 79).

Nevertheless, harbor engineers, navigators, hydrographers, and others involved in contemporary maritime pursuits continue to recognize and employ functional port types because they do convey useful information. Morgan states,

> the activity we ascribe to [ports] in this way is real, if the degree to which it is a complete statement of this or that port's activities may vary enormously (1958: 79).

Conversely, although some overlap may exist in the general meaning of "harbor," "port," and "anchorage," each of these terms reflects a distinct sense of topography and function.

CONCLUSIONS

Ancient Greek terms such as ἐπίνειον, ἐμπόριον, λιμήν, ὅρμος, ὕφορμος, and πρόσορμος, as well as the Latin terms *portus* and *statio,* constitute capsules of information within the larger context of Greco-Roman geographical texts. Examination of the topography of Cypriot and Cretan coastal sites reveals that λιμήν, ὅρμος, ὕφορμος, and πρόσορμος, in particular, represent distinct terms employed by Strabo, Stadiasmus, Josephus, and other Roman authors to distinguish between maritime facilities of diverse natural or artificial topography. In using such terms, Roman writers of Periploi, especially Stadiasmus, produced navigational guidebooks that were probably intended, like *Mediterranean Pilots* today, to promote the safety and convenience of shipping (Haslam 1976: 1). The present study of Roman Periploi and harbor terminology holds particular relevance for coastal surveys and the excavation of Roman harbors, since the topographical information contained within ancient Greek and Latin harbor terms (Tables 1, 2) may affect the way in which archaeologists approach particular coastal sites or features.

λιμήν

The term λιμήν, based upon textual and topographical evidence, means either a natural or artificial harbor, in a general sense, or a relatively large or important port, in a specific, commercial sense. A λιμήν site may contain the architectural remains of breakwaters, quays, and warehouses. Λιμήν should be translated "harbor," unless additional literary or archaeological evidence invokes the term's more specific meaning of "port."

ὅρμος

Ὅρμος denotes a natural or artificial harbor of relative medium or small size and/or importance, with a generally circular or ring-like shape. Ὅρμος may also mean an internal harbor basin. A ὅρμος site may contain the remains of breakwaters and natural or artificial divisions between internal basins. The hinterland of a ὅρμος is probably less extensive than that of a λιμήν. Ὅρμος is commonly translated "haven," "anchorage," or "roadstead" (see above), but the preferable translation is "harbor or "basin."

Ὕφορμος

ὕφορμος and πρόσορμος denote minor, natural anchorages.[25] The natural topography of these coastal sites, like that of λιμήν sites, remains indeterminate and may never have been predictable based upon the terms themselves. It is worth noting, however, that the verb ὑφορμέω (hyphormeo) has the meaning "to lie at anchor in wait for (others)" or "to anchor under" (Liddell and Scott, s.v. ὑφορμέω). Perhaps the noun ὕφορμος, then, also denotes an anchorage that is somewhat concealed (within a narrow cove, for example) or that lies below an overlooking headland. The verb προσορμέω (prosormeo), on the other hand, means "to come to anchor at," while προσορμίζω (prosormizo) means "to anchor at or near" (Liddell and Scott, s.v. προσορμέω, προσορμίζω). Perhaps—as topographical evidence also indicates—the noun πρόσορμος further signifies an anchorage that lies beside a distinct natural feature, such as a peninsula, coastal eminence, or small island. Additional study may eventually be able to provide greater support for such terminological precision, but in the meantime ὕφορμος and πρόσορμος should be translated "natural anchorage" or simply "anchorage."

ἐπίνειον, ἐμπόριον

ἐπίνειον and ἐμπόριον are both functional terms, of which only ἐπίνειον refers exclusively to harbors. Ἐπίνειον denotes the commercial port of an inland city or town, or at least a harbor economically dependent upon a separate inland settlement.[26] An ἐπίνειον may have been either a natural or artificial facility. Furthermore, although an ἐπίνειον may have also been a city or town in its own right (e.g., Cherronesos in Crete), separate residential areas were often located inland at a distance from port facilities (e.g., Corinth, Lechaion, and Kenchreai). Morgan suggests:

> Malarial coastal plains were in part responsible for this dualism, but the arrangement also reflected the prevalence of piracy, a recurrent feature of Mediterranean maritime life (1958: 152).

An ἐπίνειον site may contain the remains of breakwaters, quays, and warehouses, as well as traces of a road that once connected the coastal site with its principal inland ally. Ἐπίνειον is most precisely translated, "commercial port."

Although frequently found in descriptions of natural or artificial ports, ἐμπόριον denotes primarily a commercial center in the general sense. A port site designated in ancient texts as an ἐμπόριον may contain the remains of breakwaters, quays, and warehouses, the last perhaps evincing a distinct commercial precinct within the port. Ἐμπόριον is most precisely translated "commercial center" or "emporium."

Other harbor terms that have less archaeological significance, either because of their textual infrequency or their topographical imprecision, include the Latin terms *portus* and *statio,* the ancient Greek terms ναύσταθμος, ναύσταθμον (naustathmos, naustathmon), σάλος (salos) and ἀγχυροβόλιον (angkhurobolion) and Latin transcriptions such as *emporium* and *salum.*[27]

Portus

Portus denotes a natural or artificial port that may have handled primarily wholesale commercial transactions and provided accomodation for long-term layovers, such as during the winter off-season. *Portus* sites may contain the remains of breakwaters, quays, warehouses, and shipyards. *Portus,* like λιμήν, should be translated "harbor" in a general sense, unless additional literary or archaeological evidence supports the term's more specific meaning of "port."

Statio

Statio denotes a natural anchorage largely exposed to the wind and waves, which provided primarily short-term accommodation. The term *statio,* like ὕφορμος and πρόσορμος, may be translated "natural anchorage" or simply "anchorage."

Ναύσταθμος

Ναύσταθμος signifies a harbor or anchorage in a general sense, although Lehmann-Hartleben suggests that Roman authors use the term almost exclusively in the military sense of a "naval station" (Liddell and Scott, s.v. ναύσταθμος; Lehmann-Hartleben 1923: 108, n. 1).

---

[25] Mlynarczyk suggests that a ὕφορμος and a πρόσορμος were "small havens of unequal importance, apparently intended only for local coastal navigation" (1990: 30).

[26] Revere, in his discussion of ancient "ports of trade" in the eastern Mediterranean, equates such centralized trade centers with the ἐπίνειον (1957: 52). The main functions of a "port of trade," exemplified by Alexandria in Egypt, were to guarantee neutrality and a constant supply or exchange of goods (Revere 1957: 52, 61).

[27] For discussion of other similarly obscure terms, see Rougé (1966: 112).

Σάλος

Σάλος denotes the tossing or rolling swell of the sea (which can lead to sea sickness), but the term also appears occasionally (Stadiasmus, 25) in the sense of an open natural anchorage (Rougé 1966: 110–12; Liddell and Scott, s.v. σάλος).

Ἀγχυροβόλιον

Ἀγχυροβόλιον, like σάλος, signifies a temporary natural anchorage largely exposed to the elements (Rougé 1966: 112).

Emporium, Salum

The Latin transcriptions *emporium* and *salum* generally convey the same meaning as their original Greek counterparts (Rougé 1966: 108, 111). *Salum,* however, may also denote an anchorage that can accommodate large ships with drafts too great to pass freely into the shallower *portus* itself (Rougé 1966: 111–12).

* * *

The foregoing catalogue (summarized in Tables 1 and 2), while intended to represent the most commonly encountered harbor terms in ancient Greek and Latin texts, does not include the entire array of single words or less succinct phrases used by ancient authors in describing maritime localities. The interpretation of ancient harbor terminology, furthermore, is full of potential pitfalls: particular terms may have had different meanings in various contexts, or evolved in their meaning with the passage of time. Of even greater concern, individual authors may have used various harbor terms indiscriminately or according to their own personal interpretation. Λιμήν, for example, is the only harbor term used by Pseudo-Scylax to describe Cypriot harbors, while Strabo and Stadiasmus employ λιμήν along with a variety of other seemingly specific terms. Whether this is a case of a general term that later assumes a specific meaning as well, or an example of authors' individual tastes in vocabulary remains open to debate.

The difference, however, between harbor descriptions of Roman date (written in Greek) and those of earlier periods, illustrated by a marked increase in the number and variety of harbor terms in use during the Roman period, does suggest some degree of evolution in the particular term λιμήν, as well as in Greek harbor terminology in general. Furthermore, Ptolemy's exclusive, indiscriminate use of λιμήν in his description of Crete, Dio Cassius's use of ὅρμος to mean a harbor in the general sense, and the use of ἐπίνειον

to mean a naval station in the *Suda* may testify to continued evolution (or later devolution) in ancient Greek terminology—or may simply represent additional examples of authors' individual preference or interpretation.

The comparative study of contemporary harbor terminology and classification in English reveals that today's harbor engineers, as well as hydrographers, navigators, and others involved in maritime pursuits, strive to describe maritime facilities systematically and with a certain degree of precision. Literary, archaeological, and geomorphological evidence indicates that a similar system of specialized harbor terminology may have existed in Roman times, when ship traffic was extensive and coastlines were even more intensively exploited for maritime purposes than they are today.

The island of Cyprus, in particular, offers clear evidence of both widespread coastal exploitation during the Roman period and of the terminological specificity with which Roman authors such as Strabo and Stadiasmus identify various coastal places. Furthermore, the marked diversity of single terms and the distinctiveness of individual coastal descriptions evident in the Cypriot Periploi of Strabo and especially Stadiasmus may be a reflection of the sources from which these authors originally gathered their information. In designating particular localities as λιμένες, ὅρμοι, ὕφορμοι, or ἀνάπλοι, for example, or as having been entirely ἀλίμενοι (harborless) or ἔρημοι (deserted), or additionally as having good water, dangerous shoals, seasonally tricky winds, or sufficient space only for smaller ships, Stadiasmus is almost certainly relying (directly or indirectly) upon the reports of sailors and other sea travelers familiar with eastern Mediterranean coasts. Likewise, Strabo's use of the rare term πρόσορμος, which appears only in his descriptions of southern Anatolian, Cypriot, Levantine, and North African anchorages (see above, note 3), may also be a trace of a particular informant's dialect or individual knowledge of the eastern Mediterranean basin. This seeming immediacy of past sailor-informants, in addition to the array of topographical details and our ability to compare the ancient descriptions with coastal features apparent today, are several of the factors that contribute to the intriguing nature and archaeological significance of Roman Periploi. Nevertheless, Periploi, like other ancient literary sources, must be approached with caution, not only with respect to terminological questions, but also in attempting to date a particular harbor's foundation or earliest period of use. The Periplous of Stadiasmus seems the most informative and reliable of the coastal accounts discussed in this paper, but even this Periplous may have been compiled from information that was occasionally outdated, garbled, or otherwise erroneous. Just as Ptolemy (*Geog.* 5.14.1–2), for example, transposes Capes Zephyrion and Drepanon in his description of the southern Cypriot coast, so does Stadiasmus (312–313) mistakenly report Kyrenia as lying west of Lapethos, instead of east, in his description of the island's north coast.

As additional archaeological studies are undertaken along the coasts of Cyprus, the occasional inconsistencies between the literary and archaeological records may eventually be resolved. Coastal surveys may also be able finally to locate those places mentioned in the texts whose exact whereabouts today remain uncertain, such as Palaia, Leukolla, Kargaiai, and the Arsinoe between Cape Zephyria and Nea Paphos. Furthermore, numerous smaller harbors and anchorages remain to be identified, which are omitted completely in the Periploi, such as that recently documented at Drousha-Kioni on the west coast of the Akamas Peninsula (Leonard 1995b). In studying these smaller, less familiar sites, we can begin to categorize them according to our understanding of both ancient harbor terms, in Greek and Latin, and the contemporary terminological practices of today's engineers.

To strive for terminological precision and consistency within the ongoing study of Roman harbors, however, several final points on contemporary English terms appear worthy of consideration: The term "harbor" corresponding to the general terms λιμήν, *portus,* and occasionally ὅρμος denotes a coastal or riverine location in general where ancient ships may have found shelter or at least were able to anchor. The term "port," on the other hand, (corresponding to the specific terms λιμήν and *portus*) refers to a distinct, functional type of harbor or maritime facility (i.e., a commercial harbor), and should be avoided in referring to a harbor in general. The internal area of a port where ships were protected from the elements is most precisely described using the specific terms "harbor" or "basin" (corresponding to ὅρμος). Lastly, the simple term "anchorage" corresponding to ὕφορμος, πρόσορμος, and *statio*) appears sufficiently precise for describing isolated natural harbors, such as Dhrousha-Kioni, or those areas outside larger facilities, such as Nea Paphos, where ships may have dropped anchor and received at least some protection from the elements. As archaeological study does continue in Cyprus, Crete, and elsewhere around the greater Mediterranean area, the terminological and topographical information contained within ancient Periploi may become even more of a useful, instructive tool in coastal survey and the excavation of Roman harbors.

REFERENCES

Allain, M. L.
  1977   *The Periplous of Skylax Karyanda.* Ph.D. Dissertation. Ohio State University.
Bown, A. H. J.
  1955   *An Introduction to Port Working.* London: C.R. Heiser.
Bouzek, J.
  1988   Preliminary Prospecting on the Site of Akrotiri (Knidos) in Cyprus, 1972. *Report of the Department of Antiquities, Cyprus,* Part 2: 71–75, esp. 73.
Calvet, Y.
  1993   Kition, Travaux de la Mission Française: le port de guerre (epoque classique). Pp. 125–27 in *Kinyras: L'Archéologie Française à Chypre; Table-rond tenue à Lyon, 5–6 novembre 1991, sous la direction de M. Yon.* Travaux de la Maison de l'Orient 22. Lyon, Paris: Maison de l'Orient, Diffusion de Boccard.
Christodoulou, D.
  1959   *The Evolution of the Rural Land Use Pattern in Cyprus.* Herts, England: Geographical Publications.

Cornick, H. F.
  1960– *Dock and Harbor Engineering,* Vols. 1–4. London: Charles Griffin & Co.
  1969
Cunningham, B.
  1908   *A Treatise on the Principles and Practice of Harbor Engineering.* London: Charles Griffin & Co.
Des Gagniers, J., and Tinh, T. T.
  1985   *Soloi: Dix Campagnes de Fouilles (1964–1974), Vol. I.* Sainte-Foy: L'Université Laval.
DuBois, C.
  1907   *Pouzzoles Antique.* Fasc. 98. Paris: Bibliothèque des École Françaises d'Athènes et de Rome.
Du Plat Taylor, F. M.
  1934   *The Design, Construction and Maintenance of Docks, Wharves and Piers.* 2nd ed. London: Ernest Benn.
du Plat Taylor, J.
  1980   Excavations at Ayios Philon, the ancient Carpasia, Part I: The Classical to Roman periods. *Report of the Department of Antiquities, Cyprus:* 152–216.
du Plat Taylor, J., and Megaw, A. H. S.
  1981   Excavations at Ayios Philon, the ancient

Carpasia, Part II: The Early Christian buildings. *Report of the Department of Antiquities, Cyprus*: 209–50.

Empereur, J.-Y.
1995   Le Port Hellénistique d'Amathonte, in *Proceedings of the International Symposium, Cyprus and the Sea, Nicosia, 25–26 September, 1993*, eds. V. Karageorghis, D. Michaelides. Nicosia.

1985   Rapport sur les Travaux de L'École Française à Amathonte de Chypre en 1984: le port. *Bulletin de Correspondance Hellénique* 109: 984–89.

Empereur, J.-Y., and Verlinden, C.
1986a   Rapport sur les Travaux de L'École Française à Amathonte de Chypre en 1985: le port. *Bulletin de Correspondance Hellénique* 110: 899–907.

1986b   Le port antique d'Amathonte à Chypre. *Archeologia* 215: 32–37.

1987a   Rapport sur les Travaux de L'École Française à Amathonte de Chypre en 1986: le port. *Bulletin de Correspondance Hellénique* 111: 755–59.

1987b   The underwater excavations at the ancient port of Athamus in Cyprus. *International Journal of Nautical Archaeology* 16: 7–18.

Flemming, N. C.
1974   Report of preliminary underwater investigations at Salamis, Cyprus. *Report of the Department of Antiquities, Cyprus*: 163–73.

Ford, P., and Bound, J. A.
1951   *Coastwise Shipping and the Small Ports*. Oxford: Blackwell.

Frost, F. J., and Hadjidaki, E.
1990   Excavations at the Harbor of Phalasarna in Crete: The 1988 Season. *Hesperia* 59.3: 513–27.

Gifford, J. A.
1985   Post Bronze-Age Coastal Change in the Vicinity of Kition. Pp. 375–87 in V. Karageorghis and M. Demas, et al., *Excavations at Kition V: the pre-Phoenician levels; areas 1 and 2; part I*. Nicosia: Department of Antiquities.

Green, J. N.
1973   An Underwater Archaeological Survey of Cape Andreas, Cyprus, 1969–1970: a preliminary report. Pp. 141–78 in *Marine Archaeology*, Colston Papers 23, ed. D. J. Blackman. London: Butterworths.

1969   *Cape Andreas Expedition*. Oxford: Research Laboratory for Archaeology.

Hadjidaki, E.
1988   Preliminary Report of Excavations at the Harbor of Phalasarna in West Crete. *American Journal of Archaeology* 92: 463–79.

Haslam, D. W.
1976   *Mediterranean Pilot, Vol. 5: The Coasts of Libya, Egypt, Syria, Lebanon and Israel; The Southern Coast of Turkey and the Island of Cyprus*. 6th ed. Taunton: Royal Navy.

Hermary, A.
1993   Les Fouilles Françaises d'Amathonte: le port. Pp. 172–74 in *Kinyras: L'Archéologie Française à Chypre; Table-rond tenue à Lyon, 5–6 novembre 1991, sous la direction de M. Yon*. Travaux de la Maison de l'Orient 22. Lyon, Paris: Maison de l'Orient, Diffusion de Boccard.

Heywood, H. C.
1982   The Archaeological Remains of the Akrotiri Peninsula. Pp. 162–75 in *An Archaeological Guide to the Ancient Kourion Area and the Akrotiri Peninsula*, H. W. Swiny, ed. Nicosia: Department of Antiquities.

Hill, G.
1940   *A History of Cyprus, Vol. I: To the Conquest by Richard Lionheart*. Cambridge: Cambridge University.

Hohlfelder, R. L.
1995a   Ancient Paphos Beneath the Sea: A Survey of the Submerged Structures. Pp. 191–210 in *Proceedings of the International Symposium, Cyprus and the Sea, Nicosia, 25–26 September, 1993*. eds. V. Karageorghis, D. Michaelides. Nicosia: University of Cyprus.

1995b   The cave of the amphoras. *Biblical Archaeologist* 58: 49–51.

Hohlfelder, R. L., and Leonard, J. R.
1994   Underwater explorations at Paphos, Cyprus: The 1991 preliminary survey. *ASOR Annual* 51: 45–62.

Karageorghis, V.
1989   Chronique des fouilles et découvertes archéologiques à Chypre en 1988: Kition-Bamboula. *Bulletin de Correspondance Hellénique* 113: 824–26.

1981   Minor Excavations: Akhelia. *Annual Report of the Department of Antiquities for the Year 1980*: 43. Nicosia, Cyprus: Department of Antiquities.

Leatham, J., and Hood, S.
1958–   Submarine Exploration in Crete, 1955. *Annual*
1959   *of the British School at Athens* 53–54: 263–280.

Lehmann-Hartleben, K.
1923   Die antiken Hafenanlagen des Mitellmeeres. *Klio* Beiheft 14. Wiesbaden: Klio.

Leonard, J. R.
1995a   Evidence for Roman Ports, harbors and anchor-

ages in Cyprus. Pp. 228–46 in *Proceedings of the International Symposium, Cyprus and the Sea, Nicosia, 25–26 September, 1993*, eds. V. Karageorghis, D. Michaelides. Nicosia: University of Cyprus.

1995b   The Anchorage at Kioni. Pp. 133–70 in *Ancient Akamas I: Settlement and Enviornment*, ed. J. Fejfer. Aarhus, Denmark: Aarhus University.

Leonard, J. R., and Hohlfelder, R. L.
1993   Paphos harbor, past and present: The 1991–1992 underwater survey. *Report of the Department of Antiquities, Cyprus:* 365–79.

Leonard, J. R.; Tuck, S. L.; Hohlfelder, R. L.; and Nicolaou, I.
1995   Evidence for a Lighthouse at Nea Paphos? *Report of the Department of Antiquities, Cyprus*: 237–48.

Myers, J. W.; Myers, E. M.; and Cadogan, G. (eds.)
1992   *The Aerial Atlas of Ancient Crete*. Berkeley: University of California.

Mlynarczyk, Y.
1990   *Nea Paphos III: Nea Paphos in the Hellenistic Period*. Warsaw: Wydawnictwa Geologiczne.

Morgan, F. W.
1958   *Ports and Harbors*. 2nd ed., revised by James Bird. London: Hutchinson University Library.

Müller, C.
1855   *Geographi Graeci Minores, Vol. I*. Paris: A. Firmin Didot.

Nicolaou, K.
1976a   *The Historical Topography of Kition*. Studies in Mediterranean Archaeology 43. Goteborg: Åströms.

1976b   Ancient fishtanks at Lapithos, Cyprus. *International Journal of Nautical Archaeology* 5.2: 133–42.

Papageorghiou, A.
1991   Chronique des fouilles et découvertes archéologiques à Chypre en 1990: Kition-Bamboula. *Bulletin de Correspondance Hellénique* 115: 812–13.

1990   Chronique des fouilles et découvertes archéologiques à Chypre en 1989: Kition-Bamboula. *Bulletin de Correspondance Hellénique* 114: 962–67, esp. 964–65.

Peristianis, I. K.
1910   Γενική Ἱστορία τῆς Νήσου Κύπρου. Nicosia.

Pirazzoli, P. A.
1988   Sea-Level Changes and Crustal Movements in the Hellenic Arc (Greece). The Contribution of Archaeological and Historical Data. Pp. 157–84

in *Archaeology of Coastal Changes: Proceedings of the First International Symposium "Cities on the Sea—Past and Present," Haifa, Israel, September 22–29, 1986*, ed. A. Raban. BAR International Series 404. Oxford: B.A.R.

Pirazzoli, P. A.; Ausseil-Badie, J.; Giresse, P.; Hadjidaki, E.; and Arnold, M.
1992   Historical Environmental Changes at Phalasarna Harbor, West Crete. *Geoarchaeology* 7.4: 371–92.

Quilici, L., and Quilici, S.
1972–   Ricerche Intorno a Melabron: la perlustrazione
1973   della penisola di Kormakiti. *Revista dell'Instituto Nazionale d'Archeologia e Storia dell'Arte,* 19–20: 7–102.

Quinn, A. DeF.
1961   *Design and Construction of Ports and Marine Structures*. New York: McGraw-Hill.

Raban, A.
1995   The Heritage of Ancient Harbor Engineering in Cyprus and the Levant. Pp. 139–89 in *Proceedings of the International Symposium, Cyprus and the Sea, Nicosia, 25–26 September, 1993*, eds. V. Karageorghis, D. Michaelides. Nicosia.

Revere, R. B.
1957   No Man's Coast: Ports of Trade in the Eastern Mediterranean. Pp. 38–63 in *Trade and Market in the Early Empires,* eds. K. Polanyi, C. M. Arensberg, and H. W. Pearson. Glencoe, Ill.: Free Press.

Rickman, G. E.
1985   Towards a Study of Roman Ports. Pp. 105–14 in *Harbor Archaeology, Proceedings of the First International Workshop on Ancient Mediterranean Harbours, 24–28 June, 1983*, ed. A. Raban. BAR International Series 257. Oxford: B.A.R.

Rougé, J.
1966   *Recherches sur L'Organisation du Commerce Maritime en Méditerranée sous L'Empire Romain*. Ports, Routes, Trafics 21. Paris: École Pratique des Hautes Études.

Rupp, D. W.
1981   Canadian Palaepaphos survey project: preliminary report of the 1979 season. *Report of the Department of Antiquities, Cyprus:* 251–68.

Salles, J. F. et al.
1993   *Kition-Bamboula 4: Les Niveaux Hellénistiques*. Paris: Editions Recherche sur les Civilisations.

Sanders, I. F.
1982   *Roman Crete*. Warminster, England: Aris & Phillips.

Shaler, N. S.
  1895   *Sea and Land; Features of Coasts and Oceans with Special Reference to the Life of Man.* London: Smith, Elder.

Shield, W.
  1895   *Principles and Practice of Harbor Construction.* London: Longmans, Green.

Soren, D.
  1986   The Apollo Sanctuary at Kourion: Introductory Summary of the Excavation and its Significance. Pp. 393–404 in *Acts of the International Archaeological Symposium, "Cyprus Between the Orient and the Occident," Nicosia, 8–14 September, 1985,* ed. V. Karageorghis. Nicosia: Department of Antiquities.

  1981   Earthquake: The Last Days of Kourion. Pp. 117–33 in *Studies in Cypriot Archaeology,* eds. J.C. Biers, D. Soren. Monograph 18. Los Angeles: Institute of Archaeology, University of California.

Soren, D., and Lane, E.
  1981   New Ideas About the Destruction of Paphos. *Report of the Department of Antiquities of Cyprus:* 178–82.

Swiny, H. W. (ed.)
  1982   *An Archaeological Guide to the Ancient Kourion Area and the Akrotiri Peninsula.* Nicosia: Department of Antiquities.

United Nations, UNCTAD Secretariat.
  1969   Conference on Trade and Development, Geneva. *Development of Ports; Improvement of Port Operations and Connected Facilities.* Preliminary report, No. E.69 II.D 17. New York: UNCTAD Secretariat.

Vigarié, A.
  1979   *Ports de Commerce et Vie Littorale.* Paris: Hachette.

Wallace, P. W., and Orphanides, A. G.
  1990   *Sources for the History of Cyprus, Vol. I: Greek and Latin Texts to the Third Century A.D.* Albany, N.Y.; Nicosia, Cyprus: Institute of Cypriot Studies, State University of New York; Cyprus College.

Yon, M.
  1995   Kition et la Mer a l'Époque Classique et Hellénistique, in *Proceedings of the International Symposium, Cyprus and the Sea, Nicosia, 25–26 September, 1993,* eds. V. Karageorghis, D. Michaelides. Nicosia: University of Cyprus.

Table 1
Ancient Harbor Terms, Suggested Meanings, Expected Topography
GREEK

Term (sing./plural) and Transliteration	Suggested Meaning	Expected Topography
ἀγχυρόβλιον (-α) angkhurobolion (-a)	Temporary natural anchorage; exposed to the elements (Rougé 1966: 112).	Natural facility Open coastline; natural inlet offering little to no protection; water area outside port or other well-protected maritime facility. Poss. remains: Pottery scatter on seabed or adjacent shore; anchors [NOTE: these same poss. remains are represented elsewhere in Table 1 by an asterisk (*)].
ἀλίμενος (-οι) alimenos (-oi)	Harborless	(Innumerable possibilities)
ἀνάπλοος (-οι) anaploos (-oi)	"Sailing upstream"; "canal (from the sea to an inland harbor)"; "putting out (to sea)"; a "sailing back"; a "return" (Liddell and Scott, s.v. ἀνάπλοος).	Natural or artificial facility Canal or other distinct passage or inlet leading inland away from sea? Channel or passage between islets, in the lee of which shelter may be found? Poss. remains: warehouses; inter-site road(s); pottery scatter.
ἐμπόριον (-α) emporion (-a)	Commercial center, emporium; not necessarily a harbor (Rougé 1966: 108–9).	Coastal/riverine: Natural or artificial facility Poss. remains: breakwaters, quays, warehouses (possibly forming distinct commercial precinct within port). Inland: Poss. remains: warehouses; inter-site road(s).
ἐπίνειον (-α) epineion (-a)	Commercial port (of another town), satellite harbor; dependent economically upon a town located some distance away (Rougé 1966: 109–10).	Natural or artificial facility Poss. remains: breakwaters, quays, warehouses, main road leading inland; *.
λιμήν (λιμένες) limen (limenes)	Harbor (in general sense) Port; relatively large or important	Any natural or artificial harbor site Substantial port site Natural or artificial facility Poss. remains: breakwaters, quays, warehouses; *.
ναύσταθμος (-οι) naustathmos (-oi) or ναύσταθμον (-α) naustathmon (-a)	Harbor or anchorage (in general sense), naval station (Liddell and Scott, s.v. ναύσταθμος; Lehmann-Hartleben 1923: 108, n.1).	Any natural or artificial harbor site Poss. remains: breakwaters, shipsheds, armament.
ὅρμος hormos (-οι) (accus. pl.: ορμους	Harbor; of relative medium or small size and/ or importance, with generally circular shape Internal basin of harbor	Natural bay or cove enclosed by headlands Man-made harbor of gen. circular shape Poss. remains: breakwaters, natural or artificial divisions between internal basins; *.
πάνορμος (-οι) panormos (-oi)	All-weather harbor; provides safety from any wind and even the largest storms (Rougé 1966: 113-14).	Natural bay, generally circular, with narrow entrance oriented away from locally predominate wind. Poss. remains: *.
πρόσορμος (-οι) prosormos (-oi)	Minor natural anchorage	Natural facility Anchorage beside distinct natural feature (e.g. peninsula, coastal eminence, small island)? Poss. remains: *.
σάλος (-οι) salos (-oi)	Tossing, rolling swell of sea; open natural anchorage (Rougé 1966: 110-12; Liddell and Scott, s.v. σάλος)	Natural facility Open coastline; natural inlet offering little to no protection; water area outside port or other well-protected maritime facility. Poss. remains: *.
ὕφορμος (-οι) hyphormos (-oi)	Minor natural anchorage	Natural facility Concealed anchorage (e.g. within narrow cove)? Anchorage below overlooking headland? Poss. remains: *.

Table 2
Ancient Harbor Terms, Suggested Meanings, Expected Topography
LATIN

Term (sing./plural)	Suggested Meaning	Expected Topography

Emporium (-a)	Commercial center, emporium (not necessarily a harbor)
	
	Latin term generally conveys same meaning as original Greek counterpart (Rougé 1966: 108–9); see Table 1: ἐμπόριον.
		Coastal or riverine:
		    Natural or artificial facility
		    Poss. remains: breakwaters, quays, warehouses (possibly forming distinct commercial precinct within port); pottery scatter on shore or adjacent shore, anchors (NOTE: these last two types of possible remains are prepresented elsewhere in Table 2 by an asterisk (*).
		Inland:
		    Poss. remains: warehouses; inter-site road(s); pottery scatter.

Portus (-i)	Harbor (in general sense) Port; large, enclosed Primarily for wholesale transactions Also provided accommodation for long-term layover (Rougé 1966: 117–18).	Any natural or artificial harbor site Port site Natural or artificial facility Poss. remains: breakwaters, quays, warehouses, evid. of shipyards; *.
Salum (-a)	Tossing, rolling swell of sea Open natural anchorage Exterior anchorage; located outside port, for large ships with drafts too deep to enter port (Rougé 1966: 111–12). Latin term generally conveys same meaning as original Greek counterpart (Rougé 1966: 108-9); see Table 1: σάλος.	Natural facility Open coastline or natural inlet offering little to no protection Somewhat protected water area outside/near a port site Poss. remains: *.
Statio (-i)	Natural anchorage; unenclosed, for temporary layover; served as subsidiary market, and gathering place for merchants of similar origin (Rougé 1966: 117–18).	Open coastline Natural bay or cove, somewhat exposed Poss. remains: quays, warehouses; *.

The Distribution of Cypriot Sigillata as Evidence of Sea-trade Involving Cyprus

JOHN LUND

Collection of Near Eastern
and Classical Antiquities
The Danish National Museum
Frederiksholms Kanal 12
1220 Copenhagen K
DENMARK

Cypriot Sigillata is a ceramic fine ware that was in use in the Late Hellenistic and Early Roman periods. It was presumably made in Cyprus; the author argues that the kilns were probably located in the Nea Paphos area. The distribution of the ware suggests that Crete, Rough Cilicia, the Nabatean Kingdom and part of the Mediterranean coast of Egypt were major trade partners of Cyprus. Only a few examples have been found at Antioch, probably because a rivalling product, Eastern Sigillata A Ware, was manufactured in northwestern Syria. A peculiar form of Cypriot Sigillata, bowls with astragal shaped feet, have been found in higher numbers outside the island than on it. Also, this form was copied locally in Israel and in the Persian Gulf region. Its popularity may have been due to its function: the bowls may have been used as containers of incense. Production of Cypriot Sigillata culminated in the second half of the first century C.E., and came to a near stand-still in the second half of the second century C.E. The reason for this may have been that the kilns were all but wiped out by an earthquake.

The present paper is a case study of the geographical and chronological distribution outside Cyprus of a specific product that was—in all likelihood—made on the island. It is offered in the hope that the results may increase our knowledge of the exportation of perishable and hence archaeologically invisible Cypriot goods.

Cypriot Sigillata is a fine red-slipped ceramic ware manufactured from the first century B.C.E. to the second century C.E. and perhaps longer. J. W. Hayes was the first to define and describe the ware in an article that appeared in 1967. Eighteen years later the same scholar published what has become the standard work on Cypriot Sigillata with a typology of fifty-nine shapes, mostly dishes, bowls, kraters and closed forms (fig. 1; Hayes 1967 and 1985a). Since then, several publications of material from excavations and surveys have enriched our concept of Cypriot Sigillata.[1] A few new forms—and variants of the previously recognized ones—have been added to the repertoire, and some of the questions raised by Hayes and those who follow his views have been answered. Also, the increasing number of finds enables us to study the ware using quantitative methods, although the question of how representative the material is, should always be kept in mind.

The problems involved in a study such as this concerning questions of pots and trade are formidable, and work based on distribution maps runs the danger of documenting

[1] (Kenrick 1985; Abadie-Reynal 1987: 52–53; Burkhalter 1987: 358 and 391–94; Williams 1989: 1–8; Hayes 1991: 37–50; Sackett 1992: 152; Malfitana 1992: 233–35; Lund 1993: 99–105; Malfitana 1993: 299–301). References to finds from sites mentioned in the text or shown on the figures may be found there or in Hayes (1967; 1985a) unless other publications are quoted.

Form P 11 (188 examples)

Form P 40 (126 examples)

Form P 22 A (90 examples)

Form P 12 (79 examples)

Form P 37 (71 examples)

Form P 28 (51 examples)

Form P 10 (48 examples)

Form P 4 B (34 examples)

Form P 5 (30 examples)

Form P 19 (23 examples)

Form X 38 (11 examples)

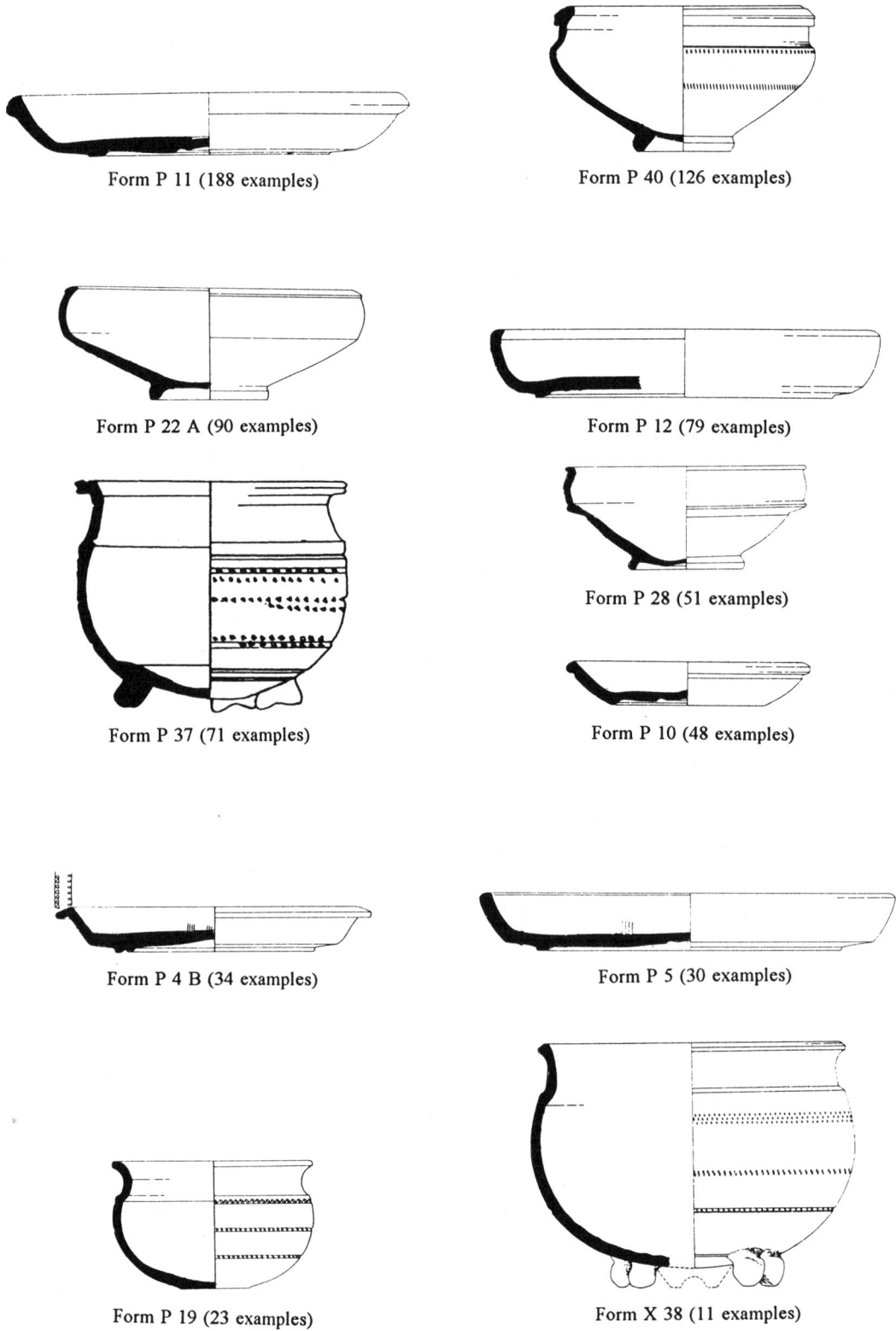

Fig. 1. Cypriot Sigillata: the forms most commonly represented in and outside Cyprus.

"areas of scholarly research, rather than actual distribution patterns" (Bilde 1994: 192); indeed, H. Meyza (1995) has recently underlined the difficulties involved in a study of the distribution of Cypriot Sigillata. Still, if the pitfalls are recognized, it is surely legitimate at any time to gather the evidence and to interpret the material based on our current knowledge.

THE QUESTION OF ORIGIN

Hayes (1967: 74) originally noted that the ware is "likely to have come from the Soli region, though the possibility that it is not from Cyprus at all cannot be altogether ruled out." Then, in 1972, A. Negev published a selection of Cypriot Sigillata found near pottery kilns at Oboda in Southern Israel, and he suggested a local, Nabatean, origin for the ware, but this theory was not accepted (Negev 1972; Negev 1986, XIX; cf. Lund 1993a: 100).

The question was raised again by two publications presenting results of Neutron Activation Analyses of specimens mainly from Israel, Cyprus (Gunneweg et al. 1983, 14–15; 109–10) and Petra in Jordan (Amr 1987). Both stressed the uniformity of the composition of the clay and its similarity to Cypriot Base Ring Ware from the Late Bronze Age, but one of them opted surprisingly for a source for Cypriot Sigillata in southwestern Asia Minor (Gunneweg et al. 1983, loc. cit.). The latter hypothesis has been rejected by most scholars (cf. Slane 1989: 222 note 20), who continue to regard Cyprus as the probable location of the production center(s) of the ware. The material presented below supports this view.

But where was the production center located on the island? If we are justified in assuming that a ceramic ware is more likely to occur in higher quantities close to its source than in more remote regions (cf. Peacock 1982: 167–68), then the chronological distribution of Cypriot Sigillata on the island itself becomes relevant. Regrettably, sufficient documentation is only available from a few sites. However, evidence from the on-going excavations at Aradhippou *Panayia Ematousa* in the Larnaca district suggests that the ware was relatively poorly represented in eastern Cyprus in the first century B.C.E. (fig. 2a).[2] The situation in northwestern Cyprus is far from clear; the material from Ayia Irini certainly testifies to the presence of Cypriot Sigillata in this part of the island in the first century B.C.E., but only a few such finds have been published from Soli. The ware was relatively well-represented at Amathus on the south coast (Burkhalter 1987; fig. 2b here). However, the highest number of finds datable to the first century B.C.E. has occurred in the Palaipaphos area (Lund 1993a: 99–105; fig. 2c here), and especially in Nea Paphos (Hayes 1991; fig. 2d here). This suggests that the production center(s) could have been located in the southwestern part of the island.

Two pieces of evidence may throw light on the question. First, Polish scientists who analyzed the clay of Cypriot Sigillata reached the conclusion that its composition is more or less similar to that of the Late Roman Cypriot Red Slip Ware (Meyza 1995; Daszkiewicz and Raabe 1995). Secondly, M. Rautman and his collaborators have recently published results of Neutron Activation Analysis of Cypriot Red Slip Ware suggesting two possible locations for the source of the clay: either the area between Nea Paphos and Polis in western Cyprus or the Cape Greco region in eastern Cyprus (Rautman et al. 1993; Rautman 1995: 335–36). When these results are combined it follows that the source of Cypriot Sigillata should also be sought in one or the other of the two said regions. And if the above-mentioned distribution of the latter in Cyprus is taken into account, it is reasonable to assume that the kilns were probably located in the Nea Paphos area. This conclusion makes eminent sense from a historical point of view.

Nea Paphos was the capital of the Roman province (Maier and Karageorghis 1984: 249–83), and archaeological evidence indicates that this city and its territory experienced an economic boom in the Late Hellenistic and Early Roman periods (Lund 1993a: 140–41; Alcock 1994a: 180–81). Conditions were apparently less favorable in the vicinity of modern Polis (Alcock 1994b, 169 with reference to Raber 1987). Also, a larger number of different forms—including some rare ones—has been brought to light in Nea Paphos than at any other single site. Moreover, J.-P. Morel (1983: 70) has stressed the urban character of certain "grandes productions céramiques, comme la sigillée claire." Finally, the city possessed an excellent harbor (Hohlfelder and Leonard 1993; Leonard and Hohlfelder 1993), and it has been noted that "the presence of an important harbor and hence a flourishing trade may ... have been a vital stimulus for an intensive pottery production" (Bilde 1994: 200–1 with reference to Fulford 1987). Looked at from these angles, the Nea Paphos region is an ideal candidate, although the question cannot be clinched until the actual workshops have been identified.[3]

---

[2] The evidence presented here is based on the author's preliminary assessment of the finds from the 1993 and 1994 campaigns directed by L.W. Sørensen (cf. Sørensen and Grønne 1992).

[3] For other harbors and anchorages in western Cyprus from where Cypriot Sigillata might have been shipped, cf. Leonard (this volume; 1995a and b).

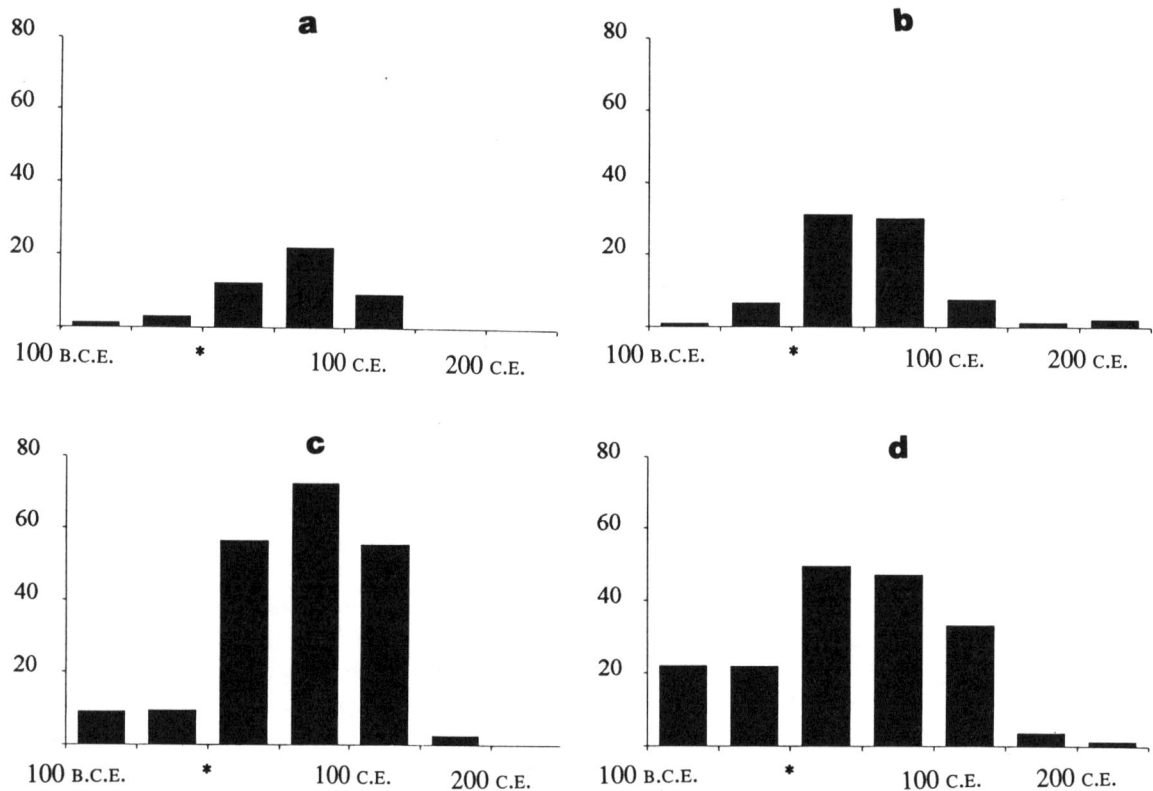

Fig. 2. a) The chronological distribution of Cypriot Sigillata found at Aradhippou in 1993 and 1994 (48 examples); b) the chronological distribution of Cypriot Sigillata found at Amathous based on Burkhalter (1987) (80 examples); c) the chronological distribution of Cypriot Sigillata from the Palaipaphos Survey Project based on Lund (1993) (205 examples); d) the chronological distribution of Cypriot Sigillata from the excavations of the House of Dionysos in Nea Paphos based on Hayes (1991) (178 examples).

THE QUESTION OF CHRONOLOGY

The chronological framework for Cypriot Sigillata was established by Hayes, chiefly on the basis of deposits in the House of Dionysos at Nea Paphos. His chronological scheme has remained virtually unchallenged (Lund 1993a: 100–1), but chronological evidence has recently emerged from Marina el-Alamein in Egypt necessitating a slight revision of the date of some of the forms.[4] The corrections in question have been taken into account below.

Also, the Polish excavations at Nea Paphos seem to suggest that production of Cypriot Sigillata could have continued beyond the second century C.E. Meyza now argues that there may have been a measure of continuity between Cypriot Sigillata and Cypriot Red Slip Ware (Meyza 1995).

Nonetheless, it is clear that production figures of the former decreased sharply in the second half of the second century C.E. The reason for this is a matter for speculation. Perhaps the ceramic industry was all but eliminated by one of the severe earthquakes that struck Cyprus in the second century C.E. (cf. Lund 1993a: 142).

THE DISTRIBUTION OF CYPRIOT SIGILLATA OUTSIDE CYPRUS

Cypriot Sigillata was widely distributed outside the island already in the first century B.C.E. (fig. 3), when Crete may have been the largest "consumer" of the ware, to judge by the finds from Knossos (Sackett 1992: 152 and passim; cf. also Blackman and Branigan 1975: 31 fig. 9). Relatively

---

[4] W.A. Daszewski has noted that the find contexts suggest that Form P 9 "can be assigned to the second quarter or, at the latest, around the middle of the first century C.E.," and that Form P 22 B began to be produced in the second half of the first century C.E. Forms P 10 and P 12 occurred in contexts dated to the second half of the first century C.E., and the most likely period for smaller bowls of form P 40 was "between mid-first and early second century C.E.," cf. Daszewski (1995: 29–30).

few such finds have otherwise been made in the Aegaean: in Tenos (Etienne 1986: 226 no. Fa 11 pl. 122; 229 no. Ga 6; 231 nos. An 12–13 pl. 125; 231 no. 15 pl. 126), Rhodes, Amorgos (Παππά 1989: 102 pl. 93:Μ/πδ 133) and Kenchreai (Adamscheck 1979: 63 nos. ER 37, ER 38a pl. 16; 63 no. ER 38b pl. 17 and no. P 596; 63–64 nos. ER 39–40). The second largest concentration has been brought to light at Oboda in Israel, and there are scattered finds from other parts of Israel (Riley 1975: 44–46 no. 88; 46 no. H4037; Gunneweg et al. 1983: passim). The ware likewise occurred in some quantity at Hama in Syria (Lund 1995: 138–39) and Petra in Jordan ('Amr 1987). Corresponding finds have not been reported from Western Asia Minor,[5] but Anemurium in Rough Cilicia is a major find spot (Williams 1989: 1–8). Smaller amounts were brought to light at Kaunos, Tarsus and Derbe. Similar evidence comes from sites along the North African coast, from Alexandria and Marina el-Alamein in Egypt (Daszewski 1990; 1995) to Berenice in Libya and Carthage in Tunisia. A few examples have been identified in Italy, but occurrences in the western Mediterranean are negligible in comparison with those from the eastern Mediterranean.

Before the first century C.E. the so-called Eastern Sigillata A Ware, which is now thought to have been produced in the Antioch region in northwestern Syria,[6] was the dominant fine ware throughout most of the eastern Mediterranean, including Cyprus. However, in the first century C.E. Cypriot Sigillata became predominant at Anemurium in Rough Cilicia and Marina el-Alamein in Egypt (Daszewski 1995). The ware had its widest distribution in this century, but the distribution pattern shows no break with that of the previous century (fig. 4). Apart from Rough Cilicia, the largest amount of such finds has occurred in Crete, Israel, and Jordan, where Cypriot Sigillata was popular at the Nabatean sites of Oboda, Nessana and Petra. Interestingly, the ware is now also documented at Aqaba (Whitcomb, n.d., 1 fig. 12:r) and at Quseir al-Qadim in Egypt (Whitcomb and Johnson 1982, 64–65 pl. 29–30:b, c, i and z). Numerous finds have also been made in North Africa, especially at Marina el-Alamein and Berenice;

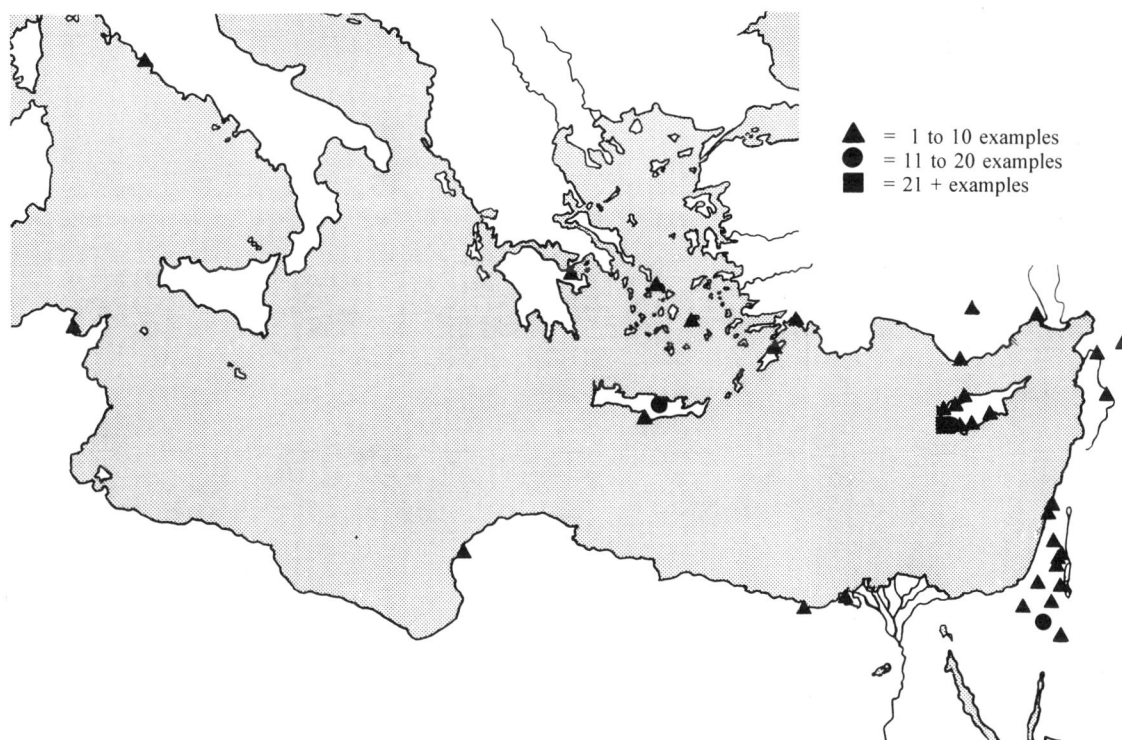

Fig. 3. The geographical distribution of Cypriot Sigillata in the first century B.C.E.

---

[5] The ware is not represented among the finds from the basilica in Ephesos published by Mitsopolulos-Leon (1991).
[6] For the standard classification of the ware see Hayes (1985b); for recent additions to the bibliography see Lund (1993: 90–96; 1995: 136–37) and Schneider (1995).

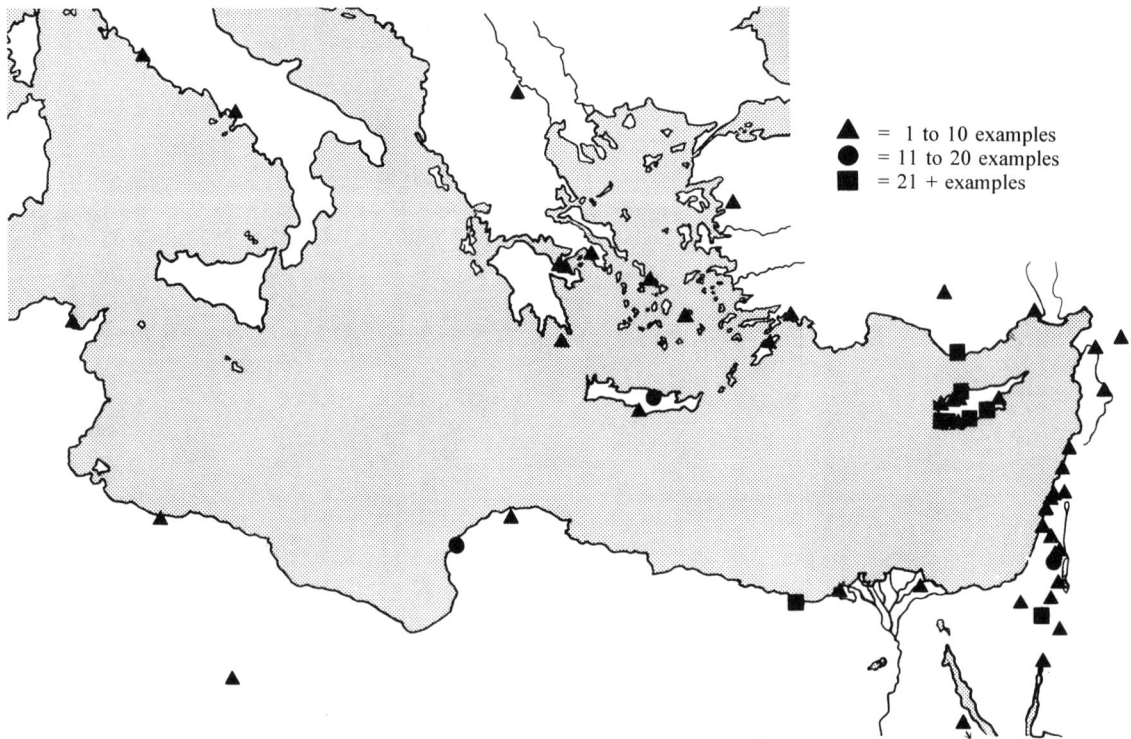

Fig. 4. The geographical distribution of Cypriot Sigillata in the first century C.E.

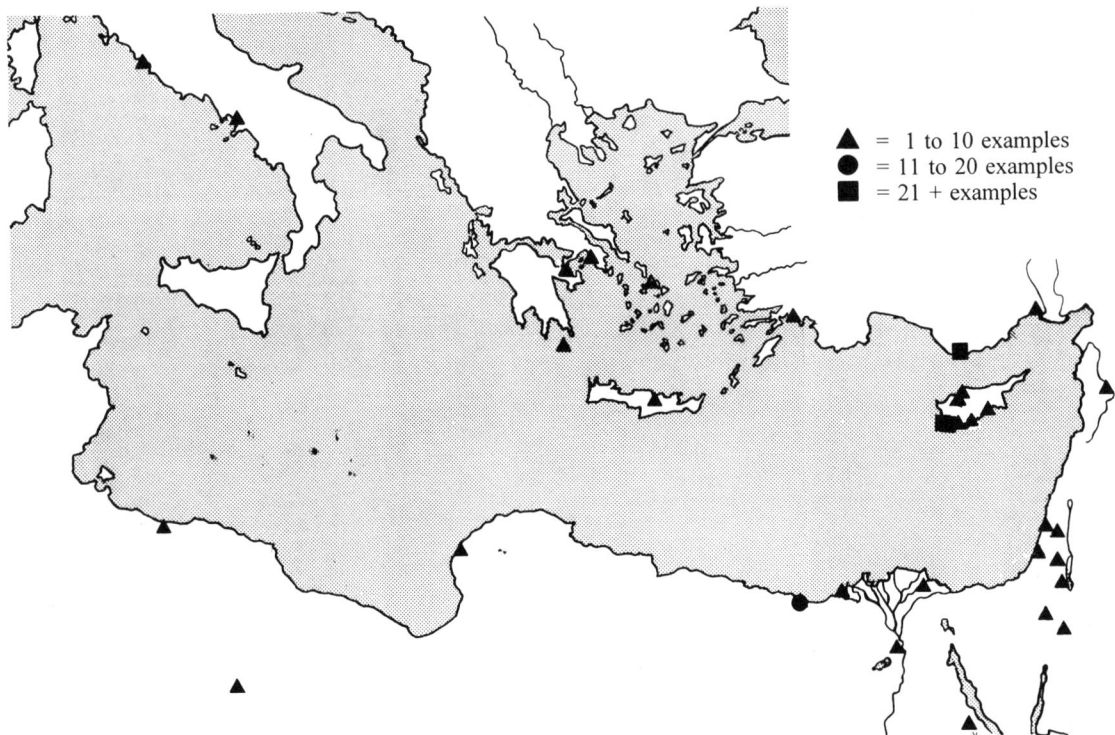

Fig. 5. The geographical distribution of Cypriot Sigillata in the second century C.E.

however, a few new find spots are documented for the first time: Cyrene and Sabratha (Kenrick 1986: 135, 155 and 166).

The situation was basically unchanged in the second century C.E. (fig. 5), until the number of finds declined everywhere after about 150 C.E. At Marina el-Alamein, for instance, "importation of Cypriot Sigillata died out in the course of the late 2nd century" (Daszewski 1995: 31). In fact, nearly all of the specimens found outside Cyprus date from the first half of the second century C.E.

THE CHRONOLOGICAL DISTRIBUTION OF CYPRIOT SIGILLATA

Judging by the finds made in Cyprus, production of Cypriot Sigillata reached its peak in the second half of the first century C.E. (fig. 6). This was followed by a pronounced decrease after about 100 C.E., and a dramatic one in the second half of the second century C.E. The material brought to light outside Cyprus suggests more or less the same pattern (fig. 7).

It is notable that certain forms were more popular outside the island than within it, especially bowls of the forms P 37 and X 38 with their characteristic astragal feet. The twelve examples of form P 37 found in Cyprus are dwarfed by the fifty-nine specimens hitherto found in other parts of the eastern Mediterranean. Remarkably, it seems that only one bowl of form X 38 is among the published finds from Cyprus, in contrast to ten examples found outside the island (cf. also Meyza 1995: 180). All of this suggests that part of the production was made especially for export.

IMITATIONS OF CYPRIOT SIGILLATA

Cypriot Sigillata was imitated at several places, and a pottery kiln in which such imitations were produced has been excavated at Oboda in Israel (Hayes 1985a: 79; Williams 1989: 2). Also, a bowl with astragal feet imitating form P 37 or X 38 was brought to light at Kypros near Jericho (Rosenthal 1978: 19), and a local version of form P 40 has been found at Kôm el-Hawaga in the vicinity of Bouto in Egypt (Ballet and von der Way 1993: 20 no. 59 fig. 9 pl. 2:c).

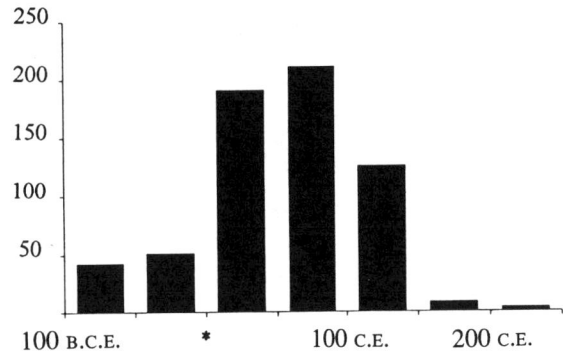

Fig. 6. The chronological distribution of Cypriot Sigillata found in Cyprus (631 examples).

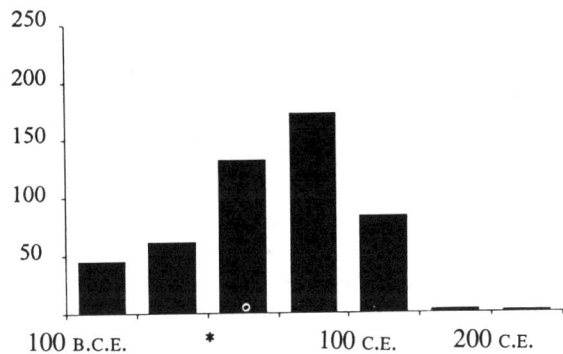

Fig. 7. The chronological distribution of Cypriot Sigillata found outside the island (499 examples).

Copies of form P 37/X38 complete with astragal feet, made in the so-called BI-Ware, have turned up in the Danish excavations at Failaka (Hannestad 1982: 26–27 nos. 175–176 pl. 14) and at Ed-Dur in the United Arab Emirates (Potts 1989: 26 fig. W; Salles 1990: 321 fig. 7:h). J.-F. Salles has recently discussed these finds together with other bowls with feet moulded in the form of shells. The latter are copies of bowls with shell-shaped feet known to have been manufactured in Athens as well as in Rhodes in the Late Hellenistic period.[7] Only the examples from Failaka and the specimen from Ed-Dur seem to have the characteristic astragal feet, and it is reasonable to assume that knowledge

[7] Salles (1990); S. Rotroff dates some Attic mouldmade bowls with feet in the form of moulded shells to the last quarter of the third century B.C.E., cf. Rotroff 1982: 16 and 45 no. 2 pl. 1. Corresponding finds have been made elsewhere in Greece, for instance in Aegina (Smetana-Scherrer 1982: 83 nos. 662–663 pl. 50), in Eretria (Metzger 1969: 62 no. 2 pl. 41), and in the Kabeirion near Thebes (Heimberg 1982: 107 nos. 868:a–s pl. 60). There is now evidence that black-slipped bowls with such feet were also produced in the city of Rhodes: moulds and wasters of shell-shaped feet were among finds from a ceramic workshop now on display in the Palace of the Grand Masters.

of the Cypriot prototypes—or actual specimens—could have been transmitted to the Persian Gulf via the trade route along the Euphrates or that following the Red Sea; the route may be traced by the examples of Cypriot Sigillata found at Aqaba and Quseir al-Qadim.

It is possible that the bowls with astragal feet were widely distributed outside Cyprus simply because the unusual shape caught the fancy of the consumers. However, it is, perhaps, more likely that they owed their popularity to the fact that they fulfilled a special function. A tomb stele in Munich from the Late Hellenistic or the Early Roman Period may give a hint of the use to which the form was put. It seems to depict a man holding a bowl of this form in his left hand; he scatters incense over an incense-burner with the other.[8] Incidentally, the hypothesis that the bowls—at least occasionally—could have functioned as incense-containers, may go some way in explaining the unusual form of the feet.

DISTRIBUTION OF OTHER CYPRIOT PRODUCTS

It would be interesting to compare the distribution of Cypriot Sigillata with a wide range of other products made in Cyprus in the Late Hellenistic and Early Roman Periods. However, this cannot be done at present due to lack of sufficient information about other wares manufactured in Cyprus, apart from transport amphoras. Hayes singled out two such amphora types current in the late first and second centuries C.E. Both belong to the amphora-producing tradition of the southern part of Asia Minor and the Dodecanese.

"Type I" is an amphora of Sub-Koan shape with characteristic long double-roll handles.[9] The west Mediterranean version is usually referred to as "Dressel 2–4" (see Martin-Kilcher 1993: 274–77). This type is part of a large family of Sub-Koan amphoras manufactured at several places in the Dodecanese and along the southwestern and southern coast of Asia Minor (Empereur and Picon 1989: 225–30). The shape of the Cypriot version may differ somewhat from that produced in the other workshops, but it is impossible to attribute an individual find—especially a fragment—to a particular workshop without scientific analysis of the clay.

"Type III" is an amphora with a near-cylindrical body and with characteristic pinched handles. It is also known under the name "Mid Roman amphora 4," "Mau XXVII–XXVIII" and "pinched-handle" amphora.[10] A kiln producing such amphoras has been excavated at Anemurium in Asia Minor (Williams 1989: 94–95), but there is little doubt that the type was also manufactured in Cyprus. Unfortunately, it is impossible to distinguish clearly between products from the various places of origin, and this question will probably not be resolved until clay analyses of the specimens are available.

It is likely that future research will demonstrate that the distribution of Cypriot-made amphoras of "Type III" is largely congruent with that of the Cypriot Sigillata: the latter was "definitely the most frequent foreign amphora" at Marina el-Alamein in Egypt, where a large amount of Cypriot Sigillata has been brought to light (Majcherek 1993: 215), and corresponding finds have been reported from Crete, which is likewise a major find spot for Cypriot Sigillata.

CYPRIOT SIGILLATA AS EVIDENCE OF TRADE

There is a growing realization—due mainly to the influential work of M. Vickers and D. Gill—that pottery did not have as high a status in the ancient world as many scholars previously believed. Moreover, it has been asserted that "there has yet to be found a shipwreck which has conclusively been shown to have contained pots alone,"[11] and it is now believed that fine ware pottery was mainly supplementary merchandise in cargoes of perishable goods, "not ex-

---

[8] Pfanner (1989: 171 pl. 28:1 note 6). I am grateful to P. G. Bilde for drawing my attention to this publication.

[9] Hayes (1991: 90–91); cf. also Peacock and Williams (1986: 105–6 Class 10); Empereur (1987: 42 no. 2 pl. 26:2); Böttger (1992: 333–35); Lund (1993: 122–24).

[10] Hayes (1991: 91–92); cf. Mau (1909 pl. 2 forma XXVII and XXVII)I; Riley (1979: 186–87); Williams (1989: 91–95); Daszewski et al. (1990: 46–49): Type 4; Böttger (1992: 340–41 nos. 65–66 fig. 3:2 pl. 99:6: Unbenannter Typ2); Lund (1993: 126–27). Cf. also Leonard (1995a: 144–45) with new information about the ware and chronology. To the evidence cited there may be added references to a few isolated finds: Sackett 1992: 178 and 2L5 no. U139 (Crete, Knossos, the Unexplored Mansion); Zemer (1977: 52) (Israel, Hadera); Parker (1992: 234 no. 567) (Sicily, Lampedusa A); Sciallano and Sibella (1991): unpaginated (from the gulf of Fos). Could this be the type of transport amphora from Carthage seen on Martin-Kilcher (1993: 289 fig. 8:9)?

[11] Gill (1994: 105); Vickers and Gill (1994); for the question of "pots and trade" see also the recent contribution of Small (1994).

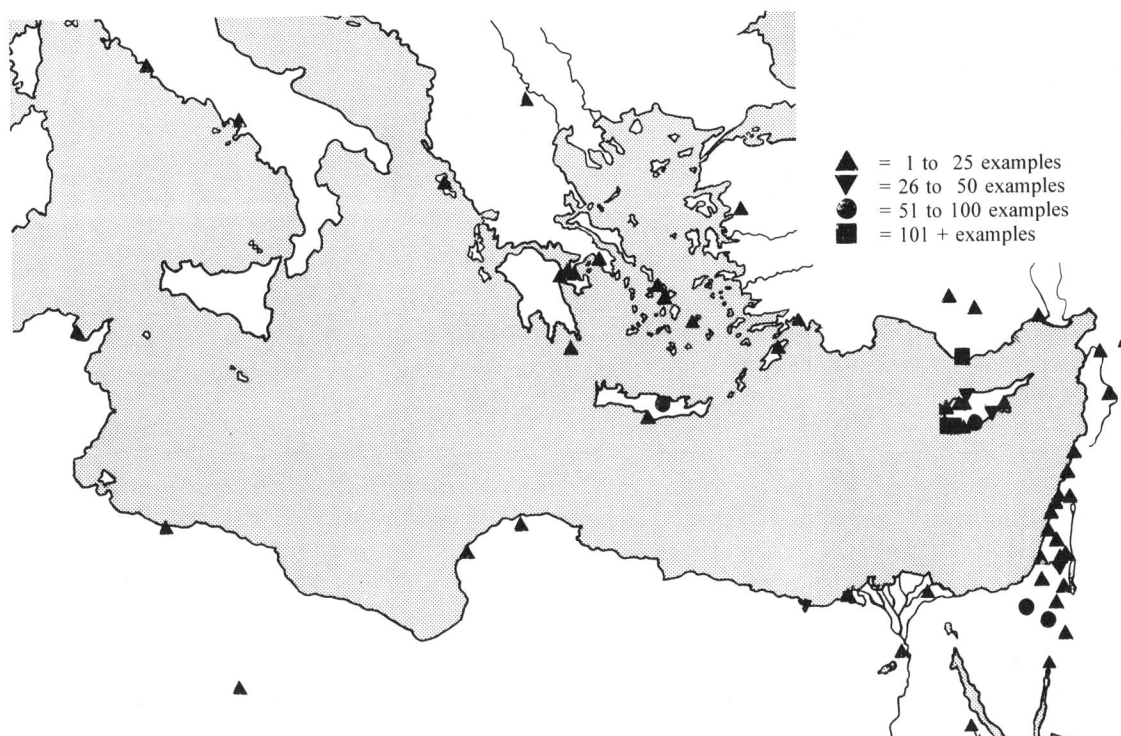

Fig. 8. The geographical distribution of Cypriot Sigillata from the first century B.C.E. through the second century C.E.

ported as part of a trade strategy, but rather following other goods, mainly wine amphorae .... It was the perishable goods, mainly grain, but also oil, wine, cattle and slaves, that constituted the economic basis for trade" (Bilde 1994: 193).

Still, few will presumably deny that even undecorated fine wares such as Cypriot Sigillata did play a positive role—albeit a minor one in comparison with the other commodities mentioned—in the economy and contributed to the welfare of the potters, the owner(s) of the kilns, the community in which they lived, and the merchants who sold the products in—and outside the island. Otherwise, it is hard to see what their incentive could have been to make the effort.[12]

As a matter of fact, the huge output of certain Late Hellenistic and Roman ceramic fine wares implies that the pottery industry and trade may have been more important to the ancient economy than Vickers and his disciples allow for. But even if the theory that pottery played an insignificant role in ancient trade as a whole is accepted, the dis-

tribution of ceramic finds does have a value as "an *index* of the frequency with which different routes were plied ... and a few sherds could be all that remains of a very considerable trade in foodstuffs, for example" (Peacock 1982: 154; cf. also Morel 1983; Fulford 1987; Tomber 1993: 142–43).

Generally speaking, the overall distribution of Cypriot Sigillata supports the notion of pottery as an index of trade (fig. 8). Nonetheless, there may be at least one exception to this rule, i.e. the scarcity of the ware in northwestern Syria, an area with which Cyprus certainly had close relations both before and after the Hellenistic period. The lack of relevant finds from there may be explained by the fact that the Antioch region was the source of Eastern Sigillata A ware.[13] However, it cannot be excluded that the situation reflects historical developments in the eastern Mediterranean in the Late Hellenistic period. Eastern Sigillata A was certainly the ceramic fine ware *par excellence* of the Seleucid Kingdom (Lund 1993b: 39–40), whereas Cypriot Sigillata was mostly distributed in an area that used to be part of what may be called the Ptolemaic Commonwealth (cf. Hölbl

---

[12] *Contra* the view expressed by Morel (1983: 70–71) without supporting evidence.

[13] A corresponding situation has been documented with the distribution of the late Roman Oxford and New Forest pottery in England, cf. Peacock (1982: 167–68).

1994). Still, in view of this suggestion, it is surprising that Cypriot Sigillata appears to be relatively poorly represented in Alexandria, but this may be a faulty impression, due to the scarcity of up to date publications of ceramic finds from this metropolis.[14]

In the first century C.E., Cypriot Sigillata became the dominant fine ware at Marina el-Alamein in Egypt and in Rough Cilicia, but it came second to Eastern Sigillata A Ware at Tarsus further to the east.[15] If the theory of pottery as an index of trade holds true, then Rough Cilicia and a part of the North African littoral must have been major trade partners of Cyprus in the Early Roman period. This accords well with the fact that Cilicia and Cyprus originally consti-tuted a single province in the Roman Empire, ruled from Cilicia, until the island became a separate province under Augustus.

Cypriot Sigillata had a less prominent position in other overseas markets, but the numerous finds from Crete, Israel and Jordan are surely evidence of trade connections between these parts of the world and Cyprus.

The available material yields no information about the ethnicity of the merchants who transported Cypriot Sigillata—and other products from the island—to the har-bors along the eastern Mediterranean. The mechanisms in-volved in the further transportation and distribution of the ware from there are also largely undocumented. Many ques-tions concerning the modalities of the ancient pottery trade will probably never be answered based on archaeological evidence alone, but it can be noted that Cypriot Sigillata was at times carried for relatively long distances overland, a fact that tends to underline its value to the consumer.[16]

SUMMARY AND CONCLUSIONS

It is highly likely that Cypriot Sigillata was made in western Cyprus, probably in the Nea Paphos area. The im-portance of this ceramic industry to the economy of Late Hellenistic and Early Roman Cyprus cannot be gauged, but common sense dictates that it must have had a positive im-pact, at least on a local level.

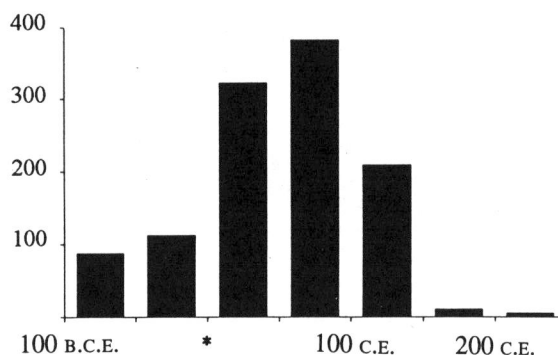

Fig. 9. The geographical distribution of Cypriot Sigillata found in and outside the island (1130 examples).

The ware made its appearance in the first century B.C.E. and production seems to have culminated in the second half of the first century C.E. (fig. 9). A steep decline followed in about the middle of the second century C.E., perhaps as the result of one of the earthquakes that devastated the western part of Cyprus at that time.

A considerable amount of the Cypriot Sigillata pro-duced—perhaps nearly half of the total output—seems to have been sold on overseas markets. Clearly, the geographi-cal position of Cyprus in the eastern Mediterranean facili-tated the diffusion of the ware, and the harbor of Nea Paphos could well have been an important factor in this, especially since it has been argued that the presence of an important harbor was—generally speaking—a vital stimulus for an intensive pottery production.

If the theory of pottery as an index of trade holds true, then Rough Cilicia and sites along the Mediterranean coast of Egypt could have been major trade partners of Cyprus in the Early Roman period, followed by Crete, Israel and the Nabatean city of Petra. However, Cyprus certainly also had close connections with Antioch and Alexandria, where Cyp-riot Sigillata seems to be poorly represented. The fact that northwestern Syria was the homeland of Eastern Sigillata A Ware, the fine ware *par excellence* of the Seleucid King-dom, presumably accounts for the almost total absence of

[14] However, see Rodziewicz (1976: 45): "on peut affirmer que la dite *Cypriot Sigillata* apparaît à Kôm el-Dikka sous les formes reconnues par Hayes comme les plus anciennes, par contre plus tard cette catégorie existe constamment mais dans des proportions relativement modestes." Cf. also Meyza (1995: note 6) and Daszewski (1995). Examples of the ware are not included in Kadous (1988).

[15] According to H. Meyza (1995: 179) "haphazard visits to the remains of Roman cities there" (i.e., along the south coast of Asia Minor) "suggest, that sites with numerous CS are frequent ... Tarsus ... should be noted as the possible eastern limit of this Anatolian area."

[16] For long-distance exchange in general see Tomber (1993: 145–48) and the references there cited. Concerning the overland transportation of Cypriot Sigillata, cf. Lund (1995: 138).

Cypriot Sigillata at Antioch. The scarcity of such finds in Alexandria is probably to be explained by the scarcity of up-to-date publications of ceramic finds from that city.

Part of the production of Cypriot Sigillata, especially many bowls with astragal feet, was apparently manufactured especially to cater for overseas customers. This, in turn, suggests that the trade was well-organized, and was not, or at least not normally, in the hands of merchants who happened to pass by western Cyprus and picked up—almost coincidentally—a consignment of Cypriot Sigillata as a "parasitic" ware.

The overall distribution of Cypriot Sigillata (fig. 8) probably reflects the routes and ports of call of ships carrying Cypriot goods, but we cannot determine if the ships in question were owned by Cypriots or not (cf. Gill 1994: 105–6).

One is left with the impression that the distribution of Cypriot Sigillata is more or less congruent with that of Cypriot pottery in the Late Bronze Age, the Iron Age and the Late Antique period. If this notion of a recurring pattern of Cypriot exports from one period to another can be substantiated, the reasons for this phenomenon might be a fruitful topic for future research in the ancient sea trade involving Cyprus.

ACKNOWLEDGMENTS

I wish to thank P. G. Bilde for constructive criticism of a draft version of the paper and L. Hannestad for enlightening me about the finds from Failaka. Also, I am grateful to C. Abadie-Reynal, B. Schmaltz and D. S. Whitcomb for permission to mention unpublished finds from Argos, Kaunos and Aqaba. W.-A. Daszewski and H. Meyza generously gave me access to their papers in press, and I benefitted from discussing some of the problems connected with Cypriot Sigillata with the latter during his visit to Copenhagen in 1994.

REFERENCES

Abadie-Reynal, C.
1987   Céramique romaine. Pp. 45–65 in *Études chypriotes VIII, La nécropole d'Amathonte Tombes 113–367 II: Céramiques non-chypriotes.* Nicosia: Service des Antiquités de Chypre, École Française d'Athènes and Fondation A. G. Leventis.

Adamscheck, B.
1979   *Kenchreai. Eastern Port of Corinth IV: The Pottery.* Leiden: Brill.

Alcock, S. E.
1994a   Breaking up the Hellenistic world: survey and society. Pp 171–90 in *Classical Greece: ancient histories and modern archaeologies,* ed. I. Morris. Cambridge: Cambridge University.

1994b   Surveying the Peripheries of the Hellenistic World. Pp. 162–75 in *Centre and Periphery in the Hellenistic World,* eds. P. Bilde, T. Engberg-Pedersen, L. Hannestad, J. Zahle and K. Randsborg. Aarhus: Aarhus University.

'Amr, Kh.
1987   *The Pottery from Petra. A Neutron Activation Analysis Study,* BAR International Series 324. Oxford: B.A.R.

Ballet, P., and von der Way, Th.
1993   Exploration archéologique de Bouto et de sa région (époques romaine et byzantine). *Mitteilungen des Deutschen Archäologischen Instituts Abteilung Kairo* 49: 1–22.

Bilde, P. G.
1994   Mouldmade Bowls, Centres and Peripheries in the Hellenistic World. Pp. 192–209 in *Centre and Periphery in the Hellenistic World,* eds. P. Bilde, T. Engberg-Pedersen, L. Hannestad, J. Zahle and K. Randsborg. Aarhus: Aarhus University.

Blackman, D. J., and Branigan, K.
1975   An Archaeological Survey on the South Coast of Crete, between the Ayiofarango and Chrisostomos. *The Annual of the British School at Athens* 75: 17–36.

Burkhalter, F.
1987   La céramique hellénistique et romaine du sanctuaire d'Aphrodite à Amathonte. *Bulletin de Correspondance Hellénique* 111: 353–95.

Böttger, B.
1992   Die kaiserzeitlichen und spätantiken Amphoren aus dem Kerameikos. *Mitteilungen des Deutschen Archäologischen Instituts Athenische Abteilung* 107: 315–81.

Daszewski, W.-A.; Majcherek, G.; Sztetyllo, Z.; and Zych, I.
1990   Excavations at Marina al-Alamein 1987–1988. *Mitteilungen des Deutsches Archäologischen Instituts Abteilung Kairo* 46: 15–51.

1995   Cypriot Sigillata in Marina El Alamein. Pp. 27–39 in *Hellenistic and Roman Pottery in the Eastern Mediterranean—Advances in Scientific*

Studies, eds. H. Meyza and J. Mlynarczyk. Warsaw: Polish Academy of Sciences.

Daszkiewicz, M., and Raabe, J.
1995   Cypriot Sigillata and Cypriot Red Slip ware—a preliminary report on technical investigations. Pp. 183–84 in *Hellenistic and Roman Pottery in the Eastern Mediterranean—Advances in Scientific Studies,* eds. H. Meyza and J. Mlynarczyk. Warsaw: Polish Academy of Sciences.

Empereur, J.-Y.
1987   Les amphores. Pp. 42–43 in *Études chypriotes VIII, La nécropole d'Amathonte Tombes 113–367 II: Céramiques non-chypriotes.* Nicosia: Service des Antiquités de Chypre, École Française d'Athènes and Fondation A. G. Leventis.

Empereur, J.-Y., and Picon, M.
1989   Les régions de production d'amphores impériales en méditerranée orientale. Pp. 223–48 in *Amphores romaines et histoire économique: dix ans de recherche,* Collection de l'école française de Rome 114. Paris and Rome: École française de Rome.

Fulford, M.
1987   Economic interdependence among urban communities of the Roman Mediterranean, *World Archaeology* 19: 58–75.

Gill, W. J.
1994   Positivism, pots and long-distance trade. Pp. 99–107 in *Classical Greece: ancient histories and modern archaeologies,* ed. I. Morris. Cambridge: Cambridge University.

Gunneweg, J.; Perlman, I.; and Yellin, J.
1983   The Provenience, Typology and Chronology of Eastern Terra Sigillata. *QEDEM Monographs of the Institute of Archaeology* 17. Jerusalem: The Hebrew University of Jerusalem.

Hannestad, L.
1982   *Ikaros: The Hellenistic Settlements 2:1: The Hellenistic Pottery from Failaka. With a Survey of Hellenistic Pottery in the Near East.* Aarhus: Jutland Archaeological Society Publications, XVI: 2.

Hayes, J. W.
1967   Cypriot Sigillata. *Report of the Department of Antiquities. Cyprus:* 65–77.
1985a   Sigillata Cipriota. Pp. 79–91 in *Enciclopedia dell'arte antica classica e orientale, Atlante delle forme ceramiche* II. Roma: Istituto poligrafico e zecca dello stato.
1985b   Sigillata Orientale A (Eastern Sigillata A). Pp. 9–48 in *Enciclopedia dell'arte antica classica e*
        orientale, Atlante delle forme ceramiche II. Roma: Istituto poligrafico e zecca dello stato.
1991   *Paphos III: The Hellenistic and Roman Pottery.* Nicosia: The Department of Antiquities.

Heimberg, U.
1982   *Das Kabirenheiligtum bei Theben III: Die Keramik des Kabirions.* Berlin: Walter de Gruyter & Co.

Hölbl, G.
1994   Geschichte des Ptolemäerreiches: Politik, Ideologie und religiöse Kultur von Alexander dem Großen bis zur römischen Eroberung. Darmstadt: Wissenschaftliche Buchgesellschaft.

Hohlfelder, R. L., and Leonard, J. R.
1993   Underwater Explorations at Paphos, Cyprus: The 1991 Preliminary Survey. *Annual of the American Schools of Oriental Research* 51: 45–62.

Kadous, E. Z. H.
1988   *Die Terra Sigillata in Alexandria.* Trier: Inaugural-Dissertation zur Erlangung des Doktorgrades im Fach Klass. Archäologie im Fachbereich III am der Universität Trier.

Kenrick, P. M.
1985   Excavations at Sidi Khrebish Benghazi (Berenice) III 1: The Fine Pottery, *Supplements to Libya Antiqua* V. Tripoli: Socialist People's Libyan Arab Jamahiriya, Secretariat of Education, Department of Antiquities.
1986   Excavations at Sabratha 1948–1951. A Report on the Excavations Conducted by Dame Kathleen Kenyon and John Ward-Perkins. *Journal of Roman Studies, Monograph No. 2.* London: The Society for the Promotion of Roman Studies.

Leonard, J. R.
1995a   The Survey of the Anchorage at Kioni. Pp. 133–70 in *Ancient Akamas I,* ed. J. Fejfer. Aarhus: University Press.
1995b   Evidence for Roman Harbors and Anchorages in Cyprus. Pp. 191–208 in *Cyprus and the Sea,* eds. V. Karageorgis and D. Michaelides. Nicosia: University of Cyprus.

Leonard, J. R., and Hohlfelder, R. L.
1993   Paphos Harbor, Past and Present: The 1991–1992 Underwater Survey. *Report of the Department of Antiquities. Cyprus:* 365–79.

Lund, J.
1993a   Pottery of the Classical, Hellenistic and Roman Periods. Pp. 79–155 in *The Land of the Paphian Aphrodite II: The Canadian Palaipaphos Survey Project. Artifact and Ecofactual Studies,* Studies in Mediterranean Archaeology CIV:2, eds. L. W. Sørensen and D. Rupp.

1993b The Archaeological Evidence for the Transition from the Persian Period to the Hellenistic Age in Northwestern Syria. *Transeuphratène* 6: 27–45.

1995 A Fresh Look at the Roman and Late Roman Fine Wares from the Danish Excavations at Hama, Syria. Pp. 135–61 in *Hellenistic and Roman Pottery in the Eastern Mediterranean—Advances in Scientific Studies,* eds. H. Meyza and J. Mlynarczyk, Warsaw: Polish Academy of Sciences.

Maier, F. G., and Karageorghis, V.
1984 Paphos: History and Archaeology. Nicosia: The Leventis Foundation.

Majcherek, G.
1993 Roman Amphorae from Marina el-Alamein. *Mitteilungen des Deutschen Archäologischen Instituts Abteilung Kairo* 49: 215–20.

Malfitana, D.
1992 Ceramica Romana. Pp. 229–37 in F. Giudice et al., Paphos, Garrison's Camp, Campagna 1988. *Report of the Department of Antiquities. Cyprus* 1992: 205–50.

1993 Terre *Varia* Sigillate. Pp. 297–304 in F. Giudice et al., Paphos, Garrison's Camp, Campagna 1989. *Report of the Department of Antiquities. Cyprus* 1993: 279–327.

Martin-Kilcher, S.
1993 Amphoren der späten Republik und der frühen Kaiserzeit in Karthago. Zu den Lebensmittelimporten der Colonia Iulia Concordia. *Mitteilungen des Deutschen Archäologischen Instituts Roemische Abteilung* 100: 269–320.

Mau, A.
1909 Pp. 619–95 in *Tituli vasis fictilibus inscripti. Corpus Inscriptionum Latinarum IV, supplementum 2.* Berlin.

Metzger, I. R.
1969 *Eretria II Ausgrabungen und Forschungen: Die hellenistische Keramik in Eretria.* Bern: A. Francke.

Meyza, H.
1995 Cypriot Sigillata and Cypriot Red Slip Ware—problems of origin and continuity. Pp. 179–202 in *Hellenistic and Roman Pottery in the Eastern Mediterranean—Advances in Scientific Studies,* eds. H. Meyza and J. Mlynarczyk. Warsaw: Polish Academy of Sciences.

Mitsopoulos-Leon, V.
1991 *Forschungen in Ephesos IX 2/2: Die Basilika am Staatsmarkt in Ephesos Kleinfunde, I. Teil: Keramik hellenistischer und römischer Zeit.* Wien: Schindler.

Morel, J.-P.
1983 La céramique comme indice du commerce antique (réalités et interprétations). Pp. 66–74 in *Trade and Famine in Classical Antiquity,* eds. P. Garnsey and C.R. Whittaker. Cambridge: Cambridge University.

Negev, A.
1972 Nabatean Sigillata, *Revue Biblique* 79: 381–98.
1986 The Late Hellenistic and Early Roman Pottery of Nabatean Oboda, Final Report. *QEDEM Monographs of the Institute of Archaeology* 22. Jerusalem.

Παππά
1989 Ερυθροβαφής κεραμεική από την Αμοργό. Pp. 97–108 in Α 'Συνάντηση για την Ελληνιστική Κεραμεική Δεκέμβρης 1986, eds. Λ. Μαραγκού, Ι. Α. Παπασποτόλου and Β. Παππά. Ιωάννινα.

Parker, A. J.
1992 *Ancient Shipwrecks of the Mediterranean & the Roman Provinces,* BAR International Series 580. Oxford: B.A.R.

Peacock, D. P. S.
1982 *Pottery in the Roman world: an ethnoarchaeological approach.* New York: Longman.

Peacock, D. P. S., and Williams, D.F.
1986 *Amphorae and the Roman economy: an introductory guide.* New York: Longman.

Pfanner, M.
1989 Ein Relief in der Münchner Glyptothek und Überlegungen zu einigen bemerkenswerten Aspekten hellenistischer Grabreliefs. *Mitteilungen des Deutschen Archäologischen Instituts Athenische Abteilung* 104: 165–96.

Potts, D.
1989 Ed Dur—The Danish Excavations. *Mesopotamia* 24: 13–27.

Raber, P.
1987 Early Copper Production in the Polis Region, Western Cyprus. *Journal of Field Archaeology* 14/3: 297–312.

Rautman, M.
1995 Neutron Activation Analysis of Cypriot and Related Ceramics at the University of Missouri. Pp. 331–49 in *Hellenistic and Roman Pottery in the Eastern Mediterranean—Advances in Scientific Studies,* eds. H. Meyza and J. Mlynarczyk. Warsaw: Polish Academy of Sciences.

Rautman, M. L.; Gomez, B.; Neff, H.; and Glascock, M. D.
1993 Neutron Activation Analysis of Late Roman Ceramics from Kalavasos-*Kopetra* and the Environs of the Vasilikos Valley. *Report of the Department of Antiquities. Cyprus* 1993: 233–64.

Riley, J.
1975   The Pottery From the First Session Of Excavation in the Caesarea Hippodrome, *Bulletin of the American Schools of Oriental Research* 218: 25–63.

1979   The Coarse Pottery from Berenice. Pp. 91–467 in Excavations at Sidi Khrebish Benghazi (Berenice) II, *Supplements to Libya Antiqua* V. Tripoli: Socialist People's Libyan Arab Jamahiriya, Secretariat of Education, Department of Antiquities.

Rodziewicz, M.
1976   *Alexandria I: La céramique romaine tardive d'Alexandrie.* Varsovie: Centre d'archéologie méditerranéenne de l'académie polonaise des sciences et centre polonais d'archéologie méditerranéenne dans la république arabe d'Égypte au Caire.

Rosenthal, R.
1978   The Roman and Byzantine Pottery. Pp. 14–19 in Excavations at Tel Mevorakh (1973–1976), Part one: From the Iron Age to the Roman Period, ed. E. Stern. *QEDEM Monographs of the Institute of Archaeology* 9. Jerusalem.

Rotroff, S.
1982   *The Athenian Agora XXII: Hellenistic Pottery, Athenian and Imported Moldmade Bowls.* Princeton, New Jersey: The American School of Classical Studies at Athens.

Sackett, L. H.
1992   The Roman Pottery. Pp. 147–256 in Knossos from Greek City to Roman Colony. Excavations at the Unexplored Mansion II, *The British School of Archaeology at Athens Supplementary Volume* no. 21, ed. L.H. Sackett. Oxford: Thames and Hudson.

Salles, J.-F.
1990   Questioning the BI-Ware. Pp. 303–34 in *Failaka, fouilles françaises 1986–1988, sous la direction d'Yves Calvet et Jacqueline Gachet.* Lyon: Maison de l'Orient Méditerranéen.

Sciallano, M., and Sibella, P.
1991   *Amphores. Comment les identifier?* Aix-en-Provence: Édisud.

Schneider, G.
1995   Roman red and black-slipped Pottery from NE-Syria and Jordan. First results of chemical analysis. Pp. 415–22 in *Hellenistic and Roman Pottery in the Eastern Mediterranean—Advances in Scientific Studies,* eds. H. Meyza and J. Mlynarczyk. Warsaw.

Slane, K. W.
1989   Corinthian Ceramic Imports: the Changing Pattern of Provincial Trade in the First and Second Centuries A.D. Pp. 219–25 in The Greek Renaissance in the Roman Empire, ed. S. Walker and A. Cameron. *Bulletin of the Institute of Classical Studies, Supplement* 55. London: University of London Institute of Classical Studies.

Small, J. P.
1994   Scholars, Etruscans and Attic painted vases, *Journal of Roman Archaeology* 7: 34–58.

Smetana-Scherrer, R.
1982   Spätklassische und hellenistische Keramik. Pp. 56–91 in *Alt-Ägina* II,1, ed. H. Walter. Mainz: von Zabern.

Sørensen, L. W., and Grønne, C.
1992   Report of Archaeological Soundings at Panayia Emathousa, Aradhippou, Cyprus 1991, *Report of the Department of Antiquities. Cyprus* 1992: 185–203.

Tomber, R.
1993   Quantitative approaches to the investigation of long-distance exchange, *Journal of Roman Archaeology* 6: 142–66.

Vickers, M., and Gill, D.
1994   *Artful crafts: ancient Greek silverware and pottery.* Oxford: Clarendon.

Whitcomb, D. S.
n.d.   *Excavations in Aqaba: Preliminary Report on the 1986 Season.* Unpublished.

Whitcomb, D. S., and Johnson, J. H.
1982   Quseir al-Qadim 1980: Preliminary Report. Malibu, *ARCE Reports* 7.

Williams, C.
1989   Anemurium: The Roman and Early Byzantine Pottery, *Subsidia Mediaevalia* 16. Toronto: Pontifical Institute of Mediaeval Studies.

Zemer, A.
1978   *Storage Jars in Ancient Sea Trade.* Second Printing Revised. Haifa: the National Maritime Museum Foundation.

Ziegenaus, O., and de Luca, G.
1975   *Altertümer von Pergamon XI.2: Das Asklepieion. Teil der nordliche Temenosbezirk und angrenzenden Anlagen in hellenistischer und frührömischer Zeit.* Berlin.

* * * * *

Since this paper went to press an important publication of Roman pottery found at Perge in Pamphylia has appeared:

Atik, N.
1995   Die Keramik aus den Südthermen von Perge, *IstMitt Beiheft* 40. Tübingen: Wasmuth.

The relatively few examples of Cypriot Sigillata shows conclusively that Pamphylia was not the source of the ware: 76–77 nos. 120, 121, 123, 127–29; 90 no. 147.

A few other relevant recent publications are listed below, together with some older ones, that I had overlooked:

Ballet, P.
1995   Relations céramiques entre l'Égypte et Chypre à l'epoque gréco-romaine et byzantine. Pp. 11–25 in *Hellenistic and Roman Pottery in the Eastern Mediterranean—Advances in Scientific Studies,* eds. H. Meyza and J. Mlynarczyk. Warsaw: Polish Academy of Sciences.

Lauffray, J.
1940   Une fouille au pied de l'Acropole de Byblos. *Bulletin du Musée de Beyrouth* 4: 14 fig. 6.

Papuci-Wladyka, E.
1995   *Nea Pafos. Studia nad ceramikq hellenistycznq z polskich wykopalisk (1965–1991).* Kraków: Nakladem Uniwersytetu Jagiellońskiego.

Pucci, G.
1977   Le terre sigillata italiche, galliche e orientali. P. 21 in *Quaderni di cultura materiale 1, L'instrumentum domesticum di Ercolano e Pompei nella prima età imperiale.* Roma: "L'erma" di Bretschneider.

Unterkircher, E.
1983   Terra Sigillata aus dem Heraion von Samos. *Athenische Mitteilungen* 98: 189 fig. 5.

Coastal Changes in Corinthia, Greece

Hampik Maroukian
Kalliopi Gaki-Papanastassiou

Department of Geography and Climatology
National University of Athens
157 84 Athens
GREECE

Dimitrios Papanastassiou

Seismological Institute
National Observatory of Athens
118 10 Athens
GREECE

The area around the gulf of Lechaeon in the northern Peloponnesus, is well-known for its numerous archaeological finds. There are archaeological sites that date from the Neolithic period, but the most important ones extend from Classical to Roman times.

Four important coastal archaeological sites, the ancient ports of Lechaeon and Kenchreai, the Diolkos and Heraeon were studied in order to determine the coastal changes that have taken place in this area since ancient times.

At Lechaeon and the Diolkos raised beachrocks have been observed overlying ancient structures. In the area of Heraeon there is a wide notch as well as uplifted beachrocks containing potsherds eroded at three levels, whereas at Kenchreai ancient structures have been submerged.

These observations of vertical land movements, attributed to active tectonism and intense seismicity, have caused significant coastal changes in the broader area of Corinth.

INTRODUCTION

The area under investigation is located in the south eastern part of the gulf of Corinth, especially the narrow strip of land that joins the Peloponnesus with mainland Greece, the well-known Isthmus of Corinth.

Geomorphologically, this region is bounded in the south by the fault zone of Ancient Corinth-Kenchreai extending along the northern slopes of Mount Onia, and in the north by the fault zone of Heraeo-Perachora-Loutraki, located along the southern slopes of Mount Gerania (fig. 1). Due to the presence of these two parallel and antithetic fault zones, a tectonic depression, represented by the Gulf of Lechaeon, has been formed.

It should be noted that north of the fault zone of Heraeo-Perachora-Loutraki, there is a large offshore fault that is responsible for the overall uplift of the area under study as well as the northern Peloponnesus. This uplift is not con-

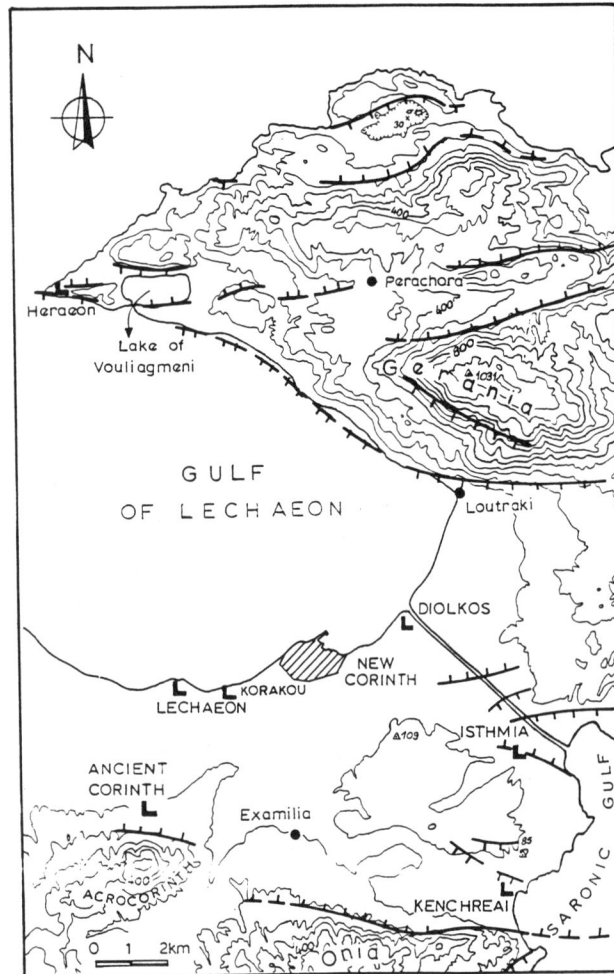

Fig. 1. Topographic map of the area under study showing the location of archaeological sites. The main faults are also indicated.

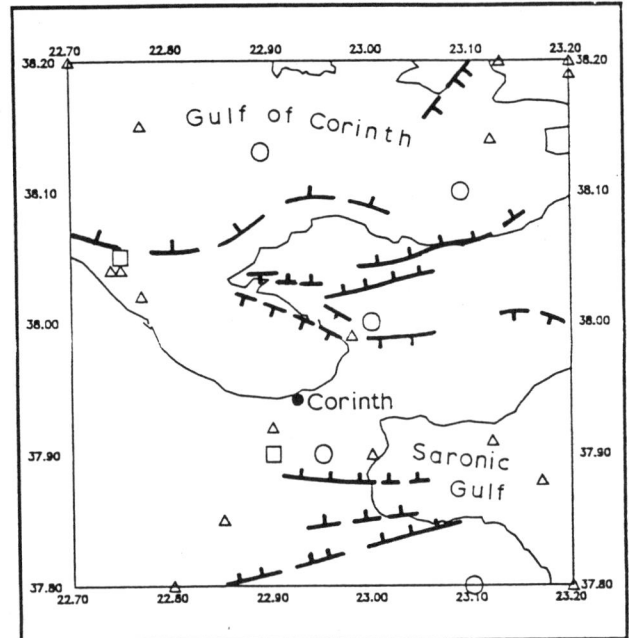

Fig. 2. Seismotectonic map of the southeastern Corinthian Gulf. Squares represent earthquakes that have occured, and circles denote earthquakes associated with the reactivation of specific faults, while triangles are other earthquakes, having a magnitude greater than 5, instrumentally recorded in this century.

tinuous, however, and thus the morphology of the northern Peloponnesus is characterized by a step-like arrangement with marine terraces having elevations from a few meters to hundreds of meters, (von Freyberg, 1972; Dufaure et al., 1975; Sebrier, 1977; Vita-Finzi and King, 1985; Keraudren and Sorel, 1987). Geological observations imply that the northern coast of the Peloponnesus is uplifted at a rate of 0.3 mm/yr, (Collier et al., 1992). Due to the complex tectonism caused by the numerous faults, this area is affected by two movements: uplift by the action of the large submarine fault and sinking by the action of the two marginal fault zones of ancient Corinth-Kenchreai and Heraeo-Perachora-Loutraki.

Geologically, the area under study is composed of Mesozoic limestones forming the Gerania and Onia mountain masses, while the terraces are composed of Plio-Pleistocene lacustrine, brackish, marine and fluvial deposits. Low-lying areas are characterized by alluvial deposits.

Due to its geographical importance this region has undergone intense housing development since prehistoric times in spite of high seismicity risks. The presence of numerous coastal archaeological sites (fig. 1; Papahatzis, 1977; Wiseman, 1978) provides the opportunity to correlate cultural remains with the interpretation and, if possible, the dating of the movements that have lead to the submergence or emergence of the sites. This was undertaken through coastal geomorphologic observation, the tectonic setting of the area and with information provided by major earthquakes.

SEISMICITY AND SEISMOTECTONICS OF THE AREA

The eastern Gulf of Corinth is characterized by high seismicity rates with frequent reports of destructive earthquakes from antiquity onwards. Local earthquakes are thus reported in 420 B.C.E., 227 B.C.E., 77 C.E., 160, 365, 375, 524, 543, 551, 580, 1307, 1312,. 1858, 1876, 1887, 1928, 1930 and 1981 C.E.

Written reports of historical authors, findings, and indications from excavations of archaeological sites in Corinthia, combined with modern evidence, observations and instrumental recordings lead us to single out those earth-

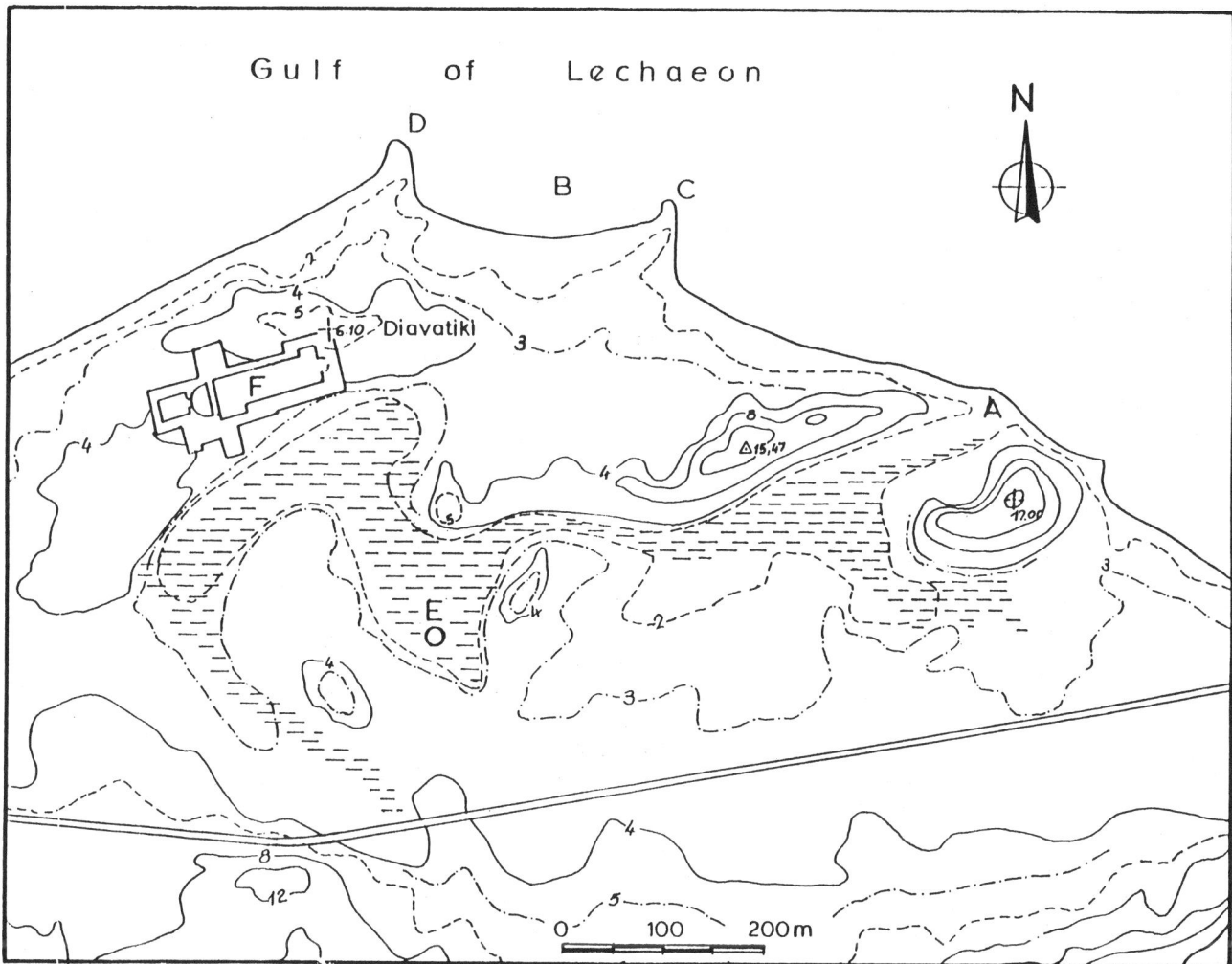

Fig. 3. Topographic map of Lechaeon, where parts of the ancient harbor are still visible. (A = the eastern entrance to the inner port; B = the outer port; C = the eastern jetty; D = the wester jetty; E = an artificial island (monument?) in the inner port; F = a large paleo-christian basilica.)

quakes that caused significant destruction and had their epicenters in the area under study. These are the 420 B.C.E., 227 B.C.E., 77 C.E., 524, 543, 580, 1857, 1887, 1928 and 1981 C.E. earthquakes, (Galanopoulos, 1961; Papazachos and Papazachou, 1989; Makropoulos et al., 1989; Guidoboni, 1989).

The correlation of these earthquakes with the activation of known fault zones in the examined area is neither thoroughly understood nor complete. Based on recent research work and the reevaluation of available data we can associate some of the strongest earthquakes with the reactivation of specific faults, such as the earthquakes of 227 B.C.E. and 1887 with the big Xylokastro fault located offshore northwest of Corinth; those of 524 and 1858 with the zone of Onia (north of Kenchreai), that of 1928 with the zone of Loutraki, and that of 1981 with the faults of the northern

slopes of Gerania (Kousta, 1858; Aiginitis, 1928; Tanakadate, 1928; Jackson et al., 1982; Abrasseys and Jackson, 1990; Papanastassiou and Gaki-Papanastassiou, 1994). The epicenters of these earthquakes are shown in fig. 2. It is important to note that most of the earthquakes, with a magnitude greater than 5 that have occurred and were instrumentally recorded in the present century, could be associated with some of the active faults.

The absence of information regarding earthquakes that took place in the Corinth area between the sixth and nineteenth centuries C.E. is noteworthy. According to historians studying this period, these areas were economically and politically far from important centers at the time and destructive earthquakes were perhaps not reported. Evidently, this gap hinders a complete reconstruction of the seismic history of Corinthia.

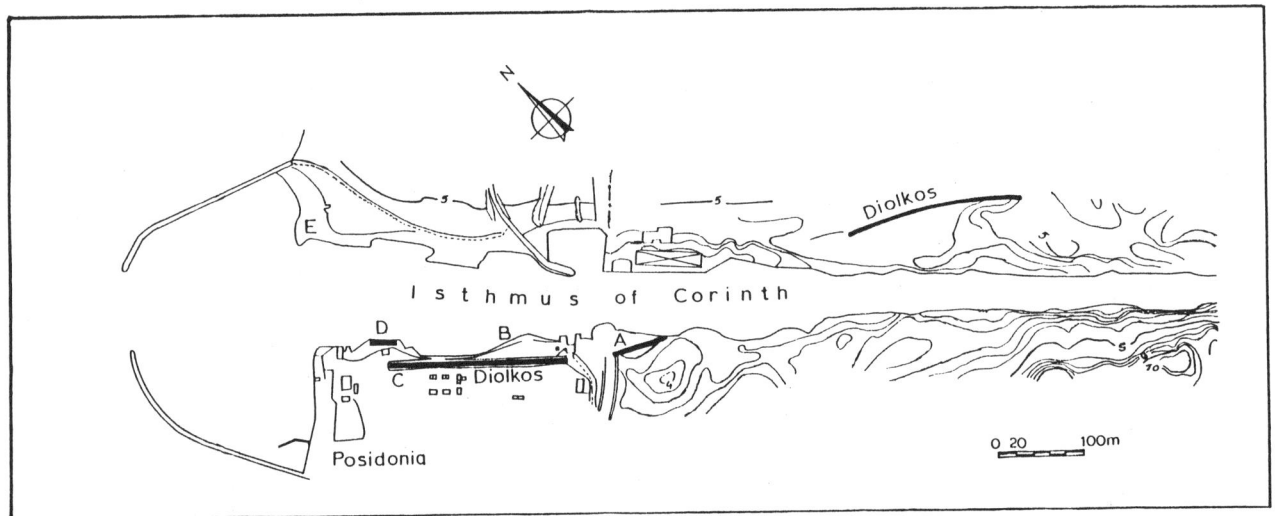

Fig. 4. Topographic map of the Isthmus Canal's west entrance, where the remnants of the western extremity of the Diolkos are located.

ARCHAEOLOGICAL SITES

As mentioned, this area has been inhabited since ancient times. In the Bronze Age, there were at least eight settlements located in the triangle of Kenchreai, Isthmia and Corinth. Some, like the settlement of Korakou (fig. 1), have been excavated (Blegen, 1921; Rutler, 1974). Korakou was more important than Corinth in Mycenaean times. The city-state of Corinth gained great economic power during the eigth century B.C.E., and in the fifth century B.C.E. it was one of the three most powerful city-states of Greece.

Lechaeon: Corinth's northern port on the shores of the Gulf of Corinth was important to the city in pre- classical times, in the seventh century B.C.E. (fig. 3). Later, the Corinthians continued to show considerable interest in Lechaeon, as it was the port nearest to the city. The port was mostly man-made, being the result of excavation and dredging. In the fifth century B.C.E., the Corinthians connected Corinth and Lechaeon with long walls. There has not as yet been any systematic excavation or research of the harbor installation.

The port of Lechaeon was made up of two parts, with inner and outer basins. The inner one was artificial, forming three sections joined by canals. Georgiadis (1906) shows only one canal (A) connecting the inner port with the sea. According to Paris (1915) and Roux (1958) there were in fact two canals (A and B), leading to the sea. The eastern one (A) is connected directly with the sea while the western one joins to outer port (B). The latter had two jetties (C, D), remnants of which are seen today, not only on land but also in the sea. The final form of the harbor installation, which included a little artificial island (E) in the west basin were attained as a result of extensive earth works, during Imperial Roman times.

On the Diavatiki hill, situated between the western inner port and the coastline, lie the ruins of a large palaeochristian basilica (F) of the fifth century (Palas, 1956; 1960; 1965), whose foundations are at an elevation of about 3 m. This church was destroyed by an earthquake and fire in the sixth century.

Diolkos: At the western entrance of the modern canal of Corinth lie the remains of the Diolkos (fig. 4). In 1956 and later, Verdelis (1956; 1960; 1962) excavated a section of paved road, the "Diolkos," built by the Corinthians to connect the Corinthian coast to the Saronic Gulf in order to haul ships from one side of the isthmus to the other. The name "Diolkos" derives from a Greek verb meaning "to drag." The excavations near the west end of the modern canal revealed that a paved road was used as a passage for a wheeled vehicle upon which the ship was lashed having been relieved of its cargo at the docks of Kenchreai or Lechaeon. The Diolkos was particularly useful for transporting warships that did not contain a cargo.

The Diolkos was constructed by Periander (625–585 B.C.E.), the great tyrant of the house of Cypselus and one of the Seven Sages of the ancient world, while its last mentioned usage was by the Byzantine admiral Nicetas Ooryphas in C.E. 883 during the reign of Basil I, the Macedonian.

Heraeon: The small harbor of Heraeon is located at the westernmost end of the Perachora peninsula, just west of Lake Vouliagmeni near the ruins of the sanctuary of Hera (fig. 5). The harbor area was excavated and studied by the British Archaeological School of Athens from 1930 to 1933 (Payne, 1940).

The sanctuary, located at the head of the harbor, is believed to have been founded in the eighth century B.C.E., and around 700 B.C.E. was destroyed and moved to another location. There is evidence that this area has suffered from

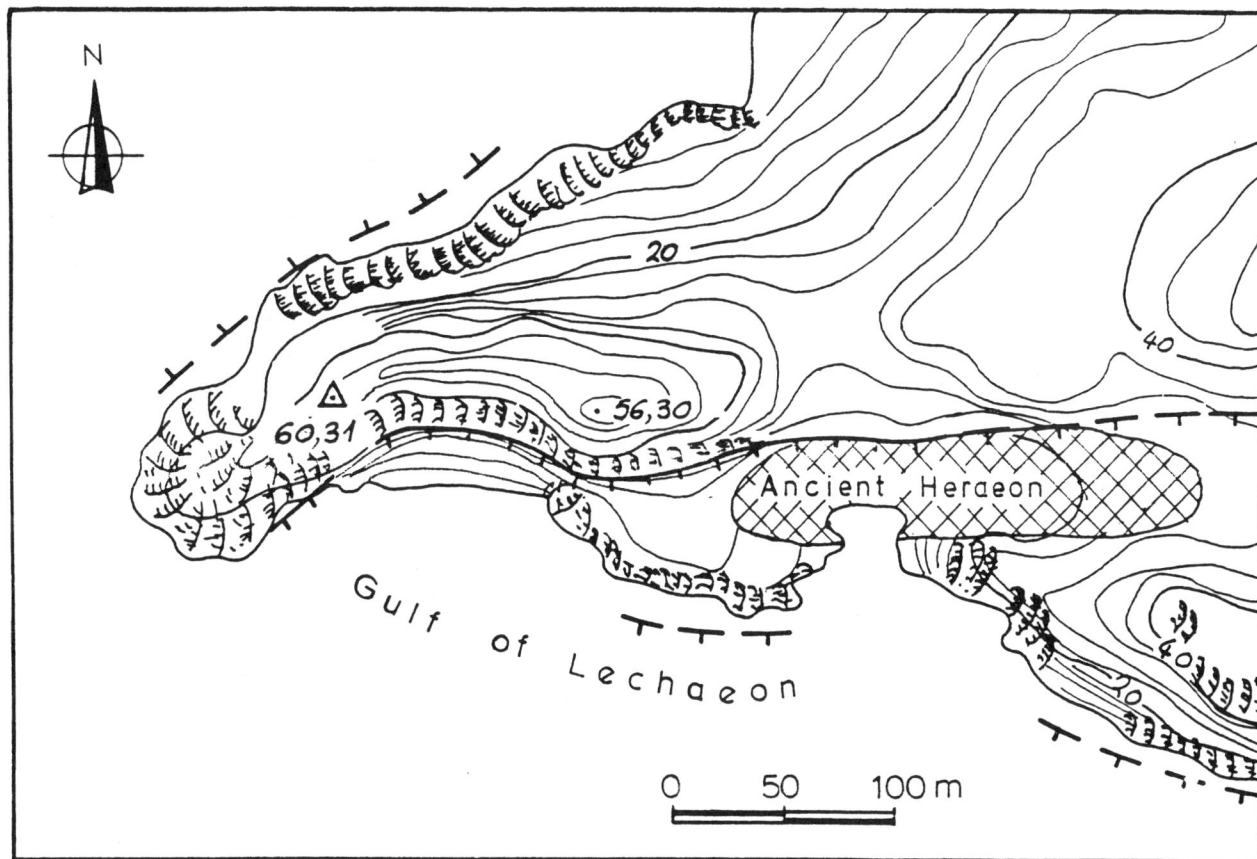

Fig. 5. Topographic map of the harbor of Heraeon. The main faults are indicated.

a number of earthquakes; the first occurring in the sixth century B.C.E., as dated by sherds found in a landslide west of the harbor. In the middle of the fourth century B.C.E., the whole of the harbor was remodelled. In the early Roman period, the northern part of the sanctuary of Hera was covered by the debris of a landslide. In the second century C.E., an earthquake was responsible for its final destruction.

It should also be noted that in the area of Lake Vouliagmeni a prehistoric settlement was discovered (Fossey, 1969). It is believed to have been destroyed by an earthquake during the Early Helladic I period.

Kenchreai: Corinth's east port on the Saronic gulf was situated on a bay still known as the Bay of Kenchreai (fig. 6). This harbor is seldom referred to by ancient authors despite the fact that it was of great importance to Corinthian communications with the Greek islands and the east.

The half-moon shaped natural anchorage had been converted into a fine harbor by the construction of moles as early as the Hellenistic period. They extended into the sea at the north and south ends of the port and supported various structures. The south mole was the widest. At some points their foundations remain visible though most of them are now submerged.

Excavations begun in 1963, sponsored by the American School of Classical Studies at Athens and the Universities of Chicago and Indiana (Scranton and Ramage, 1967; Scranton et al., 1976), have brought to light foundations of structures both on land and underwater. Most of the buildings belong to the Roman period. The south mole (A, fig. 6b) included a variety of installations, specifically a group of warehouses with a length of 135 m. The warehouses were extended to the east by a jetty of 80 m. On the northeastern side, towards the harbor, at depths of 0.8 m to 1.3 m, foundations of warehouses were found, while towards the sea and at a depth of 1.5 m, a fish tank had been constructed. All this building activity was dated to the first century C.E. and later. Southeast of the warehouses, at a depth of 0.75 m, a structure of the second century C.E. is believed to belong to the temple of Isis. Parts of the temple at the base of the mole are covered by a fourth century Christian church that was used until the mid-sixth century.

At the landward extremity of the 106 m long north mole (B), are the ruins of a tower, and a little farther inland, the foundations of mudbrick structures of late Roman and early Christian date.

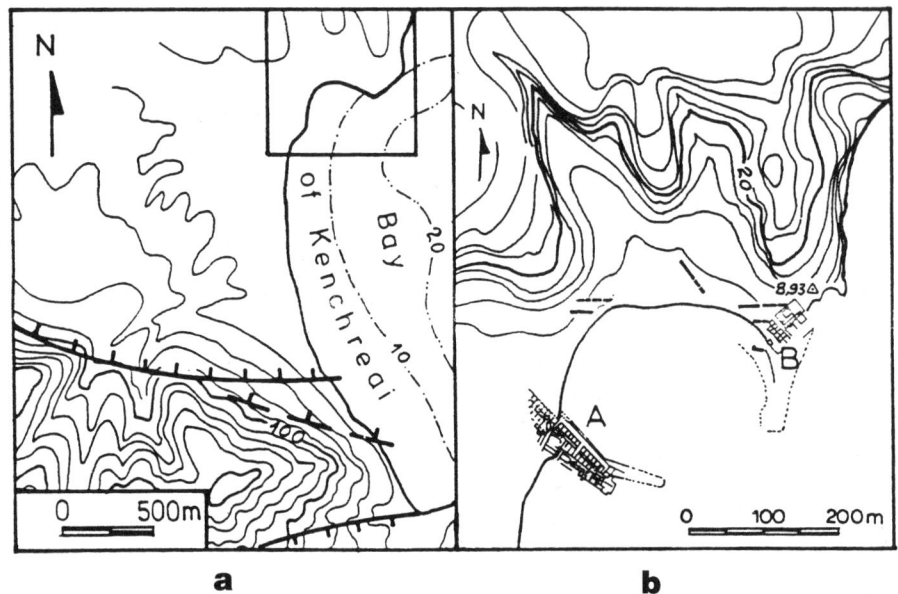

Fig. 6. a) Topographic map of the bay of Kenchreai and environs. The observed faults are shown. Inset is map b; b) Detailed amp of Kenchreai harbor and the excavated structures.

The excavators recognized three levels of destruction in this area and attributed them to earthquakes which occurred in 77 B.C.E., 365 C.E. or 375 C.E., and the sixth century C.E., with a corresponding sea level rise of 0.70 m, 0.80 m, and 0.80 m.

ARCHAEO-GEOMORPHOLOGICAL OBSERVATIONS

Korakou: The prehistoric settlement of Korakou is located a few hundred meters east of the ancient port of Lechaeon (fig. 1), on top of a coastal hill at an elevation of approximately 30 m. The hill is composed of marls capped by conglomerates. At present it is eroding, forming a bluff towards the sea. Consequently, huge blocks of conglomerate have fallen at the base of the bluff carrying with them parts of the northern section of the settlement. Based on this archaeological evidence it is reckoned that the coastline has retreated about 10 m since Mycenaean times.

Lechaeon: The ancient port of Lechaeon is located 3 km west of modern Corinth and covers an area of 0.5 km². Two hills dominate the landscape with elevations well over 15 m (fig. 3). One is situated north of the inner port and the other east of the eastern artificial entrance to the inner port. The area of the inner port was a marsh in prehistoric times owing to the presence of springs. This marsh was separated from the sea by a natural sandy spit and coastal sand dunes.

Today, borings of lithophaga organisms are visible at a height of 0.70 m above sea level on the walls of the quay forming the inner port, on the little island of the western inner port and on the *in situ* stones located southeast of the artificial eastern entrance of the port, indicating an earlier sea level about 70 cm above the present one.

Immediately west of the eastern entrance beachrock, up to 0.80 m thick, covers an ancient structure (fig. 7). This structure extends into the sea in a northeasterly direction, and is 50 m from and parallel to the *in situ* southeast wall of the entrance. Within the sandy and cobbly material of the beachrock, there are potsherds of Hellenistic to Roman date.

Similar formations of uplifted beachrock are observed on the west side of the western jetty of the outer harbor, which is devoid of beachrock.

The palaeochristian basilica (fig. 3.F) just west of the ancient port of Lechaeon, on Diavatiki hill, was excavated in the late 1950s by D. Pallas, who made some deep cross-sections at the northeastern foundations of the church. The deepest one reached 3.20 m. At 40 cm below the church floor, a thin destruction layer rich in ash was found and attributed to the burning of the port of Lechaeon and the city of Corinth by the Roman Momius in 146 B.C.E.

Diolkos: On the western end of the canal of the Isthmus of Corinth are found the remnants of the western extremity of the Diolkos (fig. 4). The general morphology of this area is very low, not exceeding heights of 5 or 6 m above sea level.

At a distance of 300 m from the western entrance, on the southern shore of the canal (position A), a formation of old, partially cemented beachrock was observed reaching up to a height of 0.80 m above sea level and dipping to the northwest (fig. 8). It is made up of limestone pebbles and cobbles having a mean size of 20 cm or less, but most of them are within a range of 4 to 6 cm. This material becomes sparser within an even less cemented matrix of sandy marine material above the beachrock. Its thickness is about 3 m and includes several marine shell fragments. No archaeo-

Fig. 7. Ancient harbor of Lechaeon. Roman structures covered by beachrocks.

logical sherds were found therein. On top of these marine sediments, the pavement of the Diolkos is constructed.

As we move towards the entrance of the canal, away from the Diolkos to undisturbed deposits, we see that the sandy marine deposits become more and more affected by terrestrial pedogenic processes. In this area (B), the Diolkos slopes towards the sea until it comes into contact with the old beachrock underneath and near the present sea level.

At a distance of 50 m northwest from position B is the beginning of the Diolkos (C) with a separate pavement on the side of the sea (D). The last one is covered by younger beachrock (Photo 2) up to a height of 0.80 m. Across the canal (E), similar beachrock is observed, with a width of about 150 m.

Following the excavations of the Diolkos and the removal of large quantities of material, serious erosion has been observed in the last thirty years with retreat of the coast at an accelerated rate, particularly in the last ten years.

Heraeon: The area is escarped with steep limestone cliffs (fig. 5). It is currently in a state of uplift due to active

Fig. 8. The western section of the Diolkos covered by beachrock.

Fig. 9. Raised mushroom-type notches in the Heraeon area.

tectonism. Distinctive 1.2 and 3 m wave erosion notches are observed on the rocks of both sides of the harbor entrance. The 1 m and 2 m wave marks form a wide notch (fig. 9). This indicates that it is not the product of just one movement but the result of two or three events of lesser magnitude. In the general area of Heraeon, on both sides of the entrance to Lake Vouliagmeni, raised beachrocks were observed having been eroded at three levels, namely 0.40 m, 1 m and 2 m corresponding to former sea levels. Within the 2 m level potsherds were found. The beachrock at the 1 m level is the wider and the most distinctive. It is also observed around the shores of Lake Vouliagmeni. Very clear also is the 2 m mark, while the lower one of 0.40 m is eroded and not very distinct. Finally, remains of older sea levels were observed at 6 and 10 m elevations in the form of coastal caves.

Kenchreai: The area of Kenchreai is located in a tectonic depression bounded to the south by the great fault zone of Onia (fig. 6), and to the north by smaller local faults of the Isthmus. In this basin, a dendritic type of drainage network has evolved. The streams are seldom active today, and as a consequence negligible quantities of fluvio-torrential deposits reach the sea.

In the coastal zone of Kenchreai, south of the submerged ancient structures, the sandy beach stops abruptly and continues as an alluvial cone. Remnants of marine depostis were found on the lower parts of the cone and traces of an old strandline were observed at an elevation of 0.60 m above sea level.

The contact between the sandy beach and the cone corresponds to the extension of the Onia fault zone towards the sea, that is to say, the Kenchreai Bay. According to a recent study of the Saronic Gulf (Papanikolaou et al., 1988) using the seismic reflection method and the construction of lithoseismic sections, the offshore extension of the Onia fault towards the east is confirmed (fig. 6).

On the beach south of the fault on a limestone exposure, well-defined 1 m-wide wheel ruts were observed slopping diagonally into the sea.

There are strong indications of coastal submergence, erosion and retreat all along the harbor area.

DISCUSSION AND CONCLUSIONS

On the western end of the Corinth canal, where the Diolkos starts, and sloping to the northwest, two different beachrock formations were observed. The oldest one, at 1 m above sea level, underlies the Diolkos, while the other runs over it with its highest point at 0.80 m above sea level.

The presence of these two distinct beachrock formations indicates that the region has undergone two uplifts, one before and the other after the construction of the Diolkos.

Provided that the formation of beachrock requires a calm coastal environment for the sand to accumulate and consequently become cemented within the intertidal zone, we are lead to the conclusion that the overlying beachrock was formed during a period when the Diolkos saw very little to no use. This suggests that it must date to the post-Roman period. Moreover, the great width of the younger beachrock indicates that a slow but limited submergence preceded its cementation, which could correspond to the last two submergence events at Kenchreai in the fourth and sixth centuries C.E. It should be noted that vertical tectonic movements caused by the reactivation of faults are greater near the fault zone and diminish as the distance from the fault increases. A submergence of 70 or 80 cm at Kenchreai could have produced a submergence of a few tens of centimeters further away, as at Lechaeon and the Diolkos.

The port of Lechaeon, like the Diolkos, also exhibits terrestrial beachrock incorporating sherds. These confirm the supposition that they were formed in post-Roman times overlying Roman structures, then a rather rapid uplift lead to the emergence of the beachrock.

Similar uplifted coasts are found in the Heraeon-Vouliagmeni area with a distinctive 1 to 2 m notch at Heraeon and eroded beachrock at 0.40, 1 and 2 m levels at Lake Vouliagmeni. These heights are greater here than those observed at the Diolkos and Lechaeon.

Considering the fact that the east Corinthian gulf is characterized by intense seismicity and high uplift rates, it is possible to attribute the previous geomorphological observations to relatively recent seismic activity accompanied by tectonic uplifting movements. Such simultaneous uplifting movements at Lechaeon, the Diolkos and Heraeon could only be caused by the reactivation of the fault located offshore, north of Heraeon.

The relatively wide lower notch at Heraeon indicates that it was not formed by just one uplift event but by several of smaller magnitude. Thus in the period between the sixth and nineteenth centuries C.E., when we start having historical records about earthquakes, there should have been seismic activity due to the activation of the great offshore east-west fault.

The region of Kenchreai is situated in a local tectonic depression bounded in the south by the Onia fault. The observed submergence of the Kenchreai harbor should be attributed to the activation of this fault and not to the big offshore fault, which is situated relatively far away.

It becomes evident from this study that the combination of archaeological information together with the tectonic regime, the seismic activity, and the geomorphological observations of the area are indispensable for a better understanding of its palaeogeographical evolution.

REFERENCES

Aiginitis, D.
  1928   Ο σεισμός της Κορίνθου της 22 Απριλίου 1928 και τα αποτελέσματα αυτου. Πρακτικα της Ακαδημίας Αυηνών 3: 369–81.
Ambraseys, N. N.; and Jackson, J. A.
  1990   Seismicity and Associated Strain of Central Greece between 1890 and 1988. *Geophysical Journal International*. 101: 663–709.
Blegen, C.
  1921   *Korakou, a Prehistoric Settlement Near Corinth*. Athens: American School of Classical Studies at Athens.
Collier, Re. L.; Leeder, M. R.; Rowe, P. J.; and Attkinson, T. C.
  1992   Rates of Tectonic Uplift in the Corinth and Megara Basins, Central Greece. *Tectonics* 11/6: 1159–67.
Dufaure, J. J.; Keraudren, B.; and Sebrier, M.
  1975   Les terrasses de Corinthie: chronologie et deformations. *Comptes rendus, Academie des Sciences* Paris, section D, 281: 1943–45.
Fossey, J. M.
  1969   The prehistoric settlement by Lake Vouliagmeni, Perachora. *Annual of the British School of Athens*. 64: 53–69.
Galanopoulos, A.
  1961   *A Catalogue of Shocks with Io≥VII for the Years Prior to 1800*. Athens: Seismological Laboratory, Athens University.
Georgiades, A.
  1906   *Les ports de la Grece dans l' antiquité qui subsistent encore aujourdhui*. Athénes: Imprimerie N. Taroussopoulos.
Guidoboni, E.
  1989   I terremoti prima del mille, in Italia e nelle area Mediterranea. Bologna: *Instituto Nazionale di Geofisica*.
Jackson, J.; Gagnepain, J.; Houseman, G.; King, G. C. P.; Papadimitriou, P.; Soufleris, G.; and Viriex, J.
  1982   Seismicity, Normal Faulting and the Geomorphological Development of the Gulf of Corinth (Greece): The Corinth Earthquake of February 1981. *Earth and Planetary Science Letters* 57: 377–97.
Keraudren, B.; and Sorel, D.
  1987   The Terraces of Corinth (Greece). A Detailed Record of Eustatic Sea-level Variations During the Last 500,000 Years. *Marine Geology* 17: 99–107.
Kousta, K.
  1858   Ο σεισμός της Κορίνθου 202: 22–229.
Makropoulos, K.; Drakopoulos, J.; and Latoussakis, J.
  1989   A Revised and Extended Earthquake Catalogue for Greece Since 1900. *Geophysical Journal International* 99: 305–6.

Pallas, D.
1956   Ανασκαφή Βασιλικής εν Λεχαίω.
        Πρακτικά Αρχαιολογικής Εταιρίας 112:
        164–78.
1960   Ανασκαφαί εν Λεχαίω. Πρακτικά
        Αρχαιολογικής Εταιρίας 116: 144–70.
1965   Ανασκαφαί εν Λεχαίω. Πρακτικά
        Αρχαιολογικής Εταιρίας 121: 137–66.
Papahatzis, N.
1977   *Ancient Corinth*. Athens: Ekdotike Athenon.
Papanastassiou, D., and Gaki-Papanastassiou, K.
1994   Γεωμορφολογικές παρατηρήσεις στην
        περιοχή Κεγχριών—Αρχαίας Κορίνθου και
        η συσχέτισή τους με σεισμολογικά
        δεδομένα. Πρακτικά ΙΙΙου Συνέδριου
        Ελληνικής Γεωγραφικής Εταιρίας. II:
        210–23.
Papanikolaou, D.; Lykousis, V.; Chronis, G.; and Pavlakis,
P.
1988   A comparative study of neotectonic basins across
        the Hellenic arc: the Messiniakos, Argolikos,
        Saronikos and Southern Evoikos gulfs. *Basin Re-
        search*. 1: 167–76.
Papazachos, B. C,; and Papazachou, C. B.
1989   Οι σεισμοί της Ελλάδας. Εκδόσεις Ζήτη.
        Θεσσαλονίκη. Thessalonica: Zeti.
Paris, J.
1915   Contributions á l'étude des Portes antiques du
        monde Greque, I, notes sur Lechaion. *Bulletin
        de Correspondence Hellèniques* 39: 6–16.
Payne, H.
1940   *Perachora, the sanctuaries of Hera Akraia and
        Limenia*. Oxford: Clarendon.
Roux, G.
1959   *Pausanias en Corinthie*. Paris: Editions Les
        Belles Lettres.

Rutler, J.
1974   *The late Helladic IIIB and IIIC periods at
        Korakou and Gonia in the Corinthia*. Ph.D. the-
        sis. Philadelphia: University of Pennsylvania.
Scranton, R., and Ramage, E.
1967   Investigations at Corinthian Kenchreai.
        Hesperia. 36: 124–86.
Scranton, R.; Shaw, J.; and Ibrahim, L.
1978   *Kenchreai, Eastern Port of Corinth*. I. *Topogra-
        phy and Architecture*. Leiden: Brill.
Sebrier, M.
1977   *Tectonique recente d'une transversale à l'Arc
        Egéen: le Golfe de Corinthe et ses regions
        peripheriques*. Thèse, Univ. de Paris-Sud, Cen-
        tre d'Orsay. Paris.
Tanakadate, H.
1928   Some Remarks on the Earthquake in Korinthos
        1928. Πρακτικά της Ακαδημίας 3: 413–19.
Verdelis, N.
1956   Ανασκαφή του Διόλκου. Αρχαιολογική
        Εφημερίς, Παράρτηγα, 95: 1–3.
1960   Ανασκαφή του Διόλκου. Πρακτικά
        Αρχαιολογικής Εταιρίας 116: 136–43.
1962   Ανασκαφή του Διόλκου. Πρακτικά
        Αρχαιολογικής Εταιρίας 118: 48–50.
Vita-Finzi, C., and King, G.
1985   The Seismicity, Geomorphology and Structural
        Evolution of the Corinth Area of Greece. *Philo-
        sophical Transactions of the Royal Society of
        London*. Ser. a. 314: 379–407.
1972   Geologie des Isthmus von Korinth. *Erlanger
        Geologische Adhandlungen*. 95: 1–183.
Wiseman, J.
1978   *The Land of the Ancient Corinthians*. Studies in
        Mediterranean Archaeology, Vol. 50. Göteborg:
        Åströms.

Late Holocene Coastal Evolution
of the Southwestern Euboean Gulf
in Relation to Ancient Coastal Settlements

Hampik Maroukian,
Kosmas Pavlopoulos,
and Sotirios Leondaris

Department of Geography-Climatology
University of Athens
Panepistimiopolis
157 84 Zografou
GREECE

Coastal habitation has been a vital element of settlement in Greece since ancient times. The south Euboean gulf has numerous coastal archaeological sites that have played a significant role in the development of the area. These sites, together with the prevailing geomorphic processes and important coastal landforms, have enabled us to provide a picture of the Late Holocene coastal changes that have taken place in the southwestern Euboean gulf.

In the last two millenia, most coastal archaeological sites have been submerged down to about 1.5 m, indicating a sea level rise of at least 2 m. This is believed to be due mainly to eustatic movements and less so to tectonism. Coastal erosion has been prevalent in most zones except in the deltaic plains, where stability is more common. Human agency and a rise in sea level are predicted to affect seriously the coastal environment in the coming decades.

INTRODUCTION

Greece has been a favored area for human habitation. The presence of the sea has played a role in determining the location of ancient settlements. One such place is the coastal zone of Attica, Boeotia and Euboea (fig. 1).

The western part of the south Euboean gulf is an area of particular interest regarding the evolution of the coastal zone in the Late Holocene period, both from the geomorphological and the archaeological points of view.

Geomorphologically, the south Euboean gulf presents a variety of coastlines (sandy, gently sloping to rocky cliffs), landforms (beachrocks, spits, dunes), longshore drifts as well as anthropogenic interventions (coastal structures, jetties, piers, moles) that provide valuable information on the evolution of the coastal environment during the Late Holocene. It also provides information on the future environmental pressures that the area will experience.

The area contains a number of coastal archaeological sites (fig. 2). Starting from the north along Euboea's coast and from west to east there is Chalkis, Lampsakos, Haghios

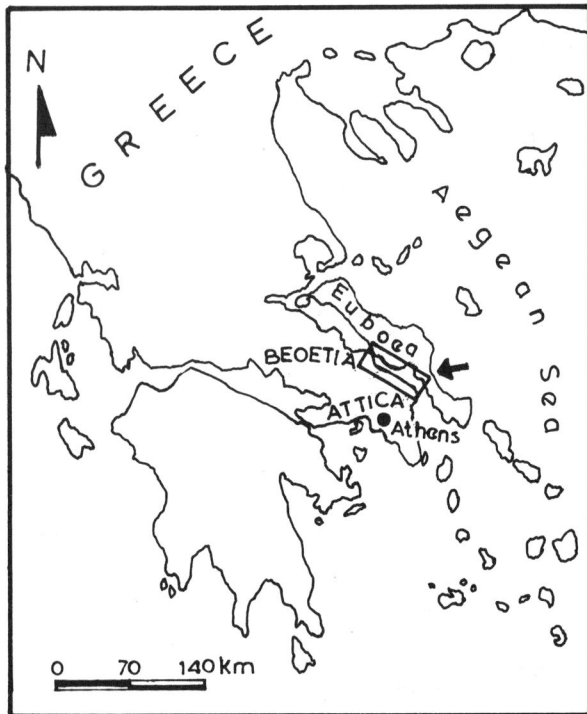

Fig. 1. Topographic map of the area under study showing the location of archaeological sites.

Nikolaos, Lefkandi, Linovrochi, Seimen Mnima (Malakonda), Eretria, and Liani Ammos (Magoula). On the side of Attica-Boeotia and from west to east the following sites are listed: Glypha, Avlida, Dilessi (Delion), Skala Oropou, Delphinio, and Psaphis.

GEOMORPHOLOGY AND GEOLOGY

There are two important drainage networks in the study area: Lilandas on the side of Euboea and the Boeotian Asopos on the side of Attica-Boeotia. Their deltaic deposits cover extensive low-lying stretches in the area of Lampsakos and Haghios Nikolaos for Lilandas and that of Chalkoutsi and Skala-Oropou for Asopos.

One additional region of Holocene fluvio-torrential deposits covers a large area near Avlida without exhibiting, however, an active drainage network.

Coastal geomorphological mapping was conducted in the study area of the South Euboean Gulf for a better understanding of the geomorphological processes and landforms encountered in the coastal environment. Leondaris and Maroukian (1988), and Kambouroglou (1989) have already mapped parts of the coastal zones of this area.

The symbols used in the coastal geomorphological mapping are divided into groups of processes, landforms and other elements of the coastal environment (fig. 3). There

are three symbols in the first group that show the coastal slope (gentle, steep, medium). In the second group, the symbols designate whether the coastline is stable, advancing (depositing) or retreating (eroding). There follows the third group indicating the particle size of the coastal sediments. In the fourth group belong the symbols that relate to the coastal and submerged beachrocks and the coastal dunes. The symbol of prevailing longshore drift is next. If terrestrial sediments are recorded without rock formations, they are designated as consolidated or unconsolidated. The remaining symbols determine the type and location of manmade structures or human interference on the coastline. Finally, there is a group of symbols dealing with coastal and/ or submerged archaeological sites. Needless to say, these symbols are not the only ones used in coastal geomorphological mapping. There are many more used to describe satisfactorily all the elements present in the coastal environment.

The geological formations encountered in this area are Mesozoic limestones, Neogene marls and conglomerates, Quaternary conglomerates and clay deposits, as well as recent fluvio-torrential deposits (Katsikatsos, 1986).

COASTAL ARCHAEOLOGICAL SITES

The coastal archaeological sites found in the western south Euboean gulf are spread along Euboea and Attica-Boeotia.

The Euboean Coastline

Chalkis (Haghios Stephanos): This site exhibits the remains of large public buildings found during an excavation in 1984 whose foundations are at today's sea level. They are dated to the fourth or third centuries B.C.E. (Kambouroglou et al. 1988: 75). The site is situated near coastal and submarine springs that issue from limestone outcrops. A large coastal zone has been filled in with earth in recent years thus altering the morphology of the area.

Lampsakos: This is a burial ground covered with a number of tiled tombs eroded by the sea due to human interference in the coastal environment. Their orientation is north-south. The area is found within the old deltaic deposits of the Lilandas river.

Haghios Nikolaos: The site consists of a late Roman coastal cemetery, partially eroded by the sea. As a result, several tiled tombs have been exposed at sea level (Kambouroglou et al. 1988: 75). This area comprises part of the western edge of the deltaic plain of the Lilandas River. The delta extended into the sea in older times but the coastline is re-

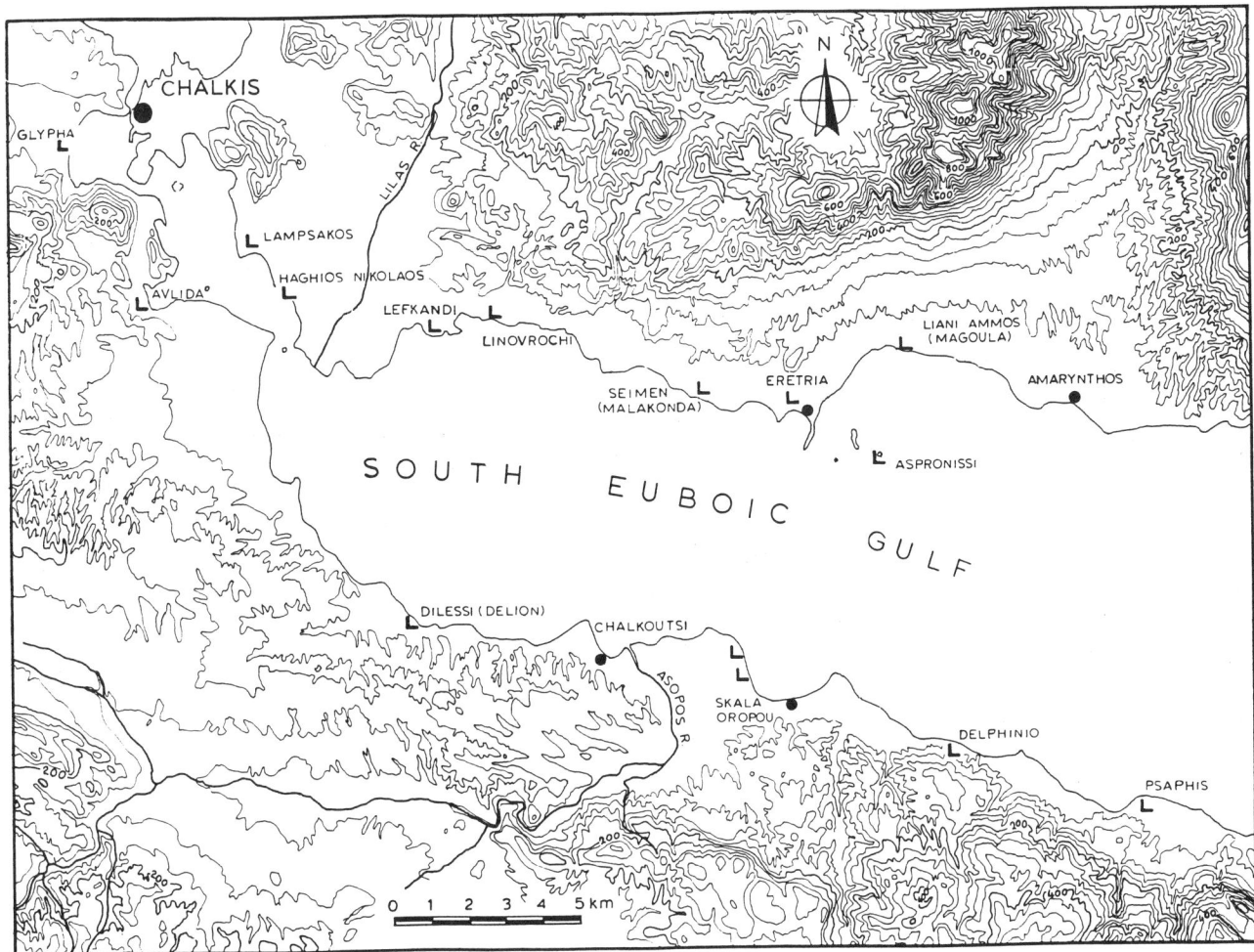

Fig. 2. Coastal archaeological sites in the western section of the south Euboic Gulf.

treating today due to river mouth changes to the southeast and the reduction of sediment discharge.

Lefkandi: A prehistoric settlement of Early Helladic III age (2450–2350 B.C.E.) to the end of the Geometric period (700 B.C.E.). It prospered immediately after Manika in the north. Following the end of the Geometric period, Lefkandi declined while Chalkis prospered (Popham and Sacket 1967: 60). The site is on an eroded hill having a height of 17 m, and composed of conglomerates of fluvial provenance of Pleistocene age. The coastline is slowly retreating today. Parallel to it, submerged beachrock is observed down to a depth of 1.5 m below the surface (fig. 4). The coast is steep and the coastal sediments are coarse.

Linovrochi: There are underwater and coastal springs at this site at which Bronze Age pottery has been discovered (Psychoyos, 1988, p. 86). The coast is steep and made up of coarse marine sediments. A spring issues through conglomerates and marly sandstones.

Seimen: The site consists of a neolithic coastal settlement dating from the younger Neolithic II (4300–3800 B.C.E.). It was excavated in 1976 but work stopped for technical reasons when it reached 70 cm below the present sea level despite the continuation of archaeological deposits (Sampson 1981: 129–31). The settlement is situated a few meters from the eastern jetty of "Eretria Hotel," where a low cliff defines today's coastline. About 100 m farther east, archaeological remains of the Classical period suggest that at that time the sea level would have been more than 1 m lower.

Eretria: Semi-submerged harbor structures of Early Archaic date (sixth century B.C.E.) indicate a sea level rise of about 1.5 m. Beachrock was observed down to a depth of 4.70 m.

Isle of Aspronissi (Eretria): On the southwestern coast of the island a wall was located, partially covered by the sea and a beachrock formation. The associated pottery belongs to the Hellenistic period (third to second centuries B.C.E.). The evidence suggests that this area has been eroded at an

LEGEND

LAND | SEA

Gently sloping coast
Medium to steep coast
Steep coast or cliff
Steep coast or cliff with talus
Stable coastline
Retreating coastline
Advancing coastline
Sandy Beach
Shingle Beach
"Mixed" Beach
Beachrock
Underwater or cut off Beachrock
Coastal dunes (active)
Coastal dunes (inactive or eroding)
Vegetated stable dunes
Longshore drift (prevailing)
Coast composed of unconsolidated material
Coast composed of consolidated material
Artificially filled-in coast
Built-up coastal zone
Sewer
Wharf, waterfront
Jetty, pier
Pier on pillars
Breakwater
Anchorage
Damaged or destroyed man-made structure
Archaeological site (on land)
Archaeological site (in sea)
Archaeological site (underwater)

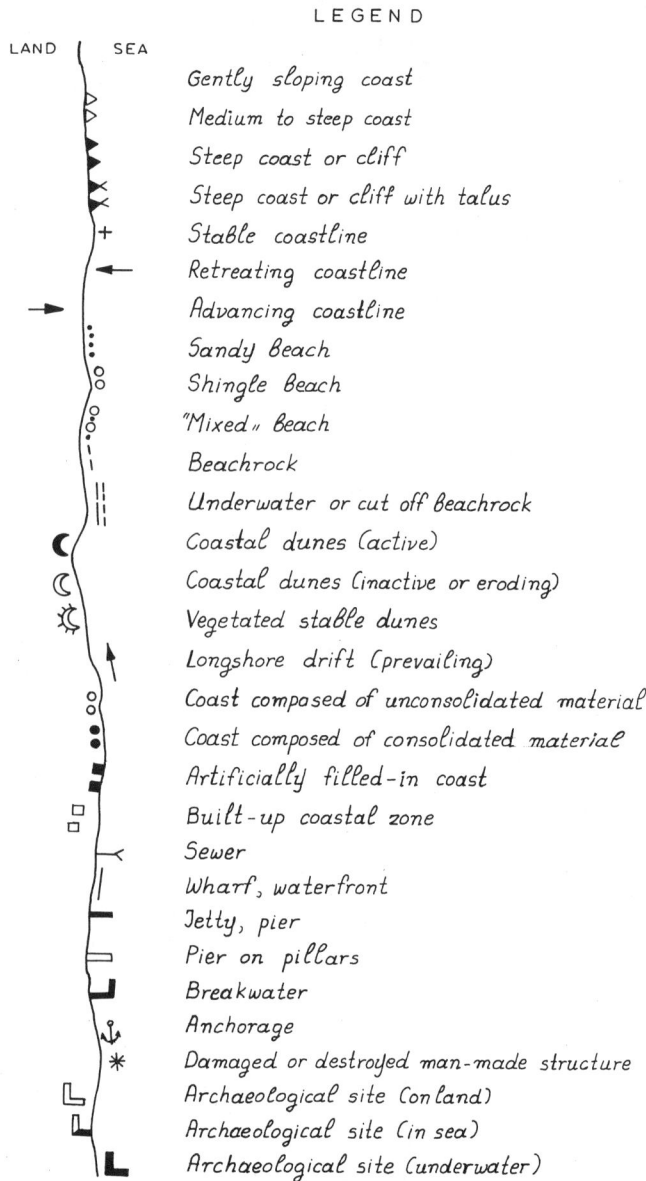

Fig. 3. Symbols used in the coastal geomorphological mapping.

accelerated rate in the last two millennia. The presence of the Hellenistic wall indicates that the sea level has risen more than 1 m during this period (Kambouroglou 1989: 95).

Liani Ammos (Magoula): This area is characterized by continuous habitation from the Late Neolithic through the Roman period. Many cemeteries have been found, one of which was partly on land and partly submerged to a depth of 1 m (Kambouroglou et al. 1987: 25). The site is located 5 km east of Eretria and today due to marine erosion forms a 4 m cliff.

The Attica-Boeotian Coastline

Glypha: It consists of a prehistoric site on a low hill. Founded in the Early Helladic II period, it was mainly inhabited during the Middle Helladic and Mycenaean periods. An excavation conducted in 1976 along the southern flanks of the hill uncovered some buildings and a wall of Mycenaean date (thirteenth century B.C.E.) (Kambouroglou et al. 1988: 75). The wall, perpendicular to the coastline, ends by the water's edge.

Avlida: According to Psarianos (1948: 270) the Avlida deposits are of Holocene date. In this area, there used to be a wide bay capable of receiving the "armada" that assembled for the expedition to Troy. No archaeological remains have been recorded.

Dilessi (Delion): This coastal town is today a summer resort. Near the town square, there are ruins of Late Classical and Hellenistic buildings (fourth century B.C.E.) partially covered by the sea to a depth of about 1 m. The buildings are related to the well-known temple of Delios Apollon, and there was also a spa in the same area (Kambouroglou et al. 1988: 75). The gently sloping coast, which consists mostly of coarse sediments, is currently eroding (fig. 5).

Skala Oropou: Ruins (one is circular) on land and submerged down to about 1 m are located just northwest of the town (fig. 6). Other archaeological remains found in the area date to the third–fourth centuries B.C.E.

Delphinio: This is the sacred harbour of Amphiario, of the fourth century B.C.E. The harbor breakwater is submerged at a depth of 2 m below the present sea level. The coastline consists of a cliff, and the associated sediments are coarse. The presence of a coastal fault accentuates the steep morphology of the coast.

Psaphis: An old harbor of Classical date has been reported (Petrakos 1968: 11) but no coastal archaeological remains have been found. The coastline is smooth and gently sloping with coarse sediments. Underwater springs are located northeast of this area.

CONCLUSIONS

It can be concluded with certainly that the coastline of the western South Euboean gulf is retreating. This is confirmed not only by submerged beachrock down to -4.70 m but also by coastal archaeological finds that are eroded by the sea and often submerged.

Fig. 4. Part of Lefkandi hill and geomorphological map of the area.

Fig. 5. Dilessi and geomorphological map of the area.

Fig. 6. Archaeological ruins near Skala Oropou and geomorphological map of the area.

The retreat of the coastline during the Late Holocene in the last 2000 years is believed to be due to sea level rise (eustatism), although land movements (tectonism) of a local character should not be ruled out as a mechanism for coastal submergence or emergence. As an example, we could mention the presence of a wave notch on limestone rocks at a height of 0.60 m, indicating an uplift of that magnitude, in the area of Avlida.

Whenever we have archaeological sites, coastline retreat is observed. Some are not only eroding but are at a lower level than the present sea level (Liani Ammos, Eretria, Dilessi, Skala Oropou, Delphinio)—which could mean that an unknown number of undiscovered archaeological sites may be submerged.

Evidently, the South Euboean gulf did not have its current configuration. Near the end of the Pleistocence period (16,000–18,000 B.P.) the gulf did not exist, as the sea level was more than 100 m below the present one. Five thousand years ago, sea level was 4–5 m below and in Classical to Hellenistic times it was about 1 m below the present level. Since then, it has risen to the present level, not excluding some undulations of a few tens of centimeters within this time period.

Human interference during the last decades has accentuated the changes that have been taking place in the Late Holocene. Moreover, if the accelerated sea level rise due to global climatic change occurs as predicted, then the coastal zone of the western South Euboean gulf will undergo significant changes, particularly where deltaic plains exist. Coastal archaeological sites, near or at sea level, will be dramatically affected by an expected additional sea level rise. Unfortunately, very little can be done to save them other than to undertake detailed studies before the sites are lost forever.

REFERENCES

Guernet, C.
1971   *Contribution à l'étude géologique de l'Eubée et des régions voisines.* Doctorat d'Etat, Université de Paris.

Kambouroglou, E.
1989   *Eretria, paleogeographic and geomorphologic evolution during the Holocene.* Ph.D. thesis, University of Athens (in Greek).

Kambouroglou, E.; Maroukian, H.; and Sampson, A.
1988   Coastal evolution and archaeology north and south of Chalkis (Euboea) in the last 5000 years. *Proc. of the 1st International Symposium "Cities on the Sea—Past and Present," Haifa, Israel (Sep. 1986).*

Kambouroglou, E.; Karapaschalidou, A.; and Manolis, S.
1988   Αρχαίο παράκτιο νεκροταιφείο στην περιοχή Ερέτριας (Ν. Εύβοια) και η συμβολή του στη μελετη της γεωμοργολογικής εξέλιξής της. *Ανθρωπολογικά Ανάλεκτα* 49: 21–27.

Karapaschalidou, A.
1985   Old World Archaeology Newsletter, IX/3: 14.

Katsikatsos, G.
1979   La structure téctonique de l'Attique et d'Eubée. Pp. 211–28 in *Proceedings of VI Colloquium of the Geology of the Aegean Region, Athens 1977,* Vol. I.

Leondaris, S., and Maroukian, H.
1988   Προβληματικές για τον άνθρωπο ακτές Νότιου Ευβοϊκού κολπου, περιοχή Αυλίδας - Σκάλας Ωρωπού. Πρακτικά του Συνεδρίου Ελληνικής Γεωλογικής Εταιρίας Μάϊος 1986, Αθήνα, Δελτίο Ελληνικής Γεωλογικής Εταιρείας, ΧΧ: 383–98.

Petrakos, V.
1968   Ο Ωρωπός και το Ιερόν του Αμφιαρίου. Εκδόσεις Αρχαιολογικής Εταιρείας Αρ. 63, Αθήνα.

Popham, M. and Sackett, H. L.
1967   *Excavations at Lefkandi, Euboea, 1964–1966.* British School of Archaeology at Athens, Supplementary vol. 11, London: Thames and Hudson.

Psarianos, P.
1948   Αι προσχώσεις της Αυλίδος. Πρακτικά της Ακαδημίας Αθηνών 23: 268–74.

Psychoyos, O.
1988   *Deplacements de la ligne de rivages et sites archaéologiques dans les régions côtieres de la mer Egée au Néolithique et l'Age du Bronze.* Thèse, Univ. de Paris I.

Sampson, A.
1981   *The Neolithic and Early Helladic I in Euboea.* Ph.D. thesis, University of Athens.

The Uluburun Shipwreck

Cemal Pulak

Institute of Nautical Archaeology
Texas A & M University
P.O. Drawer HG
College Station, TX 77841-5137
U.S.A.

Excavation of a late fourteenth century B.C.E. shipwreck off Uluburun in southern Turkey has revealed one of the largest assemblages of Bronze Age trade goods found in the Mediterranean. The ship's cargo consisted of ten tons of copper ingots and a ton of tin ingots, but also terebinth resin, glass ingots, hippopotamus and elephant tusks, ostrich eggshells, and ebony logs. Among the manufactured goods were Cypriot ceramics, glass beads, faience cups, musical instruments, and ivory containers. Galley wares, tools, fishing implements, and some foodstuffs were for shipboard use, while some jewelry, cylinder seals, weapons and balance weights were probably personal effects. The ship probably sailed from a Canaanite or Cypriot port, and certain personal and shipboard items suggest a similar origin for the ship, but a pair of swords and seals reveal that Mycenaeans were also on board. Some refinement of Late Bronze Age chronology is suggested by a number of finds.

Between 1984 and 1994, the Institute of Nautical Archaeology (INA) at Texas A & M University excavated a Late Bronze Age shipwreck off Uluburun,[1] or "Grand Cape," 8.5 km southeast of Kaş in southern Turkey.[2] The wreck lay 60 to 70 m off Uluburun's east face, and about 400 m from the terminus of the cape (fig. 1). It was brought to the attention of INA as a result of the Institute's annual shipwreck surveys along the Turkish coast. These surveys had been designed in part to locate a Late Bronze Age shipwreck that included a cargo of copper ingots because, since the 1960 excavation of the Cape Gelidonya (Gelidonya Burnu) wreck where copper ingots had been discovered, there were hopes that a similar site

might be found and excavated in order to test hypotheses presented by George Bass in his publication of that site (Bass 1967: 163–67; 1973).

The wreck at Uluburun was discovered in the summer of 1982 by sponge diver Mehmet Çakır, who promptly informed archaeologists from INA and the Bodrum Museum of Underwater Archaeology. Shortly thereafter a group of archaeologists from INA and the museum proceeded to the site and found the wreck lying between 44 and 52 m deep on a steep, rocky slope. A single copper "oxhide" ingot was raised for dating purposes.

As part of INA's 1983 survey between Bodrum and Antalya, the author directed a ten day investigation of the

---

[1] The now preferred spelling of the site as one word is in keeping with proper Turkish grammar.

[2] Over the years, the project was generously funded by the INA Board of Directors and by grants from the National Endowment for the Humanities, the National Science Foundation, the National Geographic Society, Texas A&M University, and the Institute for Aegean Prehistory. Fuel for the project was donated by Shell of Turkey, Ltd., while Cressi-sub of Italy not only donated diving equipment outright, but also provided significant concessions for its purchase for the duration of the excavation.

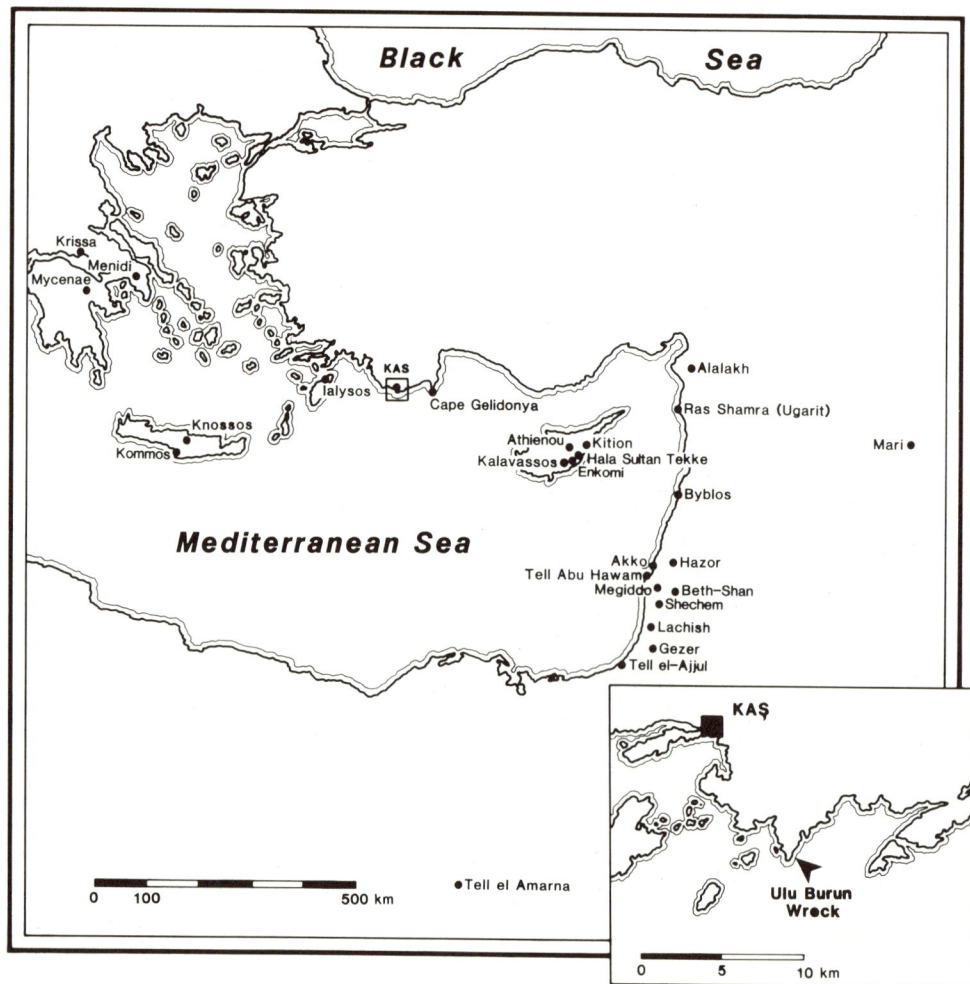

Fig. 1. The Uluburun shipwreck and Late Bronze Age sites in the eastern Mediterranean.

Uluburun wreck in order to assess the logistical factors involved in planning a full-scale excavation campaign for 1984 (Pulak and Frey 1985; Bass, Frey, and Pulak 1984). During inspection of the site a sketch plan was made of all visible artifacts. Some eighty-four copper ingots were visible in at least three distinct rows, although it was clear that more lay buried beneath these ingots and the sand. The arrangement of the ingots showed that the wreck was oriented approximately east to west, its western extremity being uppermost on the slope, with the rows of ingots running athwartships. Additionally, a group of six large storage jars (pithoi) lay mostly to the south of the ingots, indicating the direction in which the ship had listed after it struck the sea bed. Noted also were two large stone anchors, one of which, lying at the deeper end of the site, suggested that that end of the wreck represented the ship's bow. Pottery was scattered among the copper ingots and elsewhere on the site, including more than half a dozen Canaanite amphoras situated near the center of the site just upslope of the group of pithoi.

We raised for study a Canaanite jar, a pilgrim flask, a wall bracket, and a discoid copper ingot, all seemingly of Syro-Palestinian and Cypriot origin. At that time these objects suggested the end of the fifteenth or the first half of the fourteenth century B.C.E. as a tentative date for the wreck.

Why the wreck occurred at Uluburun will probably never be known with certainty, but it is possible that the ship, sailing in a northwesterly direction, drew dangerously close to the point before tacking and failed to clear it. It also is conceivable that the vessel was dashed against the rocky promontory by an unexpected south wind, which seldom blows during the summer, or that it experienced some difficulty steering while trying to round the cape.

The Uluburun wreck appears to be another indicator of a sea route for the east-west transport of copper, tin and other raw materials in the eastern Mediterranean during the Late Bronze Age. While navigating this route, ships apparently hugged the southern coast of Turkey, as evidenced by copper ingots recovered from a probable fifteenth century

B.C.E. wreck reported near Side, in the Bay of Antalya (Buchholz 1959: 27, pl. 3:5–6, 30; 1966: 63, fig. 2b, 65), sailed past Gelidonya Burnu, as shown by the ship that sank there around 1200 B.C.E. with copper and tin ingots aboard, and then rounded Uluburun before passing Deveboynu Burnu, the westernmost tip of the Datça Peninsula on Turkey's southwestern coast, where a copper ingot is reported to have been netted in water more than 100 m deep by a sponge dragger (Bass 1986: 272). An additional shipwreck with copper ingots is reported to have been seen in the Straits of Samos in the 1960s by a sponge diver, but this site has not been located. How the oxhide ingot on the western Black Sea coast near Sozopol, Bulgaria (Dimitrov 1979: 70, 73, fig. 3; Bouzek 1985: 21, pl. 4:2; Gale 1989: 248, fig. 29:1), a hoard of nineteen copper ingots from Kyme, Euboea (Buchholz 1959: 35–37, pl. 5:3–4; Buchholz 1966: 62); and the scattered finds of "oxhide" ingots south of Haifa, as well as the tin ingots found there (Galili, Shmueli, and Artzy 1986: 25–34, figs. 7–8) relate to the trade in metals remains to be established.

Under the directorship of George Bass in 1984 and 1985 and Cemal Pulak since that time, the excavation of the Uluburun shipwreck was concluded in 1994 (fig. 2).[3] During the course of the excavation, 22,413 dives totaling 6,613 hours on the sea bed have revealed one of the most spectacular Late Bronze Age assemblages to have come from the Mediterranean region.

The ship's cargo consisted mostly of raw materials—items of trade that before the excavation were known primarily, or sometimes only, from ancient cuneiform texts or Egyptian tomb paintings. The primary cargo comprised ten tons of copper and nearly a ton of virtually pure tin.

The bulk of the copper cargo on the Uluburun ship consisted of ingots of two major types: 354 ingots of the so-called "oxhide" type, each averaging about 25 kg (fig. 3),[4] and more than 130 ingots of the plano-convex discoid, or bun, type (fig. 4; Bass 1986: 275–77, pl. 17:1; Pulak 1988: 6–8). Among them are five smaller, pillow-shaped ingots of the general "oxhide" form (fig. 4; Pulak 1988: 7, fig. 3), usually considered an earlier type, a small-sized oxhide ingot of unique shape, and several plano-convex oval ingots. By far the most numerous are those with four handles, in the shape termed "oxhide" when it was believed, errone-

ously, that such ingots were cast to resemble dried ox hides. The discovery on the wreck of at least thirty-one similar but two-handled ingots helps to disprove this notion (fig. 5). Less than a third of the two-handled oxhide ingots have been cleaned. Of these the heaviest registers 25.23 kg, the lightest 22.00 kg, with an average of 22.88 kg. The four-handled ingots also have been called "Keftiubarren" in the belief that Egyptian artists associated them mainly with people from the land of Keftiu, or Crete (Buchholz 1959: 1). They are, in fact, more frequently associated with Syrian merchants and tribute-bearers in their Egyptian representations (Bass 1967: 62–67). Almost all of the Uluburun ingots are of a shape in use from the fourteenth to the late thirteenth or early twelvth centuries B.C.E. The five pillow-shaped ingots, however, appear to be of a type more common in the sixteenth and fifteenth centuries B.C.E., although they are depicted in Egyptian art into the fourteenth century. Clearly, dating ingots by shape alone is not always valid.

The pillow-shaped ingots from Uluburun appear to be smaller than the examples found elsewhere and may represent a distinct category, perhaps fractional units that did not require handles to facilitate porterage. Within the five ingots in this group are two pairs of mold siblings, as revealed by identical mold impressions on the ingots' surfaces. These pairs, therefore, must have been cast in reused stone or clay molds, rather than in perishable sand molds.

A total of 121 intact bun and oval ingots, with additional fragments that would add up to another nine ingots, were recovered. As with the oxhide type, these ingots vary in size, but five complete ingots of oval shape and large fragments of two more are the largest among the group. Most of the copper ingots are still being cleaned and conserved, but preliminary examination has shown that at least 160 oxhide ingots, or about one-half of the total found, are incised with one or more marks, almost always on the upper or rougher surface opposite the mold side. Only twenty-eight of the bun ingots appear to be marked. Unlike their oxhide-shaped counterparts, with one exception, these are marked only on their lower, or smoother, mold sides.

Originally stowed in four distinct rows across the ship's hold, many ingots either slipped down the slope after the ship sank or were displaced as the hull settled under the tremendous weight of the cargo, but the basic arrangements

---

[3] Yearly reports have appeared in *The INA Quarterly* (*INA Newsletter* prior to 1992) and *The Proceedings of the International Symposium of Excavations,* vols. 7–16 (Ankara, Turkey); vols. 10–16 in Turkish.

[4] Of the fifty-six oxhide ingots cleaned and weighed to date, only thirty-four are reasonably well-preserved with all their corner projections or "handles" intact. Among the latter group, the heaviest weighs 25.85 kg and the lightest 20.75 kg, with the average of the thirty-four being 24.61 kg. On the other hand, one ingot that has lost a handle weighs 26.97 kg. How much of this weight variation is due to the differing original weights of the ingots themselves and how much is due to corrosion remains to be determined.

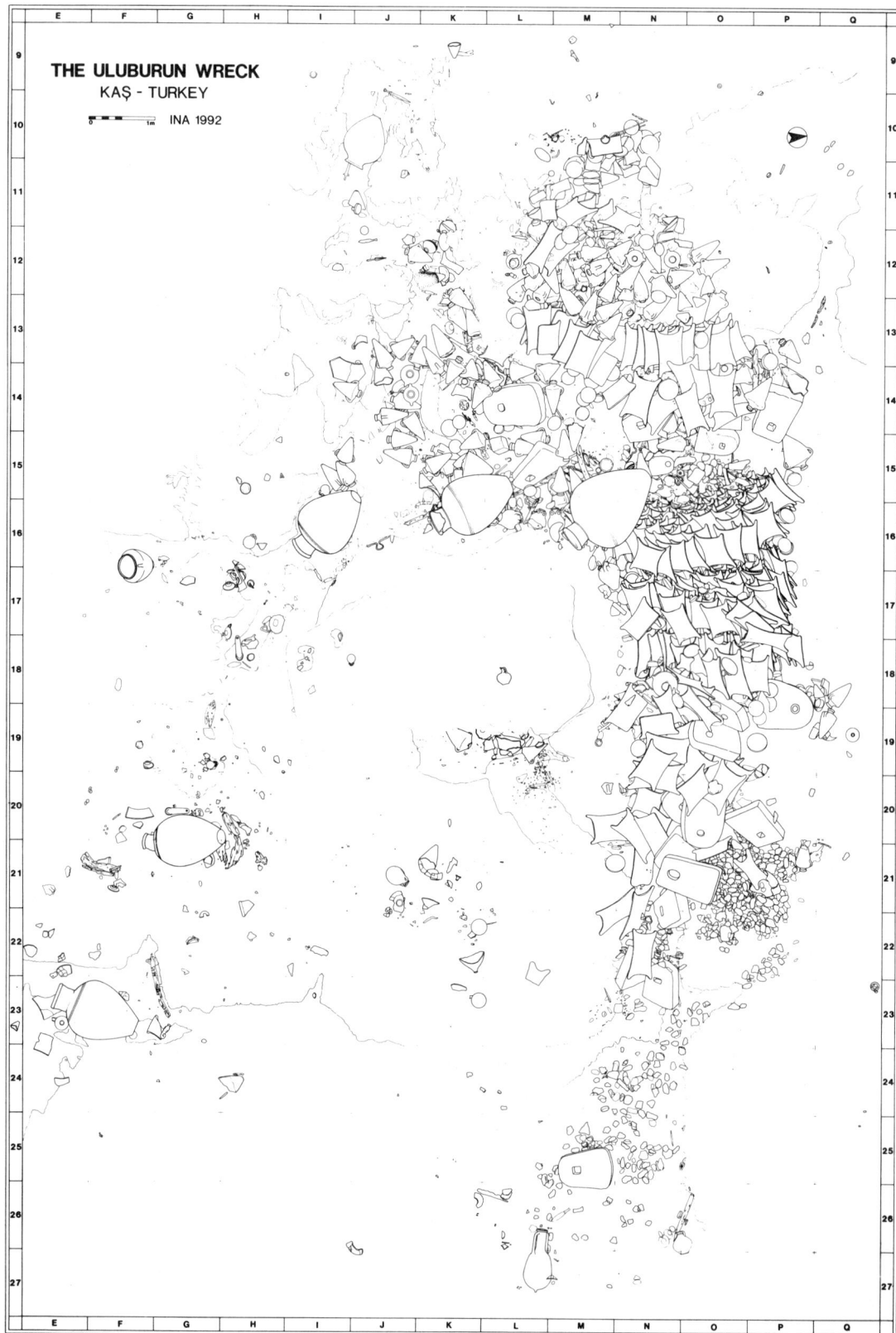

Fig. 2. Excavation plan of the site.

Fig. 3. Typical copper oxhide ingot (KW 2175) with incised mark on lower right corner, before cleaning. Maximum length: 81 cm.

Fig. 4. Copper plano-convex discoid or bun ingots of two sizes (top left and bottom center), pillow-shaped ingot (top right; maximum length: 30 cm), tin ingot of plano-convex shape (bottom left), and tin quarter oxhide ingot (bottom right).

of the rows survived. This displacement of ingots, evident in all four rows, but particularly pronounced in the first row (the sternmost, highest on the slope) and the fourth (lowest on the slope), makes it impossible to ascertain any ingot's original position. Those still in place, however, revealed that the ingots, stretching from one side of the hull to the other, overlapped one another in each row like roof shingles (fig. 6). With one exception, the direction of overlap alternated from layer to layer, apparently to prevent slippage during transit. Each row of ingots was made up of eight to eleven layers with, on average, twelve ingots in each layer; the bottom layers were placed on beds of brushwood and branches (or dunnage, in nautical terminology) to protect the hull timbers. All the ingots appear to have been stowed with their smooth, mold sides down, probably to facilitate handling by providing a natural purchase for fingers around the ingots' beveled edges, or to provide better "grip" between ingots by ensuring that no two smooth sides contacted one another. This arrangement may also have allowed the ready viewing of ingot marks, which almost invariably appear on the surface opposite the mold side.

Metallurgical studies of the Uluburun ingots have not been completed, but analyses of the Cape Gelidonya ingots have shown that the oxhide ingots and at least some of the bun ingots from that wreck were cast by the same process and from the same, nearly pure copper (Muhly, Wheeler, and Maddin 1977: 357–58, table 1). The two main ingot shapes, therefore, do not appear to reflect differing copper compositions or purity. The different shapes may be attributable instead to different production techniques or areas, or to the need for smaller units of copper.

Recent analytical work on copper ingots from different sites in the Mediterranean has raised hopes of determining the sources of copper from which the ingots were cast. Such work is invaluable for suggesting patterns for the trade in

Fig. 5. Two-handled variety of the oxhide ingot (KW 2761), before cleaning. Maximum length: 73 cm.

metals. Grouping various ingots through common trace-element signatures allows the ingots to be compared with known copper sources having similar trace-element signatures. When a grouping appears to center upon a region that is a known source of copper, a reasonable conclusion is that those ingots were made of copper from that specific source.

Eighteen oxhide ingots and one bun ingot from the Uluburun wreck were subjected to atomic absorption analysis by R. Maddin. According to his study, the Uluburun ingots differ sufficiently in elemental composition from the Cape Gelidonya wreck ingots to suggest separate groupings for the two. The elemental composition of the ingots from Cape Gelidonya closely approximates that of Cypriot ingots, which suggests that Gelidonya ingots were made from Cypriot copper. Maddin concludes, therefore, that the Uluburun ingots either did not derive from the same ores as those from Gelidonya, or that they came from a different

Fig. 6. Oxhide ingots in their original overlapping stowage in the ship's hold running from one side of the hull to the other. The direction of overlap alternates in each layer to prevent shifting of the heavy ingots during transit.

location in the same ore body, or were produced by a different smelting technology than that used to produce the Gelidonya ingots (Maddin 1989: 101; Muhly 1991: 188).

Despite such helpful comparisons, it must be remembered that the elemental composition analyses of samples from ingots are subject to a host of errors and effects that make it extremely difficult to relate ores to ingots on this basis alone. Therefore, at present, the use of lead isotope analysis coupled with trace element analysis to determine the source of the copper ore deposit from which a copper ingot was cast seems to be more reliable, because the isotopic composition of lead is usually homogeneous in a sample. It should be kept in mind, however, that because it is nearly impossible to sample exhaustively all ore bodies from which a specific metal could be won, lead isotope analysis may be used only to exclude certain ore sources from a group of possible sources. It cannot determine the specific ore body from which a copper was smelted, and, as such, similar analytical results for both a metal and an ore mean only that the properties of the copper are consistent with those of the ore

body, and that the ingot may have been derived from that ore body. Therefore, as with most analytical studies, lead isotope data must be used carefully and critically, and concerns already are being expressed, although some of it appears to be unfounded, as to its applicability in determining sources of metal ingots (Budd et al. 1995: 1–32).

Samples from fifteen oxhide ingots from the Cape Gelidonya wreck and samples from four oxhide, five bun, and one pillow-shaped ingot from the Uluburun wreck have been subjected to lead isotope analysis by N. Gale (1991: 228–31). The results indicate that the lead isotope properties of the copper in all of the Gelidonya oxhide ingots appear to be consistent with those of Cypriot copper ores, as currently characterized for the island (Stos-Gale, Gale, and Zwicker 1986: 125–28; Gale 1989). The four oxhide ingots from Uluburun, along with three of the bun ingots and the pillow-shaped ingot, on the other hand, form a cluster separate from that of the Gelidonya ingots. Yet this cluster, although occupying a somewhat peripheral position, lies within the limits of the field determined for Cypriot copper ores and so can be considered provisionally as being consistent with the Cypriot ore field. But, as more Uluburun ingots are analyzed and revisions are made to the Cypriot field, we may have to modify our interpretation. The two remaining bun ingots have lead isotope ratios that deviate significantly from those of Cypriot copper and, therefore, suggest a different and hitherto unknown source of ore. The implications of these preliminary results are that further work on various ingots from both shipwrecks will reveal a copper cargo of more complex distribution than previously recognized, probably one that was drawn from multiple ore sources.

The widespread occurrence of the basic oxhide ingot shape, from Sardinia to Mesopotamia, and from Egypt (as representations only) to the Black Sea, has suggested to some a central authority exercising control over the production of and trade in this important commodity. The recurrence of differing weights for the oxhide ingots, even after taking into account the change in weight due to corrosion, probably indicates that these ingots were not intended for use as currency but rather constituted a quantity of "blister," or raw copper, subject to weighing and evaluation during each commercial transaction. Their broadly common weight standards would have simplified accounting procedures by allowing a rough but quick reckoning of a given quantity of raw metal prior to weighing (Parise 1968: 128; Zaccagnini 1986: 414–15). The shape itself probably evolved merely for ease of transport over long distances by pack animals. A theory that this shape also developed because it was more practical for shipboard stowage than that of discoid ingots, however, has been weakened by the discovery of large quantities of the latter on both the Gelidonya and Uluburun shipwrecks.

Fig. 7. Tin oxhide ingot (KW 1932), before cleaning. Maximum length: 62.5 cm.

The tin ingots from the Uluburun wreck are the earliest known with secure dates. Five other tin ingots, three of them marked with seemingly Cypro-Minoan syllabary, were found in the sea off Haifa, Israel, presumably from a shipwreck (Galili, Shmueli, and Artzy 1986: 25–32). Two unprovenienced tin ingots were dated to the Late Bronze Age based on the similarity of their incised marks to Cypro-Minoan script (Maddin, Wheeler, and Muhly 1977: 46), and two others, claimed to have been bought from a fisherman who had found them on a shipwreck, are of the same shape and even bear some of the incised marks evident on the first pair. A fifth century date also has been proposed for the two latter ingots, which would date all four to that century if they came from the same source (Artzy 1983: 51–55). The ingots in oxhide and bun shapes from Uluburun show clearly that at least some tin was traded in the same shapes used for copper ingots (fig. 7). They remind us of Egyptian tomb paintings showing stacks of similar metal ingots previously identified as silver or lead, but later suggested to be tin (Bass 1967: 62, fig. 63; 63, nos. 2–3, fig. 65; 64, fig. 69). Other tin ingot types include rectangular slabs, sections of large, thick disks, and a unique example similar in shape to a stone anchor with a large hole at one end (fig. 8). This last ingot, if its shape is original and not a result of deterioration, is similar to a blue ingot from the tomb of Amen-em-opet at Thebes, which is shown on the shoulders of two Syrians in the company of others who carry pink copper oxhide ingots (Bass 1967: 65, no. 9, fig. 75). Much of the tin on the wreck had been converted to another tin phase by a complex change in its crystalline structure. This transformation, which results in a larger volume, often had resulted in the loss of an ingot's recognizable shape (Maddin 1989: 102–4). In a number of instances the tin had assumed the consistency of toothpaste which, when disturbed during excavation, disintegrated. We attempted to collect all the tin from the site, regardless of its condition, for later evaluation and study. It is not yet possible to report

Fig. 8. Tin ingot resembling a stone anchor (KW 3935) with a circular hole at its upper end filled with encrustation. Maximum length: 32 cm.

the exact amount that was being carried on the ship, but we estimate a ton which, when alloyed with the copper, would have yielded eleven tons of bronze.

Most of the tin ingots had been cast in the oxhide form, but had later been cut into quarters (fig. 4, bottom right), each retaining one "handle." Whether these partial ingots represent exact quadrants of the ingots from which they were cut in antiquity cannot be ascertained, but it seems reasonable to assume that at least some attempt was made to maintain the uniformity of the pieces. Several half-oxhide sections were also recovered. In any case, whole oxhide ingots probably represent the form in which tin, like copper, was transported from primary smelting areas at the mines or from nearby processing centers to distribution and/or manufacturing centers. Moreover, because descriptions of the tin trade in ancient texts from western Asia hint at a tin source located somewhere to the east (perhaps in Iran or even Afghanistan or central Asia), oxhide ingots also presumably represent the preferred form in which tin was transported overland by donkey caravans. This lends weight to the supposition that the oxhide type was designed for ease of handling and for transportation by animals. Hence, it is unlikely that tin ingots aboard the Uluburun ship were cut into smaller quarter-oxhide sections for convenient handling, as the ship also carried more than 350 complete copper oxhide ingots. Similarly, it seems unlikely that they had been cut into pieces *en route* for trading purposes during the voyage, as that would not explain the near absence of intact tin ingots among the many cut fragments on the wreck. Surely, these ingots were cut up as needed, and not all at once during or at the beginning of the voyage. Tin ingots may have been cut down to smaller sizes at their point of receipt, however, perhaps for use in various transactions. If this is the case, then we may assume that the Uluburun tin ingots do not represent ingots of a shipment procured directly from a single or primary source, but rather a collection gathered by barter, levies, taxes or gifts.

At least one tin ingot among the few that have so far been cleaned and that retain their original surfaces is marked with an incised sign that also appears on some of the copper ingots. Copper and tin are usually mined in different geographical regions, so the presence of the same mark on ingots of these different metals may suggest that the marks were incised at a common point of receipt and/or export rather than at the places of production. That the marks are more or less centered on the tin oxhide ingot fragments may also indicate that they were incised after these ingots were cut into pieces.

The actual sources of Bronze Age tin remains one of the greatest enigmas of the period, even though some tin may have been obtained from the east, as mentioned above. Now, because we have tin ingots in forms that probably represent the way tin was conveyed from primary production centers, we could be a step closer to solving the problem. Several tin samples from the Uluburun wreck were submitted to K. A. Yener of the University of Chicago for lead isotope analysis, in an effort to assess their similarity to the tin ores she has discovered in the Taurus mining districts of Bolkardağ in south-central Anatolia. Unfortunately, it seems that the Uluburun tin is virtually devoid of lead as an impurity, and thus several attempts at lead isotope analysis have yielded unsatisfactory results. Work in this direction, however, continues. Yener's recent archaeological work at Bolkardağ has shown that tin in that region had been mined during the Early Bronze Age (Yener and Vandiver 1993a:

221–22; 1993b: 261), but had become exhausted by the beginning of the Middle Bronze Age (Yener: personal communication). If this is the case, that region appears to be an unlikely source for Uluburun tin, although lead-isotope ratios of two lead fish-net sinkers from the wreck reveal a high probability that one and a low probability that the other were manufactured from lead originating in the Taurus mining districts (Yener, et al. 1991: 558, 574). There is, on the other hand, a high probability that the lead of six other lead objects, mostly net sinkers, was mined at Laurion in Greece (Sayre et al. 1992: 101, 105). This result, which has yielded several sources for the net sinkers, is to be expected of lead, as this metal is virtually indestructible and easily lends itself to continued reuse. Sinkers that were lost during the use of a net could have been replaced with those picked up at various ports of call, and those from old nets would have been salvaged and used on new nets. Over time, therefore, a net could end up with lead sinkers from an assortment of sources.

At least 149 Canaanite amphoras were on the Uluburun ship. Canaanite amphoras are widely distributed in the eastern Mediterranean, in Greece, Cyprus, Syria-Palestine, and Egypt, but those from the Uluburun wreck are known as the northern type, probably made somewhere to the north of modern-day Israel, perhaps in Syria. The amphoras from the wreck appear to fall into three general size groups, with the smallest size (representing ca. 75% of the jars) having an average capacity of 6.7 liters (fig. 9a), the medium size about twice that volume (fig. 9b), and the largest examples (ca. 14% of the jars) 26.7 liters, or four times the smallest value.[5] This last value may correspond to a *bath,* the ancient unit of liquid measure used, for instance, to describe the capacity of the "molten sea" that Hiram of Tyre made for Solomon's temple.

One amphora was filled with glass beads, and several others with olives, but the great majority contained a yellowish material chemically identified by J. S. Mills and R. White of the National Gallery, London, as *Pistacia* resin, probably from *Pistacia atlantica,* a tree that grows in much of the Mediterranean region (Mills and White 1989). The identity of this material as terebinth resin had been suspected by C. Haldane, the project archaeobotanist, after her discovery of *Pistacia* leaves and fruits inside the jars (Haldane 1991: 219). This resin cargo of approximately one ton is second in weight only to the eleven tons of raw copper and tin on the ship providing the first instance of its identifica-

---

[5] The jar volumes were measured with polystyrene beads, but repeated measurements were not taken to determine the mean experimental error. While this method is a practical way of taking capacity measurements, one cannot obtain a true absolute value for a jar's capacity because the polystyrene beads do not fill the jar uniformly (Koehler and Wallace 1987: 57).

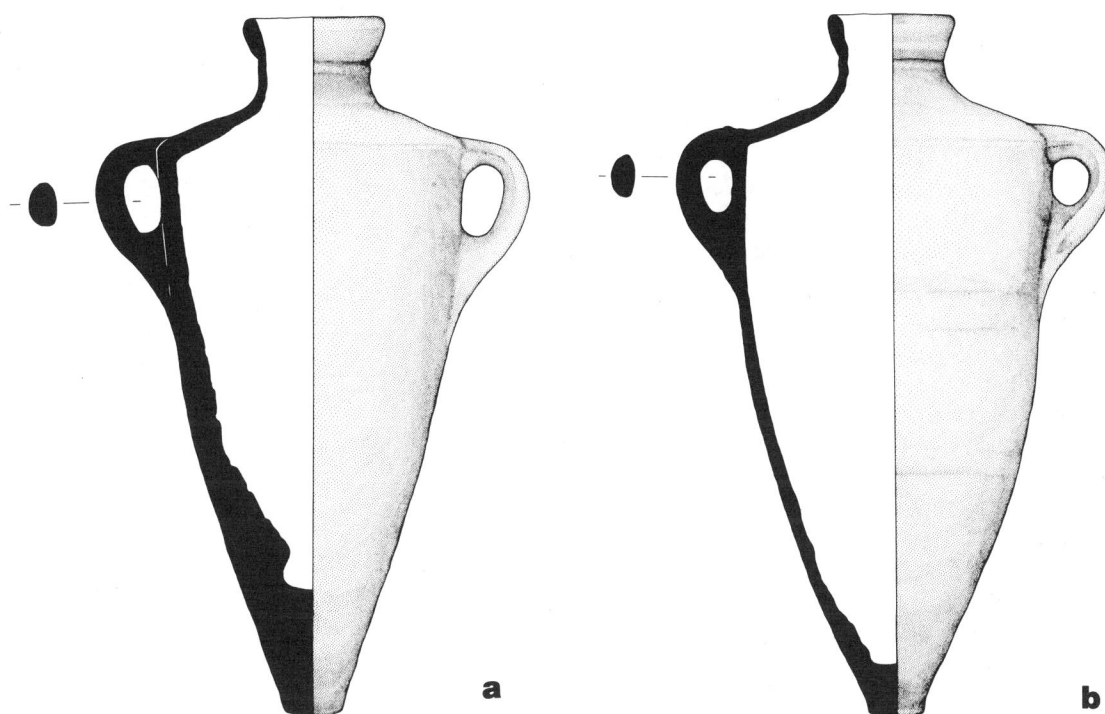

Fig. 9. Canaanite amphoras of 7.8 liter (a: KW 612) and 13.0 liter (b: KW 214) capacity; both contained terebinth resin.

tion by modern analytical methods; it is the largest ancient deposit of this material ever found. Recent analysis of resin from the Eighteenth Dynasty site of Amarna has revealed that it is virtually identical to the terebinth resin from the Uluburun shipwreck (Haldane 1993: 353). With the discovery of such a large quantity in an unmistakably commercial context, there is no doubt that terebinth resin can be added to the list of raw materials, luxury goods, and other commodities that were a part of the complex trade activity that took place in the eastern Mediterranean in the Late Bronze Age.

Terebinth resin may be the Egyptian *sntr* brought in Canaanite jars from the Near East to the pharaoh (Loret 1949: 21–23), as depicted in the tomb of Rekh-mi-re in Thebes, where an amphora in a royal storeroom displaying Canaanite tribute is labeled *sntr* (Davies 1943: pl. 48). Baum (1994),[6] however, has recently suggested that while the word *sntr* denoted primarily frankincense (olibanum), a *Boswellia* spp., the Egyptians occasionally substituted for *Boswellia* various resins from *Commiphora* spp. (both of Burseraceae) and those of the Anacardiaceae family, which includes *P. atlantica*. The total liquid volume of *sntr* received by Tuthmosis III is recorded for five of the years in his annals: year 24 (12,345 liters), year 33 (12,420 liters), year 34 (10,395 liters), year 35 (1,260 liters), year 38 (9,840 liters). Loret (1949: 20–23) notes that the amount imported averages 9,250 liters per year. It is noteworthy that the annals for year 35 record only 1,260 liters, which is close to the amount calculated to have been carried on the Uluburun ship and may, therefore, correspond to a single shipment of resin. Loret's estimated annual total, then, is the approximate equivalent of the annual receipt in Egypt of nine cargoes of *sntr*, each the size of the terebinth cargo found at Uluburun. The Linear B word *ki-ta-no*, found on a few tablets from the palace at Knossos, Crete, has been translated as a *Pistacia* product, probably terebinth fruits (Melena 1976: 177–90).[7] Based on the finds from the Uluburun wreck, however, we may now suggest terebinth resin as an alternate translation for this word, which refers to a commodity brought to the palace as payment in very large quantities: some 18,400 liters, which probably represents payments made during all or some portion of the year in which the destruction at Knossos preserved the tablets.

[6] I thank Christine Lilyquist for bringing this reference to my attention.

[7] Melena equates *ki-ta-no* with κρίτανος defined by Hesychius as τέρμινθος or terebinth; Melena believes *ki-ta-no* refers to terebinth fruits.

Approximately 175 glass ingots shaped like discoidal truncated cones were found on the wreck. These are the earliest intact glass ingots known. Cobalt blue (Bass 1986: 281–82, figs. 15–16), turquoise and lavender in color, they probably are the *mekku* and *eḫlipakku* listed on Ugaritic and Amarna tablets as trade items from the Syro-Palestinian coast (Oppenheim 1973: 259–63). They also may be the cakes of "lapis lazuli" and "turquoise" (as opposed to "genuine lapis lazuli" and "genuine turquoise") tribute from Syria shown in a relief from the time of Tuthmosis III at Karnak.[8] R. Brill of the Corning Museum of Glass reports that those of cobalt-blue are chemically identical to blue glass in Eighteenth Dynasty Egyptian core-formed vessels and in Mycenaean pendants beads (Bass 1986: 282), which suggests a common source for all.

Logs of what the Egyptians called ebony (Bass, et al. 1989: 9, fig. 17), now known as blackwood *(Dalbergia melanoxylon)* from tropical Africa, are unique archaeological finds. Other logs found on the wreck recently have been identified as cedar, a well-attested commodity in Late Bronze Age texts. Other raw materials include ivory in the form of one whole elephant tusk and a section of another and thirteen hippopotamus teeth (Bass 1986: 282–85, figs. 18–19; Bass, et al. 1989: 11, fig. 20; Pulak and Bass 1992: 64, fig. 3, 65); murex opercula, a possible ingredient of incense (Pulak 1988: 5); tortoise carapaces, possibly intended as sound-boxes for musical instruments; and three ostrich eggshells that probably were to be transformed into ornate containers by the addition of faience or metal components.

The excavation was completed only recently, and most artifacts are still in need of treatment, sorting, and at least partial reconstruction before we can start definitively quantifying the various manufactured goods that also were on the ship. But it is worthwhile at this stage of our investigations to give an idea, even if provisionally, of the size of the Cypriot pottery cargo, which comprised the largest group of manufactured items carried on board. At least three of the ten pithoi (fig. 10) contained Cypriot pottery including oil lamps (Bass 1986: 282, ill. 4), Base Ring II (Bass 1986: 280, ill. 11), White Slip II (Bass 1986: 279, ill. 10), White Shaved juglets (Bass 1986: 281, ill. 12), and Bucchero jugs (Bass 1986: 281, ill. 13). The most common Cypriot vessels in the assemblage are the White Shaved juglets with thirty-five examples, while the White Slip II milk-bowls

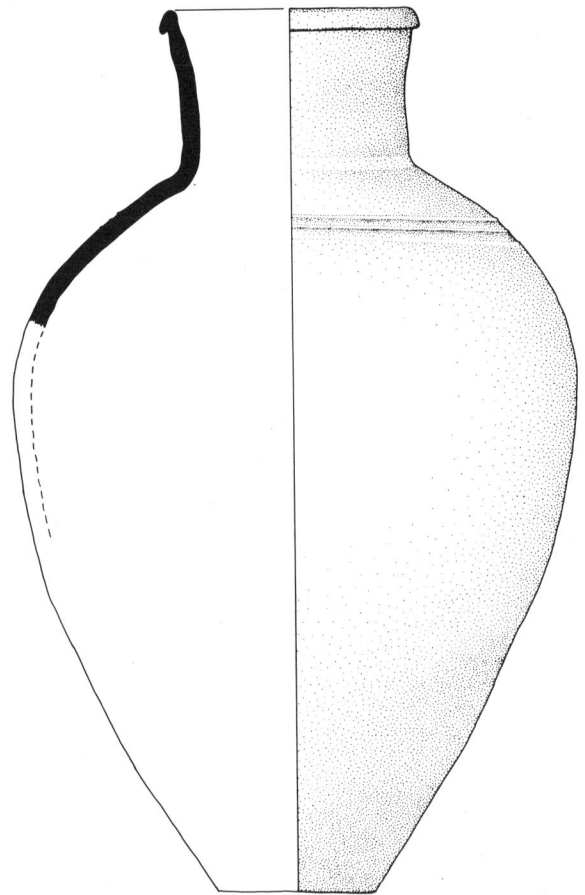

Fig. 10. Large Cypriot pithos (KW 255). Height: 130 cm.

are close behind with twenty-nine. There are also nineteen Base-ring II bowls, three Bucchero jugs, and twenty-two oil lamps, all representing types recovered from some of the pithoi. To these we may add ten wall brackets, at least four trefoil-mouth pitchers, ten pithoi, and several other vessels (presumably all of Cypriot origin), the corpus totaling no less than 135 vessels, of which eighty-six are fine wares.

If the intended destination of this ceramic cargo was the Aegean, then the sheer quantity of the Uluburun Cypriot wares contrasts with what so far has been found in the Aegean. Until recently, Cypriot artifacts were thought to be scarce in the Late Bronze Age Aegean, but Cline (1994:

---

[8] G. F. Bass, "Beneath the Wine Dark Sea: Underwater Archaeology and the Phoenicians of the *Odyssey,*" paper read at Cornell University on 23–25 April 1993: *Greeks and Barbarians: A Conference on the Classical Origins of Eurocentrism.* The blue and green "glass ingots" called lapis lazuli and turquoise in the relief of Tuthmosis III are reproduced in Sherratt and Sherratt 1991: 386, fig. 2. The Akkadian "genuine" (literally "from the mountain") and "artificial" (literally "from the kiln") lapis lazuli are in Oppenheim, *et al.* 1970: 10.

60) has compiled a list of some 176 objects of Cypriot origin dating to LH/LM I–IIIC, as well as additional examples not included because of their imprecise dating. If one subtracts from the list the seven objects from the Cape Gelidonya shipwreck and the forty-five from the Uluburun wreck that have been included in his tally, we are left with 124 objects, of which only sixty-eight are ceramic vessels. This is a small number in comparison with the Uluburun Cypriot ceramic assemblage comprising at least 135 vessels. The Uluburun ship, in other words, was carrying twice the amount of Cypriot pottery presently known from all phases of the Late Bronze Age over the entire Aegean region. Cypriot milk-bowls represent the most popular type of ceramic vessel imported into the Aegean, preceded only by the Canaanite jar, which almost certainly was imported exclusively for its contents rather than for the vessel itself. Cline mentions forty-four milk-bowls for the Aegean (Cline 1994: 60), only fifteen more bowls than the total number carried by the Uluburun ship. If the Uluburun ship had reached the Aegean and dispatched its cargo of Cypriot pottery, then the quantity of Cypriot ceramics from the Aegean would have tripled, which serves to demonstrate clearly that the archaeological record, even with respect to non-perishable goods, does not necessarily represent the true nature and magnitude of the trade in question. Cline's breakdown of the ship's cargo in terms of places of origin (an evaluation based only on the limited information then published about the site), which is claimed to correlate remarkably well with the breakdown of worked Near Eastern goods found in LH/LM IIIA–B contexts in the Aegean (Cline 1994: 100, 103, figs. 20–21), is now altered significantly.

Copper and/or bronze vessels of several types also appear to have been part of the cargo. Although these thin-walled vessels had mostly disintegrated through corrosion, their sturdier parts such as rims and handles have survived to reveal their numbers, sizes, and shapes. Among them are two sets of bowls. Although fragmentary, it is clear that each set comprises three bowls of graduated sizes nested one inside another (fig. 11), suggesting that other scattered fragmentary bowls may originally have been carried in this manner. Furthermore, these bowls appear to have been stored in large caldrons, which are represented on the wreck mostly by their handles; although the handles have not yet been studied and matched as pairs, it seems that at least half a dozen were aboard the ship. Elements of other vessels—a riveted spout, for example—hint at the variety of metal forms that were present, but which we may never be able to reconstruct fully. Furthermore, more tin vessels than had previously been found throughout the entire Bronze Age Near East and Aegean (Bass et al. 1989: 11, fig. 22) have surfaced from the wreck. As some of these vessels are fragmentary, we have yet to determine their exact numbers and

Fig. 11. Innermost bowl (KW 2130) of a set of three graduated bowls nested one inside the other; reflection of bowl on top. Diameter: 15.5 cm.

the variety of shapes represented, but a conservative estimate would be not less than five pieces.

An astonishingly rich collection of both usable and scrap gold and silver Canaanite jewelry was recovered during the course of the excavation. Among the thirty-seven gold pieces discovered—a few being of Egyptian origin—are pectorals, medallions, pendants, beads, a small ring ingot, and an assortment of cut and deformed fragments (Bass 1986: 287–88, pl. 17:3; Pulak 1988: 26–27, fig. 32; Bass et al. 1989: 4–6, figs. 5–6). One of the pendants bears a repoussé figure of a nude female holding a gazelle in each hand (Bass et al. 1989: 2, 4, fig. 3). She wears an unusual wigged crown on her head, four bangles on each wrist, and pairs of anklets. The figure is almost certainly that of a fertility deity, as yet unidentified, but probably representing one of the three great goddesses of the Canaanite pantheon, Ashera, Anat, or Astarte. Their similar fertility functions appear to have frequently caused confusion among their followers, making their identification on plaques and other objects im-

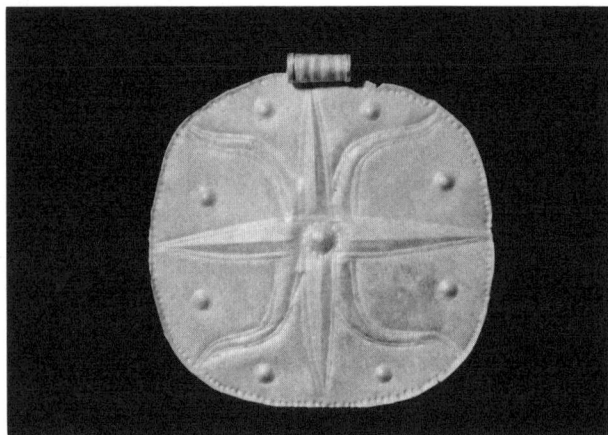

Fig. 12. Large Canaanite gold medallion (KW 1672). Maximum diameter: 11.8 cm.

possible. Among the four gold medallions from the wreck, which are decorated in repoussé with a four-pointed star exhibiting curved rays between the straight rays (Bass 1986: 289–90, pl. 17:4; Bass et al. 1989: 4, fig. 4), is perhaps the largest example of a gold Canaanite medallion of its type (fig. 12). A poorly preserved silver parallel, similar both in shape and size, was found at Shiloh in Palestine (Finkelstein and Brandl 1985: 23–24; Finkelstein, Bunimovitz, and Lederman 1993: 243–44, fig. 9.12:1–2). A gold pectoral, in the shape of a falcon with outstretched wings clutching a hooded cobra in the talons of each foot, is worked both in repoussé and granulation; it is in the tradition of the well-known falcon earrings from Tell el-Ajjul (Bass 1986: 287–88, pl. 17:3).

A biconical chalice, the single largest gold object from the wreck, is of uncertain origin (Bass 1986: 286, 289, ill. 24). While biconical footed cups or goblets of ceramic and stone do occur in the Near East (Tufnell, Inge, and Harding 1940: pl. 47A and B:222, 232; Yadin et al. 1960: 57, Pl. 93:21; Finkelstein, Bunimovitz, and Lederman 1993: 225, figs. 9.15:4, 9.18:2), none appears to display the full-body form of the cup section of the Uluburun chalice. Likewise, the Uluburun chalice has no exact parallels in the Aegean, but because of its similarity to cups from that area, an Aegean origin has been suggested (Lolos 1989). The cup's centrally located raised band with its rounded section is strongly reminiscent of those on some Vapheio cups (Davis 1977: figs.

102, 112, and 136), but a second band on the cup, placed directly below the first band, has a carinated profile, which, with its pedestal base, sets the Uluburun chalice apart from the typical Aegean shapes.

Egyptian objects of gold, electrum, silver, steatite, and other stone were also found (Pulak 1988: 27–28, figs. 33–34; Bass et al. 1989: 17–29, figs. 29–30, 32–33). Undoubtedly, the most significant is a unique gold scarab inscribed with the name of Nefertiti, wife of the Egyptian pharaoh Akhenaten. It is considered to be one of the most important Egyptian objects ever discovered in the eastern Mediterranean outside Egypt. Based on the partial reversal of Nefertiti's long name, Weinstein suggests that sometime late in Akhenaten's reign or shortly after his death, Nefertiti was pharaoh of Egypt (Bass et al. 1989: 29), although his interpretation is not shared by all (Weinstein: personal communication). The scarab is also the single most important object for establishing the wreck's *terminus post quem,* or its earliest possible date: 1376–1358 B.C.E. or 1339–1327 B.C.E., depending on the chronology used. Other scarabs from the wreck, mostly of the Second Intermediate Period, display either unreadable combinations of signs or good-luck and/or prophylactic signs. One scarab bears the name of Thutmosis I.

No less than four faience drinking cups were crafted in the shape of ram's heads (Bass et al. 1989: 7–8, fig. 12) and, in one case, the head of a woman (Pulak 1988: 32, fig. 40). The three Near Eastern ram-headed faience cups published so far, all dated to the thirteenth century, were found associated with female-headed cups. That these cups were found in temple and tomb contexts and were used as diplomatic gifts exchanged by kings, as suggested by the Amarna letters, would argue that they were used together for ritual purposes (Zevulun 1987: 92–93, 100, 102). They are generally believed to have originated from a single manufacturing center, probably in north Syria (Zevulun 1987: 93). Peltenburg (1991: 168, 170) identifies the animal-headed cups from the wreck as Near Eastern *bibru,* and states that these were "value-laden gifts" often dispatched from court to court. The presence of these cups suggests, therefore, that the ship's cargo was not merely commercial.

Other artifacts from the site include two duck-shaped ivory cosmetics boxes with hinged-wing covers (fig. 13),[9] an ivory cosmetics or unguent spoon with a handle terminating in a clenched fist, and a trumpet in the form of a

---

[9] Because many of the Uluburun objects mentioned in this article have been treated elsewhere, I have included discussions and parallels mostly for those objects being mentioned for the first time, as is the case with these ivory containers. Although of differing shapes and styles, each of the Uluburun duck containers has pivoting wings that served as a lid for the body cavity, which presumably contained a cosmetic or other material. They seem typical of Syro-Palestinian craftsman-

Fig. 13. One of two duck-shaped ivory cosmetics boxes with hinged-wing covers (KW 2818). Maximum length of body: 14.6 cm.

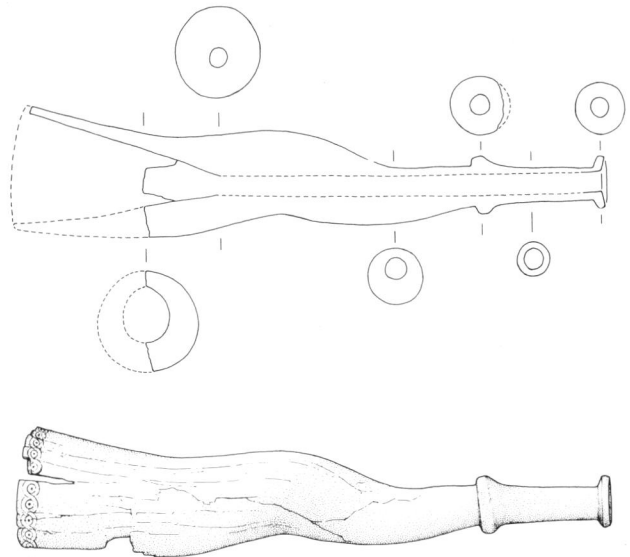

Fig. 14. Trumpet in the form of a ram's horn carved from a hippo-potamus incisor (KW 3526). Length: 24 cm.

ram's horn carved from a hippopotamus incisor (fig. 14; Gates 1994: 258–59, fig. 4; Pulak 1992: 7–8, fig. 4). A section of an elephant tusk from Ras Shamra-Ugarit that is pierced at its narrower anterior end, and with the pulp cavity of the tusk comprising its hollow core, has been suggested to represent a trumpet (Caubet 1987: 737–39). A fragmentary object similar to the Uluburun example, presumably also carved from a hippopotamus incisor into the likeness of a ram's horn, comes from Tell Abu Hawām (Hamilton 1935: 61, pl. 32:376); it is identified as an ivory handle in the form of a twisted horn. As is the case with the Uluburun horn, the bell of the Tell Abu Hawām piece is decorated around its bell, but with a band comprising three incised parallel lines rather than the more ornate enclosed twist/cable or *guilloche* pattern seen on the Uluburun horn. A. Caubet kindly informs me that based on the example found on the Uluburun shipwreck, a fragmentary piece from Ras Shamra-Ugarit that she previously published as a possible (furniture) leg (Caubet and Poplin 1987: 302, no. AO 14797), may now also be identified as a part of a trumpet. It is surprising that horns or trumpets are not found among the Megiddo ivories. Several pieces reported as being "pierced from end to end" do occur there, but their short length and

general shape make it more likely that they were used as flask spouts (Loud 1939: 18, nos. 187–89, pl. 43:188–89). Ivory, according to the Amarna letters, also belongs to the reciprocal gift exchange sphere whether as worked objects or tusks (Peltenburg 1991: 170). Additionally there were found more than two dozen sea-shell rings, each with a band of Mesopotamian bitumen that once held inlays (Pulak 1988: 26–27, fig. 31; Bass, et al. 1989: 11–12, fig. 20). J. Connan, of Elf Aquitaine (Production), recently has analyzed by LC-GC the bitumen from three Uluburun shell rings. He informs me that the bitumen on the rings is from a single source probably somewhere in Iraq, perhaps one of the natural seepages in the region of Hit (Connan 1988). Beads of amber, agate (Pulak 1988: 25, fig. 27; Bass, et al. 1989: 6–8, fig. 11), carnelian, quartz (Pulak 1988: 25, fig. 28), gold, bone, seashell, ostrich eggshell, faience (Bass 1986: 286, 289, ill. 26) and glass were found by the thousands. The amber has been identified chemically by C. Beck of Vassar College as being of Baltic origin (Bass 1986: 286, 289, ill. 25 for the shape of one of the beads).

---

ship, but double-winged containers are not found as frequently as are their single-winged counterparts. For one of the Uluburun wings, see Pulak (1990a: 54, fig. 2). Double-winged containers are found throughout Syria-Palestine and Cyprus. There are at least six examples from Megiddo (Loud 1939: pl. 12:45–53, pl. 24:129, pl. 30:157, pl. 31:158, with various duck's heads in pl. 45, and duck's feet similar to those from Uluburun in pl. 25:143–45); two from Tel Dan in Israel (Biran 1971: pl. a; Biran 1970: 119); two from Kamid el-Loz (Hachmann 1983: 163; 1966: pl. 20:9); and, one each from Tell Qasîle (Mazar 1975: 81, pl. 7:C); Meskéné-Emar, a site on the Euphrates (Beyer 1982: 123); Alalakh (Woolley 1955: pl. 75); an undated example from Nimrud (Barnett 1975: 238, pl. 149); and, probably from Ugarit (Gachet 1987: 263–64, 271, pl. 6:53). On Cyprus: at Kition (Karageorghis and Demas 1985: pl. 121), and two from Enkomi (Gallis 1973: figs. 4–5; Courtois 1984: 576, fig. 18:12, pl. 6:11).

An important find was a bronze female figurine with the head, neck, hands, and feet covered with sheet gold (fig. 15; Gates 1994: 259, fig. 5; Pulak 1992: 10, figs. 10–11). A narrow headband and a multi-strand necklace adorn her head and shoulders, respectively. Shoulder-length plaits of hair, as well as a braided central lock that terminates in a loop halfway down her back, resemble those on several statuettes from Syria-Palestine (Negbi 1976: 70, 73, 181, pl. 42; Loud 1939: 18, pl. 39) and on a gold plaque from Lachish (Clamer 1980; Metropolitan Museum of Art 1986: 118–20). Such fine figurines produced by the lost wax process were probably items that only royalty and the aristocracy could afford. Most metal figurines are thought to have been votive idols in the form of deities, rather than images of ordinary human beings. The archaeological contexts in which such statuettes have been found on land sites suggest that they were used in domestic and funerary cults, perhaps as objects with magical powers (Seeden 1982: 119–20). The statuette found on the Uluburun wreck may also have served to protect the ship and all aboard from peril at sea. Alternately, among the items listed on the Amarna tablets as gifts to the pharaoh are gold-clad bronze statuettes made in the likeness of the kings or their wives and daughters.[10] It is possible that the Uluburun statuette represents an article of such gift exchange. The position of her hands, with the left extended and open and the right raised as if clutching a symbol of divine power, however, makes this last possibility unlikely, as this gesture is typical of a blessing god or goddess, in whom is embodied the hope that what has been asked in prayer may be granted in real life (Seeden 1982: 119).

Weapons on board included arrowheads (Pulak 1988: 23, fig. 25, 26), spearheads, maces (Bass 1986: 274, ill. 4; Pulak 1988: 24, fig. 26), daggers (Pulak 1988: 22–23, fig. 23), a shaft-hole axe with lugs, a single armor scale of Near Eastern type, and swords of Canaanite, Mycenaean, and possibly Italian types. Of great interest are four swords whose proveniences are unrelated. All are about the same size and, being shorter than conventional swords of the period, should properly be referred to as short swords. The best preserved is a heavy Canaanite weapon cast in one piece (fig. 16). Its excellently preserved pointed blade becomes widest about mid-length, and the edges of the hilt are flanged for the encasement of hilt plates of ivory and ebony (African blackwood), probably originally affixed with glue (Pulak 1988: 20–22, fig. 20). Two daggers with shapes nearly iden-

Fig. 15. Bronze female figurine with the head, neck, hands, and feet covered with sheet gold (KW 3680). Overall height: 16.4 cm.

tical to each other, only one of which is preserved with its hilt inlays of ivory and ebony, resemble the Canaanite sword and may be companion pieces to it. Similar daggers from Cyprus are attributed to a Syro-Palestinian origin. A good parallel for the Uluburun daggers comes from a fourteenth century tomb near the "Persian Garden" in Akko, Israel (Ben-Arieh and Edelstein 1977: 33, 40, fig. 18:1). Daggers seem to have been fairly common weapons on the Syro-Palestinian coast during the Late Bronze Age.[11] In addition to the example mentioned above, several daggers appear to be Canaanite versions of wide-bladed Egyptian daggers (Bass 1986: 282–83, ill. 17; Pulak 1988: 22–23, fig. 24). A group of knives with curved blades, in contrast, are of an

---

[10] See, for example, EA 14 I.55, 59 and II.13, 14 (Moran 1992: 28, 29).

[11] For a convenient listing of weapons of this type see Ben-Arieh and Edelstein (1977: 33 with n. 43). To this we may add another example from Aphek-Antipatris (Kochavi 1977: 9).

Aegean type found in coastal areas, including Rhodes, south-western Turkey, and mainland Greece (Bass, et al. 1989: 6–7, n. 23, fig. 10).

Two incomplete swords slightly different in size are Aegean products (figs. 16–17; Pulak 1993: 11, fig. 13; 1988: 21–22). Their single-piece construction, finely ribbed blades, flanged grips, and cruciform shoulders with rounded lobes are typical of a type that existed during the fourteenth century B.C.E. Holes in the hilts indicate that rivets once secured plates of some material to the hilts, but those plates have not survived. Nor have we recovered any of the swords' pommels (pommels were usually fashioned from semi-precious stone, metal, ivory, or wood). These swords are shorter than average for their class and their blades have a broad flattish midrib with fine grooves instead of the distinctive high midrib. It has been suggested that the finest specimens of such swords were made at Knossos during the LMII period until its fall, but the possibility of other mainland production centers has been proposed (Driessen and MacDonald 1984: 64–65). In any case, during the fourteenth century, elaborately decorated pieces were replaced by more efficient and utilitarian types, of which the Uluburun weapons appear to be examples. Although the variants of this sword type without pronounced midribs are mainly confined to weapons not exceeding 50 cm in length, the loss of the midrib is recognized as a development leading to moderately thickened double-convex blades without true midribs. Typologically, therefore, the variants of this sword type, which stand at the end of the ornamental sword-making tradition of the fifteenth and early fourteenth centuries B.C.E., and to which we may add the Uluburun examples, constitute a transition to later sword forms.

The last and the most poorly preserved sword is of yet a third type (Pulak 1988: 21–23, fig. 22). Although most of its tang and blade edges are missing, the positions of its three large hilt rivets and its "lozenge-shaped" blade section have led to comparisons with a type found in southern Italy and Sicily that is fairly common in the local Middle to Late Bronze Age. This type, especially its Sicilian variety, is supposed to have derived from remote Aegean or Cypriot prototypes. The blade section of the Uluburun sword appears to resemble those of the swords from southern Italy, while its heavy rivets (each with two conical ends) recall examples from Lipari (Vagnetti and Lo Schiavo 1989: 222–24; Jones and Vagnetti 1991: 137).

A large number of tools, including sickles, awls, drill bits, a saw, a pair of tongs, chisels, axes, a plowshare, whetstones, and adzes were found on various parts of the wreck (Bass 1986: 274–76, ill. 6; Pulak 1988: 14–20, figs. 11–13, 15–19; Bass et al. 1989: 5, 7–10, figs. 7–8, 18), but mostly in what is believed to have been the after section of the ship. All but a group of six broad-chisel blades, and possibly two double axes, are either of Near Eastern types or are shapes ubiquitous in the eastern Mediterranean. The six broad-chisel blades, which may in fact be adze blades, have no parallels or are very rare in the Near East, but many examples occur in the Aegean (Pulak 1988: 17, fig. 14). Double axes are also associated primarily with the Aegean and while they may be uncommon in the Levant they do, unlike the broad-chisels, occur there, as evidenced by the four found on the Cape Gelidonya wreck (Bass 1967: 94–95, fig. 107:101–3) and a few from other sites including those in Israel (Miron 1992: 80–86, pl. 19).

The largest set of zoomorphic weights from the Bronze Age was recovered at Uluburun (Pulak 1988: 30–32, figs. 37–38; Bass, et al. 1989: 8–9, fig. 14). It includes a sphinx, bulls, cows, a calf, ducks, frogs, lions, and a fly; one ornate weight bears the figure of a cow herder kneeling before three of his calves. The complete study of these weights and the more than 120 weights in geometric forms found on the wreck will broaden significantly our understanding of Bronze Age weight sets and metrology. The geometric-shaped weights are of bronze and a variety of stones, including hematite (fig. 18). Two pairs of thin, circular, copper or bronze objects, one pair of which is encased in a wooden sleeve, appear to be pans for pan-type balances with which the weights would have been used.

Nearly all of these Uluburun balance weights have been cleaned and weighed, but in a preliminary attempt to determine the unit mass of the weight standard represented, only those weights in an excellent state of preservation have been considered; just over 60 percent are preserved in a state that seems to reflect accurately their originally intended masses. Those remaining are either damaged or, in the case of the bronze weights, have lost significant portions of their original weight due to corrosion, rendering them useless for metrological analysis. Several hematite weights have lost their lead plugs, which in antiquity allowed for the adjustment of the weights to the required value of a given standard. Separated into four groups comprising hematite sphendonoid (i.e., sling-bullet shaped), stone sphendonoid, hematite domed, and stone domed weights, each group was examined with a non-inductive approach as outlined by Petruso in his study of the weights from Ayia Irini, Keos (Petruso 1992: 71–75). The analysis yields as the most probable standard unit a mass of 9.1 g to 9.3 g. Exactly how each individual weight relates to this unit remain to be investigated, and the unit mass may increase slightly after the few weights that may represent other systems are excluded from the set. Precisely how the two major weight shapes, the sphendonoid and the domed, pertain to this system has yet to be determined, although a cursory examination of the domed weights suggests that the group probably was based

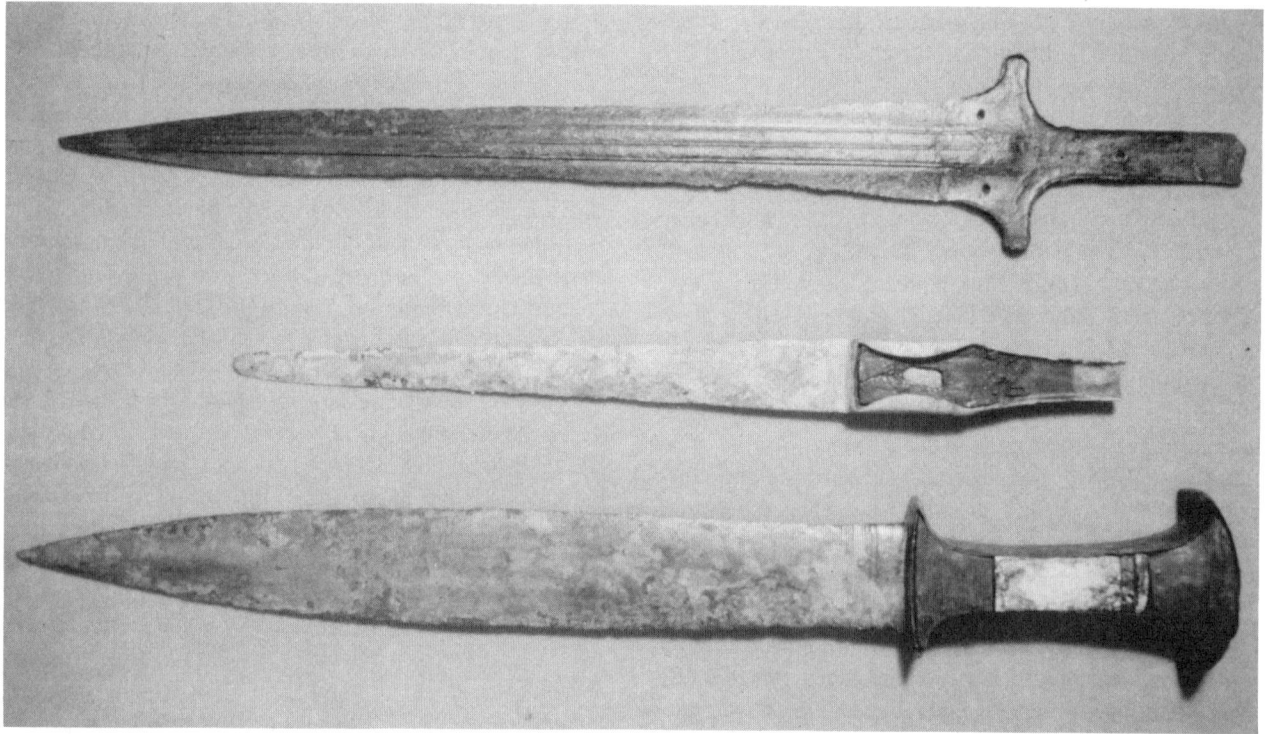

Fig. 16. Mycenaean sword (top: KW 301, preserved length: 45.5 cm), Canaanite sword with ivory and ebony inlaid hilt (bottom: KW 275, length: 45.4 cm), and Near Eastern dagger with wooden hilt plates (middle: KW 296, preserved length: 33.5 cm).

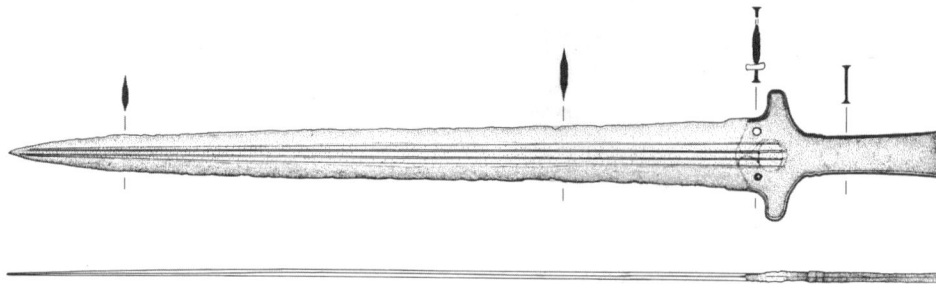

Fig. 17. One of two Mycenaean swords from the wreck (KW 4193). Preserved length: 51.3 cm.

on the weight of the Egyptian *deben* (= 10 *qedet*), a decimally factored system. Suffice it to say at this point that the dominant weight standard on the Uluburun shipwreck is well within the limits of the Ugaritic shekel of 9–9.9 g, with a peak at 9.3–9.5 g (Petruso 1984: 296; Liverani 1972: Parise 1971: 13), which also appears to be the system used on Cyprus (Petruso 1984: 302–3).

Foodstuffs, whether as cargo or for shipboard consumption, include almonds, pine nuts, figs, olives, grapes (or raisins or wine), safflower, black cumin, sumac, coriander, and whole pomegranates, along with a few grains of charred wheat and barley (Haldane 1993: 352; 1991: 218–21; 1990:

57–60). Lead net sinkers, netting needles, fishhooks (Bass, et al. 1989: 5, fig. 9, 7–9, fig. 13), a fish spear, and a bronze trident (fig. 19) are evidence of fishing from the ship.

The Uluburun ship was constructed in the "shell-first" technique with pegged mortise and tenon joints holding its planks together and to the keel (Bass 1989: 25). Used in Greco-Roman ships, this edge-joined planking technique contrasts with the more familiar "skeleton-first" construction technique, whereby the ship's planking is formed around and fastened to the pre-erected skeleton of a vessel. The earliest example of the "shell-first" method of ship construction for seagoing vessels prior to the Uluburun excavation

Fig. 18. Domed and sphendonoid balance weights of hematite.

had been detailed through the excavation and detailed study of the late fourth-century B.C.E. merchantman discovered near Kyrenia, Cyprus (Steffy 1985; 1994: 42–59). The Kyrenia wreck remained the earliest well-documented example of a ship built with this method prior to the discovery of the shipwreck at Uluburun. Except for larger mortise and tenon joints used for the edge-fastening of the planks on the Uluburun ship, the joinery method is virtually the same as that seen on the Kyrenia hull. But, in spite of our detailed examination of the hull remains, unlike what was found on the Kyrenia ship, no evidence for any framing has emerged. At this time we reason that perhaps the preserved hull section is not wide enough, or perhaps not long enough, to include frames or bulkheads or evidence for securing such elements to the planking, especially if they were not affixed to the first few strakes they spanned. The sided (inner) dimension of the keel is larger than its molded (side) dimension. Although the latter dimension is somewhat uncertain due to the poor preservation of the keel's outer surface, it appears, nevertheless, that the lower surface of this timber originally protruded beyond the outer planking surface by only a few centimeters. The timber would have served as the ship's spine, as well as to protect the planks and support the vessel when beached or hauled ashore, but unlike keels of much later sailing ships, it would have done little to help the ship hold course or point nearer the wind under sail. In other words, it appears that we have a rudimentary keel, perhaps more of a keel-plank than a keel in the traditional sense. The ship, with its planks and keel of cedar (*Cedrus* spp.; previously incorrectly identified and published as fir, Bass 1989: 25) and tenons and pegs of oak, is estimated to have been about 15–16 m long. Remains of what we believe to have been a fence of wicker call to mind the fencing on Syrian ships depicted in nearly contemporary Egyptian tomb paintings (Davies and Faulkner 1947: pl. 8; Davies 1963: pl. 15; Säve-Söderbergh 1957: pl. 23; Basch 1978:102,

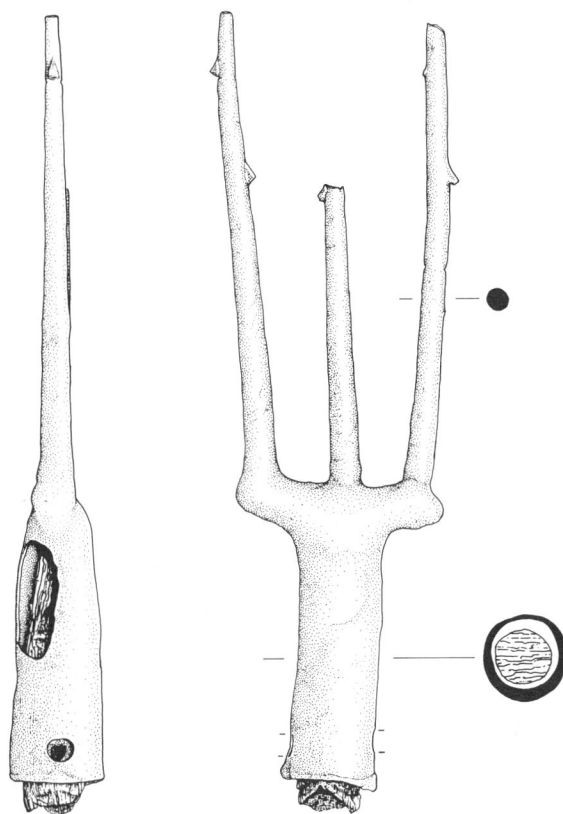

Fig. 19. Bronze trident with multiple barbs (KW 4160). Preserved length: 24.6 cm.

figs. 4–6; 1987: 63–65, with figs.), and of the wicker fence constructed by Odysseus to keep the waves out of his craft (*Odyssey* 5.256). A recent cursory re-examination of the scanty evidence of the Cape Gelidonya hull shows that it was similarly constructed with pegged hard-wood tenons of about the same size.

In the hope of obtaining an absolute date for the ship, seven wood samples taken from the ship's keel-plank, planking, and cedar dunnage were submitted to P. Kuniholm of Cornell University for dendrochronological dating. While some samples did not have a sufficient number of tree rings to match the established master sequence, others with more rings appeared not to match at all. One small root or branch, presumably fresh-cut firewood or dunnage, however, yielded a date of 1356 B.C.E. ±37 years, with an additional unmeasurable ring on the exterior, and a larger log-like piece of undetermined purpose, but with its outer layers trimmed, yielded a date of 1441 B.C.E. ±37 years, the uncertainty factor arising from the carbon dating of samples constituting the floating master conifer-ring sequence. Kuniholm further reports that recent callibration curves along with several other factors allow for the modification of these dates by shifting the entire floating sequence to the extreme recent end of the ±37 years (Kuniholm 1996), which would then date the most recent sample on the wreck to 1317 ±2 B.C.E. or 1316 ±2 B.C.E. after taking into account the unmeasurable ring. It would appear, therefore, that the ship sank sometime after that date, but probably not much later.

What, if anything, does the Uluburun material tell us about eastern Mediterranean relative and absolute chronologies? The unique gold scarab of Egypt's Queen Nefertiti, Akhenaten's beloved wife, is by itself of little help, as it appears to be fairly worn from use, which suggests that it had been around for some time before it was taken on board the ship. Furthermore, it may have been part of a jeweler's hoard, as it was discovered in the midst of complete, cut, and folded jewelry pieces and other bits of scrap precious metals (Bass, et al. 1989: 17–20, 23–29). If the scarab was a part of the scrap hoard, which is debatable, it almost certainly arrived on the ship after Nefertiti's time, when her scarab would have been worthless except for its gold value.

If, however, the scarab, the collection of Mycenaean pottery from the wreck, and the absolute dendrochronological date established for the sinking of the ship are addressed in concert, they bear important implications for Aegean chronology. According to the so-called "traditional chronology," the LH/LM IIIA:2 period begins during the reign of Amenhotep III and lasts until the time of Horemheb (c. 1360–1330 B.C.E.), while in the "revised chronology" the same period commences some time before the end of Amenhotep III's rule and closes near the end of or just after Akhenaten's reign (c. 1400–1365 B.C.E.) (as summarized with dates in Cline 1994: 5). Cline's (1994: 7, table 1) own "modified revised chronology," on the other hand, which uses Kitchen's absolute chronology for Egyptian rulers, places the LH/LM IIIA:2 period between Amenhotep III's rule and near the end of Akhenaten's reign (c. 1360–1340 B.C.E.). A synchronism between Akhenaten, the 18th Dynasty rulers who succeeded him, and the LH/LM IIIA:2/ IIIB:1 period is suggested by the quantities of LHIIIA:2, and to a lesser extent of IIIB:1, pottery found at Amarna, Akhenaten's capital city (Hankey 1987: 48–50). Although there is no published evidence for dating any of this LHIIIB:1 pottery at Amarna more precisely than to the period from Akhenaten to Horemheb, Hankey (1987: 48–49) favors a date in the reign of Horemheb. Weinstein (Bass, et al. 1989: 24–25, n. 123), however, rightly points out that on the basis of the Egyptian evidence, we can only place the transition from LHIIIA:2 to LHIIIB:1 within approximately the last three-quarters of the fourteenth century B.C.E.

J. Rutter, who is studying the Mycenaean pottery from Uluburun for publication, notes the relative chronological homogeneity of the assemblage and dates it mostly to the LHIIIA:2 period (Bass 1986: 285, 288 fig. 23, 289, 291–93, figs. 30, 34; Pulak 1988: 13–14, figs. 8–9; Bass, et al. 1989:

12 fig. 23). Of the fourteen fine-wares on board, at least two of the vessels exhibit stylistic features of the early LHIIIA2 phase, which suggest that they may have been about a half-century old when the ship sank. Although Rutter has yet to personally examine the pottery, much of which is still in need of cleaning and mending, he further notes that with one exception none of the Uluburun vessels appears to have any morphological or decorative features that require a LHIIIB:1 dating. A concreted fragment of a round-mouthed jug, however, is likely to be of early LHIIIB date (personal communication). If, after this jug has been cleaned and mended, a LHIIIB dating for it proves to be accurate, this vase will become an important piece of evidence for the absolute dating of the beginning of the LHIIIB period. Until such time then, the Uluburun evidence appears to indicate that in 1316 ±2 B.C.E. or some time shortly thereafter, LHIIIB:1 style pottery had not yet come into common use, if it is assumed that the Mycenaean pottery from the wreck is representative of its time and was not a collection consisting exclusively of heirlooms. With Kitchen's (1987: 52) absolute chronology for Egyptian rulers, it would seem that the Uluburun ship sank sometime during Horemheb's reign (1323–1295 B.C.E.), which would corroborate Hanky's contention that the LHIIIB:1 pottery at Amarna is from Horemheb's time. Even when we consider Helck's (1987: 26) ultra-low chronology, it appears that the Uluburun ship could not have sunk before his dating of Tutankamun's reign (1319–1309 B.C.E.), again moving forward, but to a lesser degree, the date of the LHIIIB:1 pottery at Amarna from Akhenaten's time to nearer the end of the 18th Dynasty.

Here we may insert an inference from the Nefertiti scarab. If we employ Kitchen's dates, the scarab would have been about thirty years old before it arrived on the Uluburun ship during Horemheb's reign. While this is by no means an impossibility, it does seem unlikely that a scarab naming Nefertiti would have survived for that length of time without being destroyed or melted down, especially after Tutankhamun's abandonment of Amarna for Memphis. On the other hand, Helck's ultra-low chronology places the scarab in the first several years of Tutankhamun's reign or just before his third regnal year when Tutankhamun left Amarna. The actual date of the scarab probably lies between these two extreme positions.

What the Uluburun evidence suggests is that the high chronology for the Egyptian rulers is too early if they are to agree with the evidence provided by the Uluburun ship, and that the lower chronologies seem to fit the overall picture better. It appears, therefore, that the LHIIIA:2/LHIIIB:1 transition must date to a period after Akhenaten's reign and some time before the end of Horemheb's rule. In absolute terms, we submit that a date between 1320 and about 1295 B.C.E. does not seem unreasonable for this transition.

The Uluburun shipwreck, therefore, belongs to a well-documented segment of ancient history, and inferences from the Amarna letters as well as evidence from Egyptian tomb paintings can aid us in better understanding the nature of the Uluburun vessel's voyage. The only extant depiction of a Mediterranean merchant venture from the fourteenth century B.C.E. is a scene in the tomb of Kenamun at Thebes that illustrates the arrival of a Syrian merchant fleet in an Egyptian port (Davies and Faulkner 1947; Davies 1963: 14, pl. 15). Porters unload cargo including Canaanite amphoras and a pilgrim flask that are similar to those found on the Uluburun wreck. The roundels on the necks of some of the crew may represent star-disk pendants of the type recovered during the excavation. The Uluburun pithoi recovered with their contents of mostly intact Cypriot pottery allow us to speculate about the pithoi depicted on the ships' decks. Perhaps they too were filled with pottery as well as other goods. Other Egyptian tomb paintings show tribute bearers carrying not only elephant tusks, ebony logs, Canaanite amphoras, and vessels of the types found on the wreck, but also copper and perhaps tin ingots.

If we assume an average weight of 25 kg for each copper oxhide ingot on the Uluburun ship, then 354 ingots would correspond to about 325 talents of copper in the oxhide shape alone, reminding us of the Amarna letters that mention the shipment of one hundred (*EA* 34) and two hundred (*EA* 33) units of copper from Alashia to Egypt.[12] The five hundred (*EA* 35) units of copper mentioned in one Amarna letter—believed by some to represent 500 shekels instead of 500 talents because of its high number—and an accompanying apology for the small quantity of copper sent, clearly need not be regarded as unreasonably inflated in light of the amount of copper that has been found at Uluburun. The Amarna letters also mention elephant tusks, ebony logs, gold jewelry, silver, valuable statuettes, weapons, and what seem to be glass ingots, among other royal gifts, all of which are also matched by the finds on our wreck.

As a high-risk endeavor, long-distance trade would necessitate extensive preparations, provisions for security during the voyage, and substantial capital investment for the procurement of goods. All of these services could best be provided by the state, which came to dominate nearly all aspects of social, economic, political, and military life (Liverani 1987; Foster 1987; Peltenburg 1991: 167–70). It appears likely, therefore, that while there were private merchants engaged in retail trade in domestic markets, nearly all international exchange during the Late Bronze Age in the Near East was controlled or influenced to some extent by the palaces. Such being the case, could the Uluburun cargo represent a royal shipment of the type exchanged between the Syro-Palestinian coast, Egypt, and Alashia, as is vividly revealed by the Amarna letters, but one whose ultimate destination lay farther to the west, in the Aegean?

Where exactly this Aegean destination was can only be surmised by studying the distribution of objects matching those she was carrying. Due to its variety and wealth the Uluburun cargo may be seen as evidence for directional trade where intra-Mediterranean voyages involved specific destinations rather than simply "tramping" between minor ports. Moreover, this notion of distribution appears to be a working example of the concept of "gateway communities," in which imported goods came directly to a few major centers and were characterized by long-distance trade connections (for a summary of trade mechanisms see Cline 1994: 87–88). Such communities were usually sites of transportational significance (for example Kommos) and often had large populations that included resident specialist craftsmen and occasional foreign merchants (such as at Mycenae). Ialysos on Rhodes, Knossos, and Tiryns also fit this description. Some of the Mycenaean objects from the Uluburun ship have close parallels from Rhodes, an island that seems to have played an important role as a commercial redistribution center for the Aegean (Sandars 1963: 128; Portugali and Knapp 1985: 52–53). Alternately, the recent discovery of Cypriot pottery, copper ingot fragments, and Canaanite jars at Kommos on Crete suggests that the ship's primary cargo could have been destined for Crete. We already know that Ugaritic ships visited Crete during this period as evidenced by a ship returning from Crete to Ugarit with a cargo of grain, a fermented beverage, and oil (Nougayrol 1955: 107–8; Portugali and Knapp 1985: 66). Or could the ship, or perhaps part of its cargo, have been destined for the northern Aegean and even beyond into the Black Sea, as hinted by some of the finds on the wreck that seem to originate from this region? This possibility will be discussed further below.

Almost all the items on the ship, cargo or otherwise, could have been taken on at a Cypriot or Syro-Palestinian port, with some of the goods probably in transshipment, which makes it impossible to determine the ship's precise point of departure. It is plausible that ports in both areas were visited before the ship sailed westward. What is certain is that the ship set sail from one or both of these areas,

---

[12] C. Zaccagnini, noting the variations in phraseology in references to copper in the Amarna letters, translates the passages as "(ingots of) copper," "(talents of) copper," or "copper (ingots) weighing (one) talent," according to their formulation (1986: 414). See also Moran (1992: 105, note 5).

probably even from one of their northern ports, undoubt-edly intent on making port in a region west of Cyprus and Uluburun via the southern Anatolian coast.

At this early stage of our investigation it is difficult to ascertain the nationality of the ship, but it is clearly worth seeking. It should be pointed out, however, that the nation-ality of a single vessel is insignificant in the overall picture and does not allow sweeping generalizations about the na-ture of Late Bronze Age trade in the Mediterranean. Assyrian and Syrian cylinder seals do not necessarily represent the presence of merchants from those lands on the ship, as col-lections of seals were sent as tribute or gifts from Near East-ern rulers to both Egyptian and Aegean rulers (Bass, et al. 1989: 12–16, figs. 24–28). It is clear that most of the cargo comes from the Syro-Palestinian coast and Cyprus, but cargo alone does not identify the nationality of the ship that car-ried it. Better evidence comes from the ship's twenty-four stone anchors (fig. 20), which are of a type virtually un-known in the Aegean, but are often found in the sea off the coast of Israel[13] and also in the walls of temples and tombs at Ugarit and Ugarit's port at Minet-el Beida (Schaeffer 1978: 371–75, 387; Frost 1969b; 1991), Byblos (Frost 1969a), and Kition on Cyprus (Karageorghis 1976a: 875–78; 1976b: 60, 69, 72, 78, 169; Frost 1985), as well as on the Cape Gelidonya ship (Pulak and Rogers 1994: 20–21). Such anchors seem to have been manufactured at Tell Abu Hāwam and Tel Nami (Bass 1991: 74). A box-wood diptych (Bass, et al. 1989: 10–11; Bass 1990; Payton 1991; Warnock and Pendleton 1991; Symington 1991) found in a pithos that had contained whole pomegranates may have been the ship's manifest, perhaps a list of intended destinations and the cargo to be off-loaded at specific ports of call, or even a royal message. Whatever text the diptych may have contained has disappeared along with its wax writing surfaces. A wooden leaf of a second diptych found during the last campaign in 1994 is also of no help (fig. 21), as it too has lost its wax surface. Although of the type mentioned by Homer (*Iliad* 6.169) in his only reference to writing, these wooden writing boards most likely are Near Eastern in origin,[14] as is the partly gold-clad bronze statu-ette of a female that perhaps represents the ship's protective deity. Furthermore, a preliminary examination of the pan-

balance weights from the ship indicates that a great major-ity of them correspond most closely to a unit of weight measurement in use at Syria and Cyprus. Moreover, many of the personal effects of those on board, including a razor and amulets, along with the shipboard tools, suggest that the ship, too, may have been of Near Eastern origin, a view that will be reinforced if the sandstone from which the ship's anchors are made, and which currently are undergoing pet-rographic studies, proves to be from the Near East.

Perhaps the best indicator of a ship's origin or nation-ality is the source of its galley ware. After having excavated and studied in Turkey six shipwrecks from various periods of antiquity, I maintain that galley ware is reliable evidence of a ship's nationality and/or crew. Certainly, additional pots may be picked up at various ports of call to supplement or replace those that could have broken during a voyage, but the majority of the pottery in use on a ship will be of types from the region in which the ship originated. When the gal-ley wares of the Uluburun ship are identified and studied in detail we will be in a much better position to evaluate its origin, but until such time one can venture to say only that based on the available evidence, albeit sparse, a case can be made for a home port on the northern Levantine coast. Two types of saucer-shaped ceramic oil lamps were found on board. Most of the lamps of the larger and more heavily built type (Bass 1986: 285, 287, ill. 22; Pulak 1988: 12–13, fig. 6), presumably of Syro-Palestinian origin, are charred around their nozzles, suggesting use aboard the ship. Oil lamps of the second type, some of which were found along with Cypriot export pottery inside the large pithoi, on the other hand, are in pristine condition. Neither Mycenaean oil lamps nor any Egyptian vessels have been found on the site. Scanty as this evidence is, the lamps may provision-ally be taken as an indicator of the ship's Syro-Palestinian origin. Furthermore, it is at Minet-el Beidha, one of the two ports servicing Ugarit, that we find a storeroom containing some eighty Canaanite amphoras, possibly awaiting export by sea (Schaeffer 1949: pl. 31:1, 209). A second storeroom not far from the cache of Canaanite jars contained more than a thousand vessels, mostly Cypriot, which according to Schaeffer (1939: 19; Bass 1986: 295, n. 163) were ready for export. As for Ugarit itself, in the first floor of a build-

[13] Several groups or clusters of stone anchors discovered off the coast of Israel in recent decades may belong to wrecked Bronze Age ships (Galili 1985: 143–53; Galili, Shmueli, and Artzy 1986: 33, 35, figs 9–10; and more recently: Galili, Sharvit, and Artzy 1994: 93–107).

[14] Designated only as "cylindrical objects," four ivory pieces from Megiddo (Loud 1939: 20, nos. 305–308, pl. 58:305–308) are similar to the hinge sections of the Uluburun diptych. Hinges of this type also could have been used on small boxes, but if the Megiddo examples are from wax-surfaced writing boards, then this may be taken as further evidence for the use of such boards in the Late Bronze Age eastern Mediterranean.

Fig. 20. View of the site from west. Six anchors are in the foreground with two additional anchors visible above the last row of copper ingots.

Fig. 21. Wooden leaf of second diptych (KW 4863). A now-detached three-part ivory hinge would have affixed its two leaves. Maximum length: 12.4 cm.

ing, eight Cypriot pithoi of the type carried on the Uluburun ship were discovered (Schaeffer 1937: 128, pl. 20:3), and in another room there were twenty-eight oil lamps and seventeen other vessels contained in a large storage jar (Schaeffer 1962: 100, figs. 83–84, 119), which seems to parallel the stowage of the Cypriot pottery inside the large pithoi on the Uluburun ship. It is possible, then, that the Uluburun ship embarked on its ill-fated journey from Ugarit, the largest international emporium in Syria.

On the other hand, Mycenaean glass pendant beads from at least two separate necklaces (Bass, et al. 1989: 8–9, fig. 15), amber beads, a bronze long pin (Pulak 1988: 29–30, fig. 36), razors (Bass 1986: 292–93, ill. 33; Pulak 1988: 14–15, fig. 10), knives, spears, a pair of swords, two seals (Bass 1986: 283–84, 285, ill. 20, pl. 17: fig. 2; Pini 1993: 453–54), tools (Pulak 1988: 17, fig. 14), and nearly two dozen pieces of pottery that include utilitarian wares, point to a near-certain Mycenaean presence aboard the ship, if

only as a passenger or passengers. J. Rutter notes that none of the Uluburun utilitarian shapes (cup, dipper, kylix, flask, and pitcher), aside from the kylix, is generally attested as an import in the Levant or Egypt (personal communication). Because such drinking services evidently were not popular in the Near East, the owner or owners of this pottery on board the Uluburun ship was or were most likely Mycenaean. Rutter further suggests that if such services were indicators of rank, the presence of one on the wreck might be viewed as evidence for the Mycenaean origin of the captain or of an important official on board. But, if the ship was sailing to the Aegean, as has been suggested already, then the presence of Mycenaean passengers does not seem unusual. It is, perhaps, even to be expected that Mycenaean officials or envoys would be aboard ship to accompany such an important cargo presumably destined for their homeland. But an Aegean connection that extends as far as the northern Balkans, as suggested by the recovery from the wreck of a stone ceremonial scepter-axe (fig. 22; Pulak 1990b: 11, fig. 6), comes as something of a surprise. The scepter-axe finds its best parallel, albeit of bronze, in a hoard dis-covered at Drajna-de-Jos in the northern Danube region (in modern Romania), a hoard that also includes a sword frag-ment with Late Helladic affinities (Vulpe 1970: 59, pl. 41:565). Another stone parallel and a stone mold for cast-ing such a scepter-axe are known from Bulgaria.[15] Unlike their typologically similar counterparts, which are functional axes, these scepter-axes probably were of cultic and/or ceremonial use; Tončeva (1982: 180) sees the scep-ter-axe as a symbol of royal power held by a tribal chief who also was the head priest.

This possibility of a northern Balkan connection may also help explain the seemingly anachronistic presence of the long pin of bronze mentioned earlier. At one time, pins of this type were generally thought to have been introduced into Greece at the end of the LH IIIC period from regions to its north, possibly associated with the influx of a new popu-lation. Most scholars now tend to believe it more likely that they were produced locally, but with influences that appear to have come from the north (Pulak 1988: 29–30 for refer-ences). Arguments have also been advanced for a purely indigenous origin and production in southern Greece of the long pins found there (Kilian-Dirlmeier 1984a: 288–89; 1984b: 77), a view that is not supported by Bouzek (1994: 230), and that the direction of diffusion could have been from south to north and northeast Greece (Dakoronia 1992: 296–97). Although they do not constitute very close paral-lels to the Uluburun example, these late pins from the north-west Balkans do seem analogous. A general derivation of the Greek long pins from the northwest Balkan pins, there-fore, appears likely, but the relation seems to have been in-direct and Greek pins more autonomous in character. Even so, size aside, the Uluburun pin is closer in shape to the more developed pin forms seen in Submycenaean times in Greece than to their predecessors of the LH IIIC period. In turn, those most similar to the Greek Submycenaean pins are those from southern Italy, Sicily, and Albania. It is note-worthy that southern Italy and Sicily are regions proposed as the origin for one of the swords on the Uluburun wreck, as indicated above. While it is tempting to associate the Uluburun pin and sword, and suggest a common source for both in southern Italy or Sicily, there are chronological dif-ficulties that prevent such an attribution. Pins of this "north-ern" type seem to spread to these areas from the north at

Fig. 22. Stone scepter-axe (KW 2742) of northern Balkan origin. Maximum length: 19.4 cm.

about the same time as they appear in Greece (Bouzek 1985: 164, fig. 84:10 and 12, 166). They constitute a parallel to the Greek long pins, but in many ways they are an indepen-dent group. It seems, therefore, that these pins had not yet reached southern Italy and Sicily during the time that the sword was in use there. Nearly all of the Submycenaean

---

[15] The Bulgarian stone mold is from Pobit-Kamak (Cernykh 1978: 244, fig. 67:7, 246, fig. 69; 1979: 62, nos. 81–82), the stone scepter-axe from Sava-Zoneva (Tonceva 1982: 180, not illustrated). Another example, seemingly of the same group but with a circular tang or projection for mounting rather than the typical shaft hole or socket, is reported from southwest Russia (Cernykh 1976: 246, pl. 42:9). A color photograph of the scepter-axe appears in the Geographica section of *National Geographic* 181.6 (May 1992).

pins from Greece, on the other hand, find analogies in the northwest Balkans and northeastern Italy (Bouzek 1985: 166–67 with many references).

It is not my intention here to discuss in detail the evolution of the Greek long dress pin and its associated problems, but suffice it to say that such pins were most popular in the northwestern Balkans during the time that our ship sank, and that they would not be seen in Greece for nearly another two centuries. A reasonable assumption for the Uluburun example is that it represents an original pin coming directly from the northern Balkan region, and that it belongs to a type that, at some later time, would play a role in the development of the Greek long pin. The Uluburun pin would not have been out of place farther north in Europe, where such pins were popular during the fourteenth and thirteenth centuries B.C.E. (Bouzek 1985: 161, 166). Had our ship in fact reached Greece, our pin would have been by far the earliest of its type to be discovered there.

Another northwestern Balkan connection for the Uluburun ship is suggested by the recovery from the wreck of at least six spearheads (fig. 23) thought to be associated with that region or, more accurately, like the Greek long pin, to represent a type that probably evolved in northwestern Greece, but was inspired by spearheads from areas to its north (Bouzek's type B3 [1985: 138, 141], and Höckmann's group KII [1980: 69, fig. 15:K18–K19, 70]). These spearheads have distinct, leaf-shaped blades and solid-cast sockets that seem to have developed in the north, whereas most of the sockets on the remaining fifteen spearheads from Uluburun apparently have split sockets. Many are extremely fragile and need to be cleaned, however, before we can be certain of these attributions. In other words, the northwestern Balkans, the apparent center of dispersion for spearheads related to Aegean types, had a genetic relationship with Greece, but most spearheads found in Greece, with only a few exceptions, most likely were local products (Bouzek 1985: 141; Höckmann 1980: 70). As with the long pin, this spear type appears late in Greece, and all dated examples come from the late thirteenth and twelvth centuries (Wardle 1992: 130; Bouzek 1985: 139; Höckmann 1980: 68, 149), although a stone mold for a spearhead of this type from Macedonia dates to the beginning of the LH IIIB period (Wardle 1992: 130). This "northern" type, however, appears to have many analogies with those from the Early Urnfield cultures of the fourteenth and thirteenth centuries B.C.E. in Europe (Bouzek 1985: 141, n. 64 with many references).

It is noteworthy that while Mycenaean pottery seems to be absent in areas to the north of the Rhodope range, bronze weapons and tools with Mycenaean affinities found in that region mostly come from inland sites, a fact that appears to argue against a Mycenaean cultural penetration into

the northern Balkans by ships sailing along the Black Sea coast (Hiller 1991: 208–9). It may be more than a mere coincidence, therefore, that one of the Mycenaean lentoid seals from the Uluburun ship finds its closest parallel at Krisa near Delphi (Bass 1986: 283–84), a site more northwesterly than any of the great Mycenaean centers on the mainland. Could this, then, be taken as an indication that once our ship had reached and off-loaded its cargo at a "gateway community" on the Greek mainland, some of the goods would then have been shipped to the northern Balkans, either directly or indirectly through Mycenaean intermediaries who were operating out of Mycenae or Tiryns, and working their way north via Krisa and the western Balkans rather than Thrace or the Black Sea?

Naturally, the problem lies in the difficulty of establishing the route by which these goods would have been distributed after they had arrived by sea and were unloaded. It is possible that both the Uluburun pin and the "northern" type of spears on the ship, which, in fact, are more like Mycenaean examples than those of purely northern origin, would have been the earliest examples of their types found to date in Greece, had the ship indeed made port there. In such a case, the suggestion of any connection with the north would be superfluous. In fact, I would have hesitated to make any association between these two groups of items from the Uluburun ship and the northern Balkans, had it not been for the curious scepter/axe. This rare object, along with its related axe types, has an unequivocally central and northern Balkan distribution.

Why, then, could not the Uluburun ship have been bound directly for a port somewhere in the northern Aegean that would have had more direct access to the northern Balkans, or even for the western shores of the Black Sea? This, again, may be in the realm of possibility, but the lack of any known major "gateway communities" there that could receive a cargo of such magnitude and wealth, and the virtual absence from that region of some of the cargo items carried on the ship, such as Cypriot pottery, make an indirect connection to the region, perhaps through Mycenae, more likely. While the evidence for a mainland Greek destination for the Uluburun ship seems to be growing, why then are we suggesting connections with the north, even if it may have been an indirect one through Mycenae? Could these so-called "northern" objects simply have belonged to mercenaries from the north who were in the service of the Mycenaeans on the ship? Certainly this is one suggestion, along with the possible migration of populations from this region, that could account for the proliferation of "northern" weapons and other related elements in Greece during the LHIIIC period (Höckmann 1980: 68). But, chronological considerations aside, even though this perhaps may explain the presence of the pin and spears on the Uluburun

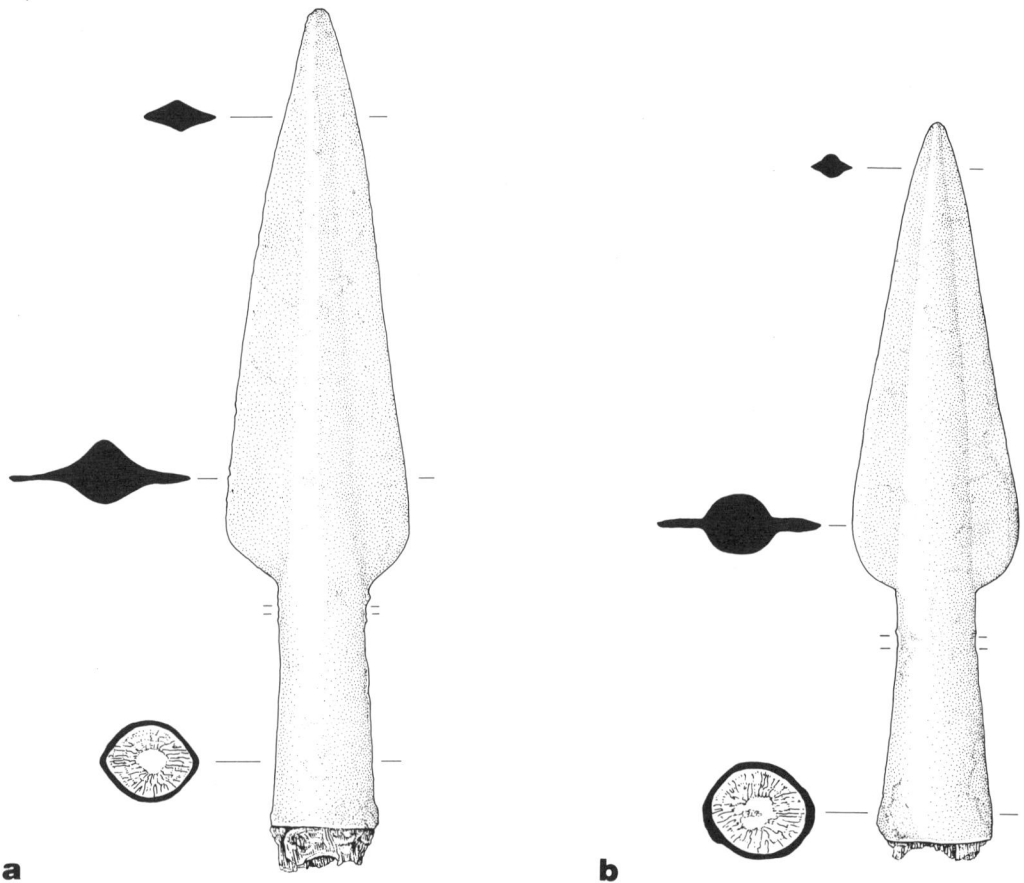

Fig. 23. Spearheads of a "northern" type: a) KW 309, maximum length 23 cm; b) KW 360, maximum length 20.2 cm.

ship, it does not explain the scepter/axe, an object that in all likelihood was entrusted to an individual of rank or power. That the Mycenaeans aboard also were not simply military personnel, on the other hand, is clearly revealed by the quantity and value of their personal possessions as well as the two pairs of glass pendant or relief beads, which usually were associated with individuals of some rank or nobility. Such a view, which must be regarded only as a tentative suggestion, would therefore have some or all of the Uluburun ship's cargo destined for the Greek mainland rather than Crete, but it does not negate the possibility that Crete could or would have been visited on a subsequent stop, before the ship sailed farther south to reach the African coast, perhaps via Bates' Island off Marsa Matruh (Pulak 1988: 37), *en route* to the Syro-Palestinian coast.

In summary, the Uluburun ship epitomizes the various means by which Near Eastern goods reached the Late Bronze Age Aegean. New implications for the dynamic and far-reaching trade activities in the Late Bronze Age are just beginning to emerge. The stunning diversity of artifacts found on the wreck represents products of at least nine or ten cultures: Canaanite, Mycenaean, Cypriot, Egyptian, Nubian, Baltic, Northern Balkan, Old Babylonian, Kassite, Assyrian, eastern Near Eastern, and possibly Sicilian. The ship and its cargo appear to represent an official dispatch of an enormously rich and valuable cargo of raw materials and manufactured goods largely intended for a specific destination. In addition to utilitarian objects and raw materials, the presence of prestige goods would appear to indicate that the Late Bronze Age Aegean was not so far removed from the international trade that was based on royal gift-giving in the Near East, and which is reflected vividly in the Amarna letters. As was the practice in such ventures, the ship's cargo was probably placed in the care of an official or a semi-official who represented the king's interest, but who may have engaged in some private trade of his own on the side. This emissary also was entrusted with a contingent of prestige goods that he would present personally to the royalty receiving the cargo.

ADDENDUM

The date of 1316 B.C.E. was given in a preliminary report by Peter Kuniholm (1996), as the year of the last observable (but not measurable) ring on a piece of timber from the Uluburun shipwreck (supra, p. 252). As the timber in question did not show any evidence of modification by man, it was believed to be missing only a few rings on its exterior. The timber is probably a twisted branch intended for use as dunnage or firewood and, as such, must have been taken aboard shortly before the ship began its voyage.

After this paper was submitted for publication, a re-examination of the timber by Kuniholm and L. Steele at the Laboratory for Aegean and Near Eastern Dendrochronology at Cornell University has revealed the presence of ten additional rings, almost all of which occur on a node on the reverse side of the timber. Accordingly, the final ring on the timber is now placed at 1306 B.C.E., which suggests that the Uluburun ship sank some time after that date. This new date for the ship's sinking changes little the conclusions reached in this paper regarding the transition date of LHIIIA:2 pottery to that of LHIIIB:1.

REFERENCES

Artzy, M.
1983   Arethusa of the Tin Ingot. *Bulletin of the American Schools of Oriental Research* 250: 51–55.

Barnett, R. D.
1975   *A Catalogue of the Nimrud Ivories.* London: British Museum Publications, Ltd.

Basch, L.
1978   Le navire *mnš* et autres notes de voyage en Egypte. *Mariner's Mirror* 64: 99–123.
1987   *Le musée imaginaire de la marine antique.* Athens: Hellenic Institute for the Preservation of Nautical Tradition.

Bass, G. F.
1967   *Cape Gelidonya: A Bronze Age Shipwreck. Transactions of the American Philosophical Society* 57, Part 8. Philadelphia: American Philosophical Society.
1973   Cape Gelidonya and Bronze Age Maritime Trade. Pp. 29–38 in *Orient and Occident: Festschrift Cyrus H. Gordon (Alter Orient und Altes Testament* 22), ed. H. A. Hoffner, Jr. Neukirchen-Vluyn: Neukirchener.
1986   A Bronze Age Shipwreck at Ulu Burun (Kaş): 1984 Campaign. *American Journal of Archaeology* 90: 269–96.
1989   The Construction of a Seagoing Vessel of the Late Bronze Age. Pp. 25–35 in *Tropis* I: *1st International Symposium on Ship Construction in Antiquity,* ed. H. E. Tzalas. Athens: Hellenic Institute for the Preservation of Nautical Tradition.
1990   A Bronze-Age Writing-Diptych from the Sea off Lycia. *Kadmos. Zeitschrift für vor- und frügriechische Epigrafik* 29: 168–69.
1991   Evidence of Trade from Bronze Age Shipwrecks. Pp. 69–82 in *Bronze Age Trade in the Mediterranean,* ed. N. H. Gale. Studies in Mediterranean Archaeology 90. Jonsered: Åströms.

Bass, G. F.; Frey, D. A.; and Pulak, C.
1984   A Late Bronze Age shipwreck at Kaş, Turkey. *The International Journal of Nautical Archaeology* 13: 271–79.

Bass, G. F.; Pulak, C.; Collon, D.; and Weinstein, J.
1989   The Bronze Age Shipwreck at Ulu Burun: 1986 Campaign. *American Journal of Archaeology* 93: 1–29.

Baum, N.
1994   *Snṯr:* Une révision. *Revue d'égyptologie* 45: 17–39.

Ben-Arieh S., and Edelstein, G.
1977   *Akko. Tombs Near the Persian Garden.* ʿAtiqot (English Series) 12. Jerusalem: Ahva.

Beyer, D.
1982   *Meskéné-Emar: Dix ans de travaux 1972–1982.* Paris: Éditions Recherche sur les Civilisations, A.D.P.F.

Biran, A.
1970   Notes and News: Tel Dan. *Israel Exploration Journal* 20: 118–19.
1971   Laish-Dan: Secrets of a Canaanite City and an Israelite City. *Qadmoniot* 4: 2–10.

Bouzek, J.
1985   *The Aegean, Anatolia and Europe: Cultural Interrelations in the Second Millennium B.C.* Studies in Mediterranean Archaeology 29. Göteborg: Åströms.
1994   Late Bronze Age Greece and the Balkans: A Review of the Present Picture. *The Annual of the British School at Athens* 89: 217–34.

Buchholz, H. G.
1959   Keftiubarren und Erzhandel im zweiten vorchristlichen Jahrtausend. *Praehistorische Zeitschrift* 37: 1–40.
1966   Talanta, Neues über Metallbarren der

ostmediterranean Spätbronzezeit. *Schweizer Münzblätter* 16/62: 58–72.

Budd, P.; Pollard, A. M.; Scaife, B.; and Thomas, R. G.
1995   Oxhide Ingots, Recycling and the Mediterranean Metals Trade. *Journal of Mediterranean Archaeology,* 8: 1–32.

Caubet, A.
1987   La musique à Ougarit. *Académie des Inscriptions & Belles-Lettres: Comptes-Rendus des Séances de l'Année 1987:* 731–54.

Caubet, A., and Poplin, F.
1987   Les objects de matière dure animale: Étude du matériau. Pp. 273–306 in *Le centre de la ville: Ras Shamra-Ougarit* III *38e–44e campagnes,* ed. M. Yon. Paris: Éditions Recherche sur les Civilisations, A.D.P.F.

Cernykh, E. N.
1976   *Drevnjaja metallo-obrabotka na jugo-zapada SSSR.* Moscow: Academy of Sciences.
1978   *Gornoe delo i metallurgiia v drevneishei Bolgarii.* Sofia: Bulgarian Academy of Sciences.
1979   *Gold der Thraker: Archäologische Schätze aus Bulgarien.* Mainz am Rhein: von Zabern.

Clamer, C.
1980   A Gold Plaque from Tel Lachish. *Tel Aviv* 7: 152–62.

Cline E. H.
1994   *Sailing the Wine-Dark Sea: International Trade and the Late Bronze Age Aegean.* BAR International Series 591. Oxford: B.A.R.

Connan, J.
1988   Quelques secrets des bitumes archéologiques de Mésopotamie révélés par les analyses de géochimie organique pétrolière. *Bulletin des Centres de Recherches et d'Exploration-Production d'Elf-Aquitaine* 12: 759–87.

Courtois, J.-C.
1984   *Alasia* III: *Les objects des niveaux stratifiés d'Enkomi.* Paris.

Dakoronia, P.
1992   Chrērē kai Proeleysē Makrōn Peronōn YM kai PG Epochēs. Pp. 292–97 in *Diethnes Synedrio yia tēn Archaia Thessalia stē mnēmē tou Dēmētrē R. Theocharē (International Congress on Ancient Thessaly in memory of Dimitris R. Theochares).* Athens: Ministry of Culture, Publication of the Archaiologikon Deltion. In Greek with English summary.

Davies, Nina de G.
1963   *Scenes from Some Theban Tombs. Private Tombs at Thebes* IV. Oxford: Griffith Institute.

Davies, N. de G.
1943   *The Tomb of Rekh-mi-rē at Thebes.* New York: Metropolitan Museum of Art.

Davies N. de G., and Faulkner, R. O.
1947   A Syrian Trading Venture to Egypt. *Journal of Egyptian Archaeology* 33: 40–46.

Davis, E. N.
1977   *The Vapheio Cups and Aegean Gold and Silver Ware.* New York: Garland.

Dimitrov, B.
1979   Underwater Research Along the South Bulgarian Black Sea Coast in 1976 and 1977. *The International Journal of Nautical Archaeology* 8: 70–79.

Driessen, J. M., and MacDonald, C.
1984   Some Military Aspects of the Aegean in the Late Fifteenth and Early Fourteenth Centuries B.C. Part II: Aegean Swords and Warrior Graves: Their Implications for Knossian Military Organization. *Annual of the British School in Athens* 79: 56–74.

Finkelstein, I., and Brandl, B.
1985   A Group of Metal Objects from Shiloh. *The Israel Museum Journal* 4: 17–26.

Finkelstein, I.; Bunimovitz S.; and Lederman, Z.
1993   *Shiloh. The Archaeology of a Biblical Site.* Monograph Series of the Institute of Archaeology. Jerusalem: Institute of Archaeology of Tel Aviv University.

Foster, B.
1987   The Late Bronze Age Palace Economy: A View from the East. Pp. 11–16 in *The Function of the Minoan Palaces,* eds. R. Häag and N. Marinatos. Skrifter utgivna av Svenska institutet i Athen 35. Stockholm: Svenska institutet i Athen.

Frost, H.
1969a   The Stone Anchors of Byblos. *Mélanges de l'Université St. Joseph* 45: 425–42.
1969b   The Stone Anchors of Ugarit. Pp. 235–45 in *Ugaritica* VI, ed. C. F. A. Schaeffer. Institut français d'archéologie de Beyrouth 81. Paris: Imprimerie Nationale.
1985   Appendix 1: The Kition Anchors. Pp. 281–321 in *Excavations at Kition* V. *The Pre-Phoenician Levels,* eds. V. Karageorghis and M. Demas. Nicosia: Department of Antiquities, Cyprus.
1991   Anchors Sacred and Profane: Ugarit-Ras Shamra, 1986; The Stone Anchors Revised and Compared. Pp. 355–410 in *Ras Shamra-Ougarit* VI: *Arts et industries de la pierre.* ed. M. Yon. Paris: Éditions Recherche sur les Civilisations, A.D.P.F.

Gachet, J.
1987 Objets en os et en ivoire. Pp. 249–72 in *Le centre de la ville: Ras Shamra-Ougarit* III: *38e–44e campagnes (1978–1984)*, ed. M. Yon. Paris: Éditions Recherche sur les Civilisations, A.D.P.F.

Gale, N. H.
1989 Archaeometallurgical Studies of Late Bronze Age Oxhide Copper Ingots from the Mediterranean Region. Pp. 99–105 in *Archäometallurgie der Alten Welt. Beiträge zum Internationalen Symposium: Old World Archaeometallurgy*, eds. A. Hauptmann, E. Pernicka and G. A. Wagner. Der Anschnitt, Beiheft 7. Bochum: Deutschen Bergbau-Museums.
1991 Copper Oxhide Ingots: Their Origin and Their Place in the Bronze Age Metals Trade in the Mediterranean. Pp. 197–239 in *Bronze Age Trade in the Mediterranean*, ed. N. H. Gale. Studies in Mediterranean Archaeology 90. Jonsered: Åströms.

Galili, E.
1985 A Group of Stone Anchors from Newe-Yam. *The International Journal of Nautical Archaeology* 14: 143–53.

Galili, E.; Sharvit, J.; and Artzy, M.
1994 Reconsidering Byblian and Egyptian Stone Anchors Using Numeral Methods: New Finds from the Israeli Coast. *The International Journal of Nautical Archaeology* 23: 93–107.

Galili, E.; Shmueli, N.; and Artzy, M.
1986 Bronze Age Ship's Cargo of Copper and Tin. *The International Journal of Nautical Archaeology* 15: 25–37.

Gallis, K.
1973 Duo Nēoschēmoi Pyxides Ex Engkomēs. *Archaiologike Ephemeris:* 120–29.

Gates, M.-H.
1994 Archaeology in Turkey. *American Journal of Archaeology* 98: 249–78.

Hachmann, R.
1966 *Bericht über die Ergebnisse der Ausgrabungen in Kamid el-Loz [Libanon] in den Jahren 1963 und 1964.* Bonn: Habelt.
1983 *Frühe Phöniker im Libanon.* Mainz am Rhein: von Zabern.

Haldane, C. W.
1990 Shipwrecked Plant Remains. *Biblical Archaeologist* 53.1: 55–60.
1991 Recovery and Analysis of Plant Remains from some Mediterranean Shipwreck Sites. Pp. 213–23 in *New Light on Early Farming: Recent Developments in Palaeoethnobotany*, ed. J. M. Renfrew. Edinburgh: Edinburgh University.
1993 Direct Evidence for Organic Cargoes in the Late Bronze Age. *World Archaeology* 24: 348–60.

Hamilton, R. W.
1935 Excavations at Tell Abu Hawām. *The Quarterly of the Department of Antiquities in Palestine* 4: 1–69.

Hankey, V.
1987 The Chronology of the Aegean Late Bronze Age. Pp. 39–59 in part 2 of *High, Middle or Low? Acts of an International Colloquium on Absolute Chronology Held at the University of Gothenburg 20th–22nd August 1987*, ed. P. Åström. Göteborg: Åströms.

Helck, W.
1987 Was kann die Ägyptologie wirklich zum Problem der absoluten Chronologie in der Bronzezeit beitragen? Chronologische Annäherungswerte in der 18. Dynastie. Pp. 18–26 in part 1 of *High, Middle or Low? Acts of an International Colloquium on Absolute Chronology Held at the University of Gothenburg 20th–22nd August 1987*, ed. P. Åström. Göteborg: Åströms.

Hiller, S.
1991 The Mycenaeans and the Black Sea. Pp. 207–16 in *Thalassa, L'Egée préhistorique et la mer*, eds. R. Laffineur and L. Basch. Liège: Université de Liège.

Höckmann, O.
1980 Lanze und Speer im spätminoischen und mykenischen Griechenland. *Jahrbuch des romisch- germanischen Zentralmuseum Mainz* 27: 13–158.

Jones, R. E., and Vagnetti, L.
1991 Traders and Craftsmen in the Central Mediterranean: Archaeological Evidence and Archaeometric Research. Pp. 127–47 in *Bronze Age Trade in the Mediterranean*, ed. N. H. Gale. Studies in Mediterranean Archaeology 90. Jonsered: Åströms.

Karageorghis, V.
1976a Chronique des fouilles et découvertes archéologiques à Chypre en 1975. *Bulletin de Correspondance Hellénique* 100: 839–906.
1976b *Kition: Mycenaean and Phoenician Discoveries in Cyprus.* London: Thames and Hudson.

Karageorghis, V., and Demas, M.
1985 *Excavations at Kition. The Pre-Phoenician Levels.* Nicosia: Department of Antiquities, Cyprus.

Kilian-Dirlmeier, I.
1984a Der dorische Peplos: ein archäologisches

Zeugnis der dorischen Wanderung? *Archäologischer Korrespondenzblatt* 14: 281–91.

1984b   *Nadeln der frühelladischen bis archaischen Zeit von der Peloponnes. Prähistorische Bronzefunde* 13.8. Munich: C. H. Beck.

Kitchen, K. A.
1987   The Basics of Egyptian Chronology in Relation to the Bronze Age. Pp. 37–55 in part 1 of *High, Middle or Low? Acts of an International Colloquium on Absolute Chronology Held at the University of Gothenburg 20th–22nd August 1987,* ed. P. Åström. Göteborg: Åströms.

Kochavi, M.
1977   *Five Seasons of Excavations at Tel Aphek-Antipatris (1972–1976).* Tel Aviv: Institute of Archaeology, Tel Aviv University.

Koehler, C. G., and Wallace, M. B.
1987   Appendix. The Transport Amphoras: Descriptions and Capacities, in C. Pulak and R.F. Townsend, The Hellenistic Shipwreck at Serçe Limanı, Turkey: Preliminary Report. *American Journal of Archaeology* 91: 31–57.

Kuniholm, P. I.
1996   Long Tree-Ring Chronologies for the Eastern Mediterranean. *Archaeometry* 94, eds. Ş. Demirci, A. M. Özer, and G. D. Summers. Ankara: Tubitak.

Liverani, M.
1972   Il talento di Ashdod. *Orientis Antiqui Collectio* 11: 193–99.

1987   The Collapse of the Near Eastern Regional System at the End of the Bronze Age: the Case of Syria. Pp. 66–73 in *Centre and Periphery in the Ancient World,* eds. M. Rowlands, M.T. Larsen, and K. Kristiansen. Cambridge: Cambridge University.

Lolos, Y. G.
1989   The Gold Chalice from the Late Bronze Age Wreck at *Akroterion* (Ulu Burun) in Lycia. *Enalia (Annual English Edition of the Hellenic Institute of Marine Archaeology)* 1: 8–9, 46.

Loret, V.
1949   *La résine de térébinthe (sonter) chez les anciens Égyptiens.* Recherches d'archéologie, de philologie et d'histoire 19. Cairo: L'Institut français d'archéologie orientale.

Loud, G.
1939   *The Megiddo Ivories.* Chicago: University of Chicago.

Maddin, R.
1989   The Copper and Tin Ingots from the Kaş Shipwreck. Pp. 99–105 in *Archäometallurgie der Alten Welt. Beiträge zum Internationalen Symposium: Old World Archaeometallurgy,* eds. A. Hauptmann, E. Pernicka and G. A. Wagner. Der Anschnitt, Beiheft 7. Bochum: Deutschen Bergbau-Museums.

Maddin, R.; Wheeler, T. S.; and Muhly, J. D.
1977   Tin in the Ancient Near East: Old Questions and New Finds. *Expedition* 19.2: 35–47.

Mazar, A.
1975   Excavations at Tell Qasîle, 1973–1974 (Preliminary Report). *Israel Exploration Journal* 25.2–3: 77– 88.

Melena, J. L.
1976   La producción de plantas aromáticas en Cnoso. *Estudios clásicos* 20: 177–90.

Metropolitan Museum of Art
1986   *Treasures of the Holy Land: Ancient Art from the Israel Museum.* New York: The Metropolitan Museum of Art.

Mills, J. S., and White, R.
1989   The Identity of the Resins from the Late Bronze Age Shipwreck at Ulu Burun (Kaş). *Archaeometry* 31: 37–44.

Miron, E.
1992   *Axes and Adzes from Canaan. Praehistorische Bronzefunde* 9.19. Stuttgart: Steiner.

Moran, W. L.
1992   *The Amarna Letters.* Baltimore: The Johns Hopkins University.

Muhly, J. D.
1991   The Development of Copper Metallurgy in Late Bronze Age Cyprus. Pp. 180–96 in *Bronze Age Trade in the Mediterranean,* ed. N.H. Gale. Studies in Mediterranean Archaeology 90. Jonsered: Åströms.

Muhly, J. D.; Wheeler, T. S.; and Maddin, R.
1977   The Cape Gelidonya Shipwreck and the Bronze Age Metals Trade in the Eastern Mediterranean. *Journal of Field Archaeology* 4: 353–62.

Negbi, O.
1976   *Canaanite Gods in Metal: An Archaeological Study of Ancient Syro-Palestinian Figurines.* Tel Aviv: Tel Aviv University, Institute of Archaeology.

Nougayrol, G.
1955   *Le palais royal d'Ugarit* III. Paris: Klincksieck.

Oppenheim, A. L.
1973   Toward a History of Glass in the Ancient Near East. *Journal of the American Oriental Society* 93: 259–66.

Oppenheim, A. L.; Brill, R. H.; Barag, D.; and von Saldern, A.
1970   *Glass and Glassmaking in Ancient Mesopotamia.* Corning, New York: Corning Museum of Glass.

Parise, N. F.

1968   I pani di rame del II millennio A.C.:
        Considerazioni preliminari. Pp. 117–33 in *Atti e
        memorie del 1° Congresso internazionale di
        Micenologia*. Roma: Edizioni dell'Ateneo.

1971   Per uno studio del sistema ponderale ugaritico.
        Dialoghi di Archeologia 4–5 (1970–71): 3–36.

Payton, R.

1991   The Ulu Burun Writing-Board Set. *Anatolian
        Studies* 41: 99–106.

Peltenburg, E.

1991   Greeting Gifts and Luxury Faience: A Context
        for Orientalising Trends in Late Mycenaean
        Greece. Pp. 162–79 in *Bronze Age Trade in the
        Mediterranean,* ed. N.H. Gale. Studies in Medi-
        terranean Archaeology 90. Jonsered: Åströms.

Petruso, K. M.

1984   Prolegomena to Late Cypriot Weight Metrology.
        American Journal of Archaeology 88: 293–304.

1992   *Ayia Irini: The Balance Weights. Keos* 8. Mainz:
        von Zabern.

Pini, I.

1993   *Corpus der minoischen und mykenischen Siegel.*
        Vol. 5 supplement 1B. Berlin: Gebr. Mann.

Portugali, Y., and Knapp, A. B.

1985   Cyprus and the Aegean: A Spatial Analysis of
        Interaction in the Seventeenth to Fourteenth Cen-
        turies B.C. Pp. 44–78 in *Prehistoric Production
        and Exchange,* eds. A.B. Knapp and T. Stech.
        Institute of Archaeology Monograph 25. Los
        Angeles: University of California.

Pulak, C.

1988   The Bronze Age Shipwreck at Ulu Burun, Tur-
        key: 1985 Campaign. *American Journal of Ar-
        chaeology* 92: 1–37.

1990a   The Late Bronze Age Shipwreck at Ulu Burun,
        Turkey: 1989 Excavation Campaign. Pp. 52–57
        in *Underwater Archaeology Proceedings from
        the Society for Historical Archaeology Confer-
        ence,* ed. T. Carrell. Tucson, Arizona: Society
        for Historical Archaeology.

1990b   Ulu Burun: 1990 Excavation Campaign. *INA
        Newsletter* 17.4: 8–13.

1992   The Shipwreck at Ulu Burun, Turkey: 1992 Ex-
        cavation Campaign. *The INA Quarterly* 19.4:
        4–11, 21.

1993   The Shipwreck at Uluburun: 1993 Excavation
        Campaign. *The INA Quarterly* 20.4: 4–12.

Pulak, C., and Bass, G. F.

1992   The Shipwreck at Uluburun, Turkey: 1991 Ex-
        cavation Season. Pp. 62–67 in *Underwater Ar-
        chaeology Proceedings from the Society for His-
        torical Archaeology Conference,* eds. D. H.

Keith and T. L. Carrell. Kingston, Jamaica: So-
        ciety for Historical Archaeology.

Pulak, C., and Frey, D. A.

1985   The Search for a Bronze Age Shipwreck. *Archae-
        ology* 38.4: 18–24.

Pulak, C., and Rogers, E.

1994   The 1993–1994 Turkish Shipwreck Surveys. *The
        INA Quarterly* 21.4: 17–21.

Sandars, N. K.

1963   Later Aegean Bronze Swords. *American Jour-
        nal of Archaeology* 67: 117–53.

Säve-Söderbergh, T.

1957   *Four Eighteenth Dynasty Tombs. Private Tombs
        at Thebes* 1. Oxford: Oxford University.

Sayre, E. V.; Yener, K. A.; Joel, E. C.; and Barnes, I. L.

1992   Statistical Evaluation of the Presently Accumu-
        lated Lead Isotope Data from Anatolia and Sur-
        rounding Regions. *Archaeometry* 34: 73–105.

Schaeffer, C. F. A.

1937   Les fouilles de Ras Shamra-Ugarit: huitième
        campagne (printemps 1936). *Syria* 18: 125–54.

1939   *The Cuneiform Texts of Ras Shamra-Ugarit.*
        Schweich Lectures of the British Academy for
        1936. London: Oxford University.

1949   *Ugaritica* 2. Institut français d'archéologie de
        Beyrouth, 47. Paris: Imprimerie Nationale.

1962   *Ugaritica* 4. Institut français d'archéologie de
        Beyrouth, 74. Paris: Imprimerie Nationale.

1978   *Ugaritica* 7. Institut français d'archéologie de
        Beyrouth, 99. Paris: Imprimerie Nationale.

Seeden, H.

1982   Peace Figurines from the Levant. Pp. 107–21 in
        Archéologie au Levant, Recueil R. Saidah. Col-
        lection de la Maison de l'Orient méditerranéen
        12, Série archéologique 9. Lyon: P. Guichard.

Sherratt, S., and Sherratt, A.

1991   From Luxuries to Commodities: The Nature of
        Mediterranean Bronze Age Trading Systems. Pp.
        351– 86 in *Bronze Age Trade in the Mediterra-
        nean,* ed. N.H. Gale. Studies in Mediterranean
        Archaeology 90. Jonsered: Åströms.

Steffy, J. R.

1985   The Kyrenia Ship: An Interim Report on Its Hull
        Construction. *American Journal of Archaeology*
        89: 71–101.

1994   *Wooden Ship Building and the Interpretation of
        Shipwrecks.* College Station, TX.

Stos-Gale, Z. A.; Gale, N. H.; and Zwicker, U.

1986   The Copper Trade in the South-East Mediterra-
        nean Region. Preliminary Scientific Evidence.
        Report of the Department of Antiquities, Cyprus:
        122–44.

Symington, D.
  1991   Late Bronze Age Writing-Boards and Their Uses: Textual Evidence from Anatolia and Syria. *Anatolian Studies* 41: 111–23.

Tončeva, G.
  1982   Thracia Pontica à l'âge de Bronze Recent. *Thracia Pontica* I: 176–82.

Tufnell, O.; Inge, H. C.; and Harding, L.
  1940   *Lachish* II: *The Fosse Temple*. London: Oxford University.

Vagnetti, L., and Lo Schiavo, F.
  1989   Late Bronze Age Long Distance Trade in the Mediterranean: The Role of the Cypriots. Pp. 217–43 in *Early Society in Cyprus,* ed. E. Peltenberg. Edinburgh: Edinburgh University.

Vulpe, A.
  1970   *Die Äxte und Beile in Rumänien* I, *Prähistorische Bronzefunde* 9.2. Munich: C. H. Beck.

Wardle, K. A.
  1992   Mycenaean Trade and Influence in Northern Greece. Pp. 117–41 in *Wace and Blegen: Pottery as Evidence for Trade in the Aegean Bronze Age 1939–1989,* eds. C. Zerner, P. Zerner, and J. Winder. Amsterdam: J. C. Gieben.

Warnock, P., and Pendleton, M.
  1991   The Wood of the Ulu Burun Diptych. *Anatolian Studies* 41: 107–10.

Woolley, L.
  1955   *Alalakh: An Account of the Excavations at Tell Atchana in the Hatay, 1937–1949.* Oxford.

Yadin, Y., et al.
  1960   *Hazor* II: *An Account of the Second Season of Excavations, 1956.* Jerusalem: The Magnes Press of the Hebrew University.

Yener, K. A.; Sayre, E. V.; Joel, E. C., Özbal, H.; Barnes, I. L.; and Brill, R. H.
  1991   Stable Lead Isotope Studies of Central Taurus Ore Sources and Related Artifacts from Eastern Mediterranean Chalcolithic and Bronze Age Sites. *Journal of Archaeological Science* 18: 541–77.

Yener, K. A., and Vandiver, P. B.
  1993a   Tin Processing at Göltepe, an Early Bronze Age Site in Anatolia. *American Journal of Archaeology* 97: 207–38.
  1993b   Reply to J. D. Muhly, "Early Bronze Age Tin and the Taurus." *American Journal of Archaeology* 97: 255–64.

Zaccagnini, C.
  1986   Aspects of Copper Trade in the Eastern Mediterranean During the Late Bronze Age. Pp. 413–24 in *Traffici micenei nel Mediterraneo.* Taranto: Instituto per la storia e l'archeologia della Magna Grecia.

Zevulun, U.
  1987   A Canaanite Ram-Headed Cup. *Israel Exploration Journal* 37: 88–104.

Who Were the Cilician Pirates?

NICHOLAS K. RAUH

Department of History
Purdue University
West Lafayette, IN 47907
U.S.A.

This paper tests the source tradition for the Cilician pirates against parallels provided by recent, innovative studies of Anglo-American piracy in the eighteenth century C.E. The vast majority of Cilician pirates neither came from Cilicia, nor were they connected in any manner with the bandit chieftains of its hinterland. Rather they emerged from a vast international substratum of displaced naval warriors from maritime regions under stress. By name and language they would appear to have been mostly Hellenistic Greeks and Levantines, rather than Latins, and to a large degree they drew their manpower from the provincial elements of the collapsing Hellenistic and expanding Roman realms. In many respects, the Cilician pirates represented a common man's response to decades of authoritarian oppression.

The rise and fall of Cilician piracy between 139 and 67 B.C.E. presents one of the most poorly understood problems of the late Hellenistic era, in part because the sources address it with a high degree of hyperbole.[1] The accounts of Plutarch, Dio, and Appian sound so exaggerated, so sententious, yet so similar, that their authority can be questioned justifiably, especially if, as Strasburger has suggested, they ultimately derive their knowledge from one common source (the stoic philosopher Poseidonius) (Strasburger 1965: 40–53). In this paper, I will test the source tradition for the Cilician pirates against parallels provided by recent, innovative studies of Anglo-American piracy in the eighteenth century C.E.[2] Evidence for the social and cultural origins of early modern piracy as well as for the attitudes and behavioral patterns generally of these pirates appears to corroborate much of what the ancient sources tell us about the Cilician pirates. If these parallels are proven effective, they may help to confirm the authenticity of the ancient source tradition and perhaps enable us to assess more properly the significance of the Cilician pirates to late Hellenistic events.

In view of the exaggerated character of the ancient discussion of the pirates, a number of questions arise. Did pirates calling themselves Cilicians truly originate from Cilicia, and had they the capacity to seize control of the Mediterranean sea lanes between 88 and 67 B.C.E. with the

---

[1] Ancient pirate bibliography: See Ormerod (1987: 190–91); Benabou (1985: 60–69); Brandt (1992: 83–84); Briant (1976: 212–13); Brulé (1978); Clavel-Leveque (1979: 17–32); Dell (1967: 344–58); Garlan (1978: 1–16); Gianfrotta (1981: 227–42); Kaletsch (1986: 484–85); Marasco (1987a: 129–45); Marasco (1987b: 122–46); Maroti (1961: 32–41); Maroti (1962: 187–94); Maroti (1969–70: 24–42); Maroti (1970: 481–93); Pohl (1993).

[2] Early modern pirate bibliography: See Rediker (1987: 254–87); Sherry (1986); Rankin (1969); Thomson (1994: 22–26, 43–54, 69–76, 105–18); Burg (1995); Earle (1970); Gosse (1946); Lydon (1970); Ritchie (1986); Senior (1976); Williams (1962); Wolf (1979). Rediker, Sherry, and Thomson employ theoretical models of Hobsbawm (1969). Where possible, I have tried to refer to the principal primary source for transatlantic piracy, [Capt. C. Johnson] (1724), generally acknowledged to be the work of Daniel Defoe. For discussion see Sherry (1986: 368–70).

cohesiveness and manpower that the ancient sources insist? If so, what unique qualities about their cultural background and social organization may account for this? Precisely who were the Cilician pirates, anyway, and how did they project the stength to dominate the Mediterranean basin for a full generation or more? The focus of my paper requires that I provide a brief outline of the historical experience of Cilician piracy before turning to questions of origin, social background, mentality, and behavior.

HISTORICAL OUTLINE
OF THE CILICIAN PIRATES

The Cilician pirates emerged from the dynastic disputes of various pretenders to the Seleucid throne c. 146–138 B.C.E., having been organized by Diodotus Tryphon, a former Seleucid military officer from Apamea, during his conflicts with Demetrius II and Antiochus VII Sidetes (fig. 1; see Fischer 1972: 201–13; Maroti 1962: 187–94). Before his death in 138, Tryphon managed to install "naval forces" at a number of impregnable fortresses along the eastern Mediterranean corridor—most particularly at Coracesium (Korakesion) in western Rough Cilicia (Cilicia Tracheia or Aspera) and Dora in Phoenicia.[3] In the aftermath of Tryphon these naval elements continued to launch naval assaults on Syria and Cilicia, apparently acting as independent autonomous pirate bands. In a short time, a number of pirate chiefs (*tyrannoi, strategoi, archipiratae*) carved out small principalities for themselves, particularly along the remote mountainous coast of western Cilicia.[4] At first their marauding activities were tolerated by other powers of the region—the republic of Rhodes, the Attalid kings of Pergamum, the Ptolemies of Egypt and Cyprus, and Roman commercial elements active in the Aegean, since they not only directed the thrust of their assaults against Seleucid assets but they benefited the illicit commerce of the region by generating

Fig. 1. Diodotus Tryphon. Drawing by Peter Butler.

sales of captured pirate booty (slaves and luxuries) at notorious harbors such as Aegean Delos, Phaselis, Attaleia, and Side (the last three on the bay of Pamphylia).[5] However, the pirates soon grew increasingly indiscriminate and predatory in their selection of prizes. A sufficient quantity of evidence indicates that non Seleucid shipping likewise fell prey to their ambuscades.[6]

By 102 B.C.E., the indiscriminate attacks of the Cilician pirates finally outweighed the benefits of their illegal traf-

---

[3] Coracesium: Strabo 14.5.2 (668); Plut. *Pomp.* 27.1; Dora: Jos. *A.J.* 13.223; 1 *Macc.* 15.1–25; cf. Grainger (1991: 123).

[4] For the initially limited range of their depradations, see Flor. 1.41.3; App. *Mith.* 92; Strabo 14.1.32 (644).

[5] For Delos, Phaselis, Attaleia, and Side: Strabo 14.3.2 (664); 14.5.2 (669); 14.5.7 (671); Cic. *Verr.* 2.4.21; *De Leg. Agr.* 1.5, 2.50; Alciphr. 1.8; with Marasco 1987b: 137 n. 70. Strabo 16.2.14 (754) implies that the refusal of Arados in Phoenicia to cooperate with pirates was exceptional; cf. Plut. *Luc.* 3.2; Marasco (1987b: 141 n. 91); Garlan (1978: 8). For the attitude of neighboring realms, Strabo 14.5.2 (669). Marasco (1987b: 135) suggests that Rome intervened at the insistence of Rhodes. Another possibility is that Romans themselves were attacked, or their Phoenician contacts. Note the connection of the Granii at Delos with Antioch, for example Rauh (1993: 66–67).

[6] For pirate assaults on Roman shipping, see Macr. 3.6.11; Serv. in *Aen.* 8.363; Rauh (1993: 118–19); cf. Plut. *Cat. Mai.* 21, for evidence of Roman cargo fleets traveling in convoys. Gianfrotta (1981), has suggested recently that the remains of decapitated sailors found in shipwrecks in the waters off Sicily and Sardinia, with their skulls still strapped to military helmets, marked the violent trail of pirates. For the evidence of problems posed by piracy at Delos, see Couilloud (1973: nos. 337–350, 475); *ID* 1661, 2305, 2401, 2433. For further discussion, see Rauh (1993: 68–69).

Fig. 2. Mithradates VI Eupator. Drawing by Peter Butler.

fic and provoked the Romans to act against them through a combined program of diplomatic pressure, legal prohibition, and main force.[7] These measures proved minimally effective. The pirates survived the naval assault of the pro-

consul, M. Antonius "the Orator" (who apparently got as far as Side), and soon gained new-found support from Rome's greatest adversary in the region, King Mithradates VI Eupator of Pontus (fig. 2). By aligning themselves with Mithradates at the outset of his war against Rome (88–84 B.C.E.), the pirates greatly enhanced their naval capacities and expanded their sway to new territories. For example, they participated in the king's assaults on Delos, Rhodes, and Lycia and harassed the Roman proquaestor L. Licinius Lucullus as he sailed from Crete to Cyrene to Egypt raising naval forces for his commander, L. Cornelius Sulla.[8] Unwisely, Sulla resolved to let these assaults go unpunished. His pressing need to return to Italy to defeat his internal adversaries compelled him to make an imperfect peace with Mithradates, a peace that left the pirates not only unscathed but in a better position than they had been prior to the war.[9]

Pirate realms now dominated the entire gulf of Pamphylia. By 78 B.C.E. a pirate chief named Zenicetes appears to have carved out an independent territory for himself in eastern Lycia, centered in a castle near the eternal fires that dominated the harbors of Olympus, Corycus, and Phaselis.[10] Further east other pirate chiefs had constructed impregnable fortresses at Coracesium (fig. 3) and the "Kragos mountain" (fig. 4), complete with well-stocked harbors, warehouses, shipsheds, and skilled artisans and laborers chained to their stations.[11] Independent cities along the Pamphylian coast appear to have cooperated fully.

From this point onward the sources describe the pirate menace in highly sensational terms:[12] pirates reportedly stormed the Sanctuary of the Kabeiroi at Samothrace, plundering its temple of ornaments valued at 1000 talents, even as Sulla, during a brief visit, helplessly looked on. Accord-

---

[7] For the Roman Piracy Law of 102–100, see Riccobono (*FIRA*, 1.121, no. 9); Hassal et al. (1974: 195–220); Blümel (1992: 13–14, no. 31).

[8] For the assault on Delos, see Rauh (1993: 68). For Rhodes, Lycia, and Lucullus, Plut. *Luc.* 2.6; App. *Mith.* 27, 56.

[9] Mithradates funded them and left them huge quantities of naval supplies: App. *Mith.* 63, 92.

[10] The eternal fires burn from the heights of a jagged coastal ridge above Olympus and are visible from the sea. See Diler (1991: 161–76).

[11] For the Kragos and the Antikragos, φρούρια μέγιστα, see App. *Mith.* 96. Appian is the only source to mention this bastion in connection with piracy and he clearly states that Pompey assaulted it upon his arrival "in Cilicia." The place name is frequently confused with the mountains Strabo describes in western Lycia (modern Yediburun), despite the remoteness of the latter place from known pirate enclaves (14.3.5[665]; 14.5.3[669]; Ormerod 1987: 240 n.1). One suspects that the places were simply synonymous. Strabo 14.3.2 (664) asserts, for example, that the inhabitants of western Lycia abstained from piracy, and while he mentions both places (neither in connection with piracy), he was obviously more impressed with the "Kragos" in Cilicia, a πέτρα περίκρημνος Θαλάττη. Small wonder: its Roman-Byzantine topography includes an acropolis citadel on a precipitous cliff 250 m above the sea, and a lower more heavily fortified bastion on a rocky promontory out in front (the Antikragos?). The lower citadel is in turn flanked by a second crest of rock sheltering two hidden sea coves. For the site see Erdemgil and Özoral (1975: 55–71); Huber (1964: 143–44); Rosenbaum et al. (1967: 18–29, 49–52, 67–68, 90–91); Hild and Hellenkemper (1990: 322).

[12] App. *Mith.* 92–93; Dio 36.20–23; Plut. *Pomp.* 24; Eutrop. 6.3, 6.12.1; Oros. 5.23, 6.4; Sall *Hist.* 2.47.7 M.; Flor. 1.41.

Fig. 3. Castle Walls of Alanya (Coracesium). Drawing by Peter Butler.

ing to Plutarch and Appian, the pirates organized themselves into fleets that eventually wielded a combined armament of several hundred warships and 30,000 combatants.[13] Operating from more than a hundred fortresses, castles, and hidden coves (fig. 5), the pirates engaged in widespread depradations throughout the Mediterranean, although their principal theaters of operations prior to 78–75 B.C.E. remained the Aegean and the Levant.[14] Allegedly they stormed more than four hundred cities and pillaged as many as twelve sanctuaries of the Greek world. But they also roved the western Mediterranean, aiding and abetting Sulla's recalcitrant en-

emy, Q. Sertorius, in Spain, and perhaps marauding commerce in and around Sicily, Sardinia, and Corsica.[15]

Cognizant of the seriousness of this threat, the Romans dispatched a number of promagistrates against them. The most successful prior to Cn. Pompeius Magnus was unquestionably P. Servilius Vatia (Isauricus), cos. 79, who in a three-year campaign stormed the pirate empire of Zenicetes, restored Roman rule in Pamphylia, and conquered the Isaurians and other bandit tribesmen in the mountainous interior of Cilicia.[16] For some reason, however, he failed to assault the pirate headquarters of Cilicia, Coracesium and

[13] For the manpower see App. *Mith.* 93 (*muriades*); 96 (10,000 slain in 67 B.C.E.); Plut. *Pomp.* 28.2 (20,000 captured in 67); with discussion in David Magie 1950: 1180 n. 42. For the size of the pirate fleets see Strabo 14.3.3 (665) (1300 ships in all); App. *Mith.* 96 (Pompey captured 377 ships in 67 B.C.E.); Plut. *Pomp.* 28.2 (ninety of these possessed bronze rams). Most of these warships will have been small sleek *hemioliai,* but the ninety were presumably decked. For the insistence that the pirates sailed in large organized fleets, see Dio 36.21.1; App. *Mith.* 63, 92; Plut. *Caes.* 1.2; *Pomp.* 24.4; Cic. *Verr.* 2.5.97.

[14] For pirate activities in Syria, Phoenicia, and Judea, Strabo 16.2.14 (754), 16.2.28 (759); 1 *Macc.* 15.23; Plut. *Luc.* 3.2; Jos. *AJ* 14.43; Marasco (1987a: 133; 1987b: 141 n. 91). In Egypt and Cyrene: Dio 36.35.3; Flor. 1.41.3, Plut. *Luc.* 2.6; App. *Mith.* 56; Reynolds (1974: 19–23).

[15] For some archaeological evidence, see Gianfrotta (1981).

[16] Ormerod (1922: 35–56) remains worthwhile; cf. Hall (1973: 568–71).

Fig. 4. Byzantine Castle (the Antikragos?), Antioch on the Kragos. Drawing by Peter Butler.

"the Kragos." The effectiveness of Isauricus' campaign, combined with the likelihood of further assaults, did probably convince the Cilician pirates to redirect their campaigns toward the western Mediterranean, hoping in this manner to draw Roman attention as far from the bases in Cilicia as possible (Flor. 1.41.4–6; Marasco 1987b: 139). As a component of this strategy, they entered into close diplomatic relations with Mithradates and Sertorius, an arrangement culminating in the "Unholy Alliance" that converged on Rome from all points of the Mediterranean in 75–74 B.C.E.[17] Piratical assaults on Italy proper were highlighted by inland raids and scorched earth campaigns in southern Italy, firings of fleets (military and commercial) in Ostia and Caieta, and a series of sensational kidnappings of Roman dignitaries and very important persons.[18]

Roman counter offensives remained desultory until 67 B.C.E, when the Roman popular assembly commissioned a proven young general, Cn. Pompeius Magnus, with an extraordinary command to eradicate the pirates once and for all throughout the entire Mediterranean (fig. 6; Broughton 1986: 2.146; Magie 1950: 1179 n. 41). With some fifteen to twenty-four legates, 270 ships, and the authority to draw upon a potential complement of 120,000 infantry, 4000 cavalry, and 8000 talents of revenue, Pompey swept the Mediterranean from west to east in a three-month campaign, cornering the last holdouts in their bases in Cilicia and defeating them, ultimately, in the waters off Coracesium. Through lenient terms Pompey was able to persuade the majority of the pirates to surrender, and after dismantling the walls of the feared pirate bases, he resettled his former adversaries

[17] For sources and discussion, see Magie (1950: 1203 n. 1). Contrary to current opinion, Sallust's use of the expressions *res novae* and *tumultus* suggests that in 75 B.C.E. the Cilician pirates succeeded in bringing the Sullan establishment to the brink of political collapse (Sall. *Hist.* 2.45, 2.47.7, 2.50 M).

[18] Harbors: Dio 36.22.2; Cic. *De imp. Cn. Pomp.* 33. Kidnappings included the praetors Sextilius and Billienus and the daughter of M. Antonius the Orator (Plut. *Pomp.* 24.6; Cic. *De imp. Cn. Pomp.* 32–33), Julius Caesar (Suet. *Iul.* 4; Plut. *Caes.* 1.4), P. Clodius (Dio 36.17.3; 38.30.5; Cic. *Har. Resp.* 42; Strabo 14.6.6 [684]), various Roman *legati quaestores praetoresque* (Cic. *De imp. Cn. Pomp.* 53), and foreign embassies to Rome (Cic. *De imp. Cn. Pomp.* 32). Pirate ransoms remained a popular theme of Roman rhetorical exercises (ps. Quint. V, VI, IX; Sen. *Contr.* 1.6, 1.7; *Ben.* 1.5.4, 7.15.1; cf. Long. *Daphnis and Cloe* 1.30).

Fig. 5. Pirates' Cove (?), Antioch on the Kragos. Drawing by Peter Butler.

Genuine understanding of this problem calls for a sensitive appreciation of regional developments in the eastern quadrant of the Mediterranean world—for example, the unique social and cultural system that prevailed locally in Cilicia—as well as for the peculiar conditions of maritime society that tend to generate piracy in any historical period. The emergence of Cilician piracy in Rough Cilicia largely conforms with behavorial patterns of that region. Brent Shaw and others have demonstrated that no imperial power successfully dominated the tribal chieftains of these mountains, no matter how much the Assyrians, the Persians, the Seleucids, or the Romans claimed to have done so.[20] The tyrants of Rough Cilicia viewed their right to engage in banditry as a code of honor, a code that regarded collaboration with any outside power as a sign of lost face and illegitimacy. Inaccessible, hostile, and outcast, the Cilician tyrants loomed over and peered down on the Mediterranean *oikumene* of Flat Cilicia (Cilicia Pedia), plundering its coastal cities and farmlands but otherwise holding aloof from its social and economic order. Accordingly, the degree to which any of these elements involved themselves in the affairs of the Cilician pirate bases on the western coast becomes difficult to assess.

Some sort of interaction clearly occurred between the Cilician pirates settled on the shore and bandit tribes of the mountainous hinterland, regardless of how little we are able to identify this at present. Appian, for example, alludes to the existence of "Mountain Cilicians" (οἱ ὄρειοι Κίλικες) who supported the pirates against Pompey.[21] He and other sources refer repeatedly to the leaders of the Cilician pirates as tyrants (τύραννοι), the Greek term traditionally used to identify the bandit chieftains of the interior, and he adds that Pompey led many such tyrants in his triumph in 62 B.C.E. (App. *Mith.* 117). The matter remains complicated, however. Tryphon appears to have selected the remote western coastal stretches of Cilicia Tracheia as his headquarters precisely because they were inaccessible from traditional sources of power in Seleucid Cilicia. The largest concentrations of Seleucid settlements lay in eastern Rough Cilicia, for example, the colony Seleucia on the Calycadnus River, and the cities of Soli, Tarsus, Mopsuestia, and Adana in neighboring Cilicia Pedia. This is undoubtedly the region where the Seleucids recruited the Cilician troops so often mentioned in this period—from the cities of eastern Cilicia and to some degree from the independent mountain peoples

as colonists in Cilicia Pedia and elsewhere.[19] With that, Mediterranean piracy subsided for a generation, or until Pompey's son, Sex. Pompey, renewed the pirate wars in his rivalry with the triumvirs, Antony, Octavian, and Lepidus. But that is a another story. With Pompey's settlement of the Cilician pirates in 67 B.C.E., their menace to the Mediterranean world came to an end.

UNLIKELIHOOD OF A CILICIAN ORIGIN

While the impact of the Cilician pirates on Mediterranean affairs seems clear, their points of origin are less so.

---

[19] At Pompeiopolis and elsewhere in eastern Cilicia, at Dyme in Achaea, and apparently even in Tarentum. For sources and discussion, see Magie (1950: 1180 n. 43); Ormerod (1987: 240–41).

[20] Bibliography for Cilician banditry: Shaw (1984: 3–52; 1990: 199–233); Desideri (1991: 299–304); Hopwood (1983: 173–88; 1986: 343–56; 1989: 191–92; 1990: 171–87; 1991: 305–9); Lewin (1991: 167–84); Russell (1991: 283–97); Syme (1986: 159–64).

[21] Florus 1.41.5 notes a similar connection.

that loomed directly behind (see Launey 1949: 476–80, 586; Bar-Kochva 1976: 49, 51–52; Russell 1991: 283–85). More than one Seleucid pretender—Alexander Balas in 147 B.C.E., Demetrius II in 145, Seleucus VI in 95, a son of Antiochus X, possibly, in 75 B.C.E., and Philip I in 67/66 B.C.E.—resided in eastern Cilicia after being expelled from Syria, and others continued to wage war in the region throughout the era of the pirates.[22] The distinction between the settlements and hinterland peoples of eastern Cilicia and the Cilician pirate bases in western Cilicia may be significant, therefore. Even as the pirates flourished from 139 to 67 B.C.E., Seleucid pretenders dominated and resided in the east. Collusion between these two elements (especially maritime elements) is likely, but equally so the risk of direct confrontation. Strabo indicates that the province's chief city, Seleucia on the Calycadnus, one of the closest in proximity to the pirate bases, refrained from the "manners" (τρόπος) of its neighbors in Cilicia and Pamphylia.[23] This suggests that the pirates exerted little influence, coercive or otherwise, on its inhabitants. Although the pirates undoubtedly recruited manpower from the harbor towns of eastern Cilicia, quite possibly the cape of Anemurium marked the extent of their sway in this direction, much as it did the limits of Seleucid naval authority in the west.

The western coast of Rough Cilicia was narrower (hemmed in closely by mountains with few passes), more remote, and far less populated.[24] While it probably harbored a dozen small urban settlements at this time,[25] several, including Hamaxia, Coracesium, Laertes, and Charadrus, were little more than fortified waystations garrisoned by Ptolemaic and Seleucid mercenaries to provide safe havens for coasting traffic and to exploit the mountainous region's natural abundance of timber and naval supplies.[26] Neither can it be shown that the Cilician tyrants of the interior exerted influence over these tiny harbors, in most cases inaccessible from the mountains.

Fig. 6. Cn. Pompeius Magnus. Drawing by Peter Butler.

The intense degree to which the ancient sources refer to the pirates as *Kilikes,* and to their chieftains as *tyrants,* seems to imply that the pirate commanders drew on the mountain peoples of the Taurus hinterland for manpower, or that the mountain chieftains themselves somehow dominated the pirate bands. Many scholars point to a relationship between the two.[27] In this regard one can correctly point to analogous relationships between coastal pirates and moun-

[22] Jos. *AJ* 13.112, 145, 368; Just. 40.12.3; cp. Cic. *Verr.* 2.4.27; Diod. 40.1a. For campaigns in Cilicia in 116, see Pomp. Trog. *Prol.* 39; Liv. *Per.* 62; Just. 39.2.7–10; App. *Syr.* 69; cf. Bevan (1966: 2.220, 259, 263).

[23] 14.5.4 (670)—referring undoubtedly to his immediately preceding discussion of the part played by the inhabitants of both regions in piracy: 14.3.2 (664); 14.5.2 (668). Strabo adds, 14.5.2 (669), that during Tigranes' invasion of Cilicia in 83, the King of Armenia left the sea to the Cilicians, thus indicating that he did not meddle in Cilicia Tracheia (Marasco 1987a: 131). For the limits set on Seleucid naval authority by the treaty of Apamea (the promontories of the Calycadnus), App. *Syr.* 39.

[24] Rightly noted by Launey (1949: 476); cf. Hopwood (1991: 305–9).

[25] In Strabo's time only Selinus and Arsinoê qualified as cities: Strabo 14.5.3 (669). Syedra is conspicuously absent.

[26] See Strabo 14.5.2–3 (668–9) for Hamaxia, "a *katoikia* on a hill with a *huphormon* where shipbuilding timber is brought down." He describes Coracesium and Laertes as *phrouria* and Charadrus as an *eruma.* Cf. Bagnall (1976: 114–16); Bommelaer (1987: 5–6); Jones and Habicht (1989: 334–35).

[27] Ormerod (1922: 36–41; 1987: 205); Marasco (1987b: 129); Benabou (1985: 66); Garlan (1974: 2); Dell (1967: 357).

tain bandits in regions such as Illyria, Aetolia, and Crete. Pierre Brulé (1978: 117–84) has convincingly portrayed the emergence of Cretan piracy in the Hellenistic era as a downward and outward progression of bandit populations from secure mountain fastnesses to neighboring coastal harbors, and then to piracy. Scholars such as Marcel Benabou and Yvon Garlan argue for a general fluidity between mountain bandits and pirate elements throughout the Mediterranean (see note 27). However much the terminology employed by the ancient sources for the Cilician pirates and their chiefs seem to confirm such a pattern, these models appear inappropriate to Cilicia. Evidence to demonstrate a population movement from the Taurus hinterland to the remote western shore of Cilicia Tracheia is altogether lacking. Indeed, the more natural lines of communication between mountain tribes and coastal elements flowed eastwardly, toward Seleucia, following the natural decline of the Calycadnus River.[28] Even then, the bandit tribes of the Rough Cilician hinterland and the maritime inhabitants of its coastal cities remained socially and culturally distinct.[29] A number of sources point to the existence of a smoldering state of resentment between the Cilician mountain and coastal populations that endured to the end of the Roman imperial era.[30] In western Rough Cilicia the jagged ridge of the Taurus formed a sharp barrier between the tribes of the interior and the harbor settlements along the narrow coastal strip, allowing limited means of access between the two.[31] It seems unlikely, therefore, that Tryphon or his pirate successors drew to any significant degree on Cilician bandit tribesmen for manpower in their naval operations, however much the two elements coexisted and cooperated.[32]

Ormerod (1922: 51) seems to have sensed this disjunction between Cilician mountain and shore when he wrote, "in the days when piracy had its headquarters in Cilicia Tracheia, the name Cilician was largely applied to all pirates, whatever their origin, much as 'Algerian' frequently included at a later date all Mediterranean corsairs who were not Christian." While somewhat misconstrued, his point remains well-taken. Recent scholarship has demonstrated that by the eighteenth century the majority of the "Algerian," or Barbary pirates were not only Christian, but European.[33] By the same token, the pirates of Cilicia may have originated far from the mountainous hinterlands of the Taurus. To understand this, we must probe beneath the peculiar character of Mediterranean maritime society. This is where parallels from the early modern era have something to offer.

MARITIME CULTURE AS A PROVING GROUND FOR PIRACY

One of the difficulties for a mountain-bandit origin for piracy is the certain fact that the Cilician pirates, as all later pirates, were skilled seamen, in fact, the most skilled seamen of their times (Rediker 1987: 264). "Landlubbers" such as mountain bandits traditionally lack the essential skills and familiarity with the sealanes that piracy requires.[34] In addition, pirates tended to be well-financed—at the very least they possessed small sleek warships, something that mountain bandits would first have to acquire, as well as a preexisting network of commercial contacts willing to purchase stolen pirate goods.[35] As we shall see, the ancient

[28] Strabo 14.5.6 (671), for example, includes his discussion of Cilician banditry "both on land and on sea" in connection with this eastern watershed.

[29] By the very manner that Appian refers to the mountaineers as *oreioi Kilikes,* he differentiates between these peoples and the pirates on the shore.

[30] As late as 52 C.E., marauding mountain bands attacked the coastal cities and were resisted specifically by *mercatores* and *navicularii* (Tac. *Ann.* 12.55; cf. Dio 55.28.3; Tac. *Ann.* 6.41). Similar tensions emerged in the fourth century C.E. (Amm. Marc. 14.2.1–20; Lewin 1991: 171–77; Shaw 1990: 230–31).

[31] See Ormerod (1921: 49) for the difficulties posed by P. Servilius Vatia's ascent into Isauria in 75 B.C.E. Even today there is no direct paved road from Konya (Iconium) in the interior to Alanya (Coracesium) on the shore.

[32] The mountain realms possibly provided places of refuge for the pirates when they came under assault by sea (as indicated by Florus 1.41.5–6), or perhaps the bandit leaders of the mountains participated in the slave trade of the pirates by conducting raids into the interior regions of Anatolia and by exchanging these with the pirates for goods from abroad.

[33] Mainly displaced French and English sailors (Thomson 1994: 44, citing Earle 1970: 30–31).

[34] Bandit chiefs of Cretan aristocratic society probably gained skilled naval manpower by recruiting sailors already resident in neighboring coastal settlements at the time of their synoicism. This would conform well with Brulé's thesis regarding the expanding size of the underclasses in the Cretan *damoi* as well as with the absence of any expressed pirate chieftains in Crete (Brulé 1978: 173–82).

[35] Rightly noted by Brulé (1978: 161, 183).

sources report that Cilician piracy emerged from a broad spectrum of Mediterranean maritime elements, that the unique qualities of western Cilicia induced pirates to settle there, and that the unparalleled circumstances of the late Hellenistic era caused this piracy to escalate beyond the proportions of any historical antecedent.

The emergence of "pirate commonwealths" in the early modern era offers a suitable parallel to the rise of Cilician piracy (Thomson 1994: 22–26, 43–54, 69–76, 105–18). While piracy localized and otherwise plagued the European "Great Powers" throughout this era, a series of related developments caused piracy to erupt to unheard proportions between 1690–1750, when tens of thousands of pirates chose to "declare war on all mankind." The problem emerged with a sustained population of irregular sea warriors, the consequence of an increasing reliance on privateers by the colonial powers England, France, Holland, and Spain, as well as with the harsh social and economic conditions that drove destitute young men to service aboard merchant men, warships, and privateering vessels in the first place. Once at sea, harsh discipline and equally severe living conditions frequently culminated in mutiny and desertion. One factor seems to have compounded the other.[36] In the brief period cited above, each of the Great Powers repeatedly initiated naval operations by recruiting privateers to supplement their military capacities; however, at the close of each conflict these same powers as readily demobilized privateering forces and expected them to return to peaceful lifestyles. Trained as privateers, it was simpler and far more profitable for these elements to continue their activities by shifting over to piracy, especially in the English colonies in America, where authority was lax and where the tendency prevailed for the same people who financed legal privateering ventures during wartime to continue to fund active piracy during peacetime. The governors and merchant communities of the English colonies notoriously tended to look the other way when elements of this maritime flotsam and jetsam turned to piracy, time and again offering refuge to pirate outlaws in exchange for shares of booty or for the opportunity to purchase expensive, otherwise scarce luxuries for resale in the colonies. Typically, the only way for the Great Powers to curb piracy was by offering blanket amnesties that allowed pirates to keep their captured goods so long as they agreed to abandon life "on the account." However, the European powers mostly offered these amnesties at times of renewed conflict, when their real object was to recruit privateers.

This revolving pattern of renewed conflict and of recruitment of privateers followed by mass demobilizations, outright piracy, and connivance of colonial officials and communities in the commerce of piracy, resulted in the emergence of a sustained pool of privateersmen, mutineers, and deserters, many of whom were armed and dangerous, equipped with sleek warships, potentially well-financed, yet, cut adrift from prevailing elements of society. As Thomson notes (1994: 117), large numbers of deep-sea pirates came to reject "any ties to their home state and gave their allegiance to pirate 'commonwealths,' with their radical democratic, even anarchical, mode of governance." Strange pirate confederacies, whose populations were frequently interrelated, emerged at places such as Hispaniola, Jamaica, Tortuga, Madagascar, the Bahamas, and the Guinea coast of Africa.[37] Contemporary estimates of the pirate population of this period placed the number between one and two thousand at any one time, and Rediker concludes that in all some 4,500 to 5,500 men went "on the account."[38] In a short span of time the unique circumstances of early modern European naval warfare had culminated in an international piracy of unprecedented proportions.

It is possible to evaluate the rise of the Cilician pirates in a similar light. While the distinction between privateers and pirates is not clearly recognizable in the ancient experience, there is no doubt that the Hellenistic kings developed a long standing practice of recruiting pirates to fill out their navies.[39] Apart from the Rhodian republic and the Ptolemies (before 256 B.C.E.), most Hellenistic realms lacked large standing navies, relying heavily in times of war upon naval

[36] Indeed, one of the attractions of privateering was the prospect of better treatment, since discipline on privateers was lax and incentives for violence greater because the only profits sailors stood to gain were portions of booty seized through naval combat.

[37] Many of the pirate elements driven from Jamaica and Tortuga moved to Madagascar; when driven from Madagascar, they moved to the Bahamas, and when driven from the Bahamas some moved back to Madagascar, and others to the Guinea coast. Indeed, pirate voyages between the Carribean or the ports of the American colonies and Madagascar were so commonplace that they came to be known as the "Pirate Round." For a graph of interrelationships among pirates, see Rediker (1987: 268).

[38] Rediker (1987: 256), who adds that the pirates' chief military enemy, the Royal Navy, employed an average of only 13,000 men in C.E. 1690–1750.

[39] See Launey (1949: 34–35). For the Seleucid fleet and its heavy reliance on pirates see Bickerman (1938: 98–100, 100 n. 9). In accordance with the Treaty of Apamea, the Seleucid fleet was reduced to ten warships by 162 (Polyb. 21.42.14 =

requisitions from maritime subject states and allied cities.[40] What little is known about the Seleucid navy suggests that Diodotus Tryphon assembled his motley forces from the available warships of the Seleucid maritime cities and interested neighbors. Having created the impregnable bases in the remote western corner of Rough Cilicia, Tryphon left these elements positioned to continue on their own, in an area remote from any formal naval supervision, yet straddling the important sealanes between Egypt and the Aegean. His surviving forces consisted of naval veterans long accustomed to service under Hellenistic dynasts and hence skilled and equipped to adapt to independent piracy.[41] Aiding in this development was the assistance these pirates received from Seleucid rivals—the Rhodians, the Attalids, the Ptolemies, and the Romans—who all turned a blind eye toward them so long as they focused their assaults on the commerce, countryside, and cities of the rival Seleucid realm. But the decision of neighboring cities such as Side, Attaleia, and Phaselis to open their harbors to the pirates proved equally detrimental since it enabled the pirates to exploit sales of captured booty to outfit their ships with the necessary men and material to continue their depredations elsewhere.[42] A similar relationship existed between the pirates and the Roman and Italian merchants newly established at the duty-free *emporium* of Delos (Strabo 14.5.2 [669]; Rauh 1993: 41–68). Finally, the behavioral pattern of the Cilician pirates—serving Tryphon in 145–139 B.C.E., then turning to independent piracy; aligning with Mithradates VI in 88–84

B.C.E., then returning to independent piracy; and aligning with Mithradates once again in 75–67 B.C.E.—parallels the ebb and flow of early modern privateering and piracy. In short, the same ingredients for sustained piracy in the early modern era were visible in Cilicia—ingredients that enabled Cilician piracy to attain the unprecedented proportions that distinguished it from its Illyrian, Aetolian, and Cretan antecedents.

PIRATE MENTALITY

The mentality of early modern European piracy offers another important comparison with the Cilicians. Like early modern pirate commonwealths, the Cilician pirates appear to have formed a unique social order (see Rediker 1987: 254–87; Rankin 1969: 22–41; Sherry 1986: 67–148). Rediker argues that piracy in the eighteenth century represented "crime" on a massive scale. "It was a way of life voluntarily chosen, for the most part, by large numbers of men who directly challenged the ways of the society from which they excepted themselves."[43] Through fair, egalitarian treatment and just behavior within pirate bands and active efforts at cooperation externally between bands, pirates formed their own unique social order, with a sense of maritime ethos and "consciousness of kind."

Many standard generalizations about Anglo-American piracy hold significance for the Cilicians. For example, the emergence of Rough Cilicia as an independent pirate com-

---

Liv. 38.38.3; Polyb. 31.2.9–14, and 8.4–8; App. *Syr.* 46). For the reliance of the Ptolemies on pirates and Cretan mercenaries, see Paus. 1.7.3; Launey (1949: 199, 248–86, 1068–72); Brulé (1978: 162–63). After 256 B.C.E., the Ptolemaic navy declined from a high of perhaps 400 decked warships to the thirty that supported the army at the Battle of Raphia in 218 (Athen. 5. 203 d; App. *Proem.* 10; Polyb. 5.68; Préaux (1939: 39); Van 'T Dack and Hauben (1987: 60–93, esp. 66–67). Heavy Ptolemaic reliance on "freebooters"—note, for example, the movement in the Levant of the fleets of Ptolemy IX Lathyrus c. 116–80 B.C.E., as described by Stieglitz (this volume)—may help to explain the king's reluctance to support Lucullus against the pirates in 86–85 (App. *Mith.* 23; Plut. *Luc.* 2.5–6; Cic. *Acad.* 2.11, 61).

[40] For the heavy reliance of the Seleucid navy on the maritime cities of Phoenicia and Pamphylia, see Bickerman (1938: 100); Bevan (1966: 236). The Ptolemies amassed their navy through a combination of intensive naval construction, alliances, and subjection of traditional eastern Mediterranean naval elements (Theoc. 17.86–92; Van 'T Dack and Hauben 1978: 72). In any event, they relied extensively on Greek manpower to run their fleets (Van 'T Dack and Hauben 1987: 79).

[41] Lewin (1991: 168), correctly emphasizes the Hellenistic power vacuum within which the Cilician pirates emerged; cf. Liebmann-Frankfort (1969: 188). In essence, Tryphon's installation of naval forces at Coracesium violated the terms of the Treaty of Apamea, but by 139 B.C.E. this hardly mattered and, as an renegade commander of mercenary pirate bands, he would hardly have cared.

[42] Side and Phaselis had long skirted the boundaries of Greek and Near Eastern authority, and in this instance formed open alliances with the pirates (Cic. *De Leg. Agr.* 1.5, 2.50; *Verr.* 2.4.21; Strabo 14.3.2 (664), 14.5.7 (671); Alciphr. 1.8).

[43] Rediker (1987: 255). Cf. Thomson (1994: 46): "Piracy was not simply or always an economic crime—the theft of private property. It was also a political act—a protest against the obvious use of state institutions to defend property and discipline labor."

monwealth. As Rediker notes (1987: 257–58), "as bases sea robbers sought and usually found bases near major trading routes, as distant as possible from the powers of the state. ... In fact, some authorities feared that pirates might set up a sort of commonwealth in uninhabited regions, since no power in those parts of the world could have been able to dispute with them." Frank Sherry insists (1986: 90–94) that this was particularly evident for the pirate commonwealths that emerged at Madagascar.

> Another element that made Madagascar especially attractive to pirates was the fact that the native population was usually friendly, if not forced to conform to European laws or customs. But by far the most important factor was its status as a political orphan. No European nation owned it. Despite hollow claims and pitiful attempts to colonize the island, there was no legitimate western presence on Madagascar. Furthermore, none of the numerous squabbling local tribes dominated more than a few square miles of the huge island. Madagascar was unclaimed territory: pleasant, impregnable, and—above all—lawless ... Because the Madagascar pirates shared similar economic interests, similar personal backgrounds as authority-hating ordinary seamen, and a common geographic center in Madagascar, they began to experience a kind of "gravitational force" that, within a brief period, pulled them into a rough outlaw confederacy—out of which, many thought, an authentic state might emerge.

As we have seen, Rough Cilicia stands at precisely such a juncture, situated as it was on the fringe of Seleucid, Ptolemaic, and Attalid empires, cut off from its hinterland by giant mountains, and ruled in tribal fashion by petty tyrant chieftains who appear to have cooperated with the pirates so long as they were otherwise left alone. As the pirates gradually expanded their range of operations, they selected similarly hidden locales, seizing control of promontories, desert islands, and roadsteads along crucial Mediterranean shipping lanes. By the end of the second century B.C.E. they converted these into fortified harbors (ναύσταθμα πειρατικὰ) and signal stations (φρυκτώρια), and extended their marauding capacity throughout the seas (Plut. *Pomp.* 24.3; App. *Mith.* 92). Instead of intermittent hit-and-run piratical raids on merchantmen, by the 70s B.C.E., the Cilician pirates had developed the capacity to shut down sea lanes altogether, even during the quiet winter months.

Rediker (1987: 260) and Sherry (1986: 111–12) note that owing to the lucrative nature of piracy, pirates represented an elite breed of seamen, recruited from the best crews of merchantships, privateers, and warfleets. Likewise, Plutarch informs us (*Pomp.* 24.3) that "the fleets which put in at the Cilician pirate bases were admirably equipped for their own work with fine crews, expert pilots, and light fast ships," and the sources generally report that the pirates drew their manpower from the socially displaced elements of neighboring maritime regions, or as Appian notes (*Mith.* 92), "sailors from Cilicia, Syria, Cyprus, Pamphylia and Pontus and those of almost all the eastern nations, who on account of the severity and the length of the Mithradatic War, preferred to do wrong rather than to suffer it, and for this purpose chose the sea instead of the land." The likelihood that most of the pirates who called themselves Cilicians and are referred to as such by the sources were not in fact from Cilicia proper seems very real, therefore. Cilicia was their chief military base; it was not necessarily their place of origin (cf. Marasco 1987a: 134).

According to Rediker (1987: 267), pirates constructed their society in defiant contradistinction to the ways of the world they left behind. Though viewed as outcasts and criminals by established orders of society, they themselves acted as "revolutionary traditionalists," searching for a world in which men were justly dealt with, and the rich and the oppressors avenged. As one of their most eloquent spokesmen, Captain Charles Bellamy, exclaimed while berating the captain and crew of a captured merchantman:

> Damn ye, you are a sneaking puppy, and so are all those who will submit to be governed by Laws which rich men have made for their own security, for the cowardly whelps have not the courage otherwise to defend what they get by their knavery. But damn ye altogether. Damn them for a pack of crazy rascals, and you, who serve them, for a parcel of hen-hearted numbskulls. They villify us, the scoundrels do, when there is only this difference: they rob the poor under the cover of Law, forsooth, and we plunder the rich under the protection of our own courage. Had you not better make one of us, than sneak after the arses of those villains for Employment?[44]

In the same manner the ancient sources speak in stern moral tone about the military and social oppression that drove the peoples of the eastern Mediterranean into piracy.

---

[44] [Capt. C. Johnson] (1724: 482). Or, as a captured pirate chief supposedly replied to Alexander the Great when ordered to defend his behavior (Aug. *Civ. Dei* 4.4; cf. 6.6), "I do it for the same reason that you conquer the known world. But when I go plundering with a small ship, I am called a pirate. You do the same thing with a great fleet and are proclaimed *imperator!*"

Having lost both livelihood and country by reason of war and having fallen into extreme destitution, the pirates harvested the sea instead of the land. (App. Mith. 97)

The disturbed condition brought about in Asia by the Mithradatic Wars engendered a spirit of daring in these abandoned and desperate robbers, who, under the cover of the disturbances of a foreign war and the hatred of a foreign prince, ranged over the seas with impunity. (Flor. 1.41.2)

Piracy had always existed in certain locals, but at this time, ever since war had been carried on continuously in many different places at once, and many cities had been overthrown, sentences hung over the heads of all the fugitives. Since there was no freedom from fear for anyone anywhere, large numbers took to plundering... (20.4) For while the Romans were occupied with their opponents, the pirates made great headway, sailing about to many quarters, and adding to their band all of like condition, until a small number of them, in the manner of allies, were able to assist many others. (Dio 36.20.1)

Plutarch (*Sull.* 25) comments specifically on the harsh conditions prevailing in the province of Asia in the wake of Pontic and Roman reprisals during the Mithradatic War, and he concludes that "some men of wealth and of good family and of exceptional intelligence began to join the pirate fleets and to share in their enterprises, regarding piracy as a profession in which honor could be attained and ambition satisfied" (*Pomp.* 24).

These descriptions suggest, at least potentially, that the Cilician pirates forged an identity for themselves based on some conception of social justice, retaliation against provincial abuse, resistance to domination by external imperial powers (by this time focusing principally on the Roman Republic), and perhaps both ethnic and class liberation. What began as a military component of a Seleucid dynastic dispute gradually evolved into a full-scale maritime resistance movement.

In place of the harsh realities of established maritime society, Anglo-American pirates of the eighteenth century C.E. governed themselves according to a strict code of egalitarianism and social brotherhood, or as Rankin describes it, "a practice of democracy that bordered on anarchy" (Rankin 1969: 28; Rediker 1987: 261–67; Sherry 1986: 85–100). Pirate crews elected their captains and expected them to act as bold leaders in combat and fair administrators of justice. Crews formed themselves with written articles of agreement and cemented the loyalty of all new members by swearing oaths on bibles or axes. Discipline in work and in battle was tightly regulated; booty was distributed according to a premodern notion of maritime shares; and some portions of the booty were set aside as a common fund for the needs of the permanently disabled.[45] As Sherry asserts:[46]

> In the late seventeenth and early eighteenth centuries there was only one true democracy on earth: the pirate brotherhood forged in Madagascar. Incongruous as it might appear, the cutthroats who brutalized captives and who scoffed at the rules of society, were passionately democratic. They had a high regard for individual rights—and a burning hatred for the tyranny that had oppressed them in their days of "honest service." Unlike privateer crews, who were still only hired hands despite the fact that they received fair shares of their ship's plunder, pirates regarded themselves as self-employed, collective owners of their own ships. They believed that since the crew of a pirate ship had acquired their vessel by their common effort, all should participate equally in making decisions aboard her. For this reason pirates evolved a system that called for virtually all matters regarding life aboard their ship—whether to fight, where and when to anchor, division of spoils, even courses to be followed—to be subjected to a referendum, with each man, regardless of his rank, race, religion, or previous employment, entitled to an equal vote in the decision, as well as an equal right to voice his opinion. Only during battle did the pirates abandon this referendum system.

Available evidence for the internal dealings of Cilician pirate bands suggests the existence of similar lines of community and discipline. That members of pirate bands dealt fairly with one another, even to the extent of codifying their behavior is certain: Plato had Socrates assert that like a city or an army, "bandits, and thieves and all other groups of people joined together for bad intentions could hardly succeed if they began committing injustices against one another" (*Rep.* 1.351 C). In the *De Officiis* (2.40), Cicero wrote, undoubtedly with contemporary examples of piracy and banditry in mind:

---

[45] Rediker (1987: 261–67). Rankin (1969: 37) observes that pirates exercised greater cruelty in maintaining discipline among themselves than in their treatment of prisoners. One of their constant anxieties was that a member of their company might desert and provide damaging evidence to the authorities.

[46] Sherry (1986: 122). As an example, Sherry adds that the crew of one particular pirate ship elected thirteen captains during a cruise of only a few months.

The importance of justice is so great that not even those who live on criminal earnings could survive without some canons of justice among themselves. If, for example, one member of a gang of robbers were to steal from another, he would not even be considered fit to be a member of society such as that, and if the archipirata could not give the others a fair share of the loot, he would be abandoned or even killed by his comrades. Hence the rule "honor among thieves" which they are all obliged to observe.

St. Augustine (*Civ. Dei* 4.4 and 6), may likewise have envisioned the Cilician pirates when he asserted,

Are not bands of robbers themselves like small realms? Are they not groups of men commanded by a chief, drawn together by a social contract or by conventions that determine their distribution of booty?

With respect to care of the Cilician pirates for their disabled and dependents, Plutarch calls attention to the numerous women and children, and "the large disabled crowd" that the pirates of Coracesium concealed in scattered mountain fortresses and citadels when Pompey assaulted the region in 67 B.C.E. (*Pomp.* 28.1; cf. Sen. *Contr.* 1.6). The internal discipline of the Cilicians is possibly revealed by the cultivation of the religious cult of Mithras by the pirate chief Zenicetes at the eternal fires above Olympus. The ascetic character of this religion, calling the initiates to extreme levels of self-discipline in their commitment to the cause of righteous order of the universe, not only made it popular among the pirates, but caused it to appeal as well to the Roman soldiers who defeated them and who conveyed the cult to Rome.[47]

As compassionate and just as Anglo-American pirates of the eighteenth century were in their treatment of their own community, they behaved harshly and vengefully toward the oppressive elements of established society that hunted them down. As Rediker notes (1987: 273), "to a pirate, vengeance was justice. Hence pirate justice was extremely violent, in part to inspire fear in the hearts of those elements responsible for the oppression by engaging in a system of reciprocal terror." To punctuate this sentiment, pirates frequently christened their ships with names conjuring messages of vengeance and resistence—*Vengeance, Holy Vengeance, Black Revenge, Revenge's Revenge, Queen Anne's Revenge, New York's Revenge, New York Revenge's Revenge, Defiance,* and *Liberty*.[48] "The black flag itself," observes Sherry (1986: 136), "with its skull and crossbones, spoke of hatred and retribution." To confront the general ban imposed by authorities on all sea outlaws (and its certainty of execution), pirate crews supported and protected one another by making threats and by engaging in acts of vengeance when fellow pirates were captured or executed.

The same is certainly true of the Cilician pirates who at their peak in the 70s B.C.E. engaged in successive waves of terrorist-styled kidnappings of prominent Roman political and social figures, striking fear into the hearts of the Roman elite. By the late 70s pirate assaults and the names of pirate captains were feared throughout the west from Spain to Italy. In 73 B.C.E., for example, the pirate chieftain, Heracleo, terrorized the inhabitants of Syracuse, apparently because the provincial governor of the time, Q. Verres, had taken pirate money toward the release a fellow *archipirata* and had failed to deliver.[49] While criticizing Verres for failing to display this prisoner publicly, Cicero demonstrates not only the dread these pirates provoked in maritime communities but the satisfaction people derived from the sight of their executions:[50]

[47] Plut. *Pomp.* 24.5. Zenicetes possibly exploited this cult to gain magical authority over his followers. Rather than surrender in 76 B.C.E., he set himself and his entire household ablaze in his castle beneath the fires (Strabo 14.5.7 [671]). See below, note 51, for Blackbeard's similar use of fire to inspire wonder and dread.

[48] Rankin (1969: 28); Sherry (1986: 138). It should be noted that British men-of-war also bore names such as *Vengeance* and *Defiance*. Other pirate ships carried names intended to ridicule the religious values of honest society—*Prophet Daniel, Happy Delivery, Most Holy Trinity, Blessings, Mayflower, Childhood, Amity, Merry Christmas, Morning Star, Peace, Black Angel, Charming Mary*. Still others—*Jolly Shark, Black Joke, Sudden Death*—employed lugubrious gallows' humor (Sherry 1986: 138).

[49] Cic. *Verr.* 2.5.63–79, 86–100. Cicero accuses Verres of having taken a bribe from the pirates to spare the life of the *archipirata* (2.5.64, 73, 75, 79, 106, 136) and additional bribes from sailors seeking to avoid naval duty, thus leaving the province ill prepared against pirate reprisals. Heracleo's pirate band attacked shortly thereafter. Heracleo's little display in the Syracusan harbor was apparently followed up by a thorough assault by the pirate chief Pyrganio, who was eventually driven off, though not eliminated, by L. Metellus: Oros. 6.3.6; Liv. *Per.* 98. Cf. Marasco (1987a: 135), who suggests that Roman authorities imprisoned pirate chiefs to exchange them for captured notables.

[50] Cic. *Verr.* 2.5.65–67. For Verres' execution of the ordinary pirates from this ship see 2.5.71.

The homines maritimi of Syracuse, who had often heard and often trembled at the name of this archipirata, longed to feast their eyes and satisfy their souls with the spectacle of his torture and execution, yet no one was allowed to see him. P. Servilius (Isauricus) captured more pirate chiefs alive than all his predecessors together, and was anyone forbidden to enjoy the exhibition of these prisoners? Far from it. Wherever Servilius journeyed, he provided the public with the delightful sight of its captured enemies in chains. Crowds gathering to see the spectacle came from every quarter to greet him, not only from the towns through which the prisoners passed, but from neighboring towns as well.

In essence, the Anglo-American and Cilician pirates attempted to turn the tables on imperial authorities, making them the victims and the pirates themselves the arbiters of justice. After seizing merchant vessels, Anglo-American pirates liked to try the ships' captains with testimony elicited from their crews. Harsh captains were humiliated, tortured, and/or executed; yet fair honest captains were often rewarded. These incidences "reveal how pirates attempted to intervene against—and modify—the standard brutalities that marked the social relations of production in merchant shipping" (Rediker 1987: 273). In this regard a strange anecdote about the visit of a number of ancient pirate chiefs (conplures praedonum duces) in warships to the seaside villa of the popular Roman general, P. Scipio Aemilianus, at Liternum, points to similar notions of piratical justice and fair play. "For they shouted to him from outside that they had not come to plunder his household or seize his person, but simply to gaze upon his countenance, to shake his hand, and to honor the man they so universally admired as a divine gift to humanity" (Val. Max. 2.10.2).

Aristocrats, generals, and senators were not the only persons victimized by pirate justice. As Sherry observes (1986: 137), "any prisoner who seemed to represent authority might find himself singled out for brutal treatment." The Cilician pirates, according to Plutarch, derived similar satisfaction from the mockery of ordinary Roman citizens:

But the way in which they treated their prisoners was the most outrageous thing of all. If a prisoner cried out that he was a Roman and gave his name, they would pretend to be absolutely terrified; the pirates would smite their thighs and hands and fall down at his feet begging him to forgive them. The prisoner, seeing them so humbled and hearing their entreaties, would believe that they meant what they said. They would dress him in Roman boots and a Roman toga in order, they said, that there should be no mistake about his identity in the future. And so they would play with him for a time, getting all the amusement possible out of him until, in the end, they would let down a ship's ladder when they were far out to sea and tell him that he was quite free to go, wishing him a pleasant journey. If he resisted, then they threw him overboard and drowned him. (Pomp. 24.7; cf. Cic. Verr. 2.5.147)

In this manner, explains Sherry (1986: 141), "the pirates reduced the institutions of the society they warred with to mere caricatures. By doing so they also diminished the lingering fears that they, as rebels against—but products of—that society, still bore in their hearts. Like all rebels, in order to free themselves of the past they had to laugh at it."

Cilician and early modern pirates possessed numerous additional traits in common, for example, their dress and manner. Modern bandits and pirates flaunted their escape from the norms of established society by wearing outlandish, colorful clothing.[51] Pirate chiefs gloried in the notoriety of their outrageous names and titles—*Blackbeard, Gentleman Harry, Calico Jack Rackham, Long John Avery, Black Bart (Bartholomew) Roberts, Montbars the Exterminator, Roche Brasiliano, Captain Flogger,* and *Half Bottom*[52]—and frequently asserted pretensions of imperial grandeur. The ever articulate Captain Charles Bellamy boasted, "I am a free prince and I have as much authority to make war on the whole world as he who has a hundred sail of ships at sea and an army of one hundred thousand men in the field" ([Johnson] 1724: 482). John Plantain, who dominated the pirate enclaves of Madagascar in 1720, liked to refer to himself as "The King of Ranter Bay." Senior mem-

---

[51] On the day of his last sea battle in 1722, Captain Black Bart (Bartholomew) Roberts donned "a rich crimson damask waistcoat and breeches, a red feather in his hat, a gold chain round his neck, with a diamond cross hanging to it, a sword in his hand and two pair of pistols, hanging at the end of a silk sling, flung over his shoulders" ([Johnson] 1724: 211). Blackbeard (alias Edward Teach) used the appearance of his enormous, matted, sable-colored beard to inspire terror. Reportedly, he would twist his beard into "small tails" decorated with tiny ribbons. In time of action, he would stick "lighted matches" ("slowmatch," a length of slow burning fuse) under his tricornered hat to create a swirl of smoke around his head, lending him the appearance of "a Fury from Hell" ([Johnson] 1724: 57).

[52] The last name being the result of a physical condition caused by a cannon ball passing too near the seat of his pants.

bers of Black Bart Roberts's crew took to calling themselves "The House Of Lords" and strolled about the deck addressing each other as "Your Lordship" ([Johnson] 1724: 166–67, 194, 230; Sherry 1986: 90, 138, 293, 328, 347–48).

The Cilician pirates claimed similar pretentions and dressed equally as notoriously. Plautus liked to categorize sailors generally by their broad brimmed, rust colored hats, their patches over one eye, and their short rust colored cloaks. "That's the maritime shade—be tight, be trim."[53] According to Plutarch (*Pomp.* 24.3), the Cilicians flaunted their rebellion against the established orders by ornamenting their ships with gilded sails, purple awnings, and silvered oars. Dio observes (36.21.1) that they sailed in large fleets commanded by generals (*strategoi*), and so acquired a great reputation. And Appian asserts (*Mith.* 92) that the Cilician pirate chiefs, "being elated by their gains and having given up all thought of changing their mode of life, now likened themselves to kings (*basileis*) and tyrants *(tyrannoi),* and thought that if they should all unite they would be invincible." The names of several *archipiratae*—Agamemnon,[54] Isodorus (Florus 3.6; Plut. *Luc.* 12.2), Nico (Cic. *Verr.* 2.5.77–79), Zenicetes (Strabo 14.5.7 [671]), Mena and Menecrates (Vell. Pat. 2.73; App. *BC* 5.79; Ormerod 1987: 251), Seleucus (Memnon, *FGH* 434 frg. 37, 1–4 Jac.; Plut. *Luc.* 13 f.; App. *Mith.* 76, 78), Cleochares Spado (App. *Mith.* 76, 78; Oros. 6.3.5 refers to him as a eunuch), Heracleo (Cic. *Verr.* 2.5.37, 91 and 97), Athenodorus (Phlegon, *FGH* 257 frg. 12, 13 Jac.), and Pyrganio (Oros. 6.3.5 ; cf. Liv. *Per.* 98; Ormerod 1987: 231 n.1)—were unquestionably legendary to have survived as they do. And as Plutarch noted above (*Pomp.* 24.2), refugees even from the established provincial orders came to view "piracy as a profession in which honor could be attained and ambition satisfied."

Apart from such dress and manner deliberately intended to mock the established authorities, several of the most notorious negative behavioral patterns of pirates both ancient and modern tend to reflect a momentous urge to celebrate hard-fought freedom. "While the chance to win a treasure usually supplied the initial and immediate lure that attracted honest seamen to piracy," observes Sherry (1986: 123), "an objective examination of the lives actually led by pirates makes it clear that the real lure, implicit in the outlaw nation's values, rules, and style of life, was the chance that piracy offered to ordinary sailors to live as free men." In their hidden ports pirate crews celebrated their naval victories with endless rounds of drinking bouts and wenching.

> It was the freedom to drink as much and as often as he liked, that the ordinary sea outlaw prized above all others. Pirates considered it their right to drink constantly, whether under sail or at anchor. Drunkenness was not only the great solace for the boredom that was so much a part of life aboard ship—the antidote for days of endless blue skies and empty ocean—it was also, for the ordinary pirate, the undeniable proof that he was, indeed truly free. It was the keystone of his personal liberty. (Sherry 1986: 132)

As the first article of Black Bart Robert's newly formed pirate crew makes clear, articles of agreement usually placed the right to drink at the top of the contract: "every man ... has equal title to the fresh provisions or strong liquors at any time seized, and [may] use them at pleasure unless a scarcity ... make it necesary for the common good of all to vote a retrenchment" ([Johnson] 1724: 182). Rankin (1969: 31) records one instance where the articles of agreement were "sworn to on the Bible, along with the consumption of a goodly supply of rum." Obviously, such excessive alcohol consumption occasionally impeded the abilities of pirate crews to attack prizes, to resist assaults on themselves, or to weather storms at sea (Rankin 1969: 38; Sherry 1986: 132–33). Numerous unexplained shipwrecks and groundings can probably be attributed to widespread drunkenness aboard pirate ships.

After drink, sexual indulgence was the second most cherished of personal liberties. "Among many pirate crews it was the custom, when they careened their ships on remote beaches, to sweeten this necessary interval with orgies of drinking and sex with prostitutes and captive women." Probably the most famous pirate orgy of modern times occurred in October 1718, when Blackbeard's crew joined the pirates of Captain Charles Vane on Ocracoke Island off the North Carolina coast—and enjoyed a weeklong carousal with local prostitutes especially brought in for the occasion (Sherry 1986: 134). Where sexual license was concerned, Blackbeard set brutal standards. The fearsome captain "married" fourteen women, most of them teenage beauties. The last of these was only sixteen when Blackbeard

---

[53] Plaut. *Mil. Glor.* 1176–1181, 1283; *As.* 69; *Pers.* 154–157. Obviously Plautus' depictions predate the Cilician pirates, but he was unquestionably familiar with piracy and featured it in several of his plays (Plaut. *Poen.* 897; *Mil. Glor.* 118; *Tri.* 599, 1088; *Bacch.* 282). I am assuming that, as in the early modern era, ancient sailors and pirates belonged to the same maritime subculture, the only difference between them being a pirate's decision to go "on the account."

[54] Diod. 37.16; Oros. 5.18.10. During the Social War this *archipirata* commanded Picene forces against Rome.

had Governor Eden of North Carolina perform the rites in Bath in 1718. Rumor had it the pirate regularly invited "five or six of his brutal companions to come ashore, and he would force her to prostitute herself to them all, one after another, before his face" ([Johnson] 1724: 49).

Music, provided by talented members of the crew, added another important component to these drunken revels. Pirates forced captured musicians to join their crews involuntarily, simply to satisfy their critical demand for entertainment. They would then reward these musicians with larger shares of the booty (Sherry 1986: 347). Crews of merchantships assaulted by pirates often recalled the eery sound of flutes playing as the pirate vessel approached. Recounting Black Bart Robert's infamous assault on the port of Trepassey in Newfoundland in 1720, a Boston newspaper wrote that his pirate ship came charging into the harbor with "drums beating, trumpets sounding, English colors flying, and the pirate flag at the topmast with death's head and cutlass" (cited in Sherry 1986: 329; cf. [Johnson] 1724: 187).

While our sources for the social behavior of the Cilician pirates are rarely so graphic or detailed, they provide at least a hint of proof that the same tendencies toward alcoholic, sexual, and musical license prevailed among them. Plutarch observes (*Pomp.* 24.3–4):

> [The Cilician pirates] were certainly formidable enough; but what excited most indignation was the odious arrogance of it all—the gilded sails, the purple awnings, the silvered oars the general impression that they were delighting in this way of life and priding themselves on their evil deeds. Roman supremacy was brought into contempt by their flute-playing, their stringed instruments, their drunken revels along every coast, their seizures of high ranking officials, and the ransoms they demanded from captured cities.

Cicero adds that among the crew of the pirate ship that Verres captured in 73 B.C.E. were several handsome youths *(navis plena iuventutis formosissimae)* and six musicians whom the governor kept for his own purposes. Elsewhere he accuses P. Clodius, during his ransom by the Cilicians, of having submitted to their insults and sexual gratification.[55]

The patterns of behavior for early modern European and ancient Cilician piracy, therefore, are remarkably similar even to the extent of their rebellious dress and coarse revelry. Similarities such as these entitle us to draw important inferences from the reports of collusion among the Cilicians and of their ability to forge vast maritime brotherhoods. As Rediker observes (1986: 275–76), eighteenth-century pirates did not prey on one another. Rather, they consistently expressed in numerous and subtle ways a highly developed consciousness of kind that acted as a strategy of survival and formed a collectivist ethos. Pirates showed a recurrent willingness to join forces at sea and in port. Unacquainted pirate crews exchanged greetings with cannon salutes and frequently invoked an unwritten code of hospitality to forge spontaneous alliances. One of the strongest indicators of a "psychological solidarity against a common foe" is the manifest absence of discord between different pirate crews. To some extent this was even a transnational matter: French, Dutch, Spanish, and Anglo-American pirates usually cooperated peaceably, only occasionally exchanging cannon fire.

A sufficient quantity of evidence suggests that early modern piracy was not only ethnically but racially colorblind. Africans served alongside Europeans on pirate ships even as they captured and marketed seized cargoes of fellow African prisoners.[56] As we have seen, several sources demonstrate that the Cilician pirates, likewise, drew their manpower from a broad international substratum of maritime peoples. The sources certainly hint, and modern scholars tend to believe, that the Cilicians enlisted runaway slaves among their crews.[57] If true, the inherent contradiction nonetheless remains that, according to Strabo (14.5.2 [668]), these same pirates sold thousands of prisoners to the Roman and Italian slave traders at Delos.

Apart from the multicultural tendencies of the Cilicians, Dio (36.22.4–5) demonstrates that Cilician chiefs and crews wholly unacquainted with one another and possibly roving in separate theaters of the sea communicated with and supported one another militarily and financially.

> The pirates showed such friendship for one another as to send money and assistance even to those with whom

---

[55] Cic. *Verr.* 2.5.63, 71, 73; *Har. Resp.* 42; cf. *Div. in Caec.* 55; Caes. *BC* 3.14. For homosexuality in transatlantic piracy, see [Johnson] (1724: 181, 194, 314); Burg (1995).

[56] In 1722 the captured crew of Black Bart Robert's consort ship *Great Ranger* revealed fifty-nine Englishmen, twenty-three Africans, and eighteen French ([Johnson] 1724: 218–21; Sherry 1986: 342). Of the 267 pirates serving with his combined crews, seventy were African ([Johnson] 1724: 252).

[57] Marasco (1987a: 129–30, 137). Runaway slaves were certainly visible in Roman maritime culture: Plaut. *Trin.* 1022–1027; *Poen.* 831–835; Petron. 95; Juv. 8.174; cf. Casson (1971: 322).

they were wholly unacquainted, as if they were their nearest of kin. In fact, this was one of the chief sources of their strength, that those who paid court to any of them were honored by all, and those who challenged any of them were plundered by all.

These heightened lines of communication imply the existence of an international pirate brotherhood whose members were readily capable of identifying and accepting the marks of one another's signet rings and/or letters of credit. Only the existence of a Mediterranean-wide network of pirate contacts such as this can explain the ease with which two notorious Roman military deserters, L. Magius and L. Fannius, organized the "Unholy Alliance" in 76 B.C.E., by sailing round-trip from Pontus, to Italy, to Spain on a three-month cruise aboard a *myoparo*, all the while eluding a Roman *senatus consultum* demanding their arrest.[58] As noted previously, through coercive force the pirates also compelled numerous cities to enter into alliances with them—alliances specifically referred to by the sources as *societates*—thus, providing them with markets where they could openly conduct their sales of captured prisoners and booty.[59] Plutarch offers perhaps the best proof of cooperation among the pirates when he describes their general stampede toward Cilicia during Pompey's momentous naval sweep of the Mediterranean in 67 B.C.E. (Plut. *Pomp.* 26.3, 28.1). According to Appian (*Mith.* 92), the pirates used Cilicia Tracheia as their "common anchorage and military camp" (κοινὸν σφῶν ὕφορμον ἢ στρατόπεδον).

They had forts and peaks and desert islands and retreats everywhere, but they chose for their principal rendezvous the coastal strip of Cilicia that was rough and harborless and rose in high mountain peaks. For this reason they went by the name Kilikes.

As Ormerod observed, the label *Cilicians* may be the most telling characteristic of their behavior. Rediker (1987: 278–79) and Sherry (1986: 96–97) insist that early modern pirates affirmed their unity symbolically, through common language, dress, and through use of a recognizable emblem, namely, the flag of the *Jolly Roger*. For the Cilician pirates, the unifying emblem would appear to have been the name Κίλικες itself. For it is virtually impossible that the 30,000 odd pirates captured and killed by Pompey in 67, most of whom went by and are expressly referred to by the sources as *Kilikes,* all originated from Cilicia. In essence, a *Kilix* was any seaman who "reduced himself afresh to the savage state of nature by declaring war against all mankind."[60] So-called "Cilician" pirate bands are documented throughout the Mediterranean: they cruised about Sertorius' fortified harbor of Dianium in Spain (Plut. *Sert.* 7–8, 21.5; *Pomp.* 19.6; Sall. *Hist.* 2.90 M.; Strabo 3.4.6 [159]; Cic. *Verr.* 2.5.146; *Balb.* 25); they tormented the inhabitants of Syracuse (Cic. *Verr.* 2.4.116); they plundered the harbor of Caieta and set fire to a Roman war fleet in Ostia (see note 18 above); they negotiated with Spartacus, seeking to convey his slave army across the strait of Messina in 71 B.C.E. (Plut. *Crass.* 10.3; Sall. *Hist.* 4.32 M). Eight thousand "Cilicians" garrisoned (and looted) King Mithradates' Black Sea bastions at Sinope and Amisus against Lucullus in 72–70 B.C.E.,[61] and numerous others appear to have manned the citadels of Crete against Q. Metellus Creticus in 68 B.C.E.[62] Rather than identify their place of origin, the appellation "Cilician" provided disparate bands of Mediterranean pirates with "a consciousness of kind" and enabled them to forge "a psychological solidarity against a common foe." As Appian observes (*Mith.* 93), the unity of purpose encoded in this name offered the Cilician pirates a momentary advantage over their more heavily armed, better-organized Roman adversaries.[63]

---

[58] An affair warranting closer attention (Cic. *Verr.* 2.1.87; *De imp. Cn. Pomp.* 46; Sall. *Hist.* 2.77–79 M.; Ps. Ascon. 244 St.; cf. Plut. *Pomp* 20; *Sert.* 27; App. *BC* 1.115; and above, note 17). As Konrad (1994: 191) notes, their *myoparo pulcher* was a vessel especially popular among pirates. Konrad suggests that Magius and Fannius were themselves pirates and that they originally came to know King Mithradates in this manner.

[59] See above, note 5. In fact, Cicero ascribes the importance of Phaselis to its use as a waystation in the Cilician "pirate round" (*Verr.* 2.4.21): *ut et exeuntes e Cilicia praedones saepe ad eam necessario devenirent, et, cum se ex hisce locis reciperent, eodem deferentur.*

[60] Rankin (1969: 22); or as Cicero states (*Verr.* 2.5.76): *hostes acerrimi atque infestissumi populi Romani, sue potius communes hostes gentium nationumque omnium.*

[61] Memnon, *FGH* 434, frg. 37.1–4 Jac.; Oros. 6.2.6, 6.3.2; Plut. *Luc.* 12.2, 13.3, 23.2–6; App. *Mith.* 78, 83; Strabo 12.545; Maroti (1970: 481–82); Marasco (1987a: 13)2. See Launey (1949: 480), for the inscription recording Epitynchanon of Tarsus, commander of a Pontic contingent, honored by Apollonia in Pontus.

[62] Plut. *Pomp.* 29.2; App. *Sic.* 6.1; Flor. 1.42.1; Diod. 40.1.3; Memnon, *FGH* 434 frg. 29.5, 33.1 Jac.; Strabo 10.4.10 (477); 12.3.33 (557); Marasco (1987a: 136); Brulé (1978: 171).

[63] Logistical difficulties posed by the remoteness of their bases and their inherent need to remain hidden tended to keep concentrations of pirate forces in any one region (apart from Cilicia proper) low and restricted to clusters of small, independent bands. Early modern pirates likewise disbanded their fleets to avoid detection (Sherry 1986: 242; Rediker 1987: 267).

It appeared to the Romans to be a huge and difficult task to destroy so large a force of seafaring men scattered every which way on land and sea, with no fixed possession to encumber their flight, sallying out from no particular country or any known places, having no property or anything to call their own, but only what they might chance to light upon. Thus the unexampled nature of this war, which was subject to no laws and had nothing tangible or visible about it, caused perplexity and fear.

While several additional parallels between early modern European and ancient Cilician piracy exist, a sufficient number have been explored to confirm the legitimacy of the tradition for the latter.[64] While the ancient numerical figures for piracy remain subject to scrutiny, there is little reason to doubt the ability of the Cilician pirates to accomplish what they did. Organized into a broad confederacy bound by its name, the Cilician pirates cruised a "pirate round" from Coracesium to Dianium, plundering sanctuaries and maritime cities, foraging inland, effectively shutting down the sealanes, and nearly starving the far-flung territories of the Roman Republic into collapse. As Rediker notes (1986: 285) however, their very strengths—independence, diversity, dispersement, and decentralization—were double-edged weapons that eventually ushered their demise:

> Pirates themselves unwittingly took a hand in their own destruction. From the outset, theirs had been a fragile social world. They produced nothing and had no secure place in the economic order. They had no nation, no home; they were widely dispersed; their community had virtually no geographic boundaries. Try as they might, they were unable to create reliable mechanisms through which they could either replenish their ranks or mobilize their collective strength. These deficiencies of social organization made them, in the long run, relatively easy prey.

CONCLUSION

To answer the questions raised at the outset, the vast majority of Cilician pirates neither arose from Cilicia, nor were they connected in any manner with the bandit chieftains of its hinterland. Rather they emerged from a vast international substratum of displaced naval warriors from maritime regions under stress. In any event, they were people who owned ships and who knew how to sail as well as fight. By name and language they would appear to have been mostly Hellenistic Greeks and Levantines, rather than Latins, and to a large degree they drew their manpower from the patiently suffering provincial elements of the collapsing Hellenistic and expanding Roman realms. Driven from their homes by the anarchy and incessant conflicts of the times and trained in warfare by their eventual adversaries, the Cilician pirates honed their martial skills to seek vengeance against their immediate persecutors and ultimately against every visible form of privilege and authority. They built fortified, well-supplied harbors to defy the threat of imperial navies. They employed gaudy dress and crude manners to flaunt their revolt against ancient hierarchical society, and violent, terrorist tactics to exact justice and to secure a means to survival. In many respects, the Cilician pirates represented a common man's response to decades of authoritarian oppression. They emitted the sound and the fury of ordinary people throughout the Mediterranean basin, bruised and battered by the senseless violence that characterized the late Hellenistic world. As Rediker concludes (1986: 286):

> The social constellation of piracy, in particular the complex consciousness and egalitarian impulses that developed once the shackles were off, provides valuable clarification of more general social and cultural patterns among seamen in particular and the laboring poor in general. Here we can see aspirations and achievements that under normal circumstances were heavily muted, if not in many cases rendered imperceptible altogether, by the power relationships of everyday life.

---

[64] Pompey's strategy of leniency towards the defeated Cilicians in 67 B.C.E. finds a direct parallel in Governor Woodes Rogers' eradication of Anglo-American piracy in the Bahamas (Sherry 1986: 218–79). Similarly, Plutarch's observation (*Pomp.* 26) that numerous hardened pirates, "conscious of having committed crimes too great to be forgiven," fought to the death.

REFERENCES

Bagnall, R. S.
1976　*The Administration of the Ptolemaic Possessions outside Egypt.* Leiden: Brill.

Bar-Kochva, B.
1976　*The Seleucid Army: Organization and Tactics in the Great Campaigns.* Cambridge: Cambridge University.

Benabou, M.
1985　Rome et la police des mers au 1er siècle avant J.C.: la répression de la piraterie cilicienne. Pp. 60–69 in *L'Homme méditerranéan et la mer.* Actes du Troisième Congrès International d'études des cultures de la Méditerranée Occidentale (Jerba, Avril 1981), eds. M. Galley and L. Ladjimi Sebai. Paris: Boccard.

Bevan, E. R.
1966　*The House of Seleucus.* Reprint of 1902 London edition. New York: Barnes and Noble.

Bickerman, E.
1938　*Institutions des Séleucides.* Paris: Librarie orientaliste Paul Geuthner.

Bommelaer, J.-F.
1987　Meydancik Kalesi, place forte de Cilicie Trachée au IIIe siècle av. J.-C. Pp. 5–13 in *Sociétés rurales dans l'Asie Mineure et la Syrie hellénistiques et romaines.* Actes du colloque organisé à Strasbourg (novembre 1985) par l'Institut et le Groupe de Recherche d'histoire romaine et le Centre de Recherche sur le Proche-Orient et la Grèce antiques, ed. E. Frézouls. Strasbourg: AECR.

Blümel, W.
1992　*Die Inschriften von Knidos, Teil I.* Inschriften griechischer Städte aus Kleinasien, Band 41. Österreichische Akademie der Wissenschaften, Rheinisch-Westfälische Akademie der Wissenschaften. Bonn: Habelt.

Brandt, H.
1992　*Gesellschaft und Wirtschaft Pamphyliens und Pisidiens im Altertum.* Bonn: Habelt.

Briant, P.
1976　'Brigandage,' dissidence et conquète en Asie achéménide et hellénistique. *Dialogues d'histoire ancienne* 2: 212–13.

Broughton, T. R. S.
1986　*The Magistrates of the Roman Republic.* Revised edition. Atlanta: American Philological Association.

Brulé, P.
1978　*La piraterie crétoise hellénistique.* Annales littéraires de l'Université de Besançon 223. Paris: Les Belles Lettres.

Burg, B. R.
1995　*Sodomy and the Pirate Tradition: English Sea Rovers in the Seventeenth-Century Caribbean.* Revised version of 1983 publication. New York: New York University.

Casson, L.
1971　*Ships and Seamanship in the Ancient World.* Princeton: Princeton University.

Clavel-Leveque, M.
1979　Brigandage et piraterie: représentations idéologiques et pratiques impérialistes au dernier siècle de la République. *Dialogues d'histoire ancienne* 5: 17–32.

Couilloud, M.-Th.
1973　*Les monuments funéraires de Rhénée,* Exploration archéologique de Délos 30. Paris: Boccard.

Dell, H. J.
1967　The Origin and Nature of Illyrian Piracy. *Historia* 16: 344–58.

Desideri, P.
1991　Strabo's Cilicians. *De Anatolia Antiqua (Eski Anadolu)* 1: 299–304.

Diler, A.
1991　Lykia Olympos Daginda Bir Ön Araştırma. *Turk Arkeologiji Dergisi* 29: 161–76.

Earle, P.
1970　*Corsairs of Malta and Barbary.* London: Sidgwick and Jackson.

Erdemgil, S., and Özoral F.
1975　Antiochia ad Cragum. *Turk Arkeologiji Dergisi* 22.2: 55–71.

Fischer, T.
1972　Zu Tryphon. *Chiron* 2: 201–13.

Garlan, Y.
1978　Signification historique de la piraterie grecque. *Dialogues d'histoire ancienne* 4: 1–16.

Gianfrotta, P. A.
1981　Commerci e pirateria: prime testimonianze archeologiche sottomarine. *Mélanges d'Archéologie et d'Histoire de l'École française de Rome. Antiquité* 93: 227–42.

Gosse, P.
1946　*The History of Piracy.* New York: Tudor.

Grainger, J. D.
1991　*Hellenistic Phoenicia.* Oxford: Clarendon.

Hall, A. S.
1973　New Light On The Capture of Isaura Vetus by P. Servilius Vatia. Pp. 568–71 in *Akten des VI.*

internationalen Kongresses für griechisch und lateinisch Epigraphik. Vestigia 17. Munich: Beck.

Hassal M.; Crawford, M.; Reynolds, J.
1974   Rome and the Eastern Provinces at the End of the Second Century B.C. *Journal of Roman Studies* 64: 195–220.

Hild, F., and Hellenkemper, H.
1990   *Kilikien und Isaurien.* Tabula Imperii Byzantini 5. Vienna: Österreichischen Akademie der Wissenschaften.

Hobsbawm, E. J.
1969   *Bandits.* New York: Delacorte.

Hopwood, K.
1983   Policing the Hinterland: Rough Cilicia and Isauria. Pp. 173–88 in *Armies and Frontiers in Roman and Byzantine Anatolia.* Proceedings of a colloquium held at University College, Swansea, in April 1981, ed. S. Mitchell. BAR International Series 156. Oxford: B.A.R.

1986   Towers, Territory and Terror: How the East was Held. Pp. 343–56 in *The Defense of the Roman and Byzantine East.* Proceedings of a colloquium held at the University of Sheffield in April 1986, eds. P. Freeman and D. Kennedy. BAR International Series 297. Oxford: B.A.R.

1989   Consent and Control: How the Peace was Kept in Rough Cilicia. Pp. 191–201 in *The Eastern Frontier Of The Roman Empire,* eds. D. H. French and C. S. Lightfoot. BAR International Series 553. Oxford: B.A.R.

1990   Bandits Elites And Rural Order. Pp. 171–87 in *Patronage In Ancient Society,* ed. A. Wallace-Hadrill. New York: Routledge.

1991   The Links between the Coastal Cities of Western Rough Cilicia and the Interior during the Roman Period. *De Anatolia Antiqua (Eski Anadolu)* 1: 305–9.

Huber, G.
1964   Vorläufige Beobachtungen über die Städteplanung in den Küstenorten des westlichen Kilikien. *Turk Arkeologiji Dergisi* 13.2: 140–48.

[Johnson, Captain Charles]
1724   *A General History of the Robberies and Murders of the most notorious Pyrates, and also Their Policies, Discipline and government, From their first Rise and Settlement in the Island of Providence, in 1717, to the present Year 1724.* London. Modern edition, London: Routledge and Kegan Paul, 1926.

Jones, C. P., and Habicht, Ch.
1989   A Hellenistic Inscription from Arsinoe in Cilicia. *Phoenix* 43: 317–46.

Kaletsch, H.
1986   Seeraub und Seeräubergeschichten des Altertums. 2000 Jahre antiker Seefahrt und Piraterie zwischen Adria und Ostmittelmeer. Pp. 469–500, in Vol. 2 of *Studien zur alten Geschichte: Siegfried Lauffer zum 70. Geburtstag am 4. August 1981 dargebracht von Freunden, Kollegen und Schulern,* eds. H. Kalcyk, B. Gullath, and A. Graeber. Rome: G. Bretschneider.

Konrad, C. F.
1994   *Plutarch's Sertorius: A Historical Commentary.* Chapel Hill: University of North Carolina.

Launey, M.
1949   *Recherches sur les armées hellénistiques.* Paris: Boccard.

Lewin, A.
1991   Banditismo e *civiltas* nella cilicia tracheia antica e tardoantica. *Quaderni di Storia* 76: 167–84.

Liebmann-Frankfort, Th.
1969   *La frontière orientale dans la politique extérieure de la République romaine depuis le traité d'Apamée jusqu'à la fin des conquêtes asiatiques de Pompée (189/8–63).* Brussels: Palais des Académies.

Lydon, J. G.
1970   *Pirates, Privateers and Profits.* Upper Saddle River, NJ: Gregg.

Magie, D.
1950   *Roman Rule in Asia Minor to the End of the Third Century after Christ.* Princeton: Princeton University.

Marasco, G.
1987a   Aspetti della pirateria cilicia nel I secolo A.C. *Giornale Filologico Ferrarese* 10: 129–145.
1987b   Roma e la pirateria cilicia. *Rivista Storica Italiana* 99: 122–46.

Maroti, E.
1956   Das Piratenunwesen um Sizilien zur Zeit des Proprätors C. Verres. *Acta Antiqua* 4: 196–210.
1961   Die Rolle der Seeräuberei zur Zeit der römischen Bürgerkriege. Ein Überblick. *Das Altertum* 7: 32–41.
1962   Diodotus Tryphon et la piraterie. *Acta Antiqua* 19: 187–94.
1970   Die Rolle der Seeräuberei zur Zeit der mithridatischen Krieges. Pp. 481–93 in *Richerche storiche ed economiche in memoria di C. Barbagallo.* Naples: Edizione scientifiche italiane.
1969–   Der Sklavenmarkt auf Delos und die Piraterie.
1970   *Helikon* 9–10: 24–42.

Ormerod, H. A.
 1922   The Campaigns of Servilius Isauricus against the
         Pirates. *Journal of Roman Studies* 12: 35–56.
 1987   *Piracy in the Ancient World*. Liverpool, 1928;
         Reprint, New York: Dorsett.

Pohl, H.
 1993   *Römische Politik und Piraterie im östlichen
         Mittelmeer vom 3. bis 1. Jh. v. Chr*. Berlin: de
         Gruyter.

Préaux, C.
 1939   *L'Economie Royale des Lagides*. Brussels:
         Édition de la fondation égyptologique Reine
         Élisabeth.

Rankin, H. F.
 1969   *The Golden Age of Piracy*. Williamsburg in
         America Series, 7. Williamsburg, VA: Colonial
         Williamsburg.

Rauh, N. K.
 1993   *The Sacred Bonds of Commerce: Religion,
         Economy, and Trade Society at Hellenistic Ro-
         man Delos*. Amsterdam: Gieben.

Rediker, M.
 1987   *Between the Devil and the Deep Blue Sea: Mer-
         chants, Seamen, Pirates, and the Anglo-Ameri-
         can Maritime World 1700–1750*. Cambridge:
         Cambridge University.

Reynolds, J. M.
 1974   A Civic Decree from Benghazi. Pp. 19–23 in
         *Society for Lybian Studies. 5th Annual Report,
         1973–74*. London Institute of Archaeology, Uni-
         versity of London.

Ritchie, R. C.
 1986   *Captain Kidd and the War against the Pirates*.
         Cambridge, MA: Harvard University.

Rosenbaum, E.; Huber, G.; Onurkan, S.
 1967   *A Survey of Coastal Cities in Western Cilicia.
         Preliminary Report*. TTKY VI/8. Ankara.

Russell, J.
 1991   *Cilicia—Nutrix Vivorum*: Cilicians Abroad in
         Peace and War during Hellenistic and Roman

Times. *De Anatolia Antiqua (Eski Anadolu)* 1:
         283–97.

Senior, C. M.
 1976   *A Nation of Pirates: English Piracy in its Hey-
         day*. New York: Crane, Russak.

Shaw, B. D.
 1984   Bandits in the Roman Empire. *Past and Present*
         105: 3–52.

Shaw, B. D.
 1990   Bandit Highlands and Lowland Peace: The
         Mountains of Isauria-Cilicia. *Journal of the Eco-
         nomic and Social History of the Orient* 33:
         199–233.

Sherry, F.
 1986   *Raiders and Rebels: The Golden Age of Piracy*.
         New York: Hearst Marine Books.

Sherwin-White, A. N.
 1976   Rome, Pamphylia and Cilicia 133–70 B.C. *Jour-
         nal of Roman Studies* 66: 1–14.

Strasburger, H.
 1965   Poseidonius on Problems of the Roman Empire.
         Journal of Roman Studies 55: 40–53.

Syme, R.
 1986   Isauria in Pliny. *Anatolian Studies* 36: 159–64.

Thomson, J. E.
 1994   *Mercenaries, Pirates and Sovereigns: State-
         Building and Extraterritorial Violence in Early
         Modern Europe*. Princeton: Princeton Univer-
         sity.

Van 'T Dack, E., and Hauben, H.
 1987   L'Apport égyptien à l'armée navale lagide. Pp.
         60–93 in *Das ptolemäische Ägypten. Akten des
         internationalen Symposions 27.–29. September
         1976 in Berlin*, eds. H. Maehler and V.M.
         Strocka. Mainz: von Zabern.

Williams, N.
 1962   *Captains Outrageous: Seven Centuries of Pi-
         racy*. New York: Macmillan.

Wolf, J. B.
 1979   *The Barbary Coast: Algiers Under the Turks
         1500–1830*. New York: Norton.

Traveling Pottery Connections Between Cyprus, the Levant, and the Greek World in the Iron Age

LONE WRIEDT SØRENSEN

Institute of Archaeology and Ethnology
University of Copenhagen
Vankunsten 5, DK-1467
Copenhagen K
DENMARK

An analysis of foreign pottery found in the eastern Mediterranean from the early part of the first millennium B.C.E. shows that, although the majority of Greek and Cypriot pottery in the Levant has been found at coastal sites in North Syria, more and more finds appear at sites towards the south, that an almost equal number of Greek and Phoenician pottery has been published from Cyprus, and that Cypriot pottery only reached specific Greek locations. Among the issues associated with pottery in a foreign context, trade and/or colonization, ethnicity, taste, and change of customs are interconnected. The analysis shows that the distribution of pottery does not necessarily reflect traders, political hostilities, or ethnicity of the owner, and that modern estimations of different types of pottery may have had little meaning in the societies in question.

INTRODUCTION

Pottery found in a non-native context has been subject to many different types of interpretations ranging from evidence of visitors or traders to either a political or cultural expansion. The present paper focuses on the distribution of various types of decorated vessels found in a non-native context in the eastern Mediterranean during the early part of the first millennium B.C.E. and the conclusions drawn from them. Information available in the present case derives from Cypriot and Greek pottery found in the Levant, Greek and Phoenician pottery found in Cyprus and Cypriot pottery found in Greece.

CYPRIOT POTTERY FOUND IN THE LEVANT (fig. 1)[1]

A series of problems is connected with the study of Cypriot Iron Age pottery found in the Levant. Little attention was paid to this specific find group during early excavations, and sometimes the material has been insufficiently published. Furthermore, the difference between Cypriot and

---

[1] Apart from the finds listed in the publications from Tell Mevorakh (Stern 1978: 52–59) and Dor (Gilboa 1989) see also: Ras el Bassit (Courbin 1982; 1983; 1986; 1990a); Al Mina (Taylor 1959); Hama (Riis 1948; 1990); Tell Sukas (Riis 1960; Lund 1986); Tell Darouk (Oldenburg 1981); Tell Michal (Marchese 1989); Sarepta (Koehl 1985; Anderson 1988); Tell Qiri (Ben-Tor and Portugali 1987); Hurbat Rosh-Zayit (Gal 1992); Tell Abu Hawam (Balensi 1985; Herrera and Balensi 1986); Tyre (Bikai 1978).

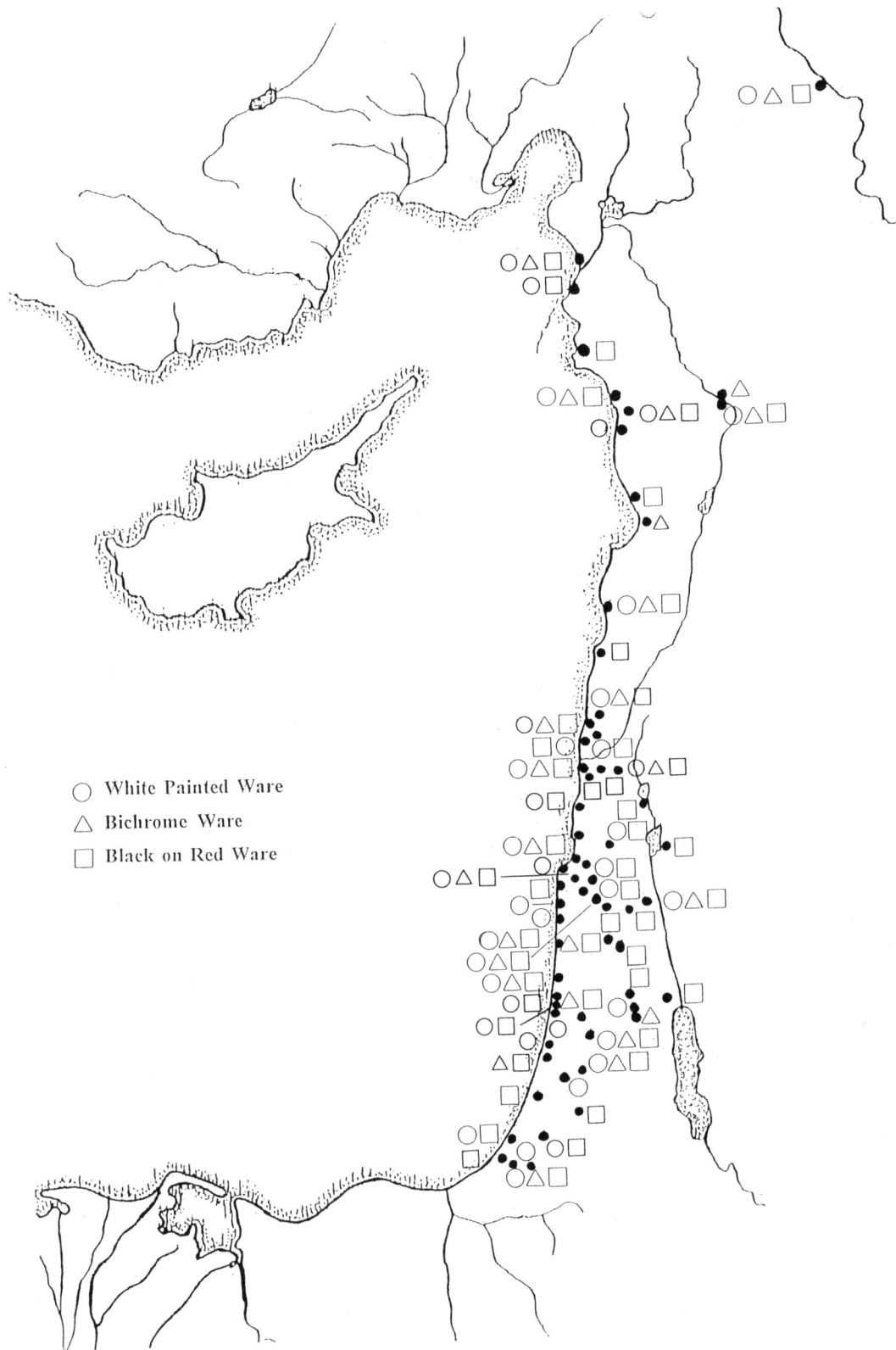

Fig. 1. Distribution of Cypriot pottery in the Levant.

Palestinian chronologies represents a serious obstacle to studies pertaining to relations between the two areas (cf. for instance Coldstream 1968: 302–3; Karageorghis 1982; Stern 1978: 53). Here, however, only Cypriot chronology is followed. Cypro-Geometric pottery appears in the Levant from about 1050 B.C.E., and Al Mina together with Tell Sukas and Ras el Bassit on the coast are so far the most prolific find spots in the North Syrian area. Cypriot pottery has also been found at the inland localities of Hama and Carchemish (Riis 1948: 110; Riis, et al. 1990: 180). In the Phoenician stronghold of Tyre a significant number of Cypriot finds are reported, and smaller assemblages have been found in many recent excavations in Israel. The finds listed show that Cypriot pottery was widely distributed not only along the coast but also at southern inland sites.

The well-known categories of White Painted Ware, Bichrome Ware and Black on Red Ware are represented in the Levant.[2] Bowls, juglets, jugs and containers like amphoras are all represented in each of the three ware types. Interest has focused on the occurrence of Black on Red Ware despite the fact that White Painted and Bichrome Ware together are represented at a larger number of sites. The find pattern concerning ware types and shapes in the Levant corresponds with the pattern noticed in Cyprus (Sørensen 1987).

A series of imitations of Greek skyphoi beginning in the late eighth century B.C.E. should also be mentioned in this context, although they represent a somewhat different case. They were first identified at Al Mina, but scientific analyses have shown that they were made in Cyprus (Jones 1986: 694). It has been convincingly argued that they were produced by local Cypriot potters rather than Greek potters residing in Cyprus (Coldstream 1979: 269), and their distribution from Tarsus to Tyre supports the picture obtained from the distribution of Cypriot pottery.

There are few discussions of the implications of Cypriot finds in the Levant, and comments have often been restricted to finds from North Syria where Cypriot pottery is briefly referred to as evidence of trade or belongings of resident Cypriots, sometimes called Cypro-Greeks (Boardman 1980). Apparently Cypriot pottery reached the Levant before Greek pottery. This is documented by finds at Ras el Bassit, Tell Sukas, Ras ibn Hani in the north, but also at Sarepta, Tyre and quite a number of sites in Israel (Courbin 1991: 257; Gilboa 1989). Even at Al Mina the earliest Cypriot pottery of the Cypro-Geometric III period (850–750 B.C.E.) is still earlier than the Greek material (Kearsley 1989: 145).

It has been suggested that certain shapes were reserved for specific usages; for instance, Stern (1978: 53) has suggested, based upon the finds from Mevorakh and Tell Abu Hawam, that Black on Red jugs and juglets were used mainly in funerary contexts, and bowls were used in settlement contexts. However, this same pattern is not seen at Beth Pelet, Byblos, Qraye and Megiddo, for example.

In some cases, find locations of Cypriot pottery have been used to identify habitation sites for Cypriots in the Levant. At Tell Sukas concentrations of Cypriot pottery were noticed in two specific areas at the periphery of the tell. This made Lund (1986: 190) propose that Cypriots had lived there from about 675 B.C.E. Such a proposal, however, would imply, that expatriate Cypriots preferred Cypriot ceramic products to both the available local and Greek pottery. In this respect they would differ from their kinsmen in Cyprus who seem to have used all types of available pottery (see below). It would also imply that Cypriots at Tell Sukas lived in separate quarters and were not fully integrated in the local society. Information from other localities does not confirm that this was the case elsewhere in the Levant.

Why and how did Cypriot pottery end up in the Levant? According to Gjerstad (1948) open vessel shapes must have been imported for their own sake, and others have later supported this point of view, seeing Cypriot pottery as an indication of the greater wealth and wider contacts of an urban center versus a village site (Lapp 1967: 37; Ben-Tor and Portugali 1987: 202). Gilboa (1989: 217), discussing the finds from Israel, rejected this explanation with reference to the comparatively small number of finds and suggested at least for the early pieces that they represent personal belongings, which were acquired directly by certain people, or were brought by Cypriots. Already Gjerstad (243–44) in 1948, expressed uncertainty concerning a Cypriot origin for some of the finds, and although some analyses indicate that the vessels in question were made of Cypriot clay (Bikai 1978: 88; Yellin and Perlman 1978: 88), others do not appear to come from the island (Yellin 1989). Imitations show that Cypriot pottery was sometimes considered worth copying or that Cypriots living abroad had their own pottery made locally, but the lack of crude imitations, which could indicate that local potters attempted to

---

[2] Cypriot chronology and pottery system consists of Cypro-Geometric I (1050–950 B.C.E.): White Painted and Bichrome I; Cypro Geometric II (950–850): White Painted and Bichrome II; Cypro-Geometric III (850–750): White Painted and Bichrome III, Black on Red I; Cypro-Archaic I(IV) (750–600): White Painted and Bichrome IV, Black on Red II, Bichrome Red I; Cypro-Archaic II(V) (600–474): White Painted and Bichrome V, Black on Red III, Bichrome Red II.

make similar products, seems to show that either they were incapable of doing so or there was no real market for such products.

GREEK POTTERY IN THE LEVANT (fig. 2)[3]

Studies of Greek pottery in the Levant have concentrated mostly on Geometric wares and sixth century Attic pottery. Analyses of the early finds have been influenced by the search for the Greek overseas hero-foundations mentioned in literary sources and have resulted in long-standing discussions of whether the Euboeans or the Phoenicians were responsible for the revival of Mediterranean contact during the early Iron Age. Interest has focused on Al Mina in particular, but also on Tell Sukas and Ras el Bassit in North Syria, while the finds from sites further towards the south have received less attention.

Apart from a few proto-Geometric finds from Ras el Bassit and Tyre (Courbin 1990a: 505; Coldstream and Bikai 1988) the earliest Greek pottery in the Levant is Geometric Euboean/Cycladic, primarily skyphoi, together with some Attic Middle Geometric II products from both North Syria and Phoenicia. Al Mina is no longer considered Posidaion founded by the Greeks after the Trojan war. Still, this locality is seen as a Greek trading station from the early levels onwards, because of the large amount of Greek pottery found here (Boardman 1990). Others have been more cautious or have even rejected the idea of the presence of a Greek establishment here or elsewhere in the Levant, including Ras el Bassit now identified as Posidaion (summed up Elayi 1987; cf. also Perreault 1993). Furthermore, the earliest graffiti on a late eighth century sherd from Al Mina and a fragment of an imitation of a Protocorinthian skyphos from Ras el Bassit with an incised Greek? letter can hardly account for Greek communities (Boardman 1982; Courbin 1991: fig. 5). The finds of Greek pottery from Tyre are a good example for caution. Here, well over a hundred pieces of Greek pottery, including not only skyphoi, but, by analogy with Ras el Bassit and Cyprus, plates with pendant semicircles and closed shapes, have also been found (Courbin 1986: fig. 16 and 19; Coldstream and Bikai 1988). On the basis of these, no one would venture to suggest that a Greek trading post was situated at Tyre, but the finds may well represent a regular Greek–Phoenician contact.

The war in Euboea about 700 B.C.E. seems to have discontinued Euboean finds overseas. East Greek pottery together with a smaller amount from Corinth and other Greek production centres replaced them in the Levant, where most of the finds have appeared at the same North Syrian localities as the earlier material. According to Perreault this shows that Greek interest was limited to this area, but both East Greek and Corinthian pottery has appeared at a number of sites in Israel, indicating that the picture may change somewhat with future investigations. The variety of shapes and styles is larger than before, but shapes connected with drinking, pouring and wine mixing still predominate.

Two Greek graffiti from Ras el Bassit, both Ionian names, are dated to the end of the seventh century B.C.E. One is written on an Ionian cup, the other on a local amphora (Courbin 1986: fig. 31 and 199; idem 1991), and among the the sixth century graffiti on locally produced ceramics from Tell Sukas is an Ionian female name on a spindle whorl and a Rhodian male name on a base that, according to Riis, belongs to a Phoenician bowl (Ploug 1973: 84; Riis 1982: 241). From this we may conclude that Ionian Greeks either visited or lived in the settlements in question, that both men and women were represented, and that they used Greek as well as local and Phoenician pottery.

Greek pottery found at the fort at the Mesad Hashvayahou has been seen as evidence of Greek mercenaries, an interpretation that agrees with the evidence of Greek mercenaries settled in Egypt and Libya (Braun 1982a: 22; 1982b: 35).

During the early sixth century the ceramic pattern did not change much. However, the finds are more widespread, and larger closed shapes also penetrated into the hinterland of Palestine. About the middle of the century Attic drinking cups, later followed by lekythoi, ousted any other shape and fabric following a pattern that corresponds with the evidence from the western Mediterranean area (Perreault 1986). Attic pottery has also turned up at an increasing number of sites in Israel, where lekythoi found primarily in fifth century tombs have been interpreted as belongings of Greek mercenaries, who had settled there after the campaigns against the Egyptians and the Persians. This interpretation has been questioned by Stern (1982: 71; 91). It is generally agreed that the advent of the Persians in the late sixth century caused an opening of this area towards the Mediterranean, and it has been suggested that the presence of Attic rhyta was dictated by drinking habits within the Achaemenid empire (de Vries 1977).

When we turn to the question of Near Easteners' opinions of Greek pottery products, there is again a diversity of opinions among archaeologists. While Cook concluded that

---

[3] Al Mina (Robertson 1940; Boardman 1990); Ras el Bassit (Courbin 1978; 1990b; 1991); Tell Sukas (Ploug 1973); Tyre (Bikai 1978; Coldstream and Bikai 1988). For general surveys see Wenning (1981), Perreault (1986; 1991), Riis (1991).

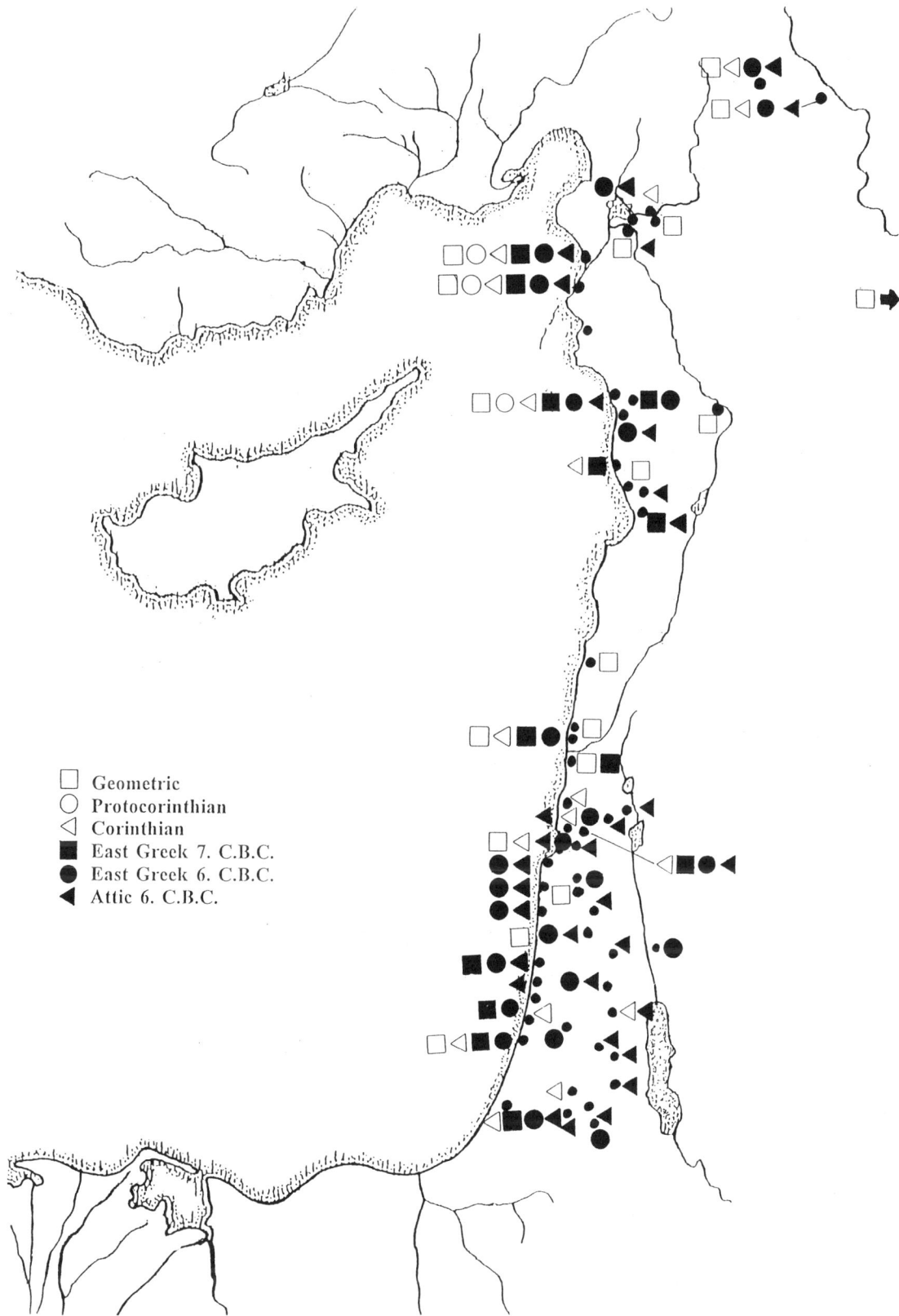

Fig. 2. Distribution of Greek pottery in the Levant.

	MG	LG	7		6.1			6.2				6.3				6.4	5.1
			EG	Cor	EG	Cor	Att	EG	Cor	Att	GR	EG	Cor	Att	GR	Att	Att
Amathus	25	26	42	2	101	10	2	29		5	1	6		23		4	5
Kition	3	1	1		3			1			1			1	1	1	3
Salamis		1	13	9	24	4	1	20		2			1	3		1	3
Marion		1			3		1	1				2		41		30	17
Central Cyprus				2	1									3		4	2
Eastern Cyprus		1	1		1			1									2
Northern Cyprus	3	2		1	3	1		1				1					2
Southern Cyprus				2									1				
Western Cyprus	2	2		2	1				2					1			
Unknown	9	10	2	7	26	7		6	7			5	2	15	1	20	28

Fig. 3. Greek pottery found in Cyprus. MG: Middle Geometric. LG: Late Geometric. EG: East Greek. Cor: Corinthian. Att: Attic. Gr: Greek. 7: 700–600 B.C.E. 6.1: 600–575 B.C.E. 6.2: 575–550 B.C.E. 6.3: 550–525 B.C.E. 6.4: 525–500 B.C.E. 5.1: 500–474 B.C.E.

people in the Near East had no taste for Greek pottery (Cook 1959: 122), an opposite view was presented by Coldstream who suggested for instance that Geometric kraters found here and elsewhere may represent objects of gift exchange (1983; cf. also Perreault 1991: 396). East Greek pottery is hardly discussed in this context, and Attic Black- and Red-figure pottery has per tradition in the archaeological literature been considered as worth possessing, although many of the finds in the Levant are of a poor quality (Boardman 1980: 53).

GREEK POTTERY FOUND IN CYPRUS (fig. 3)

After the collapse of the Mycenaean mainland palace culture, Cyprus still retained at least sporadic contact with both Greece, the Levant and the western Mediterranean (Desborough 1972: 329–30; Karageorghis 1982: 110–11; Knapp 1988; Muhly and Stech 1990: 207–8). Several analyses have shown that the pattern for Greek pottery in Cyprus resembles that observed in North Syria (Coldstream 1985; Collombier 1987; Sørensen 1988), but as mentioned above, proto-Geometric and Geometric pottery, including plates with pendant semi-circles and closed shapes known from Cyprus, is only matched by finds from Ras el Bassit and Tyre. Greek pottery has been found scattered all over the island, and the most important find places are Salamis, the so-called Eteo-Cypriot Amathus and Phoenician Kition. According to Gjerstad (1979) Tomb 1 at Salamis represents a royal Cypro-Greek intermarriage (Gjerstad 1979), while Coldstream (1983) interprets the Greek pottery found in

the tomb as gift exchange items, as mentioned above. Evidence of Greek pottery from the early part of the seventh century B.C.E. is not impressive. Later an increasing number of East Greek products reached the island together with some from Corinth, mostly aryballoi. East Greek pottery retained a strong position during the early part of the sixth century B.C.E., while Attic products, again primarily bowls and cups, predominated from about the middle of the century, just as was the case in the Levant and elsewhere (Perreault 1986: 165). The close contact between Salamis and eastern Greece has been emphazised (Calvet and Yon 1978), but most of the Greek pottery throughout the seventh and the sixth centuries B.C.E. has appeared at Amathus, which is merely considered a transit port for Greeks sailing to Egypt (Karageorghis 1982: 139; for another suggestion cf. Hermary 1987).

Based upon literary sources mentioning foundations by Greek heroes after the fall of Troy, it has been accepted generally that many of the Iron Age kingdoms originated from Achaean colonization of the island and were ruled by descendants of their elite (Gjerstad 1944; Karageorghis 1982: 114; for a different view cf. Rupp 1987). Therefore it has never been suggested that Greek pottery found in Cyprus, unlike the finds from North Syria, represents evidence of Greek colonies or trading posts. Only two Greek graffiti on Greek pottery found in Cyprus have been published. These are both from Salamis: one is a fragment of a SOS amphora carrying a graffito consisting of two letters, the other is a Greek name incised on the neck of black-figure hydria? (Calvet and Yon 1977: nos. 2 and 61).

	White Painted	Bichrome	Black on Red	Red Slip
Rhodes	23	29	7	8
Crete		3	42	1
Cos			14	
East Greece	1			1
Aegina	2	2		
Euboea	4	1		
Olynthos		1		

Fig. 4. Cypriot pottery found in Greece.

The Cypro-syllabic script, considered a survival from the Late Bronze Age Cypro-Minoan script, was used for an unknown Eteo-Cypriot language and for the local Greek dialect and represents an argument in favor of an unbroken social structure from the Late Bronze Age to the Iron Age in Cyprus. It is important, however, to note that, like the early Greek alphabetic writing, it was no longer serving administrative but personal purposes (Masson 1961: 38; Karageorghis 1983: 370; cf. also Liverani 1987). Apparently it was not commonly written on Greek pottery, as only one Attic krater from the fifth century B.C.E., with a Cypriot graffito indicating the shape and the unit cost of three, has been published (Masson 1961: no. 350; Johnston 1979: Type 26F, no. 21).

Local imitations of foreign pottery include the so-called Al Mina cups mentioned above, and Greek influence can also be seen in a number of other cases (Gjerstad 1948: 304; Karageorghis 1982: fig. 105; Maier and Karageorghis 1984: figs. 161, 164). However, the Cypriot potters did not make true copies, and only selected certain elements from the originals which they used in their own way.

CYPRIOT POTTERY FOUND IN GREECE (fig. 4)[4]

The earliest Cypriot pottery found in Greece is represented by a Bichrome II flask from Lefkandi in Euboea where local pottery also shows influence from Cyprus (Popham 1994: fig. 2.2). Two barrel-shaped jugs found at Yalysos on Rhodes may be equally as old. Cypriot pottery of periods III and IV (850 to 600 B.C.E.), Black on Red I(III) and II(IV) juglets, have been found in particular in Crete and Cos, and local imitations with Greek geometric decoration were produced at both places (Coldstream 1984). Most of the Cypriot pottery from Rhodes, together with a few finds from Athens, Aegina and Euboea, belong to White Painted and Bichrome IV Wares. Local imitations of oriental Red Slip jugs and aryballoi of the so-called circle and spaghetti style were produced in Rhodes, where a single sherd with a Phoenician graffito has also appeared (Amadasi Guzzo 1987, no. 2). According to Coldstream, Phoenicians from Kition, the so-called Cypro-Phoenicians, probably set up unguent factories in the Aegean islands; in Cos and Crete the local potters made the containers for the perfume, while resident Oriental potters produced the aryballoi that were made in Rhodes (Coldstream 1982: 268). Other evidence for Cypriot influence is present in Cretan pottery (Gjerstad 1948: 299; Bock 1957: 191; Coldstream 1977: 69) and in the so-called Cypro-jugs made in Athens and found in Cyprus (Beazley 1948: 33). These may represent an effort to increase the sales in the Cypriot market or they may have been commissioned by individual Cypriots.

PHOENICIAN POTTERY IN CYPRUS (fig. 5)

Phoenician pottery was apparently frequent in North Syria, and over six hundred pieces have been published from Cyprus (Bikai 1987). Bikai has divided the material into a set of chronological "horizons." The majority of the earliest Phoenician pottery, "the Kouklia horizon" has been found at Koukli (Palaipaphos) and is dated tentatively to 1050–850 B.C.E. This may indicate that an early Phoenician trade used western Cyprus as a stopping point. The second horizon, "the Salamis horizon," has been found along the south coast from Kouklia to Larnaca, and at Salamis and Rizokarpaso in the north. The third horizon named after Kition is absent from Kouklia, but is otherwise common along the south

---

[4] Coldstream (1969; 1984), summed up in Sørensen and Lund (1989).

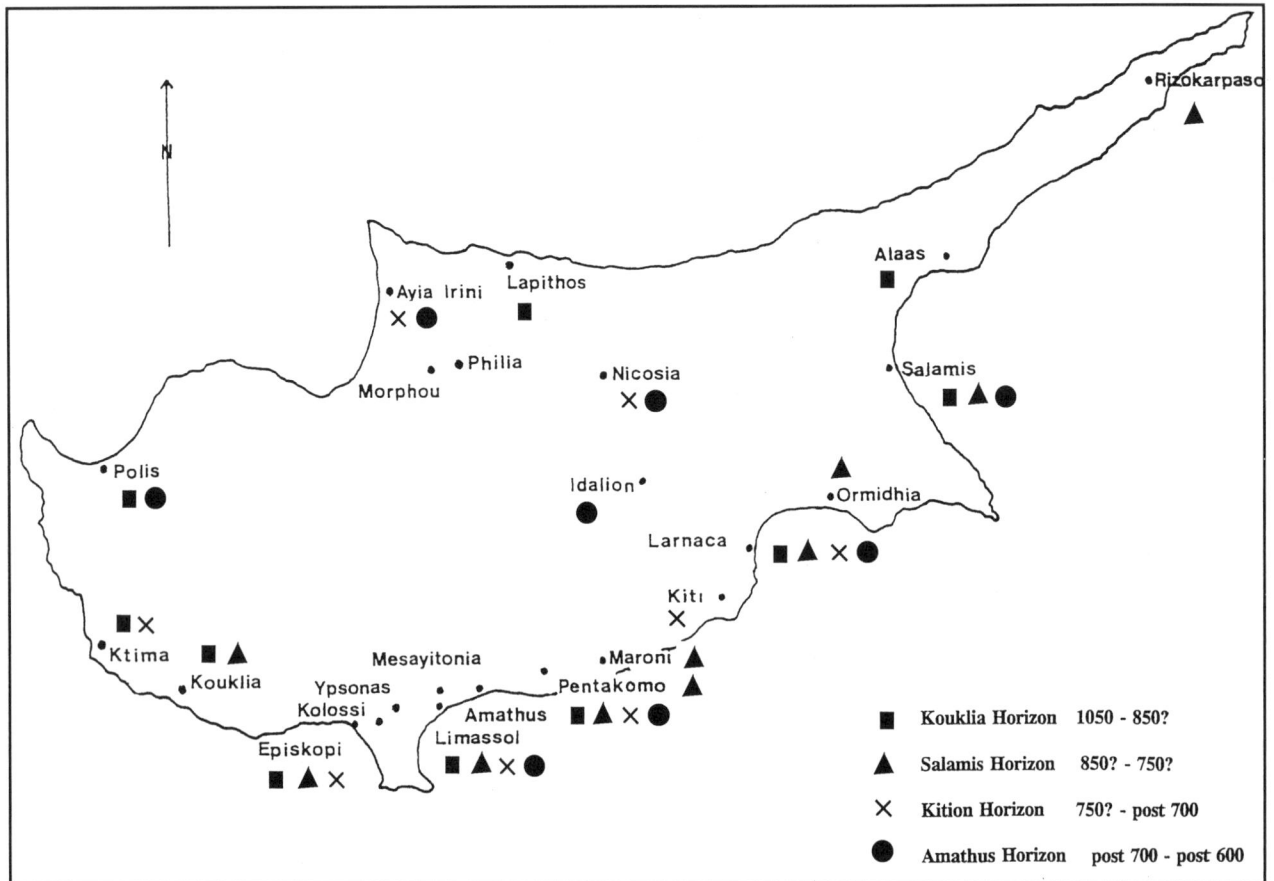

Fig. 5. Distribution of Phoenician pottery in Cyprus.

coast, and also at Ayia Irini on the northwest coast, where the quantities, according to Bikai, indicate a trading station nearby. Similarities between material from Ayia Irini and Sarepta, and pottery from Kition and Tyre, respectively, has led Bikai to suggest a division in trading spheres accordingly. The last horizon, the Amathus horizon, has also been found at Larnaca and Salamis, but is scarce in the north and west.

The variety of Phoenician shapes includes containers such as jugs and jars, but also jugs for pouring, plates and carinated shallow bowls, which we would usually associate with tableware. Phoenician pottery is considered "pedestrian and often even crude," to use Bikai's words (Bikai 1987: 48), and we may wonder what attraction it could have had to the Cypriots. The explanation could be that Phoenicians living in Cyprus simply preferred to use their own pottery. However, if Bikai's classification is followed, this would imply a certain movement of Phoenicians from one area to another within the first part of the first millennium B.C.E. This is hardly likely and far from supported by the distribution of Phoenician inscriptions (Masson and Sznycer 1972). It seems rather that Phoenician pottery was simply used alongside Greek and local pottery. The fact that

Tomb 1 of Gjerstad's Greek princess at Salamis, which contained the large number of Greek Middle Geometric pottery mentioned above, also contained thirty Phoenician vessels including various types of juglets, jugs and plates (Bikai 1987: table 1; Coldstream 1989: 93) seems to support that pottery finds cannot be used as ethnic indicators, at least in Cyprus. This is also corroborated by examples of epigraphic evidence on pottery. The appearance of an Anatolian female name scratched in Phoenician on a Red Slip jug from Kition is an eminent reminder of the need to be cautious (Adamasi and Karageorghis 1977: D6; Bonnet 1990: no. 1). Furthermore, Phoenician inscriptions also appear on Cypriot decorated pottery, for instance a graffito on a White Painted IV jug (Masson and Sznycer 1972: 94 no. 6). Phoenician names have been painted on local Cypriot pottery either before or after firing (Masson and Sznycer 1972: 112; Sznycer 1980: 128). Phoenician pottery also had an impact on the local ceramic production. Apart from the examples listed by Gjerstad (1948: 287–88) attention should be paid to the so-called Canaanite jars painted in a Cypriot manner, that have been found at Salamis and Kition (Yon 1971: pl. 23, 58; Christou 1993: 722 fig. 10).

ANALYSIS

This brief survey of the distribution of decorated pottery found in the eastern Mediterranean during the first part of the first millennium B.C.E. shows that, although both Greek and Cypriot pottery are more abundant at coastal sites in North Syria, both categories also appear at more and more sites towards the south, that an almost equal number of Greek and Phoenician pots have been found in Cyprus, and that quantities of Cypriot pottery only reached specific Greek destinations. Along with other types of objects, pottery found in a non-native context may be evidence of contact in the form of trade, colonization, or cohabitation of different ethnic groups, as well as evidence of taste and customs. However, the use of pottery finds in such contexts sometimes seems to emphasize the problem that opposing conclusions, with regard to the type of contact, have been reached. The following will describe each of these cases separately, with due consideration to the other issues.

Trade and Colonization

With regard to trade and trade routes, we are still far from having a clear picture of carriers, traders and trade routes. Several reconstructions of trade routes, either for specific commodities or in broader terms, have been suggested (Coldstream and Bikai 1988: 43; Boardman 1990; Sherratt and Sherratt 1993). For example, the belief in an early Greek colonization movement in the Geometric period has dwindled over the years, replaced by a growing tendency to consider Phoenicians and even Cypriots as carriers of the Greek material in the Levant down to the late eighth century B.C.E., when according to textual references, Greeks were raiding the coastal cities. These first active Greek enterprises in the East apparently did not yet result in Greek colonies (Braun 1982a: 15; Perreault 1991: 396 and 402; idem 1993: 81). Information about the enmity between the Greeks and the Phoenicians expressed in the literary sources (Braun 1982a: 14) has led to a focus on the differences rather that the similarities between the ceramic finds from North Syria and Phoenicia. The non-native ceramic finds in both areas would have been interpreted as evidence of one and the same process, in particular because of the similarities between the finds from Ras el Bassit and Tyre. In other parts of the world, for instance at Pithecussai on the island of Ischia, the Phoenician element in the Euboean settlement suggests an initially friendly attitude between the Greeks and the Phoenicians, and so do the even earlier finds from Sant'Imbenia in Sardinia (Ridgway 1994: 41). According to Niemeyer, the Greek agrarian colonization movement of the seventh century forced the Phoenicians to establish themselves more permanently near the centers of old

metal routes in southern Spain in order to consolidate earlier trade relations (Niemeyer 1993; cf. also Ridgway 1994). This is in keeping with the reported Greek raids on the coast of the Levant and suggests a changing relationship between Greeks and Phoenicians. How is this change reflected in the patterns of pottery finds? As mentioned above, East Greek pottery replaced Euboean and Attic geometric pottery and became the dominant foreign type at most find places in the seventh and early part of the sixth century B.C.E. In the latter part of the sixth century B.C.E. Attic pottery took over this role. There seems, however, not to be a reflection of hostilities in the distribution of the pottery, thus pottery seems to be a bad indicator of the political situation in the recipient areas (cf. Gill 1994: 106).

According to analyses of trade marks on later Greek fine ware pottery, Corinthian pottery was mostly handled by Corinthian traders or commisioners, while Attic Black- and Red-figure products were also traded by people from outside Attica, mainly Ionians (Johnston 1979; idem 1991: 219), and at least in the fifth century B.C.E., even by western Phoenicians and Cypriots (Johnston 1979: type 26F no. 21; Gill 1988: 6). Furthermore, evidence so far available from shipwrecks shows that cargoes were mixed, and contained also pottery from different production centers both in the Archaic and Classical periods (Parker 1990; Treister 1993). Unless there was a change in the carrier systems, we may assume that mixed cargoes were common during the Geometric period also. These sets of information represent yet another warning with regard to deductions based on ceramic evidence.

Ethnicity

The second issue is pottery as evidence for ethnicity. A survey of the inscriptions on pottery found in the areas dealt with here leads to an interesting conclusion: Inscriptions on pottery need not prove the existence of Greeks in the Levant until the end of the seventh to early sixth century B.C.E. when Greek inscriptions appear also on local pottery. The population in Cyprus is considered a mixture of Greeks, Phoenicians and Cypriots, the so-called Cypro-Greeks, Cypro-Phoenicians and Eteo-Cypriots, terms that do not signify well-defined population groups, but have been inferred from descriptions of specific groups of objects. As mentioned above, two different writing systems, Cypriot Syllabic and Phoenician, were used. Both scripts were either incised or painted on both local and Phoenician pottery (Karageorghis and Karageorghis 1956), but apparently neither writing system was used on Greek pottery until the fifth century B.C.E. (Johnston 1978: type 26F, no. 21). Greek graffiti have not appeared on local or Phoenician pottery, and are so far restricted to the few Greek vessels from Salamis mentioned above. According to the present evidence, both Cypriot and Phoenician pottery was owned by people speaking Cypro-Greek or Phoenician, while Greeks using the alphabet are only represented by the graffiti from Salamis, which may have been scratched on before arriving in Cyprus. This shows that in the Levant and Cyprus we have to be very careful using pottery as an indicator of ethnic relations.[5] Comparable material from Mediterranean centers believed to be points of contact support this impression. In Rhodes, where a faience factory and a local production center imitating Cypriot pottery was established by "Cypro-Phoenicians," only one Phoenician graffito, perhaps referring to wine, has appeared on a Corinthian or local bowl from Ialysos (Coldstream 1969: pl. III, h; Amadasi Guzzo 1987: 16). The majority of the aryballoi produced here have been found at Pithecussai where the evidence points toward an Oriental element in the population (Ridgway 1992: 111–12). This is supported by the use of an amphora of Greek type with Greek and Aramaic graffiti and a superimposed Semitic funerary symbol used for a child burial (cf. also Amadasi Guzzo 1987: fig. 10). Other Phoenician inscriptions are seen on a local imitation of an Early Protocorinthian kantharos and a Phoenician Red Slip plate (Amadasi Guzzo 1987: fig. 8–9; Ridgeway 1992: fig. 31). The famous Nestor inscription from Pithecussai, written on a cup from Rhodes, presents another interesting case (Ridgway 1992: fig. 26), and an amphora with a Messapian name from the late seventh or early sixth century B.C.E. may indicate that a man from Apulia was living at Pithecussai (Buchner and Ridgway 1993: tomb 285, 1). Marriages between Greeks and locals are believed to have taken place not only at Pithecussai, but also at other places situated at the frontiers of the Greek world, but in his recent analysis of various possible examples of mixed marriages Coldstream sees "no compelling evidence at this time of any intermarriage between Aegean and Cypriot Greeks" (1993: 98). However, child burials in Phoenician jars found at Salamis and Kition from the early Iron Age (Calvet 1980) may indicate that mixed marriages did take place, in this case between Cypriots and Phoenicians, since little else suggests the presence of separate Phoenician enclaves within the Cypriot communities.

Additional examples of Greek pottery used as evidence for Greek settlers in the Levant may also be questioned. An Ionian is believed to have been buried in a sixth century B.C.E. tomb at Ras el Bassit, which contained Greek pottery and an Etruscan kantharos (Courbin 1990a: 508). However, the tomb was disturbed (Courbin 1991: 264), and since the Greek pottery was from different places it could have been collected by a local inhabitant. It has also been suggested that the tombs at Tell Sukas dating from the late seventh to early fifth centuries B.C.E. belong to a mixed Greek-Phoenician population. Here drinking cups found in the tombs are exclusively Greek and fragments of tiles were found in connection with some of the tombs (Riis 1979: 31; 1982: 49). However, since only tomb 29 was certainly associated with both a tile fragment and a cup, and tiles were not generally used for burials in eastern Greece during the Archaic period, the evidence is inconclusive. We may also question whether the so-called Greek mercenaries buried in Israel with Attic lekythoi were indeed Greeks. We may assume that the majority of Greeks participating in conflicts against Egyptians and Persians came from eastern Greece. However, the significance of Attic lekythoi in eastern Greek burial contexts has not been analyzed, therefore a firm conclusion with regard to these finds must await such studies.

Taste and Customs

The third issue pertains to the evaluation of different types of pottery used for the same purposes in past societies. The assumption introduced by Cook (1959: 122) that Greek pottery was not appreciated by Near Easterners was accepted by many, not least for its usefulness in proving the presence of Greeks in the East, but the finds from Tyre in particular seem to contradict this. If Coldstream is correct in suggesting that large shapes like kraters were used as gifts among the elite, they must have been prized in the East. Coldstream's suggestion (1989: 94) that the surface treatment of the Geometric skyphoi made them more pleasant to drink from than the local products should also be taken into consideration. The lack of extensive imitations of Greek pottery in the Levant may suggest that these wares were not liked by the local inhabitants, but an alternative explanation for this could be that the local potters were unable to technically produce them considering their own rather coarse products.

In Cyprus, both Phoenician and Greek pottery was imitated, however it is a more interesting phenomenon that Greek potters in a few known cases imitated vessel shapes from the Levant and Cyprus with the apparent purpose of selling them in these areas. The geometric plate with pen-

---

[5] In this connection it is not entirely irrelevant to pay attention to the later epigraphical evidence from Al Mina, since it documents a Levantine rather than a Greek ownership. Of the fifty graffiti on late fifth to fourth century B.C.E. Attic fragments, thirteen are illegible, thirty Phoenician, seven Aramaean and one Greek? (Elayi 1987: 260).

dant semi-circles and the Attic so-called Cypro-jug are two well-known examples. Attic potters are also known to have imitated vessel shapes from Etruria, East Greece and Egypt for the very same markets (Boardman 1980). Cypriot pottery represented a source of inspiration for pottery productions in Crete, Rhodes and Cos, and Phoenician pottery did have an impact on the local pottery production of Central Italy (Rathje 1983: 7). The latter was probably connected with the influence of a new custom, the banquet, which was introduced to this area directly from the Levant, rather than from Greece (Rathje 1994). It has been suggested that western Phoenician imitations of Greek skyphoi may indicate an adoption of Greek drinking habits in western Phoenician societies (Briese and Docter 1992: 42). Imitations of Greek skyphoi are known from Cyprus and the Levant, therefore their route to the western Mediterranean might as well start from there.

The debate about the value of Attic Black and Red-figure pottery in antiquity is well-known and need not be repeated here, but notice should be paid to a recent contribution by Small (1994). She draws attention to the evidence from Etruscan tomb paintings that indicate that the wealthi-est Etruscans dined from metal ware. This brings us back to the Levant and Cyprus where these bowls were made. Although none of them has been found in Phoenicia, their presence at Nimrud and in Cyprus together with other types of metal vessels amply testify to their popularity in the Near East, as do the written sources (Zaccagnini 1984; Aubet 1993: 63). However, the fact that metal ware was preferred by those who could afford it does not exclude that foreign ceramic products were also appreciated, perhaps simply because they were foreign and not easily available or because customs had changed.

It has been the purpose of this survey of interconnections of traveling pottery—primarily from the eastern Mediterranean during the first part of the first millennium B.C.E. to stress the importance of regional analyses of material available in the Levant, Cyprus, Greece, Italy and the Iberian peninsula. Most importantly, the analysis has demonstrated a need to co-ordinate these analyses in order to obtain a coherent understanding of trade, politics, and movement of ethnic groups and customs in the entire Mediterranean area in the period under discussion.

REFERENCES

Amadasi, M. G., and Karageorghis, V.
1977   *Fouilles de Kition III. Inscriptions Phéniciennes.* Nicosia: The Department of Antiquities, Cyprus.

Amadasi Guzzo, M. G.
1987   Iscrizioni semitiche di nord-ovest in contesti greci e italici (X–VII sec. C.). *Dialoghi di Archeologia*: 13–27.

Anderson, W. P.
1988   *Sarepta I. The Late Bronze Age and Early Iron Age Strata of Area II, Y.* Beyrouth: Publications de l'Université Libanaise.

Aubet, M. E.
1993   *The Phoenicians and the West. Politics, Colonies and Trade.* Cambridge: Cambridge University.

Balensi, J., and Herrera, M.-D.
1985   Tell Abu Hawam 1983–1984. *Revue biblique* 92: 82–128.

Beazley, J. D.
1948   Some Attic Vases in the Cyprus Museum. *Proceedings of the British Academy* 33: 3–51.

Ben-Tor, A., and Portugali, Y.
1987   *Tell Qiri. A Village in the Jezreel Valley.* Qedem 24. Jerusalem: The Institue of Archaeology. The Hebrew University of Jerusalem.

Bikai, P. M.
1978   *The Pottery of Tyre.* Warminster, England: Aris & Phillips.
1987   *The Phoenician Pottery of Cyprus.* Nicosia: A. G. Leventis Foundation and J. Paul Getty Trust.

Boardman, J.
1980   *The Greeks Overseas. Their Early Colonies and Trade.* London: Thames and Hudson.
1982   An Inscribed Sherd from Al Mina. *Oxford Journal of Archaeology* 1.3: 365–67.
1990   Al Mina and History. *Oxford Journal of Archaeology* 2: 169–90.

Bock, J. K.
1957   *Fortetsa. Early Greek Tombs near Knossos. Athens.* Annual of the British School at Athens. Supplementary Paper 2. Athens.

Bonnet, C.
1990   Lés Étrangers dans le Corpus Épigraphique Phénicien de Chypre. *Report of the Department of Antiquities Cyprus:* 141–57.

Braun, T. F. R. G.
1982a   The Greeks in the Near East. Pp. 1–31 in vol. III. 3 of *Cambridge Ancient History. The Expansion of the Greek World, Eighth to Sixth Centuries B.C.,* eds. J. Boardman and N. G. L. Hammond. Cambridge: Cambridge University.

1982b   The Greeks in Egypt. Pp. 32–53 in vol. III. 3 of *Cambridge Ancient History. The Expansion of the Greek World, Eighth to Sixth Centuries b.c.,* eds. J. Boardman and N. G. L. Hammond. Cambridge: Cambridge University.

Briese, Ch., and Doctor, R.
1992   Der Phönizische Skyphos: Adaption einer Griechischen Trinkschale. *Madrider Mitteilungen* 33: 25–69.

Buchner, G., and Ridgway, D.
1993   Pithekoussai I. *Monumenti Antichi. Serie Monografica* 4. Rome: Accademia Nazionale dei Lincei.

Calvet, Y.
1980   Sur certaines rites funéraires de Chypre. Pp. 115–21 in *Salamine de Chypre. Histoire et archéologie,* ed. M. Yon. Paris: Centre National de la Recherches Scientifique.

Calvet, Y., and Yon, M.
1977   Céramique trouvée à Salamine (Fouilles de la ville). Pp. 9–21 in *Greek Geometric and Archaic Pottery found in Cyprus,* ed. E. Gjerstad et al. *Opuscula Atheniensia* 4. Stockholm: Åströms.
1978   Salamine de Chypre et le commerce ionien. Pp. 43–51 in *Les céramiques de la Gréce de l'est et leur diffusion en occident.* Paris and Naples: Centre Jean Bérard Paris; Institut Francais de Naples.

Christou, D.
1993   Chronique des fouilles à Chypre en 1992. *Bulletin de Correspondance Hellénique* 117: 719–55.

Coldstream, J. N.
1968   *Greek Geometric Pottery.* London: Methuen.
1969   The Phoenicians of Ialysos. *Bulletin of the Institute of Classical Studies* 16: 1–8.
1977   *Geometric Greece.* London: E. Benn Ltd.
1979   Geometric Skyphoi in Cyprus. *Report of the Department of Antiquities Cyprus:* 255–69.
1982   Greeks and Phoenicians in the Aegean. Pp. 261–75 in *Phönizier im Westen,* ed. H.G. Niemeyer. *Madrider Beiträge* 8.
1983   Gift Exchange in the Eighth Century b.c. Pp. 201–206 in *The Greek Renaissance of the Eighth Century b.c.: Tradition and Innovation,* ed. R. Hägg. Svenska Institutet i Athen. Stockholm: Åströms.
1985   Archaeology in Cyprus 1960–1985: The Geometric and Archaic periods. Pp. 47–59 in *Archaeology in Cyprus 1960–1985,* ed. V. Karageorghis. Nicosia: A. G. Leventis.
1984   Cypriaca and Cretocypriaca from the North Cemetery of Knossos. *Report of the Department of Antiquities Cyprus:* 122–37.

1989   Early Greek Visitors to Cyprus and the Eastern Mediterranean. Pp. 90–94 in *Cyprus and the East Mediterranean in the Iron Age,* ed. V. Tatton Brown. London: British Museum.
1993   Mixed Marriages at the Frontiers of the early Greek World. *Oxford Journal of Archaeology* 12: 89–107.

Coldstream, J. N., and Bikai, P. M.
1988   Early Greek Pottery in Tyre and Cyprus: Some Preliminary Comparisons. *Report of the Department of Antiquities Cyprus* 2: 35–44.

Collombier, A.-M.
1987   Céramique grecque et échanges en Méditerranée orientale: Chypre et la côte syro-phénicienne. Pp. 239–48 in Phoenicia and the East Mediterranean in the First Millenium b.c., ed. E. Lipinski. *Studia Phoenicia* 5.

Cook, R.M.
1959   Die Bedeutung der bemalten Keramik für den griechischen Handel. *Jahrbuch des deutschen archäologischen Instituts* 74: 114–23.

Courbin, P.
1978   La céramique de la Grèce de l'est à Ras el Bassit. Pp. 41–42 in *Les céramiques de la Grèce de l'est et leur diffusion en Occident.* Paris and Naples: Centre Jean Bérard Paris; Institut Francais de Naples.
1982   Gourdes, *Revue Archeologie* I: 9–24.
1983   Bassit. *Les annales archeologiques arabes syriennes* 33.2: 119–27.
1986   Bassit. *Syria* 63: 175–219.
1990a   Bassit-Posidaion in the Early Iron Age. Pp. 503–9 in *Greek Colonists and Native Populations,* ed. J.-P. Descoeudres. Oxford: Clarendon.
1990b   Fragments d'amphores protogeometriques grecques a Bassit. Pp. 49–64 in *Resurrecting the Past. A joint Tribute to Adnan Bogunni,* eds. P. Matthiae, M. van Loon and H. Weiss. Belgium.
1991   Bassit-Posidaion des origines à Alexandre. Pp. 257–68 in *O ELLENESMOS STEN ANATOLE.* Athens: European Cultural Centre of Delphi.

Desborough, V. R. d'A.
1972   *The Greek Dark Ages.* London: E. Benn.

de Vries, K.
1977   Attic Pottery in the Achaemenid Empire. *American Journal of Archaeology* 81: 544–48.

du Plat Taylor, J.
1959   The Cypriot and Syrian Pottery from Al Mina, Syria. *Iraq* 21: 62–92.

Elayi, J.
1987   Al-Mina sur l'Oronte à l'époque perse. Pp. 247–66 in Phoenicia and the East Mediterranean in the First Millennium b.c., ed. E. Lipinski. *Studia Phoenicia* 5.

Gal, Z.
1992   Hurbat Rosh Zait and the Early Phoenician Pottery. *Levant* 24: 173–86.

Gilboa, A.
1989   New Finds at Tel Dor and the Beginning of Cypro-Geometric Pottery Import to Palestine. *Israel Exploration Journal* 39: 3–4, 204–18.

Gill, D. W. J.
1988   Silver Anchors and Cargoes of Oil: Some Observations on Phoenician Trade in the Western Mediterranean. *Annual of the British School at Athens* 56: 1–12.

1994   Positivism, pots and long-distance trade. Pp. 99–107 in *Classical Greece. Ancient Histories and Modern Archaeologies,* ed. I. Morris. New Directions in Archaeology. Cambridge: Cambridge University.

Gjerstad, E.
1944   The Colonisation of Cyprus in the Greek Legend. *Opuscula Archaeologica* 3: 107–23.

1948   The Cypro-Geometric, Cypro-Archaic and Cypro-Classical Periods. *The Swedish Cyprus Expedition* IV. 2. Stockholm: V. Pettersons.

1979   A Cypro-Greek Royal Marriage in the Eighth Century B.C. Pp. 141–46 in *Studies Presented in the Memory of P. Dikaios,* ed. V. Karageorghis et al. Nicosia: The Lions Club of Nicosia.

Hermary, A.
1987   Amathonte de Chypre et les phéniciens. Pp. 375–88 in Phoenicia and the East Mediterranean in the First Millenium B.C., ed. E. Lipinski. *Studia Phoenicia* 5.

Herrera, M. D., and Balensi, J.
1986   More about the Greek Geometric Pottery at Tell abu Hawam, *Levant* 18: 169–71.

Johnston, A. W.
1979   *Trademarks on Greek Vases.* London: Aris & Phillips.

1991   Greek Vases in the Marketplace. Pp. 203–32 in *Looking at Greek Vases,* eds. T. Rasmussen and N. Spivey. Cambridge: Cambridge University.

Jones R. E.
1986   *Greek and Cypriot Pottery. A Review of Scientific Studies.* Greece: British School at Athens.

Karageorghis, V.
1982   *Cyprus from the Stone Age to the Romans.* London: Thames and Hudson.

1983   *Palaepaphos-Skales. An Iron Age Cemetery in Cyprus,* ed. F. G. Maier. Konstanz: Deutsches archäologisches Institut.

Karageorghis, V., and Karageorghis, J.
1956   Some Inscribed Iron-Age Vases from Cyprus. *American Journal of Archaeology* 60: 351–59.

Kearsley, R.
1989   The Pendant Semi-Circle Skyphos. *Bulletin of the Institute of Classical Studies. Supplement* 44.

Knapp, B. A.
1988   "Hoards d'Oevres: of metals and men on Bronze Age Cyprus." *Oxford Journal of Archaeology* 7: 147–76.

Koehl, R. B.
1985   *Sarepta III. The Imported Bronze and Iron Age Wares from Area II, X.* Beyrouth: Université Libanaise.

Lapp, P. W.
1967   The 1966 Excavations at Tell Ta'anek, *Bulletin of the American Schools of Oriental Research* 185: 2–39.

Liverani, M.
1987   The Collapse of the Near Eastern System at the End of the Bronze Age: the Case of Syria. Pp. 66–73 in *Centre and Periphery in the Ancient World,* eds. M. Rowlands, M. Larsen and K. Kristiansen. Cambridge: Cambridge University.

Lund, J.
1986   Sukas VIII. *The Habitation Quarters.* Historisk-Filosofiske Skrifter 12. Copenhagen: The Royal Danish Academy of Sciences and Letters.

Maier, F. G., and Karageorghis, V.
1984   *Paphos. History and Archaeology.* Nicosia: A. G. Leventis.

Marchese, R. T.
1989   Aegean and Cypriote Imports in the Persian Period (Strata XI–VI). Pp. 145–52 in *Excavations at Tel Michal, Israel,* eds. Z. Herzog, Jr., G. Rapp, and O. Negbi. The University of Minnesota, Minneapolis and Sonia and Marco Nadler Institute of Archaeology, Tel Aviv University.

Masson, O.
1961   *Inscriptions chypriotes syllabiques,* Paris: École Francaise d'Athenes.

Masson, O., and Sznycer, M.
1972   *Recherches sur les Phéniciens a Chypre.* Paris: Centre de Recherches d'Histoire et de Philologie.

Muhly, J. D., and Stech, T.
1990   Final Observations. Pp. 202–17 in Metallographic and Statistical Analyses of Copper Ingots from Sardinia, eds. F. Lo Schiavo, R. Maddin, J. Merkel, J.D. Muhly and T. Stech. *Quaderni* 17.

Niemeyer, H. G.
1993   Trade before the Flag? On the Principles of Phoenician Expansion in the Mediterranean. Pp. 335–44 in *Biblical Archaology Today. Proceedings of the Second International Congress on Biblical Archaeology, Jerusalem 1990.* Jerusalem.

Oldenburg, E., and Rohweder, J.
1981   *The Excavations at Tall Daruk (Usnu?) and Arab al-Mulk (Paltos).* Historisk-Filosofiske Skrifter 10: 3. København: Det Kongelige Danske Videnskabernes Selskab.

Parker, A. J.
1990   Classical Antiquity: The Maritime Dimension. *Antiquity* 64: 335–46.

Perreault, J. Y.
1986   Céramique et Échanges: Les importations attiques au Proche-Orient du VIe au milieu du Ve siècle avant J.-C. Les données archéologiques. *Bulletin de Correspondance Hellénique* 110: 145–75.
1991   Lés débuts de la présence effective de grecs surla côte syro-palestinienne à l'age du fer. Pp. 393–406 in *O ELLENESMOS STEN ANATOLE.* Athens: European Cultural Centre of Delphi.
1993   Les emporia grecs du Levant: Mythe ou réalité? Pp. 59–83 in *L'Emporion,* eds. A. Bresson and P. Rouillard. Paris: Pierre Paris.

Ploug, G.
1973   *Sukas II. The Aegean, Corinthian and Eastern Greek Pottery and Terracottas.* Historisk. Filosofiske Skrifter 6, 2. København: Det Kongelige Danske Videnskabernes Selskab.

Popham, M. R.
1994   Precolonization: Early Greek Contact with the East. Pp. 11–34 in *The Archaeology of Greek Colonisation. Essays Dedicated to Sir John Boardman,* eds. G. R. Tsetskhladze and F. De Angelis. Oxford University Committee for Archaeology. Monograph 40. Oxford.

Rathje, A.
1983   A Banquet Service from the Latin City of Ficana. *Analecta Romana* 12: 7–29.
1994   Banquet and Ideology. Some New Considerations About Banqueting at Poggio Civitate. Pp. 95–99 in *Murlo and the Etruscans,* eds. R. De Puma and P. Small. Wisconsin: University of Wisconsin.

Ridgway, D.
1992   *The First Western Greeks.* Cambridge: Cambridge University.
1994   Phoenicians and the Greeks in the West: a View from Pithekoussai. Pp. 35–46 in *The Archaeology of Greek Colonisation. Essays Dedicated to Sir John Boardman,* eds. G.R. Tsetskhladze and F. De Angelis. Oxford University Committee for Archaeology. Monograph 40. Oxford.

Riis, P. J.
1948   *Hama II 3. Fouilles et recherches de la Fondation Carlsberg 1931–1938. Les cimetières*

à crémation. Copenhague: Fondation Carlsberg.
1960   L'activité de la mission archéologique danoise sur la côte phenicienne en 1959, *Annales Archéologiques de Syrie* 10: 111–32.
1979   *Sukas IV. The Graeco-Phoenician Cemetery and Sanctuary at the Southern Harbour.* Historisk-Filosofiske Skrifter 10: 2. Ktbenhavn: Det Kongelige Danske Videnskabernes Selskab.
1982   Griechen in Phönizien. Pp. 237–60 in *Phönizier im Westen,* ed. H. G. Niemeyer. Madrider Beiträge 8. Mainz: von Zabern.
1991   Les problèmes actuels de l'établissement pré-hellénistique de grecs sur la côte phénicienne (lieux, dates, modalités). Pp. 203–11 in *Atti del II Congresso Internationele di Studi Fenici e Punici* 1. Roma: Istituto per la civiltà fenicia e punica.

Riis, P. J., and M. L. Buhl
1990   *Hama II 2. Fouilles et recherches de la Fondation Carlsberg 1931–1938. Les objets de la période dite Syro-Hittite (âge du fer).* Copenhague: Nationalmuseet.

Robertson, M.
1940   The Excavations at Al Mina, Sueidia IV. The Early Greek Vases. *Journal of Hellenic Studies* 60: 2–21.

Rupp, D. W.
1987   Vive le Roi: The Emergence of the State in Iron Age Cyprus. Pp. 147–61 in *Western Cyprus: Connections,* ed. D. W. Rupp. Studies in Mediterranean Archaeology 77. Göteborg: Åströms.

Shaw, J. W.
1989   Phoenicians in Southern Crete, *American Journal of Archaeology* 93: 165–83.

Sherratt, S., and Sherratt, A.
1993   The Growth of the Mediterranean Economy in the Early First Millennium BC. *World Archaeology* 24: 361–78.

Small, J. P.
1994   Scholars, Etruscans, and Attic painted vases. *Journal of Roman Archaeology* 7: 34–58. Wisconsin: University of Wisconsin.

Sørensen, L. W.
1987   Cypriote Iron Age Pottery: An Experiment Employing Simple Quantitative Analysis. Pp. 129–35 in *Western Cyprus: Connections,* ed. D.W. Rupp. Studies in Mediterranean Archaeology 57. Göteborg: Åströms.
1988   Greek Pottery found in Cyprus. *Acta Hyperborea* 1: 12–32

Sørensen, L. W., and Lund, J.
1989   Cypriot Finds in Greece and Greek Finds in Cyprus ca. 950–500 B.C. Pp. 294–96 in *Early*

Society in Cyprus, ed. E. Peltenburg. Edinburgh: Edinburgh University.

Stern, E. (ed.)

1978 *Excavations at Tel Mevorakh (1973–1976). Part one: From the Iron Age to the Roman period.* Qedem 9. The Hebrew University of Jerusalem.

1982 *Material Culture of the Land of the Bible in the Persian Period 538–332.* Warminster: Aris and Phillips.

Sznycer, M.

1980 Salamine de Chypre et les Phéniciens. Pp. 123–29 in *Salamine de Chypre. Histoire et archéologie,* eds. V. Karageorghis et al. Paris: Centre National de la Recherches Scientifique.

Treister, M. Y.

1993 Notes on International Trade in the 6th–4th Century BC. Pp. 377–89 in *Aspects of Hellenism in Italy,* eds. P. Guldager, I. Nielsen, M. Nielsen, *Acta Hyperborea* 5. Copenhagen: University of Copenhagen.

Wenning, R.

1981 Griechische Importe in Palästina aus der Zeit vor Alexander d.Gr.. Vorbericht über ein Forschungsprojeckt, *Boreas* 4: 29–46.

Yellin, J.

1989 The Origin of some Cypro-Geometric Pottery from Tel Dor. *Israel Exploration Journal* 39: 219–27.

Yellin, J., and Perlman, I.

1978 Provenance of Iron Age Pottery from Tell Mevorakh. Pp. 86–105 in *Excavations at Tel Mevorakh (1973–1976),* ed. E. Stern. Qedem 9, The Hebrew University of Jerusalem.

Yon, M.

1971 *Salamine de Chypre II. La tombe T.I. du XIe s. av. J.C.* Paris: Université de Lyon. Institut F. Courby.

Zaccagnini, C.

1984 La circolazione dei beni di lusso nelle fonti neo-assire (IX–VII sec.a.C.). *Opus* 3: 235–47.

Ptolemy IX Soter II Lathyrus on Cyprus and the Coast of the Levant

Robert R. Stieglitz

Department of Classical and Modern
Languages and Literatures
Rutgers University
175 University Avenue
Newark, NJ 07102
U.S.A.

While he was king of Cyprus, Ptolemy IX Soter II (Lathyrus) became involved in the struggle for control of the coastal strip between Phoenicia and Egypt—from Ptolemais-Akko to Gaza. His direct military intervention completely transformed the geopolitics of the region and resulted in a new alignment that lasted until the Romans imposed yet another political arrangement. This paper deals primarily with the military and naval aspects of Ptolemaic actions on the Syria-Palestinian coast during the period 108–95 B.C.E. The attribution of the bronze ram from Athlit to one of three Ptolemaic fleets of this era is also discussed.

W. W. Tarn, in his classic study of Hellenistic civilization, characterized Ptolemy IX [designated VIII by Tarn], who was nicknamed Lathyrus "Chickpea" (116–80 B.C.E.), as a "colourless" king (Tarn 1965: 45). This prosaic assessment seems to me to have missed the mark, for, as we shall see, Lathyrus was anything but bland! Indeed, during a period noted for almost continual civil upheavals, when regional and local alliances were often shifting and treachery was customary, he managed to secure for himself a rather long and eventful reign, in Egypt, on Cyprus and finally, over both. The beginning of his career was rooted in his political experience on Cyprus.

Ptolemy served as governor *(stratēgós)* of that island from 118 to 116 B.C.E., for his father, Ptolemy VIII Euergetes II (145–116 B.C.E.). Upon the death of Euergetes on 28 June 116 B.C.E., Lathyrus, who was his elder son, was recalled to Egypt to become co-regent as Ptolemy IX Soter II, sharing the throne with his mother Cleopatra III (116–101 B.C.E.). The relationship between the queen and her son can only be described as tempestuous at best. Ptolemy was twice ex-pelled from Egypt by the queen, and twice reconciled with his mother, first in 110/9 B.C.E. and again in the spring of 108 B.C.E. These episodes were merely the forerunners to the real storm.

Late in 108 B.C.E., or early the following year, he made his first military move in the Levant (Josephus, *Antiquities of the Jews* 13.278). Soter dispatched an army of six thousand Egyptian troops to aid his Seleucid ally Antiochus IX Cyzicenus (115–96 B.C.E.), who had married his divorced wife Cleopatra IV. Antiochus needed this auxiliary army to augment his recently defeated forces in the region of Samaria. The Syrian king found himself in this predicament after he had responded to an appeal for help from the city of Samaria, which was then besieged by the Hasmonaean ruler of Judaea, John Hyrcanus I (135–104 B.C.E.). This Samaritan campaign eventually ended in disaster for Antiochus, as he lost numerous troops to Judaean ambushes. He therefore returned to Syria, having appointed two generals to conduct the war on his behalf (*AJ* 13.279). The force sent by Soter from Egypt was evidently unable to deliver victory and Samaria was captured by the Hasmonaean forces late in the year 107 B.C.E.[1]

In Egypt, meanwhile, Soter found himself once again in a state of severe crisis with his mother. Their struggle culminated in an uprising in Alexandria in October 107 B.C.E., leading to a battle that forced Soter to flee the city by ship.[2] Evidently his intervention in Syria-Palestine had so angered his mother that their intermittent quarrel was now transformed into unremitting warfare. Soter was again forced into exile and found refuge on Cyprus. There seems to be no doubt that in time of need, he could rely on his Cypriot supporters, as he was well-known on the island that he had previously governed.

During the reign of Euergetes II, Cyprus was elevated to a more prominent geopolitical role in the realm. The Ptolemaic navy withdrew from its bases on the Aegean islands to Cyprus, and turned the island into the headquarters of the Ptolemaic Mediterranean fleet (Mitford 1959: 125). Soon after 142 B.C.E., the capital of Cyprus was moved from Salamis to Paphos, and the Ptolemaic governors of Cyprus were granted the title of admiral (*naúarchos*). That could only mean, as noted by Mitford (1953: 124), that Egypt and Cyprus had once again formed a united kingdom, with the admiralty now located not in Alexandria but at the port city of Paphos.

In order to retain power after his hasty exit from Egypt, Soter had to secure Cyprus, for on the island were stationed both infantry and cavalry units, in addition to the significant naval forces. His mother, of course, would have none of that, and took quick action in order to crush her difficult offspring.

In the spring of 106 B.C.E., Cleopatra III dispatched a strong expeditionary force to Cyprus in order to vanquish her son. Her forces were able to capture Cyprus for the queen, but Soter eluded them and found refuge at Seleucia-in-Pieria, located at the mouth of the Orontes in North Syria. This city had declared its autonomy in 108 B.C.E. and was willing to harbor the deposed king without a country. Cleopatra did not accept the escape of her son calmly, and proceeded to execute the commanding general who had allowed Soter to escape.[3]

After foiling a plot on his life at Seleucia,[4] Ptolemy IX succeeded in marshalling an army and navy, in a remarkably short period, in order to recapture his lost throne. His

return to power was as swift as was his demise. During the course of the following year (September 106–September 105 B.C.E.), his twelvth since being crowned in Alexandria, he attacked and reconquered Cyprus. One of his first acts was to reorganize the administration of the island and to appoint a new admiral (Mitford 1959: 129). His strategy would be to use Cyprus as a base to regain the throne of Egypt.

By the year 103 B.C.E., he was secure enough on Cyprus to intervene militarily, this time personally, in Levantine affairs. As was the case five years earlier, the *casus belli* was a request for urgent military assistance by yet another city under Hasmonaean intimidation. In the spring of 103 B.C.E., the major coastal town of Ptolemais- Akko was threatened by King Jonathan Alexander Jannaeus (103–76 B.C.E.). According to Josephus (*AJ* 13.328–31), Ptolemais first summoned Soter to its aid, but later changed its mind. Josephus attributed this vacillation to internal politics, which saw a pro-Lathyrus faction struggling against a neutral party, with the latter temporarily gaining the upper hand. Thus, the obliging king of Cyprus, probably seeing a golden opportunity to improve his geopolitical position in the encounter with his mother, set sail to the Levant. On the way, he was informed about the change of heart in Ptolemais and was, therefore, uncertain if he would even be allowed to enter the city.

Soter landed at the rather obscure port of Sycamina with a substantial force of 30,000 infantry and cavalry (*AJ* 13.333). The site of Sycamina is now identified with Tell es-Samaq at the foot of the Carmel Promontory, a location quite unsuitable for landing a large legion with horses. Furthermore, the settlement itself was then in ruins, having been destroyed in 132 B.C.E. during one of the numerous Seleucid civil wars (Elgavish 1974; 1994: 1373–78). The actual landing site was not at the tell proper, but probably nearby, in the sheltered waters of Haifa al-ʿAtiqah, at the western tip of the modern harbor of Haifa. This location provided Soter with calm waters and secure flanks, should there be an attempt to disrupt his arrival.

After he landed, Soter proceeded to camp near Ptolemais and then negotiated a treaty with his supposed enemy King Jannaeus. According to their agreement, Soter would dispose of a local ruler named Zoilos, who controlled the prominent ports of Dor and Straton's Tower just south of Sycamina, in return for 400 talents of silver.[5] Jannaeus would

---

[1] According to *Megillat Taʿanit* 20, the walls of Samaria were captured on 25 Marheshwan (November); for the text, see Lichtenstein (1931–32: 257–351).

[2] Pausanius, *Description of Greece* 1.9.1–3, states that Cleopatra incited the mob to attack Soter. After he fled, his brother Alexander was recalled to Egypt from Cyprus. See Mitford (1953: 130–71).

[3] Justin 39.4.2; see Mitford (1959: 127). The conjecture that the executed general was Chelkias (*AJ* 13.287) is baseless.

[4] Diodorus 35/39.39a. The plotter was "one of his friends," presumably recruited by Cleopatra III.

[5] *AJ* 13.334–35. On the military role of Straton's Tower, see Stieglitz (1993: 646–51).

thus receive this valuable coastal strip, while Soter would substantially endow his war chest, presumably to be used in the campaign against his mother in Egypt.

This arrangement, at the expense of Zoilos, was indeed concluded, but Jannaeus also planned to betray Soter by secretly appealing to Queen Cleopatra to attack the army of her son. Soter, however, quickly uncovered this scheme and renounced the treaty. He left part of his army to besiege Ptolemais, which had indeed refused him entry, while he himself proceeded with the rest of his forces inland through the Galilee. His strategy was to secure his supplies from a local ruler named Theodorus of Emathus, presumably a more dependable ally, whose territory was located in the mostly Hellenized Transjordan (Stern 1985: 99).

The army of Soter, led by a general called Philostephanus, engaged the Hasmonaean army in crucial combat at the Transjordanian town of Asaphon, where the Judaean army was defeated after a difficult fight. Soter then continued to ravage the countryside, wisely avoiding a needless battle over Jerusalem, and made his way back to the southern coast of Palestine. He then established his headquarters in the friendly town of Gaza, while his forces in the north had in the meantime succeeded in capturing the city of Ptolemais (*AJ* 13.347). Thus, by the summer of 103 B.C.E., the *anabasis* of Soter made him master of the entire coastal strip from southern Phoenicia to the Sinai Peninsula.

These manoeuvres of Lathyrus undoubtedly alarmed his mother greatly, and she was now more determined than ever to reverse his fortunes. She quickly dispatched her younger son and co-regent, Ptolemy X Alexander I (108–88 B.C.E.), at the head of a fleet to Phoenicia. His task was evidently to secure the allegiance and support of Tyre and Sidon, which had become autonomous some twenty years earlier. Cleopatra herself sailed with another fleet to Ptolemais, and after a short siege captured the city from Soter's army at the end of the summer of 103 B.C.E. Cleopatra then advanced to Scythopolis-Beth Shan in the Jordan Valley, where she concluded a treaty of friendship with King Jannaeus. That pact, which strengthened Judaea, was a warning to the local rulers, but was primarily aimed at depriving Soter of any influence in the region.

Ptolemy IX Soter II, at Gaza, was thus cut off from his allies and decided to attack Egypt in the hope of capturing the country while his mother and brother were absent. The army of Cleopatra was under the command of two Jewish generals, Helqiyah and Hananyah (Chelkias and Ananias

in *AJ* 13.285;349). Helqiyah was apparently stationed with his forces at the gate of Egypt—in Pelusium. When Soter advanced on the port, his effort to enter Egypt was halted. Josephus noted (*AJ* 13.351) that General Helqiyah was killed while pursuing Soter, and we can conjecture that this took place in the wake of the combat at the gateway to Egypt.

In the meantime, Cleopatra and her son Alexander hastened back to Pelusium in order to regroup their forces and secure their kingdom. In this connection, we should note the inscription found long ago in Egypt, that dated to the fifteenth year of Cleopatra's (103/2 B.C.E.) reign, the very year of the crucial conflict with Soter, which records that the queen appointed a son of Chelkias to his father's command.[6] This was presumably a posthumous reward for the fallen warrior. After all, the defeat of Soter saved the throne of Cleopatra.

It is unknown what role, if any, King Jannaeus played in this battle for Egypt. There is, however, some tantalizing testimony in epigraphic and archaeological sources that the Hasmonaeans had some naval forces at their disposal. The primary Hasmonaean harbor was at Jaffa, which was captured and annexed around 140 B.C.E. by Simon—a younger brother of Judah the Maccabee (I *Maccabees* 13:5). More significant is the report about the very lavish family mausoleum built by him for his father and fallen brothers at their home town of Modi'in. The monument was set in a prominent position high in the hills, one which made it visible from the sea, a distance of some 28 km:

> And he erected seven pyramids in a row, for his father and his mother and his four brothers. And he made devices for these, setting up great columns and putting on the columns trophies of armor for an everlasting memorial, and beside the armor carved prows of ships, so that they could be seen by all who sailed the sea (I *Maccabees* 13:28–30).

According to Eusebius (*Onomastikon* 703), this monument was still admired by visitors at the beginning of the Byzantine period. We should also note that when the Hasmonaeans began minting coins, shortly after the rule of Simon, they included naval symbols in their numismatic repertoire. This development coincides with the recruiting of Aegean and Anatolian mercenaries into their army.

The interest of the Hasmonaeans in nautical matters was certainly expanded during the reign of Jannaeus. A contemporary Jewish tomb excavated in Jerusalem (Rahmani

---

[6] Reinach (1900: 50–54); the name of the son before the patronymic *Chelkiou* is missing). Also see (Kasher 1990: 144). On Cleopatra and Alexander at Pelusium in 103/02, see Stern (1964: 332 n. 40). On the chronology, see Glanville and Skeat (1954: 45–58).

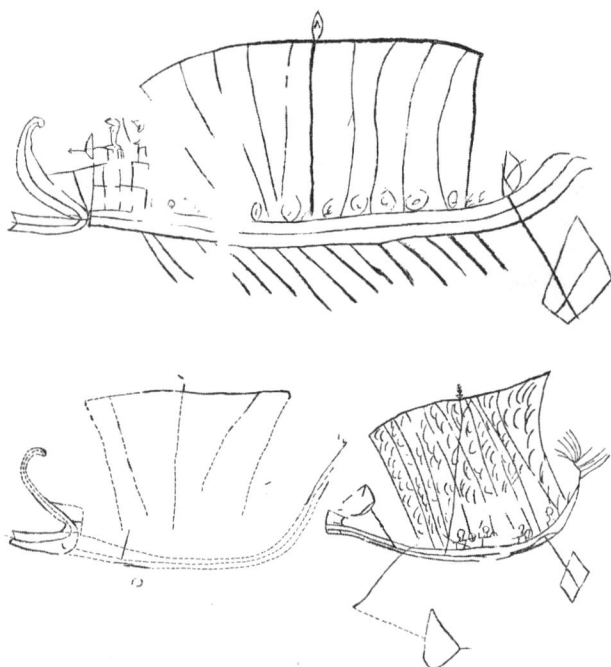

Fig. 1. Warships in the Tomb of Jason, Jerusalem, ca. 100 B.C.E. After Rahmani (1964).

Fig. 2. Model of warship from the Tomb of Jason at the National Maritime Museum, Haifa.

1964) of someone named Jason provides a valuable glimpse into the vessels of the period. In the tomb were found several ship graffiti (figs. 1, 2), clearly indicating that Jason had some nautical connection. There was also an Aramaic epitaph and a brief Greek inscription in the tomb, but unfortunately they do not shed any more light on this matter. Yet the very presence of the nautical scene in a tomb from the early years of King Jannaeus suggests a nautical involvement. Perhaps Jason was an officer in charge of a naval unit manned by Aegean mercenaries.

Of particular interest is the depiction of the two warships in action (fig. 1), both equipped with a prominent three-pronged ram. It is very tempting to connect this illustration in Jerusalem with the find of an actual bronze ram at Athlit, dated to this period. This unique find, made in 1980 off the northern harbor at Athlit, may well have belonged to a Ptolemaic vessel from one of the three fleets—those of Lathyrus, Cleopatra or Alexander—that operated along the Syro-Palestinian coast during the hectic year 103/2 B.C.E. Less likely is the possibility that the Athlit ram is from a unit in the paid service of King Jannaeus. Studies of the ram itself, the symbols on its surfaces and the wood that attached it to the hull, suggest that it was from a trireme, probably built on Cyprus (Casson and Steffy 1991).

In any event, after his defeat at Pelusium, Soter was forced to retreat to his base at Gaza, where he spent the winter of 103/2 B.C.E. Seeing that his mother and brother were firmly in control of Egypt, he sailed back to Cyprus in the Spring of 102 B.C.E. a much wiser king, substantially wealthier, and certainly more experienced. There is epigraphic evidence from Paphos that at this time, or perhaps even before his departure for the Levant in 103 B.C.E., a Ptolemaeion was founded in honor of Soter. The temple provides the earliest evidence for the existence of a ruler cult on Hellenistic Cyprus (Watkin 1988: 326).

In Egypt, Cleopatra did not savor the triumph over her eldest son for long. In the autumn of 101 B.C.E., Ptolemy X Alexander I had his mother killed (Pausanius, *Description of Greece* 1.9.3), and then reached a *modus vivendi* with his brother Soter. They evidently agreed to maintain the *status quo*, which meant that the contested coastal strip of Palestine was recognized, *de facto*, as belonging to the Judaeans.

King Jannaeus did not wait long to take advantage of the new geopolitical arrangement. After Soter left Gaza in 102 B.C.E., the city declared its autonomy, following in the footsteps of several major coastal towns in Syro-Palestine. Jannaeus now found this situation quite appropriate for his own territorial ambitions. He attacked and conquered Gaza in 100/99 B.C.E. (Kasher 1986: 1;1990: 145), thus extending his control along the Levantine littoral from Carmel to Rhinocolura (El Arish). Only the city-state of Ascalon remained free of Hasmonaean domination (Kanael 1955: 9–15). Its unique status was attained because Ascalon was a faithful ally of the rulers in Alexandria, in spite of the fact that the city had declared its autonomy in 104/3 B.C.E.

As king of Cyprus, Ptolemy IX still did not abandon his hope of regaining the throne of Egypt and clearly believed that the road to Alexandria still led through Syria. In the year 96/5 B.C.E., after the death of his ally Antiochus IX, he intervened again in the Levant. This time, he recalled another Seleucid prince, Demetrius III Eucaerus, from the island of Knidos and had him installed as king in Damascus (*AJ* 13.370). The disintegrating Seleucid kingdom was now divided between this ruler and his brother Antiochus X Philip I (Stern 1964: 329).

King Soter remained ruler of Cyprus until 88 B.C.E., when a major rebellion in Egypt, and the flight of his younger brother Alexander, resulted in his recall to Alexandria as the sole regent. During the next three years, Soter acted decisively, thereby preserving his crown. Among the noteworthy consequences of his deeds was the nearly total destruction of Thebes, as King Soter successfully put down the simmering revolt. By 85 B.C.E., he was the undisputed king of both Egypt and Cyprus. He made one final royal appearance on the coast of the Levant, albeit a numismatic one. In the year 84/3 B.C.E., the city of Ascalon issued a coin depicting the portrait of the rather colorful Soter, to commemorate the city's twentieth year of autonomy and ongoing successful alliance with the Ptolemaic Dynasty.[7]

Ptolemy IX Soter II remained on the throne of Egypt until his death in 80 B.C.E., having reigned over Egypt and Cyprus for a total of thirty-six years. During his turbulent reign, his military actions in Syro-Palestine, Cyprus and Egypt altered the geopolitical balance of power in favor of the Ptolemies, at the expense of the Seleucid kingdom, which was in its final stages of collapse.

Cyprus was the key to his success due to the Ptolemaic Mediterranean fleet's headquarters location on the island, which he skillfully used to his advantage. Yet only a generation after his eventful reign, in the year 58 B.C.E., Cyprus was taken away from Egypt and became part of the Roman sphere of influence. The new overlords from Italy had previously decided to enter the Levant to stay. Like their predecessors, the Romans too had to control the island of Cyprus, in order to protect their interests on the coast of the Levant.

REFERENCES

Brett, A. B.
1937　A New Cleopatra Tetradrachm of Ascalon. *American Journal of Archaeology* 41: 452–63.
Casson, L. and Steffy, J. R., eds.
1991　*The Athlit Ram.* College Station, TX: Texas A&M University.
Elgavish, J.
1974　*Archaeological Excavations at Shikmona, II*: The Level of the Hellenistic Period—Stratum H. Haifa: City Museum of Ancient Art.
1993　Shiqmona. Pp. 1373–78 in *The New Encyclopedia of Archaeological Excavations in the Holy Land,* vol. 4, ed. E. Stern. Jerusalem: Israel Exploration Society/Carta.
Glanville, S. R. K. and Skeat, T. C.
1954　Eponymous Priesthoods of Alexandria from 211 B.C. *Journal of Egyptian Archaeology* 40: 45–58.
Kanael, B.
1955　Notes on Alexander Jannaeus' Campaigns in the Coast Region. *Tarbiz* 24: 9–15. In Hebrew.
Kasher, A.
1986　Josephus on King Jannaeus' War against the Hellenistic Cities. *Cathedra* 41: 11–36 (in Hebrew).
1990　*Jews and Hellenistic Cities in Eretz-Israel.* Tuebingen: JCB Mohr.
Lichtenstein, H.
1931–　Die Fastenrolle. *Hebrew Union College Annual*
1932　8–9: 257–351.

Mitford, T. B.
1953　Seleucus and Theodorus. *Opuscula Atheniensia* 1: 130–71.
1959　Helenos, Governor of Cyprus. *Journal of Hellenic Studies* 79: 94–131.
Rahmani, L. Y.
1964　*The Tomb of Jason.* ʾAtiqot 4 (in Hebrew). Jerusalem: Israel Department of Antiquities.
Reinach, Th.
1900　Un prefet juif il y a deux mille ans. *Revue des études juives* 40: 50–54.
Stern, M.
1964　The Political Background of the Wars of Alexander Jannai. *Tarbiz* 33: 325–33 (in Hebrew).
1985　The Relations between the Hasmonaean Kingdom and Ptolemaic Egypt, in view of the International Situations during the 2nd and 1st Centuries B.C. *Zion* 50: 81–106 (in Hebrew).
Stieglitz, R. R.
1993　Straton's Tower: The Name, the History and the Archaeological Data. Pp. 646–51 in *Biblical Archaeology Today, 1990*: Proceedings of the Second International Congress on Biblical Archaeology, Jerusalem, June-July, 1990. Jerusalem: IES—Israel Academy of Sciences & Humanities.

---

[7] Bret (1937: 452–63). Her conclusions on the relationship between Lathyrus (designated by her as Ptolemy X), King Jannaeus and the city of Ascalon were justifiably criticized by Kanael (1955).

Tarn, W. W.

1961   *Hellenistic Civilization,* rev. 3rd ed. Cleveland and New York: Meridian.

Watkin, H. J.

1988   *The Development of Cities in Cyprus from the Archaic to the Roman Period.* Ph.D. dissertation. New York: Columbia University.

A Classification of Ancient Harbors in Cilicia

ROBERT L. VANN

School of Architecture
University of Maryland at College Park
College Park, MD 20742
U.S.A.

This paper explores the relationship between the city and its harbor and the criteria for insuring a successful combination. These criteria include the availability of fresh water, a fortifiable position, a sound economic regional base, physical connections to the interior, and the location of a suitable harbor. Examples, including cities such as Coraceseum, Selinus, Antioch on the Crag, and Pompeiopolis are drawn from the ancient region of Rough Cilicia on the south coast of Turkey.

The purpose of this paper is to explore the relationship between the city and its harbor. Once established, which combination will be successful and which will not? The focus is not on architectural infrastructure such as breakwaters, shipsheds, warehouses, or lighthouses (Blackman, 1983), nor on the position of the harbor within the city and the fortifications, streets, marketplaces, and various shops, eateries, and baths that one associates with a port facility. The principal focus of the paper is why certain positions were selected as harbors and cities and, of the many natural anchorages around the eastern Mediterranean used by sailors during the Bronze and Iron ages, why some became important classical harbors while others did not? Think about the voyage of the Late Bronze Age ship found at Uluburun (see Pulak, this volume). When she sailed along the Turkish coast it was largely uninhabited. Fifteen hundred years later there were literally dozens of harbors, some serving as ports of call for large freighters that crisscrossed the open sea while others were significant only for local or regional trade. This paper will outline ideas about a formula for success for the city and its harbor, using as examples some of the lesser known sites of Rough Cilicia where I have been carrying out a harbor survey since 1991 (fig. 1; Vann 1992, 1994). These are not large cities and their names might not be as familiar as the better-known sites of the western coast of Asia Minor. The term "city" will be used throughout the paper although most of these sites should more accurately be called towns. They were

prosperous to a limited extent, but judging from the rubble construction of their public buildings, they do not appear as substantial as the ruins in other areas of the country. Finally, there has been very little archaeological fieldwork in Rough Cilicia. The coast has been well-traveled by teams of epigraphers including Heberdey and Wilhelm (1896), Herzfeld and Guyer (1933), Keil and Wilhelm (1931), Bean and Mitford (1962, 1965, 1970), and, more recently Dagron and Feissel (1987). On the other hand, Anemurium is the only site that has been systematically excavated for an extended period of time. New work is now being carried out at Kelenderis by Konya University, but that project is only in its fifth year.

The Cilician coast of southern Turkey traditionally has been divided into two distinct zones by its topography. To the east is the broad alluvial plain of the Sarus and Pyramus rivers, known in antiquity as Cilicia Pedias or Smooth Cilicia. The second, more mountainous region, Cilicia Tracheia or Rough Cilicia, lies to the west, extending from Tarsus to Coraceseum (modern Alanya) and inland to the crest of the Taurus mountains. This coast of Rough Cilicia can be further sub-divided into three regions according to their relationship to the Taurus range. The western area, between Coraceseum and Anemurium, extended from the border with Pamphylia on the west to the southernmost point of the mainland facing toward Cyprus on the east. The coast, about 125 km long, runs northwest to southeast and is parallel to the ridges of mountains on the interior. This region

Fig. 1. Map of Cilician coast with principal harbor locations.

is characterized by steep, high bluffs with long stretches of straight shores, but is without the deep indentations necessary for excellent harbors. There are a few small coastal plains at the effluences of short seasonal streams. Ancient towns on or near this coast include Coraceseum, Iotape, Selinus, Cestrus, and Antioch on the Crag (fig. 1).

The Central Zone between Anamur and Silifke features a 140 km coastline crossing the grain of the mountain range at an angle, thus creating numerous indented bays separated by projecting rocky headlands. There are also many islands along this coastal stretch. Although the terrain offers better sites for harbors, the rugged landscape and lack of open land for farming has resulted in this section being more sparsely populated than areas farther east. Towns in this zone are Anemurium, Celenderis, Aphrodisias-Zephyrium, and Seleucia on the Calycadnus (fig. 1).

The eastern Zone from Silifke to Mersin, a distance of 90 km, is once again parallel to the range of mountains with no direct access across the rugged Taurus, other than the Calycadnus river. It too has a relatively smooth coast with small inlets to serve as natural harbors. Seasonal streams created a rugged terrain of deep ravines along this coast that made land communication difficult through the first half of this century. A wider coastal plain emerges at Evanlı, gradually increasing in width toward Mersin and Tarsus. Ancient sites in this zone include Coraseum, Corycos, Eleausa-Sebaste, and Soloi-Pompeiopolis (fig. 1).

Why did settlements appear where they did in Cilicia? What forms did their harbors take? How were harbors and cities related? There are general criteria to consider—requirements necessary for settlements throughout the ancient world. But there is also a regional character to be taken into account based upon local conditions. For example, in Rough Cilicia, one must look first to the few coastal plains that are of sufficient size to support large populations. Next, there is the region's natural wealth, specifically its ancient forests. Finally, we have the reputation of its citizens for brigandry on land and piracy at sea.

GENERAL CRITERIA

Obviously the formula varied considerably from time to time and place to place, but must have always included critical items such as (1) the availability of fresh water, (2) an area that might be fortified, (3) a sound economic base whether it be the agricultural wealth of inland territory or the existence of nearby raw materials, (4) physical connections to the interior, and (5) the location of a suitable harbor. All of these would have been major considerations for locating a city, but the lack of one or more of these features would not necessarily mean an urban center would fail. For example, some cities were located away from the coast for protection against seaborne invaders, and had separate harbor facilities.

Water

Local water might have been provided by aqueduct systems such as those in Selinus or Elaeusa-Sebaste (fig. 2). Such amenities were almost expected during the Roman Imperial period to serve its major consumers like the public baths and ornamental nymphaea. But wells, springs, or rivers might have provided the public water supplies for most cities until these later Roman building types multiplied throughout the provinces. Another major water source throughout antiquity was the storage of winter rains in large underground cisterns like those from Kanytelleis (fig. 3) or Andriake. Concerns about the availability of water certainly changed according to the strategic stability of a region. Obviously there were greater problems with a secure water supply during the unsettled Late Hellenistic period when the safest supply would be local cisterns, wells, or springs within the city walls. By the same token, during the quieter Imperial period, aqueducts carried on impressive bridges could deliver water from more distant springs. Water was a special requirement for the larger harbors that would need fresh supplies to provide ship stores.

Fortifications

Secondly, the city's position should be fortified. Once again, the degree of this concern varied from the Hellenistic through the Roman period, only to come full circle during late antiquity when this same stretch of coast included the frontiers of the shrinking Byzantine empire and the expanding Arab world. Often the selection of a strongly defensible position was the single most important consideration during periods when the majority of these cities were founded in either the eighth or seventh centuries B.C.E., or the early Hellenistic period. An excellent example is Seleucia on the Calycadnus, one of the few larger cities of the region. The city developed around its acropolis, now identified by a formidable late antique castle, commanding a view across the broad Calycadnus delta. Seleucia's harbor was within the navigable river but we do not know exactly where it was located. A team of Dutch scholars studying the hydrology of the Göksu delta suggested to me that the site might have been a low lying area a few kilometers southeast of the modern city of Silifke. Its situation was similar to that they found at Tarsus, just beyond the border of Rough Cilicia in the plains of Smooth Cilicia, where a grove of extremely tall poplars might mark the rich soil that now fills the ancient harbor basin.

Other examples of sites obviously selected with their defensive positions in mind are Coraceseum and Selinus. At the former, a steep hill over 200 m high emerges from the coastal plain (figs. 4, 5). Its sheer cliffs and elevated position provided an easily defensible site with excellent views up and down the coast. Extensive circuit walls seen today belong to the early Turkish period when the city was a harbor for the Selçuks. Higher on the acropolis significant remains of Hellenistic masonry are visible that must have stood there during the first century B.C.E. when we know the city served as headquarters of the Cilician pirates. Even the strength of this position did not insure success but could have provided its inhabitants with a good view down on the decisive battle between Pompey and the pirate fleet that took place in 67 B.C.E.

Selinus or Trajanopolis, about 45 km to the southeast, was situated at the base of another steep hill over 200 m

Fig. 2. Aqueduct at Selinus.

Fig. 3. Cistern at Kanytelleis.

high (fig. 6). Once again to the south are sheer cliffs and even the more gentle northern approach would tire anyone climbing up to lay siege to the walls. Most of the fortifications here are of a later date but I assume that the location of an earlier settlement during the Hellenistic and Roman pe-

riods included at least some degree of enclosure. Selinus is most famous as the city where Trajan died on his way back to Rome from campaigns in the East. After that event the city took the name of Trajanopolis for a short while.

Not all acropoli were so imposing as Coraceseum and Selinus. On a smaller scale we can see the same concern for

Fig. 4. General view of acropolis at Coraceseum.

Fig.5. Rugged terrain of Corceseum.

a secure position at nearby Iotape where the city is set on a small fortified headland forming a harbor on its eastern side (figs. 7, 8). Like most settlements of this region, practically nothing is known about the site. Seen here from the east, Iotape is the first anchorage one approached when sailing

west from Selinus, some 10 km away. The tiny cove is well-protected from the southwesterlies by its acropolis. Overlooking the anchorage to the east is a Roman bath of row-type plan, and just above it a prostyle marble temple. Iotape was a small town that remained small. Its harbor was ad-

Fig. 6. Acropolis of Selinus-Trajanopolis.

Fig. 7. Distant view of Iotape from the west.

equate for local trade but there is no reason to believe that it was ever anything more than a modest port that might be visited on the way from Coraceseum to Selinus. Yet three inscriptions associated with Trajan found at the site have suggested to Bean and Mitford (1965: 27–29; Dio 68.17)

that the emperor stopped here on his way to Syria on his final campaign.

The next site is Antioch on the Crag where the town is set out on hilltops at least 300 m above the sea (fig. 9). Continuous city walls were not necessary but several hill-

Fig. 8. Harbor and acropolis of Iotape.

Fig. 9. View of twin anchorages at Antioch on the Crag.

tops were heavily fortified. We will return to this site below to discuss its role as the ideal small scale pirate anchorage. Finally we have the opposite condition at Soloi-Pompeiopolis where the city stands on a flat plain and with the only hillside used to position its theater. The defense of this town always depended on its walls rather than on a naturally strong position. Obviously there were other reasons for the location of the city and I return to this site later.

Economic Base

The third general criterion is the availability of an economical base, including sustenance and the proximity of raw materials. A rapid survey of Rough Cilicia shows that there are very few coastal plains. From west to east these are: Coraceseum, Selinus, Anemurium, Charadrus, Seleucia on the Calycadnus and Soloi-Pompeiopolis. There are other minor valleys and plains where the location of a village or town and its harbor becomes almost predictable once the researcher becomes well-acquainted with the countryside. An example is found at Charadrus (fig. 10).

The major coastal plains were probably most important for raising food for local consumption, and one would expect to find a bartering system that allowed one town or village with excellent vineyards or productive fields to exchange goods with its neighbors. Other sites might have depended mostly on fishing for their subsistence. Small towns probably had natural anchorages that needed few, if any, improvements. Perhaps a timber quay like those seen

along the coast today would have facilitated loading and unloading, but without careful surveying these perishable materials would be difficult to identify by archaeologists (fig. 11). One of Cilicia's few natural resources was the excellent timber from its mountains, suitable for ship construction. It is possible that some of the smaller anchorages were employed to gather timber locally and load it on vessels for transport. A convenient parallel to these would be the small havens along the Cypriot coast mentioned by Blue (this volume) that facilitated the exportation of copper.

Connections with the Interior

The fourth criterion for a successful harbor would be its connections with the wider range of markets of the interior. To limit oneself to the products of a local region would result in a harbor of only minor importance. If, on the other hand, harbors along the south coast were transshipment points for a wider territory of the Anatolian plateau or Taurus uplands, their significance would naturally increase. Drawing upon the information provided by Burnet (this volume) on the forest products of Cyprus, we might expect a similar range of exports form the Cilician harbors.

Harbor Location

Finally, and most critical for our interest in siting coast settlements, was the position of a suitable harbor. An excellent solution would be to have a natural harbor either formed

Fig. 10. Plain at Charadrus.

by a promontory or set within a cove that was alongside an easily fortified position. Because prevailing winds in this region are from the southwest, the best anchorages will be to the eastern sides of these promontories. On the other hand, a shift of wind would make an anchorage on the opposite (west) side more advantageous. Small scaled versions of this can be seen at Iotape and Söğük Su where protruding landmasses create protected anchorages on their eastern flanks (fig. 12). The latter is one of the clearest diagrams of a harbor along the Cilician coast. The area, now marked

Fig. 11. Timber Quay at Knidos.

Fig.12. Harbor at Söğük Su.

only by very late antique walls, occupies a headland connected to the shore by a narrow isthmus. To the east is a well-protected harbor, while to the west lies a more exposed position.

A much larger version of the same scheme is seen at Aphrodisias, perhaps the best natural harbor along the entire coast (figs. 13, 14). The site occupies a large peninsula approximately 2.5 km across. Only on the north, in the direction of a tiny isthmus that joins it to the mainland, is there a low-level approach to the island. The best anchorage is on the northeast, the same location as the early Christian church of St. Pantaleon excavated by Budde (1987) more than a decade ago. Aphrodisias is another example of a double harbor on opposite sides of a peninsula joined to the mainland by a narrow isthmus and in this case, because of the size of the promontory and the height of its peaks, there is likewise a protected anchorage on the west side.

There is no evidence for a natural harbor at Selinus-Trajanopolis but it does not seem likely that goods would be off-loaded on a beach exposed to the southwesterlies. Two other possibilities seem more compelling. First, the harbor might have been east of the acropolis. The land behind the peak is low and could have been the site of a now silted-in harbor. Remains of a colonnaded street have been reported running from the forum toward this location. A second possibility is that the city's anchorage was within the river (fig. 15). The site remains unexcavated although plans have been produced by both Beaufort (1817) and Rosenbaum (1967: 32). Partially visible along the left bank

of the stream are an open forum, a bath, and a colonnaded enclosure 80 m square with a later Selçuk structure built on ancient foundations. The location of the forum and a bath in this area is consistent with the proximity of a river harbor but with the exception of some stonework found by Beaufort still facing the internal angles of the river banks, no additional evidence exists at this time.

A large trading harbor in Cilicia is best-illustrated by Soloi-Pompeiopolis, where a spacious new basin was constructed in the second century C.E. (figs. 16, 17). Soloi was badly damaged by Tigranes of Armenia during the Mithradatic wars, and many of its citizens were removed. The city remained deserted until 67 B.C.E. when, following his successful campaign against the Cilician pirates, Pompey settled some of the survivors here. In gratitude the city took the name of Pompeiopolis and initiated a new era date.

Boyce (1969) proposed that the harbor illustrated on coins of Antoninus Pius of 143/44 C.E. should refer to the dedication of the port. She further suggests that Hadrian might have initiated this project during his journey though Cilicia on the way to Egypt (Boyce 1958: 72). This makes a lot of sense. The emperor was continually at the center of building projects, whether as patron or honoree. The rounded end is visible to the left, and a two-story structure surrounded the interior basin where a reclining figure identified as a harbor god fills the central field. A male figure stands on the base at the upper (eastern) terminus; a higher tower on the opposite (western) side might have been the lighthouse. There has been no excavation at Pompeiopolis other than

Fig. 13. Isthmus connecting peninsula to mainland at Aphrodisias.

the probes made by Beaufort and his sailors in the silted harbor. They reported finding large quantities of tile, broken pottery, and ancient glass before being compelled to stop because of the high level of ground water (Beaufort 1818: 249).

The concrete breakwaters at Pompeiopolis are the best-preserved in Asia Minor and were the subject of a University of Maryland survey in 1993 (Vann 1994). Although badly silted and now partially blocked with beachrock, the basic lines of the basin are recognizable. It is enclosed by

Fig. 14. Eastern harbor at Aphrodisias with Church of St. Pantaleon in foreground.

Fig. 15. Location of possible river harbor at Selinus-Trajanopolis.

two parallel breakwaters 180 m apart and almost 300 m long. This rectangular space is expanded by two large semicircular ends, that to the northwest carved into the land, and to the southeast open on its central axis to serve as the entrance from the sea. Its overall length is almost 500 m and the central axis of colonnaded street and harbor is one of the most impressive relationships of city and harbor in the Roman period (Vann 1993).

Finally, and very important for Cilicia during the first century B.C.E., was the use of local harbors by the pirates described by Rauh (this volume) and their associates from Crete described by Frost (this volume). Both Side and Phaselis were harbors known to have been used by the pirates, as well as the markets on the island of Delos. Their local stronghold was Coraceseum, which we have already discussed in terms of its siting and fortification. For its harbor we are unfortunately less certain. Beaufort's plan shows a breakwater in approximately the same location as the modern deep water berth for cruise ships that has probably obliterated any earlier evidence. But it is not certain that the Beaufort plan shows the ancient breakwater. In fact the harbor of Coraceseum was rebuilt by the Selçuks who added the fortification walls, the great Red Tower, and the vaulted ship sheds. We have no firm evidence about the size or position of the ancient harbor except to say that it must have been in this same approximate location at the foot of the fortified city.

A second site to consider as a pirate harbor is Antioch on the Crag. There are two tiny anchorages hidden beneath the seaside cliffs. To the right is a small beach open through a deep vertical cut between two fortified hilltops and to the left a second, hidden anchorage approached by way of a natural cave communicating with the sea. Both inlets are very small and would not allow much traffic. Their location was not convenient to the city, more than 300 m above it. In other words, these anchorages at Antioch would not have served well as a commercial harbor with significant amounts of traffic, but would have been superb as hidden harbors with excellent visibility from easily fortified positions. Sailors familiar with the coastline could slip into their protected anchorages while being defended by allies on the crags above. Antioch was an ideal site for Cilician pirates interested in preying on the shipping that utilized this section of the channel between Cilicia and Cyprus.

CONCLUSION

The earliest anchorages were in natural coves where ships might stop for the night protected from the prevailing southwest seas. The excellent natural harbor at Aphrodisias, or the small headland at Söğük Su might be included in this category. A second harbor type was located in navigable rivers. We know, for example, that Seleucia on the Calycadnus and Tarsus, both inland cities, were served by harbors on their rivers within the inland delta regions. A third river harbor was probably at Selinus, also known for a time during the second century C.E. as Trajanopolis for it was here that Trajan came ashore and then died on his jour-

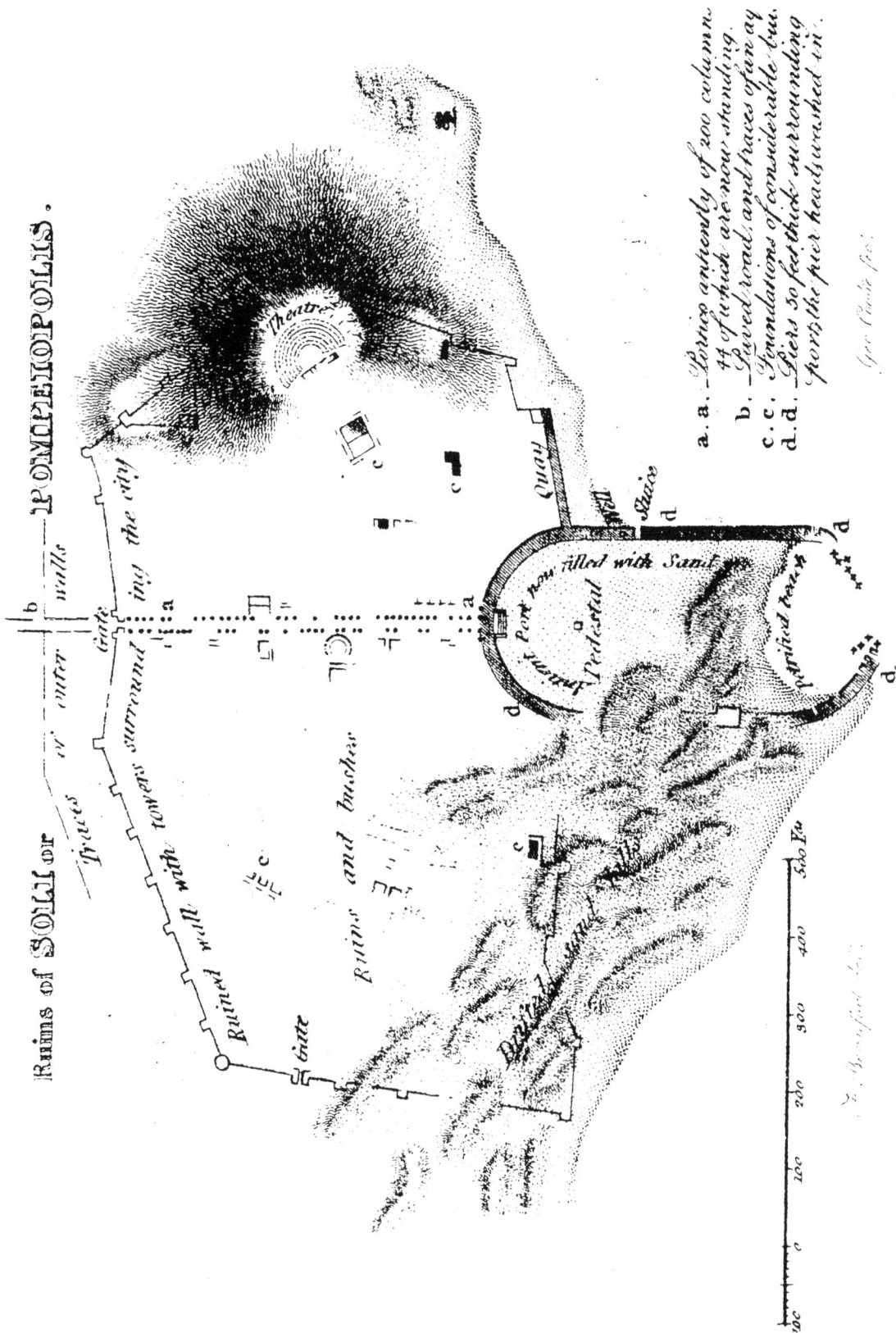

Fig.16. Plan of Pompeiopolis and its harbor.

ney from Syria back in the direction of Rome. The site today has no visible evidence of a harbor but its position on
one of the few large coastal plains would suggest that some
type of port existed. Its exposure to the southwest seas, seen
dramatically in the breakers along its coast, would lead me
to believe that vessels would seek the shelter of the quieter
river rather than offload in the heavy surf zone (fig. 6). Fi-

nally, there were harbor locations that were either partially
or wholly man-made, intended to meet the demands of larger
vessels in the Hellenistic and Roman periods. The most
impressive example of this category was the second century Roman Imperial harbor at Pompeiopolis. The site, now
just west of the major city of Mersin, was near the natural
borders between Rough and Smooth Cilicia, where the
coastal plain begins to widen noticeably to the east.

REFERENCES

Bean, G. and Mitford, T. B.
    1962   Sites Old and New in Rough Cilicia. *Anatolian
            Studies* 12: 185–217.
    1965   Journeys in Rough Cilicia in 1962 and 1963.
            *Österreichische Akademie der Wissenschaften,
            Wien, Philosophisch-historische Klasse,
            Denkschriften*, 85: 3–44.
    1970   *Journeys in Rough Cilicia in 1964–1968.*
            Österreichische Akademie der Wissenschaften,
            Wien, Philosophisch-historische Klasse,
            Denkschriften, 102.

Beaufort, Sir F.
    1817   *Karamania.* London: R. Hunter.

Blackman, D. J.
    1983   Ancient Harbours in the Mediterranean. *Inter-
            national Journal of Nautical Archaeology* 11.2:
            79–104; 11.3: 185–211.

Boyce, A. A.
    1958   "The Harbor of Pompeiopolis: A Study in Ro-
            man Imperial Ports and Dated Coins," *Ameri-
            can Journal of Archaeology* 68: 67–78.
    1969   The Foundation Year of Pompeiopolis in Cilicia:
            the Statement of a Problem. *Homages à M.
            Renard, vol. 3 Collections Latomus* 103. Brus-
            sels.

Budde, L.
    1987   *St. Pantaleon von Aphrodisias in Kilikien.
            Beiträge zur Kunst des Christlichen Ostens,*
            Band 9. Recklinghausen: Bongers.

Dagron, G. and Feissel, D.
    1987   *Inscriptions de Cilicie.* Paris: de Boccardi.

Heberdey, R. and Wilhelm, A.
    1896   *Reisen in Kilikien.* Österreichische Akademie der
            Wissenschaften, Wien, Philosophisch-
            historische Klasse, Denkschriften, 44.6.

Herzfeld, E. and Guyer, S.
    1933   *Meriamlik und Korykos, Monumenta Asiae Mi-
            noris Antiqua* ii. Manchester: University of
            Manchester.

Keil, J. and Wilhelm, A.
    1931   *Denkmäler aus dem Rauhen Kilikien,
            Monumenta Asiae Minoris Antiqua* iii.
            Manchester: University of Manchester.

Vann, R. L.
    1992a   A Survey of Classical Harbors in Cilicia. *Ameri-
            can Journal of Archaeology* 92: 337.
    1992b   Ancient Harbors in Cilicia (Turkey). Pp. 75–79
            in *Underwater Archaeology: Proceedings from
            the Society for Historical Archaeology, Kingston,
            Jamaica 1992,* 75–79, eds. D. H. Keith and T.L.
            Carrell. Uniontown: Society for Historical Ar-
            chaeology.
    1993   Street and Harbor: The Urban Axis of Soli-
            Pompeiopolis (Rough Cilicia). *American Jour-
            nal of Archaeology* 97: 341–42.
    1984   Cilician Harbor Survey: 1993 Survey of Soli-
            Pompeiopolis. Pp. 68–73 in *Underwater Ar-
            chaeology Proceedings from the Society for His-
            torical Archaeology Conference, Vancouver
            1994,* eds. R. P. Woodward and C. D. Moor.
            Uniontown: Society for Historical Archaeology.

The Cypro-Mycenaean Wreck
at Point Iria in the Argolic Gulf:
First Thoughts on the Origin
and the Nature of the Vessel

YANNIS VICHOS AND YANNOS LOLOS

Hellenic Institute of Marine Archaeology
4 Al. Soutsou Street
Athens 106 71
GREECE

This paper considers the preliminary results of the underwater excavation at the Cypro-Mycenaean wreck at Point Iria in the Argolic Gulf (1990–1994), conducted by the Hellenic Institute of Marine Archaeology under the direction of the archaeologist Charalambos Pennas.

In the first part of this paper we examine the finds raised from the wreck site at Point Iria in 1991–1994. These finds include Late Cypriot IIC/IIIA, Late Minoan IIIB2 and Late Helladic IIIB2 vases and one stone anchor of composite type.

In the second part, we try to detect the route of the Iria ship along its last voyage, on the basis of the provenance of the finds deriving from our study and also from the preliminary results of the petrographic analyses of the clay of the vases.

Finally, based on contemporary iconographical evidence and relevant material from other LBA III shipwrecks, we attempt to identify the type of the ship.

The wreck at Point Iria was a chance discovery by the present president of the Hellenic Institute of Marine Archaeogy (H.I.M.A.), Nikos Tsouchlos, in 1962.[1] In 1971 Tsouchlos paid a second visit to the wreck with the archaeologist Charalambos Kritzas, Peter Throckmorton and Bruno Vailati, who filmed and photographed the site. Their first impression at the time was that it was a cargo ship of the Geometric or Archaic period. In 1990 the archaeologist Charalambos Pennas (1992) directed a survey that was organized and carried out by the Institute.

It took four continuous excavation periods under the direction of Charalambos Pennas, from 1991–1994 (Pennas, Vichos and Lolos 1995; 1996; also Karageorghis 1993a, 584–88) to plan and excavate the area of the wreck (figs. 1,

[1] We would like to thank Professor Vassos Karageorghis most warmly for his valuable help and collaboration, and also the A. G. Leventis Foundation and the Institute for Aegean Prehistory, which have been the principal financial supporters of the Iria excavation. We are also especially indebted to our colleague Dr. Lucia Vagnetti for generously supplying information during our preliminary study of the pottery from the wreck. Our warm thanks also to Professor Spyros Iakovides for useful advice on the material from the wreck, and to Dr. William Phelps for translating this paper and for his interest in our excavation. Lastly, we thank the archaeologists Tonia Koutsouraki and Stella Demesticha for drawing the finds from the wreck.

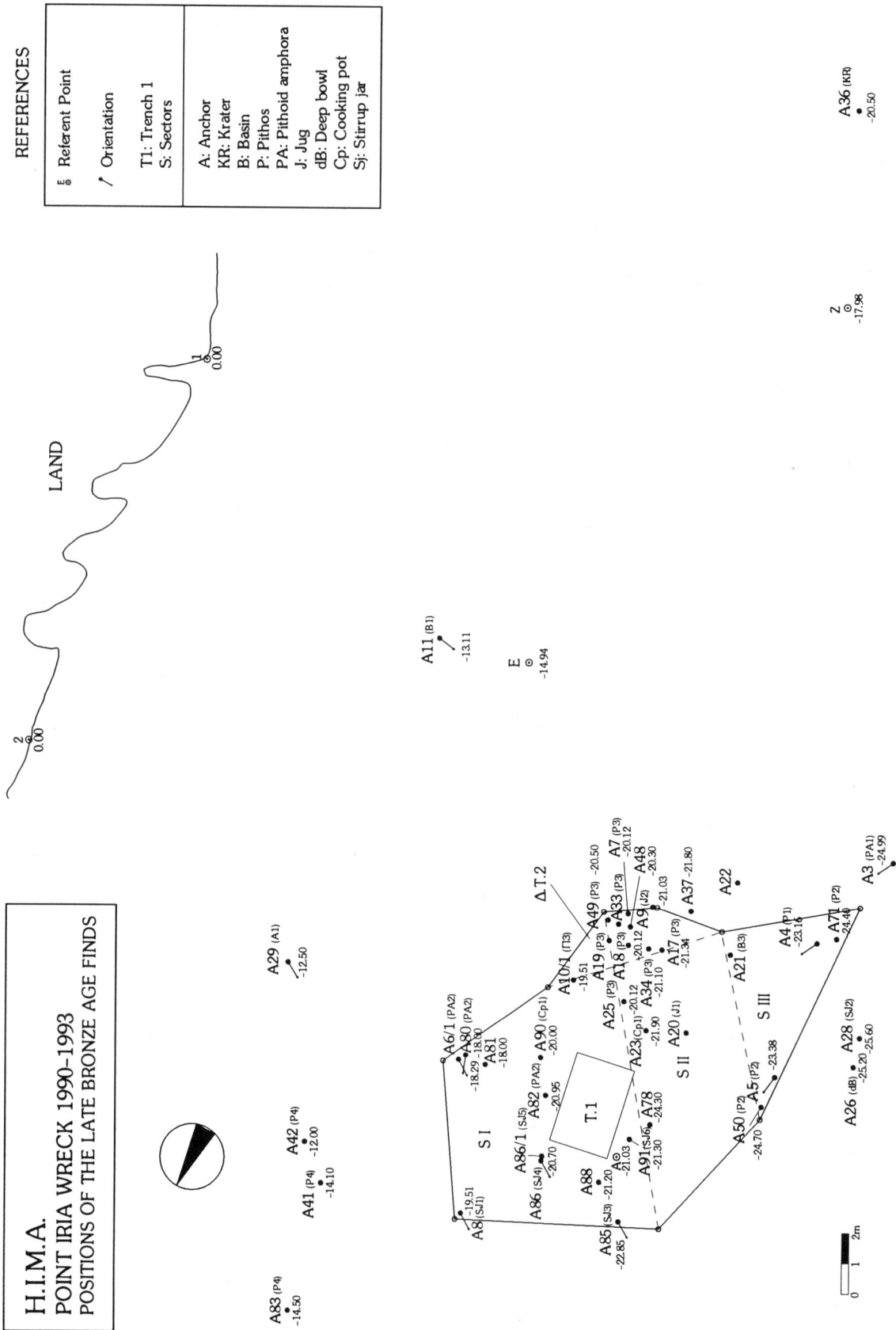

Fig. 1. Point Iria wreck. Plan of the wreck-site, with positions of Late Bronze Age III finds. Drawing by Y. Vichos.

2), which was spread over some hundred square meters on a sloping bottom with sandy intervals and patches of concretions and rocks. The areas northwest and southeast of the wreck were also investigated, and many finds of earlier, contemporary and later periods were located, from which we concluded that the locality was a highly dangerous one for shipping. The objects we discovered and raised consisted chiefly of pottery, but we also found a stone anchor and different sized stones and river stones that may have formed part of the ship's ballast, as well as small pieces of wood and some organic remains.

The Iria wreck lies about 10 m from the rocky shore and about 100 m before the tip of the promontory. Point Iria, known in ancient times as Point Strouthous, is on the north coast of the Gulf of Argolid, west of the Mycenaean site of Mases, which is mentioned in the Iliad in the catalog of Mycenaean cities that sent ships to take part in the Trojan War. A short distance north of the point, at Iria, there is another Mycenaean settlement site, and further west again stands Asine (fig. 3), a major site also mentioned in the catalog of ships.

A preliminary study of the pottery from the Iria wreck shows that it comprises one of the rarest and most important assemblages of pottery to have been found so far in Greek waters (fig. 4). The petrographic examination of the clay of the vases by Peter Day is expected to produce valuable supplementary evidence for the origins of the ship's cargo. His preliminary study, parts of which we present here, reinforces our initial observations about the provenance and date of a large part of the finds.

The large pottery fragments from the site of the wreck, which will probably make up four complete pithoi (e.g. fig. 5), and a large intact jug (fig. 6), have so many close parallels in Cyprus that there can be no doubt about their Cypriot origin.[2] The closest parallels to the Iria pithoi are typical Late Cypriot IIC and early IIIA pithoi from sites like Myrtou *Pigadhes,* Pyla *Kokkinokremos* and Maa *Palaiokastro,* and also Ugarit in Syria (Catling 1957: fig. 24:359; Karageorghis and Demas 1984: pl. XXI:18A, XXII:19, XLI:19, 18A; Karageorghis and Demas 1988: pl. LXII:462, CLXXXIV:462; Schaeffer 1949: fig 86: 22, 23, 27, 29, pl. XXXI:2). Piriform and ovoid pithoi, handleless or with two handles, and decorated with a horizontal multiple relief band on the shoulder, or often with two such horizontal bands with a central wavy band on the body, have a wide distribution in Cyprus, especially during the thirteenth century B.C. (Åström 1972: 259–64: fig. LXXII: 6; Karageorghis 1992: 8). The type of Late Cypriot IIC–IIIA pithos with an ovoid-conical body, cylindrical neck and multiple relief bands on the shoulder and body, is widely diffused in the Mediterranean, from Ugarit and Cyprus to Sicily and Sardinia (Schaeffer 1949: fig. 86: 21, 22, 23, 27, 28, 29; Ferrarese

Fig. 2. Point Iria wreck. Excavating with the air-lift around stirrup-jar A86 (1993). Photograph by K. Jachney.

[2] Petrographically these vessels have parallels in typologically similar examples from Kommos, Sardinia and southern Cyprus (Peter Day, personal communication, July 1994).

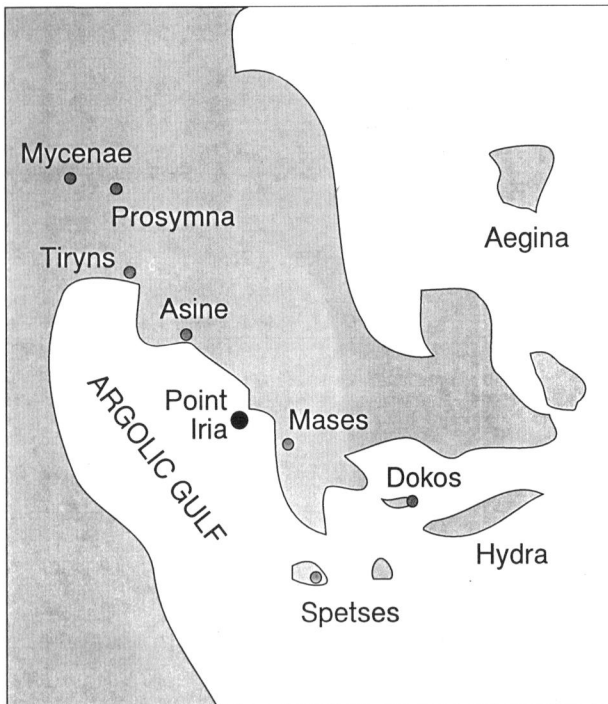

Fig. 3. Point Iria wreck. Map of Southern Argolid, with main Mycenaean sites mentioned in the text. Drawing by Y. Vichos.

Fig. 4. Point Iria wreck. Cargo of pottery (1990–1994).

Ceruti, Vagnetti and Lo Schiavo 1987: 19, 36, fig. 2.5 [from Antigori]; Karageorghis 1992: 8; 1993a, 584, fig. 3 [from Agrigento]). The Iria examples, however, are the first to be found in the Aegean (e.g. fig. 7).

To the four pithoi from Iria one more may be added, which was found intact by Nikos Tsouchlos in 1971. There was nothing inside it, according to Tsouchlos, and this also applies to the pithoi recovered from the bottom in 1991, 1993 and 1994. We have therefore no evidence for their contents. On the other hand, similar Cypriot pithoi found among the cargo of the Uluburun wreck of ca. 1300 B.C. contained olive oil, pomegranate fruit and collections of small Cypriot vases of characteristic types (Bass 1987, 710–11; Pulak 1993a).

The tall undecorated jug no. A20 (fig. 6) is distinctive for its considerable weight, massive body, wide base and relatively narrow neck. Its particular shape, which is quite different from the repertoire of Late Mycenaean pottery, as well as its general appearance, closely relate it to exact parallels among Late Cypriot IIC or IIIA jug-types from Cypriot sites like Ayios Iakovos, Myrtou *Pigadhes,* Kition, Pyla *Kokkinokremos* and Maa *Palaiokastro* (Gjerstad 1934: pl. LXVI: 1 [top row, no. 2]; Catling 1957: fig. 22: 305–7 [Plain White Jugs]; Karageorghis and Demas 1985: pl. LXII: 230/ 2; Karageorghis and Demas 1984: pl. XXXVII: 1, 24, 45, 50, 88A; 128; Karageorghis and Demas 1988: pl. LX: 550, CXCI: 550, CXCV: 615, Bothros 1/2, CXCVI: 432; also Åström 1972: fig. LXXII: 5).

There is also a second example of a Cypriot jug of this type, but smaller, in the cargo of the Iria ship (A9). It consists of the base and lower body of a jug of Late Cypriot IIC/IIIA type.

Two partly preserved vases with open shapes, the large deep bowl or basin A14 and the basin A11, which came from points outside the main concentration of pottery, may also prove to be Cypriot, once they have been properly cleaned and their clay has had the necessary laboratory examination. It should be noted that their particular shapes, which bear no similarity to those of Late Helladic IIIB plain basins from Peloponnesian sites, are very close to the shapes of contemporary, generally large deep bowls or basins from Cypriot sites, especially certain shapes from the sanctuary at Myrtou *Pigadhes* and from Pyla *Kokkinokremos* (Catling 1957: figs. 21 and 22, Plain White Bowls; Karageorghis and Demas 1984: pl. XXI: 18, XXXVI: 18).

It is probable that a partly preserved juglet (fig. 8) was inside the Cypriot pithos A5/A92 at the time the ship sank, since it was found directly underneath the pithos fragments. We can presume that the rim of the juglet, only part of which is preserved, was circular or circular with a small pinched spout or a rudimentary trefoil. The body would have been biconical-spherical or ovoid-spherical. In its general shape the juglet is closer to well-known types of Late Cypriot jugs (Åström 1972: fig. LVIII: 1, LXVII: 3, 7–9, LXIX: 9, LXX: 9–10). To judge from the type and color of the clay and the general appearance, the juglet must be a Cypriot product.

A find that stands out from the rest is the upper part of an amphora (A99) with neck slightly expanding towards the top. The rim is well-formed and rounded on the outside. The body could be restored as either spherical or ovoid/ spherical. It has two sturdy, expanded vertical handles from the rim to the shoulder. The amphora is generally well-made,

type of tall commercial stirrup-jar with an ovoid body and were probably undecorated (e.g. fig. 11). The type was popular in the Late Helladic/Late Minoan IIIA and IIIB periods, during the fourteenth and thirteenth centuries B.C. (Furumark 1941: fig. 9, shape 164).

The general shape of these stirrup-jars can be compared with coarse-ware stirrup-jars from the House of the Wine Merchant at Mycenae, dated to Late Helladic IIIA–B, and with others from the end of the Late Helladic IIIB1 period from the House of the Oil Merchant at Mycenae, as well as many inscribed stirrup-jars from sites on the Mainland and in Crete, which between them span the Late Helladic/Late Minoan IIIA2–IIIB or IIIB periods (Haskell 1981: 225, 230, no. 10952, fig. 3d, pl. 43b; Catling et al. 1980; cf. also Blegen and Rawson 1966: 403, shape 65a, fig. 329, no. 402, 389, no. 402, 390, no. 402 [from the Palace of Nestor in Messenia]).

As underwater finds, commercial stirrup-jars of the tall type occur from *Akroterion* (Uluburun) in Lycia to the island of Filicudi, north of Sicily (Bass 1987: 715; Cavalier and Vagnetti 1982: 138, no. 11, pl. XLVII: 11).

The eighth stirrup-jar from the Iria wreck (fig. 12) is of broader shape, with an ovoid-conical body; it has a painted

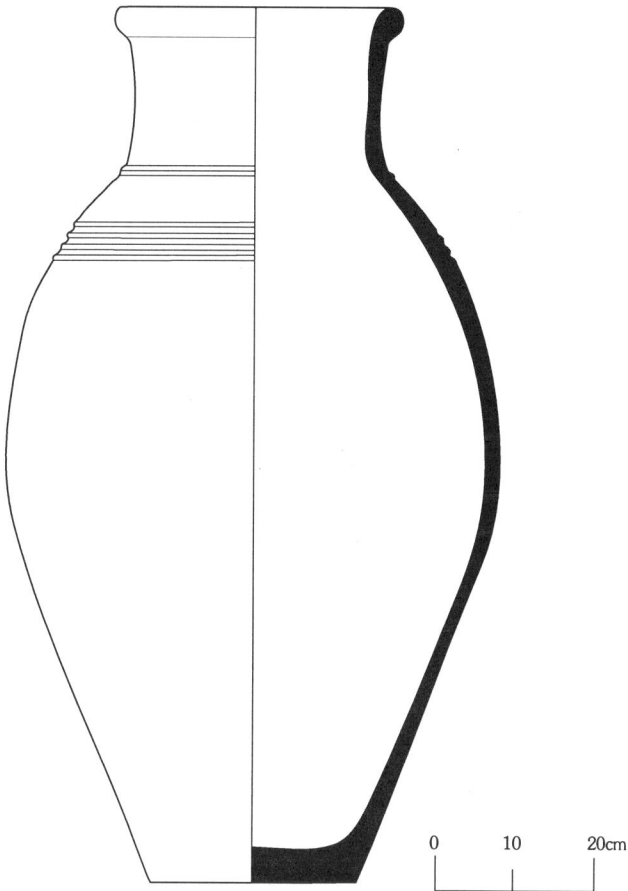

Fig. 5. Point Iria wreck. Cypriot pithos A4. Drawing by T. Koutsouraki.

and the outside is covered with a whitish pale yellow slip. This particular type of amphora is not unknown among the vase-types of the Late Helladic IIIB period (Furumark 1941 shape 69; also Blegen 1937: fig. 177: 316, 303, 289, 455:134, 116, 118). There is a large incised linear mark like the Arabic numeral "1" on the upper part of each handle (fig. 9). It could be either a linear sign with a syllabic value or a simple potter's mark. Such relatively large incised marks, singly or in groups, often occur on the bodies or handles of Late Cypriot, Late Mycenaean and Syro-Palestinian vases. A large incised mark, related to ours but not the same, and still undeciphered, appears on the body of a Canaanite amphora from the Tholos Tomb at Kato Englianos in western Messenia (Blegen et al. 1973: 94, fig. 174: 4a–b; Åkerström 1975: 187, fig. 2, 5). It is worth noting, however, that our mark finds its closest parallels in incised linear marks on the handles of two Late Mycenaean vases from Tomb VI at Minet el-Beida in Syria (Schaeffer 1949: fig. 59: 1e, j).

A find of decisive importance for the precise date of the wreck is the group of eight Mycenaean coarse-ware stirrup-jars (fig. 10). Seven of them lack only the vertical tubular mouth, while the upper half of the eighth is preserved with its rim intact. Seven belong to the well-known Aegean

Fig. 6. Point Iria wreck. Cypriot jug A20. Photograph by N. Tsouchlos.

Fig. 7. Point Iria wreck. Body sherd of Cypriot pithos A49 bearing multiple relief band. Photograph by N. Tsouchlos.

Fig. 9. Point Iria wreck. Incised linear marks on handles of amphora A99. Drawing by Ch. Kritzas.

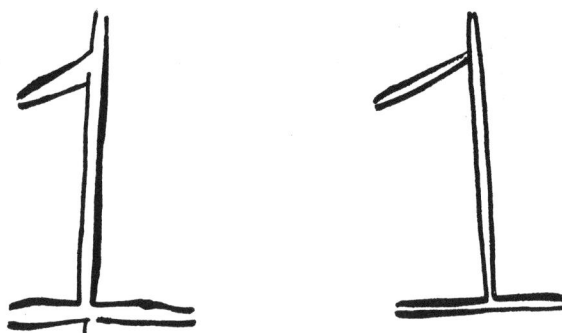

Fig. 8. Point Iria wreck. Upper part of Cypriot juglet A97. Photograph by S. Garbari.

spiral decoration on the disk of the false mouth and painted bands on the base of the false mouth and on the shoulder. The simple spiral is a usual decorative theme on the false mouth disk of stirrup-jars, both large and small. The spiral on the Iria vase has a close parallel on the disk of a commercial stirrup-jar from the cemetery of Armenoi at Rethymnon,[3] as well as from Kommos, and on the disks of other examples from the Greek mainland.

On the basis of the parallels already referred to and in view of their particular ovoid shape and general appearance,

the eight stirrup-jars from Iria should be dated to the later thirteenth century B.C., and probably towards, if not exactly at, its end. From the evidence of the preliminary petrographic examination of the clay, the Iria stirrup-jars appear to have come from Central Crete (Peter Day, personal communication, February 1995).

As a unit, the group of Aegean stirrup-jars from the Iria wreck can be compared quantitatively with that from the Uluburun wreck, which consisted of ten examples, according to C. Pulak (Pulak, personal communication, October 1994). In other words, it is the second largest group of "maritime" stirrup-jars from the Mediterranean known so far.

The cargo of the Iria wreck also includes three large undecorated pithoid jars of general Minoan/Mycenaean appearance (although no exact parallels have yet been found), with two horizontal cylindrical handles on the shoulder. The upper part of the first one has survived and five fragments of the second; the third one was recovered intact during the 1994 season (fig. 13). The three examples of this shape can fairly safely be assigned to the late thirteenth century B.C. The occurrence of two horizontal cylindrical handles on the shoulders of large vessels of this kind, although much rarer than the usual three or four horizontal or vertical handles, is not unknown on Late Mycenaean pithoid jars. It should be noted that the shape of the three pithoid jars from Iria closely resembles that of a pithos from a Mycenaean tomb at Prosymna in the Argolid (Blegen 1937: fig. 430).

The almost complete deep bowl krater A36 (figs. 14a, 14b), although found at a certain distance from the main concentration of the pottery, must also belong to the cargo of the ship. The spouted deep bowl krater is a relatively rare Late Mycenaean shape. Its general form has close parallels with painted deep bowl kraters from Prosymna in the

---

[3] Unpublished example in the Rethymnon Museum, no. 2336 (mentioned here by kind permission of Dr. Y. Tzedakis).

Fig. 10. Point Iria wreck. LM IIIB 2 stirrup-jar A85 *in situ*, underneath a pointed amphora of later date. Photograph by K. Jachney.

Argolid, Enkomi *Ayios Iakovos* in Cyprus, Souda in Crete and other sites (Blegen 1937: fig. 124: 231; Catling and Karageorghis 1960: 114, no. 15, pl. 27c; Furumark 1992, pl. 166:3031; Godart and Tzedakis 1992, pl. LIX:1). Our krater has an exact counterpart from the Lower Akropolis at Tiryns in the Argolid (Kilian 1988: 108, fig. 8).

A good example of fine ware from the cargo is the concreted deep bowl fragment A26. The painted decoration, if it has survived, may well give us important evidence for an even closer dating of the wreck. Nevertheless, a painted deep bowl sherd (fig. 15) found in the pithoid jar A98 could be part of the same bowl. This sherd (A100), the first example of a fine Mycenaean vase with painted decoration to be identified among the cargo of the Iria wreck, can be dated to the Late Helladic IIIB 1 or early IIIB 2 period, to judge from its profile and diagnostic decoration (panelled pattern-triglyph) (Furumark 1941: motif 75; Mountjoy 1986: 121, 123, fig. 148: 24, 159: 1, 161: 9). A cooking pot with two vertical handles, in two pieces (fig. 16), was also found (A23 and A90).[4] Sherds from coarse and semi-coarse LH IIIB utility vessels (tripod cook-pots and other household utensils) made from clay of the same kind are found in abundance on Late Mycenaean sites in the Argosaronic gulf, like Kastelli Vourlia, east of Point Iria, Myti Kommeni on the island of

Dokos, Ayii Anargyroi on Spetses and Ayios Nikolaos-Bisti on Hydra.

A number of fragments of pots of later periods that were found in the general area of the site should be interpreted as occasional jettisoning by passing ships or parts of cargoes from other shipwrecks, and they have no connection with the major Cypro-Mycenaean body of material. A similar situation was observed at Myti Kommeni at Dokos and other wrecks, especially when they are in localities where there is a high risk of shipwreck, like Point Iria.

A small stone anchor (fig. 17) of composite type with three holes was found at a depth of 13 m just above the main pottery concentration. It weighs some 25 kg and is made from conglomerate rock. Its position a little higher up than the main concentration of the cargo is a possible indication that it belonged to the Cypriot ship, but it cannot be dated with certainty from its type and shape. The petrological analysis that will be made may produce more evidence for its provenance.

Two more stone anchors, one with a single hole and the other with three, were found close to Point Iria, but their considerable distance from the site of the wreck (about 150 m) eliminates any possibility that they belong to it.

A few small pieces of wood (e.g. fig. 18) that were found may have come from the ship, but the hull itself has

---

[4] It is petrographically consistent with an origin in Aigina (Peter Day, personal communication, July 1994).

Fig. 11. Point Iria wreck. LM IIIB 2 stirrup-jar A93 (complete except for vertical tubular spout). Photograph by S. Garbari.

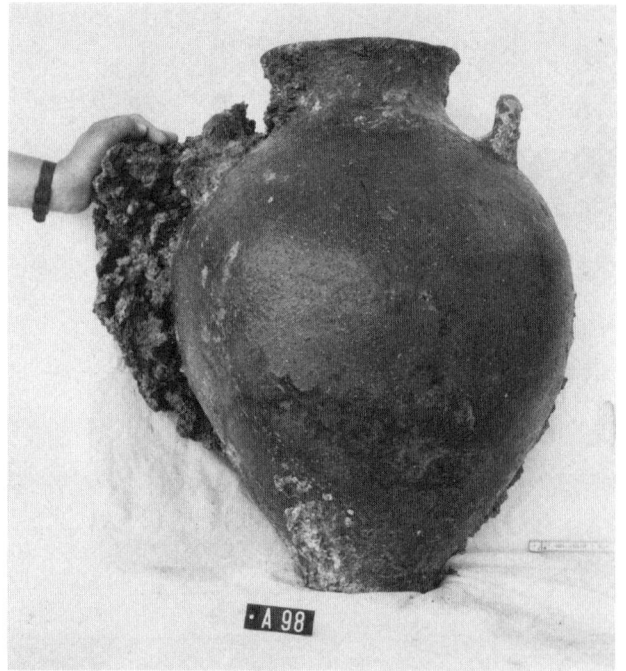

Fig. 13. Point Iria wreck. LH/LM IIIB 2 pithoid jar A98. Photograph by S. Garbari.

Fig. 12. Point Iria wreck. Point Iria wreck. LM IIIB 2 decorated stirrup-jar A86/1 (complete except for vertical tubular spout). Photograph by N. Tsouchlos.

not survived. Three organic remains are of considerable interest; when they were found buried in the sand, they were cylindrical, but they lost all their shape when they were brought to the surface. They were probably pieces of rope like those found in the Cape Gelidonya wreck (du Plat Taylor 1967: 160–62, BM 5, 6, 7; Haldane 1991: 11; Sibella 1993: 86–87). An examination of the wood and probable pieces of rope hopefully will tell us what they were and their date. The complete absence of metal objects, in spite of careful excavation and surveying the whole wreck area with a metal detector, is curious.

The ship, which was wrecked shortly before it was able to round Point Iria, was carrying a mixed cargo of pottery consisting chiefly of large transport vessels (Cypriot pithoi and LH/LM IIIB 2 pithoid jars) and medium size ones (Cretan stirrup-jars, Cypriot jugs and an amphora with incised linear signs). The various small pots, like the cooking pots and juglet, may have belonged to the crew. Lastly, the cargo also included a few decorated Mycenaean vases in fine ware (a deep bowl krater and one or two deep bowls). Dates for all these finds, irrespective of their provenance, of around 1200 B.C. leave no doubt that they all belonged to the cargo of the same ship.

The provenance of the cargo, as far as we know it to date, gives us an idea of at least some part of the ship's last voyage (fig. 19). After loading Cypriot pithoi, probably containing food or fruit, at a harbor on the south coast of Cyprus,

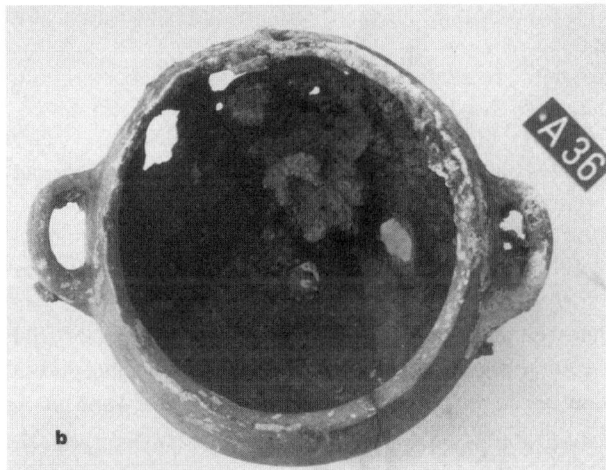

Fig. 14. Point Iria wreck. LH IIIB 2 spouted deep bowl krater A36 (complete except for horizontal side spout). Photograph by N. Tsouchlos.

Fig. 15. Point Iria wreck. Rim and wall fragment of LH IIIB 1–2 decorated deep bowl A100. Photograph by S. Garbari.

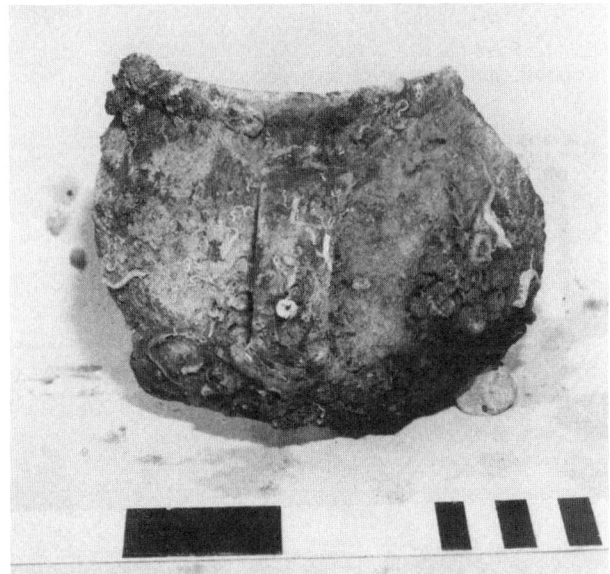

Fig. 16. Point Iria wreck. Part of coarse two-handled LH IIIB 2 cook-pot A23. Photograph by N. Tsouchlos.

the ship sailed to the north coast of Central Crete, perhaps to a point near Knossos; there it took on board at least eight stirrup-jars with oil and perhaps other jars with unknown contents or empty, and proceeded on its way to the west end of the island. When the weather allowed, it set out on the difficult crossing northwards, probably passing by Kythera and arriving at the southern tip of Cape Malea. Sailing north along the east coast of the Peloponnese, it may have put in at some Mycenaean harbors (like Tiryns and Asine) and unloaded part of its cargo. It then continued on its voyage, which perhaps ended at Mases or Hermione or one of the Argosaronic islands like Dokos, Hydra or Aegina

(fig. 3). The likelihood that it sailed directly from Crete or via the Cyclades to the Gulf of Argos can be ruled out, because both of the great distance of these routes without any intermediate land and of the northerly winds that made such a route almost impossible. The evidence we have suggests

Fig. 17. Point Iria wreck. Stone anchor A29, with three holes, of composite type. Photograph by K. Jachney.

Fig. 18. Point Iria wreck. Pieces of wood (one with a semicircular hole), probably belonging to the ship's hull.

that the Iria ship's final voyage must have been something like the above.

If the final destination of the Iria ship cannot be traced with certainty, as well as its home port, the starting-point of its last voyage, we think, is clear: Cyprus. The question that arises is the vessel's "nationality": was it Cypriot, Mycenaean or Cretan-Mycenaean? The existing evidence is probably insufficient for us ever to know for sure. It has never in fact been possible to know the nationality of any ancient wreck with certainty, especially a prehistoric one. Possibly an analysis of the small pieces of wood and rope that were found may produce evidence that can help. But here again, we cannot say for sure whether the ship was built in Cyprus, Crete or Mycenaean Greece, or whether the crew were Cypriots or Mycenaeans.

The case for its being a Cretan or, better, a Cretan-Mycenaean ship is perhaps the least probable. Why would a ship have left Crete to transport olive oil to Mycenaean Greece and have first gone to Cyprus, unless, of course, the Cypriot pithoi and jugs had been carried previously in another ship from Cyprus to Crete.

The case for a ship setting out from a Mycenaean harbor on the Greek mainland and sailing to Cyprus, perhaps with a cargo of fine painted Mycenaean pottery and oil, and then returning to Greece via Crete, is much more probable. This would explain the presence of the fine Mycenaean vases and the cooking pots, either as the remnants of a cargo that had not been all disposed of, or as vessels that belonged to the crew. The cooking pots might have been used for cooking during the voyage.

It is equally likely that the ship was Cypriot. The relatively poor cargo may be more understandable if we imagine a ship setting sail from Cyprus, loaded, in addition to the pithoi, with some of the organic products, either contained in the pithoi or separately, and not traceable today, that we know from Linear B sources were exported from Cyprus to mainland Greece at that time: these included wool, wool cloth, spices, sesame, cumin, clothing alum and purple dye (Palaima 1991: 276–84). The ship would have had two destinations:

First, Crete, where it may have unloaded a part of its cargo, perhaps raw copper in the form of ingots. There it took on a cargo of stirrup-jars and possibly pithoid jars which, along with the Cypriot pottery, it was going to try to sell in some of the many Mycenaean harbors it would find on its voyage to the Gulf of Argos. A Cypriot origin would also explain the presence of the two jugs, which could have held drinking water for the crew.

Whatever the provenance of the ship, the basic conclusions are the same:

1. It confirms the links between the Argolid and Cyprus at the end of the thirteenth century B.C. Such contacts and commercial transactions must have been frequent, because we are not dealing here with a special shipment ordered by some central authority, but with a

Fig. 19. Map of eastern Mediterranean, showing possible route of Iria ship. Drawing by Y. Vichos.

humble, "everyday" trading expedition. Crete forms a natural intermediate stopping point on the Argolid-Cyprus sea-route, from the point of view of both navigation and trade, given the close relations between what was now Mycenaean Crete and the Argolid and the traditional Cyprus-Crete connection. A similar conclusion was reached by Thomas Palaima in his important paper, "Maritime matters in the Linear B Tablets."[5]

2. We are dealing with a wreck within the context of close Cypro-Mycenaean contact without the presence of objects coming from other civilizations. In contrast to the ships of Uluburun and Cape Gelidonya, the Iria ship made its final voyage, at least, from Cyprus to the Argolid in the midst of a predominantly Mycenaean environment.

TYPE OF SHIP

From the known contemporary iconographical evidence for the "round" Mycenaean and Cypriot ships and boats, various types of vessel emerge (see list below). However, there is a general prevailing type of hull that is symmetrical in form and has different variations.

The evidence for Late Bronze Age ship construction provided by the Uluburun and Gelidonya wrecks (fig. 20), as well as iconographical evidence, demonstrates that at least from the fourteenth century B.C. onwards, one of the building techniques, if not the principal one, was that of shell-first construction with all its main features as we know them from the later Greek and Roman shipwrecks (Vinson 1990: 15, 16; Pulak 1993b: 5–8, figs. 4, 5). From the Late Bronze Age to the Classical period this method of building ships

---

[5] Palaima (1991:309): "Cypriote potmarks and references to 'Cypriote' goods in the Linear B Tablets indicate that a special directional trade probably existed between that island and the Argolid and Crete. It is impossible to make any deduction from the Tablets about the degree to which such trade would have been either palatially controlled or entrepreneurial."

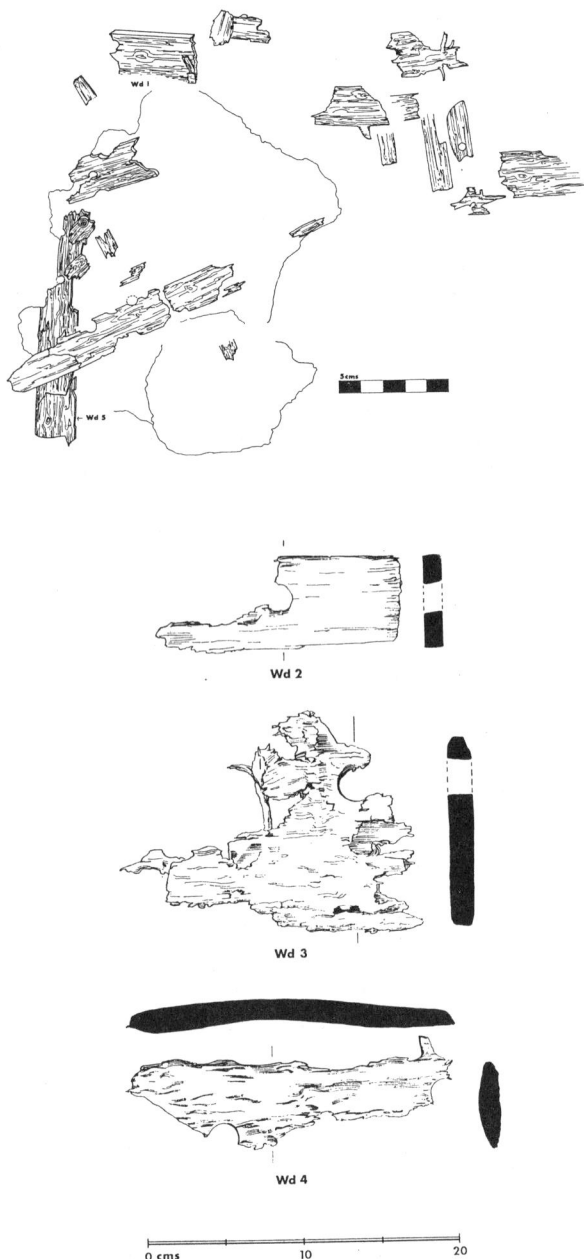

Fig. 20. Cape Gelidonya wreck. Wood remains from the ship's planks (some with peg holes). After Bass (1967: figs. 46, 51).

evolved continuously into late Roman times, when it began to be replaced by the skeleton-first method. By then, however, ships already had a keel, keelson, planking joined by mortises and tenons held in place by wooden pegs, frames, wales and stringers. At the same time there must also have been other ship-building techniques, such as tied ships and ships made of skins over a wooden frame. However, we must suppose that around 1200 B.C. a seagoing boat, however small it may have been, in order to cover the distance from Cyprus to the Argolid that required a long sea cross-

ing, must have been built by the shell-first method, a method that proved so effective that it continued to be used for over 1500 years. It would not be wise to draw any conclusion about the method of constructing the Iria hull from the few small pieces of wood found in the excavation, at least before they are analysed and dated, but in one of these fragments, a worked semicircular hole is visible that perhaps indicates the former existence of a wooden peg (fig. 18; Bass 1967: 48, figs. 46, 51 (wd 2); Pulak 1987: 130, fig. 73).

ICONOGRAPHICAL EVIDENCE

Mycenaean Ships

–   Clay ship model from a tomb at Mycenae, ca. 1300 B.C. National Archaeological Museum, Athens (Basch 1987: 141: fig. 292). The model has a symmetrical shape with raised prow and stern. It had two benches or frames, and because of its half-moon outline may belong to the Minoan tradition.

–   Two clay ship models from Tanagra, thirteenth century B.C. Archaeological Museum of Thebes (Basch 1987: 141: fig. 293) The first is symmetrical in shape with a raised prow and stern. It has dark painted decoration inside and out. Fifteen frames and the keelson are indicated on the inside. The second is a small boat model, one end of which is terminated in a bird's head. The frames and keelson are also shown on the inside.

–   Clay ship model from Asine, twelvth century B.C. Archaeological Museum of Nauplion (fig. 21). As restored, it has a symmetrical shape. Three, out of six or seven frames, are painted on the inside, while a small depression in the center of the hull may indicate the mast step. On the outside the gunwale, a wale, and the keel are indicated.

–   Painted representation of a ship on a small stirrup-jar from Skyros, early twelvth century B.C., Archaeological Museum of Skyros (fig. 22; Parlama 1984: 146–51, pl. A, 62–64, ill. 31–32; Basch: 1987, 142, fig. 295). The hull is round and the prow ends in a bird's head. It has a central mast with a masthead, forestay, and backstay. There may have been bulwarks on the side.

–   Clay ship model from Phylakopi, island of Melos, thirteenth century B.C. National Archaeological Museum, Athens. There is a skeg on the stern to prevent leeway, and a painted eye. On the

Fig. 21. Asine. Clay ship model. Photographs by S. Garbari, by kind permission of Mrs. Pahiyanni, Ephor of the Argolid.

inside and outside are painted representations of seven frames. The mast step is shown one-third of the length from the prow (Basch 1987: 142: fig. 296).

– Rock carvings from Dramesi, Boeotia, ca. 1200 B.C. Archaeological Museum of Schimatari. A long fighting ship is depicted above and a round merchant ship below (see Basch fig. 2, this volume). This is the first time in antiquity that these two basic types of vessel appear together. The round ship has two towers, one forward and one aft, and a curving hull. The rigging is not shown. It has far fewer frames than the long ship, perhaps because the planking is stronger and the construction generally stouter (Basch 1987: 144: fig. 301; Basch 1991: pl. X).

– Clay ship model from Argos, LH IIIA2–IIIB2. Archaeological Museum of Argos, fig. 23 (Palaiologou 1989: 227–28). The ends are more or less symmetrical, with the prow being more pointed. Two frames are shown fore and aft of the mast step. There is also part of the attachment for a steering-oar.

– Painted representation showing two ships on a LH IIIB amphoroid krater from Enkomi *Ayios Iakovos* (Tomb 3) in Cyprus, thirteenth century B.C., in Medelhavsmuseet, Stockholm. They are two round ships seen from the side. Two levels can be distinguished: the deck and the hold. The warlike activity of the ship shows that in the eastern Mediterranean round ships could be used for military purposes (Basch 1987: 148: fig. 311).

Cypriot Ships

– Clay ship model from Kazaphani, LC I–II. Cyprus Museum, Nicosia (Westerberg 1983: 11–12: fig. 5; Karageorghis 1993b: 54: fig. 47, pl. XXXVI: 1a–1b). Ship possibly made of hide stretched over a wooden frame, or else a mixed construction using wooden planking to just above the waterline and stretched hide from there to the gunwale. In the center of the hull is a reconstruction of the mast step and on either side a system for attaching the shrouds. The stern ends in a fork, probably to hold a steering-oar.

The same type of ship is also represented in two more clay models from Maroni *Zarukas* in Cyprus (Westerberg 1983: 13–14: fig. 7; Karageorghis 1993b: 74, fig. 62, pl.

Fig. 22. Skyros. Representation of ship on small LH IIIC 1 stirrup-jar. After Parlama (1984: ill. 32).

XXXII: 2–3).

– A clay ship model from the sea of Amathus (fig. 24), LCIII or Cypro Geometric I has a rounded hull with pointed ends, two cross-beams on both bow and stern, and the mast step is indicated in the center of the hull (Westerberg 1983: 14–15: fig. 8; Karageorghis 1993b: 74: fig. 62: pl. XXXII: 7). Below the gunwale on both sides a row of seven and eight holes, respectively, closely resembles those on the models from Maroni *Zarukas*.

– Clay ship model from Enkomi *Ayios Iakovos*, Cyprus, end of the Bronze Age. Musées Royaux d'Art et d'Histoire, Bruxelles, no A1240 (Basch 1987: 73–74: fig. 146). Its shape is symmetrical except for the stem, which features a cutwater for better hydrodynamics.

The lack of evidence for contemporary parallels to the Iria ship (e.g. LBA hulls) makes it necessary to use our imagination and to hypothesize that it was a rather small

Fig. 23. Argos. Clay ship model. After Palaiologou (1989: 227).

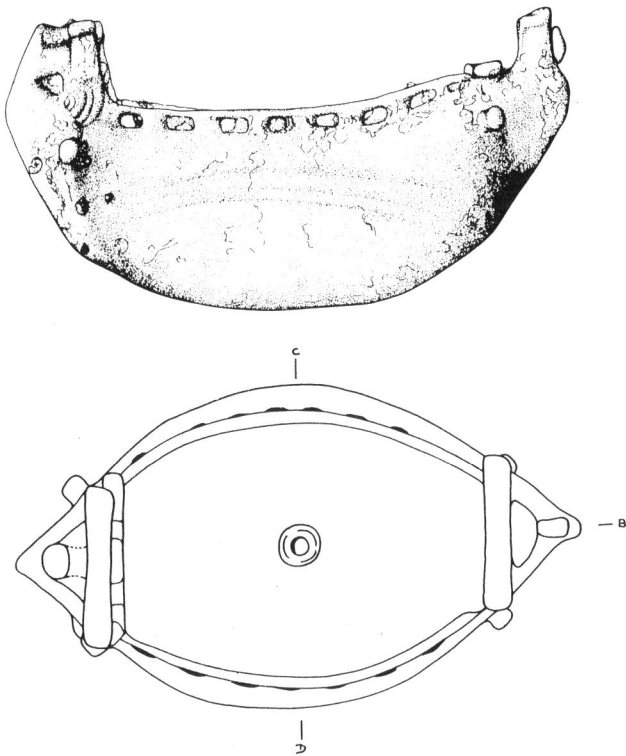

Fig. 24. Sea off Amathus, Cyprus. Clay ship model. After Karageorghis (1993: fig. 62).

vessel, not more than 10 m in length, no doubt built by the shell-first method, having a slender keel and sparsely spaced frames. It would not have had a deck, but we cannot rule out the possibility that the stem and stern were decked over and that it may have had bulwarks. It was probably propelled only by a squaresail and had no oars. It would have had either a side steering oar or one mounted in a fork formed by the stern; but the latter is less probable for a seagoing vessel.

CAUSES OF THE SHIPWRECK

The Iria ship must have been wrecked by the sudden onset of bad weather, which drove it onto the rocky shore

before it was able to weather Point Iria. This is concluded from the fact that the wreck lies only some 10 m from the shore and that the cargo is scattered about haphazardly. Our own personal experience during the four months we were working on the wreck, in the course of which we had heavy seas and high winds that twice snapped the cables holding our floating platform, as well as the information supplied by the local fishermen, confirmed that the locality of the wreck is very dangerous for vessels approaching from the west. The force with which the ship struck the rocks as it was driven by the west wind is perhaps indicated by the position of the deep bowl krater 50 m to the south of the main concentration of the cargo. The deep bowl krater, an open, relatively light vase, must have been carried some distance away before it slowly filled and sank to the bottom.

This hypothesis perhaps tells us something about the final route of the ship. After leaving the harbors at the northwest end of the Gulf of Argos, it was sailing in an easterly direction.

CONCLUSION

As a single-period underwater cargo find, the pottery so far known from the Iria wreck, of Cretan-Mycenaean, Helladic-Mycenaean and Cypriot origin, presents a remarkable chronological homogeneity. It is also interesting to note that this body of pottery includes typical forms of Cretan-Mycenaean and Cypriot transport vases that were commonplace during the thirteenth century B.C., namely the stirrup-jars and pithoi, and widespread within the Mediterranean. Within the framework of long-distance trade of the period, their distribution can now be followed from the coast of Syria (Ugarit), to Cyprus and Uluburun in Lycia, as far as Agrigento in Sicily, the Aeolian Islands north of Sicily, and Sardinia. The Cypro-Mycenaean wreck of Iria provides valuable material evidence for trade and navigation during the Late Mycenaean period in the Aegean and beyond. It also throws light on one of the most crucial periods of Greek and Cypriot prehistory, during which the breakdown of the Mycenaean *Koine* in the eastern Mediterranean commenced.

REFERENCES

Åkerström, A.
1975 More Canaanite Jars from Greece. *Opuscula Atheniensia* XI: 185–92.

Åström, P.
1972 *The Swedish Cyprus Expedition,* Vol. IV, Part 1C: *The Late Cypriote Bronze Age (Architecture and Pottery).* Lund: The Swedish Cyprus Expedition.

Balmuth, M. S. (ed.)
1987 *Nuragic Sardinia and the Mycenaean World, Studies in Sardinian Archaeology III.* B.A.R. International Series 387. Oxford: B.A.R.

Basch, L.
1987 *Le musée imaginaire de la marine antique,* Athens: Hellenic Institute for the Preservation of Nautical Tradition.
1991 Carènes égéennes à l'âge du bronze. Pp. 43–54 in *AEGAEUM 7, Thalassa, l'égée préhistorique et la mer,* Université de Liège.

Bass, G. F.
1967 *Cape Gelidonya: A Bronze Age Shipwreck, Transactions of the American Philosophical Society,* vol. 57, part 8.
1987 Oldest Known Shipwreck Reveals Splendors of the Bronze Age. *National Geographic* 172.6: 693–733.

Blegen, C. W.
1937 *Prosymna.* Cambridge: Cambridge University.

Blegen, C. W., and Rawson, M.
1966 *The Palace of Nestor at Pylos in Western Messenia,* Vol. I, Princeton: Princeton University.

Blegen, C. W.; Rawson, M.; Taylour, W.; and Donovan, W. P.
1973 *The Palace of Nestor at Pylos in Western Messenia,* Vol. III. Princeton: Princeton University.

Catling, H. W.
1957 The Bronze Age Pottery. Pp. 26–59 in *Myrtou-Pigadhes: A Late Bronze Age Sanctuary in Cyprus,* J. du Plat Taylor. Oxford.

Catling, H. W., and Karageorghis, V.
1960 Minoika in Cyprus. *BSA* 55: 109–27.

Catling, H. W.; Cherry, J. F.; Jones, R. E.; and Killen, J. T.
1980 The Linear B Inscribed Stirrup Jars and West Crete. *BSA* 75: 49–113.

Cavalier, M., and Vagnetti, L.
1982 Filicudi. Pp. 136–38 in *Magna Grecia e Mondo Miceneo: Nuovi Documenti,* ed. L. Vagnetti. Taranto: Istituto per la storia e l'archeologia della Magna Grecia.

du Plat Taylor, J.
1957 *Myrtou-Pigadhes: A Late Bronze Age Sanctuary in Cyprus.* Oxford.
1967 Basketery and Matting. Pp. 160–63 in *Cape Gelidonya: A Bronze Age Shipwreck, Transactions of the American Philosophical Society* vol. 57, part 8, ed. G. F. Bass.

Ferrarese Ceruti, M. L., Vagnetti, L., and Lo Schiavo, F.
1987 Minoici, Micenei e Ciprioti in Sardegna alla luce delle piu recenti scoperte. Pp. 7–37 in *Nuragic Sardinia and the Mycenaean World, Studies in Sardinian Archaeology III,* ed. M.S. Balmuth. B.A.R. International Series 387. Oxford: B.A.R.

Furumark, A.
1941 *The Mycenaean Pottery: Analysis and Classification,* Stockholm: Skrifter utgivna av Svenska, Institutet I Athen, 40, 20:1.
1992 *Mycenaean Pottery III: Plates,* Stockholm: Åströms.

Gjerstad, E.; Lindros, J.; Sjöqvist, E.; and Westholm, A.
1934 *The Swedish Cyprus Expedition,* Vol. I (Plates), Stockholm: The Swedish Cyprus Expedition.

Godart, L., and Tzedakis, Y.
1992 *Témoignages archéologiques et épigraphiques en Crète occidentale du néolithique au Minoen récent IIIB,* Roma: Gruppo Editoriale Internazionale.

Haldane, C. W.
1991 Organic Goods from the Ulu Burun Wreck. *INA Newsletter* 18.4: 10–12.

Haskell, H. W.
1981 Coarse-Ware Stirrup-Jars at Mycenae. *BSA* 76: 225–38.

Karageorghis, V.
1992 Μυκηναίοι και Κύπριοι στην Ιταλία. *Η Καθημερινή,* 27 May 1992: 8.
1993a Le commerce Chypriote avec l'occident au bronze récent: quelques nouvelles découvertes. *Académie des Inscriptions & Belles-Lettres, comptes rendus 1993,* fasc. II: 577–88.
1993b *The Coroplastic Art of Ancient Cyprus II: LCII–CGII,* Nicosia: A. G. Leventis.

Karageorghis, V., and Demas, M.
1984 *Pyla-Kokkinokremos: A Late 13th-Century B.C. Fortified Settlement in Cyprus.* Nicosia: Department of Antiquities.
1985 *Excavations at Kition V; The Pre-Phoenician Levels (plates).* Nicosia: Department of Antiquities.
1988 *Excavations at Maa-Paleokastro 1979–1986,* Nicosia: Department of Antiquities.

Kilian, K.
1988   Ausgrabungen in Tiryns 1982/83. *Archäolo-gischer Anzeiger* 1988: 105–51.

Mountjoy, P. A.
1986   *Mycenaean Decorated Pottery: A Guide to Iden-tification,* Göteborg: Åströms.

Palaima, T. G.
1991   Maritime Matters in the Linear B Tablets. Pp. 273–310 in *AEGAEUM 7, Thalassa, l'égée préhistorique et la mer,* Université de Liège.

Palaiologou, E.
1989   Aegean Ships from the 2nd Millennium B.C. Pp. 217–28 in *TROPIS I,* ed. H. Tzalas. Athens: Hellenic Institute for the Preservation of Nauti-cal Tradition.

Parlama, L.
1984   *Η Σκύρος στην Εποχή του Χαλκού.* Ath-ens.

Pennas, Ch.
1992   Point Iria Wreck. *ENALIA Annual 1990,* vol. II: 39–41.

Pennas, Ch.; Vichos, Y.; and Lolos, Y.
1995   The 1991 Underwater Survey of the Late Bronze Age Wreck at Point Iria. *ENALIA Annual 1991,* vol. III: 4–16.

1996   Point Iria Wreck (1993). I Excavations and re-sults; II The Stone Anchors; III The Pottery. *ENALIA Annual 1992,* vol. IV: 6–31.

Pulak, C.
1987   *A Late Bronze Age Shipwreck at Ulu Burun: Pre-liminary Analysis,* MA Thesis. College Station, TX: Institute of Nautical Archaeology.

1993a   The Late Bronze Age Shipwreck at Ulu Burun. Pp. 4–12 in *TROPIS V,* ed. H. Tzalas. Athens.

1993b   The Shipwreck at Ulu Burun: 1993 Excavation Campaign. *INA Newsletter* 20.4: 4–12.

Schaeffer, C. F.-A.
1949   *Ugaritica II: Nouvelles études relatives aux découvertes de Ras Shamra (Mission de Ras Shamra, t. V. Bibliothèque archéologique et historique, t. XLVII),* Paris: Librairie Orientaliste Paul Geuthner.

Sibella, P.
1993   *La mer dans le monde égéen préhistorique et protohistorique: navigation et commerce mari-time à l'époque Mycénienne,* thèse de Doctorat de l'Université de Paris I.

Vagnetti, L. (ed.)
1982   *Magna Grecia e Mondo Miceneo: Nuovi Documenti,* Taranto: Istituto per la storia e l'archeologia della Magna Grecia.

Vinson, S.
1990   Ships in the Ancient Mediterranean. *Biblical Archaeologist* 53: 13–18.

Westerberg, K.
1983   *Cypriote Ships from the Bronze Age to c. 500 B.C.* SIMA, Pocket-Book no. 22. Göteborg: Åströms.

Were the Sea Peoples Mycenaeans?
The Evidence of Ship Iconography

SHELLEY WACHSMANN

Institute of Nautical Archaeology
Texas A & M University
P.O. Drawer HG
College Station, TX 77841-5137
U.S.A.

The origin of the Sea Peoples remains one of the most perplexing questions pertaining to the great migrations that marked the end of the Bronze Age. Little attention has been given, however, to the possible contribution of their seagoing ships in determining Sea Peoples' origins.

Study of the Medinet Habu naval battle scene reveals that the prototypical Sea Peoples' ship depicted there was a galley that finds its closest parallels in contemporaneous Aegean (Mycenaean) ships. Additionally, the bird-head device capping the stems of the Medinet Habu ship depictions is similar to Aegean stem devices.

The Medinet Habu ships are unique among twelfth century B.C.E. Mediterranean ship depictions, however, in having an additional bird-head device facing outboard from the sternpost. This makes them similar to the central European "bird-boat" (Vogelbarke), and suggests a more northern origin for parts of the Sea Peoples' coalition.

The geographical and ethnic origins of the groups of foreign invaders that washed over the Levant in the waning years of the Late Bronze Age and beginning of the Iron Age remains tantalizingly enigmatic. To the Egyptians they were known as "Sea Peoples" (Redford 1992: 243 note 14). This term is echoed and amplified in a document uncovered in Ugarit and addressed to the prefect of Ugarit from the king of Hatti, who describes one group—the Sekels who later settled at Dor—as "those who live on their ships" (RS 34.129; see Deitrich and Loretz 1978; Lehman 1979; Rainey in Wachsmann 1982: 304 n. 1; Hoftijzer and Van Soldt 1998: 343). Presumably, these are the "alien enemies" (as opposed to local enemies?) mentioned in at least one other Ugaritic text (RS 20.162; Izre'el 1991: 100; Hoftijzer and Van Soldt 1998: 341).

We hear of these groups of ship-based marauders as early as the fourteenth century B.C.E., when the king of Alashia (Cyprus) complains of seasonal raids on his land by the Lukka (EA 38: 10–12; Wachsmann 1982: 298). Later, these periodic raids evolved into a land and sea-based migration that delivered the deathblow to a number of Late Bronze Age cultures and, in doing so, changed the face of the Levant forever.

Actual Mycenaean warriors may have served as Egyptian mercenaries as early as the Amarna period (Parkinson and Schofield 1993a; 1993b; 1995; Schofield and Parkinson 1994). The "*miši*-people," a group appearing repeatedly in the Amarna tablets, seem to have a connection with ship-based warfare (EA 101: 4, 33; 105: 27; 108: 38; 110: 48[?]; 111: 21[?] and 126: 63). Säve-Söderbergh (1946: 65–66 n. 1) proposes that they were early forerunners of the Sea Peoples.[1]

Who were the Sea Peoples? What were their ethnic origins and where did they come from? Archaeologists, not-

---

[1] See, however, the comments by Lambdin (1953). More recently, Moran (1992) translates them as "ships of the army."

Fig. 1. Ramses III's naval battle scene as portrayed on his mortuary temple at Medinet Habu. From *MH* I: pl. 37.

ing remarkable similarities between the material culture of the Mycenaean Greeks and the Sea Peoples—from the way they built cities and houses, to the type of pottery they used—have proposed an intimate connection between these cultures (Dothan 1982; Dothan and Dothan 1992; Stager 1995 and there additional bibliography). Notes Stager (1991: 14):

> As a logical inference from the archaeological evidence, we may add the following: If the makers of the local monochrome Mycenaean pottery (IIIC:1) settling along the coast from Cilica in Anatolia to Cyprus and Israel are not Mycenaean Greeks themselves, then we must conclude that they studied their potmaking in Mycenaean workshops. And then they somehow convinced all of their "barbarian" consumers that this pottery is what they should use. Throwing caution to the wind, I am willing to reject these possibilities and state flatly that the Sea Peoples, including the Philistines, were Mycenaean Greeks.

> I am willing to speculate even further: When we do discover Philistine texts at Ashkelon or elsewhere in Philistia (and it's only a matter of time until this happens), those texts will be in Mycenaean Greek (that is in Linear B or some related script). At that moment we will be able to recover another lost civilization for world history.

Could these foreign invaders indeed be Mycenaean Greeks who had fled in the wake of the turmoil that affected their homeland at the end of the Bronze Age?

This question may be approached from numerous directions of research. In the following pages I propose to examine it from one—admittedly narrow—aspect: a comparison of the ships used by the Mycenaeans and the Sea Peoples based on contemporaneous iconography.

THE SHIPS OF THE SEA PEOPLES AT MEDINET HABU

Let us first examine the ships used by the Sea Peoples. The most detailed depiction of ships that can be assigned definitely to Sea People contingents are engraved on the outer wall of Ramses III's mortuary temple at Medinet Habu. Here the pharaoh's artists portrayed two engagements in which Ramses repulsed the northern invaders: one by land, the other by water (*MH* I: pls. 33–34, 36–37, 39).

The latter scene consists of nine ships arranged in three vertical rows (fig. 1). Four of the ships are Egyptian, the remaining five are crewed by contingents of Sea Peoples. In and around the combatant ships are the bodies of the dead and the dying invading warriors.

To the eye of the casual observer there is a distinct "snapshot" quality to the scene, suggestive of a single moment in the mêlée of battle. Nelson (1943), however, has admirably demonstrated that this scene is structured around three distinct conceptual themes: spatial, ideological and temporal (fig. 2).

The Egyptian ships have their sails furled, but are propelled by oarsmen, protected behind a screen placed above the caprail. The ships of the Sea Peoples are also depicted with their sails furled, but no rowers—nor oars—are visible; in other words, they are stationary in the water. The

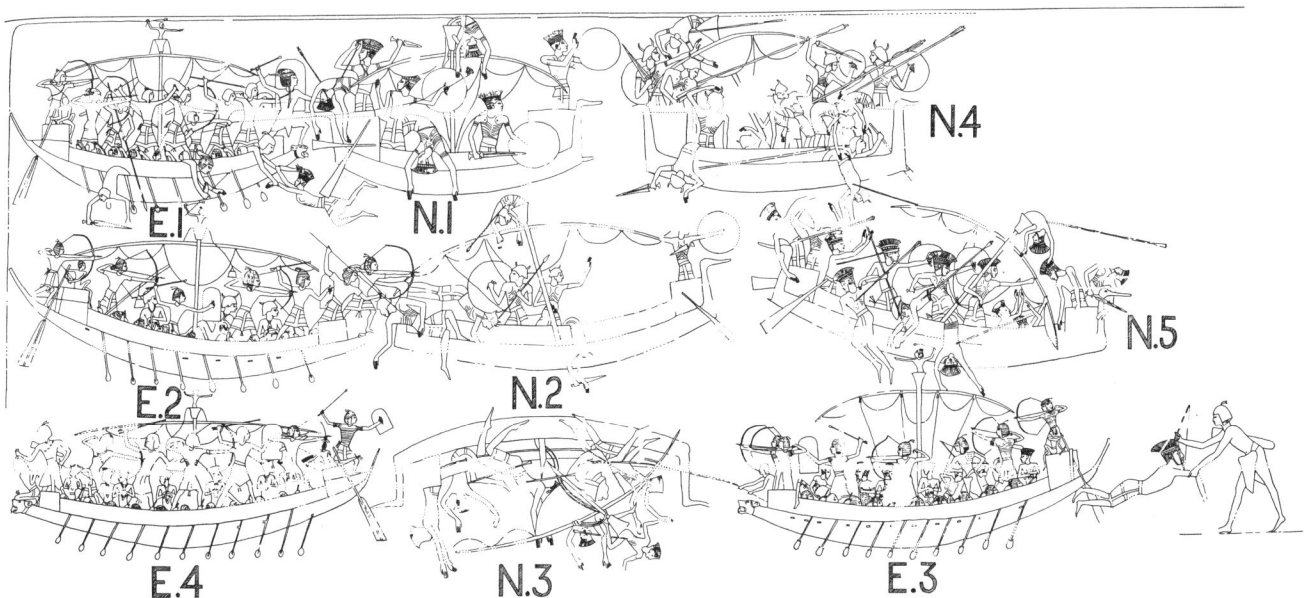

Fig. 2. The naval battle with the floating bodies removed. From Nelson (1943: fig. 4).

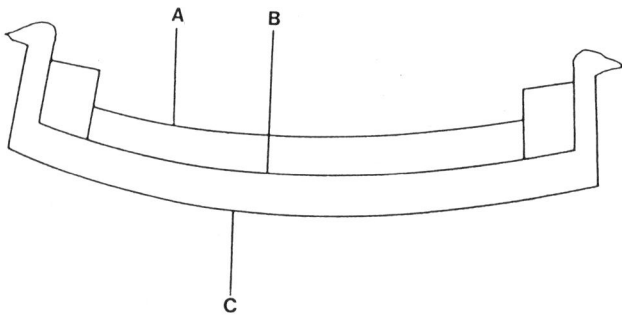

Fig. 3. The horizontal lines on ships N. 1–2, 4–5.

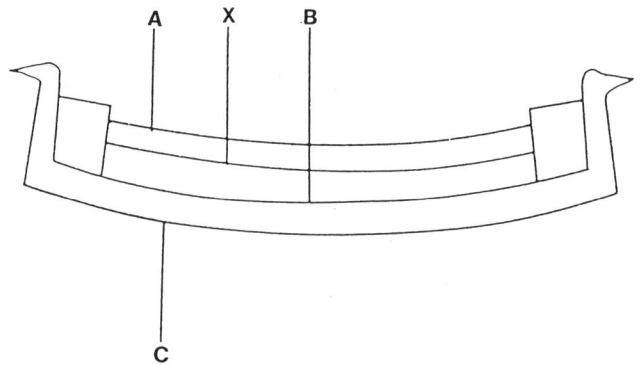

Fig. 4. The horizontal lines on ship N. 3.

accompanying inscription conveys the sense of a surprise attack sprung by the Egyptian forces on the invading fleet, perhaps when they were at anchor (*BAR* 4: § 65; Casson 1995: 38).

In 1981 I proposed that at Medinet Habu the ancient Egyptian artists had supplied us with invaluable clues for understanding the construction of the Sea Peoples ships.[2] The hulls of four of the ships—Nelson's N. 1, N. 2, N. 4 and N. 5—are defined by three horizontal lines (figs. 1–3). Were these ships our sole evidence, these lines could easily be misconstrued as a hull (Area BC), surmounted by a screen attached above the caprail (Area AB). If such were the case, then the invading ships would be similar to those used by the Egyptians.

These ships have curious anomalies, however. In one (N. 4), the helmsman and a dead shipmate protrude above line B which would, according to this interpretation, indicate the juncture of the caprail and the bottom of the screen (Wachsmann 1981: 193 fig. 6: B, C). Furthermore, in ship N. 2, one crew member sits on this same line, while another seems to be "falling" into it (Wachsmann 1981: 192 fig. 4: A, B). Curiously, something seems to be missing in these ships.

The missing component is an additional horizontal line that is *now* present in only one ship, the one that has capsized, N. 3 (fig. 4). A study of how the warriors are positioned—which body parts are visible, and which disappear behind parts of the hull's structure—teach us about the ship's construction.

Three crew members are wound around the upper and lower horizontal parts of the ship (AX and BC), but their limbs reappear in the central area (XB) (figs. 4, 5: A–D). These three independent clues clearly indicate that Area XB

was open to view. In other words, these ships must have had *an open rowers' gallery* (figs. 6, 7). Furthermore, the manner in which the three warriors are contorted around the ship's parts indicates that the ship had only a partial deck; it probably ran the entire length of the hull, but not its entire breadth.[3]

Stanchions would have been needed to support the screen and the deck beams, yet they are nowhere to be seen at Medinet Habu. Why are they missing?

Nelson (1929: 22–31) emphasizes that much of the final version of this scene no longer exists, having fallen victim to the vicissitudes of time. This scene belongs to the form of Egyptian art that is both carved and painted. In this art form carving had a status equal to, or even lesser than, painting. Thus, many details existed solely in paint and, with its loss, these details have disappeared. The stanchions, together with at least some of the other missing details on the Sea Peoples' ships originally may have existed only in paint at Medinet Habu.

Additionally, corrections to the drawing were made by plastering the wall and carving details into it (Nelson 1929: 22–31). Through time, the plaster has crumbled, and together with it, the final versions of the ships.

The degree of detailed information that may have been lost is considerable. This is vividly illustrated by the following description of another battle scene from Medinet Habu that has been better-preserved. Writes Nelson (1929: 22):

> Here, in the upper portions of the relief, even the watercolor paint is unusually well preserved, and we find that the bare sculpture has been extensively supplemented by painted details distinctly enriching the composition.

---

[2] See also supplemental materials in Wachsmann (1982).

[3] Compare this with Casson's reconstruction of an Attic Greek Geometric galley (1995: 71–74, fig. 69).

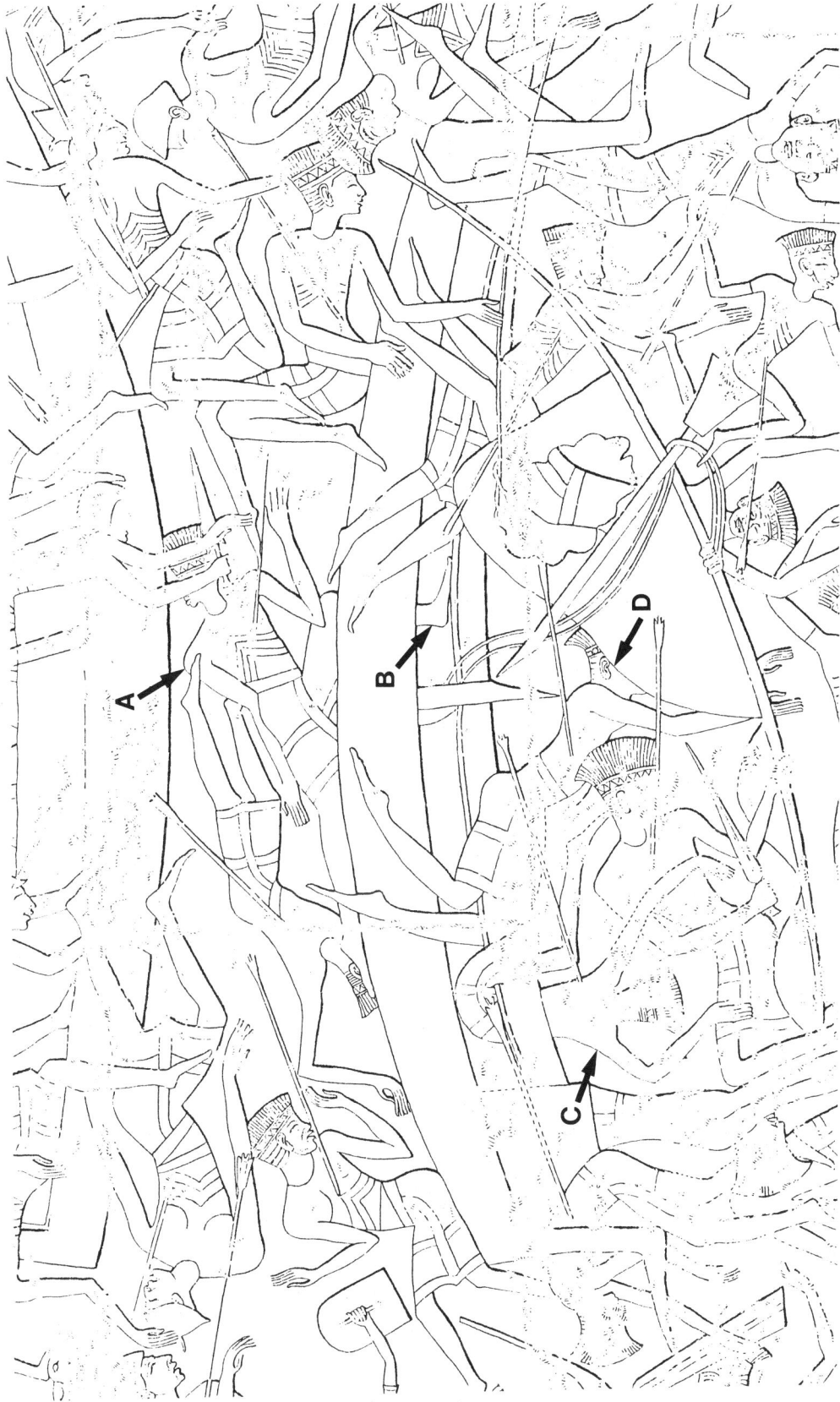

Fig. 5. Ship N. 3. Detail from *MH* I: pl. 39.

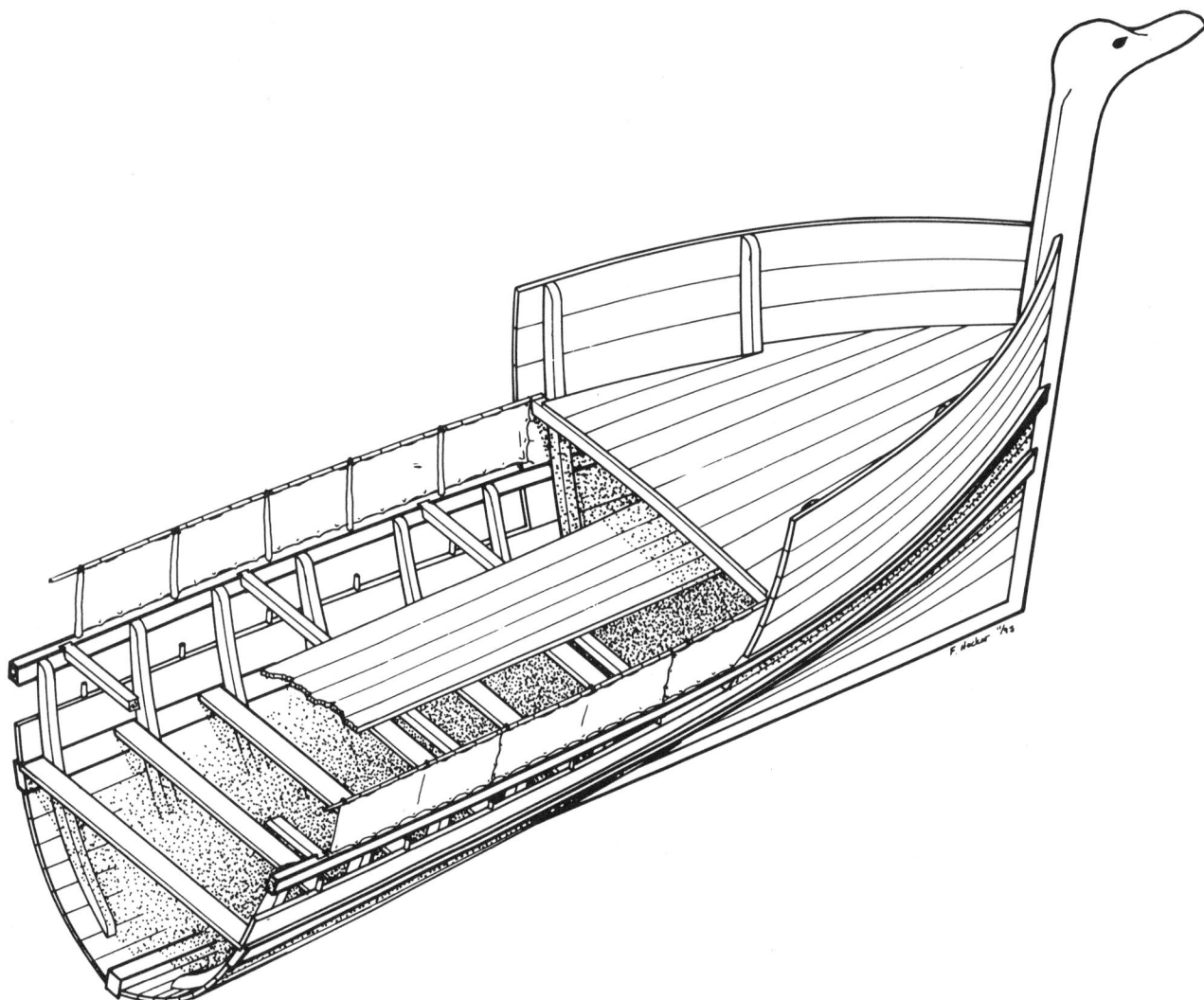

Fig. 6. Tentative isometric reconstruction of a Sea Peoples' ship. Drawing: F. M. Hocker. Courtesy Institute of Nautical Archaeology (INA).

The colors of the garments worn by the Libyans stand out clearly. Between the bodies of the slain as they lie upon the battlefield appear pools of blood. The painter has suggested the presence of the open country by painting in wild flowers which spring up among the dead. Moreover, it is apparent that the action takes place in a hilly region, for streams of blood run down between the bodies as the enemy attempt to escape across the hills from the Pharaoh's pursuing shafts. The details of the monarch's accouterments are indicated in color, relieving him of the almost naked appearance often presented by his sculptured figure when divested of its paint. It is not infrequent to find such details as bow strings or lance shafts partly carved and partly represented in paint. The characteristic tattoo marks on the bodies of the Libyans are also painted in pigment only. When all these painted details have disappeared, though the sculptured design may remain in fairly good condition, much of the life of

the original scene is gone and many aids to its interpretation are lost.

There are numerous indications that much is missing in the naval battle scene. Thus, for example, the helmsman in ship N. 4, holds the loom of the quarter rudder with his right hand while his left wraps around a now nonexistent tiller that must have been painted but not carved (fig. 8). Cases of asymmetry of the ships' accouterments are perhaps also due to a loss of painted detail. On ship N. 5, for example, the bird head stern device lacks an eye, while on N. 2 and N. 4 the stem device has one and the brails (the lines used to raise and lower the loose-footed sail) are depicted on only one side of the mast.

How do these compare with contemporary Mycenaean ships?

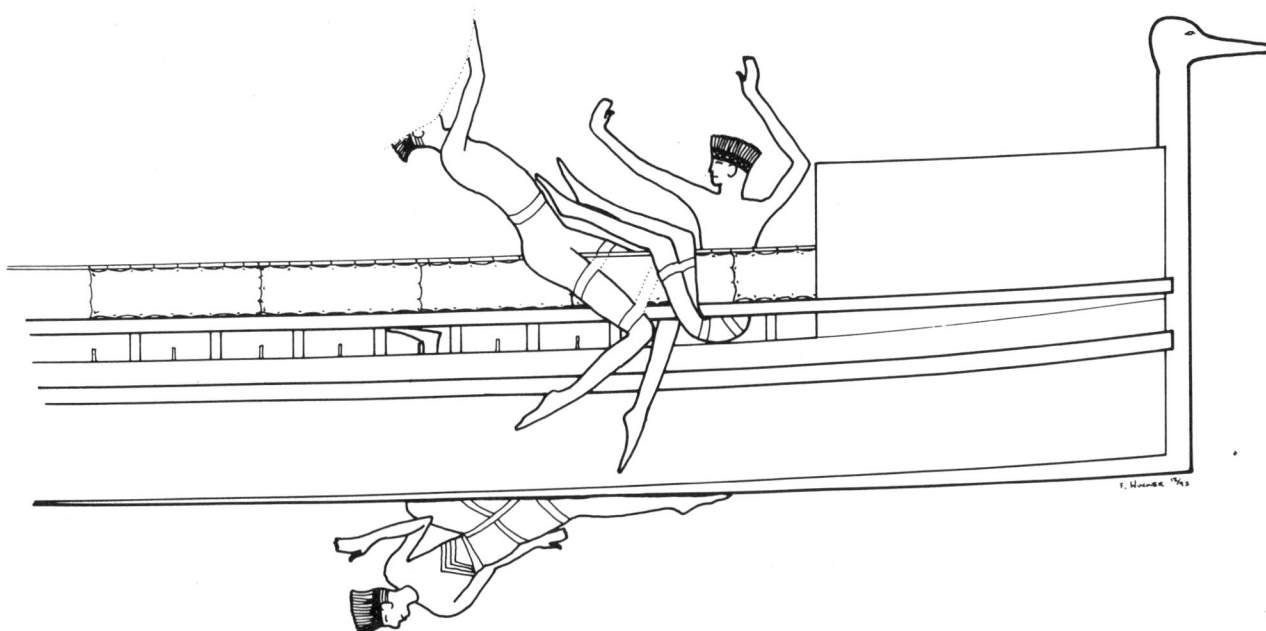

Fig. 7. Sheer or profile view of a Sea Peoples ship showing the manner in which the bodies of the warriors depicted by the Egyptian artists are situated in relation to the ship's structural details. Note that the human figures are drawn to a scale larger than that of the ship. Drawing by F. M. Hocker. Courtesy Institute of Nautical Archaeology.

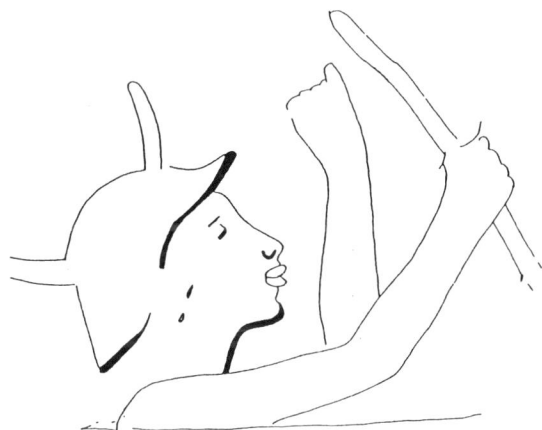

Fig. 8. The helmsmen of ship N. 4. Detail after *MH* I: pl. 39.

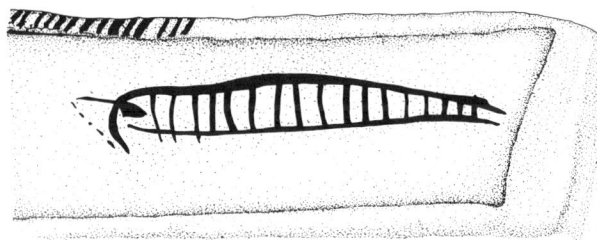

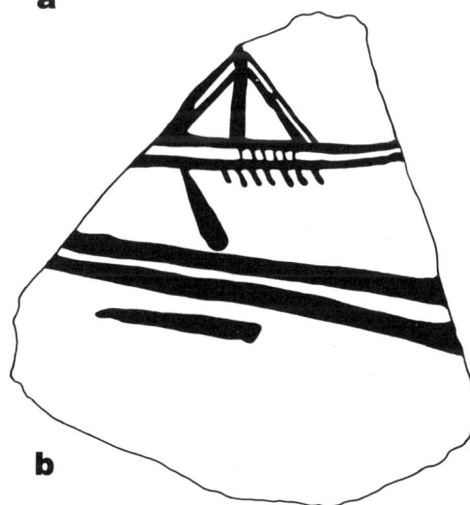

Fig. 9. a) Ship drawn upside down on the interior of a Late Minoan larnax. After Gray (1974: G47, Abb. 11); b) Galley under oar painted on a sherd from Phylakopi on Melos. After Marinatos (1933: pl. XIII: 13).

MYCENAEAN SHIPS:
THE CASE OF THE HEADLESS OARSMEN

Artists of all ages tend to focus on certain specific elements of the ships' structure or rigging that most caught their eye. For example, during the Bronze Age, artists were at pains to depict the lines that were used to support the yard and boom, called lifts, in the boom-footed sail used during that period (Naville 1898: pls. LXXII-LXXV; Säve-Södebergh 1946: 14, fig. 1).

If we were standing on an Aegean shore, gazing out over the water some 3,200 years ago—give or take a cen-

Fig. 10. Ship painted on the side of a *larnax* from Gazi, Crete. Late Minoan IIIB.

tury—at a Mycenaean vessel, the predominant element of
the ship's structure would most certainly have been something that looked rather like a ladder lying horizontally on
its side:

We know this because the majority of depictions in our large
corpus of Mycenaean ships bear this element. At times the
entire ship "becomes" this quintessential element, as for
example on a schematic graffito of a ship painted upside
down inside a Mycenaean *larnax* or a ship painted on a sherd
from Phylakopi on Melos (fig. 9; *Larnax:* Gray 1974: G19
no. 40a; Phylakopi: Marinatos 1933: 172 no. 13). Instances
of the appearance of this "horizontal-ladder motif" are numerous on Late Helladic/Minoan IIIB and IIIC ship depictions, like those from Gazi, Tragana and Hyria, for example
(figs. 10, 11; Gazi: Alexiou 1970: 253–54, 1972: 90–98;
1973; Hyria: Blegen 1949; Basch 1987: 143–44, figs.
300–2). This same motif is also painted on Mycenaean ship
models, as on a Late Cypriot III *askos* and two terracotta
ship models from Tanagra (Buchholz and Karageorghis
1973: 470 fig. 1720; Basch 1987: 141 fig. 293: 1–2). In the

latter two models, the vertical lines inside the hull do not
coincide with the frames painted inside the hull, indicating
that the external vertical lines do not represent the ships'
frames in an "X-ray" view as proposed by Basch (1987:
141).

What then does this ubiquitous "horizontal-ladder motif" represent? Until relatively recently it was impossible to
answer this question definitively because, despite the large
corpus of Mycenaean ship depictions, not one was sufficiently clear to indicate the purpose of this architectural element. This situation changed when Dakoronia (1990; 1993;
1995), excavating at Pyrgos Livanaton, a site identified as
the Homeric Kynos, found several ship depictions painted
on Late Helladic IIIC sherds. One representation contains
sufficient detail to permit an interpretation of the horizontal-ladder design.

The ship faces left (fig. 12). Three horizontal bands
define its features (fig. 13). Area BC, which represents the
hull from the line of its keel/keel-plank to the caprail, is
depicted in dark paint. Above this is a horizontal unpainted
area (XB) intersected by nineteen vertical lines next to each
of which is positioned a lunette with its convex side facing
aft. One additional line represents the mast.

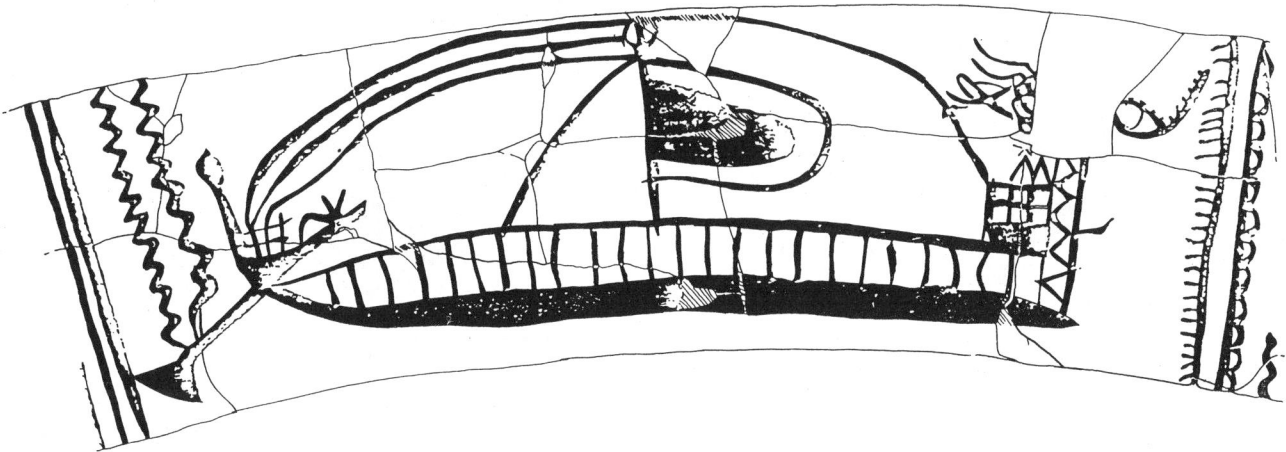

Fig. 11. Ship painted on a ceramic pyxis found at Tragana, near Pylos. Late Helladic IIIC. After Korrés (1989: 200).

Above Area XB, the third and final horizontal one, Area AX, is decorated with two bands of semicircles. Perhaps this indicates that the screen was made of leather for this motif commonly appears in Mycenaean art on the hide of bulls as well on the (leather) sides of chariots (Furumark 1941: 245 fig. 27: 6, 8; 332 fig. 18.). Line X continues forward, across the bow, possibly representing a strong freestanding wale; this would have been required to support the beams bracing the partial deck upon which the central figure stands.

Three figures stand on, or above, the ship. Two armored warriors—one positioned on a light forecastle, the other abaft the mast—brandish short throwing spears and shields. In the stern, a helmsman sitting (?) on a stern castle, hunkers over his single quarter rudder. Unless these figures are portrayed having a particularly bad hair day, all three appear to be wearing helmets with numerous protuberances. Such helmets are reminiscent of the feather (?) helmets worn by contingents of the Sea Peoples at Medinet Habu (figs. 1, 2, 5) as well as by seafarers depicted on Late Helladic IIIC sherds from the Seraglio at Kos (Morricone 1975: 360 figs. 356, 357a-c, 358–360).

The artist supplies several compelling clues indicating that the lunettes in Area XB represent oarsmen seen through an open rowers' gallery intersected by vertical stanchions that support the ship's superstructure:

- Each of the nineteen lunettes is "attached" to an oar.
- The oars' blades are angled towards the stern, indicating that the oarsmen are depicted at the end of their stroke, when they are leaning backwards as they pull on their oars. In this position, later Geometric artists depicted rowers with their far shoulder jutting forward (fig. 14).

Fig. 12. The most detailed published depiction of a Mycenaean ship appears on a LH IIIC sherd from Kynos. After Wachsmann (1988: 131 fig. 8:A). Drawing by K. Bowling.

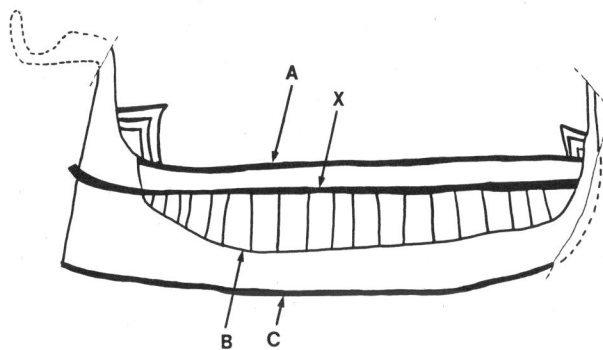

Fig. 13. Constructional details of the Kynos ship.

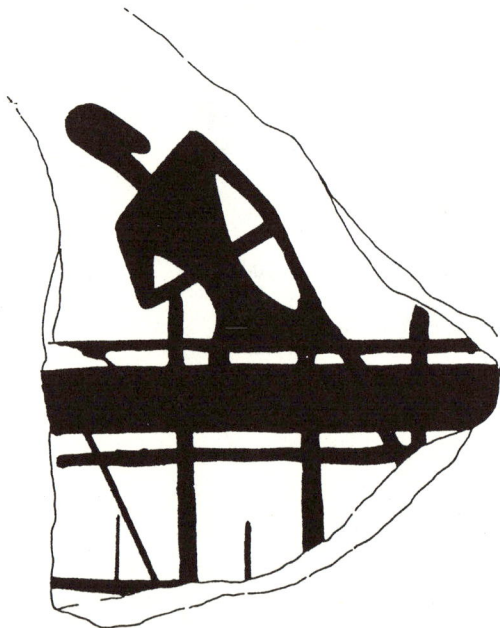

Fig. 14. A rower, depicted on an Attic Late Geometric I sherd, reaches the end of his stroke. After Basch (1987: 166 fig. 338).

Fig. 15. Detail of the helmsman on the Kynos ship.

- Furthermore, the manner in which the helmsman is portrayed indicates that the artist depicted the *unarmored* male body in a curvilinear and sinuous manner (fig. 15).

Thus, we may identify the "lunettes" as rowers' torsos—from the neck to the waist—albeit represented in a very schematic form. The oarsmen's lower body parts are hidden behind the hull while *their heads disappear behind the screen* (fig. 16).

Ideally, it would be possible to find parallels to these "headless oarsmen" in the numerous depictions of oared ships in Geometric art, which, authorities agree, are derived from Mycenaean prototypes. Any parallel to Geometric art would be suspect, however, as none of the experts who have dealt with the oared ships in Geometric art agree as to how they are to be interpreted (Kirk 1949: 123–31; Morrison and Williams 1968: 12–17; Casson 1995: 71–74; Basch 1987: 161–70).[4] Fortunately, towards the end of that period, in the closing decade of the eighth century B.C.E., a new type of oared ship appears, which, all agree, represent the *dieres*: a type of ship bearing two superimposed banks of oars on either side of the hull.

One of the earliest depictions of a *dieres,* on a Proto-Attic sherd from Phaleron, is analogous to the Kynos ship;

the rowers' torsos in the lower banks appear in the open rowers' gallery while their heads disappear behind the superstructure (fig. 17; see also, Morrison and Williams 1968: pl. 7: e–f). Thus, we may conclude that this ship depiction from Kynos indicates that the ubiquitous "horizontal-ladder pattern" on Mycenaean ship iconography represents an open rowers gallery crossed by numerous vertical stanchions.

A deck, situated above this probably ran the length of the hull from stem to stern. It could not, however, have run across the entire breadth of the ship. Some room must have been left out along the sides, to allow space for the rowers. Similarly, Casson (1995: 51 n. 58) notes that in some Greek Geometric depictions of oared warships, warriors are seen standing on the rowers' benches in an area not covered by a raised deck.

From the above considerations we may conclude that in all major discernible architectural aspects, the hull structures of Mycenaean ships were identical to those of the Sea Peoples' ships depicted at Medinet Habu. That is, the Sea Peoples were either using actual Mycenaean oared ships, or had adopted/adapted the Mycenaean galley design to the degree that today we are unable to differentiate—in macro terms—between them vis-à-vis their hull construction.

---

[4] The interpretation given here to galleys of both the Mycenaeans and the Sea Peoples agrees completely with, and further supports, Casson's interpretation of Greek Geometric galleys.

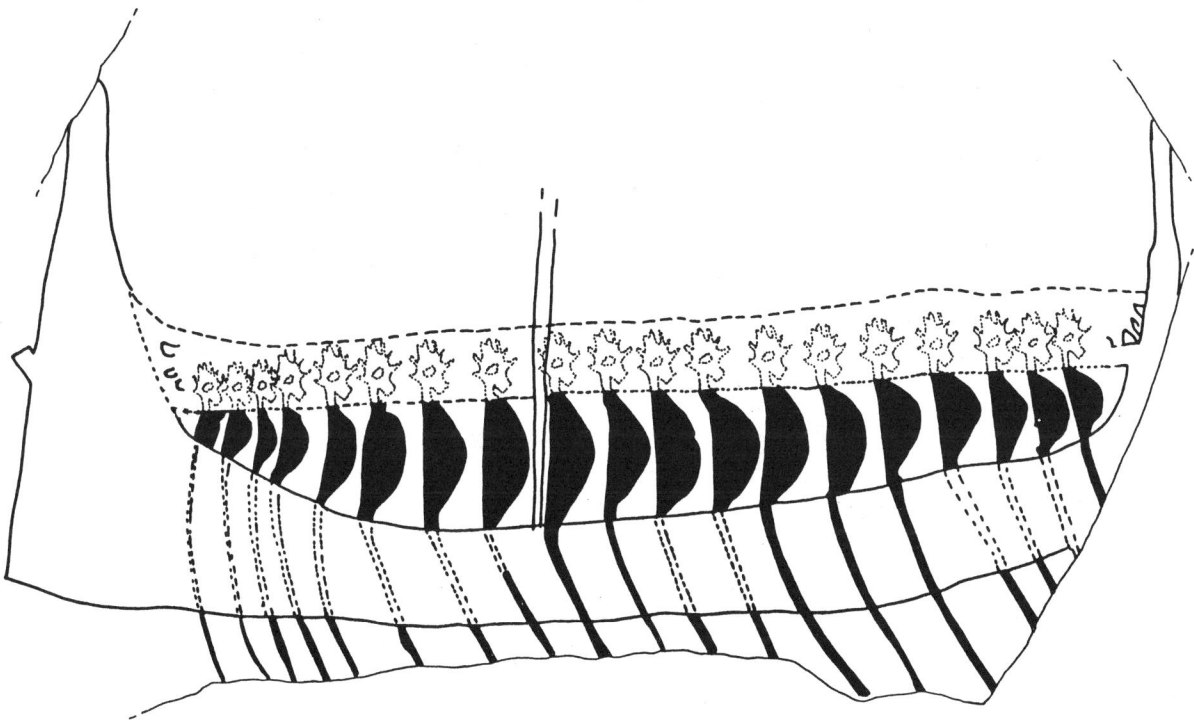

Fig. 16. A hypothetical reconstruction of the Kynos ship in fig. 12, illustrating the position of the rowers. Assuming that Area AX in fig. 13 is a screen beginning at deck level, then it would hide the heads of the oarsmen.

Using hull construction to determine ethnic identity is speculative at best, however. Peoples bearing no ethnic, or regional connection could adopt and adapt ship types to their own uses. In later times, for example, the pragmatic Romans were particularly noted for adopting foreign ship designs (Casson 1995: 105 n. 41, 141–42).

BIRD HEADS

There is, however, an additional similarity between the ships of the Mycenaean and those of the Sea Peoples. On all five of the invading craft depicted at Medinet Habu, water-bird head devices cap the stem and stern posts (fig. 18; Wachsmann 1996). During the Late Bronze Age, similar bird-heads are a distinctly Aegean, and more specifically Mycenaean, characteristic on Mediterranean ships.

The earliest bird-head known appears on Middle Helladic sherds from Aegina (Buchholz and Karageorghis 1973: 301 fig. 869). Thereafter, particularly from the thirteenth century B.C.E. and later, the head of a water bird, often with a strongly up-curving beak, appears regularly facing forward on the stems of Mycenaean ships (figs. 19, 20).[5]

Fig. 17. Proto-Attic sherd from Phaleron bearing part of a *dieres*. Note how the heads of the oarsmen in the lower bank disappear behind the superstructure. After Williams (1959: 160 fig. 1).

[5] A Late Helladic IIIC: 1b sherd of a bird-head ship ornament with the legs of a man standing on the curving post was found in an unstratified context at Ashkelon. My thanks to Dr. Stager for bringing the sherd to my attention. See Wachsmann (1998: title page, 201–2; in press).

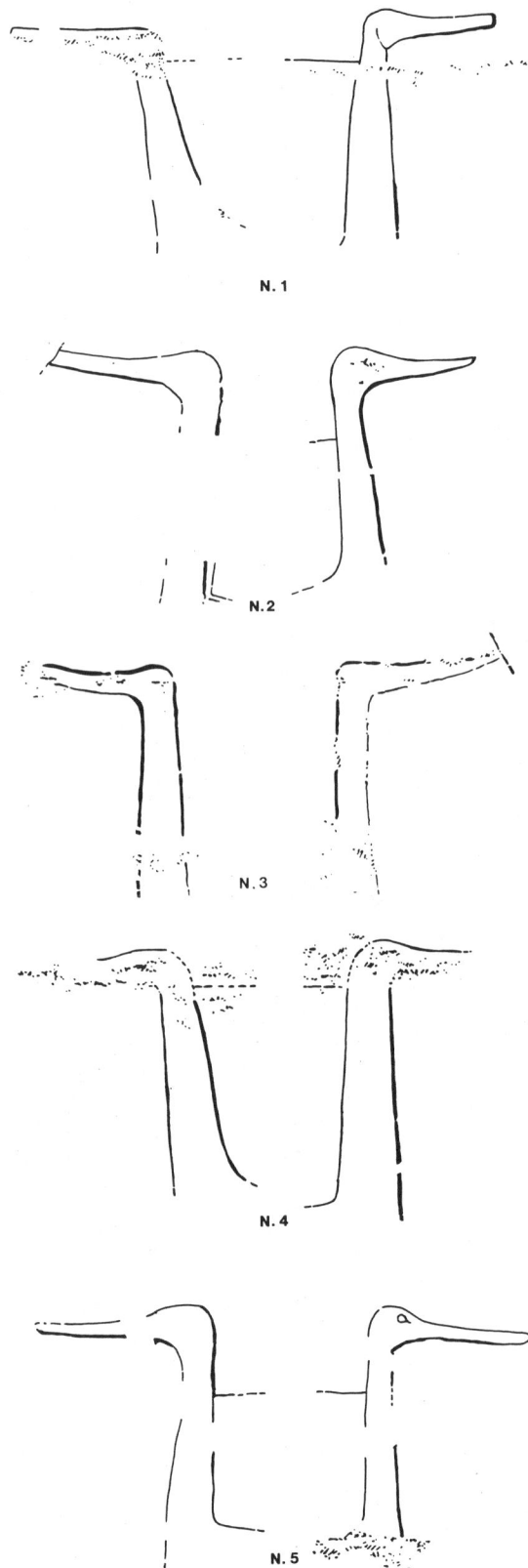

Fig. 18. The bird-head devices on the Sea Peoples' ships at Medinet Habu. After Nelson, et al. (1930: pl. 39).

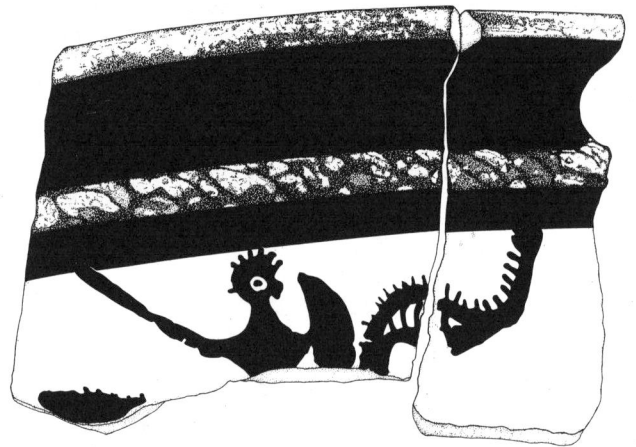

Fig. 19. Bird-head stem device painted on a sherd from Kynos. Late Helladic IIIC. After Wachsmann (1998: 134 fig. 15). Drawing by K. Bowling.

Fig. 20. A ship painted on a stirrup jar from Skyros bears the typical bird-head stem device. After Hencken (1968: 537 fig. 486).

At times, in place of a bird-head the actual body of a bird is placed on or near the stem, as for example, on the Late Helladic IIIC Tragana ship, or on one of the Mycenaean ships painted on an Late Helladic IIIB amphoroid krater from Enkomi (figs. 11, 21).

Inevitably, this device represents water fowl: the same type(s) of bird(s) that are commonly depicted on contemporaneous Mycenaean and Philistine ceramics (Furumark 1941: 253 fig. 30, 255 fig. 31: nos. 36–52; Benson 1961; Dothan 1982: 201–2 figs. 61–63).

Despite the obvious similarities, however, there is one significant difference between the manner in which the bird-heads are arranged on ships represented on Late Helladic/Late Minoan IIIB/C pottery as opposed to the manner in which they appear on the Sea Peoples' ships at Medinet Habu. On representations of Mycenaean ships the bird-head/birds are always positioned atop, or near, the stem. At first they inevitably face forward; subsequently, bird-head de-

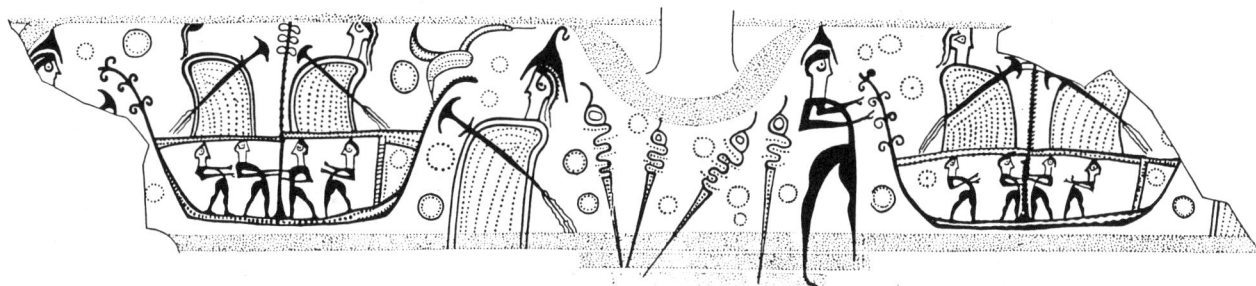

Fig. 21. Scene of ships depicted on a Late Helladic III amphoroid krater from Enkomi. Note the bird device surmounting the (stem) post of the ship on the left. After Sjöqvist (1940: fig. 20: 3).

vices also appear atop the stem facing inboard (Göttlicher 1978: 35 no. 149).[6]

In the case of the Sea Peoples' ships at Medinet Habu, however, the bird-heads are situated *on both the stem and the stern, facing outboard.* For (numerous) exact parallels to this configuration we must search farther afield: to the Urnfield cultures of Central Europe.

THE URNFIELD CULTURE CONNECTION

The striking similarity between the manner in which the bird-head devices are positioned on the Sea Peoples' ships at Medinet Habu to the "bird-boats" (Vogelbarke) of the central European Urnfield Cultures was first discussed by Hencken (1968: 568–70, 625–28).

Bouzek (1985: 178), who also notes this parallel, dates the earliest bird-boat ornaments, from the Somes River at Satu Mare in northern Rumania and from Velem St. Vid in Hungary, to the European Br D period (ca. 1250–1200 B.C.E.; figs. 22, 23).[7] A bird-boat ornament from Grünwald, Bavaria, dating to the Halstatt A1 (ca. twelvth century B.C.E.) is only slightly later (fig. 24). Subsequently, the bird-boat motif continues to appear in Urnfield and Villanovan art (fig. 25). Bird-boats are not commonly a Mycenaean symbolic device, although a bird-boat-like decoration does appear on a Late Helladic IIIC krater fragment recovered at Tiryns (fig. 26). In this case, however, the artist may have been unaware of its prototype (Bouzek 1985: 178).

Thus, although the invading *ships* depicted at Medinet Habu are built in what appears to be a Mycenaean tradition, they bear a prophylactic "bird-boat" *symbology.* This argues strongly for the ship's crew having religious beliefs associated with bird-boats, thus reflecting an Urnfield ethnicity. This does not mean, however, that the entire fleet was made up of ships manned by Urnfielder warriors. Far from it.

In attempting to put the Medinet Habu naval battle scene into its proper historical perspective it is imperative to be aware of a schematizing tendency on the part of its artists. The tableau supplies us with a "fleet" of five ship images attributable to the Sea Peoples. This is misleading, for all five images are almost certainly reproductions derived from a single prototype ship (Wachsmann 1981: 191). Similarly, only one type of Egyptian ship is represented in the scene— albeit four times—even though three types of Egyptian ships are recorded in the accompanying inscription (*BAR* 4: § 65).

Furthermore, two groups of Sea Peoples, distinguishable by their different head-gear—horned-helmeted in N. 2 and N. 4, while feather(?)-helmeted in ships N. 1, N. 3. and N. 5—are depicted in this single type of ship. This in itself, seems highly unlikely.

It is also imperative to understand the likely source for these images. Presumably, following the battle an Egyptian army artist sketched studies of one such ship. These studies would have served as a resource for the artists creating the naval battle scene.[8] We have examples of artists accompa-

---

[6] Ultimately, such inboard curving bird-heads evolved into the curved stem and sternpost finials on Greek Geometric ships (Wachsmann 1998: 185–86). Homer, in describing his warships, uses the adjective κορωνίς, which most probably means "having curved extremities." A similar word, however, is the name of a seabird: κορώνη. It is possible that this is a deliberate play on the two similar words, and that κορωνίς is intended to imply "having curved extremities that are bird-shaped" (Lenz 1998).

[7] The chronology of the Br D, to which most of the classical comparisons with the Late Helladic IIIB materials are found, may be slightly higher than previously thought (Bouzek 1994: 217).

[8] On the use of source materials in Egyptian tomb art see Wachsmann (1987: 12–26).

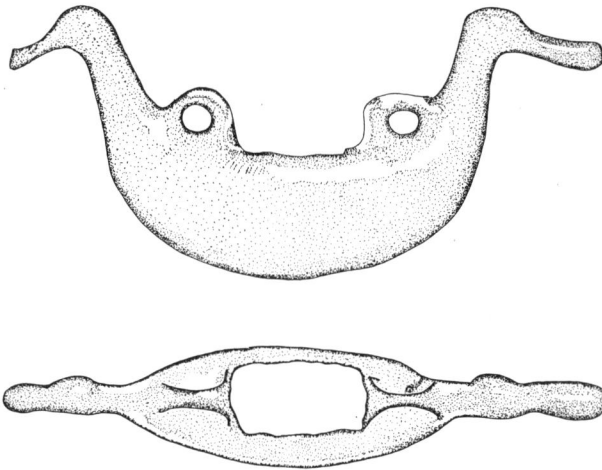

Fig. 22. Bronze bird-boat found in the Somes River, at Satu Mare in northern Romania. European Br D (?). After Göttlicher (1978: Taf. 33: 439).

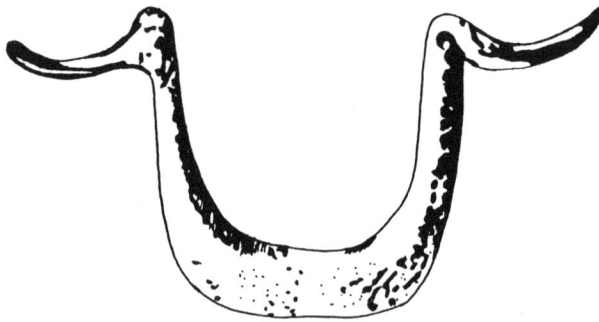

Fig. 23. Bronze bird-boat ornament from Velem St. Vid in Hungary. European Br D (?). After Göttlicher (1978: Taf. 34: 440).

nying army and trade expeditions, as witnessed by the Red Sea fishes swimming beneath Hatshepsut's Punt ships at Deir el Bahri and the Syro-Canaanite flora and fauna in Thutmose III's botanical garden; furthermore, details in the scene of how the Egyptians capsized at least one of the enemy ships with a grapnel suggests that artist(s?) were present during the action itself (Wachsmann 1987: 5–16; 1995: 22, 33–34; 1998: 19, 22, 55, 317–19).

Thus, following a minimalist approach, we may conclude that the tableau at Medinet Habu supplies us with information pertaining to *only one ship belonging to the defeated invading fleet*. It is not necessarily clear that this was a common type of vessel in the fleet. The choice of which ship to record may have been based on any number of considerations that we cannot, at a distance of over three mil-

lennia from the event, determine. Indeed there may be a degree of serendipity in the artist's decision to record this particular ship.

Turning to the *archaeological* evidence of Sea Peoples settlement in the Levant, the impression is clearly that stated by Stager. In other words, Mycenaean cultural traits predominate. This evidence argues for Urnfielders comprising a relatively limited aggregate within the mass of moving peoples who reached eastern shores. Nevertheless, there is one additional component in this equation worthy of contemplation: the urnfield cremation cemeteries at Hama.

Hama F (early phase, equivalent to Period I of the cremation cemeteries) contained nearly 1100 urns related to cremation burials (Ingholt 1940: 69–84, pls. XXI–XXVI; Riis 1948). This manner of burial is intrusive and entirely exceptional to local traditions. Components of the material culture of this group, such as fibulae, flang-hilted swords, and the urnfield burials themselves, are clearly of European tradition and indicate the arrival of an intrusive element at Hama. The Danish excavators connected the urnfield level at Hama to the migratory upheavals that ended the Late Bronze Age. Of particular interest is a typical Mycenaean/ Sea Peoples ship—complete with the ubiquitous "horizontal-ladder design" and a bird-head stem ornament—which is painted on one of the cremation urns (fig. 27; Ingholt 1940: 71, pl. XXII: 2; Riis 1948: 48 fig. 25, 97 fig. 130B: 112, 105-106, pl. 12C—no. G VIII, 551 [5B902]; Hencken 1968: 627).

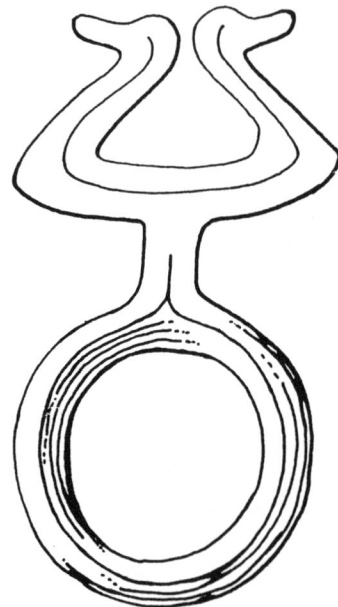

Fig. 24. Bird-boat ornament from Grünwald, Bavaria. Halstatt A1. After Hencken (1968: 516 fig. 478: f).

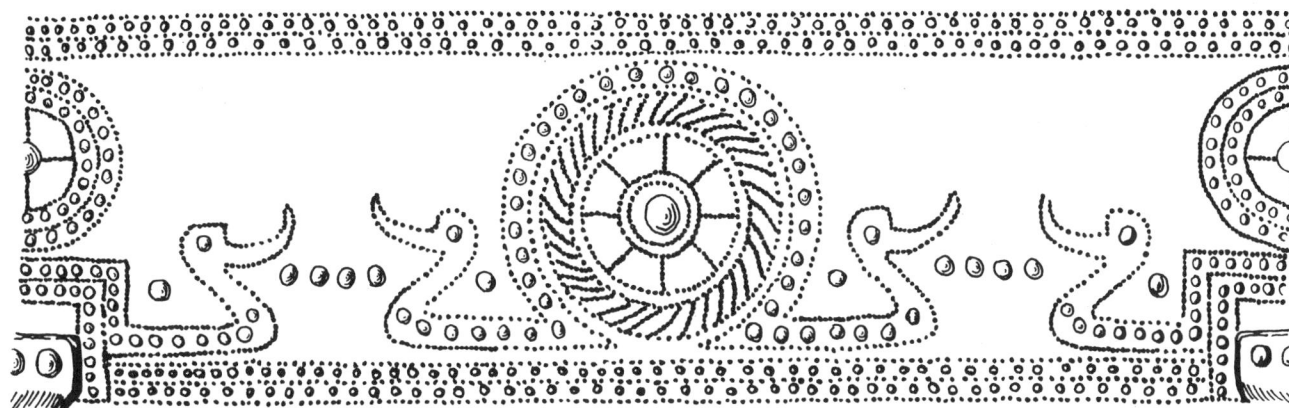

a

b

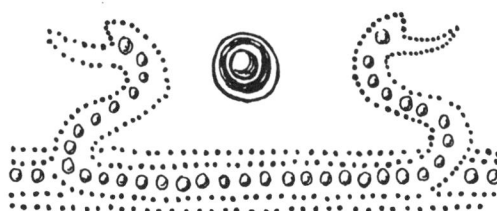

c

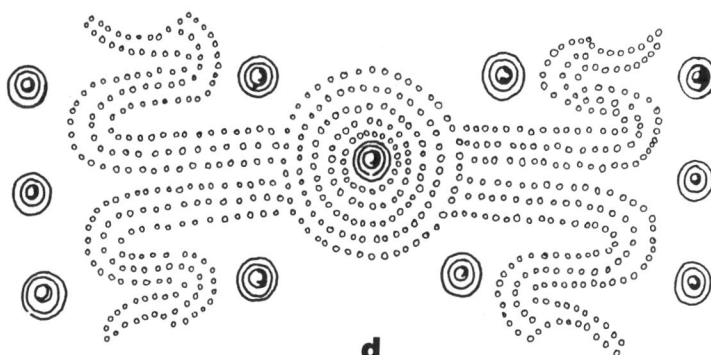

d

Fig. 25. Single and double bird-boats represented in embossed Urnfield ornaments; a) from Lavindsgaard, Denmark. Halstatt A2.; b) from "Lucky," Slovakia. Halstatt A2.; c) from Rossin, Pomerania. Halstatt B; d) from Este, Italy. Este II (= Villanovan II). After Hencken (1968: 516 fig. 478: a, b, e and g).

Fig. 26. Bird-boat (?) painted on a krater sherd from Tiryns. Late Helladic IIIC. After Bouzek (1985: 117 fig. 88: 6).

Fig. 27. Ship with a bird-head device capping the stem depicted on a funerary urn found at Hama. *Ca.* 1200– 1075 B.C.E. After Ingholt (1940: pl. XXII: 2).

CONCLUSION

This review of ship iconography confirms the strong inter-relationship between Mycenaeans and Sea Peoples, so well-documented in other manifestations of material culture. However, it indicates in addition that, together with Mycenaean elements, the invading fleet of the Sea Peoples included persons whose origins are to be sought farther north. This consideration should not prevent us, however, from an awareness that there may have been additional ethnic groups, some perhaps of Anatolian descent, that participated in the coalition.

Indeed, the absorption of polyglot elements into the Sea Peoples naval coalition may have been its hallmark. This is eloquently documented in an Ugaritic text in which Eshuwara, the chief prefect of Alashia informs the king of Ugarit that men and ships of Ugarit committed undefined transgressions against their own kingdom, perhaps indicating that they had joined the enemy (RS 20.18; Hoftijzer and Van Soldt 1998: 343).

One receives the impression of something akin to a snowball rolling down a hill and taking up along the way various elements until, by the time it reaches the bottom of the hill, it has become something more—and different—than the sum of its aggregate parts.

REFERENCES

Alexiou, S.
   1970   Mikrai Anaskaphai kai Perisulloge Arxaion eis Kreten. *Praktika tes en Athenais Archaeilogikes Etaireias:* 252–255, pls. 354–55 (in Greek).
   1972   Larnakes kai Aggeia ek Taphou Para to Gazi Irakliou. *Archaiologiki Ephemeris*: 86–98 (in Greek).
   1973   Nea Parastasis Ploiou epi Minoikis Larnakos. Pp. 3–12, pin. 1–2 in *Anatupon ek tou a Tomou ton Pepragmenon tou Gama Diethnous Kritologikou Sunedriou, "En Rethumno, 18–23 September 1971, Athens* (in Greek).
BAR
   1988   *Ancient Records of Egypt* I–V., ed. J. H. Breasted. Chicago: Histories and Mysteries of Maw. Reprint of 1906–1907 edition.
Basch, L.
   1987   *Le musée imaginaire de la marine antique.* Athens: Institut hellénique pour la préservation de la tradition nautique.
Benson, J. L.
   1961   A Problem in Orientalizing Cretan Birds: Mycenaean or Philistine Prototypes. *Journal of Near Eastern Studies* 20: 73–84, pls. III–VI.
Blegen, C. W.
   1949   Hyria. *Hesperia: Supplement* 8: 39–42.
Blegen, C. W.; Rawson, M.; Taylor, L. W.; and Donovan, W. P.
   1973   *The Palace of Nestor at Pylos in Western Messenia* III: *Acropolis and Lower Town Tholoi, Grave Circle, and Chamber Tombs Discoveries outside the Citadel.* Princeton: Princeton University.
Bouzek, J.
   1985   *The Aegean, Anatolia and Europe: Cultural Interrelations in the Second Millennium B.C.* Studies in Mediterranean Archaeology 39. Göteborg: Åströms.
   1994   Late Bronze Age Greece and the Balkans: A Review of the Present Picture. *Annual of the British School at Athens* 89: 217–34.
Buchholz, H.-G., and Karageorghis, V.
   1973   *Prehistoric Greece and Cyprus.* London: Phaidon.

Casson, L.
1995   *Ships and Seamanship in the Ancient World.*
        Reprint with Addenda and Corrigenda. Balti-
        more: Johns Hopkins University.

Dakoronia, F.
1990   War-Ships on Sherds of LH III C Kraters from
        Kynos. *Tropis* II: 117–22.
1993   Homeric Towns in East Lokris: Problems of
        Identification. *Hesperia* 62: 115–27.
1995   War Ships on Sherds of LHIII Kraters from
        Kynos? Editor's Note. *Tropis* III: 147–48.

Dietrich, M., and Loretz, O.
1978   Das 'Seefahrende Volk' von Šikila (RS 34.129).
        Ugarit-Forschungen 10: 53–56.

Dothan, T.
1982   *The Philistines and Their Material Culture.* New
        Haven: Yale University.

Dothan, T., and Dothan, M.
1992   *People of the Sea: The Search for the Philistines.*
        New York: MacMillan.

Furumark, A.
1941   *The Mycenaean Pottery: Analysis and Classifi-
        cation.* Stockholm: Svenska Institutet i Athen.

Göttlicher, A.
1978   *Materialien für ein Corpus der Schiffsmodele im
        Altertum.* Mainz: von Zabern.

Gray, D.
1974   *Seewesen. Archaeologia Homerica* Band I
        Kapital G. Göttingen: Vandenhoeck & Ruprecht.

Hencken, H.
1968   *Tarquinia, Villanovans and Early Etruscans* I–II.
        Bulletin of the American School of Prehistoric
        Research 23. Cambridge: Peabody Museum.

Hoftijzer, J., and van Soldt, W. H.
1998   Appendix: Texts from Ugarit Pertaining to Sea-
        faring. Pp. 333–43 in S. Wachsmann, *Seagoing
        Ships and Seamanship in the Bronze Age Levant.*
        College Station: Texas A&M University.

Ingholt, H.
1940   *Rapport préliminaire sur sept campagnes de
        fouilles à Hama en Syrie (1932–1938).*
        Copenhagen: Ejnar Munksgaard.

Izre'el, S.
1991   *Amurru Akkadian: A Linguistic Study* I–II.
        Harvard Semitic Studies 40–41. Atlanta: Schol-
        ars.

Kirk, G. S.
1949   Ships on Geometric Vases. *Annual of the Brit-
        ish School at Athens* 44: 93–153, pls. 38–40.

Korrés, G. S.
1989   Representation of a Late Mycenaean Ship on the
        Pyxis from Tragana, Pylos. Pp. 177–202 in

Tropis I (*Proceedings of the First International
Symposium on Ship Construction in Antiquity,
Piraeus 30th August–1st September 1985*), ed.
H. Tzalas. Athens.

Lambdin, T. O.
1953   The Miši-People of the Byblian Amarna Letters.
        Journal of Cuneiform Studies 7: 75–77.

Lehmann, G. A.
1979   Die Šikalāju—ein neues Zeugnis zu den
        'Seevölkern'-Heerfahrten im späten 13. Jh. v.
        Chr. (RS 34.129). *Ugarit-Forschungen* 11:
        481–94.

Lenz, J.
1998   Appendix: Homeric "νηυσὶ κορωνισίν." Pp.
        199–200 in S. Wachsmann, *Seagoing Ships and
        Seamanship in the Bronze Age Levant.* College
        Station: Texas A&M University.

MH I = H. H. Nelson
1930   *Medinet Habu* I: *Earlier Historical Records of
        Ramses III.* By the Epigraphic Survey; Field
        Director, H. H. Nelson. The University of Chi-
        cago, Oriental Institute Publications 8. Chicago:
        The Oriental Institute of the University of Chi-
        cago.

Moran, W. L.
1992   *The Amarna Letters.* Edited and translated by
        W. L. Moran. Baltimore: John Hopkins Univer-
        sity.

Morricone, L.
1975   Coo-Scavi e scoperte nel "Serraglio" in località
        minori (1935–43). *Annuario della Scuola
        Archeologica di Atene*: 50–51 (1972–73; N.S.
        34–35): 139–96.

Morrison, J. S., and Williams, R. T.
1968   *Greek Oared Ships: 900–322 B.C.* Cambridge:
        Cambridge University.

Naville, E.
1898   *The Temple of Deir el Bahri* III: *End of the North-
        ern Half and Southern Half of the Middle Plat-
        form.* London: Egyptian Exploration Fund.

Nelson, H. H.
1929   The Epigraphic Survey of the Great Temple of
        Medinet Habu (Seasons 1924–1925 to
        1927–1928). Pp. 1–36 in *Medinet Habu
        1924–28.* Oriental Institute Communications 5.
        Chicago: The Oriental Institute of the Univer-
        sity of Chicago.
1943   The Naval Battle Pictured at Medinet Habu.
        Journal of Near Eastern Studies 2: 40–45.

Parkinson, R., and Schofield. L.
1993a   Mycenaeans Meet the Egyptians at Last. *Art
        Newspaper* 24 (January): 10.

1993b   Akhenaten's Army? *Egypt Archaeology* 3: 34–35.

1995   Images of Mycenaeans: A Recently Acquired Painted Papyrus from El-Amarna. Pp. 125–26, pl. 8 in *Egypt, the Aegean and the Levant: Interconnections in the Second Millennium B.C.*, eds. W.V. Davies and L. Schofield. London: British Museum.

Redford, D. B.

1992   *Egypt, Canaan and Israel in Ancient Times.* Princeton: Princeton University.

Riis, P. J.

1948   *Hama: les cimetières a cremation.* Copenhagen: Foundation Carlsberg.

Säve-Söderbergh, T.

1946   *The Navy of the Eighteenth Egyptian Dynasty.* Uppsala: Harrassowitz.

Schofield, L., and Parkinson, R. B.

1994   Of Helmets and Heretics: A Possible Egyptian Representation of Mycenaean Warriors on a Papyrus from el-Amarna. *Annual of the British School at Athens* 89: frontispiece, 157–70, pls. 21–22.

Stager, L. E.

1991   *Ashkelon Discovered.* Washington: Biblical Archaeology Society.

1995   The Impact of the Sea Peoples in Canaan (1185–1050 B.C.E.). Pp. 332–48, 583–85 in *The Archaeology of Society in the Holy Land*, ed. T. E. Levy. New York: Facts on File.

Wachsmann, S.

1981   The Ships of the Sea Peoples. *International Journal of Nautical Archaeology* 10: 187–220.

1982   The Ships of the Sea Peoples (*IJNA* 10.3: 187-220). *International Journal of Nautical Archaeology* 11: 297–304.

1987   *Aegeans in the Theban Tombs.* Orientalia Lovaniensia Analecta 20. Leuven: Peeters.

1995   Earliest Mediterranean Paddled and Oared Ships to the Beginning of the Iron Age. Pp. 10–35 in *Conway's History of the Ship: The Age of the Galley.* London: Conway Maritime.

1996   Bird-head Devices on Mediterranean Ships. Pp. 539–72 in *Tropis* IV *(Proceedings of the Fourth International Symposium on Ship Construction in Antiquity, Athens 28th–31st August, 1991)*, ed. H. Tzalas.

1998   *Seagoing Ships and Seamanship in the Bronze Age Levant.* College Station: Texas A & M University.

in press   To the Sea of the Philistines. In *Cultural Interconnections in the Ancient Near East: The Sea Peoples (Seminar held at the University of Pennsylvania Museum, Spring 1995)*, ed. E. Oren.

Williams, R. T.

1959   Addenda to "Early Greek Ships of Two Levels." *Journal of Hellenic Studies* 79: 159–60.

Ougarit et le port de Mahadou/Minet el-Beida

MARGUERITE YON

Mission française de Ras Shamra-Ougarit
Maison de l'Orient Méditerranéen
Université Lumière Lyon 2 – C.N.R.S
7 rue Raulin, F-69007 Lyon
FRANCE

The commercial importance of the Late Bronze Age kingdom of Ugarit on the Syrian coast was based (dependent) on the presence of commercial harbors (maritime trading centers). The main harbor in the bay of Minet el-Beida, 1 km from the capital located on the tell of Ras Shamra-Ugarit, was excavated from 1929 to 1935. Although the site is now an inaccessible military area, the nature of the evidence from Minet el-Beida appears controversial when compared with that from the capital nearby, and a reassessment seems necessary.

The climatic conditions and geography of the site, as well as its location in relation to nearby Ras Shamra and Ras Ibn Hani, emphasize its strategic role.

From the excavation reports published in Syria, Minet el-Beida is described as an urban center, with streets and houses, similar to those on the tell, as well as warehouses, but there was no specific mention of harbor installations.

According to the texts from Ugarit the ancient name of the settlement was Ma'hadou, which usually appears on tablets with lists of men and ships, suggesting that the inhabitants were businessmen, ship owners, artisans and the like. Minet el-Beida was remarkable for the wealth of material excavated as well as for the presence of a cosmopolitan population and cultural environment that promoted the exchange of goods not only with the Mediterranean world but also with the Syrian hinterland and Euphrates valley.

Le royaume d'Ougarit, sur la côte méditerranéenne de Syrie, est connu par des textes de la fin du Bronze Récent (XIVe—début XIIe s. av. J.-C.). Et pour cette période, l'archéologie confirme que l'importance de son activité commerciale repose en grande partie sur l'existence d'un ou plusieurs ports de commerce.

La localisation du port principal est bien établie (fig. 1) depuis la fouille par C. Schaeffer du site de Minet el-Beida il y a environ 60 ans. Mais depuis cette période, les circonstances ont fait qu'on s'en est un peu désintéressé. En effet, les fouilles menées dès 1929 sur le site de la capitale (tell de Ras Shamra) avaient donné des résultats qui ont bouleversé en quelques années ce que l'on savait de l'histoire du Proche-Orient levantin au Bronze Récent, et les archéologues ont très vite fait porter leur effort principal sur la capitale au détriment du port.

Plus de cinquante campagnes de fouille sur le tell de Ras Shamra ont continué à faire découvrir de nouveaux textes, des monuments spectaculaires comme le Palais royal, mais aussi toute une ville avec son habitat ordinaire, et toutes sortes de mobilier archéologique divers. Au cours de ces années les travaux se sont poursuivis sur l'histoire et l'archéologie du royaume d'Ougarit et sa capitale, et de nombreux programmes de recherche sont actuellement en cours.[1]

---

[1] Fouilles françaises: rapports préliminaires dans la revue *Syria* depuis 1929. Voir les publications de la mission: *Ugaritica* I–VII, Paris 1939–1979, sous la direction de C. Schaeffer; *Ras Shamra-Ougarit* I–XI, Paris 1981–1995 (d'autres volumes sont en préparation), sous la direction de M. Yon. Voir également *SDB* (1979): s.v. *Ras Shamra*; Saadé (1979); Yon (1997).

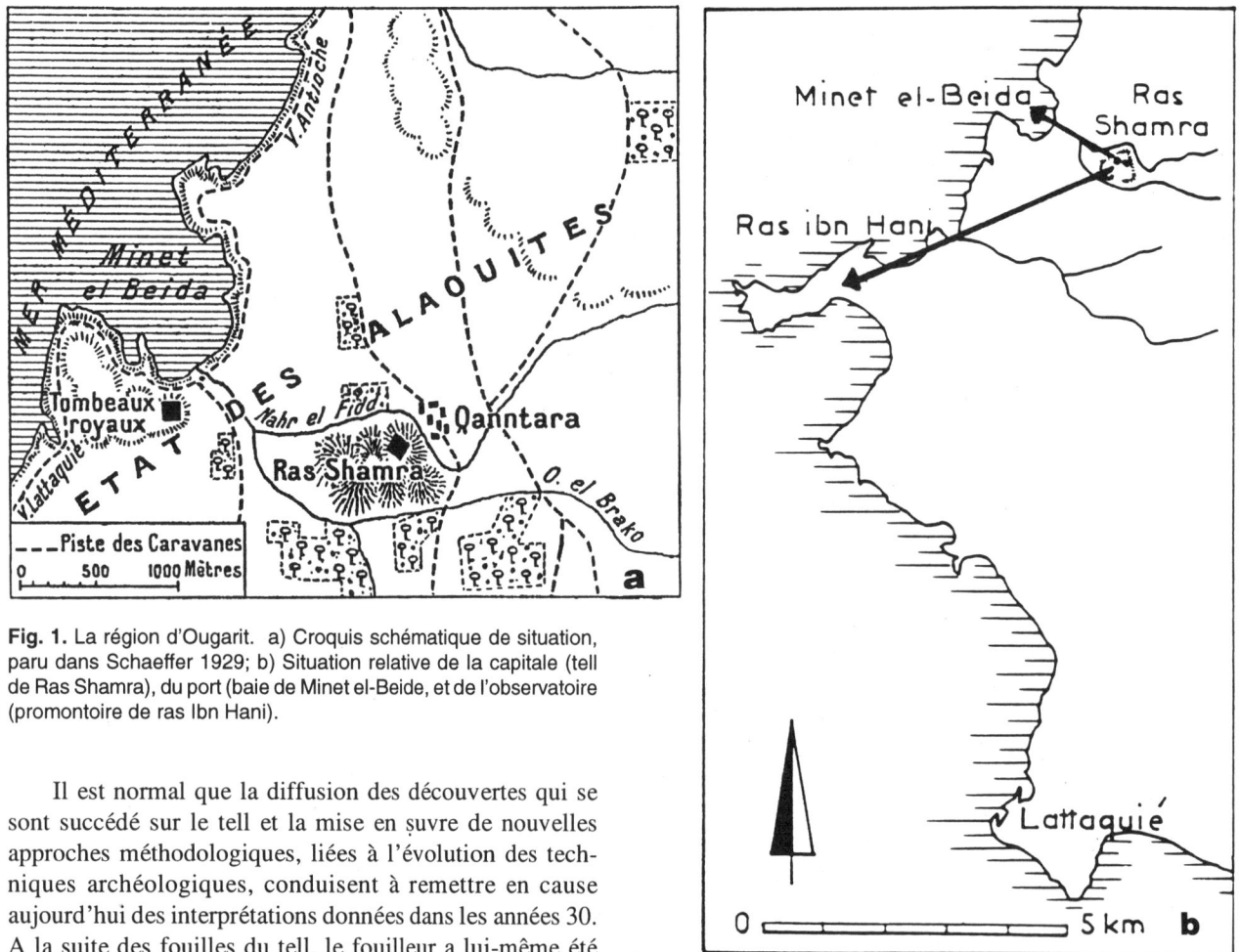

Fig. 1. La région d'Ougarit. a) Croquis schématique de situation, paru dans Schaeffer 1929; b) Situation relative de la capitale (tell de Ras Shamra), du port (baie de Minet el-Beide, et de l'observatoire (promontoire de ras Ibn Hani).

Il est normal que la diffusion des découvertes qui se sont succédé sur le tell et la mise en œuvre de nouvelles approches méthodologiques, liées à l'évolution des techniques archéologiques, conduisent à remettre en cause aujourd'hui des interprétations données dans les années 30. A la suite des fouilles du tell, le fouilleur a lui-même été amené à modifier certaines de ses premières interprétations concernant les restes architecturaux mis au jour à Minet el-Beida. Mais l'ampleur des résultats à exploiter sur le tell de Ras Shamra a fait négliger les résultats du chantier plus modeste du port, dont le développement a été interrompu; et aucune publication synthétique n'est venue compléter ou modifier les rapports préliminaires sur le port parus dans *Syria* au fur et à mesure des fouilles. Seuls ont paru pour ce site des rapports provisoires qui ne donnent pas de plan d'ensemble des restes architecturaux.

C'est pourquoi depuis quelques années, il a paru utile de reprendre l'examen des données archéologiques dont on disposait et de leur interprétation ancienne, pour essayer de mieux comprendre les fouilles de Minet el-Beida et de tirer le maximum d'informations du travail qui a été fait. Faute de pouvoir envisager une éventuelle reprise des fouilles ou même d'accéder au site pour étude, on bénéficie au moins de la comparaison avec les résultats des analyses architecturales menées sur le tell lui-même, et des informations sur le commerce portuaire que donne l'exploitation des tablettes d'archives découvertes au cours des années.

Plusieurs études s'y sont récemment consacrées (Yon 1994b; Saadé 1995; Marchegay à paraître). Nous allons essayer ici de donner l'état de ces recherches.

HISTOIRE DES FOUILLES

En 1928 fut découvert par hasard près de la mer, au bord de la baie de Minet el-Beida, un caveau funéraire construit en pierres (fig. 2; Albanèse 1929; cf. Saadé 1979). Son mobilier qui comportait de la céramique mycénienne a permis de le dater de la dernière phase du Bronze récent (*ca.* XIVe–XIIIe s. av. J.-C.). Une mission officielle, sous l'impulsion de René Dussaud, Conservateur du Département des Antiquités Orientales au Louvre, marqua le début d'une fouille régulière, dirigée par Claude F.-A. Schaeffer.

Mais très vite, dès la première année, l'attention fut attirée sur le tell de Ras Shamra, situé à moins d'un kilomètre de la baie à l'intérieur des terres, et qui révéla des monuments et des documents écrits d'une importance historique considérable. Dès 1931, cet ensemble de sites fut identifié

COVPE LONGITVDINALE A.B.   COVPE TRANSVERSALE C.D.

PLAN

NORD

TOMBE ANTIQVE

A

MINET EL BEIDA

N.° LATTAQVIÉ

(ALAOVITTES)

ECHELLE GRAPHIQVE

BEYROVTH, VI-XII- MCMXXVIII
CH. MY. DE LA CHAVSSÉE FACIT

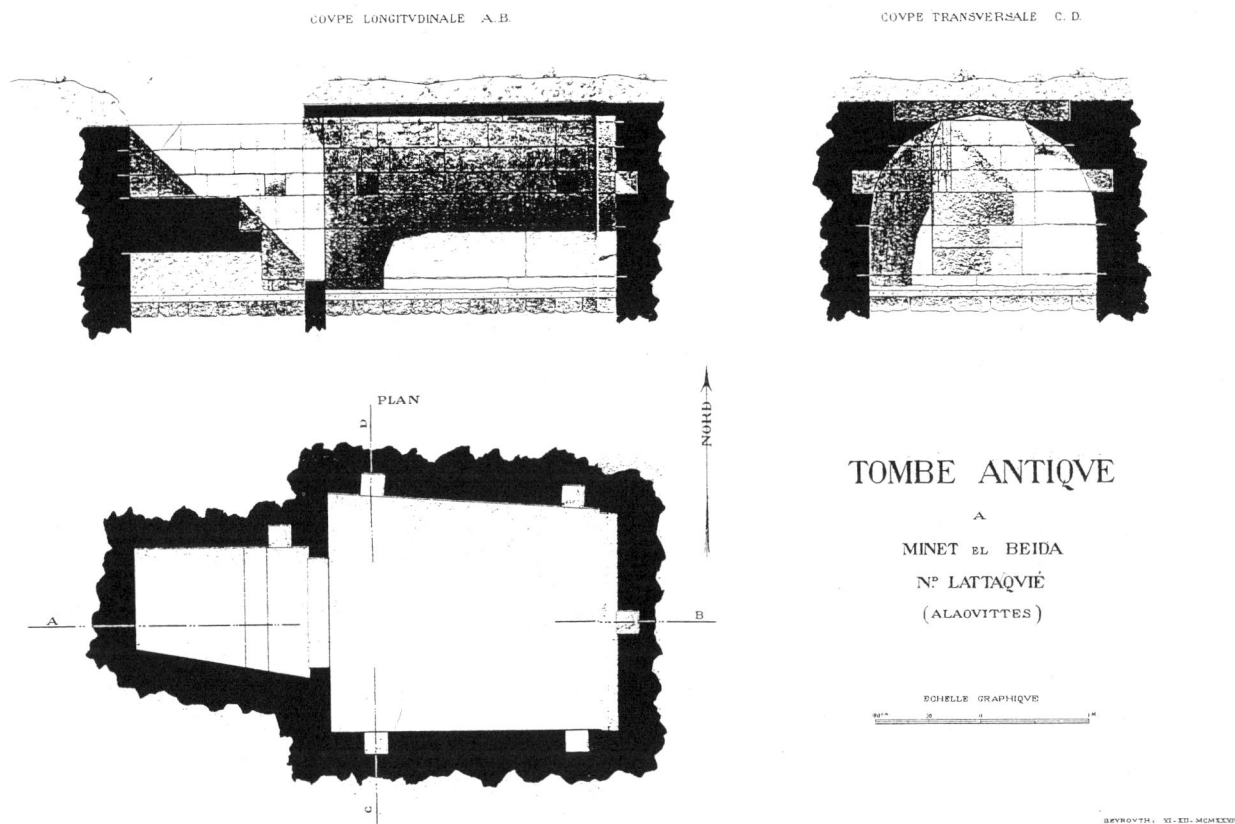

Fig. 2. Tombe découverte en 1928 à Minet el-Beida (Tombe I). Dessin de Ch. M. Y. de la Chaussée, Beyrouth, 6.12.1928.

comme la capitale (sur le tell) et le port (dans la baie de Minet el-Beida) du royaume d'Ougarit. Pour l'époque du Bronze Récent, on connaissait par des documents cunéiformes (en accadien) trouvés en Égypte (El-Amarna) ou en pays hittite (Boghazköy), l'existence de ce royaume qui a tenu alors sa place dans l'histoire de Méditerranée orientale et du Proche Orient.

Des sondages ont montré que le tell fut occupé du VIIIe millénaire jusqu'à sa destruction définitive vers 1190/80 av. J.-C.,[2] mais les fouilles ont surtout mis en évidence jusqu'ici la ville des XIVe–XIIe s. (fin du Bronze Récent), qui apparaît comme le centre culturel et administratif du royaume

d'Ougarit. Il est évident que la présence à proximité de la capitale d'un bon port, attesté pour la même période, a contribué au développement et à la richesse du royaume.

Six campagnes de fouilles ont été menées par C. Schaeffer à Minet el-Beida (fig. 1) entre 1929 et 1935.[3] Des opérations menées en 1957–58 par la Direction des Antiquités de Syrie ont surtout fait des trouvailles d'époque perse et hellénistique (cf. rapport Abdul-Hak 1958–1959: 8–9). Mais aucune activité archéologique n'a été reprise dans le site du Bronze Récent,[4] tout l'effort de la mission française ayant ensuite été porté, comme on l'a dit, sur le tell de Ras Shamra.

[2] Pour les périodes préhistoriques (avant le IIe millén.) voir Contenson (1994). Sur l'histoire du tell, voir Saadé (1979); SDB (1979); Yon (1997); pour la fin du royaume d'Ougarit, voir D. Arnaud in *SDB* (1979); Yon (1992a); Klengel (1992).

[3] Rapports préliminaires: Schaeffer (1929: 285–94; 1931: 1–4; 1932: 1–14; 1933: 3–108; 1935: 168–71). Sur l'histoire des fouilles, voir Saadé (1979: 148–52); cf. Frost (1991: 385–86).

[4] En 1994, la Direction des Antiquités a été informée par l'armée de la découverte fortuite d'une autre tombe, et Mme N. Khaskiyeh, responsable des Antiquités de Lattaquié, a pu se rendre sur place. Il semble que ce soit un caveau de pierre, pillé (Bronze Récent?), situé à l'extérieur de l'agglomération, mais nous n'avons aucune information nouvelle. Je remercie vivement N. Khaskiyeh de ses indications.

Vers 1960, le gouvernement syrien décida d'installer un port militaire dans cette baie qui paraissait le meilleur emplacement portuaire de la côte syrienne. Le premier obstacle que l'on rencontre pour étudier le port de l'Age du Bronze découle donc de cette difficulté d'accès, qui rend impossible de procéder à des sondages de vérification, voire à de simples contrôles sur le terrain. Cependant en 1988, grâce aux autorités archéologiques et militaires et à la municipalité de Lattaquié, que nous remercions vivement de leur aide, j'ai eu l'autorisation d'aller visiter le site, avec W. Mellah, alors responsable des Antiquités de Lattaquié, et O. Callot, architecte de la mission française. Nous avons pu reconnaître le site géographique de la baie tel qu'on le connaissait par les photos anciennes (fig. 3). L'emplacement des fouilles était recouvert par des constructions ou des hangars, et il semble que des aménagements fonctionnels modernes (jetée, môles, etc.) aient modifié l'aspect ancien de la baie elle-même.

GÉOGRAPHIE ET TOPOGRAPHIE

Le site archéologique portuaire se trouve à 10 km au nord de Lattaquié, et à 800 m du tell de Ras Shamra (fig. 1) situé en retrait de la côte. Le port, dont le nom arabe moderne (Minet el-Beida) signifie le «port blanc», est situé dans une profonde baie naturelle ou affleure une barre de calcaire blanc; R. Dussaud l'a identifiée avec le *Leukos Limen* du *Stadiasmos*. Le port a été utilisé aux périodes ultérieures, notamment aux VIe–Ve s av. J.-C., puis à l'époque romaine; et au Moyen Age c'est encore le «*Port Blanc*» des Croisés.

Un petit cours d'eau, désigné sous le nom de nahr el-Fidd, réunit les deux ruisseaux (nahr Chbayyeb et nahr ed-Delbé) qui cernent au nord et au sud le tell de Ras Shamra, et se jette au fond de la baie (voir fig. 1 et 3). Les restes archéologiques découverts sont situés au sud de son embouchure.

La côte de cette partie de la Syrie n'est pas rectiligne, et depuis la région d'Iskenderun/Alexandrette (le royaume de *Moukish* au Bronze Récent) jusqu'à celle de Tartous (l'ancien royaume de *Siyannou*), plusieurs abris naturel pouvaient accueillir les navires. Cependant aucune ne paraît présenter les qualités de sécurité qu'offre la baie située au voisinage immédiat de la capitale d'Ougarit: selon G. Saadé (Yon et al. 1995: 211, note 4) la plus forte tempête du siècle dans cette région de Méditerranée, le 13 janvier 1968, qui a pourtant provoqué des dégâts considérables dans les ports de Beyrouth, Tartous et Lattaquié, n'a causé aucun préjudice dans le port militaire installé à Minet el-Beida.

Le bassin est assez fermé, et il s'étendait au moment des fouilles sur environ 70 hectares; mais il faudrait reprendre une prospection géo-morphologique pour en connaître la forme et les dimensions antiques réelles. A en croire les photos aériennes de 1935 (fig. 3), le port disposait d'une grande baie principale dans laquelle s'ouvre au sud une petite baie plus fermée. Plus à l'est, là où se jette le nahr el-Fidd, la baie est bordé par une plage de sable où l'on pouvait sans doute tirer les bateaux. Son entrée à l'ouest s'ouvre dans une falaise de craie très blanche qui protège le bassin, et que sa nature rend visible de loin en mer. La zone fouillée se situe au sud-est de la baie, sur la rive gauche de l'embouchure du petit fleuve.

Outre la protection qu'offrait la baie profonde, la présence de sources et de puits en faisait une escale majeure de la navigation dans cette région. Plusieurs puits de l'Age du Bronze avaient été mis au jour au cours des fouilles. Mais même avant la redécouverte de l'agglomération antique en 1929, les bergers et les pêcheurs utilisaient au début du XXe s. un puits situé à moins de 200 m de la côte; au reste, les sources qui coulent au pied du tell de Ras Shamra ne sont éloignées de la baie que de 700 ou 800 m.

On est donc tenté de croire que la fonction portuaire de la baie est ici aussi ancienne que la navigation de Méditerranée orientale. Mais on n'en a pas les preuves archéologiques avant la dernière phase du Bronze Récent.

LES RESTES ARCHÉOLOGIQUES

Documents et conditions de la recherche

Nos informations sur le port antique du Bronze Récent reposent donc entièrement sur d'anciens documents d'archives dont on n'a pas la possibilité de contrôler les données sur le terrain. Le bilan de ces documents comporte d'une part des éléments publiés: ce sont les rapports parus dans *Syria* de 1929 à 1935, ainsi que des photos aériennes prises en 1935 par l'aviation française de l'Armée du Levant (fig. 3) et dont plusieurs sont publiées dans ces rapports.

D'autre part, les archives (inédites) de la mission se résument à ce qui a été conservé des notes de fouilles et des inventaires de 1929–1935, des photos, et un plan des restes architecturaux, incomplet et difficile à utiliser. Enfin, on dispose encore aussi sur place de la mémoire de ceux qui ont participé aux fouilles ou qui ont suivi les travaux ou visité le site lorsque c'était encore possible: mais ils sont de plus en plus rares.

On rappellera qu'une partie des notes de fouille a été détruite pendant la guerre de 1939–45. La perte d'une grande partie des archives rend donc impossible de connaître la stratigraphie et la chronologie du site. Quant au plan, dont nous n'avons pas retrouvé jusqu'ici l'original (qui existe peut-être encore?), dans les Archives conservées au Collège

Fig. 3. Photos aériennes de l'Armée française du Levant, 1935: a) Baie de Minet el-Beida et zone fouillée. Vers le nord; b) Partie sud de la baie de Minet el-Beida. Vers le sud.

de France, nous disposons essentiellement d'un tirage qui se trouvait dans les dossiers légués par J.-C. Courtois.[5]

Sur ce tirage de plan, sans date ni légende, il avait porté au crayon quelques indications manuscrites (le numéro de certaines tombes par exemple), mais on n'y voit ni orientation ni repère topographique reconnaissable. D'autre part, le tracé de l'architecte ne rend pas compte d'une quelconque analyse architecturale des bâtiments; ainsi, à titre d'exemple, le même graphisme conventionnel représente de façon continue les murs et les fondations, ce qui ne permet pas de déterminer facilement où se trouvent les portes puisque les fondations continuent sous les seuils.

Il est difficile de savoir si ce relevé a été établi à la fin des fouilles en 1936, ou à la reprise des travaux après la guerre à partir de 1958. Mais tel qu'il est, c'est le seul document graphique sur lequel on puisse s'appuyer. Nous renvoyons donc à l'analyse soigneuse qu'en a faite S. Marchegay[6] en le comparant aux photos disponibles et aux informations partielles dispersées dans les rapports.

Premières interprétations

Comme le disent les premiers rapports publiés, le fouilleur avait d'abord cru explorer une nécropole, puisqu'on y découvrait de grands caveaux construits en pierre (fig. 2) et les restes d'un riche mobilier funéraire.

Puis il reconnut autour de ces tombes des constructions où les installations consacrées à des pratiques religieuses lui semblaient avoir une place de premier plan:[7] et en effet, la découverte de nombreux objets reconnus comme mobilier de sanctuaires (rhytons par exemple) laissait supposer la présence de lieux de culte. On lit dans le rapport de la campagne de 1930 (Schaeffer 1931: pl. I, 3) des descriptions évoquant des «constructions votives en forme de double escalier» (fig. 4a), entourées de jarres et de mortiers, de puits, etc. Ce que l'on sait aujourd'hui de l'architecture d'Ougarit permet de voir qu'il s'agissait de maisons, avec

de simples volées d'escaliers dont la partie supérieure s'est effondrée, comme de très nombreux exemples en ont été trouvés au cours des années dans les maisons du tell de Ras Shamra.

Certes, les caractères funéraires et religieux sont présents à Minet el-Beida, mais la réalité est à la fois plus banale et infiniment plus diverse. Si l'aspect cultuel et la présence des tombes sont indubitables, ils s'intègrent dans une organisation architecturale et sociale plus large.

Il faut redire que, lorsque les fouilles ont commencé dans cette région en 1929, l'absence d'éléments de comparaison rendait difficile de comprendre immédiatement la fonction des restes architecturaux (caveaux funéraires, constructions diverses …). C'est précisément le mérite de C. Schaeffer d'avoir, en fouillant le tell de Ras Shamra, reconnu que les tombes y faisaient partie intégrante de l'habitat, et que les caveaux étaient construits *dans* et *avec* les maisons.[8] Il a donc bien donné lui-même des clés pour une meilleure interprétation de Minet el-Beida, même s'il n'en a pas repris l'étude. Depuis lors, les recherches sur l'urbanisme et l'architecture civile (ou domestique) de la fin du Bronze Récent (voir Callot 1983; Yon, Lombard et Renisio 1987; Yon 1992b; Callot 1994) menées ces dernières années sur le tell de Ras Shamra nous ont amenés à mieux comprendre les restes dégagés autrefois à Minet el-Beida, tout à fait identiques et contemporains de ceux de la capitale.

Architecture, Habitat

L'analyse interne[9] du plan de Minet el-Beida déjà signalé s'est appuyée sur la comparaison avec les photos aériennes de 1935 et avec le dessin des quelques tombes publiées dans les rapports (mais qu'il n'était pas toujours facile d'identifier sur le plan général). La première opération a été d'en retrouver l'orientation et d'indiquer ce qui paraissait être les limites de la fouille. On a pu ainsi com-

---

[5] Le regretté J.-C. Courtois connaissait bien la région et l'histoire de la mission; mais il n'avait pas participé lui-même aux fouilles de Minet el-Beida. Je remercie vivement Liliane Courtois qui, après la mort de son frère en 1992, a déposé ces documents au Département des Antiquités orientales au Musée du Louvre, et Annie Caubet, Conservateur en chef, avec qui j'ai pu trier ces documents.

[6] Article à paraître dans un prochain volume des publications *Ras Shamra-Ougarit*; on y trouvera le plan et l'interprétation qui en a été faite.

[7] «L'hypothèse [...] que la nécropole de Minet el-Beida était doublée d'un lieu de culte a été confirmée par nos découvertes et observations de cette année» (Schaeffer 1933: 108).

[8] Cette découverte faite sur la côte syrienne l'a du reste conduit à reconnaître par la suite le même principe architectural sur le site du Bronze récent à Enkomi de Chypre, là où les fouilles menées au début du XXe s., puis en 1930, et reprises par C. Schaeffer lui-même (fouilles anglaises: Murray, Smith et Walters 1900: 1–54; fouilles suédoises: Gjerstad 1937: 467–575; fouilles françaises: Schaeffer 1936: 107), n'avaient vu d'abord qu'une nécropole.

[9] Pour toute cette analyse, je renvoie à l'article de S. Marchegay, à paraître.

mencer à différencier des espaces de circulation et à localiser des rues, mais on reconnaît mal les ensembles dont parle le fouilleur: cependant certains bâtiments (maisons?) prennent peu à peu leur individualité, et on a proposé une analyse des espaces intérieurs.

C'est le cas par exemple d'une construction fouillée en 1930 que le rapport avait isolé comme un bâtiment autonome, désigné comme une «construction aux 13 chambres et couloirs». Mais le plan schématique publié[10] ne montre ni porte ni analyse de l'organisation: seule la comparaison avec les documents photographiques anciens, et d'autre part avec des maisons analysées sur le tell, lui donnent un sens. C'est en fait une habitation de type ordinaire, avec un vestibule donnant accès à la cour qui distribue la circulation vers les différentes parties de la maison, et un escalier menant à l'étage où sont d'ordinaire les appartements.

Les fouilles ont dès le début mis au jour de très nombreux objets abandonnés sur le sol, comme on en trouve aussi dans les maisons semblables de la ville. Dans les rapports, le fouilleur parle de «Dépôts», comme s'il s'agissait de dépôts volontaires. A lire le premier rapport paru (Schaeffer 1929: 288), il s'y mêle «sans aucune protection» des vases de luxe en céramique mycénienne, des bijoux (bagues et pendentifs en or figurant Astarté, perles en quartz, en cornaline), des objets de faïence très raffinés, des figurines en terre cuite, des statuettes de grand prix comme le Baal en bronze recouvert d'or; mais on y trouve aussi de la céramique utilitaire («grands vases mal cuits»), des mortiers pour la cuisine, etc. Le mobilier des maisons a été abandonné sur le sol au moment de l'invasion qui a vu la fin d'Ougarit vers 1190/1185, tout comme on le constate dans la ville. Les photos d'archives, et la comparaison avec ce que l'on a constaté dans les dernières fouilles sur le tell, suggèrent qu'il s'agit du mobilier de ces bâtiments, mêlé à celui des lieux de culte qui avoisinent les maison du quartier, et probablement aussi à des objets provenant de tombes pillées.

On sait que l'arrivée brutale des envahisseurs s'est traduite sur le tell par de violents combats. Comme les ennemis arrivaient de la mer, les habitants du port étaient au premier rang pour recevoir le choc: ils ont peut-être fui vers la capitale pour s'y réfugier en abandonnant leur biens, mais les combats ont commencé là, et les maisons incendiées se sont écroulées. L'effondrement des superstructures et des toitures a dû recouvrir définitivement le sol des maisons abandonnées par leurs habitants: ainsi ont pu rester sur le sol, au milieu d'un outillage domestique de faible valeur (en terre cuite ou en pierre), des objets précieux d'or ou de bronze (e.g. figurines ou pendentifs) cachés sous les décombres.

Hydraulique et aménagements utilitaires

Les canalisations avaient d'abord été interprétés à tort dans les rapports comme des aménagements de lieux sacrés, évoquant de mystérieux rites de libations et de culte des morts. En réalité, les descriptions publiées dans le premier rapport,[11] aussi bien que les quelques photos disponibles (fig. 4b), correspondent simplement aux installations utilitaires d'évacuation des eaux usées, menant à des puisards couverts d'une plaque percée d'un trou, comme on en a trouvé ensuite dans beaucoup des maisons du tell (Calvet and Geyer 1987; Callot 1994).

Ainsi les «enclos rituels» carrés ou rectangulaires, sans portes, longuement décrits (Schaeffer 1933: 106–8) ne sont dans bien des cas que des pièces de maisons dont on a dégagé les fondations continues (y compris au dessous du niveau des seuils de portes); les «rigoles menant l'eau des libations» sont les canalisations d'évacuation des eaux sales vers le puisard des cabinets; les «tables à offrandes» sont des dalles de pressoirs domestiques semblables à toutes celles que l'on trouve dans des maisons du tell.

Ancres

Quant aux «pierres percées» qui se trouvaient à proximité — et qui avaient d'abord été désignées comme des «stèles trouées» ou des «idoles percées de trois trous» (Schaeffer 1929: 293; 1932, pl. V 2) liées aux même cérémonies que les canalisations—, leur identification comme ancres a été confirmée par Honor Frost, venue les étudier en 1963. Le fouilleur lui-même a reconnu l'intérêt de découvrir des ancres de pierre dans un site portuaire (Frost 1969; Schaeffer 1978: 371–81; l'étude en a été reprise dans Frost 1991).

Lieux de culte

Il est évident que la ville portuaire possédait aussi des lieux réservés aux activités religieuses, voire des temples. Ainsi, un ensemble de constructions fouillé en 1931 (Schaeffer 1932: 4), intégré en pleine agglomération au

---

[10] Schaeffer (1931: 3, fig. 1): « l'absence complète de toute trace d'habitat nous a frappé».

[11] Schaeffer (1929: 291): «une sorte de cascade votive: deux pierres pourvues d'une rigole semblaient amener l'eau dans un fond de jarre, d'où elle devait couler par une pierre percée à l'intérieur de la terre, monument fort curieux dont je ne connaît pas l'analogue».

Fig. 4. Photos de fouille: a) Canalisations et dalles de puisard à Minet el-Beida, 1929; b) Escalier écroulé à Minet el-Beida, 1930.

milieu des maisons, atteste l'existence d'un lieu où se déroulaient des cérémonies utilisant tout un mobilier religieux spécifique: on y retrouve en particulier des rhytons (fig. 5a) et vases à libation caractéristiques.[12] Mais on manque d'éléments pour localiser précisément ces lieux sacrés et pour en reconnaître l'architecture.

Les cultes domestiques sont attestés par les petites figurines de terre cuite trouvées dans les maisons, ou qui accompagnent le défunt dans sa tombe.

Tombes

Comme les travaux ultérieurs l'ont montré dans la capitale (tell de Ras Shamra), certaines des maisons de Minet el-Beida possédaient une zone funéraire. Les fouilles ont mis au jour sept caveaux voûtés en pierre, construits sous les maisons, et auxquels on accède par un dromos en escalier. Mais si la plupart des tombes du tell, pillées dès l'antiquité probablement, ont été retrouvées vides, plusieurs tombes de Minet el-Beida, même si elles ont reçu la visite de pillards, ont livré un très riche mobilier funéraire.

Il est notable que, dans bien des cas, l'accès aux tombes ait été rendu impossible par l'effondrement des maisons. Parfois, l'emplacement de la chambre funéraire devait être repérable encore au milieu du bâtiment détruit, même si l'entrée normale par le dromos était inaccessible. Les pillards ont dû pratiquer un trou dans la couverture de la tombe pour y pénétrer par le toit (Schaeffer 1929: 291) et en retirer ce qui les intéressait, en particulier tout ce qui est en métal. C'est le cas de la grande tombe III, où les fouilleurs ont retrouvé ce qui avait été jugé sans valeur par les pillards de l'antiquité: céramique de luxe mycénienne et chypriote, faïence, vases en albâtre, objets de toilette en ivoire (par exemple le couvercle de pyxide représentant la déesse aux bouquetins: fig. 5b); et ce qui est plus rare, on y a même recueilli quelques bagues en or, en argent (et même en fer selon les rapports), oubliées dans les coins: preuve que la tombe avait été pillée par des gens pressés.

Mais pour d'autres tombes l'effondrement des murs a été plus complet, empêchant les pillards de les repérer: c'est ce qui a protégé le mobilier funéraire, ainsi conservé pendant trois millénaires.

Entrepôts

Enfin, le site a commencé à révéler de vastes entrepôts le plus spectaculaire, dit dans les rapports «dépôt aux 80 jarres» (Schaeffer 1932: pl. III; 1939: 31, pl. IX), contenait des jarres[13] soigneusement placées en rangées régulières (fig. 5). On peut les considérer comme liés plus spécifiquement aux activités commerciales du port.

Le rapport indique que les jarres ont été trouvées sous un sol de «béton dur»; dans ce cas faut-il croire qu'elles n'appartenaient pas à la dernière phase d'occupation du site? Cependant, on imagine mal que les habitants aient reconstruit ou réaménagé un bâtiment, et fabriqué un sol pour y circuler, en s'appuyant sur un sous-sol fait de jarres bien ordonnées. Par comparaison avec les maisons du tell, dont l'effondrement des étages et des toitures recouvre le sol du rez-de-chaussée d'un magma assez résistant à la pioche (Yon, Lombard & Renisio 1987: 11–128), on peut proposer d'interpréter le «béton dur» qui recouvrait le «dépôt des 80 jarres» comme les débris des étages supérieurs du bâtiment au moment de sa destruction au début du XIIe s. Cependant, comme il n'est pas possible d'aller vérifier la stratigraphie sur le terrain, on doit en rester au stade de l'hypothèse.

Quant à des aménagements qui seraient proprement portuaires, les rapports ne nous disent rien, et il est probable que la fouille n'a pas encore pu en repérer (en admettant qu'ils aient laissé des traces).

LE PORT DE *MAHADOU* D'APRÈS LES TEXTES

L'identification du site de Minet el-Beida avec le nom de *Mahadou* cité dans les textes est généralement admise depuis les travaux de M. Astour il y a plus d'une vingtaine d'années.[14] Ces recherches toponymiques s'appuient sur de très nombreux documents écrits trouvés à Ougarit: listes de villes et de villages, listes de personnes, allusions à certains lieux, etc.

Parmi les noms de sites côtiers connus dans les textes, le nom que l'on s'accorde à reconnaître comme celui du port situé à Minet el-Beida est *Ma'hadou* (terme qui désigne un «port»). Il est mentionné en particulier sur quelque 18 tablettes portant des listes d'hommes ou de navires, dont 16

---

[12] Rhytons de type conique ou en forme de tête d'animal, en céramique chypriote ou mycénienne (Schaeffer 1932, pl. II–IV).

[13] L'une de ces jarres (inventaire RS 3.257) est conservée au Musée du Louvre (AO 14876) (Caubet 1994: 259, n° 356; Yon, 1997, n° 30).

[14] Voir l'article fondamental de M. Astour 1970 (cf. Astour 1995); cf. Amadasi-Guzzo 1982. Pour un examen récent des différentes attestations du nom (et références), cf. Saadé (1995).

Fig. 5. Mobilier découvert à Minet el-Beida: a) Couvercle de pyxide en ivoire, tombe III (1929); b) Rhyton coniques mycénien et minoen (1931).

ont été trouvées à Ras Shamra, et à Ras Ibn Hani le site ougaritique voisin. D'après ces listes, les résidents apparaissent comme des hommes d'affaires, des propriétaires de navires marchands, des artisans, etc.; on possède un texte qui fait mention de «bateaux de Mahadou» (RS 11.770).

La diversité et la richesse du mobilier attestent d'autre part du caractère cosmopolite de l'emporium où vivaient à la fois des résidents ougaritiens et des communautés étrangères. Ainsi une liste mentionne un homme de Mahadou avec un homme d'Ashdod; une liste évoque à Mahadou des gens d'Arouad, d'Acco, d'Ashkelon (RS 16.249); une liste de distribution (RS 15.039) parle d'«une jarre de vin pour les Hittites de Ma'hadou»: il est bien établi que le port était fréquenté par des marins et des commerçants chypriotes, levantins, égyptiens, hittites, hourrites. Et même si l'on manque encore d'indications épigraphique concernant la Grèce et la Crète, la nature du mobilier archéologique atteste bien aussi de liens constants avec les pays de l'Égée (Caubet et Matoïan 1995).

Intérêt commercial

Dans l'économie ougaritique, la présence d'un excellent port situé à moins d'un kilomètre de la capitale était un élément fondamental de la prospérité du royaume, comme le démontrent les documents fournis par l'archéologie et les témoignages épigraphiques.

Tout d'abord, Ougarit était par là en relation avec le monde de la navigation méditerranéenne, c'est-à-dire avec l'Égypte, les pays égéens et Chypre, la côte du Levant, les côtes d'Anatolie.

D'autre part, depuis la plaine côtière qui entoure Ma'hadou, le royaume disposait de voies d'accès vers l'intérieur, au sud par la trouée de Homs et la route côtière, et surtout au nord-est par la vallée du Nahr al-Kabir (*Rahbanou*) menant vers la Syrie du nord et les régions de l'Euphrate. Le matériel découvert sur le site aussi bien que les allusions dans les textes confirment en effet que le port assurait une fonction d'ouverture sur la mer occidentale et les pays riverains, pour le commerce des régions de Syrie intérieure et de l'Euphrate.

A en croire certains textes, il apparaît même qu'il servait de port pour des navires qui appartenaient à des royaumes de l'intérieur sans ouverture sur la mer, comme celui d'Amourrou (au sud-est), ou celui de Carchemish sur l'Euphrate (au nord-est) (Malbran 1991: 25).

Fonction stratégique

On peut aussi rappeler l'intérêt stratégique que présente le dispositif topographique de surveillance maritime, tel que les rois d'Ougarit paraissent l'avoir organisé à la fin du Bronze récent; j'ai déjà eu l'occasion de montrer comment des communications optiques (relais de signaux par des feux) étaient possibles entre le port de Minet el-Beida, le tell de Ras Shamra, et le promontoire de Ras Ibn Hani (fig. 1b).[15]

En effet, la capitale située sur le tell est proche de la mer, mais un peu en retrait. Quant au port de Minet el-Beida, assez profondément enfoncé à l'intérieur des terres, il ne dispose pas d'un angle de surveillance très large vers la mer (le regard est arrêté vers le nord par un petit cap, au sud par le promontoire de Ras Ibn Hani).

Au contraire, à 4 km au sud, la presqu'île de Ras Ibn Hani avance fortement en mer et constitue un observatoire remarquable par sa largeur de visibilité du nord au sud, puisque c'est la pointe extrême vers l'ouest de toute la façade côtière du royaume. Cette disposition topographique favorable a été mise à profit par les Ougaritiens, et a dû jouer un rôle dans la décision de construire au début du XIIIe s. un vrai établissement sur la presqu'île, avec de grands bâtiments de type palatial.[16] Les documents archéologiques et épigraphiques montrent que cette période de stabilité politique en Méditerranée orientale,[17] qui assurait notamment des conditions favorables à la navigation et au commerce maritime, a été celle d'une grande prospérité économique pour le royaume d'Ougarit: le roi[18] y disposait alors à la fois du pouvoir de lancer un grand programme de constructions hors de la capitale, et des moyens financiers pour le réaliser. Il s'agissait donc en même temps d'une

construction de prestige dépendant de la capitale, de l'agrément d'une nouvelle résidence royale au bord de la mer, et du développement d'installations techniques utilitaires pour faciliter la navigation.

Les tours des temples de Baal et de Dagan occupent le sommet du tell. Et même aujourd'hui, alors qu'il n'en reste que des ruines au ras du sol, on voit clairement de là la côte et le port. Si l'on restitue les bâtiments eux-mêmes, leur élévation en fait des tours de près de 20 m de haut, qui dominent de loin le paysage; ils deviennent du reste un repère visible de loin en mer, que les marins pouvaient voir depuis le large. Et leur terrasse haute est un lieu d'observation incomparable en direction de la côte.

De même, les agglomérations de Minet el-Beida et de Ras Ibn Hani comportaient probablement des constructions à terrasse haute où pouvaient se poster les veilleurs. Leur situation respective explique l'importance stratégique de ce dispositif de surveillance maritime.

CONCLUSION

La comparaison avec Ras Shamra a bien confirmé que le site n'était pas seulement celui d'une simple nécropole. Ma'hadou est une véritable agglomération aux caractères urbains, avec des rues bordant des maisons (présentant les même caractères que celles du tell, y compris la présence des tombes), des temples, des installations commerciales, des ateliers. L'importance des entrepôts dans les mêmes quartiers où habitaient des marchands et des marins convient à la fonction de ce site qui assurait les importations et les exportations du royaume.

C'est un établissement remarquable par sa richesse, à en juger par le mobilier des tombes qui pouvaient être celles de riches négociants. Il se caractérise aussi par la présence d'une population et d'un environnement culturels cosmopolites.

Cette phase urbaine de l'occupation portuaire a duré au moins du XIVe s. jusqu'à la destruction au début du XIIe s. av. J.-C. Mais on ne peut rien dire des phases qui ont précédé celle-là.

---

[15] Cf. Yon (1992a: 113, schéma fig. 14.2). On peut rappeler que c'est par des signaux de feu de ce genre, transmis depuis Troie par relais de sommet en sommet, que selon la tradition grecque le retour d'Agamemnon a été annoncé à Mycènes; le message a été reçu par un veilleur posté sur le toit du palais. Le récit d'Eschyle (*Agamemnon*, v. 281–316), quelques siècles plus tard, renvoie probablement à une technique des relations maritimes beaucoup plus ancienne.

[16] Sur l'établissement de Ras Ibn Hani voir Bounni, Lagarce, et Saliby (1987); Lagarce (1995). Cf. aussi Caubet (1992) (pour la destruction du site).

[17] Grâce à l'accord d'équilibre des influences entre les pouvoirs du roi hittite (suzerain de la partie nord de la côte du Levant, y compris le royaume d'Ougarit) et ceux du pharaon égyptien (côte phénicienne et palestinienne), établi entre Hattousili III et Ramsès II en 1259, à la suite de la bataille de Qadesh (cf. Klengel 1992: 111).

[18] Sur les circonstances de politiques intérieures et de dissensions familiales (sur lesquelles il n'est pas le lieu de s'attarder ici) qui ont peut-être aussi contribué à la décision d'y construire la résidence dite « Palais nord», voir Lagarce (1995).

La fouille du site a été à peine commencée. Une reprise des recherche, lorsqu'elle sera possible, apportera probablement des réponses aux questions que l'on se pose sur l'extension de l'agglomération portuaire du Bronze Récent, aussi bien que sur l'organisation du port lui-même et peut-être sur les techniques proprement maritimes.

REFERENCES

Abdul-Hak, S.
1958– Leukos Limen, in Découvertes archéologiques
1959 récentes, *Annales Archéologiques de Syrie* VIII–IX: 83–86.

Albanèse, L.
1929 Note sur Ras Shamra. *Syria* 10: 15–20.

Amadasi-Guzzo, M.-G.
1982 Il vocabolo M'HD / MHZ in ugaritico e fenicio, Pp. 31–36 in *Materiali lessicali ed epigrafici* I. *Collezione di Studi Fenici* 13, Roma.

Astour, M.
1970 Ma'hadu, le port d'Ugarit, *JESHO* 13: 113–27.
1995 Pp. 55–72 in *La topographie du royaume d'Ougarit*, RSO XI.

Bounni, A.; Lagarce, J.; Lagarce, E.; and Saliby, N.
1987 *Ras Ibn Hani: archéologie et histoire*. Damas.

Callot, O.
1981 *Une maison à Ougarit*, RSO I.
1994 *La tranchée Ville Sud*, RSO X.

Caubet, A.
1992 Reoccupation of the Syrian coast. Pp. 123–31 in *The Crisis Years: the 12th century B.C. from Beyond the Danube to the Tigris*, eds. W. A. Ward and M. S. Joukowsky. Dubuque, Iowa: Kendall/Park.
1994 P. 259 in Catalogue *Pharaonen und Fremde Dynastien im Dunkel*. Vienna.

Caubet, A., and Matoïan, V.
1995 Pp. 99–112 in *Ougarit et l'Égée*, RSO XI.

Contenson, de H.
1994 *Préhistoire d'Ougarit*, RSO VIII.

Dussaud, R.
1927 *Topographie historique de la Syrie antique et médiévale*, Paris.

Frost, H.
1969 The stone anchors of Ugarit. *Ugaritica* VI: 235–45.
1991 Pp. 355–410 in *Anchors sacred and profane*, RSO VI.

Gjerstad, E.
1937 *The Swedish Cyprus Expedition* vol. I. *Finds and Results*. Lund.

Klengel, H.,
1992 *Syria, 3000 to 300 BC, A Handbook of Political History*. Berlin: Akademie.

Lagarce, J. and Lagarce, E.
1995 Pp. 141–54 in *Ras Ibn Hani*, RSO XI.

Malbran-Labat, F.
1991 Pp. 17–23 in *Listes*, RSO VII.

Marchegay, S.
in press *Un plan inédit des fouilles de Minet el-Beida*, RSO.

Murray, C. S.; Smith, A. H.; and Walters, H. B.
1900 *Excavations in Cyprus*, Londres.

RSO
1981– Série *Ras Shamra-Ougarit*, Édition Recherche
1995 sur les Civilisations, Paris.

Saadé, G.
1979 *Ougarit, Métropole Cananéenne*, Lattaquié.
1995 Pp. 211–26 in *Le port d'Ougarit*, RSO XI.

Schaeffer, C. F.-A.
1929 *Syria* 10: 285–94.
1931 *Syria* 12: 1–4.
1932 *Syria* 13: 1–14.
1934 *Syria* 14: 93–108.
1935 *Syria* 16: 168–71.
1936 *Missions en Chypre 1932–1935*. Paris.
1939 *Ugaritica I*. Paris.
1978 Remarques sur les ancres de pierre d'Ugarit. *Ugaritica* VII: 371–81.

SDB
1979 Col. 1295–1348 in *Supplément au Dictionnaire de la Bible*, s.v. *Ras Shamra*. Paris: Letouzey et Ané.

Stieglitz, R. R.
1974 Ugaritic Mhd—the Harbor of Yabne-Yam? *Journal of the American Oriental Society* 94: 137–38.

Teixidor, J.
1983 Palmyrene MHWZ and Ugaritic MIHD. *Ugarit-Forschungen* 15: 309–11.

Yon, M.
1992a The End of the Kingdom of Ugarit. Pp. 111–22 in *The Crisis Years: the 12th century B.C. from Beyond the Danube to the Tigris*, eds. W. A. Ward and M. S. Joukowsky. Dubuque, Iowa: Kendall/Park.
1992b Ugarit: the Urban Habitat. The Present State of the Archaeological Picture. *BASOR* 286: 19–34.

1994a   Ougarit et ses relations avec les régions maritimes voisines (d'après les travaux récents). Pp. 421–39 in *Proceedings of the International Symposium on Ugarit and the Bible, Manchester, September 1992*, eds. G. J. Brooke, A. H. W. Curtis and J. F. Healey. Münster: Ugarit-Verlag.

1994b   Minet el-Beida. Pp. 213–15 in *Reallexicon für Assyriologie*, Band 8.3/4. Berlin: De Gruyter.

1997   *La cité d'Ougarit.* Paris: Editions Recherche sur les Civilisations.

Yon, M.; Lombard, P.; and Renisio, M.

1987   L'organisation de l'habitat: les maisons A, B et E. Pp. 11–128 in *Le Centre de la ville, 38–40e campagnes (1978–1984)*, RSO III.

Yon, M.; Sznycer, M.; and Bordreuil, P. (eds.)

1994   *Le Pays d'Ougarit autour de 1200 av. J.-C.*, RSO XI.

Appendix
Some Brief Thoughts on the Ancient Harbor of Kourion

DEMOS CHRISTOU

Director, Department of Antiquities
Republic of Cyprus
Nicosia
CYPRUS

The exact location of the ancient harbor at Kourion remains unknown, a fact that casts doubt on its very existence. Excavations undertaken at the main city site of the Hellenistic, Roman and Early Christian periods, situated on the well-known and commanding hillock 3 km west of Episkopi village, as well as the localities of *Bamboula* and *Kaloriziki* to the east and south of the same village, resulted in the discovery of various domestic remains and tombs that date back to the Late Bronze Age, Geometric and Archaic periods. No harbor traces were found at all. Moreover, the present day topography of the coastline from the precipitous cliffs south of the Sanctuary of Apollo to Cape Zevgari on the Akrotiri Peninsula excludes the existence of a natural harbor in the vicinity.

The absence of a natural harbor at Kourion is supported by the fact that the coastal locality of *Ayios Ermoyenis,* adjacent to the Kourion hill, was continually used as a cemetery from the Cypro-Archaic to the end of the Early Christian periods.

Nevertheless, a series of huge blocks, symmetrically arranged in a slightly curved line extending about 50 m into the sea (Leonard 1995), opposite the lower part of the southeastern corner of the Kourion bluff, indicates the probable remains of an artificial harbor.

In the 1994 trial excavations in an area about 300 m northwest of the aforementioned alignment of rocks and 150 m north of the first coastal restaurant, near the foot of the Kourion acropolis, revealed the central apse and parts of the two lateral apses of an Early Christian church. Systematic excavations that resumed in March and April 1995 uncovered most of the eastern half of this monumental sacred building.

The archaeological data suggest that this is a three-aisled Christian basilica dating to the early sixth century C.E. The spacious nave and the two aisles of the main part of the church are separated by twin marble colonnades, ten intact columns of which, along with their bases and capitals, have been uncovered. The east end of the nave is joined with the sanctuary or *bema,* which has a semicircular apse once crowned by a semidome and flanked by two smaller apses. The floors of the nave and aisles are paved with multicolored mosaic compositions while the floor of the sanctuary consists of colored marble *opus sectile*. A large quantity of tesserae and fragments of wall mosaics found above the floors of the building indicate that the upper parts of the walls of the nave and the semidome of the central apse were probably decorated with elaborate mosaics. The tesserae were in some cases capped with gold or made of mother-of-pearl.

A rectangular room adjacent to the south aisle seems to constitute the *catechumenon,* that part of the church where the unbaptized converts remained during the communion. The western extremities of the nave and aisles are linked with the *narthex,* the main vestibule of the church, part of which has been uncovered. Hopefully, the remainder of the *narthex* and the entire *atrium* will be excavated in 1996.

The location of this newly uncovered basilica suggests that it was connected with the postulated artificial harbor nearby and, like the basilicas discovered close to the three ancient ports of Salamis, Amathous and Nea Paphos, was the protector of the installations at Kourion.

REFERENCES

Leonard, J. R.
  1995   Evidence for Roman Ports, Harbours and Anchorages in Cyprus. Pp. 227–46 in *Cyprus and the Sea,* eds. V. Karageorghis and D. Michaelides. Nicosia: University of Cyprus.